"UNTIL YOU ARE DEAD"

# "UNTIL YOU

### STEVEN TRUSCOTT'S LONG RIDE INTO HISTORY

# ARE DEAD"

# JULIAN SHER

## Research Associate: Theresa Burke

VINTAGE CANADA

*To Myriam and Daniel*

## VINTAGE CANADA EDITION, 2002

Copyright © 2001 Julian Sher
Chapters 44 and 45 copyright © 2007 Julian Sher

Published in Canada in 2002 by Vintage Canada, a division of Random House of Canada Limited, Toronto. Originally published in hardcover in Canada by Alfred A. Knopf Canada, Toronto, in 2001. Distributed by Random House of Canada Limited, Toronto.

Vintage Canada and colophon are registered trademarks of Random House of Canada Limited.

Photographs courtesy of the London Free Press are from the Collection of Photographic Negatives, D. B. Weldon Library, University of Western Ontario.

The verse quoted on p. 104 is from the poem "The Rose beyond the Wall" by A. L. Frink.

### National Library of Canada Cataloguing in Publication Data

Sher, Julian, 1953–
    Until you are dead : Steven Truscott's long ride into history / Julian Sher ;
    research associate, Theresa Burke.

Includes index.

ISBN-13: 978-0-676-97381-5

1. Truscott, Steven, 1945–        —Trials, litigation, etc. 2. Murder—Ontario—Clinton. 3. Trials (Murder)—Ontario—Goderich. 4. Criminal justice, Administration of—Ontario—Case studies. I. Title.

HV6535.C33C55 2002        345.71'02523'0971322        C2002-901866-8

www.randomhouse.ca

Text design: Daniel Cullen
Map: CS Richardson

Printed and bound in the United States of America

9 8 7 6 5 4 3 2

# AUTHOR'S NOTE

All italics in quoted material are mine, unless otherwise attributed; minor grammatical and spelling mistakes in some quotations have been corrected. Imperial, rather than metric, terms of measurement are used since many of the original police and court files refer to feet, miles and pounds. A map is provided on the next two pages for ease of reference.

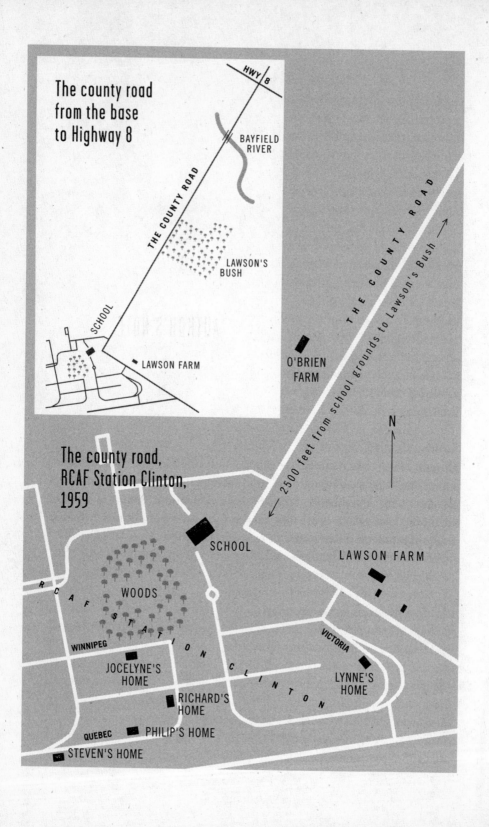

The county road from the base to Highway 8

HWY 8

BAYFIELD RIVER

THE COUNTY ROAD

LAWSON'S BUSH

SCHOOL

LAWSON FARM

The county road, RCAF Station Clinton, 1959

THE COUNTY ROAD

O'BRIEN FARM

2500 feet from school grounds to Lawson's Bush

N

SCHOOL

LAWSON FARM

WOODS

RCAF STATION CLINTON

WINNIPEG

VICTORIA

JOCELYNE'S HOME

LYNNE'S HOME

RICHARD'S HOME

QUEBEC    PHILIP'S HOME

STEVEN'S HOME

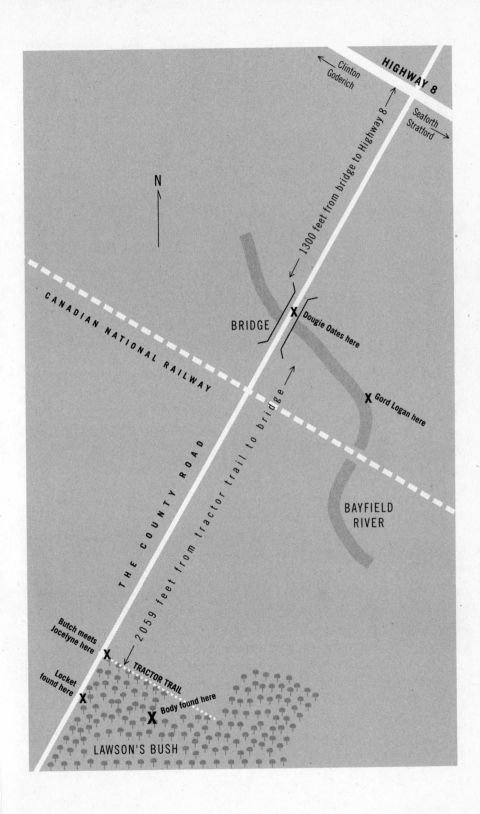

# CONTENTS

# PROLOGUE

The tall, broad-shouldered man who greeted me at his door had lines of grey running through his hair and wrinkles etched on his face. For a fifty-five-year-old, he stood remarkably fit and trim. Only the smile in his eyes betrayed a hint of the boy he had once been, in that fateful summer of 1959.

We shook hands. His grip was firm and I thought about those hands, which had built model airplanes out of balsa wood on air force bases in the '50s; hands that had grown tough and callused in machine shops as the teenage boy grew to manhood behind prison walls; hands that, once out of jail, laboured for thirty years in factories in Guelph; hands that caressed three children, and later, three grandchildren.

These hands were also the ones that the police, a jury and the Supreme Court of Canada said had strangled a young girl to death.

Steven Truscott was Canada's most famous convicted murderer. In a case that made national and world headlines, Truscott was sentenced to hang in

1959 at the age of fourteen for the rape and murder of a twelve-year-old classmate, Lynne Harper. After the federal cabinet commuted his death sentence, he spent ten years in prison, and once paroled, he spent three decades living under an assumed name in the relative obscurity of small-town Ontario.

Like many of my generation, I remember the photograph on the cover of the *Star Weekly*, a smiling boy my age standing by his racing bike. A boy who would grow up in prison for a crime he would always claim he did not commit.

Now, for the first time in forty years, Steven Truscott was willing to tell his story in his own words, revealing a face he had for the most part kept hidden from the public. There had been three books, one fictional movie, a TV courtroom re-enactment and a radio interview. But few people had seen the man the boy had become.

For the first time, too, boxes of police files and military records had been uncovered that had remained hidden or buried in government vaults for decades. There were disturbing clues—many of them revealed in this book for the first time—about an investigation and a trial the authorities had always claimed was beyond reproach.

Steven and his wife, Marlene, had chosen to speak out on *the fifth estate*, the flagship investigative documentary program of the Canadian Broadcasting Corporation. I was the segment producer. It would be the longest and hardest assignment I ever completed. The story dominated my life for two years—and it would completely change Steven's.

There were no deals, no commitments and no promises. If *the fifth estate* was going to investigate one of Canada's most controversial murder cases, we had to have unfettered access.

"If you want to prove yourself innocent, hire a defence lawyer," I told Steven. "Our job is not to prove people innocent, but to find out the truth and go down any alleys, no matter where they lead."

"That's fine," Steve replied quickly. "I'm not afraid. Talk to anyone you find, investigate wherever things lead you. I know I'm innocent and I'm not afraid of what you'll turn up."

It was an important moment. A healthy dose of skepticism, if not outright cynicism, is almost a badge of courage for journalists. Over the years, I had interviewed convicted murderers and drug dealers in maximum-security Canadian prisons, con men on the run in Latin America and war criminals from Africa. All protested their innocence or blamed someone else for their misfortunes. Steven Truscott's claim of innocence was nothing new. But his willingness to let journalists probe into the deepest corners of his life was.

When Steven Truscott went on trial for the rape and murder of Lynne Harper, Canada was a much more innocent country. It was three decades before we heard about Clifford Olson or Paul Bernardo, before sex crimes became highly publicized. Yet it would also be decades before many Canadians came to realize that the police and the courts all too often put innocent people behind bars.

Few cases in Canadian legal history have spanned so many political generations. Prime Minister John Diefenbaker wrestled with and commuted Truscott's death sentence in 1959; a young justice minister named Pierre Trudeau confronted the Truscott controversy in 1967 and, as prime minister, abolished the death penalty nine years later; and today—in the wake of revelations by *the fifth estate* and new information in this book—successive Liberal and Conservative governments had to grapple with a new and final appeal for justice from Steven Truscott and his lawyers.

Steven Truscott was convicted in the final year of the conservative 1950s, a decade when concerned parents watched their teenagers flock to the movies of James Dean and sway to the music of Elvis Presley. The presiding judge at trial warned the jurors they were "the screws that hold the lid down" on anything that threatened society's respectability.

The story of Steven Truscott is the story of Canada growing up, shedding illusions about the justice system and learning to live with doubt, fear and judicial uncertainty. It is also the story of a boy growing up behind bars, first in the shadow of the hangman's noose, then in the confines of a reform school for "juvenile delinquents," and finally behind the walls of a penitentiary. And it is the story of girl who never got a chance to grow up, a bright, lively child who never saw her thirteenth birthday.

# PART ONE

## THE BATTLE IN THE COURTROOM: 1959

*"It is with confidence that I leave
the fate of this boy in your hands."*

—Defence lawyer Frank Donnelly,
to the jurors

# JUNE: MURDER AND ARREST

1

CRIME SCENE

Nine-year-old Karen Daum was uneasy. "Be very quiet," she remembers Miss Beacom warning the grade Four pupils as they pointed to the air force men and whispered nervously. "One of the girls from school is missing and they are trying to find her."

It was a sweltering afternoon on Thursday, June 11, 1959, so hot that Edith Beacom allowed Karen and the other children to do their lessons outside on the school field. Suddenly, along the county road, they saw rows and rows of men from the Clinton air force base marching in formation. Around lunchtime, about 250 officers and airmen had rallied in the parade square on the base. They formed three search parties: one to look down by the river, one along the highway and a third group in the nearby woods.

Inside the school, the older students in Maitland Edgar's grades Seven/Eight classroom also spotted the search parties. Edgar remembers that the tall boy sitting at the back of the row of desks closest to the windows did not react differently than his classmates. Like all of his friends, Steven Truscott stared at the strange sight of dozens of men looking for a girl.

News of the young girl's disappearance had spread beyond the confines of the Clinton air force base to the surrounding towns and throughout southern Ontario. "Twelve-year-old Lynne Harper Missing Since Tuesday," read the headline in Clinton's small weekly paper, the *News-Record*, in a small article on Thursday's front page. "She was apparently last seen on the highway where she had ridden with another youngster." The story was dramatic enough to make the news in Toronto and nearby London.

Still, the paper in Clinton devoted more space to the news that the town had finally finished putting up street numbers on all the homes. In many ways, Clinton was still the small rural enclave it had been since the late nineteenth century. Except for a brief wartime boom, the town had never had more than 2,600 residents. Up until the late 1940s, horse-drawn ploughs cleared the snow from sidewalks. Clinton was also a deeply religious place; the first log school built one hundred years earlier had doubled as a house of worship, and Sunday church attendance remained strong. The Temperance Act was still in force—Clinton was a dry town. Order and discipline were ingrained both in the community and in the nearby air force base.

It was her shoes he saw first. Small, brown loafers.

"They were kind of lined up even. One was turned on its side and they were just lying perfectly side by side," George Edens recalls.

At 1:50 p.m., the sun was high overhead, unrelenting in the week-long heat wave it had inflicted upon southern Ontario. Shafts of sunlight shot through the leaves on the towering maple and ash trees as Cpl. George Edens and his fellow airmen pushed away branches and bushes, hoping they would not find what their search party had been sent out to look for: a body.

Like many on the base, Edens knew of the rumours that perhaps twelve-year-old Lynne was a runaway. "I had heard that she was hitchhiking . . . to be with her grandmother because she had a tiff at home," he remembers.

Edens was in the group assigned to search the heavily wooded area known as Lawson's bush, on a farm next to the base. The men walked in a straight line, twenty feet apart, sweating under the sun and swatting at the mosquitoes.

For thirty minutes, the air force men slowly beat their way through the bush. Then, pushing some branches and undergrowth away, Edens spotted the shoes and, moments later, the clump of clothes lying in a little depression of earth: "They were lying there, rather neatly. And I thought: 'Why would a little girl be out here without any clothes on?'" He turned and saw the body. "I thought: 'Oh my heavens, no!' I knew then that she was dead." Edens froze, too stunned to even cry out. His companion, Lieut. Joseph Leger, came up

8

behind him and his yell pulled Edens out of his stupor. "Here she is!" came the shout, and with a sickening certainty everyone now knew that the little girl was not at her grandmother's or in the safe refuge of any home. She had been murdered and it appeared she had been sexually assaulted.

Her corpse lay in a small hollow about six feet long and fifteen inches deep, behind a group of five trees growing out of a single stump. Around the stump there were about a dozen other smaller trees or saplings. Three branches from an ash tree lay across her body. Six to eight feet away, the searchers spotted three freshly broken limbs from small ash trees. South of the body was another broken branch, not entirely severed from a maple sapling. Her body was about eighty-three feet from a tractor trail and 280 feet from a busy county road.

She was lying on her back, her right leg slightly turned, bent at the knee; her left leg was straight. Her left arm lay across her chest; the right arm was bent at the elbow, palm up, next to her head. The only clothing covering the little girl was her blood-smeared undershirt, pulled up on her chest. The sleeveless white blouse she had been wearing had been ripped and yanked off; a couple of buttons were missing. Her right arm was still caught in the armhole. The ends of the blouse were rolled up and tied tightly around the girl's neck, with a knot under the left side of her jaw. A small pool of blood, just enough to fill a tablespoon, coagulated underneath her left shoulder.

The discovery of a twelve-year-old's nearly naked body was too gruesome for even some of the seasoned men in Canada's armed forces to stomach. Her face and body were swollen, and maggots and insects oozed out of the nose, mouth and genitals. In shock and horror, the searchers covered the body with their shirts and jackets. "Nobody knew what to do," Edens remembers. "You never run into this. You are in a quandary about what to do."

The well-meaning airmen wanted to protect the young victim's dignity. But in doing so, they compromised the crime scene and destroyed potential evidence. From the start, the investigation into the murder of Lynne Harper was a botched affair.

It did not take long for the Ontario Provincial Police to arrive. By 2:08 p.m., Cpl. Harry "Hank" Sayeau was on the scene, joined seven minutes later by Const. Donald Trumbley. Even for the police, the slaying of a young girl was a shock. Sayeau, a careful and considerate officer who prided himself on being "a fact finder," had seen only two murders—both domestic disputes—since he had been first stationed in Huron County in 1953. "When they told me they found her, I went into a little body shake. I was hoping against hope that she had run away," he recalls. "Up there, you didn't have much violence. It was an emotional thing—something that I had never encountered and that the community had never encountered."

Still, the officers carried out their work diligently, and they were all the more determined to catch the culprit who could commit so brutal a crime. "Police clamped down a heavy wall of secrecy as soon as the body was found," the local papers reported. "Airmen from the searching party were stationed around the outside perimeter of the woodlot to keep curious spectators out. Newsmen, too, were barred from the scene."

The local Clinton coroner, Dr. Fred Thompson, arrived by 2:35 p.m., but was instructed not to do anything until the regional pathologist arrived from nearby Stratford. A second doctor on the scene, Dr. David Hall Brooks, formally identified Lynne's body. Brooks was the senior medical officer at the base and lived across the street from the Harpers. Lynne was his daughter's Girl Guide patrol leader.

The authorities promptly notified Lynne's parents. For almost two days they had hoped that their sometimes brash, determined little girl was perhaps just acting out, running away, or at worst, simply lost. Now Leslie and Shirley Harper realized their only daughter would never blow out the candles on her thirteenth birthday cake. The chaplain from the base remained with the parents most of the afternoon and evening. According to newspaper accounts, doctors placed both parents under sedation.

While the Harpers grieved, the police began examining the crime scene. The person in charge of cataloguing the information was Cpl. John Erskine, the district identification officer for the OPP. A tall, thin man with a youthful grin, Erskine approached his job with something of a passion. "He was a perfectionist in everything he did," says his widow, Dee Harris. "It had to be done right or it wouldn't be done at all." A fellow identification officer in the nearby London district, Cpl. Dennis Alsop, agreed. He describes his colleague Erskine as "a meticulous man."

Erskine began snapping pictures of the body, the clothes and the surrounding woods. He measured precisely where everything was and took notes of any marks or indentations he found near Lynne. Her turquoise shorts lay right next to her elbow, her shoes about a foot away. Fifteen inches above her head was a cluster with two white socks and a red hairband. Her underpants, curiously, were much farther away: thirty-three feet, eight inches, northeast of the body.

Police also found a black comb seventy-eight feet away, and, in the field near the bush, three pieces of Kleenex and two Coke bottles, one empty and one full, and part of an uneaten hotdog from "what appeared to be where someone had eaten a picnic."

What was surprising was the neat, almost ceremonial appearance of the scene. The leaves and earth around Lynne's body were undisturbed—no piles of dirt, scraped earth or broken branches to suggest a violent struggle. Her shoes and socks lay "in a fairly orderly manner," the police noted, the white sockettes carefully rolled up. Her underwear had no rips or tears. Her shorts were zipped up, no tears or cuts, just a slight rent in the seam near the crotch.

There were no apparent wounds to her body, except for a gash in her left shoulder and the strangulation marks on her neck. Her assailant had not broken her neck or bloodied and bludgeoned her head. The police found no apparent weapons of any kind.

Two of the branches that lay across her body criss-crossed over her chest and extended up alongside her cheeks, framing her face in a sort of "V." At trial, the prosecution would paint the branches as a primitive attempt by a frightened boy to cover up his foul deed. Given the tidy death scene, the branches could also be interpreted as a twisted tribute or reverential covering of the victim by her disturbed assailant.

The police found no fingerprints on her body, her clothes or the tree branches, but they had no technology to spot those prints, at any rate. Today, lasers can identify prints on skin and clothes. In 1959, the only hope the police had were Lynne's shoes, because certain types of leather could reveal prints.

Corporal Erskine did not find any footprints either—at least, none he was able to distinguish. At 4:48 p.m., Erskine took pictures of marks just below Lynne Harper's feet: one ten inches long, the other eleven inches, both of them about one-eighth to one-quarter inches deep. He later described them as "scuff marks," so indistinct that he could not get a proper measurement on them. None of the police reports on file mentioned footprints found near the body.

Strangely, though, three months later at the trial, Flying Officer Glen Sage, supervising the air force men at the site, said that he spotted a print about two or three inches from Lynne's left heel. "You could see the heel, wavy lines, as if from a crepe shoe," he recalls. "I thought at the time, 'There is a footprint that probably is from the person that killed this girl.'" Sage said he even stopped a policeman from inadvertently trampling over the evidence.

"Lookit! Be careful where you're stepping because there's that footprint," he insists he called out. "I was waiting for the police to take a plaster cast of it—and they never did. I was a little disillusioned with the police at that point."

Sage's story would play a crucial part in the trial and subsequent conviction of Steven Truscott. In the minds of several of the jurors, it was the one piece of solid physical evidence that put the teenage boy at the scene of the crime.

At about 4:45 p.m., as Erskine was taking his pictures, Dr. John Llewellyn Penistan from Stratford, the district pathologist, made his entrance. Penistan had the distinguished grey hair, handsome face and deep eyes that reinforced his friendly image. The pipe he held constantly in his hand seemed to add to his aura of dignity. A graduate from the University of London, in England, with a degree in medicine and surgery, he had been the region's pathologist for the attorney general's department since 1949.

Penistan found the girl's nose and mouth covered with "innumerable maggots." Her undershirt was soiled with bloodstains. There was a small circle of blood on the front seam of her shorts, another stain on her underpants and a spot on her left shoe. "There was a pool of blood, still wet, approximately a tablespoonful, beneath the left shoulder," Penistan noted. When the body was moved, Penistan spotted some dandelion leaves with blood spatters and a twig "ringed with blood over an area approximately one inch in length" that had been just below Harper's crotch. Penistan did not examine the corpse at the scene for any foreign hairs or fibres.

The pathologist spent an hour collecting his evidence. He completed his work by 5:45 and waited for a vehicle to arrive to take the young girl's body away to a local funeral home for examination.

The men who had surrounded the lifeless body of Lynne Harper for more than four hours slowly began making their way out of the woods toward the county road. Along the dirt tractor trail that ran along the bush, the police and air force officers found two different kinds of tracks: a set of fresh tire skid marks and some old bicycle tracks.

How the police handled this evidence says a good deal about the tunnel vision that quickly enveloped the investigation. On the one hand, bicycle tire marks that by all accounts were at least a week old would become, in the eyes of the police and prosecution, incriminating evidence against Steven. On the other hand, they ignored—and kept hidden from the defence—testimony about fresh skid marks that possibly pointed to an adult killer in a vehicle.

The earth along the laneway leading to the bush was dry and cracked. With no significant rainfall since the previous month, the ground was parched. So it was hardly surprising that, at the outset, the police were not very excited about bike tire marks they found about 122 feet away from the body in the laneway. "These marks appeared to have been made quite some-time previous, when the earth was wet," the officer in charge, Corporal Sayeau, noted bluntly.

Meanwhile, as George Edens, the airman who had first found Lynne's body, walked out of the bush along the tractor trail, he caught sight of a much fresher set of tracks where the dirt trail met the pavement of the county road. "There were skid marks, maybe three or four feet long. Someone definitely spun their tires there," he said.

Two other airmen saw the same thing. Joseph Leger told police he saw a foot-long mark "which appeared to have been made by a car spinning." Corporal Harold Pudden described them as "quite deep and wide . . . as if someone got their front wheels up on the pavement and gunned it and the rear tires had spun and dug in."

No police cars had entered the laneway. The ambulance had not yet arrived. It sounded like a promising lead. Certainly, the newspapers thought so. "[George] Edens said the murderer then backed his car out of a field and his skidding tires dug holes in the laneway in a hasty flight upgrade to the road," one of the local papers reported.

That was the last public mention of the mysterious tire tracks, except for a brief reference to them by Edens at the trial. There is no indication the police ever pursued that lead. The tire tracks spotted by Edens and his fellow airmen—like much other evidence—quickly fell by the wayside as the police began their single-minded pursuit of their only suspect: the last person seen with Lynne—Steven Truscott.

**2**

WEEKEND FUN

Six days before they found her body, Lynne was dancing with the boy police soon fingered as her murderer. The party at Lorraine Wood's house on Friday, June 5, was a lot of fun. Lorraine's parents had a reputation for being unusually liberal. The cute boys were there, and the music made romantic dancing easy. Connie Francis's "Lipstick on Your Collar" and Frankie Avalon's "Bobbie Sox to Stockings" had just entered the Top 40 charts; "Lonely Boy" by Canada's own Paul Anka was soon to become Number 1.

Despite the sad look on her face, the small girl with the dark hair and dark eyes was thrilled to be invited to the party. At five foot three and 100 pounds, Lynne Harper was just two months shy of her thirteenth birthday. She was in a combined grade Seven and Eight group, which meant many of her classmates were more mature thirteen- or even fourteen-year-olds.

"Lynne really wanted to be in that crowd [of older teenagers]," recalls one of her closest friends and neighbours, Yvonne Danberger. "We were starting to get interested in boys."

The chaplain at the military base saw Lynne as a sweet girl who attended Sunday school and youth Bible class. Her Girl Guide leaders saw her as an ambitious organizer. But her friends saw another side. "She was a lonely person, kind of on the fringes," says Catherine O'Dell, who lived just a few houses down the street from Lynne. "She was kind of self-conscious about a scar on her face."

As a child, Lynne had cut her lip. Her friends heard different stories for the injury—either falling on a bottle of shampoo or falling through a window. "I didn't think it was that noticeable but a lot of people thought she had a harelip," recalls O'Dell. "It made her very self-conscious and she thought that people didn't like her because of that. You know what kids are like at that age."

Meryann Glover had moved onto the same street as Lynne a year before and was surprised when the spunky girl walked up to her door on her first day in the neighbourhood. "I remember her telling me that she didn't have too many friends and she asked if she could be friends with me," Meryann recalls. "She said she wasn't too popular. But she wanted to fit in—she really did."

Lynne was trying desperately to fit in on the night of the June 5 party, according to the teenage hostess, Lorraine Wood. "Lynne didn't have a special boyfriend and she kept asking the other boys to dance," Lorraine recounted. Lynne was particularly disappointed because her sometime companion, George Archibald, was not paying much attention to her that evening. "I took her out two or three times," explained George. "We went to the house parties and dances at the kids' houses." But he did not dance with her that night.

So Lynne turned her eyes to one of George's pals, a lanky athlete who never had to worry about being a "Lonely Boy." On the dance floor or on the football field, he was often the centre of attention. If Lynne was eager to be part of the "in" crowd, there was no boy more "in" than Steven Truscott.

"Steven was the kind of fellow who would stand out," remembers classmate Richard Gellatly. "He was the best at everything." Steven had light brown hair, hazel eyes and an almost impish grin that stretched from one ear to the other. He literally stood head and shoulders over most of his schoolmates in school photos: at five feet eight and a half inches, he was a towering, wiry figure who rapidly earned a reputation as an athlete of some skill. When the school's Ticat football team took home the Little Grey Cup in late November, the local paper ran a picture of the proud players. No one's smile was bigger than that of the tallest boy in the back row—Steven Truscott, identified as "the star of the team."

The smaller children liked Steve for his kindliness and tomfoolery. "He was nice, even though he was older," recalls Bill MacKay, who was just ten at the time. "In winter, when he had his toboggan, he'd throw me on the back of it and take me for a ride." The girls on the base saw Steven as a friendly boy, someone you felt safe around. "There was never any talk among the girls that he was a guy you had to watch out for," remembers a fellow pupil, Gail Coombs. Karen Daum remembers him as "the jock of the school; he was good-looking, good in sports and the girls liked him."

They did indeed. Karen Allen was the lucky one who called herself Steve's girlfriend, but back in 1959 small-town Ontario that didn't count for very much. "Boyfriend and girlfriend back then was just somebody you had a crush on," Karen says today. "I kind of liked him and he was a nice guy, so we'd play outside sometimes or talk through lunch hour."

Karen lived in a small village near Clinton and took a bus in every day to the school on the base. "Steve biked out to my village once," she remembers fondly. "Then we sat outside and talked for about fifteen minutes." Steven even sent her a Christmas card one year but was so shy he added a good friend's name beneath his own to make it look less intimate. A black-and-white photograph of the time shows Steve, sporting a crewcut and a beaming smile, sitting on a swing in the middle of winter with a long-haired, rosy-cheeked Karen.

On the last Friday night of her life, Lynne walked up to Steve and asked him to dance. Ever polite, the boy consented—but only danced with her briefly. He then partnered up with Lorraine, the party organizer, as a convenient escape.

"He just asked me if I would mind dancing with him as he didn't feel like dancing with Lynne any more," Lorraine later remembered. "She seemed to be following him around and he didn't specially care for her."

Lynne and Steve found themselves awkwardly dancing together in June of 1959 because of an accident of geography and history. They belonged to that special category of children that would eventually become known as "military brats": girls and boys who were bounced around the country, changing schools and friends every few years as their families followed their fathers' endless transfers to various bases across Canada and around the world. You made friends fast because you knew you were going to lose them quickly.

Clinton is nestled in the flat farmlands of southern Ontario, a three-hour drive west of Toronto. Just fifteen miles from town, the waves of Lake Huron cascade against the high cliffs that line the shore. In 1940, with war raging across the Atlantic, those cliffs held a special attraction to wartime planners because they resembled the white cliffs of Dover, where Britain was waging—and at the time, losing—a deadly air battle with the German Luftwaffe. The cliffs made Clinton an ideal location to build a secret air base to train airmen in a new technology known as radar.

After the war, as Cold War fever fuelled the need for more communications technology, RCAF Station Clinton became the largest radar and telecommunications training centre in the country. At one time, more than three thousand people lived and worked at the base, most of them unmarried, enlisted men holed up in the base barracks. To accommodate the growing number of airmen with families—this was, after all, the decade of the baby boomers—the air force built a small bedroom community next to the base, known as the Permanent Married Quarters (PMQs).

Most of the streets in the tiny community were named for Canada's provincial capitals. On his bike, Steven could circle the entire neighbourhood from Halifax Road to Winnipeg Road to Victoria Boulevard and Quebec Road in less than five minutes. The streets, never too busy with traffic, were filled with tricycles and scooters, plastic Hula Hoops and metal roller skates. But the clutter of childhood was the only disorder tolerated. Residents had to keep their lawns trimmed and neat according to military regulations; the station warrant officer could enforce this edict through the National Defence Act. Not surprisingly, the air force never had to mete out punishment for an unruly rose bush or chaotic marigolds; in the strict law-and-order atmosphere of the times, even the flowers and the blades of grass in Clinton seemed to stand at attention.

Where you lived depended, quite simply, on what insignia your father wore on his uniform. Officers and their families lived in a separate neighbourhood, segregated, in a manner of speaking, from the families of the lower ranks. While the children largely ignored the military hierarchy when it came to dances or sports, the caste system left its mark on daily life. "We didn't really hang around with the officers' kids much," recalls Karen Daum, whose father was a butcher on the base. "They seemed to be better off. They always had the best clothes; they always had money to buy stuff."

The Harpers were one of the more privileged families, their status confirmed by their proximity, on Victoria Boulevard, to the home of the base commanding officer. Flowered verandahs and large lawns were the perks of higher rank. Tall trees in front and back of the two-storey house offered Lynne's family shade in the hot summer months. Lynne's father, Leslie, at forty-two, was a successful flying officer. He had been a teacher before joining the air force in January 1940.

He and his wife, Shirley, had three children before they moved to Clinton in July 1957: Cheryl Lynne, born in New Brunswick on August 31, 1946; her older brother, Barry, sixteen by 1959; and five-year-old Jeffrey.

A dutiful daughter, Lynne always impressed her friends by spending time helping her mother, whose rheumatic hands made housework difficult. Still, Lynne sometimes yearned to break free of the confines of home. "Her home was always orderly and quiet. She loved to hang out at our house," her neighbour Yvonne recalls. The Danberger residence was the bustling beehive typical of a large family; Lynne was enthralled in particular by Yvonne's mother's talent for cooking restaurant food on the stove. "My mom made french fries quite a bit and Lynne thought that was quite neat," says Yvonne. "She wanted to spend time in our rowdy family. She used to enjoy the busyness of the house."

At the other of the end of the PMQs, past the wide homes and tall trees on Victoria Boulevard, down Regina Road and across Toronto Boulevard, along Quebec Road's simpler houses, lived another rowdy family, the Truscotts. Just up the way from the convenience store, their plain clapboard house had a small wooden porch, inevitably hidden by bikes, baseball bats and hockey sticks. The aluminum screen door was always banging as the Truscott boys scampered in and out. Steve shared a house with his older brother, Ken, sixteen, and two younger siblings, Bill and Barbara. His mother, Doris, was a petite bundle of nerves and energy. She cooked, cleaned and did laundry for her boisterous family.

The air force may have imposed its rules and regulations on the base, but inside the four walls of 2 Quebec Road, Doris was the supreme commander— and she brooked no slacking or insubordination within her ranks. "We were not overly strict," she insists, "but the children knew when they were told something, that was the way it was going to be." Steve's father, Dan, was a warrant officer, not a prominent rank, but Dan made up in exuberance what he lacked in stature. A jovial, slightly portly figure always willing to help organize events and play with the children, he was elected Man of the Year for doing the most for the welfare of young people at the base. "He was a prince of a man," says Margaret Coombs, the switchboard operator who was plugged in to the community in more ways than one. "He did more for the kids on the base than any other officer."

If you want to know what children are like, ask the man behind the candy counter. Back in the 1950s, Maynard Cory ran the Red and White, the convenience store on the Clinton air force base that was a favourite hangout for the children. Pop went for seven cents, a chocolate bar for a dime.

Lynne was a "tiny little thing" according to Cory. "I guess you notice people who wanted to be noticed, and she wanted to be noticed. She was pretty in a plain way. Kind of coquettish. You couldn't help but like her."

Steven, for his part, stood out because of his height—and his charm. "He was bigger for his age; he was also a better-looking chap," says Cory. "He'd be over by the pop counter and all the kids would be around him. He was never a bully, always a polite kid." Steve cherishes his memories of the candy counter. "You'd go in with maybe a quarter. Get nickel worth of this, nickel worth of that," he says. "You'd get a whole bag of goodies, Dubble Bubble gum with those comics, and blackballs—hard candy, about the size of a marble that you sucked on and watched as it changed colours."

If Steve was not hanging around the Red and White, there was always a good chance his friends would find him right across the street from the school at the sprawling, 150-acre farm owned by Bob Lawson. A rake-thin man with light blue eyes and a perpetual grin, Lawson, at twenty-two, was only a few years older than Steven and some of the teenagers, but his commanding height (well over six feet) and hard-working, no-nonsense approach to life made him seem much more senior to the children. Like all respected authority figures, Bob Lawson seemed to have lost his first name as far as the children were concerned; they simply referred to him as "Farmer Lawson." The children were always dropping by to play with the animals or watch him do chores. "Keeping them off was like keeping away the flies," Lawson says with a laugh. He sometimes feigned annoyance with the children, but in truth, he enjoyed their company.

"When I look back at it now, Bob Lawson must have had so much patience to put up with all of us kids," recalls Catherine O'Dell. "Everybody went over to Lawson's farm. Everybody. We'd hang over the fence and poke our heads in the barn. He was so good to us."

Steve was a more frequent visitor to the farm than most children, in part because of his curiosity and in part because Bob Lawson liked him so much.

Steve loved to help with the chores: picking up rocks from the fields, pulling out stumps, repairing the machinery. A whiz at mechanics and always eager to lend a hand, the strapping young boy struck Lawson as being a little more mature than the other kids. Steve was the only child Lawson ever let ride on his new Ferguson tractor. The boy and the farmer even cobbled together some discarded transmissions and other auto parts with the remnants of an old army truck and came up with a decent front-end loader. Steve spent hours working with Lawson on the farmer's classic 1929 Model A Ford.

Occasionally, some children would play in a heavily wooded area at the northern edge of the farm, commonly known as Lawson's bush. Later, when Lynne's body turned up there, the police built up a mythology about the woods as a sort of rural den of iniquity. "The bush was known as a real hangout, like the malls are now," says Dennis Alsop, one of the OPP officers who worked on the case. "Girls were being taken to the bush by the fellows in the town—that was well known." The reality was a bit more down to earth. The thick undergrowth and incessant mosquitoes made the woods fairly inhospitable for extended periods in the hot summer months. The ash, maple and elm trees, along with the small ditches, rocks and stumps, made the woods fun to explore, but it was hardly the lovers' lane of Clinton.

In terms of mating games, the closest thing the woods and the farm had to offer was the sighting of newborn calves. Lawson had forty head of cattle that year and finding a helpless young calf was always a treat for the children. Cows about to give birth often looked for an isolated corner for some privacy and protection. In late May, Steve and his friend Leslie Spillsbury found a young calf at the far end of Lawson's land, about a quarter of a mile from the road. The boys ran to show the farmer their discovery. "They were so proud," Bob Lawson remembers.

The bush was also a place of adventure. Steve and Leslie took their bikes to the edge of the bush and built a tree house in the woods. Lynne and her girlfriends were no strangers to the woods, either. "We were very familiar with all the farmers' fields around there," Yvonne Danberger explains. "We did a lot of hiking because we were in Girl Guides together. We'd cut down saplings and make them into tents. We'd light a fire and heat up a can of beans and talk."

On the weekend of June 6 and 7, Steve quickly finished his farm chores and then had the rest of the time to fool around: baseball, fishing—and a Saturday matinee. Every week, the children crowded into the theatre on the base, where a triple bill was ten cents. First, a weekly cliffhanger serial, which inevitably ended with the intrepid hero caught in a burning building or falling off a mountain peak, only to re-emerge unscathed the next week. Next, a cartoon or comedy from Our Gang or the Three Stooges. Then, to top it off, some wholesome family entertainment from Hollywood, feature films such as *The Shaggy Dog, The Ghost of Zorro* or *Gidget*.

In such glorious summer weather, however, most of the weekend fun was to be had outside. The school had wide play areas on all sides of the building, with a playground, swing sets, a football field and a baseball diamond. The school was the natural meeting point; every adventure or excursion to the farm or to the river seemed to start and end there.

Between Lawson's farm and the school lay a narrow, two-lane, paved rural route known by all as the county road. The road was the main artery that linked the school play area with the swimming hole in the Bayfield River, about one mile north. On any given summer afternoon, the county road would be crowded with bicycles, cars and pedestrians. Children were constantly walking or cycling up and down the road, carrying fishing poles, swimming trunks and towels. From the school, it was a pleasant, mainly downhill ride to the river; a bike could pick up a lot of speed as you coasted down the road. About a half mile on your journey, on the right-hand side of the road, there was a small laneway, a tractor trail where you could turn off and head into Farmer Lawson's bush. If you continued past the laneway, in a few moments you crossed the railway tracks and then the small concrete bridge that spanned the Bayfield River. From the bridge, it was only a few hundred yards to the busy Highway 8, a major provincial roadway.

The bridge was a small, cement structure with a short, forty-inch wall on either side. Bikes, baseball mitts and fishing gear would often be scattered by the railing. There were wide, rectangular holes at regular intervals all along the bridge wall, making it easy to stick a fishing rod through or watch for turtles in the water below. About six hundred feet east of the bridge, the river curved slightly and its waters deepened, forming a swimming hole where children splashed and frolicked for hours on end. It was a magical time, before pollution muddied the creeks and before holes in the ozone layer threatened the unprotected skin of youngsters. "We hung out down at the river quite a bit," recalls Douglas Oates, who was eleven at the time. "You could go down just about any time and you'd find somebody by the river."

The more adventurous children ventured past the river, down to the intersection and up the busy highway to a tiny white house where an old recluse named Edgar Hodges kept a few ponies. Hodges' quirky nature only added to the mystery and fun. "He had cysts all over his face, and his house was so tiny it was just like a dollhouse," remembers Meryann Glover, who visited the white house often with her friend Lynne. "We went over about once every two weeks or so. We couldn't ride the ponies, but we'd pat them or feed them apples."

It was a carefree time when children thought nothing of wandering a few miles from their home and sharing in the generosity of strangers. "I don't know how often me and a buddy just rode up some farm's driveway and said 'Hi' and suddenly found ourselves making new friends," remembers Mike Fisher, a nine-year-old back then, whom Lynne sometimes babysat. Lynne and her friends occasionally would make the short trip to the town of Clinton, just a two-mile walk down the highway from the base. Catherine O'Dell remembers hitchhiking into town with Lynne to go shopping or, in winter, thumbing a ride to go skating at the local rink. "Usually we'd just start walking, and then if a car went by, we'd just stick out our thumb," O'Dell says. "Everyone hitchhiked then. We weren't afraid. We never gave it a thought."

On Monday, June 8, the evening before she vanished, Lynne went to one of her favourite activities—the Girl Guides. "She was a good organizer and liked being in the public eye," recalled Isabelle White, one of the Guide leaders. "She was very intelligent and learned very quickly. Because of her strong will, she wasn't too popular with the other girls."

Lynne certainly had her run-ins with her friends. On that Monday, three days after the dance party at Lorraine Wood's house, Lynne got into an argument with her friends over her affection for Steve. One of her friends, Andrea Buck, had told another girl that Lynne had said she liked Steve.

Lynne confronted the girl. "Did Andrea tell you I liked Steven?"

"No, she didn't," came the meek reply.

Perhaps Lynne didn't believe her. At the Girl Guides meeting that Monday evening, Lynne got to hand out some prizes. Andrea wanted a red hairband but Lynne kept it and gave Andrea a scribbler instead.

When Lynne woke up the next morning, she must have placed the same band in her hair before setting off for school. Later, the police would find a red hairband just inches from her dead body.

## 3

## A BIKE RIDE INTO HISTORY

On Tuesday, June 9, the morning sunshine streamed through the class-room windows at A.V.M. Hugh Campbell School on the Clinton air base. The cool waters of the swimming hole beckoned and the excitement over the next day's county fair filled the air. Maitland Edgar could barely keep his students' minds on their work, much less their eyes focused on his blackboard. Teaching a combined class of grades Seven and Eight was hard enough at the best of times; it was next to impossible on a hot summer day. With less than three weeks left until the summer holidays, the children in Edgar's class were counting down their days to freedom.

Edgar had been vice-principal since 1951, but in a small twelve-room country school, administrative titles did not get you very far. He also had to teach history, geography, English and physical education to the military's offspring, even if he could not always impose military discipline on his rambunctious pupils.

Right by his desk, in the first seat of the middle row, sat Lynne Harper. The teacher put the twelve-year-old there for a reason. "She was a live wire, that one, a real chatterbox," Edgar says. "She was where you could keep her under control. But she never misbehaved or anything like that. I liked her a lot."

Her fellow students did not always agree. "She was pretty mouthy," says Meryann Glover, one of Lynne's few close friends. "One of those kids that always has their hand in the air—'Oh pick me, pick me, I know the answer!'"

In the last seat at the back of the classroom, at the end row right next to the windows, sat another of Maitland Edgar's favourite students, Steven Truscott. Edgar found him easygoing and responsible. "Steve wasn't strong academically, but he was average," Edgar says. "Sports were his passion, not studies."

Sitting near Steven was a more troublesome student, his friend Arnold "Butch" George. A strong, stocky boy, Butch had a well-earned reputation as a sometime brawler and a frequent fibber. Butch's aggressive push to be at the centre of attention came in part from the two obstacles that made him an outsider: he was a Native boy, and his father was an army man in an air force community.

Three seats away from Steve sat another outsider, desperate to be part of the crowd. Tall and thin, her face pockmarked with acne and her hair kept in dark Shirley Temple-like ringlets, Jocelyne Gaudet was teased by the older girls.

Unfortunately, Jocelyne's personality did not help her overcome her physical traits. "She was irritating. She was too loud," Meryann Glover recalls. "She was kind of forward—always pushing herself on people. She liked to let on she knew things." Yvonne Danberger, looking back with the perspective of an adult, wonders if Jocelyne's penchant for exaggerating or embellishing her importance came from her family. "She had a very dominant mother," Yvonne says. "A very matriarchal family with a mother who really did try to control her kids. Jocelyne always seemed to be trying to break free of something, but I didn't know what."

Vice-principal Edgar had more serious difficulties with both Jocelyne and Butch: "I recall with both of them there was just generally a problem of untruthfulness." No specific instances of misbehaviour stand out, he says, just a general tendency of untrustworthiness. A few small lies or exaggerations in school were just an annoyance; in a murder investigation, they could prove deadly.

When the school bell rang that afternoon, Lynne and Steve both dashed off to play separate games of baseball. Neither knew they would soon meet up again, back at the school. Neither of them could know that one's life would end violently and brutally, while the other's would be irrevocably shattered by what would transpire in the next few hours.

———

An eager substitute player on the baseball team, Lynne played only one inning that day when her team took on the challengers from the nearby town of Goderich. She was thrilled just the same. "Our team won and Lynne was very pleased," Helen Blair, a fourth-grade teacher who coached the team, later reported. Blair drove Lynne home. The girl talked eagerly with the teacher about her favourite sport, swimming. When Lynne came through her front door, her mother, Shirley Harper, glanced at the electric clock in the kitchen. It was 5:30 p.m.

The rest of the family had almost finished supper. "I was just getting my dessert when Lynne came in and sat down in her accustomed place," her father recalled. "I served her brown skin from the breastbone of the turkey and a four-inch slice of meat. Her mother had put just a bit of warm dressing on her plate because Lynne wasn't very fond of it, along with peas and potatoes." If Lynne wanted, there was bologna and ham in the fridge. And for dessert, her mother had on hand pineapple upside-down cake, and two other kinds of cake: chocolate with coconut icing and orange chiffon.

Her parents did not watch Lynne eat; they took their tea and coffee in the living room. Lynne bolted her meal in under fifteen minutes. It was 5:45 p.m. She desperately wanted to go swimming, not at the swimming hole where many of the children were gathering, but at the pool on the base. A neighbour was taking her younger brother, Jeffrey, to the pool, but her mother refused to ask the neighbour to take care of Lynne as well. "I couldn't ask him to take all my family," she told her daughter. Shirley Harper suggested Lynne get a pass to swim alone at the pool on the base. Lynne dashed out on her bike to try to secure the required permission from a base official, but she returned home within ten minutes, empty handed.

"She was a bit annoyed because I wouldn't let her go swimming," her mother later recounted, "but she didn't put up any fuss." Her father remembers that "she seemed resigned" to not being able to go to the pool.

Lynne promptly set about washing the supper dishes. "It must have taken about twenty minutes," Mrs. Harper estimated. Once done, Lynne walked to the back door without saying goodbye to her father, who was still sitting in the living room. Her mother was chatting with a neighbour, Betty McDougall, in the backyard. Lynne stopped for a moment to fondle Mrs.

McDougall's newborn baby and then strolled off. Her mother didn't ask Lynne where she was going and Lynne never said.

By now, it was 6:15 p.m. Shirley Harper's daughter headed down the road, wearing her turquoise shorts, a sleeveless white blouse and brown shoes. Around her neck, she proudly wore a locket sent to her by an aunt three weeks earlier. It had an RCAF crest in a heart made of Plexiglas. A gold chain looped through a hole at the top of the heart.

It was the last time her parents would ever see their daughter alive.

Like Lynne, Steve also spent the afternoon on a baseball diamond. He got home at about 5:15 and fooled around in his front yard. At about 5:50, his mother realized there was no more coffee and asked her son to go on a quick errand. "You'll have to hurry because the store closes in a few minutes," she called out. Steve returned promptly with the coffee in hand and a rip in the seat of his jeans at the top of his right leg, his mother remembers.

"How did you do that?" she asked, dismayed.

"On Bill's bike," Steve said sheepishly, trying to shift the blame to his brother's bicycle. "I also scratched myself."

"Oh, I think you'll live," his mother remembers saying. "Your pants will do; go on out and play for a few minutes until supper is ready."

Steve wolfed down his meal and darted out of the house as soon as he could. He knew he had to be home by 8:30 at the latest. He and his older brother, Ken, rotated babysitting duties; his parents were going out and it was Steve's turn to take care of his younger sister and brother. So his free time was cut short for the evening.

At about the same time Lynne was leaving her home, Steven was roaming around the base on his bike. A flashy green racer with foot-long streamers attached to the handlebars, it was a teenage boy's prized possession.

Gord Logan, a good friend, spotted Steven near the school and came up beside him. He asked Steve if he was going to go swimming.

"No, I don't think so," Steve replied. "I might be down later."

The county road was beginning to fill up with the usual after-dinner bustle of cars, bikes and strollers. Several people saw Steven around 6:30, biking up and down the road between the school and the bridge. Beatrice Geiger had borrowed her son's bike and, with her young daughter perched on the crossbar, bicycled down to the river. "I was riding slowly and Steven Truscott passed me, riding his bicycle," the air force mother said. "Steven went onto the bridge and then turned around and came back." Beatrice's son, Ken, was walking down to the river when his friend Robb Harrington picked him up on his bike and they both headed down to the river. Near Lawson's bush, they spotted Steven just sitting on his bike on the road.

"Your mother is down by the river," Steve yelled to Ken.

"I know, we're going there to swim," the youngster shouted back.

Another boy, Paul Desjardine, aged fourteen, was also heading to the river to go fishing, and remembered seeing Steve "just circling on his bicycle" on the county road near the bush. At the time, nobody thought anything of these sightings. Steve's actions appeared to be the aimless wanderings of a teenage boy on a lazy summer evening. But later, in the eyes of the police and the prosecution, Steven's journeys to the bridge and near the bush would become proof of a murderer on the prowl, plotting his crime.

For the children of Clinton, it was just another ordinary evening in an ordinary summer. Butch George was mowing Mrs. McDougall's lawn. Jocelyne Gaudet was washing the supper dishes. At the schoolyard, Bill MacKay, Stuart Westie and Warren Heatherall were throwing a baseball around. Down by the river, Richard Gellatly was thinking of biking home to change into his swimming trunks. Gord Logan was getting ready to fish, while Dougie Oates was busy hunting for turtles with Karen Daum. A ten-year-old named Philip Burns took his last dive in the river and was about to start his long hike home. Few of the children wore watches on their small wrists. None of them had any particular reason to remember specific events or exact times. "That night was nothing special," Steve recalls. "Nothing spectacular was going on. People are swimming. People are riding up and down the road. Nobody really has any reason to pay particular attention."

At 6:15 p.m., Lynne began making her way to the playground near the school. She ambled along Victoria and then onto Winnipeg Road, where she passed Genevieve Oates, on her lawn chatting with a neighbour. Lynne gave them a quick "Hello" and headed toward the end of the street. Oddly, instead of turning right and taking a direct path to the school playground, Lynne went through a small grove of trees and emerged on the other side where Winnipeg Road continued. Another resident who lived on the corner, Audrey Jackson, spotted her walking by her house.

Lynne did not arrive at the playground for twenty minutes, although it was a five-minute stroll from her house. The police and the prosecution, soon to be so meticulous in their timing of other children's activities, never seemed curious to fill these fifteen minutes of unaccounted time in Lynne's afternoon, a mystery that remains unsolved to this day. Jocelyne Gaudet, one of Lynne's friends and classmates, lived two doors down from Mrs. Jackson, and left her house around the same time, but it is not known if—by chance or by planning—Lynne bumped into her that evening.

When Lynne arrived at the school grounds around 6:35, Anne Nickerson, thirty-two, the Brown Owl for the 3rd Clinton Brownie pack, had her hands full preparing a scavenger hunt for an eager group of young girls. Lynne leapt at the chance to play big sister.

"Can I stay?" she asked.

Nickerson gladly accepted the offer. Lynne helped her organize the girls, five to a team. As the young scavengers headed out, Nickerson and Lynne talked under a tree for twenty minutes. "She just stood beside me and we chatted away," Nickerson later recounted. The girl seemed a little troubled. "She said she didn't want to go home, her mother was cross with her," Nickerson said, "but she seemed very joking about it."

"It wasn't too much longer until a young boy came by on his bike," Nickerson said. That young boy was Steven Truscott. Steve was wearing scruffy brown shoes with rubber soles, red jeans and a white shirt with a few holes near the neck for laces. The laces were missing, though; the shirt was a hand-me-down from a neighbour. "He sailed by on his bike," Dorothy Bohonus, another mother working with the Brownies, remembered. "And almost immediately Lynne went over and sat on the front wheel of his bike."

By all accounts it was Lynne who approached Steven and did most of the talking. The two Brownie mothers could not hear what they said and they paid no more attention to them. It had been just four days since Lynne had eagerly tried to dance with Steve at the house party; just twenty-four hours since she had quarrelled with her friends about her affection for the star athlete. Now Lynne had a chance to speak directly to the boy.

"What are you doing, Steve?" Lynne began, according to Steve's memory of their conversation.

"Well, I was going down to the river to see if any of the kids were there."

"Can I have a ride down to the highway?" she asked.

"Well, I'm going that way anyhow," came the simple reply.

An innocent moment, a fleeting exchange between two young people in a noisy school playground filled with Brownies and other excited children. "A tiny little moment that kind of changed everybody's life," Steven Truscott reflected forty years later.

Lynne and Steve set off for what was to become the most famous bike ride in Canadian legal history.

Their exact time of departure would be the subject of much dispute in the months and even in the years to come. The two adults supervising the Brownies, Nickerson and Bohonus, said they last saw Lynne and Steve sometime between 7:00 and 7:10. Only one of the women had a watch, and she had not looked at it for some time. Once they left the Brownie pack, Lynne and Steve still had to walk around the school to get onto the county road. At the far end of the building, the kindergarten classroom jutted out from the rest of the school. Steve says he glanced inside through the wide windows and caught sight of the clock on the wall. It was around 7:25 p.m., he remembers.

As Lynne and Steve circled the school, they passed several boys playing baseball. "Steve was pushing his bicycle and Lynne was walking up alongside him," said Warren Heatherall, who thought it was "around seven o'clock," but could not be sure. One of the other ballplayers, Stuart Westie, felt it was closer to 7:30, but also admitted he wasn't certain. Two younger boys playing in the same area gave later time estimates. One thought it was "between 7:15 and 7:30." The other put it at "about 7:25 p.m."

Once on the pavement of the county road, Lynne hopped on the crossbar of Steve's green racer. It was a slow but steady downhill ride north to the river and it did not take them much time to pick up speed. The wind swept across their faces, a refreshing relief from the day's oppressive heat. Lynne was laughing and smiling, turning her head frequently to talk to Steve. Steve would later tell police that Lynne told him she was upset her parents would not let her go swimming. She asked if he knew the person in a little white house not far from the highway, and said she might go down to see the ponies there.

On their right, they passed the golden fields of Lawson's farm. To their left, they approached a small farmhouse owned by the O'Brien family. They had only biked a few hundred feet when they passed Richard Gellatly, a classmate, heading south back toward the base. "I was down at the creek and I wanted to go swimming. So I had to go home to get my trunks and ask my parents if I could go back," Richard says. "That's when I came across Steven and Lynne." He put the time at about 7:25. It would have taken Richard only a couple of minutes to get to his house after seeing Steven, and his father later confirmed to police his son was home at about that time.

Steve and Lynne met Richard somewhere between the O'Brien farm and Lawson's bush, which ran for about nine hundred feet along the highway. At the end of the bush, Steve and Lynne came to the small tractor trail. No more than three or four minutes had elapsed since they left the school. They had travelled about 3,300 feet, three-fifths of a mile.

What next happened—or did not happen—is the crux of the entire Steven Truscott case. The events and consequences of the next few seconds would impassion and arouse the emotions and opinions of citizens, journalists, Supreme Court justices, politicians and prime ministers for the next four decades.

In the minds of the police, the prosecution and, eventually, a jury, Steven at this point made a sharp right turn, off the county road, and took Lynne—willingly or unwillingly—into the bush. There, he raped and strangled her.

According to Steven and his supporters, the teenage boy never veered off the county road at all. Instead, he continued to ride with Lynne past the bush and down toward the bridge and the river.

It was one or the other. Guilt or innocence. A teenage murderer or a helpless boy trapped on death row. The choices were stark. The evidence, either way, was not so clear.


According to Steve, he continued to bike with Lynne well past Lawson's bush, picking up speed as the road pitched down toward the river. After about fifteen hundred feet, they crossed the CNR tracks, and five hundred feet later they approached the small concrete bridge that spanned the Bayfield River.

The strongest support for Steve's account came from an eleven-year-old boy standing on that bridge. Dougie Oates had only one thing on his mind that evening, as he did most evenings: turtles. "At that time in my life I was heavy into nature. I'd go out, catch turtles and bring them home as pets for a while," he says. His memories are very precise, fixed in his mind because police questioned him within two days of the events. Dougie had left home around 6:00 p.m., but took his time getting to the river. He stopped for a few minutes along the road to observe two female cardinals. Once at the river, he watched as a friend snagged a turtle by the leg with his fishing line. Dougie then spotted a smaller turtle and went down under the bridge to grab it. He traded his small catch for the larger one. Pleased with his enterprise so far, the nature lover continued his hunt from the bridge when he caught sight of two people on a bike.

"To this day the one thing that still stands out for me is seeing both Steven and Lynne riding double across the bridge. They passed within feet of me. Couldn't see one of them without the other," he says now. "A boy and a girl riding double on a bike, you sat up and took notice." The turtle hunter said "Hi" and waved to the teenagers. Lynne smiled at him; Steve kept pedalling toward the highway. "There is absolutely no doubt in my mind I saw both of them," Doug says determinedly. "It's etched in my memory."

Dougie was not the only person who was certain he saw Steve and Lynne cross the bridge at that moment. The river was filled with children, most of them too busy horsing around to pay much attention to the traffic on the bridge. But one boy in the water did notice. Gord Logan, the boy who had asked Steve earlier at the school about his swimming plans, was at the swimming hole, about six hundred feet from the bridge. "I was standing by the river," Gord would later tell police. "I think it must have been nearly 7:30 when I saw her and Steve. I am sure it was her. She was wearing shorts, I think."

A third boy, Butch George, originally told police that as he swam in the river he also saw that "Steve and Lynne biked north." But he later recanted that statement. Steve told the police that down at the bridge he saw his friend Butch in the river. "He waved to me and I waved back," the police say Steven told them.

Once past the bridge, Steve says he rode Lynne along the final thirteen hundred feet to the highway and dropped her off at the intersection. Cars were whizzing by, going eastbound toward Seaforth and Stratford or westbound into Clinton and Goderich. A quick goodbye and the children separated. Lynne did not say anything more about where she was going. Steve turned back, heading south along the county road toward the river. Gord confirmed he saw Steve return to the bridge, this time alone, "about five minutes" after he first saw Steve cross the bridge with Lynne.

As Steve approached the bridge on his return trip, he was on the west side of the county road. He says he stopped and looked back to see if it was safe to cross the road to watch his friends in the swimming hole. As he glanced back, he says he saw what looked like a grey, 1959 Chevrolet car travelling eastbound on the highway. The car turned in slightly onto the county road, then traversed the road and stopped on the corner where Lynne was standing. The car was now parked on the county road, slightly at an angle, its rear bumper facing Steve.

He was fairly certain the car was a '59 Chevrolet because he had a teenage boy's fascination with cars. "That was the first year Chev changed the style of their car, and they had large fins going out like wings, and the tail lights looked like cat's eyes. And there was no other car around like that." (In fact, several models, such as the Ford '58 Fairlane, the '56 Victoria and the '57 T-Bird, all had prominent rear fins, but the '59 Chev was rather distinctive.)

Steve also caught a glimpse of something yellow or orange on the back bumper. The sun, slowly sinking in the western sky, was shining right on the fender and it could have been only a glare. "I couldn't tell whether it was a licence plate or a sticker or whatever," Steve says, another detail that would soon get hopelessly confused in the police records. (In 1959, Quebec plates had black numbers on a yellow background. Nova Scotia had light yellow plates; Manitoba had yellow on black. Nine American states—three of them on the border—had some kind of yellow on their plates.)

As he made his way over to the railing on the eastern side of the bridge, Steve thought nothing more about the car or Lynne. He saw several of his friends playing in the water, but he did not talk to anyone. Allan Oates, Dougie's sixteen-year-old brother, claimed he spotted Steve standing alone on the bridge around 7:45 p.m. Allan had been home watching his favourite television news program, *Panorama*, until 7:00 p.m., then wandered around the base until he found himself near the railway tracks, about eight hundred feet away from the bridge. "I remember seeing Steven. I could recognize him," Allan insists. "If you don't recognize someone you go to school with from that distance, there's something wrong with you." Steve says he lingered at the river for five to ten minutes, before heading back to the air force base where babysitting duties awaited.

Two boys, Dougie Oates and Gord Logan saw Lynne and Steve cross the bridge; two boys, Gord and Dougie's brother, Allan, saw Steve alone on the bridge a few minutes later. Over the next weeks and months, in various police grillings, courtroom testimonies and cross-examinations, the boys would never alter the details of what they saw. They would be called liars, conspirators or foolish lads with bad memories.

But they never budged.

If Gord Logan and Dougie and Allan Oates were certain they saw Steve and Lynne, or Steve alone, down by the bridge around 7:30 p.m., two other children would insist they had no luck finding Steve or Lynne that evening, despite their best efforts to track them down. But unlike the consistent and clear accounts by the Oates brothers and Gord Logan, the stories by Butch George and Jocelyne Gaudet were confusing, conflicting and constantly changing.

After he finished mowing the neighbour's lawn around 6:30, Butch George says he rode his bike to Steve's house. "Is Steve home?" he yelled from the front yard, and someone—he says he thinks it was Steve's mother—answered back, "He isn't home."

Butch rode his bike down the county road toward the river and by the time he reached Lawson's bush, he saw a young boy named Philip Burns walking up toward the air force base. "He got off his bike as he came up to me and asked me if I saw Steve or Lynne," Philip later recalled. "I said I never saw them." Philip, ten, did tell Butch that he'd just met Jocelyne Gaudet near the laneway into the bush. She had also asked him, Philip later told police, "if I saw Steve and Lynne, but I hadn't."

Butch soon caught up with Jocelyne just as she was coming out of the laneway. Jocelyne claimed she had walked about two hundred feet down the tractor trail—very close to where Lynne's body was eventually found—looking for Steve. She had a date with the boy to go looking for calves in the bush, she later told police. "I didn't tell anyone about this plan to meet because Steven told me not to tell anyone," she said.

Jocelyne and Butch agreed they met near the laneway, but they agreed on little else. In Butch's version, their brief exchange went like this:

"Have you seen Steven?" he asked her.

"No," Jocelyne said. "Have you seen Lynne?"

"No," Butch replied. "If I see Lynne I'll tell you."

"Okay," said the girl.

According to Jocelyne, *she* was the one who asked Butch if he had seen Steven, not Lynne, and Butch said no. "I . . . told him if he saw Steven to give me a whistle." By Jocelyne's account, her encounter with Butch took place shortly after 6:30; by Butch's account, it was well after 7:00. Both of them said they then proceeded—separately—down to the river. Butch says when he was by a rock pile at the river, he saw Jocelyne near the bridge, and she asked him again if he had seen Lynne and he said no. Jocelyne says that she saw Butch at the river, but did not talk with him; she only asked another boy about the fishing. Jocelyne said she was only at the bridge "for about ten minutes" before heading back toward the base—no one besides Butch would ever corroborate her claim to be at the bridge that night.

Jocelyne, Butch and Philip all told different—and at times contradictory—stories about not seeing Steve or Lynne that evening. But their testimonies would later form the centrepiece of the prosecution's eyewitness case against Steven Truscott. The three children did not see Steve, the argument went, because when Jocelyne, Butch and Philip were near the bush, Steve was in the woods less than three hundred feet away, strangling Lynne to death.

In the minds of the police, when the coast was clear, Steven emerged from the bush where he had left Lynne's lifeless body, walked along the laneway and then biked peacefully up the road until he reached the school. By Steven's account, after having dropped off Lynne at the highway, he simply left the bridge and headed home.

Either way, nobody disputes that Steven was at the school grounds around 8:00 p.m., although there would be quibbling about the exact time of his return. There would be no disagreement over the key fact that more than a dozen children saw him immediately upon his return to the school and everyone said he looked normal, as calm as he always was.

"What did you do with Harper? Feed her to the fish?" teased one of the boys playing ball.

"No, I just left her off at the highway like she asked," Steve replied.

Steve then made his way around the corner of the school near the basketball courts and headed to the swings, where an older group of teenagers were hanging out. "A bunch of the girls and I had just gone up there and we were sitting, swinging," recalled Lorraine Wood, who had danced with Steve four days before at her party. Several boys, including Steve's older brother, Ken, joined the girls. Lorraine and two of her friends estimated Steve showed up at their neck of the playground about 8:10 to 8:15. One of the boys said it was closer to 8:00 p.m. To Lorraine, Steve looked "normal." Her friend Lyn Johnston commented later: "His appearance seemed about the same as usual." John Carew said Steve looked and acted "the same as he was any other time." None of the teenagers noticed any scratches or sweat, much less any blood, on Steve's face or arms.

Ken reminded his younger brother he had to go home soon to babysit.

"Yes, I know, I'm going," Steve said.

"If you're going, you may as well leave me the big bike," Ken said jokingly. He was envious that Steve had a shiny racer, while he had to make do with an older bike.

"All right."

The Truscott boys then joked about exchanging shoes.

"You're wearing my shoes," Steve teased.

"Do you want them?" Ken asked.

"No," Steve replied good-naturedly.

"If you aren't home in a few minutes, I'll get after you," Ken taunted his brother, and Steve promptly took off across the school grounds for home.

"I made it, Mom!" he exclaimed as he barged into the house.

"You're lucky," said Doris, never one to tolerate tardiness. "Where were you?"

"Riding down past the river and up at the school with the kids," Steve explained.

She gave Steve instructions for babysitting his younger siblings. Bill had some homework to do, and Barbara had to be put to bed no later than 9:00 p.m. With Steve safe at home, his mother went upstairs to put on her earrings. Then, around 8:45 p.m., Doris and Dan Truscott joined their neighbours for an evening of food and conversation at the Sergeants' Mess.

Steven grabbed some snacks from the kitchen and prepared himself for a boring night of babysitting. There was nothing on TV he cared to watch, and in any case, the picture tube on the set was going. He slumped down and relaxed, oblivious to the trouble that was beginning to brew all around him.

**4**

A GIRL GOES MISSING

While Steve was babysitting his siblings, several of his friends lingered by the river. They dried themselves slowly in the cool evening air, gathered up their clothes and fishing rods on the riverbank and headed up the county road. Around 8:20 p.m., three boys biked back to the base together: Butch George, Richard Gellatly and Kenny Geiger. As they made their way up the hill, past the railway tracks and Farmer Lawson's bush, they chatted and bragged about the day's adventures. Richard remarked he had met Steve with Lynne on his bike. Then, Kenny remembers, Butch said something odd: "Butch said Steve and Lynne were in the bush but he didn't know what they were doing."

This was the first time anyone ever mentioned Steve and Lynne together in the woods. "Steve and Lynne were in the bush." Harmless words at the time, but words that would soon take on a much more ominous tone, and that came from the mouth of one of Steve's best pals.

By all accounts, Arnold "Butch" George was not the most popular kid at the base. A "ruffian," one classmate called him. "Loud" is how Maynard Cory, the convenience store owner, remembers him. "He was a meanie, a smartass,"

Karen Daum, Butch's neighbour, recalls, remembering his taunts and fisticuffs.

Undoubtedly, some of the hostility came from prejudice—Butch was an outgoing Native boy in a conservative, lily-white military community. His father was a lowly butcher in the supply and services department (the same section headed by Lynne's father). Arnold lived in a somewhat dilapidated house at 32 Edmonton Road with an older sister, two younger twin brothers and a teenage uncle or cousin—no one was really sure—named Mike. Karen Daum remembers them as "a bit wild. Sometimes his mother would come outside. And then his father would come out and yell at her."

Butch's buddies, Steve among them, appreciated his reputation as a bit of a rascal: hanging around Butch always meant a good time, a sense of adventure and daring. A muscular boy, Butch stood next to Steve in the back row for team photographs, with dark eyes, a mop of hair and an eager smile.

What bothered the other children the most about Butch was his untrustworthiness. "He was the biggest liar I've ever met," says Bryan Glover, a classmate and a friend of Steve's. "He lied so much that you wondered if he would even remember what he said twenty minutes later. It would drive you crazy." Catherine O'Dell has a somewhat more sympathetic take on Butch, who used to hang around her home quite often. "He changed his stories every day. He fabricated a lot. I think he was so used to making stuff up that it was just a reflex. I remember my mom asking him one day how come he lied so much. He just kind of shrugged it off and laughed," she says. "As I look back now I wonder if, as an 'Indian boy,' he did it because he wanted to be something extra special and wanted to get people's attention."

Butch certainly started getting people's attention on Tuesday evening by telling anyone who would listen that Steve had taken Lynne into the bush. It is possible Butch got the idea to start this tale by putting two and two together. Around 7:15, at the entrance to the tractor trail leading to the bush, he met Jocelyne, who he said told him she was looking for Lynne. About fifteen minutes later, according to Butch's first story to police, when he was down at the river he saw Steve and Lynne go across the bridge on Steve's bike. Less than an hour later, Richard Gellatly told Butch he also had seen Steve and Lynne on the bike. So perhaps Butch put Jocelyne's search next to the bush together with the sightings of Lynne and Steve on the road and came up with the perfect tease: Steve had taken Lynne into the bush.

In any event, Butch's story appeared to be a work in progress. At various points, Butch started telling people Steve "was going" to take Lynne there, which implied some prior knowledge of Steve's plans; or that he "heard" that Steve was in the bush, presumably from some unnamed third party; or that he "saw" Steve go into the bush with his own eyes, though he never explained where he was or what time he made this observation.

On Tuesday night, soon after saying goodbye to Kenny and Richard when they reached the base, Butch ran into Allan Durnin, another fourteen-year-old. Allan was playing with his bow and arrow set, using a cardboard box up against a post as a target.

"Truscott is in the bush with Harper," Butch called out.

"Oh, is that right?" an unimpressed Allan replied.

"Yeah," Butch said and went on his way. Allan didn't think much of it at the time. "What it meant was that he was in the bush with Harper trying to do whatever fourteen-year-old boys do," he recalls thinking. "Mess around—but nothing serious."

A few minutes later, Butch had reached Steve's house. It was around 8:45 p.m.; Steve's parents had already left for the evening. Butch first told the police the two friends never talked about Lynne that night; but then he changed his mind and said the following conversation took place:

"Where have you been all this time?" Butch claimed to have asked.

"Down by the river."

"How come you rode Lynne down there?"

"Oh, she wanted a lift down to the highway."

"What was she doing along the bush with you?" Butch asked.

"We were looking for a cow and a calf. What do you want to know that for?"

"Skip it, let's play ball."

Steve denies this conversation took place. Arnold told so many versions of the story, it is hard to make sense of what really happened. There were no independent witnesses.

There were, however, several witnesses for Butch's next performance. As darkness settled over the base, the older boys congregated at the Custard Cup, the local ice cream stand. Paul Desjardine, Tom Gillette, George Archibald and Bryan Glover met up with Butch. The stars were just starting to come out; the crickets competed with the noisy banter of the teenagers.

It was a time to relax and savour the day's adventures. Butch bought a bottle of pop and a treat called a Brown Derby. All four of the other boys told slightly different accounts of Butch's boasts that night. "We bought some custard and were just talking on the benches," George Archibald said later. "Butch said he saw Steve go into the woods with Lynne." Paul remembered it more as if Butch was somehow aware of Steve's plans: "Butch said Steve was taking Lynne into the woods. I didn't recall that he said he *saw him* take Lynne into the woods. The way I recall it is that Butch said that Steve *was going to take her* into the bush."

What everyone agrees upon is that no one took Butch's tale seriously. "I don't think we believed him or paid much attention," said George Archibald. "[We] just thought it was funny." Funny because the boys could not imagine their pal Steve, the school jock and a "hunk" in the eyes of many of the older girls, trying to make a pass at a young girl they saw as a bit of a misfit. "My only reaction to it was surprise—that Steven would be even associating with Lynne," Bryan recalls. "Steve was one of the most popular guys in the school and there were lots of girls in the school who liked him. I could imagine Lynne being attracted to Steve but I can't picture it the other way around." Tom said of Butch that he "says a lot of stuff and you didn't know whether to believe it or not." Paul was more blunt: "We didn't believe Butch." Even Butch himself conceded his Custard Cup boast was a bomb: "They said 'I bet!' and they were jeering at me."

They had good reason to jeer. The boy nobody trusted could not get his story straight. Earlier that evening Butch was right near the bush, supposedly looking for Steve, when he met Jocelyne. Yet he told her he had not seen Lynne or Steve. Within two hours, he was telling seven different boys he had indeed seen Steve go into the bush with Lynne. Over the next six days, he would change his story at least three times.

But it did not matter much whether Butch's tale was true or not. It quickly took on a life of its own. In the next two days, other children would hear his story about Steve taking Lynne into the bush and tease Steve about it; Steve would react with frustration, sometimes with what others saw as anger. The police would later seize on that reaction as yet another indication of guilt.

And it all started from a boy his friends called "the biggest liar you ever met."

While the teenagers were amusing themselves at the Custard Cup, the other residents of the Clinton air force base settled in for another quiet summer night. The constant flicker of black-and-white images danced through the small windows of the homes. Television sets were still a novelty in Canada after their introduction only six years earlier. That night, the parents enjoyed Pierre Berton and the other panelists on *Front Page Challenge* while the children watched "Wyatt Earp" mete out frontier justice, swiftly and efficiently arresting—if not killing—the bad guys.

The sun set that evening at 9:08 p.m. The coolness of a peaceful June evening was a welcome break from the heat wave. But at 15 Victoria Boulevard, no one was relaxing. Lynne Harper had still not shown up.

Most of the other children on the base were safely indoors by then. "Lynne's come-in time is 9:00 and her bedtime is 9:30," her mother later told police. "She didn't come back and we raised the alarm about 9:15 by asking [her older brother] Barry to go check. We thought she was only being naughty." Lynne's father joined in the search, while Shirley stayed behind, anxiously walking around the house several times and waiting on the back step.

Around 10:30 p.m., George Archibald, the sometime boyfriend of Lynne's, arrived at the Harpers' front yard. He had just come from the Custard Cup; perhaps his jealousy was tweaked by Butch's tale about Steve going into the bush with Lynne. Lynne had also promised to lend George her sleeping bag for a "sleep-out" he was planning.

George saw Barry outside the Harper home and asked him if Lynne was still up.

"No," said Barry, "she isn't in."

"She isn't home," Lynne's mother said. "Do you know where she is?"

George said he didn't. "I could tell already there was something seriously wrong."

Meanwhile, over at the Sergeants' Mess, Doris and Dan Truscott and their friends were wrapping up the evening's festivities. Steve's parents returned home by eleven to find him and the other children fast asleep. Doris woke up Steve's younger brother, Bill, to take him to the bathroom. Then the lights went out at 2 Quebec Road.

The first officially recorded concern of Lynne Harper's whereabouts came at 11:20 p.m. Leslie Harper went to see Flight Sgt. Frank Johnson, a neighbour who also happened to be the NCO in charge of the air force police.

According to the official military logs, Johnson notified the police with a cursory message:

> Lynne Harper, age 12 years, five foot three
> inches tall, 100 lbs. White print blouse,
> blue shorts. That she hadn't been home
> since about 1900 hrs and that it was
> possible she was hitchhiking to her grand-
> mother's in Port Stanley, Ontario.

The next few minutes saw a flurry of activity. Corporal William A. Webb was on duty at the RCAF guardhouse when he got a phone call from Lynne's father at 11:25 p.m. "Flying Officer Harper sounded very distressed," he reported. "When further questioned as to any possible place the girl might have gone to, Flying Officer Harper stated that she might have headed for Port Stanley, Ontario, where her grandmother was living."

At 11:30, Webb called the Exeter detachment of the OPP. He relayed a description of the girl and "in view of the possibility of the girl going to Port Stanley requested that all provincial police cars en route might be notified to be on the lookout." Webb sent an officer to check the swimming pool Lynne had so desperately wanted to visit. The officer reported "negative results" at 11:40 p.m.

Police cruiser 685 was on patrol in the Clinton area when the dispatcher's call came: "Proceed to RCAF guardhouse to check on the report of a missing person." Constable Donald Weston was at the base in eight minutes. At the Harper home, he obtained a photograph of the missing girl. Lynne's father reiterated his fear that their daughter had run away. "Flying Officer [Harper] believed Lynne may have gone to her grandparents' home," Constable Weston reported. He notified the Clinton police and patrolled the highway in the area.

In the space of about fifteen minutes, three OPP and air force police officers, in three separate reports, all indicated that Lynne was probably a hitchhiking runaway, information that only could have come from Lynne's parents. Clearly their first impulse was that their missing daughter had tried to flee to her grandmother's some eighty miles away. Months later, when Steven Truscott was on trial for the murder of their daughter, Lynne's mother denied under oath that as far as she knew Lynne ever hitchhiked. Friends such as Catherine O'Dell, with whom Lynne did in fact thumb rides, were not called upon to contradict Mrs. Harper. The prosecution implied that Lynne had neither the disposition nor the desire to run away.

The defence team and the jurors never saw the police reports from June 9 that suggested quite the opposite. The reports remained hidden until now.

The police broadcast Lynne's physical description to ten nearby counties over the OPP radio network, and passed on the information to radio stations in the neighbouring towns of Wingham and London. "The Harpers left the lights burning all night, the drapes open," recalled a neighbour. "I imagine [they were] wanting Lynne to know that they were waiting for her to come home."

For years to come the children of Clinton would remember where they were on June 9, 1959. Kevin Mattinson had whiled away the early evening up in his favourite cherry tree, near the ball field. "We spent a lot of time in that tree," he says fondly. "With our overactive imaginations, it was sometimes a spaceship or a pirate ship." He could see the schoolyard where Steve had met Lynne before they set off on their bike ride. He could see the county road that led down to the bush and the river. For Kevin and the other children of Clinton, it had been a summer night just like any other. But in the next few days, everything in their world would be turned upside down. Teasing comments would become serious accusations, confused memories would become set in stone as definitive accounts, and friends would become liars.

"And so it was the end of anything that could've been called childhood," Kevin recalls. "The adults had gone mad, wild in fear and deception; the children, wrenched from their innocence. A horror show beyond belief."

## 5

## THE QUESTIONS BEGIN

From their upstairs window, Lynne's parents could gaze eastward as the sun rose over the crop fields of Lawson's farm across the county road. The old barn caught the early rays; in the distance the cows were out in the pasture. Farther to the north, down toward the river, they could see the deep, thick bushes where their daughter's body would soon be discovered.

It did not take long on Wednesday, June 10, for the blazing sun to burn off the morning dew from the neatly trimmed lawns at RCAF Station Clinton. Alarm clocks clamoured, coffee pots simmered and the mercury in the thermometers inched steadily upward; it would not stop until it hit ninety degrees. In homes across the PMQs, youngsters were getting their morning fix of *Captain Kangaroo*. As the older children stumbled out of bed, they realized with relief and excitement that today they only had to sit through half a day of classes—school would end at noon because of a local fair. It had all the makings of a beautiful summer day.

But at the Harper home, there was a growing sense of dread. There was still no sign of their little girl. At 7:30 a.m., Leslie Harper went to see the father of Gary Hoyer, one of Lynne's friends. Harper learned that it was possible one of the Truscott boys had seen his daughter, so he headed to their home. On the way, he bumped into Steve's father.

"Lynne has been missing all night and I have been asking children if they saw her," he said, according to Dan Truscott. "Do you mind if I go and ask your boys if they saw Lynne last night?"

"Go right ahead," Dan replied.

On the second floor of their small house, the Truscott children were scrambling to get ready for school. "Change your clothes because I'm going to wash," Doris Truscott told her clan. She laid out fresh clothes for her two youngest, Barbara and Bill. Steve gave her the dirty red jeans he had worn the day before and put on a clean pair. In the kitchen, Doris made toast for the children; they would get their own cereal. But before Steven could sit down to eat, there was someone at the door.

Lynne's father stood outside the side door and heard footsteps on a flight of stairs. When the door opened, Mrs. Truscott was standing in the entrance-way. Ken was on the basement stairs shining his shoes; Steve was in the kitchen looking down into the stairwell.

"I was wondering if your boys had seen Lynne?" Harper asked.

"Lynne who?" Doris asked. The Harpers were an officer's family and she did not know them or their children very well.

"Lynne Harper," said her father. Doris turned to Ken and asked him.

"No," he said. Doris looked up inquiringly at her younger son.

"Yes," said Steve, "I took her to the corner on my bicycle and she hitched a ride on Number 8 Highway."

"Come here, down to the step," his mother said, so Steve could be closer to the visitor in the doorway.

"Are you sure, Steven?" asked the worried father.

"Yes."

"'Oh my God!'" Doris Truscott remembers Lynne's father exclaiming. The information seemed to confirm his fear that his impetuous daughter had taken flight to her grandmother's house. For the moment, it was the only explanation the Harpers had for Lynne's sudden disappearance. Her older brother, Barry, told a friend that morning his sister "had taken off." She was angry, he said, and might have tried to hitchhike to visit her grandparents.

For the military and police authorities, there was still no need to panic. An official air force log for that day records that "a search was not deemed necessary at that particular time," in part because the majority of the air force personnel "were busy on other important matters and were not available for a search." At the OPP station in Goderich, Lynne's absence

44

was filed under the dry police title of "General Occurrence #250-59." Constable Donald Hobbs read about the missing girl when he reported for duty that morning at eight and drove out to the air base to see if there was any news. A worried Leslie Harper told Hobbs "that his daughter was of a jealous and high-strung nature," according to the officer's report. Harper gave the constable a description of Lynne and informed him that he had learned that a young boy on the base gave his girl a ride to the highway the night before. "I then decided I would have a chat with Steven Truscott," Hobbs said.

With laughter and yells and the usual pushing and shoving, the children made their way into Maitland Edgar's classroom. Once inside, they quickly noticed something strange: there was one empty chair in the front row. Lynne Harper was not at school. It did not take long for everyone to start whispering about the rumours that their classmate had run away from home the night before.

Initially, the school day began the way it always did: a few announcements over the intercom, the Lord's Prayer and "God Save the Queen." But at 9:15, the quiet routine at A.V.M. Hugh Campbell School was disrupted by the appearance of a vehicle the children rarely saw on the school grounds—a police cruiser. On their way to the school, Constable Hobbs, accompanied by Flight Sgt. Frank Johnson of the RCAF police, had picked up Steve's father at his office on the base. Dan Truscott went in to get his son. "I had Steven come out and he sat in the front seat of the cruiser," Hobbs later recalled.

According to Constable Hobbs, the following conversation took place:

"Steven, do you know that Lynne Harper is missing?"

"Yes."

"Did you give Lynne a ride on a motorcycle?" the officer asked.

"I gave her a ride on a bicycle, not a motorcycle," the boy said.

"Where did you pick Lynne up?"

"Outside the school."

"What time was it?"

According to Hobbs, Steve answered, "Between 7:00 and 7:30," (although Johnson remembered Steve saying "at about 7:25 and 7:30.")

"Did she say anything to you?"

"She said she knew the people in the little white house along the highway—said she might go down to see the ponies. She said she had to be home by 8:00 or 8:30."

"Where did you drop her off?"

"I took her to the highway and dropped her off, and then I returned to the bridge over the river."

"Did you see Lynne again?"

Yes, he did, Steve answered. It is worth quoting the constable's later testimony at length because it is the first official police recording of Steven's story:

"I asked him if he saw Lynne again and he said he looked back and saw her get into a car. He *believed* it to be a late model Chev. He mentioned a lot of chrome and it *could have been* a Bel Air version. He said the car *appeared* to have a yellow licence. He said, 'There was no one in the rear; I am not sure how many were in the front.' At that, our conversation ended."

It was the morning right after Lynne's disappearance and presumably Steven's memory of the events of the previous evening was the freshest it would ever be. His recollection was peppered with "believed" and "could have" and "appeared"—a far cry from the definitive descriptions that the police and prosecution would later try to attribute to him. It would be the first of seven interviews with police over the next seventy-two hours—and every time, Steve told virtually the identical story.

Looking back at his first encounters with the police, Steven Truscott marvels at how quickly a child's casual comments became fixed and rigid in the eyes of the police. "You tell the police, 'I think this, I think that' . . . I did not know the difference between a Bel Air and the other Chevs. To me, a Chev was a Chev. But if you look at the [police] records, it eventually says a Chev Bel Air."

The police radio in the car crackled as Hobbs received an urgent message about another case. His short interview with the boy was over and Steve returned to his curious classmates. Meanwhile, the air force police officer Frank Johnson decided to check out the little white house Steve had mentioned. Not far east along the highway from the corner where Steve said he had left Lynne, Johnson came upon a small shack on the left-hand side of the road. Edgar Hodges, seventy-one, lived alone, doing odd farm jobs from time to time. He kept two Shetland ponies and sometimes children would drop by to pat them. Hodges told the police officer he knew

Lynne because she had visited "on previous occasions," he said, but he had not seen the girl on Tuesday night.

By recess time, the school was abuzz with excitement over Lynne's disappearance. "We were just kind of puzzled," remembers Mike Fisher. "Not really afraid for her or anything, just figuring she was in a bunch of trouble for falling asleep somewhere. She'd turn up soon."

Steve's friends were intrigued by his talk with the police officers. "We knew he was the last one to see Lynne Harper, so there were quite a few asking him all about it," said Tom Gillette. A group of children gathered around Steve, but Gillette could not hear what they were saying. As the bell rang, Tom and Steve walked into the school alone. "I turned around and he was beside me," Gillette would later testify. "He said he heard a calf in the woods and he went in to investigate." It seemed a curious detour into the bush for a boy who had insisted he gave a girl a ride straight to the highway. It would not be last time that day someone quoted Steve talking about calves in Lawson's bush.

At lunchtime, as the children left the school for the day, George Archibald said he overheard Steve talking to Butch near the horseshoe pits. Archibald readily admits he was about fifteen feet away from the two boys and only heard snatches of the conversation. To the best of his recollection, this is what was said:

"What were you doing in the woods with Lynne?" Butch asked.

"I wasn't in the woods with Lynne, was I?" Steve answered.

"No, I guess it was somebody else," Butch said.

"No, I wasn't. I was chasing a cow, wasn't I, Butch?" Steve continued.

"Yes," said his friend.

An even stranger conversation that afternoon, involving another member of the George family, was reported to police. Mike George was a fifteen-year-old relative of Butch's who lived with the Georges in their house on Edmonton Road. Karen Daum remembers Butch and Mike would frequently get into scraps and wrestling matches on the front lawn.

"Did you know that Lynne was raped?" Mike George said, according to Joyce Harrington, one of the mothers on the base. The account appears in a brief police note.

If true, it was an eerie remark. Most people still thought Lynne was only an adventurous hitchhiker. Butch had been spreading tales of seeing Steve go into the bush with Lynne, but never suggested any sort of foul play. How would Mike George know the presumed runaway had been raped?

Oddly, police records give no indication they followed up on that disturbing lead. The files show no statements from or interviews with Mike George or Joyce Harrington. Instead, the OPP seemed much more interested in questioning Steven. When Steve went home for a quick lunch, he faced his second police interview in three hours. This time there was a new man on the scene, Const. Donald Trumbley, a methodical officer who would do a lot of the legwork for the OPP on the case. Again sitting in the front seat of a cruiser, Steve repeated his story. According to Trumbley's notes, Steve insisted the car he saw at the corner was a '59 Chevrolet. This time, Steve provided more details: he said it had whitewalled tires with "a lot of chrome and with yellow markers." Trumbley asked the boy how he could tell what make of car it was. "By the shape of the rear of the car," he said. He described how the car pulled onto the county road from the highway, onto the shoulder, then crossed the road and parked on the right side, with its rear fender facing the bridge. The police officer recorded that Steve referred to seeing "something" yellow at the rear of the car.

With these details in hand, the officers left to continue the hunt for the missing girl. As far as the police were concerned, Lynne Harper was still a runaway. Constable Hobbs took a picture of Lynne to the nearest television station in Wingham and later sent a photo to the larger TV outlet in London.

At 4:00 p.m. Constable Trumbley drove to the bridge over the Bayfield River where Steve told him he had seen Lynne and the car. "I observed traffic proceeding up and down Number 8 Highway. I couldn't distinguish any licence numbers," the officer later said. The police would later say this was when they began to have their first doubts about Steve's story. But Steve had said nothing about reading any specific licence numbers on a car. He had simply told police he saw something yellow on the back of the car, possibly a licence plate. Steve also said he was looking at a car parked on the edge of the county road, not at vehicles speeding along the highway.

Trumbley went back to Steve's house, but the boy was not home. That afternoon Steve and his friends had gone to another of the children's favourite swimming holes, the gravel pits near Holmesville, between Clinton and Goderich. Stripped down to their waists in shorts or bathing suits, the boys horsed around and hopped in and out of the water under the scorching sun. No one noticed any scratches, scars or anything else unusual about their friend Steve.

By 5:00 p.m., when Constable Trumbley returned to the Truscott home, he had more luck. He found Steve there with his mother and convinced them both to accompany him down to the bridge. "I asked Steven where he was standing when he observed the car picking up Lynne Harper, and he walked over to a point ten feet south of the north end of the bridge," Trumbley later recounted. "I observed traffic going up and down Number 8 Highway. I still couldn't observe any licence numbers." It was, as before, a perplexing comment because no one—certainly not Steve, according to the police records—had talked about spotting digits on a plate. As he walked back to the car with Steve and another officer, Trumbley says he repeated the same comment about licence numbers. Doris Truscott, who had remained in the police cruiser, said: "Maybe it wasn't a yellow licence marker Steven had seen at all. Maybe it was a sticker like we have on our car." The Truscotts, like many families, had a tourist sticker from one of the local attractions on their rear fender.

According to police notes, Steve said nothing at all.

His mother was beginning to worry about the police's interest in Steve. "He was just trying to be as helpful as he could," Doris thought. "Why were they questioning him so much?"

By the time the sun was beginning to cast long shadows on the playgrounds and lawns of the air force community, even the youngest children were gossiping about Steve's role in Lynne's mysterious disappearance. Some families were already beginning to form their suspicions. "We knew that she'd last been seen at the school the evening before, riding off with Steven, and that he said she got into a car at the highway," remembers then-nine-year-old Mike Fisher. "We figured he was probably in a lot of trouble for giving her that ride; he should have known she wasn't supposed to go down there by herself. . . . She wanted to go to the pony place—so why did he let her off at the corner instead of taking her all the way? And how was she supposed to get home? And what's she doing getting into a strange car? I guess maybe it was by the end of that day that I started to think something about his story didn't make sense."

Around suppertime that Wednesday, Butch George claims he dropped by his friend Steve's house. Steve denies that the visit, much less the ensuing

49

conversation, took place. Butch, for his part, was very precise about the details—he just kept changing them. He would later testify at a preliminary hearing the encounter occurred at "about five o'clock." Five o'clock hardly seemed like a propitious moment for two teen plotters to meet, since the police called on Steven around the same time. At the trial, Butch moved the con-spiratorial meeting to a more convenient time of 6:00 p.m.

According to Butch, Steve explained that he had mistakenly told the police he had seen Butch by the river on Tuesday night. In fact, Steve now realized it was Gord Logan he had spotted in the water.

"The police would probably come down and question you. Did you see me?" Steve allegedly asked.

"No," Butch supposedly answered. "I might as well tell them that I saw you," he added, casually offering to lie to the police.

If true—and the police would certainly believe it to be—it was a damn-ing story. At best, the story indicated that Steve had innocently mistaken a friend at the river and knew Butch was going to mislead the police. At worst, a murderer was plotting with a pal to create an alibi.

But there was a major flaw in Butch's story. His tale about the hatching of a conspiracy on Wednesday was implausible because—even if the police assumed Steve was the murderer—Steve would not yet have needed anyone to lie for him. The police questioned Steve four times on Wednesday. According to their official records and later testimony, at no point did they ever ask him about any friends he spotted down by the river. In other words, *Steve had not yet mentioned Butch or anyone else to the police at all.* There was no need to—Lynne was still a runaway girl and Steve was not yet a suspect in any foul play. Apparently, Butch had invented an unnecessary conspiracy.

Whatever Butch imagined, what was undeniably real was the impact of the story he had been spreading since Tuesday about Steve taking Lynne into the bush. The teasing reached a peak Wednesday evening when three other boys—Bryan Glover, Tom Gillette and Paul Desjardine—joined Steve at the bridge. Butch was underneath the bridge, throwing rocks. Even after an afternoon at the gravel pits, the boys were ready for some more fun. Butch dared the boys to try to bicycle across the river. Steve and Paul took him up on the challenge and pedalled through the water. There was much splashing and laughing and joking. Over the next few months, the boys gave varying—and at times contradictory—accounts of what was said on the bridge that night. But there was general agreement the banter began when Paul asked Steve if he had taken Lynne into the woods.

"I didn't," Steve shot back.

"Arnold said you did," Paul told Steve.

Steve leaned over the bridge railing to Butch, standing below on the riverbank. "Did you say I took Lynne Harper in the woods?" he asked his friend.

"No," answered Butch (a lie, since he was the one who started the bush story at the Custard Cup the night before).

The police would later make much of what happened next, but the evidence from the boys is confused. Two issues were in dispute: if Steve talked about going into the woods to look for calves, and if Steve ever threatened Butch.

Two of the boys—Bryan and Tom—later reported that Steve said he thought he heard a calf in the woods while riding with Lynne and went to see if he could find it. Paul heard the same story but thought Steve might have heard the calf at another time since Steve "didn't say when he was looking." Butch, for his part, insisted it was he—not Steve—who brought up the calf story: "You had her at the side of the bush looking for the cow and the calf," Butch told Steve. It was a patchwork of snippets of conversations and memories. But the police saw in the calf story an attempt by a teenage murderer to dissemble and lie.

Only one of boys, Tom Gillette, claimed Steve "sounded as if he was threatening Butch" when he insisted he had not gone into the bush with Lynne. None of the other boys—including Butch, the supposed target of this threat—remarked on anything menacing in Steve's tone or actions. Still, the police chose to believe Tom's interpretation of Steve's "threatening manner" as proof of a guilty conscience.

A simpler interpretation was that the whole conversation was just teenage boys having fun. "It was more or less a joke" is how Steve remembers that evening. "Young kids saying, 'I saw you with a girl.' But what started off to be a joke all of a sudden when the police got hold of it, then it was no longer a joke. Then it was no longer teasing."

Bryan Glover agrees. "We were joking, teasing him. It wasn't as if someone was really trying to find out what had happened or accusing him of anything."

———

Steve's encounters with the police were not over for that day. Around 8:00 p.m., Sgt. Charles Anderson, the senior officer at the Goderich OPP detachment, dropped by the Truscott home. He asked Doris if Steve could show him the route he had biked on Tuesday night. Steve's mother agreed.

Steve took the officer to the school and showed him the path he had taken with Lynne to the county road. Steve added more details about his conversation with Lynne during their bike ride. He told the officer Lynne had asked if he knew the man who lived in the white house with the ponies. She also asked Steve where he went fishing. Anderson asked Steve if he did not think it peculiar that a young girl would be hitchhiking. Steven replied, accurately, that many children thumbed rides.

Anderson asked Steven if he should have told Lynne's parents.

"I didn't think much about it at the time," Steve answered, "but now I think I should have told them."

Was he ever on a date with Lynne, Anderson asked.

"No," Steve replied.

Ever given her a ride on his bike before?

"No."

Anderson gave the boy a lift back home and Steve went to bed.

There was little rest, though, for the police or the Harper family. It had been twenty-four hours since anyone had reported seeing Lynne alive. That evening, the air force police organized several small search parties. They looked in abandoned homes in the region and in various swimming areas. Several OPP officers joined the RCAF men to check either side of the county road near the bridge up to the Number 8 Highway.

Nothing. No sign of the little girl.

As classes started on Thursday morning at RCAF Station Clinton, Steve faced his fifth police interview in the space of twenty-four hours. OPP Constable Hobbs, the first officer to question Steven on Wednesday morning, came to the school, this time accompanied by Sgt. John Wheelhouse of the air force police. For the normally even-keeled boy, it was unsettling. "It's something that you can't even imagine," Steve says now of the repeated questioning. "All of a sudden a cop pulls you out of your classroom in school. 'Where were you? What did you do? This one said you did this. You were here?' It's mind-boggling."

The officers set up shop in the teachers' room at the school as the principal, Clarence Trott, dutifully shepherded in one student after another. Trott stayed in the room as the police questioned his young pupils.

"I started off asking Steven if there was anything more he had to tell me regarding Lynne Harper," Hobbs later reported.

"One thing," the boy answered, according to Hobbs. "She had a gold chain necklace. It was a heart with the RCAF crest on it." It was the first time anyone had mentioned Lynne's locket—a piece of jewellery that would assume more importance as the summer wore on.

"While you were cycling down the road, did you see anyone else?" the OPP officer asked.

Steve said he passed Richard Gellatly on the road and then at the river he spotted Butch George and waved to him. This was the first time, according to police records, that Steve told the police he saw his friend Butch. He made this statement only on Thursday morning—not, as Butch had implied, the day before.

Steve also told police that when he was near the bridge, an old grey Plymouth or Dodge had passed right by him on the county road—not the same car he had seen from a distance at the highway.

"Can you remember the people in the car, Steven?" Hobbs asked.

"There was a man and a lady in it." Steve added that he remembered the licence plate number: 981-666.

Hobbs then asked him to identify "any of the children he saw playing down there," presumably meaning the river, although in his account Wheelhouse remembers a vaguer question about "children he had seen in the area."

Steve rattled off some names: Doug Oates, Darrell Gilks, Allan Durnin's brother Gerry and Gord Logan.

"Did you see anyone else during that period?" one of the officers asked.

"Yes, I saw Stuart Westie and Warren Heatherall," Steve said, accurately identifying the young baseball players at the school.

"Approximately what time was it, Steven, when you left with Lynne?" the officers asked.

"Seven o'clock or shortly after" was the answer they recorded, although the day before, the police said Steven told them his departure was closer to 7:25 p.m.

How long did it take to get down to the river?

"About ten minutes." (This timing was later matched in tests done by police.)
How long did it take to get from the bridge to the highway?

"A further ten minutes," Steve answered according to the police notes. If that was his reply, it was either a poor estimate or a bad lie; the highway was only a few minutes away from the bridge.

How long to get back from the highway to the bridge?

"About five minutes." Police did not apparently ask Steven why it would take him half the time to return to the bridge.

Still, the officers seemed satisfied with the boy's demeanour and forthrightness. Wheelhouse later said Steven was open and intelligent: "He gave me the impression he wanted to be helpful and showed no signs of nervousness," Wheelhouse remarked. The principal, as well, noted that Steven was co-operative: "He gave his story the same as the other children did."

Constable Hobbs questioned several other children that day. His brief notes of the encounters are important because they are the first recorded accounts by any other witnesses of what occurred that Tuesday evening. Presumably, they reflect the students' best memories of the events that took place.

The most intriguing testimony came from Gord Logan, the twelve-year-old fishing at the swimming hole. He told Constable Hobbs he "saw both [Lynne and Steve] on a cycle going toward the highway and Truscott return and linger at the bridge." If true, it was an eyewitness account of great significance, for if Steve crossed the river with Lynne then clearly he was not in the bush murdering her.

But Gord's eyewitness account, corroborating Steven's story, was significant not only because of *what* he said, but *when* he said it. It was still only Thursday morning; searchers had not yet stumbled upon Lynne's body in the bush. As his mother, Frances Logan, later pointed out: "This was before the body was found, and that is why I have always thought for sure that there would not be much point in him making up a story or lying, when at the time no one knew there was anything so terribly wrong."

Later, when Gord's statement became central to Steve's defence, the prosecution would try to suggest he made up his story to protect Steven, conveniently forgetting Gord first made his statement before such a conspiracy was necessary.

Two other students also said they had seen Steve and Lynne that evening. Richard Gellatly informed the police he passed them on his bike near the school about 7:30, roughly the same time he would stick to in all his statements, but a time which the police and later the prosecution would find quite inconvenient for their case against Steve.

Even more inconvenient was what Butch George told Hobbs on Thursday morning. He said that when he was down at the river "he saw Lynne and Steven on the cycle going toward the highway." Butch's first statement to the police was one he was going to have to retract once he became a star witness for the prosecution.

As the children's concern for their missing classmate grew, the teasing directed at Steven increased. By now, many of the students had heard of Butch's tale that Steve had taken Lynne into the bush. At recess, tempers snapped.

In the boys' washroom, Allan Durnin told Steve he did not believe he had given Lynne a ride to the highway. Not because he thought Steve was a liar. Like the boys at the Custard Cup who had first heard Butch's tale on Tuesday evening, Allan did not believe a school sports hero like Steve would be caught giving a lift to a simple girl like Lynne. "He didn't like her that much to do her any favours," he recalls thinking.

According to three witnesses, Steve did not take kindly to the taunts. "He grabbed me and pushed me up against the wall in the washroom, and his face got all red," Allan recounted. George Archibald told the story with more dramatic flourish. "I saw Steve going right in after Allan, as if he were chasing him, and mad." In George's version, a teacher arrived just in time before anything serious happened. Allan's account was less exciting: "I didn't say anything else and I walked out of the washroom."

For those who would later believe in Steve's guilt, these incidents were proof of a killer's rage. On the other hand, they could simply reflect the typical embarrassment and anger of a teenager at being teased. "I was just basically kidding with him," Allan had always insisted.

By the end of school that Thursday, the time for kidding was over. The searchers had found the body of Lynne Harper. And an OPP inspector arrived in Clinton and moved with breathtaking speed to arrest the boy he was convinced was her murderer.

# 6

## THE INSPECTOR ARRIVES

Lynne's body was discovered on the very same day the provincial Progressive Conservatives were elected back into power. It was not a government that would tolerate any blow to Tory Ontario's image of order and decency, and the OPP knew they would be expected to act fast. They called in Harold Graham to crack the case.

Graham, like his fellow homicide inspectors, worked out of the Criminal Investigations Branch (CIB). He was a tall, heavy-set man of imposing stature with an equally imposing record. He started as a lowly constable in London and then in Sarnia, but in 1949, after solving several major crimes and murders, Graham, at thirty-three, became the youngest inspector with the CIB at Toronto headquarters. He was a fast-rising star in the police ranks, and the celebrity he would gain on the Truscott case would help propel him all the way to the top. By 1973, the man who jailed Steven Truscott as Lynne Harper's murderer would become commissioner of the provincial police, Ontario's top cop.

"He was a very smart investigator," says Dennis Alsop, who worked under Graham as a corporal in the latter part of the Clinton murder. Graham earned the undying respect of Alsop and the other men on the force for being the stereotype of the cop's cop: gruff and determined. "He worked hard, there's no two ways about it," recalls Hank Sayeau, who did most of the work on Truscott case alongside Graham. "He knew what he wanted; he knew the ingredients to make a case and he worked accordingly."

Graham's superiors praised him as an "outstanding investigator" who had cracked dozens of murder cases. He had the slow, steady patience that is the hallmark of good police work. In 1952, Graham confronted what he called his "most brutal case." When Arthur Kendall's wife disappeared that year near Stratford, police found some of the woman's clothes but had little else to go on and no testimony from the woman's children. Kendall claimed his wife ran away. Graham persevered for nine years, waiting until Kendall's frightened children were old enough to come forward with accounts of seeing their father stab their mother to death. At the time, it was one of only three cases in Canadian legal history where authorities secured a murder conviction without ever producing the body of the victim.

When Graham started on the force, stricter rules regarding confessions came into effect. Some of his colleagues complained, but not Graham. "It was not a great problem," he later told a newspaper. "We still got confessions and statements." As events in Clinton would soon show, the no-nonsense investigator from the CIB was determined to get those statements. And instead of waiting nine years to solve this crime, he would wrap up the Harper murder mystery in less than twenty-four hours.

Harold Graham arrived in Clinton on Thursday, June 11, at 7:45 p.m. He immediately conferred with the policemen who had been handling the case so far: Corporal Sayeau, Constable Trumbley and Sgt. Charles Anderson.

"Steven Truscott was not a strong suspect originally because of the conflicting stories we had obtained in our early attempts to find Lynne Harper," Graham said later. "A heinous crime was uncovered in the bush that day near Clinton, Ontario. It was not the type of crime an investigator would automatically attribute to a fourteen-year-old boy. But whether the person is fourteen or forty-nine, the investigator has the right and in fact the responsibility to talk to anyone who he feels may be able to assist him in determining the truth."

Sometime during that evening of June 11, the OPP issued a General Information Broadcast to alert police across the province about Lynne's assailant. The only copy of that bulletin in the police files is in Graham's handwriting:

> Re: Lynne Harper—raped and strangled body found in bush near RCAF Station Clinton—*believed to have taken place about 9:00 p.m., Tues. June 10.* One witness reports Lynne was given a ride in solid grey or white '59 Chev with yellow plates on Highway 8, going east toward Seaforth. Only the driver in the car. . . . At your discretion please check white cars with yellow plates and observe occupants *especially for scratches on face, neck, hands and arms.*

This document, which remained hidden in police files for four decades until it was unearthed in the late 1990s, was a revealing snapshot of how Graham and the police initially saw Lynne's murder. It was the first bulletin the police issued after discovering the body, their first attempt to enlist province-wide support to capture Lynne's killer, so it presumably summarized their best, most accurate intelligence as of late Thursday evening. The police statement contained three noteworthy curiosities.

The first was the generic description of the car, a 1959 Chevrolet, and not specifically a Bel Air, the model that the police would later maintain Steve had narrowed down. The colour was also appropriately vague: "grey or white." Only the "yellow plates" were precise; Steve's sighting of some sort of a yellow or orange marker on the rear of the car had now been fixed in the police's minds as plates. Provincial police immediately began stopping similar vehicles. "Deluged with calls from citizens telling of cars answering the description of the one seen by the Truscott boy, London provincial police checked out thirty vehicles," the *London Free Press* reported. "All were allowed to proceed."

The second curious reference in Graham's bulletin was the police's apparent belief that Lynne's killer had scratches on his "face, neck, hands and arms." They passed these suspicions on to the media: "Face of Killer Scratched," ran the headline on June 12 in the *Globe and Mail.* "Police found evidence of a violent struggle between the schoolgirl and her attacker," another Toronto paper reported. The *London Free Press* added: "Police said the lone occupant in the car might have scratches on his face, neck, arms and hands, indicating the young victim put up a struggle."

Were the police simply assuming a desperate Lynne had scratched her assailant? Or, considering this official description was their first serious attempt to find her killer, was the reference to scratches based on something more tangible? After all, the police had spent hours next to her body in the woods and later attended the autopsy. The pathologist took fingernail scrapings. As it happened, the emphasis on scratches to the killer's face and neck would suddenly disappear once police arrested an unblemished fourteen-year-old.

The third baffling item in Graham's bulletin was the most important: the time of death he selected. Time of death is a vital clue in the early stages of a murder investigation because it helps police narrow the hunt for potential suspects. Graham was explicit that Lynne's murder was "believed to have taken place around 9:00 p.m., Tues. June 10."

Graham must have got his dates confused because Tuesday was the 9th of June, not the 10th. But selecting 9:00 p.m. as a possible time of death was going to create a big problem for the inspector. His chief suspect—the boy he was soon to arrest—was safe at home babysitting at the time when, according to Graham's bulletin, Lynne's assailant was murdering her. Once Graham jailed Steven, no further references to that 9:00 p.m. time of death were made.

Like the problematic scratches on the killer's face and arms, any reference to the 9:00 p.m. time of death vanished from the police case history once they arrested Steve. And at trial, the Crown made sure the defence and the jurors never saw Graham's General Information Broadcast.

Graham would later claim that the police got an accurate fix on Lynne's time of death when doctors performed an autopsy Thursday evening. In fact, the autopsy created more mysteries than it solved.

The room in the Ball and Mutch funeral home in Clinton was hardly ideal for a procedure of such importance. It was small and cramped, measuring only thirteen by eight feet. "Facilities for laying out instruments and equipment for collecting specimens were inadequate," pathologist John Penistan later admitted. "Light, from an overhead bulb, was inadequate and was supplemented by a standard lamp which was brought in on request."

Indeed, Penistan would have preferred to have the body transferred to his well-equipped autopsy room in Stratford, but there were concerns over the cost of transport, and the police were eager to get the results. "It seemed desirable to proceed as soon as possible in order to provide guidance for the police on the time of death," Penistan recounted.

The pathologist from Stratford had a commanding, some would say cocky, confidence that he could get the job done. "He knew it all. Whatever he said was gospel," said one police officer who admired the doctor, even if he found him to be arrogant. "You didn't argue with him. If he said it was so, it was so." By his side to assist him stood the air force base's chief medical officer, Dr. David Hall Brooks, another medical man no one ever accused of underestimating his own talents. (He signed his police statements with six different abbreviations for various degrees.) The men began their work at 7:30 p.m. and finished in just over two hours. More than anything else, what they would have to say helped convict Steven Truscott.

In his official autopsy report, Penistan was blunt and concise about the cause of death: "strangulation by ligature." Lynne's murderer strangled her with her own blouse; her thyroid cartilage was fractured at its base.

There were no other serious wounds on her body. Penistan found "no evident fracture" of her skull, spine or major bones; her scalp showed "no evident injury." There was a non-fatal "ragged laceration" of unexplained origin on the back of the left shoulder, the wound that created the small pool of blood found under her body in the bush.

Lynne's arms and feet were covered with "scratch marks" of various lengths, many of which Penistan would later attribute to her assailant carrying her body over a barbed wire fence. There were scratches around her ankles, calves and thighs; more marks on the upper part of her left and right forearm and the back of her right hand; and a circular lesion on her right elbow. On her left leg, Penistan noted a long scratch starting from the front of the thigh a few inches above the kneecap, running down the front of the lower leg to the top of her foot; there was dried blood on the scratch, suggesting to Penistan it occurred before death.

The position of Lynne's body in the bush and the fact that she was nearly naked certainly suggested some form of sexual assault, but what was the extent of the attack? Dr. Penistan called it a "blind, violent" rape; Dr. Brooks would later horrify jurors with his description of a "grossly bruised" genital area. Yet for a murder where rape presumably played such a central role, the autopsy details were sparse and confusing.

"Vagina, hymen destroyed," Penistan began, not specifying if decomposition or rape could have accounted for the absence of the hymen, or, indeed, if it was present before the attack took place. Penistan reported the "lower vagina contused." Contusion, commonly known as bruising, is defined medically as an injury without tearing of the skin and therefore no obvious bleeding. Penistan also noted "abrasion of the right labium majus posteriorly," or a scraping of the surface layer of cells or tissue from the rounded fold of the outer right side of her vaginal opening. Normally, abrasions cause oozing and perhaps minor bleeding. But in a later section of his report, Penistan revealed that the section of the lower vaginal wall he examined under the microscope "shows intense congestion of blood vessels, but no actual hemorrhage." In other words, no bleeding. It was a contradiction Penistan would have to resolve before the trial.

Try as he could, Penistan could find no traces of semen. "No spermatozoa could be identified with certainty despite careful search," he wrote. The best he could come up with was "a considerable number of ill-defined, diffusely stained bodies" that were "comparable" in size and shape with degenerating sperm heads. Penistan did find what he called "large amounts" of acid phosphatase, "a constituent of semen and not naturally found in the female." That was the common medical belief in the 1950s; nowadays, doctors accept that women do naturally produce small levels of acid phosphatase. Still, high amounts were, in Penistan's words, "very strong presumptive evidence of the presence of sperm in the vagina."

For a "blind, violent" rape, Penistan's autopsy produced disappointingly vague evidence.

"Stomach unremarkable."

Those two words opened what would become the most controversial part of Penistan's autopsy. Penistan's analysis of the contents of Lynne's stomach was the centrepiece for his exact determination of the time of her death, and his testimony about that time of death was crucial in condemning Steven Truscott.

Yet for all its importance, Penistan paid scant attention to the stomach in his autopsy report, devoting only two lines to it: "Content of approximately

1 pint of poorly masticated, only slightly digested food, including peas, onion, corn." Even more surprising is how Penistan determined this list of contents.

According to Dr. Brooks, he and Penistan poured the contents into a jar and then studied it by "holding the jar up to the light to see what we could see." It was not the most rigorous of scientific tests, but Brooks insisted it worked just fine.

"I must confess that I don't think we did all that bad a job on what we were doing," he says four decades later. "You either see things or you don't."

Penistan—with the help of an able Crown prosecutor—would easily convince jurors that, as he stood over the corpse of Lynne Harper in that autopsy room on Thursday evening and examined her stomach contents, he deduced her time of death purely on the basis of objective science. A quick visual examination supposedly was enough to give Penistan the confidence to pinpoint an eerily precise time of death, based largely on stomach contents: "This opinion," he later wrote, "would place the time of death between 7:15 and 7:45 p.m. on 9th June, 1959."

At trial, the prosecution would claim that if there was a turning point in the police investigation into Lynne's murder, this was it. Only one person was known to be with Lynne in that time period: Steven Truscott. No single piece of evidence would be more instrumental in proving his guilt—at least in the eyes of the police, the prosecution and ultimately a jury. Penistan cited two other "observations and assumptions" to support his theory about the time of death: "the extent of decomposition" of Lynne's body and the fact that rigor mortis "had almost passed off." But it was his analysis of stomach contents that was paramount.

While many people imagine pathologists are the timekeepers of crime fighting, pathology is, in fact, the science of why someone dies (the medical causes) and how (murder, suicide or accident)—but not when. A good pathologist can tell you the circumstances of death; the time can sometimes be inferred but rarely pinpointed. In the best of conditions, pathologists can only provide ballpark figures. That's because there are too many variables from one person to the next and in the environment where a death occurs.

Those variables especially come into play with stomach contents. From everyday experience, people know that two individuals can eat an identical meal but digest it at quite different speeds. The same person can eat identical food on different days and take more or less time to digest it. Moods, such as fear and anger, play a big role in how the stomach reacts.

Yet despite all these variables, Dr. John Penistan managed to pinpoint a time of death with astonishing precision. It strains credulity to believe that a doctor, holding a jar of stomach contents to a light bulb, would pick—almost to the minute—the narrow window that matched the only possible time Steven Truscott would have had to kill Lynne.

Science is good, but it is not magic. The documentary evidence would later indicate that Dr. Penistan, in coming to such impressively exact conclusions about the time of death, might very well have been overeager to help the police and prosecution.

## 7

## WANTED—"DEAD OR ALIVE"

"$10,000—DEAD OR ALIVE"

The banner headline screamed the reward offer across the front page of the Toronto *Telegram* on Friday morning, June 12. Less than twenty-four hours after Lynne Harper's body was found, Ontario Attorney General Kelso Roberts put up a $10,000 bounty for her killer, "dead or alive." It was the highest reward in the province's history.

The province's top lawman said he expected the money would "help solve this revolting and savage crime as soon as possible," and he made it clear he did not much care if the bounty was paid out for a conviction or a corpse. "If the guilty person was killed and it was proven he was the murderer, the reward would still be given," one paper reported. Another spelled it out more clearly: "Most rewards state the money will be paid for information leading to the arrest and conviction, but today's announcement was a radical departure."

Putting a price on the head of a killer was about the only radical thing the ruling government of Ontario could be accused of. In a conservative country coming to the end of a conservative decade, the government of Premier

Leslie Frost was as staid and stalwart as they came. In many ways, Steven and Lynne grew up not just in a different time, but also in a very different country from the Canada of today. In the 1950s, social issues, like television, were black and white. There was little of the fiery passion that coloured the turmoil of the sixties or the shades of grey that have characterized debates in the more cynical decades since. It was Good versus Evil; justice always triumphed and justice was never wrong. Just ask Sergeant Joe Friday in *Dragnet* or Sheriff Matt Dillon in *Gunsmoke*.

The sexual overtones of Lynne's murder made it all the more shocking. This was, after all, a time when parents on TV still slept in separate beds, when the panicky headline on the cover of the first issue of *Maclean's* magazine for 1959 asked: "Going Steady: Is It Ruining Our Teenagers?"

So it was little surprise, then, that the Ontario government's bold announcement of a hunt for Harper's killer "dead or alive" should touch a popular chord. In an editorial entitled "An Atrocity," the Toronto *Telegram* noted that the "unprecedented size of the reward the Ontario government has offered and its urgent call for the capture of the killer 'dead or alive' reflects the Province's shock at the murder of Lynne Harper."

The paper concluded ominously: "That a child should lose her life in this way is a crime that is too appalling for any consideration of charity toward the criminal." As public outrage mounted, so did the unprecedented pressure on the police to solve this "most horrible of crimes."

Most of the students and even the staff at Lynne's school were understandably in shock over the news. Grade Four teacher Edith Beacom remembers that with police coming and going, everyone was upset and saddened by the "serious business." It was no less puzzling for the older students. Every Friday morning, Maitland Edgar encouraged the pupils in his combined grade Seven and Eight class to take fifteen minutes out of their school day to discuss current events. Friday, June 12, was no exception, and there was just one topic the children wanted to talk about: Lynne's murder.

"What are the different degrees of murder?" one student asked. Edgar explained that premeditated murder in the first degree was the most serious. Throughout the discussion, Edgar recalls, Steve was as relaxed and interested as the other students.

Steve, however, did not have much time to ponder an academic discussion of murder. He was called out of class to meet Harold Graham, the new OPP inspector in town.

At 10:45 a.m., the two met for the first time: the boy who had given Lynne a bike ride and the policeman who would become his accuser. It was Steve's sixth encounter with the police in three days. Dan Truscott accompanied his son.

"I would like a detailed account," Graham told Steve's father, "because Steven was the last person known to have seen Lynne Harper."

Graham made it sound as if Steve was still only a witness. But later at trial, the judge ruled the police knew very well when they were taking Steve's statement that "he was the person who was going to be charged" and consequently a "warning ought to have been given." "There was no equality between this fourteen-year-old boy and a group of police officers who were examining him," the judge stated bluntly, and, consequently, the statement in no way was voluntary.

The OPP did not have their own stenographer; the air force supplied a woman named Dorene Jervis. Her transcription included only two of the questions asked by the police. Truscott's purported answers to the rest of the unrecorded queries were strung together as a continuous statement. At trial, Graham was later asked about this curious omission:

"Why didn't you have her [Jervis] take down what you said to him?"

"In the interests of time, and because he was a witness at the time and not a suspect," he replied.

"You think a shorthand writer can't take down the notes as fast as they are talking?"

"Just depends on who it is."

In any event, Jervis's transcription contained some odd phrases. "I heard no story about an alligator any place," Steve is quoted inexplicably at one point. In any event, her three-page, seventy-two-line transcription is the only record available of Steve's alleged statement.

"My name is Steven Truscott. I am fourteen years old," it began. "Lynne was in [the] same class. I have known her one or two years." Steven then recounted his ride down to the highway, in much the same way he had over the previous two days. "I was going toward [the] river to see some of the boys who were going fishing. She asked if she could have a ride down to [the] highway. . . . I took her to the highway and let her off. . . . She just asked if she could get off and she got off and I went back to the bridge." Steve said Lynne asked where he went fishing and if he knew the people who lived in the little white house up the highway.

The police and prosecution would later insist Steve had singled out a specific car model and a licence plate. In fact, Steve's account of the car was strikingly similar to the vague description he first gave to Constable Hobbs on Wednesday morning. "It was a grey '59 Chev, quite a bit of chrome . . . *something like* a Bel Air," Steve told Graham. "It *appeared to be* a licence plate. *Something yellow* at [the] back. Yes, I am certain. I am sure about that."

Because Graham did not have the questions recorded, it is impossible to say what Steve was certain about. From the transcript, it appears he was sure that there was "something yellow" at the back, not necessarily a plate. The police and prosecution would conveniently forget these nuances at trial.

For the first time, Steve gave the police an explanation for how he estimated the departure time for his bike ride with Lynne: "When I was up at the school, I looked at the clock and it was about twenty-five minutes after seven," he reportedly told Graham. "There is a clock just inside the school. I let her off at the highway about 7:30." (The clock Steven would have seen was through the large windows of the kindergarten classroom, a fact that would later prove significant.)

Steve also gave Graham new details about seeing Lynne depart. "She had her thumb out. A car swerved in off [the] edge of [the] road and pulled out," his statement read. "She got in [the] front seat and the car pulled away going toward Seaforth."

Steve told the OPP inspector that after returning from the highway he lingered at the bridge for "about five minutes" and that on his way back "I waved at Arnold George" at the river. (According to OPP Constable Hobbs, on Thursday Steve had said he had waved to Butch "on the way down with Lynne," not on the way back.)

Graham asked Steve about his relationship with Lynne. "Are you interested in girls?" he asked.

"Some," Steve answered.

"Were you ever out with her?"

"No," Steve is recorded as saying. "There was no one interested in her. . . . None of them liked her too much. Sort of bossy in school. . . . She didn't appeal to boys."

Steve's statement contained only a few errors of fact. Steve recounted some of the erroneous gossip he had heard in the previous days, telling the police that "quite a few kids around school" said an adult named Audrey Jackson had spotted Lynne on the base Tuesday evening around 8:30 p.m. (In fact, she spotted her about two hours earlier.)

Steve also said he saw four boys at the river: Butch, Dougie Oates, Gerry Durnin and Gary Gilks. Gary Gilks was not at the river that evening, but his brother Darrell was. The day before, Steve had told police specifically it was Darrell, not Gary, whom he saw by the river. In the typed version of Steve's statement to Graham, the first names of the boys are in parentheses, possibly because the police added them later. It is conceivable Steve named Darrell, not Gary, and the OPP got the names confused. Steve, however, was definitely wrong about one of the boys, as Gerry Durnin was not at the swimming hole on Tuesday.

In any case, the police took this matter of the names as another sign of the boy's fabrications: he was never at the river, so he guessed at some likely names and got two wrong. Steve says if he was in error, it was much more casual than calculated. "You say, 'I think I saw so-and-so,' and it was nothing special—until afterwards," Steve says. "Then all of a sudden, it becomes more important, and the police say, 'Well, you told us you saw this person.' I said 'I think.' But according to them, 'think' is definite."

Graham's interview with Steven lasted twenty minutes. Graham ended his morning encounter with Steven by informing him the police would type his statement "and that he would be given an opportunity to examine the transcription."

That opportunity came less than nine hours later—and when it came Steve would be in police custody.

The next few hours would be decisive in the building of the police case against him. What Harold Graham did on that Friday afternoon—whom he talked to, which child he chose to believe and not believe, how he decided to interpret the medical reports—would set in motion a chain of events that put Steven on death row and left the country forever debating that rush to judgment.

"It was chaotic," OPP Cpl. Hank Sayeau remembers. "A child murder is always taken more seriously than the average [murder]. Time is such an element—so much hinges on seeing everything and hoping you move on the right track."

Graham and his officers interviewed about a dozen other students that day besides Steven. In the police files, on a single sheet of paper from a notebook, are Graham's handwritten accounts of the questioning of three of the most important—Dougie, Butch and Jocelyne. There is no date or time for the interviews, but they almost certainly took place that Friday afternoon.

Dougie, the boy hunting for turtles, told the OPP inspector something Graham certainly would not have wanted to hear if he thought Steve was the murderer. Dougie said unequivocally that he saw Steve and Lynne cross the bridge: "Lynne was on [the] crossbar. I left [the] bridge about ten minutes after Steve and Lynne went north [toward the highway.]" Graham knew Dougie was the second important witness to come forward in as many days who verified Steve's story. The day before, on Thursday, Gord Logan had made an equally clear statement that he also had spotted Steve cross the bridge with Lynne.

To arrest Steve, Graham somehow had to convince himself that these "chums of the accused," as he called them, were simply lying. It was a curious logic. For one thing, at eleven years old, Dougie was too young to be anything more than an aquaintance of Steve's, hardly a close enough friend to be willing to lie and cover up a murder. For another, Graham must have relied on gut instinct to ferret out the liars among the children because at this early stage in the investigation, on Friday, June 12, he and his men had not yet made any effort to disprove the two crucial eyewitness accounts from Dougie and Gord. The police did not re-interview the boys or conduct visual tests to try to punch holes in their stories before arresting Steven.

Graham was also selective in which "chums of the accused" he chose to believe, putting much more faith in Butch's truth-telling abilities. The police interview with Butch on Friday, June 12, would later take on almost mythic proportions in the police chronicle of the case. Faced with the horror of a brutal slaying, Butch came clean. "Arnold George, Steve's Indian chum . . . lied to the police . . . to protect Steven," Graham wrote in one report on the case "but *when the body was found*, he told the truth." It had all the makings of a great crime drama. A close buddy fibs to the cops on Thursday about seeing his pal by the river but fesses up by Friday when the evil murder is exposed. Except the drama did not match the reality.

Graham's notes, from the June 12 interview of Butch, read as follows: "Had supper, cut lawn, went to swimming hole about 7:00 p.m. Was there about fifteen minutes when Steve and Lynne biked north."

This interview on Friday—twenty-four hours after searchers discovered Lynne dead—was Butch's big chance to spill the beans, and he did not. Graham's own notes show that Butch had not changed the story that he had seen his friend go over the bridge with Lynne toward the highway. Contrary to the police myth about Steve's pal cracking "when the body was found," Butch did not change his tale until at least Monday, June 15—four days after the grisly details of Lynne's death emerged.

By late Friday afternoon, Graham was just a couple of hours away from having Steven Truscott picked up. The OPP inspector has always maintained that two decisive pieces of information tipped the scales against the boy: Jocelyne's tale of a secret rendezvous with Steve in the bush and the analysis of the stomach contents from the attorney general's laboratory. "It was not until I heard the evidence of Jocelyne Gaudet and the report from the laboratory that he became a strong suspect," Graham later said.

Graham claimed that in her talk with police on Friday, what Jocelyne gave him was motive. "That afternoon . . . she said that *Steven had asked her* to go into the bush with him to see some newborn calves and *to tell no one,*" the inspector wrote. In the eyes of the police, Steve was a lustful teenager on the prowl who had tried to lure one girl into a bush; apparently Lynne was just an unfortunate substitute.

There were several confusing elements in the early renderings of Jocelyne's tale. She gave at least three different statements to police in the twenty-four hours from Friday afternoon to Saturday, each more elaborate than the previous one. A week after she signed her official police statement, she added a fourth declaration.

Her first story came in this quick, twenty-word note scribbled in Graham's handwriting sometime on Friday: "Jocelyne Gaudette [*sic*]—*said she was looking for Lynne*—came out of bush, said she was where Lynne was found (later)."

Significantly, there was no mention at all of Steve, let alone of a secret date with him. Jocelyne simply told the police she was at the bush in a quest to find her friend Lynne, not to meet a boy. This note, like so many other early police records that contradicted witness testimony on the stand, never saw the light of day at Steven's trial.

Jocelyne also had a longer chat with Const. Donald Trumbley. A statement in his handwriting begins "Jocelyne Gaudet, age 13. I am in grade 7." It is undated but almost certainly Trumbley took it from Jocelyne on Friday afternoon. Her statement goes on for sixteen more short sentences.

"I went up the county road at about 6:30 p.m. to meet Steve," she said. Jocelyne told the police their meeting place was to be at the southern tip of Lawson's bush closest to the school, on the right-hand side of the road—presumably in plain view of everyone who would be passing by. "Steve didn't show up, so I walked along the county road with my bicycle," she said. She travelled another nine hundred feet to the northern end of the bush and then turned down the laneway that led into the bush, passing the spot where Lynne's body eventually would be found. "I didn't see any bicycle or hear any noises but I had a funny feeling," she said.

Her "funny feeling" has the whiff of fantasy, as if the young girl was trying a little too hard to be helpful to police. Along the laneway, Jocelyne was more than three football-field lengths away from where she said she was supposed to have met Steve for their rendezvous. She would have no reason even to imagine Steve was in the bush at the location she found herself, much less sense any "funny feeling." Perhaps it was another example of what her classmates described as Jocelyne's "irritating" tendency "to let on she knew things."

What is striking is the complete absence in this account of any notion of a clandestine meeting with Steve. If Jocelyne did tell the police about a secret date *before* they arrested Steve, as Graham claimed, it did not show up in their notes. Only *after* Steve was in jail did Jocelyne's tale include details about whispers in school, a visit to her home and hush-hush arrangements for an adventure in the woods, according to police notes.

Equally puzzling is that Graham appeared to take Jocelyne's story at face value. Before arresting Steven, the police took no statements from any adults who could corroborate—or challenge—her story.


If Jocelyne gave the police a motive, what they still needed was opportunity. Graham had to get medical proof that Lynne must have died in the brief time she had been with Steve on that Tuesday night.

At 12:12 p.m. on Friday, June 12, Cpl. Hank Sayeau arrived at the attorney general's laboratory in Toronto, with a glass jar bearing seal number 2201. The jar held Lynne's stomach contents. A biologist named John Funk did a quick analysis and handed over the jar to his medical director, Dr. Noble Sharpe, for more examination that afternoon.

By the end of the afternoon, Sayeau telephoned the OPP in Goderich with the results. Graham would always maintain it was this oral report from the lab experts on the time of death that gave him the scientific proof he needed to pick up Steven that evening as the suspected murderer. "It was their opinion that the meal had been ingested *not more than two hours* prior to her death," Graham said in a speech he gave in 1967.

In the OPP's sanitized version of events, the lab results were another turning point in the investigation. Graham called them his "first break" in the case. Only later would internal prosecution and medical documents reveal that the official written report from the laboratory—unlike the brief phone report Sayeau gave Graham—said nothing about a two-hour time limit on Lynne's death.

But for whatever reason, on Friday afternoon, June 11, Graham became convinced that Lynne died "not more than two hours" after eating supper at 5:45—in other words, during the time she was with Steven. "It began to shape up that Steven was a suspect," Graham said.

All that remained was to arrest the boy.

## 8

# TRAPPED

**B**y Friday evening, a tumultuous week was coming to an end in Clinton. As much as they could, the children and adults in the PMQs around the air force station tried to follow life's normal pursuits. Steve was looking forward to some fun and adventure over the weekend. Some fishing, some baseball, maybe another trip into the woods to work on the tree house. As the sun dipped in the horizon, Steve headed over to one of his favourite places around the base, Lawson's farm—unaware that he was about to spend his last hour of liberty for the next ten years.

It looked like rain, Bob Lawson thought as he rushed to finish the evening chores—a godsend after the crop-scorching heat all week. Lawson was eager to get a little haying done. "If you start the lawn mower, I can cut the grass," suggested his mother, Alice Lawson.

Bob was in the barn with the cows when he heard a loud, clanging racket. A fifteen-foot metal chain attached to the farm dog had somehow got tangled up in the mower and was slowly dragging the terrified mutt toward the sharp, spinning rotors. Lawson knew he was too far away to get to the mower in time. He caught sight of Steve rushing up the driveway to the farm.

Fortunately, the mower stalled, and the chain stopped only a few feet before the dog would have had an unappetizing encounter with the rotors.

Laughing, the boy began to untangle the chain from the lawn mower. Still, the Lawsons felt that Steve was more reserved than usual. "Steve seems a little quiet this evening," Alice Lawson told her son. Perhaps Lynne's death had shaken the boy, Bob thought. The day before, Steve had dropped by the barn and appeared to be bewildered by events: "I heard they found Lynne in the bush," Lawson remembers Steve telling him. "How did she get there?"

With the Lawsons' dog safe from the marauding mower, Steve hopped on Lawson's new Ferguson 35 tractor. "He loved being on that tractor," Lawson recalls. "I would often let him ride on it. Steve was good with machines." The lanky boy stood on the tractor's floorboard, leaning against the fender, while the farmer rode across his land. When they got to the edge of the crops, Steve jumped off and perched himself on a large rock. For safety reasons, Lawson never let Steve stay on the tractor when he hooked it up to the harvester. As Lawson began haying, Steve rested on the rock, gazing out at the paths and trails where the children played hide-and-seek and picked berries. He saw the thick expanse of Lawson's bush where only a few weeks earlier he and his friend Leslie had built a tree house.

"He was sitting on that stone, but next time, when I turned the tractor around and came back, he was gone," Lawson recalls. "I guessed he had walked back to the barn."

Bored, or perhaps anxious to get home for a bite to eat, Steve headed back down to the county road.

He never made it home.


At the Goderich OPP station, Inspector Harold Graham had made up his mind. Jocelyne's story about a date and the phone call with the results from the laboratory analysis of Lynne's stomach contents pointed the finger at the Truscott boy. "At ten minutes to seven, I had him picked up," Graham said. He sent out Const. Donald Trumbley to bring in the boy—preferably without his parents' knowledge. "I asked the constable to try and get him away from home." The OPP cruiser pulled up to the gateway at the Lawson farm.

"Would you get into the car and come with me? We want you to read over your statement," Trumbley explained, referring to Steve's interview with Graham that morning.

"Yes," said the teenager, without a moment's hesitation. Looking back forty years later at that fateful moment, Steven explains that in 1959 young people had an abiding respect and trust in authority. "Back then when you're fourteen years old, you looked up to the police. When they told you to get in the car, you got in the car," he says. Steve never thought to question where Trumbley was taking him, much less to ask about his legal rights.

Trumbley pulled into the Goderich police post with his teenage passenger and took the boy into a small room at the back of the station. Steve had no reason to believe he was doing anything but signing a witness statement. The police did not tell him he was no longer simply a witness, that he had instead become their chief suspect. They did not tell him this trip to the station was, to all intents and purposes, an arrest. Certainly, they wanted his signature—but not just on a statement. What the OPP wanted from Steven was a confession and they were going to do everything they could to get one, even if that meant bending a few rules to the breaking point.

When Steven walked into that police station Friday, he was walking into what, in hindsight, can only be described as a trap, carefully planned and well executed by Harold Graham. Twenty minutes before dispatching Trumbley to pick up Steve, Graham had another officer, Sgt. Charles Anderson, obtain a search warrant for the Truscott home. Anderson then contacted Dr. David Hall Brooks, the chief medical officer on the base "and advised him of what we had planned to do."

Graham had a very specific objective in mind—get Steven alone, without any interference from his parents. Years later, at a police convention, he boasted about his well-planned strategy: "I was well aware of the judge's guidelines that it is preferable to have a parent or social worker present when you are questioning a juvenile," he explained to his appreciative audience. "I was also well aware that it would be an exercise in futility, so I chose to disregard those guides."

Graham's was a bold admission of how far the police were willing to go to get their man, even if their man happened to be a fourteen-year-old boy. "Judges can always set their own guides for prisoners, they are not laws," Graham said defiantly. And he was right. The Juvenile Delinquents Act in 1959 did not require the police to ensure a youth's parent or guardian was present; today it is the law. Still, while Graham had not strictly violated any laws, he seemed to forget that the police had not told Steven he was a "prisoner" or even officially a suspect. At the boy's murder trial three months later, the judge was unsparing in his criticism of the police's tactics that night: "The ordinary safeguard should have been taken and he should have been warned. He was undoubtedly under arrest. It was clear he would never have been allowed to go."

"Will you read this aloud," the inspector told the boy as he handed him a typed statement based on Steve's interview earlier that day. Steve read the text out loud and, according to Graham's account, asked for only one minor change. He said his return to the school was not at 8:00 p.m., but closer to 7:50 or 7:55 p.m. "That was crossed out . . . and changed, and he said then it was correct, and I asked him to sign it and he did," Graham said. Steven signed the statement at eight o'clock, ten minutes after their meeting began.

The inspector from the Criminal Investigations Bureau, a veteran of a decade's worth of homicide cases, now had the boy exactly where he wanted him: alone in a room in a police station. Every police officer hopes they can crack a murder case with a confession, thereby saving the courts time and trouble. For the next hour and a half, Graham, assisted by Constable Trumbley, probed and prodded Steven.

Graham began by questioning his story of seeing a car at the highway. "I told him it was difficult to understand that because the distance was so great and I asked him if he was sure," the inspector later recounted.

Yes, Steve said, he was sure.

Was he sure that he had seen Lynne with her thumb out at the highway?

Well, the boy said, he had not actually seen her thumb; he had seen her arm out.

Graham noticed a crescent-shaped scratch on Steven's left arm. How did he injure himself, the police officer asked.

On a tractor in Lawson's barn, came the reply.

Then Graham moved to the guts of the interrogation: "Have you ever taken a girl into Lawson's bush?" he asked.

"No," Steve said.

"Have you ever made a date to take a girl into Lawson's bush?"

"No."

"Have you ever spoken to Jocelyne Gaudet about going into Lawson's bush?"

"No."

"Were you at Jocelyne Gaudet's house on Tuesday night?"

"No, I haven't been to Jocelyne Gaudet's home since last winter," Steve answered, according to Graham's account.

"Have you ever phoned Jocelyne Gaudet?"

"No, I have never telephoned Jocelyne Gaudet." Steve said. "The only conversation I have had with her is in school." It was a strange question. Had Jocelyne told the police about a phone call to arrange the alleged secret date? If so, the police apparently considered it an unreliable claim, for the police would never again mention a phone call to Jocelyne.

There is no official record of what went on for the duration of the ninety-minute interrogation. The two police officers were the only witnesses. Graham took only a single sheet of notes. Today, Steven Truscott remembers the first hours of his slow, steady slide into the abyss of incarceration: "They would take turns questioning me and calling me a liar," he says of Graham and Trumbley. "One would come in and question you. He would leave the room. The other one would come in and he would say: 'You lied. You did this, you did that.' They keep questioning you and calling you a liar, and you just can't believe what's going on. In your mind, you can't understand what's happening. And all through the whole thing I stuck to what I had said."

If the OPP inspector was hoping the boy would crack, he was sadly disappointed. "He steadfastly maintained that his statement was true in every detail," Graham later reported.

Throughout his ordeal that night—and indeed, throughout all his forthcoming days in court—Steve never cried, at least not in public. Much like his mother, the fourteen-year-old held his emotions in close check. "I just wasn't brought up that way—it's kind of not the air force way," he says today in reflection. "I knew I hadn't done anything. I had nothing to be afraid of."

That did not mean the boy was not scared out of his wits as he sat in a police interrogation room. Why hadn't the police contacted his parents?

Doris Truscott was in a panic. It was 9:30 p.m. and there was still no sign of her son.

"Where is he?" she wondered. "He should have been home—it's very seldom he's late."

Bob Lawson was baling his final load of hay for the day in his barn when a pair of headlights lit up the driveway to his farmhouse. As he walked over to the car, he saw Doris Truscott roll down her window. The farm was the only place she could think her boy might be this late at night.

"Have you seen Steve?" she asked. "It's getting dark and it's not like Steve to stay out late."

"I saw Steve earlier, but not for a couple of hours," the farmer informed her.

Doris was filled with a sense of dread. One schoolchild had already gone missing and turned up dead in the bush. Where in heaven's name was her boy?

At the OPP station in Goderich, Graham had decided to take Steven to the RCAF guardhouse in Clinton. He ordered one of his men to find Steve's father, Warrant Officer Dan Truscott. The police got Steven to the guardhouse on the base around 9:25 p.m. Ten minutes later, his father arrived "in a hostile attitude," according to Graham. The inspector had kept Steven in custody—getting him to sign a statement and then questioning him about a murder—for two and a half hours without even informing his parents. But the OPP man could not grasp why a parent would be upset at the officers who had swept away his son without notifying anyone.

"The father asked me in a belligerent manner how and where Steven had been picked up," Graham said. Dr. Brooks painted a slightly more sympathetic picture, reporting that Steve's father "naturally was the anxious parent who wanted to know what had happened to his son and why he was there."

For his part, the frightened boy felt relieved at least one of his parents was on hand. "My dad was there, so I figured, you know, he's not going to let anything happen," Steve says.

Dan Truscott immediately wanted to know if his son had been taken into police custody with his own consent.

"I asked him to get into the car to accompany me to read the statement and he got in willingly," Trumbley reported.

Dan turned to his son: "Is that right, Steven?"

"Yes," the boy answered.

Graham attempted to allay the father's fears. "I told them that Steven had been brought in on my instructions and as a result of our investigation thus far certain suspicions had been directed toward Steven." The OPP inspector explained he wanted doctors to examine the boy.

Steve's father asked to speak with the boy alone and took him into an adjoining room. "I told him they were accusing me and calling me a liar," Steve recounts. "It was quite clear they were trying to pin this on me." Dan emerged from the chat with his son a few moments later.

"I refuse to allow Steven to be examined by a doctor," he said. "Steven says you accused him of murdering Lynne and called him a liar."

"I didn't accuse him of murdering Lynne at all," Graham replied. "I pointed out certain features from his statement that indicated he was lying. My only duty is to try to determine the truth."

"Steven never goes out with girls," his father reportedly said.

"We have information that he had a date with a girl that night," Graham replied, referring to Jocelyne's story of her rendezvous with Steven in the bush. "Will you consent to a medical examination of Steven?"

It was a pivotal moment. Ever the military man eager to do the right thing, Warrant Officer Dan Truscott was not one to question rules and regulations. He turned to his friend, Sgt. Charles Anderson of the OPP. "What do you think about it, Charlie?"

"I think you should consent to the examination," Anderson suggested. "It looks bad if you don't consent to the doctor examining Steve." (Truscott could not know that Anderson was hardly a neutral advisor. Under Graham's orders, he had already taken steps to secure a search warrant for the Truscott home, even before Steven was picked up. Lawyers would later convince a judge that Anderson's comments were an unfair police inducement.)

In any event, it is doubtful that Dan Truscott could have wrested his son away from the police, even if he wanted to. "It was apparent to me it was unlikely he would get the boy home," Dr. Brooks reported. In the end, Steve's father bowed to authority; he turned to the OPP officers surrounding his son and agreed to the medical exam. Nobody asked Steve what he thought.

Initially, there was some question about whether Brooks should conduct the exam, but after consulting with the commanding officer, it was determined it would be better if an outside, civilian doctor performed the task.

The police asked Dan Truscott for the name of his family doctor. He mentioned that in the past, they had consulted a Clinton general practitioner, Dr. John Addison. Addison had briefly seen Steven twice in October 1957 for a urinary infection, and had treated Steven's brother Bill for a threatened appendix.

Dr. Addison arrived at the guardhouse around 10:35 p.m. A graduate of the University of Western Ontario, he had been practising medicine in Clinton since 1943. A stern-looking man with dark hair, a trim moustache and black glasses, Addison was well liked by the local citizenry. Presumably, the family doctor was supposed to be more dispassionate than Dr. Brooks, the military doctor working closely with the police. But Addison's first move was to consult with the air force medical man. "I met Dr. Brooks first, who outlined a bit of the story that had transpired before as to why they wanted me to examine the prisoner," Addison said later. "I had known . . . that this boy was the possible suspect of the rape." Hardly a good start for a neutral observer.

"He accompanied me into the adjoining office," Brooks said. "An examination of Steven then took place."

A short while earlier, Steve's mother had shown up at the guardhouse. "I was dumbfounded, I couldn't believe it," she recalls. "I felt I should have been told that they were taking him and questioning him, and I should have been there. Did they not think parents would worry when their son is not home?" She glanced at her fourteen-year-old boy, alone and frightened. "I can remember him sitting in the chair. He just looked [as if he was saying,] 'What's going on?' He couldn't believe it."

All her adult life, Doris had been a law-abiding, conservative-minded military wife, respectful of authority. That was about to change. "I always respected the police," she says. "But I sure as hell learned to lose respect."

Three officers, Corporal Sayeau, Sergeant Anderson and Cpl. Helmar Snell, followed Doris back to the house. She let them in through the side door and they advised her they had a search warrant.

"You don't need a search warrant—if it proves anything, go ahead, look!" Doris told the officers.

From Steven's bed upstairs, Sayeau took one pillow slip, two white cotton sheets, a wool blanket and a pair of red flannel pyjama bottoms. From his dresser came two pairs of washed underwear; from the hamper, some dirty underwear and a red shirt; from the top of the stairs near the back door, a pair of brown shoes. From outside the house, the police took Steve's bike. In the basement, hanging on a clothesline, the police found a pair of red trousers.

"Those are Steven's trousers," Doris told the police, according to their notes. "He was wearing them on Tuesday evening. I washed them Wednesday morning. I did all the washing Wednesday morning."

Sergeant Anderson asked Doris if she noticed anything unusual with Steve's clothes when he came home Tuesday.

"No, just boy dirt."

80

"Mrs. Truscott had a guilty feeling about her son by washing his trousers the next morning," Sergeant Anderson later concluded. The police would always insist the red jeans were the only piece of clothing on the line; Doris would claim there were more clothes at the far end.

Outside the Truscott home, the flashing lights of the police cruisers created quite a stir in the normally serene and pitch-dark rural community. Bob Lawson, finally finished with his farm work by 11:00 p.m., had been troubled ever since a frantic Doris Truscott had dropped by earlier. Lawson decided to drive around the neighbourhood to search for Steven. When he saw police vehicles around Steve's house and Steve's bike—but no sign of the boy—he feared the worst. "We were all a bit jumpy. I mean, a child had just been murdered; now here's another kid missing," Lawson says.

"Did you find Steve?" Lawson asked Corporal Snell.

"Oh yeah, don't worry, we know where he is" was the cryptic answer from the officer.

Lawson was not the only neighbour to drop by the Truscott home. Lil Woodson, whose two teenage boys played with Steve and his brother Ken, had never been that close to Doris. "I knew of her, but we played bridge in different groups," she explains. She had heard that Doris had been looking for Steve and came over to see if there was any news.

"Have you found Steve?" she asked.

"Oh, yeah," Doris said without flinching. "He's in the guardhouse."

Woodson became a regular visitor from that moment on. "We became pretty close friends," Woodson explains. "What brought us together was that my boys were just about the same age as hers. There but for the grace of God, it could have been one of mine."

By now, Steven had been in police custody for nearly five hours, almost half of that time without a parent present. Still, he remained calm and relaxed when, in the presence of his father, the two doctors began their examination.

Dr. Addison chatted with Steve to put him more at ease. "I didn't want to go in and strip the boy off and examine him. I tried to talk to him and asked him what it was all about," he later said. "Steven was very co-operative." The other doctor concurred. "He was quiet and got up and took his clothes off, as he was told, and was completely co-operative," according to Dr. Brooks. "He was examined from head to foot."

The doctors found the usual war wounds collected by an active teenager in the battlefields of a playground. On Steve's left arm, there were "four little scratches," the longest about 1¾ inches. On his right elbow, three linear scratches. On his knees, "two small scratches" about an inch long. On the back of his right thigh, a circular scratch about 2½ inches long. The police later suggested this mark matched a rip in his jeans and could have been made by the barbed wire surrounding Lawson's bush.

None of the marks were recent enough to show any blood. Addison concluded: "I thought they were trivial, little things."

But as he continued to examine the boy in front of him, Addison made a disturbing discovery: "We found a very sore penis." The doctor found "little red spots where the capillaries had been destroyed" in an area about the size of the ball of his thumb or a quarter on each side of the shaft. He described it as "like a brush burn, with serum oozing from each of those large sores on the side."

Up until that moment, according to Dr. Addison, Dan Truscott had been "just a bystander." Now the father was concerned. "Both his father and I were rather alarmed at the lesion there, and we both impressed upon Steven that . . . things looked rather dark," Addison said.

"How did you get such a sore penis?" the doctor says he asked the boy.

"I don't know. It has been sore about four or five weeks."

"He has never said anything to us because it hasn't bothered him," his father said.

Addison says he pushed Steven for an explanation of the sores: "Have you been masturbating?" he asked.

No, Steven answered.

Did Steven get his penis "caught in a knothole," the doctor asked.

No, the boy replied.

Had he perhaps had intercourse with "some other girl who he was trying to protect?"

No, insisted the boy.

Addison again asked Steve if he had been masturbating. "Finally, he said he had a week ago—in his bathroom."

The two doctors left the room to tell the police about the troubling results of their examination. In a sex slaying, a sore penis on a suspect was a big break. "Here, in the officers' opinion, was incriminating evidence, circumstantial, yes, but still, in our view, very important," Graham commented later.

The police decided to take a blood sample, and Steve's father readily agreed. Dan Truscott even collected a lock of hair from his son's head at the police's request.

It was 1:00 a.m., well past Steve's bedtime. Dr. Brooks recalled that Steve's father insisted "that Steven was very tired and that Steven should be allowed to go home." But the police were far from finished with the teenager.

At one point, the police and doctors glanced at Steve sitting listlessly at a desk. "The boy was dallying on the typewriter and they thought he was tapping out some plausible theory or confession," Addison recounted. "We waited for a long time and he was still tapping away and nothing happened."

With no confession or explanation at hand, Addison turned to Inspector Graham and made a startling suggestion. "Well, he won't tell me anything about it, he won't tell his father anything," Addison said. "Do you mind if I go and question him some more?"

Graham readily agreed. After more than six hours of confinement, Steven still showed no signs of cracking. The OPP homicide investigator was only too glad to have the genial country doctor try his hand at interrogating the exhausted boy.

Dr. John Addison had completed the assignment he had been called that night to perform: a medical examination of one of his patients. Why did the doctor now decide, at 1:00 in the morning, to pursue a role more appropriate to a detective? "I didn't receive what I thought was a satisfactory explanation for his sore penis, and I wanted to see if I could get him to tell me some more of the truth," he later explained. "His stories, I didn't feel, were jibing too well and I thought I could convince him to tell me some better reason for his sore penis."

Steve had told the doctor that he'd had the sores for about four or five weeks. If Addison acted as a personal physician should, his concern should have been for his patient's health, not his criminal status. He could have taken a swab of the oozing serum, sent it to a laboratory for examination and treated Steven accordingly. If the results proved the sores came from an illness or skin condition, Addison could have laid the entire matter to rest.

Instead, Addison proceeded to question the boy for about one hour. There were no witnesses. Steven does not recall anything about the meeting. Addison's version of the events, the only existing record, came from notes he scribbled during his talk with Steven and from a lengthier account he wrote later that morning.

The doctor tried to urge his patient to come clean. "I told him that if he told the truth he would likely get off a lot easier than if it was dragged out of him in a long court procedure." Addison tried to befriend the boy in the hopes that he would open up more willingly. "Steven, there seems to me some discrepancy in our story as to how this all happened," he said. "I hear one thing from the police and one thing from you, and you haven't told us about this sore penis and things. Now let us see exactly what happened and we can put the story together."

Steve described the car he saw on Tuesday night and insisted—as he had from the start—that the yellow marker he saw on the rear fender was not necessarily a licence plate: "I think it was yellow. I am not positive whether it was a licence plate or not."

"What did you talk about when Lynne was riding with you?" Addison asked.

"She asked about our fishing places," the boy answered. "I said there was one down by the river and across the highway there was a little trout stream."

Fatigued and alone, Steve nonetheless was sticking to the story he had told police from the start. But then his tale, according to Addison, took a strange twist.

"I don't know whether I was down [by] the river or not," Steve allegedly said. "I can remember her saying something about getting a thistle. I am not sure where it was. It might have been [while we were] going down by the river. There were lots of thistles in the field."

Which field, Addison asked.

"The one just back of the bush."

"Did she get a thistle while walking through the field?"

"I think so."

"Do you think there is a possibility you may have taken her in the bush?" asked the doctor.

"I don't recall it. I remember walking in the field, but not with her."

"Are you positive you were walking through the field?"

"I am not positive but I think I was," Steve is reported to have said. "I remember letting her off at the highway. . . . I remember going down through the field, I think. I remember something about someone yelling out that they stepped on a prickle. And then I remember coming out and getting on my bike. I remember coming back to the station."

A few moments later, Steve added some more details: "I went over the fence just about two telephone poles from the middle of the field. I remember something about a big rock, sort of smooth, I think. I hit my foot on that rock. I think that was when I was going out to get my bike."

In the doctor's mind—and to the police waiting outside—it all sounded if not like a confession then at the very least a description of events before and after the murder. "I cannot help but feel that this boy did not act to me like a normal boy while I was talking to him," Addison wrote to Graham a few days later. "Even the suggestion that he may have harmed Lynne brought no angry denial or an outbreak of tears. . . . He did not protest strongly enough when I suggested he had molested Lynne. He agreed it could have happened."

To Steve's defenders, the boy's words—even assuming the doctor accurately recorded them—were no more than the confused ramblings of an exhausted teenager drained almost beyond the point of consciousness. Steve's bizarre tale of thistles, prickles and smooth rocks sounded almost dreamlike. And vague phrases such as "could have" and "might have" and "I don't know" were hardly self-condemning admissions of guilt.

Addison gave no warnings to his patient that he was, in effect, questioning him at the behest of the police. The police had not even formally advised Steve that he was their chief suspect. They were not legally required to tell him that any statements he made could be used against him. Still, a judge would later blast the police in no uncertain terms for trying to use a doctor to question a teenage boy.


But as far as Inspector Harold Graham was concerned, he now had a solid case. He had testimony from Jocelyne about a date, an oral report from the laboratory about a time of death before 7:45 p.m., a boy with penis sores and a freshly washed pair of red jeans.

Graham made no apologies for the gruelling marathon session he put the boy through to get what he wanted. "Some of the critics point to the length of time Steven was in our custody before the charge was laid," he said. "Major crimes are not always solved in time limits."

Graham consulted by phone with the Crown prosecutor. Dr. John Addison drove home and wrote up his notes.

At 2:30 a.m., Graham walked into the guardhouse and saw Steven with his head on his father's shoulder. "I told his father we were taking him to Goderich," Graham said. In other words, to jail.

At three o'clock on Saturday morning, June 13—more than eight hours after Graham had first taken Steve into police custody—the boy's arrest became official. Mabel Gray, justice of the peace, signed the arrest warrant charging Steven with murder: "Steven Murray Truscott (fourteen years of age), on or about the 9th day of June, 1959, . . . unlawfully did murder Lynne Harper, contrary to section 201 of the Criminal Code of Canada and, being under the age of sixteen years, is therefore a juvenile delinquent within the meaning of the Juvenile Delinquents Act."

Juvenile or not, within hours the Crown prosecutor would be in court attempting to get the boy tried—and, if convicted, hanged—as an adult offender.

# 9

## "LIGHTNING SPEED"

"Police Spin Speedy Web to Nab Suspect" ran the headline in the Toronto *Telegram*, reflecting the media's amazement at how quickly the OPP had cracked the sensational case. "Inspector Graham worked almost without sleep for two nights and a day in investigating the case which has shocked the air force community and surrounding towns," the paper reported. Another newspaper noted with equal surprise that the arrest came with "lightning speed."

By any standards, it was a remarkably swift operation. Harold Graham had arrived in Clinton at 7:30 Thursday evening. By Friday evening at 6:50, he had sent out a squad car to pick up Steven. In less than twenty-four hours, he had solved the headline-grabbing murder that had prompted the province to issue an unprecedented "dead or alive" reward.

"It was three o'clock [on Saturday morning] when we landed with Steven Truscott at the county jail," Graham later recounted. "Now this was only a good start on the case because there were so many witnesses to interview." It seemed oddly backwards, reflecting how rushed the entire operation had been: one would expect the police to make a "good start" in a case by interviewing the "many witnesses" *before* an arrest, not afterwards.

———

There were signs that almost from the start, Graham was convinced Steve was the killer. Graham and some of his key officers would occasionally return to the Mount Forest home of Cpl. John Erskine, the identification officer, at the end of the day to relax and discuss the case. "The officers would come back to our house," recalls Erskine's widow, Dee Harris. "I'd hear them talking about the pros and cons."

Dee remembers one of the first visits in particular, at the very beginning of the investigation. Graham came in first, up the three stairs from the side door landing toward her kitchen. "He's guilty!" the inspector declared as he turned to his men behind him. Dee did not catch the rest of the argument, but she remembers thinking to herself: "If it's so cut and dried, why bother investigating any more?" When Graham left, she discovered her husband shared her concerns. "I just can't believe Graham would say he's guilty when the case has just started," John Erskine told his wife. As Erskine continued to gather evidence on the case over the summer months, his doubts—and his conflict with Graham—would grow.

It was understandable that, as the last person known to have seen the girl alive, Steve would become a prime suspect in the eyes of the police. If Steve was innocent, there were troubling coincidences, and all good cops, for good reason, are suspicious of coincidences. His friend Butch George had been spreading rumours about seeing Steve take the girl to the area where her body later turned up. Doctors found sores on his penis days after a girl had been raped. The police thought it extremely unlikely that Lynne's assailant would return so close to her home to commit the crime or to dump the body. "Picking the person right up at Number 8 Highway and bringing her back and murdering her in the bush. My God! How realistic is that?" asks Hank Sayeau.

The police were also bothered by the fact that two children who claimed to be looking for Steve that evening, Jocelyne and Butch, could not find him between 7:00 and 8:00 p.m., and several others failed to spot him on the county road during that time. They were intrigued by his sometimes angry response to his friends' taunts about being with Lynne. They doubted he ever could have spotted the car he claimed to have seen. And eventually, they were convinced that a footprint near Lynne's body could have been made by one of Steve's shoes.

These pieces of evidence—or speculation—all pointed the police in one direction. But there were outside pressures at work as well. Dennis Alsop, who was one of the officers involved at the end of the Truscott investigation, and who knew Graham well, offers this explanation for Steve's rapid arrest: "Everything pointed to him. You're not going to let him walk. Emotions were pretty high [at the air force base]. Finding one of their own, raped and dead. There was a suspect—I don't think they could sit on it very long. That was the way when I was on the job—you moved, you didn't sit around and wait."

Emotions were indeed high, and not just at the base; the tension also existed between the air force personnel and the people in the surrounding towns and villages. The citizens of Huron County had a conflicted relationship with the several thousand military on the base. On the one hand, Clinton depended heavily on the support jobs and consumer dollars generated by the sprawling air force station. On the other hand, many civilian residents resented the isolationist attitude of the air force people. The base was, after all, legally and socially a kingdom unto itself.

All these tensions came to the fore when the grim discovery of Lynne's body would inform the air force and civilian communities that a murderous sexual predator was on the loose; each was convinced the monster could only have come from the other side.

As the farmer living right next door to the base, Bob Lawson straddled the divide between the military and the civilian worlds. He recalls that the airmen were convinced the culprit was a local civilian, and the residents of Clinton were fearful it was true. "There were some air force officers who were very outspoken about it. 'We're going to catch this person and we're going to deal with him ourselves in the most severe manner,' they said. And that kind of upset people. I mean, who do they think they are to take the law in their own hands? But when they pinned it on a young boy from the air force base, I suppose the people outside the base heaved a sigh of relief."

The rest of the province also heaved a sigh of relief. The forces of law and order had solved a gruesome sex slaying. The good people of Ontario could go back to their ordinary lives secure in the knowledge that, once again, the justice system would triumph. Steve was the perfect candidate for Lynne's murderer. He was not a civilian from town. He was not a man in uniform, which could result in a public relations disaster for the air force. He was just a teenager who could be dispensed with quickly and quietly.

Sitting on his small metal cot in the Goderich jail, Steven could not fathom what had brought him there. Looking back at his arrest much later as an adult, he concludes he was just at the "wrong place at the wrong time."

"I think it was the easiest route possible for them and they jumped on it," he says.

The trick to good detective work is not in finding a suspect, but in proving guilt methodically and scientifically while eliminating all other possibilities. The OPP had good reason to question the fourteen-year-old who last saw Lynne. But inquisitive reasoning appeared quickly to give way to blinding tunnel vision once they had the boy behind bars.

"We checked all kinds of guys around the camp and around the community," Hank Sayeau insists. "There were all kinds of names being put forward. If information came in about so-and-so being a possible suspect, we ran it down, trying to find out if there was any substance to it or if he had an alibi. Trumbley and I worked all summer trying to run down people that people had something to say about."

Sayeau and the other OPP officers did work hard all summer. And while they doubtless followed many leads, there is no indication from the official record that the police ever seriously investigated anyone as a suspect in Lynne's murder besides the fourteen-year-old boy they already had in custody.

Indeed, in the mountain of police files, the word "suspicion" is only used once to describe any other individual besides Steven. Vaughn Marshall, airman #56527, had been posted in Clinton for only ten days. He was eighteen years old and lived in the barracks with the other single men. Marshall was the only person the police questioned as a potential suspect before they arrested Steve. Only four decades later, when the long-buried police files became available, did details about Marshall's story emerge.

According to the entries in Cpl. Hank Sayeau's notebook, he spoke to the young air force recruit at 9:55 p.m. on Thursday, June 11, right after Sayeau left the autopsy. Marshall told police that at the muster parade on the base to organize the search parties, the commanding officer informed his men that Lynne—still a missing girl—might have taken a ride in a Chevrolet Bel Air. "I remember [a] two-door, '59 white hardtop, whitish grey," Marshall's statement reads. "Passed it on outskirts of Clinton about 7:05 or 7:10. Fellow and girl in it. Car going 45–50 miles per hour." Marshall said the car had "PQ plates"—in other words, yellow licence plates from the province of Quebec.

It is possible that after the muster parade Marshall told someone about spotting the car and word got back to the police. That would explain why the police might have wanted to speak to him so soon after the body was found. But far from being a casual car spotter, Marshall began telling the police some odd stories. He told Sayeau he was "introduced to Lynne about three or four weeks ago on a Friday or Saturday night" at a party, and claimed Lynne stayed at the party until midnight. He added that on the Tuesday night Lynne disappeared, he caught sight of the girl in downtown Clinton. "Saw Lynne Tuesday night on street corner in front of Tip Top Tailors—6:30 or 6:40," the police notes read. "Lynne had on (blue) shorts—just noticed from waist down. Looking down street toward Goderich."

Marshall got the description of Lynne's shorts right—police and military bulletins alternately described them as blue or turquoise. But there was no way Lynne had time after her supper to leave the base and travel to Clinton at 6:30 p.m.; she was busy helping the Brownies in the schoolyard at the time. And it was hardly likely she would have been at a party until midnight with eighteen-year-old airmen.

Retired OPP officer Hank Sayeau today has only vague recollections of questioning Marshall, but theorizes that Marshall was making up stories to get involved in a high-profile case. "Why waste your time with an individual like that?" Sayeau concludes.

Harold Graham, however, would later cite Marshall as an example of how the OPP did pursue other suspects seriously and did not go after Steven Truscott with a single-minded obsession. "My inquiry . . . during the evening of June 11th . . . included investigating the activities of an airman," he wrote in a 1966 OPP memorandum. (In an earlier draft of the memo, Graham used stronger language, writing that he questioned "an airman suspected of the murder.") He reported that Marshall "was cleared of suspicion when a . . . girl confirmed his whereabouts on the evening that Lynne Harper disappeared."

Marshall said on Tuesday evening he picked up his girlfriend, Lois Dale, and took her to Stratford, where he paid a woman twenty-two dollars because he had bumped into her fender earlier. He and Lois then went to Goderich until around 10:00 p.m.

There are no records in the available OPP files of what Lois Dale did or did not tell the police. There is no reason to believe she was anything less than truthful. Even assuming she fully corroborated her boyfriend's story, however, there seemed to be a double standard in operation; the word of a girlfriend alone was enough to exonerate an eighteen-year-old man, but the word of two boys who put Steven in the clear when they saw him at the river with Lynne were seen as suspect precisely because they were his friends—"chums of the accused," in Graham's dismissive phrase.

The case of Vaughn Marshall raised one other intriguing question. If the police believed his story about travelling with his girlfriend to Stratford and Goderich as proof that he did not abduct Lynne, they had every reason to believe his story about seeing a "whitish grey" 1959 Chevrolet with yellow plates on the highway outside of Clinton.

In other words, even if the police correctly ruled out Marshall as a suspect, he could have been a potential witness, one who said he saw the same type of car Steve claimed to have seen at around the same time and in the same area.

Marshall was not the only one who spotted a potentially suspicious car. On the night Lynne disappeared, two people saw two different cars parked near the bush late at night. By the time Steve was arrested on Friday, the authorities also knew of three other sightings, specifically of 1959 Chevrolets, in the area. Military and police officials largely ignored all but one of these five vehicle reports.

Officials at the base guardhouse initially paid Bob Lawson little heed when he told them of a car he spotted near his bush late Tuesday evening. He had finally finished a hard day's work on his farm and decided to take a late-night dip in the river. He drove down the county road toward the bridge with a friend. About halfway down, right next to the tractor trail that led into his bush—and about three hundred feet from where Lynne's body was found—he spotted something he had never seen there before: a parked car.

"There are places on that road where people park at night, mainly down between the railroad and the river. But I don't ever recall seeing anybody park there at night right beside the bush," Lawson says. It was an older maroon or red convertible, possibly a '51, '52 or '53, with a man in the front seat. "We slowed up behind it and shone the lights on it," Lawson recalls. "I thought there was a girl sitting in the car, too; you couldn't tell for sure, but I think I could see her head. She was sitting down much lower than he was. As we drove by he gave us a bit of lip."

A few minutes later, when Lawson was swimming in the river, the car whizzed by over the bridge and the driver hollered at him again. The farmer dismissed him as a local man upset because his romantic date in his fancy convertible was spoiled. Lawson did not give the matter a second thought until three days later, when Lynne's body was discovered in the bush right next to where the car was parked.

Two weeks later, the police did track down an airman who owned a dark convertible. The airman admitted he had parked on the county road at least five times when he was "with a girl" but said his late-night car romances took place nearer to the river than to the bush where Lawson had spotted the car. He said he sold his car two weeks after the murder; the police made no further investigation.

At least in that instance police had made an initial inquiry. Other car sightings made that Tuesday never even got to that stage.

A young airman had stayed behind to clean up the mess hall on the Tuesday evening, putting away beer bottles and clearing the tables. Donald Hall, who fixed radar equipment at the base, earned a little extra cash by performing some housekeeping duties. Hall lived off-base, and sometime after 11:00 p.m., he got into his car to drive home along the county road. "As I came around the bend, just after the school, I glimpsed in the distance the bumper of a car. I said to myself, 'What idiot would be parked on the side of this road? I put on my high beams so that I wouldn't hit whoever it was.'"

It was a large late-model vehicle "with heavy chrome," but Hall does not recall the make or colour. As he approached the car parked near Lawson's bush, he caught sight of the lone occupant, a young man in what appeared to be a light-coloured shirt. "He had very dark, wavy hair. A shock of wavy hair," Hall remembers. "He wasn't military for sure. Not with that hair. He was a civilian, just sitting there." He says he reported it to both the military police and the OPP. Neither force seemed terribly interested. "I talked about it in detail to the OPP. The officer took down the particulars, but when I was finished the interview I thought it was not very thorough," Hall remembers. "I was never called back about it. Never."

Another member of the air force had a disturbing encounter with a car earlier that evening. A nightly trip to the Custard Cup was a regular part of the routine for Cpl. Arlene Strauman and her girlfriends. "We used to go over there every night—it was almost without fail," she remembers fondly. "It was always crowded."

There was not much else for young single women to do at the Clinton air force base after hours. Arlene, a flight control operator, was one of three hundred women stationed there for four months of radar training. After classes ended around 4:00 p.m., she and fellow female officers would make a short trip to the mess hall, then back to the barracks for a quick shower and a change into civilian clothes. Around 7:00 p.m., they would stroll down to the Custard Cup. On Tuesday, June 9, the ritual was no different from any other night, except for one detail.

As Arlene and her friend, Beverly Bolton, left the ice cream parlour to return to the base, three men pulled up in a car.

"Would you girls like a ride?" one of them asked as he rolled down the window.

"No, thanks," the officers said demurely but firmly.

"Oh come on," the men teased, undeterred.

"I can still see the young man in the back seat who did most of the talking as vivid as anything," Arlene says today. "He was very good-looking. I remember he had really nice teeth and lots of black curly hair."

Arlene also remembers the car as a "light green or a greenish grey" Chevrolet. Just as Steven says he easily recognized the '59 Chev at the highway around 7:30 p.m. that evening, Arlene had no problem identifying a similar vehicle thirty minutes earlier at the Custard Cup. "Everybody knew what a '59 Chev looked like because they were so different," she explains. "They had those big tail fins and triangular-shaped tail lights, too."

The fancy car, though, was not enough to entice Arlene and her friend. The Chev rolled along the road beside the two air force women for about fifty feet. Then, the defeated Romeos sped away.

At the time, Arlene Strauman thought nothing of the incident: "We just walked back to the base and laughed about it." But she recalled the encounter with unease when later in the week, news about Lynne's murder was making the rounds at the base.

"Everybody was talking about it in the barracks. We heard that they'd caught a young guy and he had said that she had gotten into a '59 Chev. So right away Beverly and I looked at each other and said: 'Hey, we saw a '59 Chev. They tried to give us a ride.' So we went down to the guardhouse to tell."

But the military police at the guardhouse were not interested. "They didn't want to listen to us at all," Strauman recalls.

"You don't know your cars. What do you know?" Strauman remembers the dubious MP asking her.

"Well, I know it was a Chev!" she replied.

"I got the impression they didn't want to hear from us," Strauman remembers, the bitterness still in her voice. "We knew what a '59 Chev looked like, we definitely did. We saw it. Nobody called us. Like nobody wanted to know anything more about our information." The next week, both women finished their duties at Clinton and transferred out.

"Looking back on it now, they didn't want to know that somebody else besides Steven Truscott had seen a '59 Chev," Strauman concludes. "They already had their case and they had their suspect, and they didn't want someone to come in and mess it all up."

Strauman's account can only be confirmed indirectly, since the daily logbooks from the military police at RCAF Station Clinton are no longer available. "I know that people went to the guardhouse with information, and it was passed on to us, and we investigated cars and we investigated people," says Hank Sayeau of the OPP. The air force did issue a general call for anyone on the base with any information about Lynne's activities on Tuesday night to come forward. "As a result, numerous personnel did report to the guardhouse with various information concerning incidents occurring Tuesday night," said one official military summary of events that week. Just how many of these numerous reports the military passed on to the OPP or what the police did with them is not clear.

By the end of the week, the OPP had two more reports of 1959 Chevrolets in the area, both of them with Quebec plates. When Sayeau questioned Vaughn Marshall on Thursday, June 11, the young airman said he had spotted a man and a woman in a two-door "whitish grey" 1959 Chev with yellow plates on Highway 8 just outside of Clinton. That same evening, around 10:00 p.m., the police in Goderich stopped a man for a speeding violation. He was driving a 1959 Chevrolet with yellow Quebec plates. The officer noted the car was green but "could be mistaken for grey." The police did some checking the next morning and found that the driver had been spotted reading a paper in a local hotel, but was not registered there. He said he was on his way to Sarnia. The police had his name and licence number, but made no further follow-up. By then, they were well on their way to arresting Steven Truscott.

Ignoring potential leads was one thing. Not following rudimentary police procedures was quite another. In any sex-related murder, it was standard practice for the police back in the 1950s—and still is today—to check out the "usual suspects": the known sexual predators or recently released offenders with a history of sexual assaults. That is precisely what the OPP did three years before Lynne's murder when a five-year-old girl, Susan Cadieux, was sexually assaulted and murdered in London, Ontario, in January 1956. A police official told the newspapers they had quickly rounded up fifty known "sexual perverts," in the indelicate terminology of the times. (Cadieux's killer was never found.)

But when Lynne's body turned up nearly naked in the bush near Clinton, there is no evidence the police made any serious attempt to check out the whereabouts or activities of known sexual deviants in the region. That failure was all the more surprising because the proximity of the crime scene to the air force base gave the police both a large pool of suspects and, in theory at least, easier access to their personnel files. Several thousand young, single men moved in and out of the Clinton station on a continual basis. They were transients, often strangers to the region and to each other. Alcohol abuse was not an uncommon problem in the ranks. They constituted a much more likely group of potential suspects than teenage students.

That is certainly what some townspeople thought. Henry Lamb ran a service station in Goderich and coached a hockey team for the children. "At that base there would be a thousand men to question, but instead Steven just got railroaded," he says.

Graham did make one request of the air force brass, asking that the commanding officer hold a muster parade "for the purpose of examining the genitalia of all airmen at the school." Perhaps the prospect of his men lining up around the flagpole and displaying their private parts for all to see in the summer sun was too much for the commander to consider. He declined. "I did not pursue the matter," said Graham diplomatically.

Possibly if Graham had made a more restricted request to examine only the military records of the airmen with known criminal or sexual offences, instead of the penises of all the enlisted men, the air force might have been more compliant. That will never be known; there is no indication Graham made any more requests of the air force to investigate the sexual practices of its own men.

It was a shame. Because if he had bothered to ask, it is likely that Graham would have uncovered the case of the pedophile who had tried to pick up little girls less than three weeks before Lynne went missing.

On May 21, ten-year-old Nancy Davidson was walking back from school with two of her friends along a quiet country road outside of St. Thomas, about an hour's drive from Clinton. "We noticed a car pull up and stop when the first girl went off to her house," Nancy recalls. "He came around the corner and stopped in between two houses when the other girl went up into her driveway."

That left Nancy alone. As she neared her home, the strange man in the car pulled up beside her and first asked her if there was a creek near by, then if there was good fishing. "But then he asked me if I would get in the car. He wanted me to pick out the prettiest present. And I said no. And then he picked out these panties that he had. And he totally scared me," she remembers. "His eyes were bulgy and he had that glassy look and there were dark circles. And I knew he was drinking and I just wanted to get away."

As luck would have it, Nancy's father, Glen, approached in his car and Nancy dashed to safety. "I couldn't get in his car quick enough. And I told him what the man had done and said." Her parents called the police, who located the man not far away and brought him back to the Davidsons'. "He denied it and I called him a liar. And I said, 'Please look under the front seat,' and they did."

The police found alcohol and a bag full of panties. They arrested the man on charges of contributing to the delinquency of a minor.

The man's name was Alexander Kalichuk. At thirty-five, he was a sergeant in the air force, stationed at RCAF Station Aylmer after seven years at the Clinton base. What the OPP and the Davidsons did not know was that the troubled airman had a long history of sexual and alcohol problems. As far back as 1950, Kalichuk was charged with an unspecified "indecent act" in Trenton. He paid a ten-dollar fine and thirty-nine dollars in costs. There was a conviction for drunkenness in 1952. But military records indicate his sexual escapades continued throughout the decade. One report makes reference to a "similar incident of exposure in Seaforth." The documents also mention a case in family court that was dismissed, but not before the authorities recommended treatment "before the airman finds himself in severe difficulties."

Raised on a farm in Manitoba, Kalichuk finished grade Nine and worked briefly as a farm labourer and bulldozer operator. He never found much success in anything except military work. He was in the air force from 1941 to 1946, then again from 1950 to 1955. He briefly left the military to take a civil service examination, but failed and re-enlisted in the air force by the end of

1955. In uniform, Kalichuk never rose higher than a posting as a modest supply clerk. From 1950 until August of 1957, Kalichuk worked at Clinton; his last summer there, he quite possibly crossed paths with Lynne Harper's father, Leslie, who ran the supply department.

Even when he was transferred to Aylmer, an hour away, Kalichuk never strayed far from Clinton. He lived on a farm about twelve miles from the base, owned by his wife, Helena. Neighbours remember her as "a great cook, a wonderful woman and a hard worker," but her husband had a darker reputation as a "silent drinker." She had two older children by a previous marriage; both of them loathed their stepfather. "He leached my mother's farm for money," says the son. "She became an alcoholic because of Alec." His sister, nineteen in 1959, was equally bitter: "I found him sleazy; he gave me the creeps. It doesn't surprise me that he tried to lure girls into the car."

Together, Alec and Helena also had a young son named Mark. Ron Christensen, Mark's best friend, remembers the strange warning his pal would give him "every time without fail" before entering the Kalichuk household: "Just look at Dad and say 'Hi' but don't wait for him to say 'Hi' back," Mark would tell his friend.

"I walked into that house to be greeted by the eerie, quiet, stone-faced Alec sitting in the dark kitchen at the table with a drink in his right hand," Ron recalls. "Alec always had a bright red, glowing face with a pasted-on sort of lost stare."

One week after Kalichuk attempted to abduct Nancy Davidson, he appeared in a St. Thomas courtroom. The sergeant had spun various tales to justify his rather bizarre behaviour. "He claimed that he was on the way to the Lake Erie shore and that he was going to use the female underwear as prizes for fishermen," according to one account. "The Lake Erie shore is nowhere near where the airman was found." Kalichuk also claimed he had "decided to give some children in the neighbourhood a party" and had purchased five pairs of underwear and some boxes of candy as prizes for them.

The magistrate dismissed the charges for lack of conclusive evidence but warned the air force of his suspicions. Kalichuk paid a fine for illegal possession of liquor. Nancy's father remembers what one of the OPP officers said to him as the man who tried to abduct his daughter escaped prosecution.

"He might have got away with it here," the policeman said, "but he'll be looked after by the air force." It was wishful thinking.

It was eleven days after Alexander Kalichuk walked out of court in St. Thomas a free man that Lynne Harper disappeared.

There is no evidence Kalichuk murdered Lynne Harper. There is also no evidence that he did not. His whereabouts on the evening of June 9 are unknown. But his bizarre actions before June 9 and his rapid mental collapse afterwards suggest he was at least as likely a suspect as the boy police had scooped up and incarcerated in the Goderich jail with "lightning speed."

For starters, it was quite possible Kalichuk was in the Clinton area at the time. Though he was stationed in Aylmer, his stepdaughter remembers he came home "pretty much every night." Home was not more than a fifteen-minute drive from the intersection where Steve says he left Lynne. Kalichuk's daytime attempt to pick up Nancy Davidson also suggests it was not unusual for the wandering sergeant to be cruising the county back roads even when he was supposed to be on duty. "He was often on the road," says his stepson.

What's more, Kalichuk had a criminal record and a predisposition to luring young girls. "I could see him raping or molesting," says his stepdaughter, "but not murdering." He was a coward, she says, and if he murdered Lynne, "he probably did it while he was drunk."

Kalichuk did not own a 1959 Chevrolet. Still, even if Steven's description of the vehicle was accurate, there was no proof Lynne's murderer was in that car. It is possible Lynne got a ride in one car but met her assailant somewhere else on the road. According to his stepchildren's best memories, until 1959 Kalichuk drove a light yellow Ford. In early 1959 Sergeant Kalichuk bought a new 1959 light yellow Pontiac Stratochief, whose wide fins made it look somewhat like the flashy Chevrolets of the same year. Curiously, Kalichuk took advantage of a short trip out west in early July to sell his car. Just weeks after Lynne's murder, Kalichuk got rid of the brand-new vehicle he had owned for only a few months.

It is also possible Kalichuk had access to another car around the time of Lynne's disappearance. His stepdaughter was married in May, and family guests came from Manitoba, one of the provinces that issued yellow licence plates. The car Kalichuk used to try to pick up Nancy Davidson on May 21 was probably not his yellow Pontiac. Glen Davidson, Nancy's father, remembers "it wasn't a bright colour"—yellow or white or red. He vaguely recalls "a gunmetal grey or a light brown" vehicle. "It was big at the front end, wide," Nancy recalls. "I remember seeing wings—they were shaped up at the back."

What is certain, at any rate, is that the medical and military records portray a deeply troubled man spiralling out of control precisely around the time of Lynne's murder. On the very same morning Lynne vanished, two senior medical officers met at the St. Thomas probation office to discuss Kalichuk's deteriorating mental state. Also that day, a doctor at the air force infirmary began what would be a series of disturbing medical reports: "Lately he has been drinking to excess with increased frequency," the physician noted on Tuesday, June 9.

Eighteen days after Lynne's body was discovered, Kalichuk left Ontario on annual leave. By July 2, Kalichuk was back at the RCAF Station Aylmer infirmary with a grim prognosis. "He was . . . evasive at times and there was a definite paranoid tinge to his thinking," Dr. A. M. Beach reported. The sergeant suffered from "overwhelming anxiety, tension, depression and guilt." The psychiatrist's analysis was blunt: "sexual deviation" and anxiety reaction. "We are dealing with acute emotional disturbances so often seen in people with character disorders when they get caught," Beach concluded. It appeared to be a disproportionate overreaction if Kalichuk was bothered only by the panty incident—a charge, after all, that he had so easily beaten.

On Dr. Beach's recommendation, the air force dispatched Kalichuk to the psychiatric clinic of London's Westminster Hospital on July 22. "On admission, he was tense and nervous, and anxiety and depression were obvious," the medical staff reported. When questioned about the attempted pick-up of young girls in May, Kalichuk was "extremely vague and evasive." He also gave an "inadequate explanation" for his indecency charge in 1950. But by July 31, doctors decided the sergeant was "no longer depressed" and discharged him. The clean bill of health would prove to be premature.

What is remarkable in the Kalichuk case is not what the doctors did but what the police did not do. When the officers in the OPP's St. Thomas detachment received the general police bulletin on June 11 about the murder of a twelve-year-old girl just outside an air force base, why did no one think of Kalichuk—the air force sergeant they had picked up just three weeks prior for trying to lure a ten-year-old girl into his car? Why did no one in the military raise a red flag when they heard about the Kalichuk file at the same time an officer's daughter had been raped and murdered? It is not as if

Kalichuk's condition was a dark secret. Medical officers were reviewing his case on the morning Lynne vanished. On Monday, June 15, two days after Steven Truscott first appeared in court, an air force social welfare officer named J. J. Young wrote a confidential, two-page memorandum providing a detailed history of Kalichuk's sexual proclivities.

Kalichuk's name, however, would never appear on any police or military files concerning the Harper case. Steve's defence lawyer and the jurors would never hear about the man using panties to pick up young girls in the Clinton area in the days before Lynne's murder.

But Kalichuk's name would resurface in the 1960s; the military and the OPP could not easily escape his shadow.

Kalichuk was not the only known sexual predator in the Clinton area. Clayton Dennis, thirty-seven at the time, lived in Seaforth and had a contract to do regular electrical repairs on the air force base. "I got to know Harper because he was the head guy signing cheques," Dennis says today. "I went to his house one time. It was to repair his dryer."

Dennis admits he was involved "in a little rape case" in 1948 and served time in Collins Bay Penitentiary. He says he left Seaforth in the fall of 1959, but that his departure had nothing to do with Lynne's murder or Steve's trial. "My work was depleting and the bank was pushing me for money and I got a chance to go to the States," he says. "Nobody chased me out."

Gwen McKeller remembers it a bit differently. The former wife of Dennis's best friend, she and her daughters often saw Dennis at their home. "He talked about sexual things in a way that disturbed the girls," she says. "Disturbed me, too."

McKeller describes Dennis's departure in 1959 as "strange and sudden." She recalls talking with Dennis shortly after Lynne's death. "He made one statement that I didn't like. He said, 'She had it coming to her' or 'She was asking for it.'" To this day, McKeller wonders why the police did not check on Dennis. "He was right on the base where that girl lived and he was working there," she says. "Why wouldn't they interview everybody . . . especially ones with a record for rape?"

Clayton Dennis now lives in Florida. He dismisses such talk as "small-town gossip." "I had nothing to do with it," he says. "[The] police never came to talk with me about an alibi or about their case. Nobody ever questioned me."

Matthew Meron was a nineteen-year-old airman at RCAF Station Clinton who also worked as a lifeguard at the swimming pool, and therefore presumably knew Lynne, an avid swimmer. Shortly after Lynne's murder, he transferred out of Clinton to Goose Bay and later to Trenton. Meron married and had two daughters, but was an excessive drinker and was kicked out of the air force. He began beating his wife and sexually abusing both daughters. On one occasion, "he took [one] daughter to a secluded wooded area, and when she resisted sexual intercourse, he tried to strangle her," according to a family member. "Hunters came by and she got away."

"When his wife learned of the sexual abuse . . . she confronted her husband," the family member recounts. "He denied it at first, then with no sign of remorse, he told his wife rape was better than murdering them."

Meron never talked about the Harper murder, except to tell his wife "he knew Steven Truscott was innocent." Family members grew more suspicious when Meron seemed ill at ease anytime they were near the Clinton area. At one point, after an evening of drinking, he turned to his father-in-law and asked: "Do you think my hands could kill?"

In 1959, while stationed at Clinton, Meron had access to his mother's car, a late-model Chevrolet licensed in Montreal—in other words, with yellow Quebec plates. Meron died in 1985 without ever having been questioned by police about his activities on the night of June 9, 1959.

An air force base and a small town harbour many such ugly secrets. The fact that sexuality was more taboo in the 1950s than today did not mean that sexual problems were any less common than they are now—only that they were more suppressed. When murder strikes, it is the job of the police to turn over rocks and unearth the dark, nasty undergrowth of a community.

OPP Inspector Harold Graham, in talking about the Lynne Harper case, once said investigators had to ask themselves some tough questions. "Has the investigation been thorough and complete? Has anything been overlooked?" he asked. "Has every aspect of the case, whether favourable or unfavourable to the accused, been checked and presented to the Crown attorney?"

Excellent questions that still deserve an answer.

## 10

## "THE ROSE BEYOND THE WALL"

**A** Buddy Holly song blared over the radio. It was early Saturday morning, June 13, and twelve-year-old Catherine O'Dell was already on vacation in Alberta. A friend to both the Harpers and the Truscotts, she and her family had left Clinton for a summer holiday just a few days before Lynne's disappearance.

Suddenly, the crackle of a news bulletin shattered her vacation bliss. The police had arrested and charged a classmate with the murder of Lynne Harper. Later she found out it was Steven.

"For me it's like, 'Where were you when John Kennedy was shot?'" recalls Catherine. "I went and woke my parents up. It was really a shock. But what was even more shocking was that Steven had been accused of it."

Back in Clinton, Bob Lawson was stunned when he learned the boy who loved to ride his tractor was now sitting in jail on a murder charge. "We could hardly believe it. But in those days I guess we didn't question authority as much as we do now. We assumed somebody in their position, doctors and police and so on, were more or less above reproach."

If friends of Steven, such as Lawson, were willing to give the police the benefit of the doubt, there were plenty of others on the base who hardly needed convincing that the boy was guilty. "I don't remember anybody being surprised or insisting that it wasn't him," recalls Mike Fisher, Lynne's former babysitting charge. "Too many fingers were pointing in his direction."

Karen Allen, Steve's girlfriend of sorts, remembers the confusion a young child faced. "It was frightening to think that something like that could happen to Lynne, and then all of sudden Steve was in jail and people kept saying that he did it," she says. "It was hard to be a kid and keep saying 'but he didn't' when everybody said 'but he did.'"

Schoolteacher Maitland Edgar says most of Steve's classmates were in shock. "They didn't know what to believe," he recalls. "There was a bitter feeling that anyone could do that to Lynne." Edgar personally did not think his star athlete was guilty. "I never believed he was capable of doing something like that," the vice-principal says. "If he had had a snap temper he would have had occasion to let it explode during hockey or football games, and I never saw it."

There was less sympathy for the accused murderer in the population at large. News of the arrest flashed across the front pages of the newspapers, briefly overshadowing the upcoming visit of the young Queen Elizabeth. "CHARGE BOY, 14, GIRL'S SLAYER," the *London Free Press* announced.

"Nothing has occurred in this district for scores of years to so arouse public feeling," an editorial in the local Goderich paper said. "It was a bitter contradiction of a complacent feeling that such a thing just 'can't happen here.'"

The grief and sadness at Lynne's widely covered funeral that Saturday afternoon only heightened public fury against her accused slayer. Flowers blanketed the front of the base's Protestant chapel as the mourners filed in. Shirley Harper sobbed uncontrollably. Her husband, Leslie, and Lynne's two brothers also wept. So did the many air force officers, neighbours and dozens of children in attendance.

Squadron Leader Charles MacLaren, station padre, read a poem called "The Rose beyond the Wall":

> *Shall claim of death cause us to grieve,*
> *And make our courage faint and fall?*
> *Nay! Let us faith and hope receive—*
> *The rose still grows beyond the wall.*

The padre tried to offer a "word of hope and assurance" to what he aptly described as "a shocked and sad community." Lynne's rose still did grow beyond the wall, he assured the mourners, "because God has designed it so through immortality."

As the funeral procession left the chapel, thirty members of Lynne's Girl Guide troop, neatly dressed in uniform, formed a guard of honour on either side of the coffin. Sixteen RCAF officers served as pallbearers. Her family buried Lynne, the newspapers reported, "dressed in the Girl Guide uniform she loved."

Two families lost their children on Saturday, June 13. One, forever, to a graveyard; the other to a jail. The Harper family's loss was infinitely more tragic and final; the Truscott family's loss was nonetheless wrenching because they felt a grievous error had been committed and had no way of knowing how long their boy would stay behind bars.

"It will be over soon and he'll be out. That's the only thought I had," remembers Doris Truscott. "It would be fixed up in no time." Never in her wildest nightmares could she imagine that by the time her Steven emerged from prison, he would be a grown man.

Just two hours before Lynne's funeral began, the boy many blamed for her slaying made his first court appearance.

"His Folks Sob, but Suspect Emotionless," ran the headline in the *London Free Press*. "A pale, skinny fourteen-year-old boy, charged in connection with the murder of a twelve-year-old schoolmate, showed no emotion today as he faced a juvenile court judge," the paper reported. Dressed in a black-and-grey-striped shirt and dark sports trousers, "the boy was allowed to talk to his sobbing parents for a few minutes."

"He was scared, definitely scared," Doris Truscott remembers. To be suddenly thrown into the bowels of the justice system unnerved her as well. "It was all so different from everything that was in our lives. You're dumbfounded," she recalls.

The issue before Magistrate Dudley Holmes was a simple one: where should Steven be tried? As a general rule, a fourteen-year-old would be tried as a minor, with all the extra protection the law affords. In a juvenile court, Steve's trial would take place in camera and before a judge alone, presumably somewhat more dispassionate than a jury picked from a local population inflamed over Lynne's murder. If convicted, he would receive a sentence far short of the maximum death penalty, and his record would be sealed.

But the Crown prosecutor was determined to see Steven bumped up to adult court—and hanged as a murderer. Certain provisions of the Juvenile Delinquents Act allowed for moving the case to adult court. Two of the conditions were straightforward in Steven's case: the offence had to be indictable under the Criminal Code, and the accused had to be at least fourteen years old. The two remaining conditions were left to the discretion of the judge: trying a child in adult court had to be in the best interests of both the community and of the accused. It would take three more hearings over the next two weeks before the judge would make up his mind.

After only five minutes before the magistrate, Steven was remanded into custody until the following Thursday for another court appearance. There would be no bail for an accused murderer, even if he was a juvenile. Steve had spent the first hours of his incarceration in the early hours of Saturday morning in a detention centre. After he had appeared in court, the police now took him to his new home, the Huron County Jail. "I hope he won't be here very long," a jailer told a newspaper reporter, fully aware of the desolate and dingy conditions in the century-old cells.

The old grey bricks of the jail had not changed much since the fortress-like edifice on the outskirts of Goderich had housed its first criminals in 1841. Steve passed through the ten-foot-high wooden doors at the entrance, then down a thirty-yard corridor as dark as a tunnel, the sound of his footsteps and those of his police guards echoing off the walls. The boy undressed and stood, humiliated, as the guards frisked him and ordered him to shower. They gave him a shirt, a pair of pants and shoes—without laces. Four rows of cells radiated from the metal spiral staircase in the centre. The guards pulled a bolt to open a two-inch-thick door, then passed through two sets of metal gates to a narrow hallway lit by three light bulbs. Along one side ran a row of tiny cells with steel bars, with a common toilet at the end of the corridor.

"It really was kind of terrifying," Steven remembers. "You're doing what you want, you're free, and all of a sudden you're thrown in a four-by-eight-foot room, no friends, no family," Steve says. "It's really hard to describe the terror that you feel—especially at that age."

The boy suffered a further humiliation that afternoon when Cpl. Hank Sayeau arrived to seize his underwear. It was a puzzling move; the police had already seized underwear and other clothes from Steve's dresser and hamper at home. What did they hope to find on a pair of undershorts that the boy had worn overnight in jail? Steve, to his horror, would find out the answer in a public courtroom three months later.

"Oh, what a horrible place for him to be in," Doris Truscott says, shuddering at the memory of her first visit that Saturday. "It was just so cold. Even the people there were as a cold as the jail was. They didn't consider him being a kid." His mother and father huddled with their son, trying to assure him his ordeal would soon end. "I just thought it would all be over in a few weeks, so I wasn't worried," Doris says.

It was a curious scene: mother and son, steeled in the Truscott tradition of shielding their emotions, both unwilling to show their true anxieties and trepidations. "You could sense he was scared," his mother recalled. "I think he was putting up a front."

Of course he was putting up a front, Steve admits. He had learned from a master. "My family basically does the same thing, to show you that everything is going to be okay, and so you do the same thing. You feel it inside but you don't let it show."

Inside, though, the boy's nerves were jagged, his fears were racing. He did not sleep that first night. "I don't think your mind even grasps what's going on. It takes a long time to sink in," Steve recalls. "And all the time that it's going on you're thinking, 'They're going to realize that they made a mistake, and you know, they're going to let me go.' But it just never happened that way."

When Doris Truscott gave birth to her second son on January 18, 1945, in Vancouver, British Columbia, she could hardly expect to be visiting him in a jail before his fifteenth birthday. Just three years earlier, Doris had met a jovial young wireless operator on an air–sea rescue boat where her father was an engineer. Dan Truscott, like Doris's father, was air force; he started dropping by the house as a casual friend, but it did not take long for the wartime romance to blossom into marriage. Four children soon followed over the next decade: Ken in 1943, Steve in 1945, Bill in 1950 and Barbara in 1953. Like most military families, they played hopscotch across the country, living in bases near Vancouver, Winnipeg, Edmonton, Quebec City and River, Manitoba. "You roughed it—didn't always get what you wanted," Doris says. In the dreary cold of Manitoba, the Truscotts made do in "a little shack" with an outdoor toilet; they were grateful to be one of the families to enjoy running water.

Steve and his brothers earned extra dollars by cutting neighbours' lawns and shovelling driveways. In Edmonton, Steve and Ken delivered newspapers across the expansive base; in the dead of winter, their hands and feet were so cold that once home their father rubbed them with hot towels until the blood flowed again. But Steve would never complain; even as a child he kept his emotions in check. His mother remembers when, at the age of four, Steven fell down the stairs and a two-inch sliver of wood from a door jabbed into his back. The painful shard was extracted and some iodine was applied—and not a single tear from the boy. "I was more upset than him," his mother says.

Steve loved the adventure of new woods to explore, new rivers to skate on, with every move the family made. But military life was not without its costs. Steve was wary of striking deep friendships. "You were friends with everybody but close with nobody. Either they were moving or you were," he remembers. Steve had to repeat his third grade when one transfer meant he could not keep up with the new standards in his latest school. But school work was never Steve's forte in any case. "He was good but he would just day-dream," his mother recalls his teachers saying.

Steve preferred to get his education from the forests and streams near his many successive homes across the country. He brought bugs and snakes into the house as pets, a habit he did not abandon when he arrived in Clinton. Maitland Edgar recalls Steven enthralling his classmates with a baby screech owl and a muskrat.

As a boy, Steve dreamed of being a pilot. With his brothers, he built air-planes out of balsa wood, attaching a small gas motor and two wire lines to move the flaps. Their dreams took flight in the fields next to the real air-planes of the air force. At night, in his bedroom, Steve stared at the plastic models of Spitfires, Hurricanes and Mustangs that hung from his ceiling and cluttered his dresser.

Sports were his passion. In winter, he donned goalie pads on the skating rinks; in spring, a third-baseman's glove helped him shine on the baseball diamond. In summer, he often spent a month in Vancouver visiting with his maternal grandfather, who owned a small fishing boat in Burrard Inlet. Steve helped "Pop" put down crab traps, and sometimes, with luck, they had a lunch of fresh seafood on the boat. A faded black-and-white family photo shows a beaming Steve, no more than seven years old, holding a small floun-der and smiling with as much pride as if he had just harpooned Moby Dick himself.

The Truscotts moved to Clinton in the summer of 1956, a year before the Harpers arrived. Steve found new friends, new woods and rivers to explore—and new pranks to play. At night, with few streetlights to attract attention, Steve and his friends would hide in the pitch dark between the houses, knock on side doors and scamper off.

They did not always make a clean getaway. In April of 1959, neighbours called police when they heard a rowdy bunch of teenagers causing some property damage at the vacant farmhouse near the Clinton base. The police investigated but pressed no charges. Steve's father, Dan, organized a troop of boys to clean up the damage. "Steve said he didn't do the things they were accused of, but he was with the kids, so he had to pitch in and go back and clean it up," Doris recalled. "They knew right from wrong."

"You had a guideline—if you crossed over that, you were in trouble," Steve agrees. "If you did something, you got heck. You knew you were going to get heck."

Steve's reputation was such that even those who could hardly be accused of being in his fan club—the police—had to admit he was, by all accounts, a decent kid. "Steven was a pretty regular guy, he was well thought of," remembers OPP Cpl. Hank Sayeau. "The only thing I ever heard critical of him was that he had to win. All the kids were Steven's buddies—girls and boys. The kids liked him."


In the Goderich jail, his parents said their goodbyes and left Steven alone, on a metal cot in his cold cell. The boy who gave youngsters in Clinton rides on his toboggan, the boy who won the senior championship at the school field day, would never be a boy again.

On June 13, 1959, the Harpers buried their daughter. That same day, Steven Truscott buried his boyhood.

# SUMMER: THE SCRAMBLE TO MAKE A CASE

## 11

## TROUBLE WITH WITNESSES

Harold Graham was convinced he had Lynne's killer safely behind bars. Now all the senior OPP investigator had to do was prove it. And he had to prove it to the satisfaction of the new player who had entered the Truscott game: Crown prosecutor Glenn Hays.

The Goderich prosecutor had a reputation among police officers for being a painstaking taskmaster. "He had to satisfy himself that there were reasonable and probable grounds to put the guy on trial," Hank Sayeau remembers. "He just wanted more before he moved. You had to have things organized."

Glenn Hays, like Harold Graham, realized this case was going to be one of the most important of his career. Throughout the summer, the prosecutor and the chief investigator worked closely. Graham frequently held meetings with the Crown counsel in his Goderich offices. When the trial began, the OPP inspector sat right beside Hays, giving him advice and insight into the witnesses.

"It is the duty of the investigator to carefully weigh the facts in his mind," the inspector later remarked in a speech about the Truscott case in 1967. "Make an assessment of the facts, pursue certain theories, taking into account any new developments that might tend to support or detract from them." As it turned out, Graham and his men would stumble across many "new developments" that did detract from their original theory about Steven, facts that should have warned Hays and the police they were possibly on the wrong track. Instead, Hays ignored the inconsistencies and contradictions— and more importantly, kept them from the defence.

With Lynne buried and Steve in jail, the police began a weekend blitz of belated fact-finding: on Saturday and Sunday alone, they interviewed seventeen children and two adults. Over the next couple of weeks they would interview dozens more. For many of the children of RCAF Station Clinton, what should have been a summer of laughter and laziness became an ordeal of police queries and probes.

The police had already spoken casually to some of the children in the days after Lynne's disappearance. But now, with a murder trial looming, interviews were much more serious. They set up headquarters at the school gym and grilled the children one by one as they filed in. The police then typed up the youngsters' statements and, in most cases, got them to sign them in the days that followed. Graham was front and centre during the questioning; his signature appears as a witness at the bottom of almost all of the statements gathered that first weekend.

The children's words, their fleeting memories, the snatches of what they saw or heard, now became permanently etched in police documents. It was all standard police procedure, but for many youngsters, it was frightening. "It was pretty stressful. It was frankly terrifying," Bryan Glover, one of Steve's teenage pals, recalls. "They were always asking over and over: 'Well, are you sure, are you sure about that?' It felt like an interrogation."

Casual remarks suddenly took on a grim significance far beyond what a child could fathom. Karen Allen at first had no apprehensions when she sat down and looked up at the three police officers standing over her.

"I was not a particularly timid girl. They were asking me questions and I was answering," she says. "Then it took a turn and all of a sudden it was scary."

The turn came when Karen offered what she thought was a harmless romantic detail. "When I admitted that Steven had kissed me once at a dance party, they asked me if he had ever tried anything or if he had ever frightened me," she remembers. "I told them no, it was just a little kiss and that Steven wouldn't hurt a fly."

But Corporal Sayeau and Constable Trumbley seized on the revelation, according to Karen's memory of the event.

Had Steven ever tried bolder sexual advances, they wanted to know.

"No," Karen replied. "What are you asking me that for?"

"Did he ever frighten you?" they asked.

"No," Karen insisted.

"Then they started asking detailed questions about specific sexual acts and that's when I started to cry," Karen remembers. "Nowadays, with television, young people would probably know what they were talking about, but I really didn't. I was a kid who was green as grass. They didn't ask anything really crude but it was strange and upsetting."

Perhaps realizing they had pushed the girl too far, but determined to dig further, the police went to see Karen's mother. Mrs. Allen told the officers there was nothing sordid to investigate. Her daughter and Steven saw each other only occasionally; one time, Steve's father even drove Karen home after a dance.

"Well, why would she cry?" the police asked.

"Well, why wouldn't she cry if you're asking her questions like that?" Mrs. Allen retorted.

"So that was it. They never questioned me again," Karen says, trying to keep the anger out of her voice. "No one would allow the police to treat kids the way they did back then. If you weren't telling the police what they wanted to hear, they pretty much told you [that] you were lying. They didn't want to hear what you wanted to say."

Other children were more compliant. When strong-arm tactics did not work, the police were apparently not above exercising a little friendly persuasion to jog a child's memory. Ten-year-old Darrell Gilks told Graham and Trumbley he saw Steven on the evening Lynne disappeared, but he got some of the details wrong. "Steve had a red shirt," he said, incorrectly (Steve's shirt was white), "and red pants, and I don't know what shoes he had."

That last phrase was crossed out and, in a police officer's handwriting, replaced by the words "brown canvas shoes"—the footwear Steve wore that night.

No witnesses would need more massaging and coaxing from the police than the two children who would become star witnesses for the prosecution—

Jocelyne Gaudet and Butch George. Jocelyne had already given two somewhat confusing statements to the police, telling Graham she was at the bush looking for Lynne and telling Trumbley she went there to meet Steve, but at that time saying nothing about a secret date.

On Saturday, Jocelyne sat down with Inspector Graham and Constable Trumbley to tell them a third, more elaborate story. Graham and the prosecution seemed to have a faith in Jocelyne that her fellow classmates and teachers lacked. "She was a bragger. She was always telling people that she did this or that or what she knew—she would brag about boyfriends but no one believed she had any," recalls Meryann Glover, who was close with both Lynne and Jocelyne. "I didn't believe anything she had to say." Jocelyne's teacher, Maitland Edgar, shared that distrust. "We had some difficulties with her—school discipline, untruthfulness. She was just not reliable."

But the police needed Jocelyne to be reliable. If they were going to build an effective case against Steven Truscott, Jocelyne had to provide them with verifiable facts and times, to prove the boy was a sexual predator.

Jocelyne told the OPP officers that on the Sunday before Lynne disappeared, she dropped by Lawson's barn with a few other girls to see a newborn calf. The next day in school, during recess or social studies class, she chatted with Steve. "Some way or other we got to talking about if there might be any more calves, and Steven said he thought there would be two in the bush and asked if I wanted to go and see them."

Could she make it that night, Monday evening?

"I couldn't, I said, because I had Guides."

What about Tuesday?

"I said that I might but it wasn't set."

Jocelyne seemed confused about how often she and Steve talked about the alleged date. She told police that the next day at school they talked again, between 9:30 and 10:15 in the morning, during social studies period. At trial, Jocelyne would embellish her story, saying that there were not just two school meetings but "about four."

She was vague on the time for the date. She never claimed Steve fixed a time, only that, "I told him I might be at the bush if I could make it around six." Their rendezvous spot, according to Jocelyne, was to be "on the right-hand side of the [county] road, where the bush began. "And then I asked him to wear something I could see from a distance," Jocelyne added.

It is curious that the police did not immediately see this anecdote as somewhat fanciful. According to their star witness, the secret rendezvous was to take place in plain sight of everyone: not deep in the bush or even in the partially hidden laneway farther along the bush, but right on the road, not far from O'Brien's farm and the school. The county road at that time in the evening was a busy thoroughfare, crowded with parents and children of all ages. In fact, according to the police's own investigation, between 6:00 and 6:30 p.m., five different people—a woman named Beatrice Geiger, her son Kenneth, his friend Robb Harrington and two other teenage boys—all spotted Steven on the road. Why would Jocelyne think that special clothing was needed to spot him?

Jocelyne also added the following detail on the purported reason for the hush-hush nature of her meeting with Steve: "I didn't tell anyone about this plan to meet, because Steven told me not to tell anyone and not to bring anyone with me because *Bob didn't like a whole lot of kids on his property.*" Presumably, the police considered this excuse by Steven to be a clever lie to lure his prey into the bush. But a simple inquiry would have revealed that if Steven did use that pretence, it was a feeble one that Jocelyne should have rejected immediately. Every child on the base knew that Bob Lawson had a well-deserved reputation for openness and friendliness. "I don't think I gave the children the feeling they had to be secretive," the farmer recalls. Indeed, he explicitly told police at the time—just hours after they talked to Jocelyne—that "it was quite customary for the children of the air force station to be on my farm and in the bush."

According to Jocelyne, on Tuesday evening around 5:50 p.m., Steve came knocking on her door. "My brother, André, answered and called me to the door," she said. "I stood just inside the doorway and Steven stood outside."

"Hi," she said.

"Hi," Steve answered, then asking her if they had any homework, a strange query, considering Steve had not missed school that day and was hardly known as a studious pupil.

"I said we did and he said 'thank you,'" she recounted.

Just as he was leaving, Jocelyne added a comment: "I wasn't sure I would be able to make it to the bush at six o'clock."

"All right," he said.

The only person who could directly confirm that it was Steve who came calling was Jocelyne's seven-year-old brother. Oddly, there is no evidence in the police files that the OPP ever talked to the boy, who had presumably recognized Steve once and could do it again. The police did speak to Jocelyne's father, who said that "my son answered the door and called to my daughter that Steve was there, and she went to the door and talked to him for about a minute." In his first appearance in a courtroom, he would give a different version of how he came to know it was Steve at the door.

Evidently, the OPP were not bothered by the logical inconsistencies with Jocelyne's story. If her date with Steven was so secretive, why would Steven brazenly come calling at her house, thereby alerting her family just prior to luring their daughter into the bush for some hanky-panky? If Steve told her to "not to tell anybody" because of Bob Lawson's dislike of children, why did Jocelyne run to the barn to ask the farmer if he had seen Steve?

The OPP also never fully resolved a much more fundamental problem with Jocelyne's tale: just *who* was she looking for along the road and near the bush? The entire police case against Steven as a sexual schemer angling to get a girl, any girl, into the bush, was predicated on Jocelyne being on the road Tuesday evening hunting for Steve to meet for their secret date. While Bob Lawson confirmed to the police that she asked for Steve when she came to his barn, Jocelyne herself had *first* told police she was looking for Lynne. The only two children she spoke to on the county road that evening, Butch George and Philip Burns, *both insisted she had asked them about Lynne.* (Philip said she asked about Lynne and Steve; Butch said she was interested in Lynne alone.)

The OPP had to get around this dilemma. So ten days after her Saturday declaration to police, Jocelyne made an addendum to her story—in effect, her fourth police statement. The "further statement," as the OPP called it, was written in the third person: "She asked Philip Burns if he had seen Steven but never mentioned Lynne's name," it read. "Says she asked Butch George the same again, not enquiring about Lynne."

The OPP had no trouble getting Jocelyne to adapt her story. To get genuine corroboration, however, police needed Philip and Butch to change *their* stories to match Jocelyne's. But at the preliminary hearing and at trial, both boys would continue to insist Jocelyne had indeed enquired about Lynne.

If Jocelyne's story about the arrangements for her date had some gaps in logic, her recounting of her attempts to meet Steve on Tuesday evening was flawed by much more serious gaps in time.

Jocelyne was very definite about her times in her formal statement to the police and she stuck by those times in all of her court appearances. She said she left home around 6:30 p.m. and headed straight for Lawson's farm "to ask . . . if Steven had been around." She then biked down the county road, where she bumped into Philip and Butch. She continued on toward the bridge, where she claimed she tried to talk to Bryan Glover. "I asked him about the fishing but he didn't answer."

Jocelyne went out of her way to insist on her time at the river: "When I was down at the bridge, *it couldn't have been after seven*," she told the OPP. She then decided to return to the farm. "I stayed at Lawson's barn *rather a long time* and was home sometime between 8:30 and 9:00." Jocelyne would later specify that that "long time" was about ninety minutes.

For his key witness, Graham thus had a timeline that looked something like this:

| | |
|---|---|
| About 6:30: | Leave home, arrives shortly at Lawson's farm and stays only minutes |
| About 6:45: | Meets Philip and Butch near the bush |
| Before 7:00: | Down at the bridge |
| 7:00 to 8:30: | Leaves bridge to spend ninety minutes with Lawson |

Not a single one of the girl's times coincided with reality, a startling fact that the OPP could not have failed to notice.

Three boys confirmed that Jocelyne was near the bush. Philip, Butch and Bryan all saw her there. But they saw her around 7:15 or 7:20, not around 6:30. The police spoke to all three boys and could not have missed the fact that their key witness was seriously off in her timing.

As for her alleged visit to the bridge, it could also not have escaped the police's attention that—with the exception of Butch—not a single child or adult at the river recalled seeing Jocelyne there that evening. The police took statements from close to a dozen people at the bridge that weekend and would interview a dozen more in the days to come. No one talked about seeing Jocelyne—not even Bryan Glover, the boy with whom she allegedly tried to have a chat at the river.

Soon after Jocelyne spoke to the police on Saturday, June 13, OPP Cpl. Hank Sayeau visited Bob Lawson's farm to get a formal statement from him. Yet astonishingly, the OPP apparently did not ask the farmer to verify any of Jocelyne's times. Lawson told police Steve "appeared quite intelligent and was of good character," but Jocelyne's name did not once appear in his statement.

Only twelve days later, on June 25, did the police return to get another account from the farmer. "Jocelyne Gaudet came to my farm at 7:25 p.m.," he told police, putting her initial arrival at the barn almost one hour later than Jocelyne had. He was certain because Jocelyne asked for the time and he looked at his watch. Even more disturbingly, Lawson told the police: "Prior to leaving *she said she had been down at the bush looking for Steve and went down toward the bush again to look for him.*"

In other words, contrary to what Jocelyne had told police, *she went to the bush first*, before going to Lawson's farm.

Lawson's revelation that Jocelyne had told him a different story than she told the police should not have surprised the OPP if they had done their basic homework. They knew Jocelyne had to be near the bush between 7:15 and 7:20 when the three boys—Butch, Philip and Bryan—saw her there; and they knew she was not at the farm until around 7:25. Therefore, unless she was capable of time travel, her story had to be false: she had to have gone to the bush first and then to Lawson's barn. It was a contradiction the police either chose to ignore or dismissed as irrelevant. (If Jocelyne was at the farm around 7:25 and Steven did leave the school around that time with Lynne, it would also explain why Jocelyne never saw either of them.)

The OPP also never bothered to ask Lawson about the duration of Jocelyne's return visit, the one she claimed lasted about an hour and half from 7:00 to 8:30. The farmer would later say her stay lasted a few minutes, not ninety minutes. "It wasn't very long," he says. "I was hustling around because I wanted to get a lot of chores done on the farm."

Jocelyne seemed hard-pressed to fill up the entire two hours she was away from home—from 6:30 p.m. until around 8:30 p.m.—with her hunt for Steven. But the evidence shows that she could account for only about thirty minutes of her time that evening. There is an unexplained gap of about forty-five minutes from the time she left home at 6:30 until three boys saw her near the bush around 7:15. There is another gap of about one hour from 7:25 when Lawson said she left the barn until around 8:30 when she returned home, interrupted only by the few minutes Lawson saw her at his barn for the second time.

Whatever Jocelyne was doing that evening, it may have been something she didn't want the police or possibly her parents to know about, perhaps so embarrassing or personal that she was consistently inaccurate about her times not just with the police, but repeatedly in court. She was desperate enough that she would eventually ask an adult to help her to cover the time she could not account for.

It remains a mystery to this day what, if anything, Jocelyne was trying to hide. It also remains a mystery why the police so fervently believed a girl few of her classmates or teachers trusted.

As Graham and his officers began speaking to some of the other boys, including Steven's friends, they got their first inkling that Butch George did not have an abiding affection for the truth. Butch had told the police on the Thursday before Lynne was found and on Friday, after her body turned up, that—like Dougie Oates and Gord Logan—he had seen Steve and Lynne cross the bridge. That should have put Butch in the camp of potential defence witnesses. But on Saturday and Sunday, the police heard that he was spreading quite a different story to the boys at the base.

Allan Durnin told police that around 7:50 on Tuesday night, Butch told him that "he saw Steve Truscott go into the woods with Lynne Harper." A little more than an hour later, Butch was telling the same tale at the Custard Cup, according to George Archibald. "Butch said he saw Steve go into the woods with Lynne but I don't think we believed him or paid much attention," George told Graham. Bryan Glover, Tom Gillette and Paul Desjardine gave the police similar accounts.

These revelations must have excited the OPP investigators. A pal of Steven's who had previously given him an alibi was now changing his tune. Better still, here at last was a potentially pivotal eyewitness, someone who boldly claimed that he saw Steve Truscott take Lynne Harper into the woods where her body was later found. This was as close to the proverbial smoking gun as the police were ever going to get.

The police discovered that, as a result of Butch's tales, there was a lot of teasing of Steve in the days after Lynne's disappearance. Tom Gillette informed Graham that at school on Wednesday, Steve told him he went into the bush because "he heard a calf in the woods." That evening, Steve told a similar calf story to the boys gathered down at the bridge and "sounded as if he was threatening" Butch, Tom said. Allan Durnin told the police that on Thursday, Steve came close to fighting with him when he challenged Steve's story about giving Lynne a lift to the highway. For the police, a picture was beginning to emerge of a guilty boy, cornered by his friends and lashing out at his accusers.

The OPP formally interviewed Butch on Monday, June 15, but it was not until June 25, ten days later, that Butch signed his statement. For most children and adults, there was only a short interval of a few days, while the police typed out their handwritten notes, before they were called back in for the formal signing. Why the long delay in Butch's case? Did the police threaten Butch with the possibility that he could be charged along with Steven for trying to cover up for him? Or were the police working with him to get rid of some of the contradictions in his statement?

Clearly, the OPP were in a quandary with Butch George. If it was true he had seen Steve take Lynne into the bush, then they had a golden eyewitness. If that was not true, then one of their chief accusers against Steven was a liar. It was a seemingly stark and irreconcilable contradiction: either Butch *did* see Steve in the bush or he did not. Both could not be true. But remarkably, the police—and later the prosecution—decided they would have it both ways: they would use Butch's unverified tale of seeing Steve go into the bush to show Steve's anger when teased by his friends, while at the same time use Butch's quite contradictory insistence that he failed to spot his best friend at all on the county road that evening as proof that Steve must have been hiding in the bush. It was a stunning feat of legal gymnastics—and incredibly, they pulled it off.

In Butch's formal police statement, the OPP thus faithfully transcribed without question his account of what he told friends on Tuesday evening. "I told Allan Durnin that Steve was *at the bush* with Lynne," Butch told Graham and Const. Donald Trumbley. At the Custard Cup, he told several more boys a slightly different tale: "I had seen Steve *going into the bush* with Lynne."

Picture the scene: the OPP's top homicide investigator watches and listens as a good friend of the boy he has just jailed for the murder of Lynne Harper signs a statement declaring he saw Steve go into the bush. What more did the police need? Graham had found the eyewitness testimony he needed to put his suspect at the scene of the crime. A logical next step would have been to ask Butch a simple question. "This is very important evidence, Butch. Can you show us where and when you saw Steven take Lynne into the bush?" If police ever asked that question, there was no recorded answer to it in any of Butch's testimony to the police or the courts over the next three months. Either the police and the prosecution did not trust their chief witness enough to ask it, or, if they did ask, they were not satisfied with the truthfulness of Butch's reply.

There was good reason for misgivings. As they put together the chronology of Butch's statements, the police must have scratched their heads in bemusement, if not frustration. On Tuesday night, Butch was telling anyone who would listen he had seen Steve take Lynne into the bush. On Wednesday night when Butch, Steve and their friends gathered at the bridge, he denied that he was spreading that tale in front of the very boys to whom he had told it the night before. By Thursday morning, Butch was telling the police he saw Steve and Lynne, but not in the bush. This time, "he saw Lynne and Steven on the cycle going toward the highway" after they crossed the river. By Monday, he dramatically altered his story and swore to the police he had in fact not seen Steve or Lynne at all that evening, either at the bush or at the bridge, until he dropped by Steve's home around 9:00 p.m. Little wonder that the prosecution would make sure Butch was well prepped before testifying in court. Even then, his testimony ended up as a confusing jumble.

The OPP also seemed singularly uninterested in pursuing any other enquiries with Butch, except regarding his comments about Steve. The same day Graham sat down with Butch, the police files reveal the OPP learned that Butch's relative Mike George was claiming as early as Wednesday—the day after Lynne's disappearance—that Lynne had been raped. Not simply missing—as everyone thought at the time—but raped. Graham could have asked Butch if Mike knew more about what went on in the bush than Butch did. He could have asked Butch if he was covering for Mike or someone else. But there is no indication in the police files that the OPP asked any of these questions of Butch, Mike or anyone else.

Graham must also have noticed that Butch's statement seriously contradicted that of his other star child witness, Jocelyne. Butch gave quite a different spin to the encounter he had with Jocelyne at the laneway leading to the bush.

"I asked her if she had seen Steve," he recounted. She replied that she had not. Butch insisted that she then asked "if I had seen Lynne." Not Steve, as Jocelyne had claimed, but Lynne.

Butch said that Jocelyne then continued her quest for Lynne, not Steve, when he—but no one else—saw her down at the river. "She asked me if I had seen Lynne yet and I said no."

If the OPP had difficulty getting the changing stories of Butch and Jocelyne straight, they had the reverse problem with the two boys who claimed they saw Steve cross the bridge with Lynne on their way to the highway. In a statement witnessed by Graham and Trumbley on June 13, Gord Logan repeated the story that must have caused the police officers no end of grief, both for its consistency—the twelve-year-old never wavered in a single detail in any declaration he made to the police or in court—and in its potentially devastating impact on their case.

"I think it must have been nearly 7:30 when I saw her and Steve," he told the officers as he described what he witnessed while he was fishing and swimming in the river. "She and Steve were riding double on Steve's bike and they were going toward Number 8 Highway. . . . I am sure it was her. She was wearing shorts, I think." Gord said that about five minutes later, he saw Steve come back, this time alone, and stop at the bridge. "He hasn't talked to me about this," Gord added, perhaps in response to query from the police who were trying to determine if there had been some collusion.

Gord's statement was the single most powerful support Steve had for his innocence, because it confirmed his version of the time he left the school, and also confirmed his claim that he drove Lynne to the highway and returned without her. The police and prosecution would have to destroy Gord's credibility, by suggesting either that he lied or was mistaken about what he claimed to have seen from more than six hundred feet away.

Dougie Oates, the turtle enthusiast, posed a bigger dilemma for the police. Unlike Gord's, his story could not be dismissed because of distance. He had told Graham on Friday he had seen Lynne on the crossbar of Steve's bike as they rode right past him across the bridge, just inches away. On Saturday, he stuck to his guns. "I saw Steve and Lynne ride by. They were riding double on Steve's bike, going toward the highway," he said.

According to the police transcription of Dougie's statement, he was somewhat vague on the exact time he spotted the two older children. "I don't know the time, but I think it was a half hour either way from seven o'clock," his statement read. Dougie would later hotly contest saying those words, but they gave the police and the prosecution an opening. If Dougie's sighting was closer to 6:30, they reasoned that the boy was confused: he had seen Steven *alone*, just as several other people had seen Steven around that time along the county road. If, on the other hand, Dougie saw Steve *after 7:00 p.m.*, then he had to be telling the truth about seeing *both* Steve and Lynne crossing the bridge—and Steven was innocent. Timing, as always, was crucial.

When Constable Trumbley returned a few days after young Dougie gave his weekend statement to the police, he ran into the boy's obstinacy once again. "I took him over to a corner and we sat down in chairs and I explained to him this was the statement that was received from him on Saturday," the OPP officer recounted. "I asked him to read it over carefully. He took it in his hands."

"Is it correct? Want to make any changes?" the police officer asked the boy.

"No, it is correct," Dougie answered politely.

"Will you sign it?"

"No," the eleven-year-old said firmly, "my mother told me not to sign anything."

So the police had an unsigned statement, but one that was potentially damaging to their case just the same. Here was a classic example of what Graham called "new developments that might detract" from the police theory. Graham believed "every aspect of the case, whether favourable or unfavourable to the accused" had to be checked.

Dougie's story was clearly unfavourable to the police case, but the police seemed determined to help the prosecution prove the boy left the bridge before 7:00 p.m.—before Dougie could have seen Steven and Lynne. That meant they had to dismiss his insistence that he left for home around 7:30, after he saw Steve and Lynne. "I didn't look at the clock when I got home, but I am supposed to be home around eight o'clock," he said. The police had to ignore his mother, Genevieve Oates, who told them her son got home "around 7:20 or 7:30," although it was possible she was confused about the date.

Graham's own notes seem to support Dougie's story. According to his brief handwritten report of Dougie's first police interview on Friday, June 12, the boy said he saw "Arnold at bridge." Since by all accounts Arnold "Butch" George only got to the bridge around 7:30, Dougie must have been there at least that late on Tuesday evening to have spotted him. Most importantly, the police had to suppress important corroboration of Dougie's story that came

from a witness at the bridge, a witness who was devastating to their case—
a hidden witness the judge and jurors never got to see or hear.

While Graham and Trumbley spent the weekend questioning schoolchildren,
other officers were trying to gather other evidence. At 6:45 p.m. on Saturday,
June 13, OPP Identification Officer John Erskine went out for the fourth
time in forty-eight hours to the crime scene. This time his assignment was to
take pictures of bicycle tracks found in the laneway leading into the bush.

Erskine took pictures of three sets of tracks, encrusted in the fractured
earth, not far from where Lynne's body was found. The earth along the trail
was so parched there were large cracks breaking through the brown soil. It
had barely rained since May, and it did not take an expert like Erskine to realize the bike tracks had to have been made when the ground was damp—in
other words, at least a week before the murder took place.

Erskine was supposed to be gathering evidence against Steven Truscott.
Instead, what the corporal was accumulating were gnawing doubts about the
boy's guilt.

**12**

## "LOOK WHAT I FOUND, MOMMY"

"Our time in this investigation is being devoted to the taking of statements from various boys and girls," Inspector Harold Graham informed his superiors about the progress of his case. "The time factor being so important, I will report on this phase when the statements have been completed."

Graham was burdened by contradictory accounts about what time Steve and Lynne left the school, starting at 7:00 and going all the way to 7:30. He also had various estimates of Steve's return to the school, ranging from 7:45 to 8:15. To make their case against Steve stick, the authorities had to prove he had the time necessary to commit the crime. Steve said he had left the school around 7:25 and returned before 8:00. The police had to prove that Steven was away from the school for much longer than half an hour. It would take Steve almost five minutes to get to the laneway leading to the bush, another few minutes to walk down to the trail and enter the bush, and about ten more minutes to return, leaving him about ten minutes to hide his bike, subdue Lynne, undress her, rape and murder her, and clean himself up. A thirty-minute window made the murder technically possible but barely credible.

———

Two mothers with the Brownies at the school told police they thought Steve and Lynne left sometime between 7:00 and 7:10. But when Graham spoke to the first person Steve and Lynne met soon after they left the school and headed down the county road, the news was not good. Richard Gellatly told the police he was bicycling home when he crossed Steve and Lynne somewhere between the south end of the bush and the school. A few minutes later, at "about twenty-five minutes after seven," he got home, grabbed his swimming trunks and left. Graham and Trumbley added in their notes: "Richard's father verifies that he left about that time, as he remembers him coming home for his trunks." Richard's testimony meant that Steve and Lynne had started their bike ride much later than the prosecution needed to make a solid case. It would have taken Steve and Lynne only a few minutes—not fifteen to twenty-five minutes—to travel the short distance from the school to where they met Richard. Either he and his father were wrong or the two mothers at the school were wrong about Steve's departure time.

Once Steve and Lynne left the school, how long was Steve gone? The young boys playing baseball were the first to see him return, but they were not particularly helpful to the prosecution. Stuart Westie told Graham that Steve was gone for "about half an hour." Warren Heatherall agreed Steven returned "fifteen or twenty minutes or half an hour later." Billy MacKay put it at twenty minutes.

Three girls saw Steve pull up to the swings where the teenagers were congregating after he talked to the ball players. Lyn Johnston estimated Steve arrived around 8:15 p.m. Lorraine Wood put his return at about 8:10 or 8:15. Nina Archibald agreed.

On the other hand, two other youngsters—indirectly supported by their parents—gave earlier times. John Carew informed police he thought Steve came by the school close to 8:00 p.m. His mother and father would later reinforce his story by confirming what time John arrived home. Sandra Pleasance, meanwhile, was putting her younger sister to bed when she glanced out the window of her home near the school and saw Steve. "I am not too sure of the time, but after talking to my father about it, he thinks it would be between a quarter to eight and eight, but I think it would be closer to eight," she told police. A handwritten note by an officer at the bottom of her statement describes her as "unreliable." There is no indication the OPP ever checked with her father.

———

Graham did not fully realize it at the time, but he stumbled upon a key witness for the prosecution when he talked to a shy little ten-year-old named Philip Burns on Saturday, June 13. Philip left the bridge sometime around 7:00 and ambled home slowly, arriving at the PMQs at 7:30. Alongside the bush, he met Jocelyne and Butch George. "I walked on home and never met anyone else," he told police.

Here was a boy on the county road for a good part of the crucial half hour between 7:00 and 7:30 and he had failed to see Steven. And there was more. Philip said just as he was leaving the bridge, he spoke to a friend who was in a car driven by one of the mothers from the base, Donna Dunkin.

On Monday, June 15, when the police first talked to Donna Dunkin, she was unhelpful. She reported that on the day Lynne disappeared, she went to the river and saw "three big boys fishing on the bridge." But OPP officers Sayeau and Trumbley returned to see Dunkin a week later and, whether through police prodding or her own volition, her memory seemed to have improved. Dunkin told them she drove some children to the river in her car, parking between the bridge and the nearby railway tracks. "Just as we were slowing down to pull off to park, I met Richard Gellatly and the Burns boy," she said, referring to Philip. Her story seemed to get some support from Beatrice Geiger, who also reported seeing Philip and Richard along the riverbank at about the same time.

The police knew that Richard, travelling on his bike, met Steve and Lynne on the county road near the school. Philip, walking on foot and therefore much farther behind Richard, said he had not seen them. Now that Dunkin had told them both boys left the bridge at the same time, a simple scenario began to emerge that any juror could grasp in an instant: if Philip, travelling several hundred feet behind Richard, did not see Steve and Lynne, they must have left the road and gone into the bush.

It would become the centrepiece of the prosecution's "eyewitness" case and more than any other non-expert testimony helped convince a jury of Steven's guilt.

While the police were trying to put together a viable timeline from an array of witnesses, they also realized they faced another challenge—they had scant physical evidence tying the boy to the crime scene. Graham quickly put his men to work to find what they could.

On Monday, June 15, Cpl. Hank Sayeau brought Identification Officer Erskine the two tires he had seized from Steve's bike. Erskine began tests to see if the tires matched up in any way with the cracked marks found on the tractor trail. Sayeau also delivered the soiled pair of underwear he took from Steven in jail to a biologist at the attorney general's laboratory for further examination.

Later that evening, Erskine returned to the bridge to check out Steve's story about seeing a car at the highway. In trying to recreate the scene, the police parked a 1959 Chevrolet with various coloured licence plates at the intersection of the county road and Highway 8, while Erskine, standing at the bridge thirteen hundred feet away, snapped pictures. They concluded a yellow licence plate or marker could not be spotted on a car's rear bumper. It was the first of several visual tests the police would do, and not the last one to be seriously flawed.

The problem with photographs is that while the human eye automatically makes adjustments for focal length, a photographer must zoom in or zoom out a camera lens depending on what is being highlighted in a picture. How the OPP set the camera lens determined what the photographs looked like: a licence plate might appear much clearer than Steve could ever have seen it or much fuzzier. Only seven years later would there be a more accurate recreation, with human test subjects looking at various coloured markers—a test which produced strikingly different results than the first one.

The police also tried for fingerprints. The same day one officer showed up at Steve's jail to take his prints, another OPP officer picked up Lynne's shoes from the Toronto laboratory—presumably to check for similar prints. The police files show no records of any matches.

Finally, on Friday, June 19, a week after they jailed Steven, the police got their first piece of physical evidence, but it turned out to be an unwelcome gift.


Corporal Hank Sayeau prided himself on being a meticulous, careful investigator. Since Thursday, June 11, his men had gathered all kinds of evidence from the crime scene, from as far away as hundreds of feet from the body.

Discarded Kleenex, Coke bottles, a black comb, bits of plastic. But the one thing they could not find was the heart-shaped locket on a gold chain Lynne was wearing when she left the house. Witnesses remembered seeing her fingering the locket at the schoolyard that evening, but it was not around her neck when her body was discovered. On Tuesday, June 16, one week after Lynne's disappearance, Sayeau and several other men returned to the area to search again for the piece of jewellery, without results.

Two days later, Sayeau was back once more, along the county road. This time, he was not looking for the locket; he took a soil sample "approximately 300 feet south" of the north edge of the bush. He was standing just "four feet from the fence." He saw no trace of Lynne's locket.

The next day, however, ten-year-old Sandra Archibald had better luck. She always enjoyed picking berries along the county road, but on Friday, June 19, she spotted something shiny catching the sunlight. "I was picking strawberries and my little sister wanted to pick more, so [we] went on ahead," she later remembered. "That is when I found the locket."

On the edge of Lawson's bush, a gold locket with an RCAF crest was hanging over the lowest string of barbed wire. Part of the chain was inside the fence; the locket fell on the roadside. "I didn't know whose it was and I thought I could keep it," Sandra said. She took her prize home to her mother, Aida.

"Look what I found, Mommy!" she cried. A neighbour had told Mrs. Archibald that Lynne had a locket just like it. Aida Archibald wrapped the locket in a tissue and called the police. By 5:15 p.m., Corporal Sayeau was on the scene. Sandra later showed the officer where she made her discovery, about 280 feet south of the bush's northern tip—roughly the same spot Sayeau had stopped for soil samples and far from the tractor trail where, the police alleged, Steve had entered the bush with Lynne.

On Monday, June 22, Sayeau went back to the scene and checked the fence on the west side of the bush, where the locket had been found. From 3:25 p.m. until 4:24 p.m., he gathered evidence. He removed hair particles from the two lower strands of the barbed wire fence. He also snapped three sections of the wire. The hair samples would turn out to be animal hair. The experts at the attorney general's laboratory found nothing on the wire, though the police instructions inexplicably told the scientists, "Don't check for blood."

The next day, Sayeau showed the locket to Leslie and Shirley Harper "and they both identified it as being the one worn by their daughter on the night she went missing," according to his notes. When it came to trial, Leslie Harper would try to fudge that assessment.

And for good reason. The locket was a bothersome discovery for the police and prosecution. It could not have fallen off Lynne's neck while Steven dragged her into the bush because the police maintained they did not enter the bush directly from the county road, where the locket was found, as they would have been easily spotted. The police insisted that Steve turned down the laneway and went into the bush from the side, a distance equal to two football fields away from where Sandra stumbled upon the locket.

If Steve was innocent, on the other hand, the locket's location made sense. If a different person returned to the county road with Lynne (dead or alive) under the cover of darkness later that evening or sometime the next night, and crossed into the bush where the locket was found, it was possible the locket then fell off or was ripped off Lynne's neck. It was also possible the killer, while fleeing the scene of the crime when the murder occurred—or perhaps even days later—threw the locket into the bush, where it caught on the barbed wire fence.

Reflecting on it today, Sayeau tries to put the best possible spin on the locket's discovery, suggesting Steve may have tossed it away as he was leaving the bush. "I would like to think that maybe he did take it from the scene and he thought, 'Better not take that home.' The defence can't say that he didn't throw it there. But I can't rule out the other theory either. We certainly know he didn't throw it there from the time he was put in custody."

And that was the rub. Steve was in police custody as of Friday evening, June 12. If Steve put the locket there, he could only have done it sometime between Tuesday and Friday. That would mean the locket had to remain dangling from the fence unnoticed while police combed the area surrounding the crime scene, first when they discovered the body on Thursday, and then repeatedly in the days afterwards. It was possible everyone missed the tiny piece of jewellery for ten days after Lynne disappeared; it was possible Sayeau missed it when he was examining the same area; it was also possible someone innocently picked it up in one place and discarded it where Sandra found it. Or was it possible that the locket was not there until shortly before Sandra Archibald went picking for berries? If that was the case, Lynne Harper's locket appeared while the boy charged with her murder was locked up behind bars.

And if Steve did not put the locket there, who did?

**13**

FOR THE GOOD OF THE CHILD

The frantic police investigation was beginning to take its toll on the Clinton air force community, especially its younger members. First, the students in Maitland Edgar's class had to get used to staring at Lynne's empty desk. By the second week, there was a second vacant chair, as Steven Truscott sat in a jail in Goderich, charged with the murder of their classmate.

Doris Truscott was doing her best to cope with Steven in jail and three other children to care for at home.

"It's a bad thing for him, but it's very, very hard on the rest of the family too," she told Lil Woodson, her friend and neighbour. "You can't just let the family go."

Doris knew the tongues of some of her less charitable neighbours were wagging. "It's funny what people will think: I was a very cold person because I never cried a lot," Doris says. "It was an odd thing for people to make that remark because everybody is different. Maybe I never cried out in public, but you do at home. There was no shame in people breaking down at all, but it just wasn't my nature in public. The children took after me in that way."

Community gossip was one thing. Doris had no idea jurors would later interpret her fourteen-year-old's lack of public tears as a sure sign of guilt.

———

Soon after Steven was jailed, Dan Truscott walked in the house with news that would make defending their son all the more difficult.

"He came home and said, 'We were asked to move off the station.' The air force wanted us off the base; it was a strong suggestion," Doris remembers. "We thought, 'Now what are we going to do?'"

It was not necessarily a direct order; the brass presented it as something that would be best for everybody. Dan's son was about to go on trial for murder—a hanging offence—but the air force deemed it advisable to transfer Dan to a base near Ottawa, about 350 miles away. The Harper family would also soon depart, for England, but for them it would mean an escape from the tragic memories, the press hounds and curious onlookers.

It was hard for Doris not to think that her family was a victim of "injustice by the higher-ups," as she put it, because her boy was not an officer's son. OPP Inspector Harold Graham himself later acknowledged the problem of rank. Without providing details, he wrote to his superiors about the "difficulties" affecting his case: "There was the 'officer–men' relationship between the associates of the father of the deceased and the associates of the father of the accused."

Indeed, it did not take long for the air force to close ranks. An officer's daughter had been raped and murdered, the police had jailed the son of a non-commissioned officer, and that was it. Time to impose military discipline and show the proper respect for rank and for the chain of command.

A "confidential report" by air force police Sgt. John Wheelhouse to the training command headquarters was striking in its exuberant endorsement of the OPP case against Steven Truscott. "Steven appeared to have seen and remembered too much detail for a fourteen-year-old who was a below average student in school," the report noted somewhat caustically. "His eyesight was tested and was normal without being outstanding."

The air force official seemed more eager than the police to prove Steven guilty. "Time of death has been established as being between 19:15 hours and 19:45 hours, *more likely between 19:15 hours and 19:30 hours*," stating a narrow fifteen-minute window that even the police were not brash enough to suggest.

Despite the lack of help from the air force, the Truscotts were not going to abandon their fight for their son. Doris and the children would live in the

**14**

### THE HANGING TREE

By July 13, the day his preliminary opened, Steven had spent thirty days in jail. Three reports from Graham to his superiors on the progress of his investigation are on file from that period—June 19, July 6 and July 16—presumably representing the best police intelligence at the time. One report talked about an estimate for the time of death, but it noted that tests "to determine the actual food contents of the stomach . . . have not yet been concluded."

There was "no sperm in the vagina," Graham reported, but he took solace from the fact that "it is believed until a male is mature, no semen is found." (By trial, the prosecution would dramatically change its tune about Steve's sexual maturity.) The final report, just days before the preliminary began, noted that sperm was found on the underwear seized from Steven on the Saturday after his arrest and "fixed stains" on the knees of his red jeans. The stains would turn out to be grass, the sperm of indeterminate age.

In all of Graham's reports, there was no mention of Jocelyne's tale of a secret date or Butch's claim of a plot to lie to the police. "A brief containing statements of all witnesses is being prepared for Crown attorney Hays," Graham said.

It was remarkable how incomplete Graham's case still was—a full month after Steve had been incarcerated.

"BOY SEEMS SO CALM AND NORMAL, BUT IS HE SAVAGE MURDER-ER?" read the four-column headline in the Toronto *Telegram* when Steven's preliminary hearing began. "Was it possible that this fourteen-year-old boy in the prisoner's dock, looking so average, so typical of boys his age, could have committed a brutal murder?" asked reporter Allan Kent, in language more colourful than most of the dry courtroom accounts of the time.

"The boy sat there alone, almost expressionless, just a little shy perhaps, as the ponderous machinery of the court moved forward," Kent reported. "The boy's face, rather pale, somewhat pimpled, showed no horror, no sur-prise, nothing at all as the police evidence was given." This was the first, but far from the last time that Steven's demeanour would raise eyebrows. As is usually the case, behaviour is in the eye of the beholder. Contrary to Kent's picture of an unresponsive boy, another reporter wrote of Steven, "He lis-tened with rapt attention to every bit of evidence during the two-day prelim-inary hearing."

Everyone listened with attention when Magistrate Dudley Holmes—the same judge who had bumped Steven's case from juvenile to adult court—called the hearing into session. His first move was to order the courtroom cleared of children, who had come to testify or to watch. His words were a taste of the high drama to come: "Some of the children here are much too young to be in court listening to details that are shocking enough to adults," he warned.

The purpose of a preliminary hearing is to allow the court to decide if there is enough evidence to proceed to trial. But it is also a sort of dress rehearsal where the prosecution has a chance to try out some of its per-formers and the defence gets to size up the act. Without the benefit of dis-closure laws that defence lawyers have today, Frank Donnelly had to rely on the preliminary hearing to glean as much as possible about what Crown prosecutor Glenn Hays and Inspector Harold Graham had against his client.

To set the stage, Hays had Lynne's parents testify briefly about their slain daughter. Leslie Harper's testimony was notable for two details that would change by the time the trial began.

Lynne's father told the preliminary hearing that when he arrived at the Truscott home the morning after Lynne went missing, Steve told him in a matter-of-fact manner that he had given his daughter a ride down to the highway.

"Did he appear normal at that time?" Donnelly asked Harper.

"I wasn't concerned about Steven's condition at that time," was the non-committal reply.

"I take it you didn't notice anything about it," the defence pursued.

"No, he was very straight in his reply," Lynne's father confirmed. At trial, Harper altered his description of Steve ever so slightly. "He had the answer at the ready," he told jurors, implying a well-planned lie.

Donnelly also asked Harper about the locket found along the road, several hundred feet from the crime scene. "Do you recognize that locket positively or otherwise?" he asked.

"Yes, that is the locket that Lynne was in possession of," her father said, without hesitation. The magistrate asked him again if the locket and chain entered as Exhibit 7 belonged to Lynne. "Yes sir, that is right," her father reaffirmed. He would adjust his opinion in two months' time.

Cpl. John Erskine was the prosecution's first important expert witness at the preliminary, as he would be in the trial. The young corporal appeared reluctant to go out of his way to help the prosecution.

Erskine described the photographs he had taken of the crime scene. The marks in the earth next to Lynne's feet were "quite broken down from weeds, twigs, breakdown of earth," he said.

"Was there any imprint in it that you could find?" defence counsel Frank Donnelly asked when it was his turn to question the OPP expert.

"There was an imprint in it which appeared to be a heel, but I cannot properly say," was as far as Erskine was willing to go.

"Was it so indistinct that it could not be accurately measured?"

"That is correct, sir."

"It was so indistinct that it would be impracticable to make a comparison with the shoe? Is that a fact?"

"That is correct, sir."

"Was there any mark in this area near the right foot that could be compared with any object which might help in the investigation of this matter?"

"No sir."

Erskine could not have been more helpful to the defence. The marks next to Lynne's left foot were even more nondescript: a "quite shallow" depression less than a quarter-inch deep that was "very badly broken down." Erskine's blunt verdict: "Just an indistinct mark which I couldn't get a proper measurement on."

The prosecution knew they had to come up with something a lot better to prove Steven was in the bush with Lynne. By the trial date in September the police dutifully obliged with a surprise witness who spotted real footprints where Erskine had seen only indistinct marks.

Constable Donald Hobbs, the officer who first questioned Steve in the days after Lynne's disappearance, was also helpful to the defence in his descriptions of the accused boy.

"He appeared calm," Hobbs recalled.

"Co-operative?" defence attorney Donnelly asked.

"Yes, he was co-operative," the officer said. "He answered my questions."

"Answered them freely?"

"Yes sir."

"There was a lot of hesitation?"

"No, far from it. He was most definite. He answered right away."

Hardly the portrait of a scared or shrewd boy trying to cover up a murder. Hobbs was also clear on one other matter: he did not see "any marks or scratches" on the boy who had been sitting just a few inches away from him during the questioning.

"If there had been any visible marks or scratches on his face or hands or arms, you would have noticed them, wouldn't you?" Donnelly asked.

"On his face or hands, I would have, yes sir."

Donnelly also secured an important concession from Cpl. Hank Sayeau, the OPP's point man in charge of evidence. He was one of the first officers to arrive at the bush on Thursday afternoon, and he quickly took charge of securing the crime scene.

Donnelly queried Sayeau about the bicycle tire marks found in the laneway. "Had they been made recently?" Donnelly asked.

"No sir, not the ones I saw," the officer responded quickly and definitively. "I would say quite a time before, when the ground was soft."

"And the photograph showed that the ground was quite dry because there were big cracks where the ground was opened up."

"Yes."

"So that they certainly would be made before the 9th of June, wouldn't they?"

"Yes sir."

The OPP's second most senior officer on the case was confirming that bike tracks which supposedly could prove Steven was near the bush were "certainly" made before the murder even occurred. It was a story Sayeau would have to change by the time he presented testimony in front of a jury.

Hobbled by the frank testimony of the police officers, prosecutor Glenn Hays tried to score some points with the dark stains found on the red jeans Steven was wearing. Blood perhaps, or earth from the crime scene? But Elgin Brown, the biologist from the attorney general's laboratory who tested the clothing, offered Hays little good news.

"The staining in the knees, while appearing dark in colour, contain chlorophyll—that is, green staining pigment in plants and leaves," the scientist said. "And although they appear dark . . . the green appears dark when rubbed into this fabric." In other words, ordinary grass stains on the jeans of a teenage boy.

Brown also noted that Steven's shoes "appeared clean—generally free of soil." Corporal Sayeau, who had seized the shoes as evidence under a search warrant, said that he thought Steve's shoes were washed because of "the lack of staining" and the fading of the canvas. The biologist was less convinced than the police. "I have no evidence for or against such an observation," Brown told the judge, "other than the fact that they are definitely clean."

Glenn Hays could only hope his medical experts would put on a better show.

The prosecution's star medical witness in the preliminary hearing and in the trial would be Dr. John Penistan, the Stratford pathologist who performed the autopsy on Lynne Harper. Dr. Penistan noted that he found three superficial scratches along Lynne's legs "which could easily be obtained while climbing through a barbed wire fence." Then he moved on to describe Lynne's genital area: "There was an abrasion about between one-third and one-half inch in diameter, superficial, of the skin of the private parts on the right side. I think it is the sort of lesion which might well have been made by a blind, furious thrust of the male organ."

A blind, furious thrust? Not exactly a medically precise diagnosis. A pathologist might be able to detect the intensity of the friction during sexual intercourse, but words like "blind" and "furious" foreshadowed how the prosecution intended to sway the jury at the trial with colourful rather than scientifically accurate descriptions of the girl's final moments. Penistan's confidence that the abrasion he found was a definitive sign of a "blind, furious thrust" was all the more puzzling considering he admitted that decomposition and "a tremendous population of maggots" had obscured Lynne's anatomy.

Of all the doctor's theories, the most crucial for the Crown would be Penistan's precise determination of the time of death. Yet the preliminary hearing revealed the shaky ground upon which this vital part of the case rested.

For starters, Penistan let slip that the "very slight" rigor mortis and the large amount of eggs and maggots "were compatible with death *one and a half to two and a half days before the autopsy was done.*" That put the murder at any time between 7:00 a.m. on Tuesday, June 9, and 7:00 a.m. on Wednesday—a vastly wider window than Penistan would later describe. He would never again make that mistake.

Penistan narrowed his estimate of the time of death by relying on stomach contents. "Death would, in my view, have occurred between 7:15 in the evening of June 9th and 7:45, which would be two hours after consumption of the meal, and I would think earlier during that period rather than later," he concluded. "I think that is all I have to tell you, sir."

It was enough. If Dr. Penistan's time of death was accurate, the killer was Steven Truscott.

To try and reinforce Penistan's testimony, Glenn Hays called to the stand John Funk, the biologist from the provincial laboratory. Funk had spent the previous four weeks analyzing the jar of stomach contents police provided to him the day after the autopsy.

"Have you, as yet, completed your analysis?" Hays asked.

"No sir, I haven't," said the biologist. In other words, one month after Graham insisted the lab experts told the police Lynne had died "not more than two hours" after her supper, the expert himself was telling a court he had not yet finished his analysis.

"Are you in a position to help us [determine] how long any of this meal had been in the stomach after having been eaten?" Hays asked.

"I don't feel qualified to answer that question," Funk insisted. It was a disturbing reply, though no one in the courtroom seemed to realize just how devastating it was. After a month of examinations, the provincial laboratory's expert was not ready to speculate under oath about the time of Lynne's death. Yet on June 12, Graham claimed an oral report from the laboratory estimating time of death was enough justification to take Steven into custody. Now, in mid-July, all Funk could tell the preliminary hearing was that he would finish his analysis of the stomach in a week.

"Your Worship, if this man could have his findings in a week, I would ask that the hearing be adjourned, so we could get the findings on them," Donnelly asked. It was not an unreasonable request, considering that the Crown made stomach contents the main proof that Lynne was killed in the same half-hour she was with Steven.

"I cannot see eye to eye with you there. You will have your trial if the man is committed for trial. You will have your findings beforehand," replied Magistrate Holmes.

"We have a right to get this on discovery rather than take a handout from the Crown," Donnelly insisted, referring to the rules—much more limited in 1959 than today—that allowed the defence access to basic prosecutorial information.

"No. I can't see it. This is a preliminary inquiry, and if it should be that I am not satisfied that there is enough evidence to commit this man, then you are all right," Magistrate Holmes said firmly. "I cannot agree to any adjournment."

In effect, the judge was saying to Steven's lawyer: Don't worry about the lab report because you won't need it if I throw out the case, and if I decide to send your client to trial, you'll get the report anyway.

As it turned out, John Funk took not seven days but six more weeks to complete his analysis of the stomach contents. He filed his report on August 31. The police and prosecution saw what was in it, but not a judge or a jury. Hays never called Funk to testify at trial and he never entered the biologist's written report into evidence.

To add more weight to the medical evidence, the Crown also called in Dr. David Hall Brooks, the senior medical officer at the base, who had identified Lynne's body in the bush, assisted in the autopsy and helped examine Steven the night of his arrest. Dr. Brooks would prove to be even more enthusiastic than Penistan in helping the prosecution convict the accused boy. Sometimes, however, his zeal seemed to get the better of him.

Brooks began by describing Steven the night he was in police custody at the base guardhouse: "He was flushed and a little more emotionally charged with energy than usual. He was sitting apathetic in the chair with his head slightly bent." He was not asked how the boy could be emotionally charged and apathetic at the same time. Nor was he asked how he could know Steve had more energy than usual if he did not know the teenager or what his "usual" energy level was.

Brooks's description of Steve's body was equally puzzling. "He seemed to be very well washed in the region of his external genitalia," he remarked. "This was in rather marked contrast to the skin of his face and neck and everywhere. A child of that age, as you know, they tend to have a greasy skin, which seems to shine." Was it so unusual that Steve's face and neck would be dirtier than his private parts after spending a hot summer day on his bike and on a farm?

"The thing we discovered last," Brooks said with a dramatic flair, "and to us the most important, was that this boy had lesions on his male organ."

"Penis, is that it?" the judge asked somewhat gingerly.

"Yes," said the doctor. "Pulling the skin back sufficiently to take the wrinkle out of it, there was this lesion, one on each side. A little bigger than a quarter in size and of a degree which I have never seen."

Ordinary masturbation injuries, Brooks went on, appear to heal in one week. "This injury was still oozing serum. It would seem fairly new," he said. "I would say that this was more than forty-eight hours old and certainly less than five days old."

It was a remarkably precise dating of a sore Brooks had examined for only a few minutes. He appeared to know with certainty Steve injured his penis sometime between the previous Sunday and Wednesday evening, and not a day earlier or later. It was an impressive medical feat, but apparently not exact enough to prove Steve had raped a girl on Tuesday night. Fortunately for the prosecution, Brooks's diagnostic skills on the age of penis sores would improve by the time it came to a full trial.

———

The third doctor to complete the medical triangle of evidence against Steven was Dr. John Addison, the family doctor from Clinton who also examined the boy the night of his arrest.

Addison concurred with Brooks's description of Steve's penis. "Personally, I have never seen as sore a penis in twenty-two years of practice. It certainly wasn't a three- or four-week-old job, which Steven said it had been."

Addison testified that he did not believe Steve's reluctant admission he had masturbated a week before. "Masturbation is supposed to give every female or male offender some feeling of enjoyment," he explained, "and I don't see how it could possibly give him any enjoyment when it was as sore as the night I saw it."

But under questioning from Donnelly, Addison did not entirely rule out the possibility the wound could be self-inflicted.

"You did suggest to him that [masturbation] might be the cause of it, did you?"

"Yes sir," Addison conceded. "I suggested it as a possible reason that might cause [it]."

"How many ways do you think this could have happened, doctor?"

"In my opinion, the penis would, first of all, have to have an erection on, and it would have to be inserted between two surfaces that rub on the side," Addison explained. "Rubbing is one way. A knothole that was a little narrow from the side to side might do it. . . . An oval hole might do it, where it caught on either side."

Addison had, in effect, left the door slightly ajar to a possible explanation other than rape for Steve's penis sores. It was a door he would try to slam shut in September.

Glenn Hays knew he could not rely only on the easily coaxed testimony of police and medical experts. To convict the boy in the dock, the Crown prosecutor would have to use what one court observer aptly described as the "mixed-up recollections of children." The preliminary hearing gave Hays a taste of just how hard it was going to be to get his young charges in line.

Hays ran into his first obstacles when he tried to widen the time Steve had to carry out the crime. Warren Heatherall and Stuart Westie, playing baseball at the school, said Steve left "somewhere around 7:00," but they were not certain. Stuart said he had a watch but never looked at it: "When I am playing, I don't take much care on what time it is."

Hays hardly fared any better with the two mothers taking care of the Brownies at the school that evening. Anne Nickerson and Dorothy Bohonus.

"What time did she disappear with Steven Truscott?" Hays asked Nickerson directly.

"I didn't have a watch and, as I say, I am just going by approximate times—perhaps between five after, ten after seven," Nickerson said.

Her fellow Brownie leader was not much more specific. Dorothy Bohonus did have a watch, but the last time she glanced at it was 6:50, when she first saw Lynne. "It must have been about ten minutes after I was there that the boy came along, so it was 7:00 or shortly after when she joined him, and I didn't see them leave."

Four people, two women preoccupied with a group of Brownie girls and two boys more interested in baseball than bike-watching. Two witnesses wore watches; only one looked at her watch and that was well before Steve and Lynne left.

All in all, not a very solid array of witnesses. Hays would have to do much better at trial.

The indefatigable Crown prosecutor also had great difficulty in getting a straight story about what Steve and his friends talked about at the bridge on the Wednesday evening after Lynne's disappearance. Hays wanted to prove two things: that Steve talked about looking for calves in the bush, and that he threatened Butch about spreading the story that he had seen Steve take Lynne into the woods.

Paul Desjardine told the preliminary hearing he initiated the conversation about the bush that evening: "I asked Butch if Lynne Harper went into the woods with Steven and Butch didn't say anything, and then I asked Steven the same and I said that Butch said you had, and then Steven asked Butch if Butch said that, and Butch said he didn't."

"Was there another conversation a few minutes later?" Hays prodded, ever hopeful he could get at the story about Steve's strong words to Butch.

"I don't think so."

Dismayed, Hays pushed again. "Was there any further conversation?"

"I don't think so. I don't remember."

"Any talk of a cow or a calf?" Hays was desperate here. It would hardly do for the only boy on the bridge who questioned Steve about Lynne not to remember the calf story.

But Hays was clearly leading the witness and the judge would have none of it. "No. You may be able to do something about it later, but I smell things that aren't according to Hoyle here," he said sharply.

Bryan Glover, another boy on the bridge that evening, confirmed that he heard Paul ask Steven why he was in the woods with Lynne Harper. "He said he heard a calf in there and took her in there to show it to her."

"What was said after that?" asked Hays.

"That is all I remember."

So much for the threats exchanged between Steve and Butch. A reporter covering the hearing aptly summed up the prosecutor's dilemma: "Crown attorney Glenn Hays had a frantic and not altogether successful afternoon trying to elicit from the young witnesses the same stories they had given police earlier."

Only Tom Gillette delivered a snippet of what Hays needed. Contrary to the other boys, Tom insisted Butch told Steve he saw him take Lynne into the bush.

"I didn't go into the bush with Lynne," Steve allegedly answered, and then Tom added this editorial comment: "He sounded like he was threatening him—threatening Butch."

If Hays hoped all this confusion could be solved by the boy in the middle of the muddle—Arnold "Butch" George—he would be sorely disappointed.

The prosecution's star child witness got off to a bad start even before he began. "What do you know about swearing in court to tell the truth?" Magistrate Holmes asked as Butch George sat down in the witness box.

"You aren't supposed to tell a lie, and supposed to tell the truth," the boy answered.

"That is right, as far as it goes. Do you know what the procedure is—I am trying to get a simple word to make sure that you will tell the truth in court," the judge continued, not spelling out what word he was looking for, but clearly a bit dubious about Butch's truthfulness.

"No sir."

"Don't you?" The judge was frustrated. "I think possibly your evidence can be received but I doubt very much if you can be sworn." Holmes never hesitated to swear in many of Butch's classmates, including children younger than he was. For whatever reason, Magistrate Holmes—unlike the police—appeared to sense that Butch George was hardly a reliable witness.

"Don't add anything to it—don't put any fancy touches of your own on it, or anything that you dreamed up," the judge warned the boy in stiffer language than he used for other children.

From the beginning, Butch got things wrong.

"I did meet Jocelyne Gaudet at the end of the bush," Butch confirmed.

"Did she have a bicycle?"

"No," he answered. (According to Jocelyne, she was indeed on her bicycle that evening.)

Butch then said he went swimming until 8:30 p.m.

"And during all that period did you see Steven Truscott?"

"No," came the clear reply.

"So you saw him at no time after you left the station at about seven o'clock until you returned home about 8:30?"

"That is right."

Defence counsel Donnelly pushed the issue even further. "You didn't see him at all?"

"No," Butch said.

And then the key question: "Did you see him go into the woods with Lynne Harper?"

"No."

In other words, Butch was admitting he lied to all his friends when he told them he saw Steven go into the bush with Lynne. He kept changing other parts of his story as well. This is how he described his chat with Steve around 8:45 on Tuesday night:

"Where did you go?" Butch asked.

"I gave Lynne Harper a ride down to Number 8 Highway and then she was picked up in a 1959 Chev heading toward Seaforth," Steve told his friend.

"Why did you give Lynne a ride?"

"Why do you want to know?"

"Skip the subject," Butch replied, "and let's play catch."

It sounded like a normal chat. Gone were the juicy elements Butch had recounted to the police: his question about what Steve was "doing in the bush with Lynne" and Steve's reply that he was looking for a cow and a calf. But Butch enlivened his account of his next alleged encounter with his friend on Wednesday evening. That was when Steve supposedly told him he had made an error by telling police he had waved to Butch at the river on Tuesday evening. Butch made their conversation sound more conspiratorial by adding some exciting details to his story.

"*They are coming down. It is going to look bad for me,*" Butch now had Steve saying.

"I might as well tell them that I saw you," Butch offered.

Butch told the court he went through with that lie. "I told the police that I had seen Steven."

"What you told the police that time was not the truth?" Magistrate Holmes asked.

"Yes."

"Why did you do that?"

"To help Steven."

In his cross-examination, Frank Donnelly largely steered clear of Butch's shifting accounts of his talks with Steve. But he did probe Butch about his conversation with Jocelyne when he met her near the bush on Tuesday evening.

"I think she said she was looking for Lynne," Butch confirmed, repeating what he had told police.

"She asked you if you had seen Lynne Harper?" Donnelly stressed, to make sure there was no misunderstanding.

"Yes," Butch replied.

From Hays' perspective, given Jocelyne Gaudet's predilection for changing her story, her testimony about a secret date with Steve was mercifully brief. Even then, she managed to let slip some odd statements.

Hays asked her about the location for their clandestine get-together.

"On the county road, on the right-hand side, outside the fence by the woods," she said. "You can see it from the classroom window."

From the classroom window? That would mean their meeting point was within sight of the school. It hardly seemed the place to pick for a secret encounter. It also did not explain why Jocelyne asked Steven, according to her police statement, "to wear something I could see from a distance."

Jocelyne's father, Flight Sgt. Charles Gaudet, followed his daughter on the stand. Hays wanted him to confirm the story he had told the police: that his young son, André, had answered the door just before 6:00 p.m. on Tuesday and told Jocelyne that Steve had come calling. But in his testimony before the magistrate, the story changed. Gaudet indicated his son did open the door but did not announce the visitor. "When she came back into the dining room . . . I think my wife asked Jocelyne who was at the door." That story is not what his wife told police. (At trial, Gaudet dropped any mention of his wife, saying that only his son opened the door to someone that evening.)

"That is that," Magistrate Dudley Holmes said when the last witness left the stand. It was 5:15 p.m. on the second day of the hearing.

Holmes did not have to set the bar too high to send the case to trial. The testimony did not have to be consistent or entirely credible. He did not have even to determine the truthfulness of the testimony. All he had to decide was whether there was enough evidence for a jury to decide the truth.

He turned to the fourteen-year-old boy in the dock. "Stand up," the judge ordered, and Steven obediently rose.

"Having heard the evidence, do you wish to say anything in answer to the charge? You are not bound to say anything, but whatever you do say will be taken down in writing and may be given in evidence against you at your trial," Holmes said. It was the first time anyone had read Steven his rights. By the laws of the day, Canadian police were not obliged to spell out a suspect's rights when they were questioning or even when arresting him.

Steve looked at his lawyer. "Your Worship," Donnelly said solemnly, "the accused does not wish to make a statement."

Donnelly then proceeded to outline a defence, if it could be called that. He brought forth only Herbert and Charlotte Mellish, neighbours of the Truscotts. They testified that they had spent the evening with Steve's parents at the Sergeants' Mess the night Lynne disappeared. It was a baffling move by the defence; the Mellishes' testimony seemed entirely irrelevant to the proceedings and did nothing to establish Steve's innocence or guilt.

Donnelly called no other witnesses; his intervention was over in ten minutes. Perhaps it was indicative of Donnelly's confidence that the Crown case was so weak it needed little rebuttal. But as Inspector Harold Graham put it succinctly in a memo to his superiors after the hearing: "The evidence called by the defence was in complete agreement with the information known by the prosecution and was of little value."

At 5:30 p.m. on July 14, after hearing thirty-one witnesses and examining twenty-one pieces of evidence in two days, the judge was ready with his decision. "Well, in my opinion," Magistrate Holmes declared, "the evidence is sufficient to put the accused on trial."

"Bewildered, unhappy but most uncomprehending" was how newspaper accounts at the time described Steven's reaction. The Toronto *Telegram* reporter apparently shared Truscott's bewilderment, wondering how "out of the welter of believable and unbelievable evidence" Holmes determined there was enough evidence to proceed to trial. "The magistrate was obviously baffled by the age-old question: how do you sift out the truth from the fantasy in the mixed-up recollections of children?" the newspaper asked. "In fact, the whole area where the body was found seems to have been teeming with youngsters . . . but not one of them was able to say he or she had seen the two go into the woods."

It was a valid analysis of the weakness in the prosecution's case. The presence of reporters had allowed independent observers to explain and comment on the proceedings to the public. That probing role of the media would be entirely absent when the formal trial got underway in September.


In Clinton that evening, life went on as usual. The drive-in had a new hit on the big screen: *Love Me Tender* with Elvis Presley. The newspapers the next day would report that, south of the border, a dashing young senator named John F. Kennedy would launch what he called his "new frontier" and accept the Democratic nomination for president.

For Steven Truscott, the frontiers were limited to the walls of his cell. "You're locked up in a cell and you're on your own," he remembers. He passed the time reading magazines and walking in the small exercise yard. He felt like a bystander watching the legal storm raging all around him. Frank Donnelly visited him only twice between the preliminary and the trial. "It was more or less, 'This is a legal thing; you are a kid, you don't know anything, this is what we are doing,' and I didn't have any say in it," Steve recalls.

Donnelly and others assured him he had little to worry about. "So you believe all this," Steven says. "You don't find out until the trial that all these people haven't been telling you the right thing."

Maitland Edgar, the school vice-principal, remembers talking to Const. Donald Trumbley one day that summer while sitting in the officer's cruiser. Trumbley, who interviewed most of the children and filed the arrest papers against Steven, was frustrated that after all the hours of interrogation and weeks in a jail cell, the boy had not cracked and confessed. The policeman slapped his hands against the steering wheel in frustration. "By God, but that boy is guilty!" he exclaimed.

Edgar says he tried to explain that, to his mind, if Steven was guilty, the boy had gone through a "complete change of nature because that wasn't the kid that I knew." But he felt Trumbley was not open to doubts. "There was one train of thought for the police. You have something you grab on to and you refuse to let go."

With only a month to go before trial, the OPP was running out of time. They decided to pursue an investigation into the school's clocks. Steve had always insisted he left the school ten to fifteen minutes later than the police thought—not around 7:10 but closer to 7:25. He supported that claim by stating that as he walked across the playground with Lynne, he glanced at a clock on the wall in the kindergarten.

But in July the police discovered that an electrician had disconnected the master clock earlier in the year. Carl Lippert told them some of the clocks around the school were out five and six hours. Only on June 27—almost three weeks after Steve's bike ride with Lynne—did Lippert return to the school to synchronize all the clocks. "I had to change all the clocks," he said. "None of the readings were the same." Maitland Edgar confirmed the "clocks controlled by the master clock were not in operation."

At last, it looked as if the police had caught Steven in a direct lie—and, better still, a lie that could be exposed by incontrovertible physical evidence. A lie that exposed his attempt to narrow his window of opportunity to commit the crime.

But the truth stymied the OPP officers once again. Michael Shrepnik, the school caretaker, agreed that the school clocks hadn't run since Easter. But then he added, "Miss Irvin, who teaches kindergarten at the school, inquired if I could find her a clock. I got an electric clock and had put it up on the wall on the northwest corner of the room."

If Steven was lying, by a lucky coincidence he picked the one good clock in the school to lie about. The OPP quietly dropped the clock quest and it was never raised in court.

If officers such as Donald Trumbley had no doubts about their case, at least one of his colleagues was less sanguine. Corporal John Erskine, the identification officer who spent more time in the bush than any other police-man gathering evidence and taking pictures, had qualms from the start. "The more he looked into it, the more he was absolutely convinced the boy was not guilty," his widow, Dee Harris, recalls.

Erskine's unease was particularly worrisome because it went to the core of the chief weakness in the case so far: the lack of physical evidence from the crime scene. Corporal Sayeau had admitted in the preliminary hearing that the bike tracks were days, if not weeks old. Erskine dismissed the marks near Lynne's feet as "scuff marks." Clearly, if prosecutor Glenn Hays was going to convince a jury that Steven was in that bush with Lynne, he was going to need something more tangible.

In all of the available memos Graham sent to his superiors before the trial, the inspector never made any reference to footprints. None of the formal statements and reports by the various police officers in the file mentioned footprints. No one testified about footprints at the preliminary. But some-how, between the preliminary in July and the trial in September, footprints linking Steven to the crime scene appeared.

The prints appeared through the recollections of Flying Officer Glen Henry Sage, who took charge of the air force men at the scene of the crime. "I was standing right below the body. You look down and you saw there were two mounds," he recounted. "And you could clearly see a footprint."

The OPP were in an embarrassing situation. Flying Officer Sage was finding recognizable footprints where their own identification officer saw none. On Friday, September 11, less than a week before the trial began, Harold Graham took a dramatic step. He called in another identification officer.

Corporal Dennis Alsop was surprised when he got the call from Graham. "I was going into another officer's territory," he recalls. Alsop, who worked in the identification branch in the London district, says it was "unprecedented, definitely." Erskine must have been upset, Alsop says, know-ing Graham felt that he had blown the crime scene: "If you go to a crime scene and you miss something, you feel pretty bad." Erskine, according to his widow, called it "dirty baseball."

Upon arrival in Clinton, Alsop asked to see Steve's running shoes. He was not allowed to remove them from the premises, so he had a box of dirt brought in and then pushed down on the shoes with his hand to make a mark.

"My God—that's the impression that I saw at the scene," Sgt. Charles Anderson of the Goderich OPP exclaimed.

"Then I knew we had something," says Alsop.

"Can you do anything about this?" Graham asked.

"Well, if I get the photographs that were taken at the time, I can see what we can do." He snapped pictures of the prints in the box and planned to compare them with the photographs Erskine took of the marks at the crime scene.

Alsop thought he spotted something. "The shoe that Steven Truscott was wearing . . . had deep ribbing on the side," Alsop says. "In another picture [from the crime scene] that we enlarged quite a bit, you could see the pattern of . . . the ribbing on the side."

On the other hand, the lab expert who examined Steve's shoes seized by police the night of his arrest noted the right shoe had a split in the toe, and that there was also a break in the sole adjacent to the heel. Alsop, unfortunately, could find no similar cracks, splits or marks in the prints. "It wasn't like a footprint where you get what we call 'accidental marks,'" he recalls.

Alsop also visited London shoe stores to find out how many shoes matched the ribbing he found; he gave up, he says, when he discovered the style was all too common. "There were hundreds of them around. So we couldn't say that it was that particular shoe," he concluded. "I couldn't say that it was Truscott's shoe."

In any event, after all his work Alsop would never get a chance to present his footprint evidence at trial. Because of a legal technicality, prosecutor Glenn Hays could not call more than five expert witnesses. But seven years later, Alsop would get another opportunity in front of the Supreme Court of Canada.

The warm winds of a dying summer blessed Clinton on the mid-September weekend before the trial of Steven Truscott opened. For youngsters raised on *Dragnet* and *Gunsmoke*, the prospect of taking part in a true crime drama was enticing. "I remember it being very exciting," recalls John Carew, fourteen at the time. "Our authority figures up to that point had been school principals and teachers, and here we were confronted with a whole bunch of police and a courtroom and a judge."

John, like most of the students, assumed Steven would get off. "We had gone to the trial with a 'rally round the flag' attitude, saying: 'Let's get this sorted out because Steve wouldn't do something like that.'"

Michael Burns was a good friend of Steve's. He remembered fondly the many evenings they had spent picking up pins at the bowling alley for five cents a game. He was badly shaken by his friend's arrest. It was Michael's younger brother, Philip, who testified at the preliminary hearing about not seeing Steve or Lynne on the county road. Just days before the trial opened, the police questioned Michael himself to confirm the time his brother arrived home from the river.

Michael was chilled by the thought of taking the stand as a prosecution witness. "You tell your story and next thing you find yourself testifying against your best friend," he says. "There was a sense of doom, a real sense of doom."

If Steven was looking for an omen on the eve of his trial, it was not hard to find. Right across the street from the courthouse in Goderich, the Park Theatre announced a new feature starring Gary Cooper. The marquee spelled out the movie title in black and white for all to see: *The Hanging Tree*.

# SEPTEMBER: THE TRIAL

## 15

### THE QUEEN VERSUS STEVEN TRUSCOTT

It stood at the very centre of town, an unshakeable symbol of law and order. Other cities might have a church, a park or a fountain to serve as an anchor for its citizens. Goderich had its courthouse, a granite building in the middle of the tree-lined circle from which the entire town radiated.

On the third floor of that building, jury selection took only a few hours. They started with a pool of ninety people, including fifteen women, chosen from the voters' list of each municipality in Huron County. Doris Truscott told Frank Donnelly she thought it would be a good idea to have some women on the jury, preferably those with teenage sons. But her son's defence lawyer apparently did not agree. "He said women are too emotional," Dan Truscott recounted in a letter.

In the end, Donnelly and Hays quickly agreed on twelve men. They were simple folk: five farmers, three labourers, two merchants, a barber and a milkman, who was the foreman. They were going to decide if Steven Truscott was guilty or innocent, whether he would walk free or hang from the gallows.

All summer long, Steve's defence counsel had worked tirelessly by himself to prepare the case. Now, on the eve of the trial, Frank Donnelly recruited a young lawyer from Toronto to lend a hand. Dan Murphy, twenty-nine, had attended St. Michael's College with Donnelly and was thrilled to work on such a headline-grabbing case. "For a pretty young lawyer, it was kind of exciting," Murphy recalls. "It was my first murder trial."

Donnelly worked in a small office just across the street from the court-house. His only staff was a single receptionist. "I think he was pretty confident," Murphy says. "It's incredible how little evidence there was. There was almost none."

Frank Donnelly shared that confidence with Steve's parents. "If it was all circumstantial, you think: how can they find him guilty?" Doris Truscott says. "There just wasn't that definite proof."


On Wednesday, September 16, 1959, just over three months after Lynne Harper was murdered, the trial began. "Her Majesty the Queen, Complainant, versus Steven Murray Truscott, Accused," read the court docket.

"Place the prisoner in the prisoner's box," demanded Justice Robert Ferguson.

If the jurors were expecting to see a scene out of *Perry Mason*, where the defendant sits calmly at the same table next to his lawyer, they were in for a shock. Canadian courts took their cue from the British judicial system. As the accused, Steven sat alone in a box of dark, thick wood with a swinging gate, directly facing the judge. "I was scared to death. I hadn't seen anything like this. It's just something beyond your comprehension," Steve recalls, the fear of that first day still etched in his mind. "One part of you realizes what goes on, but you just can't believe it."

Steven's lawyer was about five feet in front of him, to the right, at a table for the defence; to the left, Glenn Hays sat at the prosecution's table, and hud-dled beside him—the standard practice in Canadian trials—was the chief investigating officer, in this case OPP Inspector Harold Graham. To the left, against a wall of tall windows where Steven could catch hints of the approaching fall colours, the jurors sat in stiff chairs, staring at the young boy they had read and heard so much about.

The spectators sat behind Steven in seven long rows of benches, much like church pews. The judge had imposed a publication ban on the trial. Journalists could have remained and recorded the proceedings for publication after the trial was over, but in 1959, reporters rarely questioned the workings of the justice system. Regrettably, that meant few independent observers would follow the trial testimony in all its intricacies.

"Upon this indictment, how do you plead?" Justice Ferguson began.

"Not guilty," said Steven in a soft voice. Those were the only words he would ever speak at his own trial. Ferguson turned toward the jurors. They were as intimidated as everyone else in the courtroom, for the judge had a reputation of being tough on just about everybody. "Hard on Crown attorneys, defence counsel, police witnesses—anything that didn't go along with him, he was critical of it," remembers Hank Sayeau. "He took slices off people."

For now, the judge started in his calmest tones. "This young lad that we are about to try is charged with murder, which is the most serious offence known to our law," the judge intoned to the jurors. "If you have read anything about it in the newspapers, please dismiss that from your mind now, because we can't try this case on newspaper comments or evidence or gossip we hear in the community."

A lofty, if somewhat unrealistic goal. It would have been hard to find anybody in Huron County who hadn't heard the rumours and gossip that had swept the community since the discovery of Lynne's "ravished body" as the press described it. "Of course everyone knew about the police case before the trial," one juror later admitted. "The police knew he was guilty. It was so obvious."

Once the judge finished his opening remarks, Glenn Hays rose to outline the Crown's case. Hays had a reputation as a powerful orator; indeed, sometimes he let his oratory get the better of him. "He was quite a talker. He liked to argue no matter what," recalls one of the jurors who knew Hays as a neighbour. "He had quite a big mouth."

Hays began by explaining the focal point of his case: the time of death based on a medical analysis of Lynne's stomach contents. "I would ask you to note what she had to eat," he said. "Also, when she finished her meal. You will later hear from a provincial pathologist who will give you an opinion of the time of her death, based on his observation of her stomach and its contents."

He then previewed the second pillar of his case: a young, lustful boy on the prowl, as evidenced by Jocelyne's testimony of a secret rendezvous in the bush. "She will tell you of arrangements she made with Steven Truscott [to go] in or near this same bush where the body was found."

The third piece of the puzzle was Truscott the liar. Hays explained that Steven claimed to have seen Lynne get into a 1959 grey Chevrolet with yellow licence plates. "You will be shown pictures taken from the bridge he was supposed to have seen this from. You will be the judges of what can or cannot be seen."

To top it all off, Hays then promised some physical proof "of very considerable significance—an item of clothing of the accused, taken from him sometime after the arrest." Hays did not give any clues, wisely planting the seed and letting the jury build up anticipation with their imaginations.

But then, less than an hour into the trial, Hays let his oratory soar a little too high and he stumbled badly. He told jurors they would not hear "of any confessions at all or anything like that." He followed with these words:

"On the Friday night, a statement was taken from the accused by Inspector Graham and the other police, signed that night by him—"

"Mr. Hays!" the judge interrupted. He was rightly furious. Nothing had been decided yet about the admissibility of Steven's statement to the police. Worse still, by slipping in a reference to a statement made by the accused as part of the Crown's case, the jurors might very well conclude that Steven had made a confession.

"I don't intend to say anything about it," Hays said, trying to recover.

"You shouldn't have said anything about it at all."

"Even the fact that it was taken at all?" Hays pleaded.

The judge would have none of it. "I may have to discharge this jury and start all over again. You shouldn't do that, you know."

Chastened, his rhythm broken, Hays limped to a conclusion in his remarks. Prompted by the defence counsel, the judge ordered the jury removed in order to discuss Hays' gaffe. "If the statement is not admitted, you have made a mistrial, Mr. Hays," said the judge sternly, in a warning he would later choose to ignore. "I can't do anything about it now."

The jury was recalled but the damage was already done. Twelve men had heard the Crown prosecutor talk about an important, perhaps damaging statement the accused had given police the night of his arrest. They could not have known that Steven's statement that night was his explanation for his innocence, not an admission of guilt.

Hays immediately called his first witness: Cpl. John Erskine, the district identification officer for the OPP. In the clipped and professional tone of an experienced policeman, Erskine quickly ran through his work when he arrived at the crime scene. Hays entered into evidence more than twenty photographs taken by Erskine. The photos showed two unidentified marks next to Lynne's feet, the bicycle tire marks in the laneway near the bush, and general views of the bridge and highway.

What is remarkable, though, is what Hays did *not* have Erskine say. Erskine spent more time at the crime scene than any other police officer, making six to eight visits in a month. His testimony lasted thirty minutes. And yet not once did the Crown have the main police identification expert tie a single a piece of evidence to the accused. In fact, the Crown's identification expert did not really identify anything, except to say which photographs he took.

This technique was to be a hallmark of Hays' well-orchestrated style—a blizzard of details and suggestions, but with little hard fact beneath it all. Hays would later make much of the alleged "footprints" found near the body, but his lead-off police identification expert was much more circumspect. Erskine would only say his photographs showed "scuff marks adjacent to and west of the feet of the deceased." That is even how Hays entered the photographs as evidence: "Exhibit 2: Photograph of scuff marks."

Hays then moved to another set of photographs. "Did you on Saturday, June 13th, make an examination of the laneway to the north of Lawson's bush?"

"I did, sir," Erskine answered.

"Did you there find any—"

"Just a moment!" defence lawyer Donnelly burst in. "I have grounds for objection to the series of pictures that my friend now has. They are not at all relevant, my lord." Justice Ferguson asked the jury to retire once again while the lawyers thrashed out their disagreements.

The photographs showed several bicycle tire marks in the dry, cracked earth of the tractor trail leading into the bush. Donnelly was outraged because Hays had assured him before the trial they would not be used as evidence.

"We are taken by surprise by this evidence," he told the judge. "My friend indicated that they were not relevant and didn't give us any copies. They were made sometime before this alleged incident. The fact that the marks were somewhat similar or similar to the tread on the bicycle tire is not material."

The judge disagreed. "Mr. Hays seems to think it has something to do with the case. I don't think I can rule it out on the grounds you put forward," he told Donnelly, and he recalled the jury.

Hays had scored a victory in getting the pictures of the tire marks entered into evidence, but his own police expert soon rendered that triumph hollow. As with the scuff marks near Lynne's body, Corporal Erskine was careful. Hays held up the two tires taken from Steven's bike.

"Did you make any tests in relation to it [the bike]?"

"I did, sir," Erskine said. "I compared the tread with the marks shown in the photograph. There was a series of vertical lines, . . . marks *on the side of the tires* similar to marks in the photograph." It was a cautious appraisal: no matching treads, no plaster casts that fit exactly.

"Can you make any comparisons with either of the other photo exhibits?" Hays asked.

"With this wheel?" Erskine asked.

"The front one."

"No sir."

"Or the rear one."

"No sir."

Not exactly a conclusive match. But by the end of the trial, Hays would turn these tire tracks into proof that Steven's bike had passed through the lane on the way to the bush; even the judge would lend weight to that theory.

Defence counsel Frank Donnelly lost his battle to exclude the photographs of the bicycle tire tracks, but he used his brief cross-examination of Corporal Erskine to score an important point about the relevancy of the tracks.

"The ground there is baked very hard?" he asked Erskine.

"It is, sir."

"There [are] wide cracks in the ground?"

"That is correct, sir."

"I suggest to you these marks would be made in these pictures when the ground was wet?" he asked.

"Yes, sir."

And then Donnelly secured his prize. "I suggest to you it would take weeks for the ground to dry out and crack like that?"

"It would take some time," the police expert agreed.

Donnelly's goal was clear. If the bike tracks were made when the ground was wet or moist and it had not rained for several weeks, then clearly the tracks were not made by Steven Truscott on June 9, in the middle of a heat wave. But Donnelly failed to make this point obvious to the jury. The cross-examination of Erskine was Donnelly's debut performance at the trial, and it demonstrated his strengths and flaws. He had a sharp mind and his precise questions often solicited gems of information. But too often, he failed to follow through on his triumphs, and stopped short of making the significance of a witness's testimony crystal clear to a jury much less familiar with the minutiae of the case than he was.

When court resumed at 10:00 the next morning, Donnelly moved on to the second piece of physical evidence—the two marks or indentations in the earth near Lynne's feet. The defence lawyer took Erskine back to his testimony at the July preliminary hearing.

"Is it still correct," Donnelly said to drive home the point, "that the marks were so indistinct you were unable to say whether they were made by a hard-soled shoe or a rubber-soled shoe?"

"That is my feeling, sir, yes."

It was an important admission. The chief police expert was conceding that the marks found near the body, in his opinion, were essentially useless in identifying a suspect.

Hays wisely did not try to counter Donnelly's work by re-examining Erskine; he quickly got the unhelpful policeman off the stand. Hays had a much better strategy: he would wait until the very end of his case to bring in his star "footprints" witness, safely assuming that by then the jury would have long forgotten Erskine's cautious words.

The second day of the trial would be dominated by the prosecution's most important expert witness, Dr. John Penistan, the pathologist who examined Lynne's body. But before the jury heard a graphic description of the corpse, Hays wanted the jury to have a sharp image of the girl when she was alive. So one of his first witnesses on Thursday, September 17, was Lynne's mother, Shirley Harper.

Hays let Lynne's mother paint a portrait of idyllic, household bliss. She described her daughter's return home after the ball game, a quick supper of peas and turkey, a pause to wash the supper dishes and then a hurried departure to go play outside.

"Have you ever known your daughter to hitchhike on any of the roads?" Glenn Hays asked.

"Not to my knowledge, sir." It was tactful response: not so much a definitive "no" as an "I don't know." It completed the portrait of an innocent Lynne, a far cry from the adventurous girl who Steve insisted had asked for a lift to the highway. It was also a far cry from the truth. Lynne's friends said they hitchhiked with her frequently. And if Lynne's mother had no knowledge of her daughter's hitchhiking habits, it was curious that Lynne's parents told the authorities on the night she disappeared that "it was possible she was hitchhiking to her grandmother's." But neither Donnelly nor the jury knew anything of this: instead, they were presented with an image of a dutiful daughter who would never run away.

Before calling his witness, Dr. John Penistan, Hays scored a dramatic point by suggesting to the judge that Lynne's mother leave the courtroom.

"I thought possibly she heard all this before," the judge said.

"No, she hadn't, my lord."

"It is better that she is out," Ferguson agreed.

Shirley Harper made a graceful exit; it must have been a poignant moment for those present, a reminder that behind all the legal sparring and medical terminology, a killer had taken a girl's life and shattered a mother's world.

The distinguished doctor then began his testimony from the witness box. "What is the pathological cause of death?" the judge asked.

"Asphyxia due to strangulation," the doctor replied. "The cause of death was strangulation by ligature of the blouse."

Penistan's testimony now turned to the central matter of his analysis of Lynne's stomach contents, upon which rested the prosecution's entire theory for the time of death. The doctor's first words on the subject were unambiguous: "I recognized peas, onions, a few pieces of meat, one bit I thought was ham and another was white meat." A little later, he said: "The food appeared to have been very poorly chewed . . . bolted and swallowed without proper chewing, which would tend to slow down the digestion." Thus, on two points Penistan seemed certain: there was meat in the girl's stomach, and her food had not been well digested.

Hays asked the doctor for his best estimate of the time Lynne's food had been in her stomach.

"I would estimate between one and two hours."

"You were in the courtroom when Mrs. Harper testified this girl finished her meal at a quarter to six," Hays continued. "On that basis, sir, you would put her time of death at—"

"As prior to a quarter to eight."

"As early as—"

"Probably between seven and a quarter to eight."

Precisely the period when Steven Truscott was with Lynne Harper. Hays' questions and Penistan's answers were intended to lead the judge and jury to believe that objective science—unsullied by the police or any other outside forces—pointed the finger at one and only one suspect—the accused boy.

"Apart from the stomach," Hays later asked his chief witness, "are there any other observations that would assist in determining the cause of death or the time of death?"

Yes, Penistan told the jury. Rigor mortis had practically disappeared, which indicated that death had occurred "some two days previously."

What the jury did not know—and Hays certainly was not going to tell them—was that two months earlier, at the preliminary hearing, the same findings led Penistan to a slightly different conclusion. In July he testified under oath that stomach contents, combined with the degree of putrefaction, might indicate a time of death *from one and a half to two and a half days* prior to his autopsy. In other words, from the physical evidence alone, Lynne could have been killed as late as Wednesday and as early as Tuesday afternoon.

Penistan's science had apparently evolved over the summer to give Hays a better time frame.

Having pinned the time of death in the jury's mind to a convenient window of the thirty to forty-five minutes when Lynne was largely with Steve, Hays now had to fill the jury's heart with disgust at how violent and brutal her rape was. The details were gory enough, but Hays had to get the doctor to do some skilful dancing around the medical facts.

From the start, Penistan admitted that the body, lying under a sweltering summer sun in an insect-infested underbrush for as long as two days, was badly decomposed. In fact, the doctor was not able to identify the hymen and could not determine "whether its absence was of recent origin or whether it had been destroyed on some other occasion." Still, the decrepit state of the body did not stop the pathologist from concluding death followed "a large degree of violence."

The defence quickly interjected: "My lord," Frank Donnelly said, "might I suggest that in view of the serious post-mortem changes that this man found, that it would be extremely dangerous for him to express any opinion at this time?" Penistan himself had stated the maggots caused considerable damage. He had acknowledged that the decomposition changes "were very severe and did completely obscure the anatomy."

But Justice Ferguson disagreed. "I think the doctor, as a pathologist, is entitled to give his opinion as to what caused these changes."

And so Penistan did. The injuries to the vagina, in particular, he said, "might possibly have been produced by a blind, violent thrust of the male organ in the direction of the entry to the vagina," using the same colourful language he employed at the preliminary. It was certainly shocking stuff for a small-town jury in the 1950s to hear. But was it scientifically accurate? The doctor did not explain how he knew the thrust was blind or violent. Presumably, even if the sex had been consensual, there might be damage to a pre-teen's genital area. What's more, the doctor had just told the court the decomposition was severe enough to "completely obscure the anatomy."

Penistan said there was an abrasion of the skin just beside the entry into the vagina, but there was no bleeding because "it was too superficial." To get around the conundrum, Penistan came up with an intriguing solution. He told the court that intercourse must have occurred after death or "while the child was dying" because the bleeding from the injuries "was extremely small."

It was a stretch. What Penistan declined to tell the jurors was that his microscopic examination of the vagina showed no hemorrhaging. The bleeding was not "extremely small"—it was non-existent.


When defence counsel Donnelly rose to begin his cross-examination, he knew he had a difficult challenge ahead. He had to shake some of Penistan's scientific certainty without confusing or boring the jury with medical jargon. Right from the start, he scored a significant point about the changes in the body following death.

"There are many factors that could contribute to the variation of time that it would take for those changes to occur, would it not?" Steven's lawyer asked.

"Yes sir," said the doctor.

"And that is not a very accurate way of estimating the time of death," Donnelly pursued. "It would be difficult to tie it down *within five or six hours* of those changes, wouldn't it?"

"Yes sir."

It was a crucial concession by the prosecution's chief medical witness. But instead of pursuing this potentially explosive line of questioning to drive the point home to the jury, Donnelly suddenly switched topics. He did not ask Penistan how he could reconcile a gap of "five or six hours" with the narrow forty-five-minute window he had fixed for the time of death. He did not ask Penistan how he could reconcile his trial testimony with his estimate at the preliminary hearing that death could have occurred as late as Wednesday. Instead, Donnelly changed the subject and proceeded to talk about blood types and knots on the blouse around Lynne's neck. Within a few minutes, the judge called for a lunch recess. Donnelly had missed his first opportunity to shatter the prosecution's theory for the time of death.

After the break, Donnelly began to poke some holes in Penistan's analysis of the stomach contents. "I thought some of it looked like ham," the pathologist testified, after admitting his examination "was simply by the naked eye."

"It was a reddish brown colour, and some looked like the white flesh of fowl," Penistan said.

Donnelly promptly pointed out that at the preliminary on July 13, Penistan said he saw "a little meat, which I feel was probably ham," but made no mention of fowl. "Why mention it now?"

"Because I am doing my best to tell you what I recall."

"You were doing your best on the 13th of July?"

"I trust so."

"You were on oath, the same as you are here?"

"Yes, indeed."

It was a testy exchange, so much so that Justice Ferguson stepped in, in an apparent attempt to save the doctor further discomfort. "I think I should, in fairness to the doctor . . ." He turned to Penistan. "If you want to refresh your memory, you may refresh it from your original notes."

"No sir." Dr. Penistan quickly declined the offer.

"You say you made a record of white meat in your notes," the judge continued. "Because I would assume you would make a record of those things in your original notes."

"I think so," the doctor replied. "I will check and see what the notes say."

"Yes, I think you should," the judge said.

Penistan paused for a few moments to look through his notes—"my dictation, my records"—taken down by Dr. David Brooks as Penistan carried out the autopsy. As he looked up to face Donnelly and the rest of the court-room, his embarrassment was palpable.

"I must say my notes say there was no meat. There was no obvious meat," the Crown's top medical expert admitted.

Donnelly could hardly believe his good fortune. "Your notes say there was—" he paused, surprised at his chance uncovering of medical flip-flops—"there was no obvious meat on your examination?"

"Yes," came the terse reply.

Donnelly did not immediately ask to see those written notes. Penistan had consulted them while in the witness box; Donnelly had every right to see them and study them as well. Perhaps Donnelly never thought of it or per-haps the oversight was typical of the deference with which lawyers in 1959 treated figures of authority. Either way, once again, Donnelly failed to capi-talize on the moment and let a key opportunity slip away.

The cornerstone of the prosecution's case was that death occurred between 7:00 and 7:45, largely because of an analysis of stomach contents. How valid was that analysis if the star medical witness had just admitted his autopsy notes said "no meat," his July testimony said the only meat was ham, and now his September testimony added fowl? These were important contradictions. Donnelly could have ensured that the jury fully grasped these glaring holes in Penistan's credibility by elaborating on each one slowly and carefully. Instead, Steve's lawyer said not another word after Penistan's embarrassed admission, and changed topics once again.

"Emotional upset or anger would lead to the slowing-down of the diges-tion process?" Donnelly went on.

"Yes," the doctor replied.

"You have no scientific data as to how much the digestive process of a twelve-year-old girl would be slowed down by improper chewing of her food?"

"No sir."

Donnelly was apparently trying to suggest that Lynne's frustration over not being able to go swimming might have delayed her digestion and there-fore altered the estimated time of death. But once more, after only a few brief questions, he moved on to another topic, and within a few minutes, his cross-examination petered out. Prosecutor Hays spent less than two min-utes in his re-examination, probably realizing it was unnecessary to do any damage control.

Donnelly had failed to shake the jury's confidence in the pathologist's neatly packaged theories that pointed the finger directly at Steven
Truscott.

The next morning, on Friday, September 18, Inspector Harold Graham got
the chance to tell his story, but most of it the jurors did not hear. Hays asked
that the jury be excused because the inspector would focus on the statement
he obtained from Steven—the same statement that Ferguson warned could
cause a mistrial because Hays referred to it before the judge had ruled on its
admissibility.

Donnelly pushed the inspector for details about his interrogation of
Steven on the night of June 11, based on that statement.

"You have been cross-examining suspects for how many years?"

"Nineteen."

"Nineteen years. And this was a boy of fourteen years of age, and you
knew that?"

"Yes sir."

"How long did you cross-examine him?"

"I talked with him."

"How long did you cross-examine him, please?" Donnelly said, evidently
losing patience with Graham's obfuscation.

"Well, there's a difference. I don't say I cross-examined him all the time.
I talked to him," Graham replied. "I can't recall how long I cross-examined
him and how long I talked to him."

"But you talked to him for an hour and a half, and you came up with this
one sheet of notes that you have?" Donnelly asked a short time later, somewhat incredulously.

"Yes sir."

"And you said a great deal more than that to him, didn't you?"

"Yes I did."

"And he said a great deal more than you have down?"

"Yes."

Donnelly was seeking to show that no one would ever know what really
was discussed between the inspector and the teenage boy if only a partial
account of their meeting was available. Steve's lawyer then tried to unravel
the OPP's tactics in trying to lure Steve into confessing. Graham was forced

to admit he had sent the officer who arrested Steven, Donald Trumbley, back home to get out of his uniform.

"Investigating a matter of this nature, it is preferable, I thought, to be plainclothes," Graham said.

The OPP's embarrassment only deepened when Trumbley himself followed his inspector on the stand. The constable first tried to argue he went home "because my pants were all dirty."

"I suggest the purpose in changing your clothes was so you wouldn't be there in uniform while the inspector was talking to this boy?" Donnelly asked.

"I would have had to go home anyway to change my clothes," the policeman insisted. "My pants were all mud."

"And you didn't want to be present with this boy of fourteen in uniform because your pants were dusty?" Donnelly asked. "Is that what you want to tell the court?"

"No," the officer conceded. "That was one reason."

"What was the main reason?"

"Because I was told by Inspector Graham to change."

"Why didn't you tell us that instead of telling us 'I went home to change my uniform because it was dirty?'"

"I have no answer." Trumbley said.

"You have no answer. No. I wouldn't think you would."

It was not the OPP's finest hour. But it was enough to confirm the judge's suspicions.

"Now just tell me," Ferguson had asked Graham earlier, "why wasn't the lad warned when you first took this statement from him? Because you were suspicious of him before you examined him the first time, and your suspicions must have been directed heavily toward that lad at that time."

"It was not until I heard the evidence of Jocelyne Gaudet and the report from the laboratory that he became a strong suspect," Graham maintained.

Donnelly told the judge he felt the police had simply not played by the rules. "The absence of a warning is fatal in this case, and the inspector very frankly admits he gave no warning." Hays, for his part, tried to suggest that the police at the time were questioning Steve "merely as a witness."

"Are we to have the situation where a boy between fourteen and fifteen just isn't available to the police?" Hays asked. "I know of these safeguards about a person's liberties and so on, but surely we can't come to the stage where the police are to be deprived of some means of getting statements, even from young people."

Judge Ferguson took the lunch break to consider the matter and came back with a swift decision.

"I have come to the conclusion that I ought not to admit this statement," he told the lawyers after the recess before the return of the jury. "I think it would be a very dangerous thing to try this boy and let that evidence go before the jury." The judge ruled that the police knew very well when they were taking the statement that "he was the person who was going to be charged" and consequently a "warning ought to have been given." For a brief moment, the justice on the bench seemed to go beyond the legal niceties and acknowledge the cold, hard power relationships as they existed in the real world. "There was no equality between this fourteen-year-old boy and a group of police officers who were examining him," Ferguson stated bluntly, and, consequently, the statement in no way was voluntary.

It was the first time in Steven Truscott's long entanglement with the legal system that a member of that system would admit he had been wronged. But the victory was only a moral one, robbed of any significance. Ferguson had explicitly warned Hays two days earlier that by telling the jurors about Steven's statement he had caused a mistrial "if the statement is not admitted." Ferguson had now barred the statement from the trial, but—as was his right—he exercised his discretion and decided not to declare a mistrial. Donnelly never pushed the issue.

Suffering what was to be his only major setback in the trial, Hays knew when to quit. When the judge recalled the jurors, the prosecutor had no more questions for Inspector Graham. Surprisingly, neither did the defence. Frank Donnelly had raised only a single line of questioning with the Crown's chief police witness.

"Did you make some investigations, Inspector, as to when the last rainfall was in the area?"

"No, I didn't, personally," answered Graham.

And that was it. In less than a minute, Steve's lawyer dismissed the man who had led the investigation against the boy, the man who had him arrested and interrogated him and more than anyone else was responsible for his incarceration. It was an omission that must have left the jury somewhat bewildered—they could only assume Steven's lawyers thought Inspector Graham had done nothing wrong.

## 16

## THE CHILDREN TAKE THE STAND

I f the Crown prosecutor wanted Dr. Penistan to convince the jury how and when Steven Truscott had killed Lynne Harper, his next witness would answer the vital question of why. Why would a fourteen-year-old brutally rape and murder a twelve-year-old? Teenage lust was the answer and Jocelyne Gaudet would provide the proof.

Jocelyne began by laying out the details of her secret rendezvous with Steve. According to her, the following conversation took place on the Monday before Lynne disappeared:

"I saw a calf at Bob Lawson's barn yesterday," Jocelyne began.

"Do you want to see two more newborn calves?" Steve offered.

"Yes."

"Can you make it today?"

"No."

"Could you make it Tuesday?"

"I'll try."

"Meet me on the right-hand side of the county road, just outside of the fence by the woods. Don't tell anyone because Bob doesn't like a whole bunch of kids on his property."

Jocelyne told the court "he just kept telling me to don't tell anybody to come with you." Then on Tuesday, at about ten minutes to six, Jocelyne explained, Steven dropped by her house and another conversation took place:

"Do we have any homework?"

"We have English homework for our test tomorrow," Jocelyne told the boy, adding a detail she told neither the police nor the preliminary hearing. As Steve was getting on his bike, she added, "I don't think I'll be able to make it [to the bush] because we're just starting supper."

"Bye," said Steven.

Jocelyne apparently finished supper quickly, because within thirty minutes, she was on her hunt for Steven. She told the jury she first went to Lawson's barn, next to the bush and then on to the river. "I stayed there for five or ten minutes and then I went back to Bob's farm."

Her testimony was short and concise, and at times so inaudible even the judge, sitting right next to her, could not hear her timid answers. But Hays had succeeded in using her tale to make two points: Steven had tried to lure another girl into the bush Tuesday night before he settled on Harper as his victim; and, since Jocelyne diligently looked up and down the county road, and Steve was nowhere to be found, presumably he was in the bushes raping and murdering Lynne.

Sensing a weakness in her grasp of time, Frank Donnelly used his cross-examination to pin down details of Jocelyne's schedule.

"What time did you leave your home on June 9th?"

"About twenty after six or six-thirty."

"What time did you get down to the bush?"

"About twenty to seven."

"What time do you think you got back to Lawson's?"

"A little before seven."

"How long did you stay at Lawson's?"

"About an hour and half."

"Doing what?

"Nothing in particular."

"Was Mr. Lawson around?"

"Yes sir."

"All the time you were there?"

"Yes sir."

Donnelly soon would get another chance to dismantle these claims, but first he needled Jocelyne on the forever-changing timings of her alleged schoolhouse chats with Steve. Her first conversation with Steve when he proposed the secret date was Monday morning "before classes . . . about five to nine," she said. A second talk to plan the meeting took place Tuesday morning.

"When?"

"A little before nine."

"Are you sure it was then? Might it have been noon?"

"Well, it was sometime during the morning. I don't know what time it was, exactly."

"When did you next talk to Steven or Steven talk to you after Tuesday morning?"

"I don't know."

"You don't know. How many conversations did you have with Steven on Tuesday?"

"About four."

"You say there was one in the morning and you don't know when the next one was?"

"No sir."

"And I suggest to you, if you don't know what time it was, you don't know where it was."

"It was in the class. He talks to me in the classroom."

"How would he talk to you in the classroom with three people sitting between you and him in the same row?"

"At nine o'clock."

"Was it not during class he was talking to you?"

"Well, when he comes up to sharpen his pencil."

"You told me a while ago you didn't know what time it was."

"Well, it is sometime before nine. . . . He came up to the front of the room to do something."

"Twice he spoke to you when the teacher was in the room?"

"Yes sir."

"I suggest to you then, he would have to whisper to you up the aisle?"

"He didn't have to. He would come by to the front and get some books or sharpen his pencil or something like that."

Jocelyne looked shaky and confused. Donnelly inflicted more damage on the prosecution's primary child witness when he was able to show that it was Jocelyne, not Steve, who seemed to be interested in looking for calves in the bushes. Was it not true, the defence counsel asked, that Jocelyne had approached another boy named Gary Gilks three weeks before Lynne's disappearance about going to Lawson's?

"I suggest that you went on and said: 'Maybe we can find some calves?'"

"Yes sir," the girl admitted.

But Donnelly did not deal the blow against Jocelyne's testimony that he could have. Shortly after Jocelyne finished testifying, Bob Lawson took the stand. One of the few people on June 9 who actually had looked at a watch, the farmer's testimony about time was more credible than most. Lawson promptly told prosecutor Hays that, yes indeed, young Jocelyne did drop by his barn looking for Steve. "She did inquire about the time just before she left."

"What time did she leave?"

"Seven-twenty-five," Lawson said. She returned to the barn about twenty to thirty minutes later.

"How long did she stay on that occasion?" Donnelly asked the farmer.

"Approximately ten minutes, I would say."

Ten minutes, not an hour and half, as Jocelyne had just claimed under oath. Lawson's undisputed testimony meant quite simply that the girl was lying. She also testified she was first at his barn around 6:30—she was off by an hour.

If Steve's lawyer missed an opportunity to impugn Jocelyne's credibility, he was also hampered by what he did not know—that Jocelyne had dropped by Bob Lawson's farm during the trial to ask a very special favour. It was around 7:00 p.m., as Lawson recalls it. Jocelyne trotted alongside the tall farmer as he hurriedly walked out to the fields. "She was really buttering up to me, chatting away, the way little girls do," Lawson says. Then she popped her big question. "She wanted me to change the time that she was over to coincide with the time that she had told them that she had been over."

"She actually pleaded with me to change the time. 'No,' I said, 'I can't do that.' I knew what time it was," Lawson continues. "We finished rounding up the cows and she kept pestering me quite a bit." Lawson never reported the incident to anyone until *the fifth estate* began probing the case in 1999. "I did think it was odd, but I thought, 'Why get a little girl in more trouble?'"

Still, it must have taken a great deal of courage—and desperation—for a young girl to approach an adult she barely knew and ask him to conspire with her in a lie. Jocelyne knew that she was badly off in her timing. She also knew eyewitnesses could only account for about thirty minutes of her activities from the time she left the house at 6:30 until the time she returned about two hours later. Wherever she was during that missing ninety minutes, and whatever she was doing, prompted her to misrepresent her timings on the stand and to ask Lawson to lie for her as well.

None of these deceptions by the prosecution's young witness ever made it into the courtroom. Jocelyne's testimony had dragged on late into the afternoon, and Justice Ferguson ordered an adjournment until the next day. He turned to the jurors fidgeting in their wooden seats. "If you find those chairs uncomfortable, mention it to me and we will see what we can do about it," he said. "County council never anticipated they would have a jury in the box sitting day after day for such a long time." The murder trial had been going on for only three days.

Jocelyne's tale of a secret date in the woods gave Glenn Hays a sexual motive to sell to the jury. Dr. Penistan gave him a precise time for Lynne's assault to have occurred. The prosecutor still had to convince the jurors that Steven was in the bush with Lynne at the right moment to do the deed.

Establishing that window of opportunity would be the prosecutor's main task on Saturday morning, September 19, as the trial moved into its first weekend sitting. It would not be easy, since no one actually ever saw Steve and Lynne enter the woods, despite the busy traffic up and down the county road all evening. Little Philip Burns was Hays' answer. Philip did not see Steve or Lynne that evening, Hays argued, but he *should* have because he left the bridge on foot at the same time that another boy, Richard Gellatly, departed on his bike. Richard met Steve and Lynne not far from the school—Philip did not, because Steve and Lynne turned off the road somewhere in between.

Nobody disputed that twelve-year-old Richard did pass Steve and Lynne on the county road near the school, so his testimony was brief and to the point.

"I came home to get my [swimming] trunks," he told the jurors. "Steve was riding Lynne Harper down toward the bridge."

"What time would it be when you met and passed them there?" prosecutor Hays asked.

"Around 7:25. I could be a few minutes out."

"Around 7:25?" Hays repeated.

"Yes," the boy confirmed.

"What time did you leave the bridge, Richard?" Hays continued.

"About 7:20," Richard replied confidently. Unlike so many of the other children, Richard's story never wavered. He gave the same approximate times in his police statement and again at the preliminary hearing. His father verified his times. Hays let the boy leave the stand unchallenged. Only much later, in his summation, would the prosecutor have to skew Richard's definitive times to make his story fit the Crown's scenario.

Donna Dunkin provided Hays with the next piece of the time puzzle by putting both Richard and Philip on the road at the same moment. The mother of two told the court she drove her children to the bridge and parked just past the railway tracks, about three hundred feet south of the bridge. She saw Richard heading home on his bike "just as I pulled off the road to park." Hays asked her when she saw Philip leaving on foot.

"At the same time as I saw Richard," Dunkin answered. "Richard would be in the lead."

"And how far behind Richard on his bicycle was Philip Burns on foot?" Hays asked.

"Oh, it would be no more than ten feet," she said. "They would both be between the railroad and the bridge."

"And what hour was that that you saw them?" the prosecutor continued.

"Oh, I would say between five after seven and a quarter after, or between seven and a quarter after," the woman replied rather vaguely.

Hays got corroboration of sorts from a second mother at the river, Beatrice Geiger, who was at the swimming hole. She said she saw both boys leave the river to head home. Philip, she told the jurors, "left from the south side of the river about the same time Richard Gellatly left the north side."

When it came time for Philip to tell his version of the story, the small boy seemed to almost disappear in the witness box as the judge peered down to question him about an oath. "It means when you ask God to come as a witness that everything that you say is true," Philip said, after dutifully informing the judge he attended Catholic Church. Judge Ferguson decided the boy "understands his obligation to tell the truth" but would testify only as an unsworn witness. That meant the jury had to consider his testimony with caution and it could not be used to corroborate what any other witness said.

Philip said he left the bridge around seven. "I took one dive and I swam to my clothes," the boy continued. "And then I went up to the river—up to the bridge."

Philip proceeded to recount the story of his slow trek back to the base along the county road, where he met Jocelyne and Butch near the entrance to the bush. "I was walking on my way home, and Jocelyne Gaudet came down and she asked me—"

"No," Hays burst in, cutting short the boy's story, "what Jocelyne would say to you isn't the kind of thing we talk about here." The prosecutor was trying to avoid hearsay evidence. But his interruption also had the added advantage of stopping Philip from blurting out an embarrassing fact. Philip had told the police and the preliminary hearing that when Jocelyne met him near the bush, she had asked if he had seen Steven *and Lynne*. It was not the kind of unsettling contradiction Hays wanted the jurors to hear.

What Hays did want the jurors to hear was Philip's assertion that he never caught sight of Steven on the road that evening. "Did you see him at all on your way from the bridge home?" the prosecutor asked, coming to the payoff for the entire day of questioning witnesses.

"No," Philip replied.

It all seemed like a neat little package. Two adults at the river see two boys set off for home at the same time. One of the boys sees Steve and Lynne, the other does not; therefore Steve and Lynne must have left the road.

Except for minor quibbles, Donnelly never challenged the underpinnings of the story. He did not suggest in cross-examination that young Philip simply might have missed seeing Steve and Lynne as they rode by (as he had failed to register Richard Gellatly, Bryan Glover, Tom Gillette and others who were on the road during his journey home). He accepted as fact that Philip and Richard left the bridge at the same time. He did not question police estimates of the times it would take to walk or bike from the bridge to the base. If he had, the entire edifice of the prosecution timing theory would have come crashing down.

Glenn Hays' work on Saturday, September 19, was not over yet. He still had to orchestrate the performance of one more major child witness. And, at times, Butch George's performance was shaky at best.

As he walked past his friend sitting in the prisoner's box and made his way to the witness stand, Butch must have sensed his fast tongue and bravado—the survival skills he had learned in the playground—might not be enough to save him in the ornate chamber of the courtroom. It was one thing for Butch to take Bryan Glover's bike without asking or borrow money from a friend without paying him back. It was quite another to lie one's way through a trial.

Butch barely made it through the usually uneventful swearing of the oath. "Do you know what happens to people when they don't tell the truth?" the judge asked perfunctorily. Even the youngest children had passed this test without too much strain.

"Yes, I guess so," came Butch's surprisingly tentative reply.

"What do you think happens to people?" Justice Ferguson queried.

"My dad told me something about that and I forget now."

"You forget," said the judge. He turned toward the prosecutor. "He doesn't seem to quite appreciate the nature of an oath and what the consequences are."

"I would like to see him sworn, my lord, if he can be," pleaded Hays, knowing full well the importance of Butch's testimony to his case. It was bad enough the judge at the preliminary hearing did not think Butch had enough of an understanding of the oath to have him sworn in July. Hays could not afford to lose Butch as a sworn witness at trial.

Justice Ferguson made another attempt. "Do you go to church, young man?"

"Well, not regularly," the teenager replied.

That didn't work. So the judge gambled with a simple question: "Do you understand you'll be punished if you don't tell the truth?"

"Yes." For some reason, that answer seemed to satisfy the judge and Butch George was at last sworn as a witness.

The trial would be Butch's third formal attempt at getting his story in order, but his testimony would be just as inconsistent and confusing as the tales he told in his police statement and at the preliminary hearing. Hays began by slowly taking Butch through his search for his friend Steve on the Tuesday evening Lynne vanished.

"I went down to the river . . . trying to find Steven," Butch recounted. "And down by the woods there I saw Jocelyne Gaudet. And I asked her if she had seen Steve."

"I don't want you to say anything that was said at all," Hays explained, moving in quickly to cut off any hearsay testimony. As with Philip Burns, Hays also wanted to silence any embarrassing revelations Butch might make about Jocelyne, telling him "she was looking for Lynne"—not Steven. Hays thus made sure the jurors would never hear anything about that.

"Had you seen Steve at any time up until you started for home?" the Crown prosecutor continued.

"No."

"Did you see him any time on your way up to the station, going home?"

"No."

The message to the jury was clear. If Steve's best friend went up and down the county road and could not find him, where else could he have been but in the bush with Lynne? In a curious way, though, Butch's admission also undermined the prosecution's case. Butch had spent much of Tuesday evening and Wednesday spreading the story that he had seen (or heard about) Steve taking Lynne into the bush. Steve's angry reaction to that story would form much of the prosecution's proof of the boy's guilty conscience. But Butch was now saying under oath that he never saw Steve in the bush.

Butch told the court he did not meet his friend on Tuesday evening until he dropped by Steve's house around 8:45. He testified the following conversation took place:

"I heard that you had given Lynne a ride down to the river," Butch said to Steve.

"Yes, she wanted a lift down to Number 8 Highway."

"I heard you were in the bush with her," adding a detail he had not reported at the preliminary.

"No, we were on the side of the bush looking for a cow and a calf. Why do you want to know?"

"Skip it and let's play ball."

Hays wanted to plant in the jurors' minds that as early as Tuesday evening, Steve was admitting he was near the bush with Lynne. But Hays wisely never asked Butch to spell out from whom he had "heard" this juicy news that Steve was in the bush with a girl. The prosecutor could only hope the jurors would not catch the gaping flaw in the story: why didn't the police find out who told Butch they saw Steve, and why didn't the prosecution produce this vital eyewitness? Because, of course, such a person never existed.

Hays quickly moved on to Butch's alleged chat with Steve the following day, on Wednesday. In many ways, this story was Butch's most important contribution to the prosecution case. It was crucial that Hays convince the jurors there was a conspiracy among Steve's friends to protect him. Hays knew the defence would present two boys—Dougie Oates and Gord Logan—who insisted they saw Steve and Lynne cross the bridge. He had to undercut the defence's case ahead of time by suggesting the boys were covering for Steve. The problem for Hays was that even Butch seemed shaky about this all-important conspiratorial plot. Steve denied the meeting ever took place, and there were no other witnesses besides Butch.

"Now, after school, Arnold, did you have [a] conversation with Steven?" the prosecutor began.

"Oh, I don't recall having a conversation with him."

Hays was irritated; this was not what he was expecting Butch to say, so he tried again: "When did you next then have a conversation with him?"

"Wait," Butch called out, his memory seemingly restored. "I did have a conversation with him."

"When was that?"

"Let us see," Butch said in an uncharacteristically formal language that made it seem as if he was rehearsing practised lines. "It was in the evening, I think."

According to Butch, Steve told the police he had seen Butch down by the river as he went by with Lynne on his bike. Steve realized later it was Gord Logan he had seen, not Butch. "He said that the police were going to go down to my place to check up, so I agreed that I would tell them I had seen Steve," Butch explained.

When would Butch tell this lie to the police, Hays asked.

"That night," Butch insisted, "because the police came to our place and asked for me."

Again, Hays wisely did not push his witness for details about his alleged Wednesday evening encounter with the police. Nor did he ever produce an OPP officer to testify about such an event. The police files contained no record of such an interview. The first time they questioned Butch, according to the police notes, was not until Thursday, the following day.

If that was the case, Butch was even lying—or mistaken—about when he lied to the police.

Frank Donnelly decided he could use Butch to his advantage. "After supper you were looking for Steve?" the defence lawyer asked at the start of his cross-examination.

"Yes," Butch replied.

"At any time, from the time you started to look for him until you found him at his home . . . that evening, did you see him anywhere?"

"No sir."

"You hadn't seen Steven near the bush at all that day?" Donnelly reiterated a short time later.

"No," Butch agreed.

Donnelly then asked Butch if he had seen any sign of his friend when he approached the laneway leading into the bush and met Jocelyne.

"Did you see his bicycle anywhere?"

"No."

"If this bicycle had been lying on the side of the road, you would have seen it, wouldn't you?"

"Yes."

Donnelly was trying to spin the prosecution theory on its head. The Crown attorney had suggested that if Butch did not see Steve, that meant Steve was in the bush. Donnelly was suggesting if Steve did go into the bush, Butch should have seen him go there.

But Donnelly knew he had to undermine Butch's testimony about the alleged plot to lie to the police to protect Steve. Butch had told the court that when he chatted with Steve on the Tuesday evening Lynne disappeared, Steve said he was near the bush with Lynne "looking for a cow and a calf." But Donnelly pointed out there had been no reported talk about calves in the bush when Butch first told the story at the preliminary hearing, held soon after the events in question.

"I forgot."

"You forgot," Donnelly said. "Why didn't you tell us that in July?"

"Well, I was nervous then," Butch tried to explain. "The first time up here in court."

"But your memory would be a whole lot better two months . . . ago than it would be today, wouldn't it?"

"Well, I stated that statement while I was—during that time," Butch mumbled somewhat incoherently.

Donnelly, with the instinct of a good trial lawyer, sensed something was afoot and played a hunch: "You have gone over this with the police since then, have you?"

Hays, his radar detecting danger here, quickly interrupted: "He didn't say that."

ABOVE: Steven, holding a Donald Duck comic book, with his older brother, Ken, at right, and friend.

A school photo of Steven at age thirteen.

**RIGHT:** Steve on board his grandfather's boat in Vancouver during summer holidays in the mid-1950s.

**BELOW:** Steven, just after his fourteenth birthday, with his friend Karen Allen in February 1959.

ABOVE: The school's football team after winning the Little Grey Cup in November 1958. Steven, identified as "the star of the team," is the tallest boy in the back row; on his right, his good friend Arnold "Butch" George.

Steven in the summer of 1959 with his green racer.

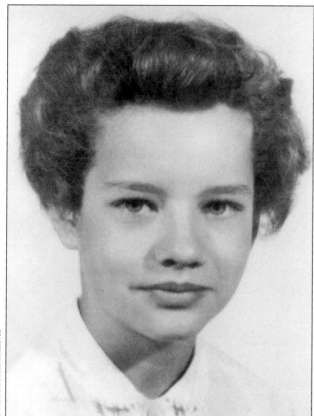

LEFT: Lynne Harper, who was murdered shortly before her thirteenth birthday.

BELOW: Lynne's body is carried out of Lawson's bush as policemen wait on the tractor trail.

ABOVE: Police photo of marks found next to Lynne's left foot. OPP Identification Officer John Erskine described them as indistinct scuffmarks, but air force Flying Officer Glen Sage insisted he could tell they were from a crepe-soled shoe.

BELOW: Cpl. Hank Sayeau at the crime scene. Stakes mark the area surrounding the body.

ABOVE: The view of the county road Philip Burns would have had as he approached the entrance to the tractor trail on his left. Philip told the court he did not see Steve and Lynne.

BELOW: The entrance to the tractor trail leading into Lawson's bush. Police say this is the path Steven took with Lynne to go into the bush.

**ABOVE:** OPP Inspector Harold Graham (left) arrives in Clinton to solve the murder.

**BELOW:** Steven is taken in for questioning.

Steven is taken to the Huron County Court House in Goderich, June 18, 1959.

But Donnelly barrelled ahead: "What did you say a moment ago about the police and a statement?"

"Well, they, like parts of my statement had been lost and they gave me another sheet," the boy offered.

"When?"

"That would be about two weeks ago."

"And how often did you read that over and study it before you came to court?"

"Oh, about ten times."

"You went over it about ten times and you couldn't memorize it in ten times?" Donnelly said a few moments later.

"I wasn't trying to memorize it."

"Why were you going over it so often?"

"Trying to make sure what I said, what I was going to say."

"And you didn't study your story too well, that is the reason you account for the difference. What is the reason why you tell a different story here today?"

The judge cut Donnelly off at this point and Butch escaped the need to answer.

Hays knew he had to do some serious damage control and he subjected Butch to the longest re-examination any witness had to endure. At times, the attempted rescue sounded almost comical.

"You gave two false statements to the police?" Hays asked.

"To the police," Butch said.

"Is that what you would call your second statement?"

"That would be my third. Well, that would be after that I would tell them the third statement."

"After the body was found you gave them the second statement?"

"No, the third one."

"Is that the true one?"

"Yes."

Even the spectators at this point thought this was a bit much. Allan Durnin, one of Steve's classmates, recalls that his father attended the trial regularly. "He told me that every time Butchie was called up to the stand to give some kind of evidence or answer a question, he changed his story. . . . You know, can this guy tell the truth or can he get his story straight, or is there something wrong with it? Because every time he told a story it was a different story."

But Hays had a definite purpose in taking his witness through his various lies.

"You say the first two statements you gave the police were false?" he asked.

"Yes."

"Why did you do it?"

"I just told them I had seen Steve at the river, *and when the body was found, I changed my story.*"

"When the body was found?" Hays emphasized.

"When the body was found," Butch agreed.

To the jurors, it must have had an angelic ring of conversion: shocked by a death of a classmate, a conniving boy decides to break ranks with his conspirator and betray his friend to the police.

At least, that was the story Hays wanted the jury to believe. But he and Graham knew there was more to it. Because buried in the police notes was Graham's handwritten account of Butch's police interview on Friday morning, June 12, after the body was found. Butch, in fact, continued to tell the police he saw Steve and Lynne at the river. He did not change his story until four days later, not "when the body was found."

But the jurors didn't know that.

The Crown prosecutor hoped that Butch and Jocelyne would convince the jurors that since two children looking for Steve could not find him, he must have been off the road and in the bushes murdering Lynne. Hays also had to convince the jurors Steve had enough time to commit the crime.

Two adults at the school, organizing a Brownie meeting, saw Lynne approach Steve. Anne Nickerson testified that she saw Steve "about a few minutes to seven, I would say. I had no watch. I am not positive about my time."

Dorothy Bohonus, the other Brownie leader, did have a watch. She appeared confused about when Lynne walked over to Steve. At the preliminary, she said, "It was 7:00 or *shortly after* that she joined him." At trial, she changed her story: "I would have said it was just *before* or around 7:00. *Not after* 7:00."

Defence lawyer Frank Donnelly asked her to explain the disparity.

"I didn't have any way of telling the time, but it seemed to me like ten minutes. It could have been longer or less. I don't know exactly how long it was." In other words, the adults were guessing as much as the children.

Prosecutor Glenn Hays used the Brownie leaders' estimates to imply that they saw Steve and Lynne leave for the river sometime between 7:00 and 7:10 p.m. In fact, all the two women were saying was that that was the time Steve and Lynne left their sight, not the time they left the school grounds. "I don't know where they went after they left me, because they only went a few yards and I dismissed it from my mind," Mrs. Nickerson told defence lawyer Donnelly.

"You only watched them a matter of a few—"

"—a few minutes."

"Two or three yards?"

"Two or three yards."

"And you paid no more attention?"

"I paid no more attention."

Mrs. Bohonus admitted the same. "What was the last you saw of Lynne?" Donnelly asked.

"When she sat down on the front wheel of the bicycle."

"Did you see her leave at all?"

"No, I did not."

"Did you see the boy on the bicycle leave?"

"No sir."

After Steve and Lynne left the Brownie leaders, they ran into children playing on the school grounds. Hays tried to use some of the young witnesses to enlarge as much as possible the time Steven was away from the school. Twelve-year-old Warren Heatherall's testimony was typical of Hays' mixed results.

"What time was that, when you saw them?" Hays asked the boy who had been playing baseball when Lynne and Steve started on their bike ride.

"I am not too sure. I think it was about 7:00," Warren said.

"Did you see Steven later that night?"

"Yes sir."

"How much later?"

"About half an hour."

Hardly enough time to leave the school, commit murder and return. A second baseball player, Stuart Westie, was even less helpful to the Crown. "I can't be sure, sir, because it all happened between seven and nine."

Both lawyers also tried to make the most of the memories of the children who saw Steve return alone to the school. John Carew gave Steve the earliest return, at around 8:00 p.m. He was able to fix the time because he remembered chatting with Steve and the other teenagers for about ten minutes, stopping by a friend's house for another ten minutes on the way home, and then arriving home in time to catch the final ten minutes of *Front Page Challenge*. The Crown prosecutor did not challenge this story, though he would try to undermine it in his summary to the jury.

"How did Steve appear to you when you saw him there?" Frank Donnelly asked John.

"Well, he appeared the same as he was any other time."

"He was just his normal self?"

"Yes sir."

"Did he talk and laugh and joke with the young people there?"

"Yes sir."

"Were there any visible marks on him that you noticed?"

"No."

"Was there any sign of blood on him?"

"No," John concluded.

Lyn Johnston, fourteen, gave a later time for Steve's return—"about a quarter after eight"—but she, too, confirmed that her classmate seemed normal.

"Did you see any marks or any blood or anything unusual about him?" Donnelly asked.

"No."

"Did he seem excited at all?"

"No."

"Flushed up?"

"No."

Lorraine Wood said she thought Steve arrived "about 8:10 or 8:15." She too reported he looked "normal" and she saw "no blood or any marks on him."

To help prove that Steve never made it to the highway with Lynne that Tuesday night, Hays brought in a young boy from outside the base. Teunis Vandendool was a Dutch immigrant who lived with his parents on a farm next to Highway 8, about a mile and a quarter from the Clinton swimming hole. He told the court he biked to the river for a swim on the evening of June 9 around 7:15. He left shortly after 7:30, he said—about the time Steve claimed he had dropped Lynne at the highway.

"Did you see any boy or girl on a bicycle at any time that night?" Hays asked.

"No," Teunis replied.

Were there any people or a car at the corner of the county road and Highway 8, Hays wanted to know.

"No persons at the corner," he said. "No car stopped at the corner."

The Crown also hoped that Steve's friends would convince the jurors he reacted with evasion and anger when asked about Lynne in the days following his bike ride with her. Glenn Hays' questions focused on the banter on the bridge at the Bayfield River on Wednesday evening between Steve and four of his friends—Butch George, Tom Gillette, Paul Desjardine and Bryan Glover. Paul asked Steve "what he was doing in the woods with Lynne Harper," Bryan told the court. "He said he didn't go into the woods."

"Did they say anything else?" Hays prodded.

"And then he said he just went in there to look for a calf."

"They say anything else?" Hays asked.

"Not that I recall, sir."

Hays expected Paul Desjardine, the boy who had initiated the conversation, to deliver more.

"I asked Steve if he had taken Lynne into the woods and he said: 'I didn't,'" Paul said.

"And was there another conversation then a few minutes later?" the prosecutor suggested. At the preliminary hearing, Paul could not recall one but his memory apparently improved with time.

"He said he had been in the woods," Paul said, "looking for a cow and a calf."

It was Tom Gillette, in the end, who gave Hays what he wanted most— an account of anger from Steve and threats directed against Butch.

Hays prompted his witness. "Did you notice anything about Steve's manner?"

"He sounded as if he was threatening him," Tom answered.

It was not much, but it was the best Hays was going to secure from the boys. Four witnesses all told somewhat different versions of the bridge talk. Butch himself testified that he did not recall any angry threats from Steve. Only one boy heard menace in Steve's words to Butch, and Donnelly moved quickly in his cross-examination to counteract Tom Gillette's interpretation.

He asked if Steve made any threatening move at all toward Butch, who was ten feet away, under the bridge playing by the river.

"No sir," Tom said.

Donnelly suggested Steve was just making an emphatic statement. "Steve said, 'I didn't go into the bush with Lynne,' and he made it pretty definite, didn't he?"

"Yes sir," the boy replied.

Forty years later, one of the boys who was on that bridge cringes as he recalls the constraints imposed by courtroom examinations. "We were joking and laughing," Bryan Glover recalls. "But lawyers don't ask you that. They just ask for exact words. You feel like you're telling about five per cent. [It's] out of context, but no one will give you a chance to tell the other ninety-five per cent."

Indeed, sitting in the witness box was a terrifying experience for most of the children. "It is very scary testifying in court when you're twelve," remembers Richard Gellatly. "They asked me things like 'Is this his bike?' and to me, a twelve-year-old kid, I'd say, 'Sure, that's his bike.' Then the lawyers come at you over and over and ask, 'How can you be sure it's his bike?' You can do that to an adult, but when you start doing that to kids—help! They just had me shaking in my boots. Those lawyers are mean, scary people when you're a kid."

As they waited their turn to testify, the children passed their time reading comics in a room at the courthouse. In a separate holding room, Steve sat with a guard when the court was not in session. He gazed out the window and counted cars going around the town square. "He was so cool," one of the officers guarding the fourteen-year-old later told a friend. "If he did it, he was the coolest kid I've ever run across."

Four days into the trial, many of Steve's friends shared his lackadaisical optimism. "Most of us kids were sure that Steve was going to go to trial and then be right home," says Catherine O'Dell. She remembers arguing with a friend's father who attended the trial regularly. He predicted things would turn out badly for Steve.

"I thought, 'He's nuts.' I just thought he was totally wrong," Catherine remembers. "Everything will be over soon and everything will go back to normal," she told her friend's father.

"They have to pin it on somebody so people can sleep at night," the man said with adult cynicism. "And they're not going to let him go."

## 17

# DUEL WITH THE DOCTORS

After a short rest on Sunday, the jurors returned to their seats on Monday, September 21. The next five days would be largely dominated by exhaustive medical testimony. But no sooner was the first doctor introduced than the judge promptly asked the jury to retire. At issue was the role Dr. John Addison played on the long night of Steve's interrogation and arrest on Friday, June 12.

Defence counsel Frank Donnelly argued that Steve's father would never have agreed to the medical examination of his son if not for the fact his friend, Sgt. Charles Anderson, the senior Goderich OPP officer, had encouraged him to do so.

Donnelly insisted, under law, any subsequent findings the doctor made on Steve's body or statements he took from the boy must be ruled inadmissible. Justice Ferguson decided he at least had to hear what Addison had to say before making up his mind, so the affable doctor stepped up to the stand, but not in the presence of the jury.

The question at hand was: did Addison act as doctor or detective?

The judge turned to the doctor in the witness box, eager to find out under what circumstances the examination took place. "Did you give any warning to the boy before you asked him any questions?" the judge asked the doctor. "Did you say to him: now what you say to me may be used in evidence?"

"Your Honour, I was examining him as a family practitioner."

"I don't care about your practice," the judge retorted.

"No, I didn't tell him it would be used against him one way or the other."

Addison then recounted his questioning of the boy. "Do you think there is a possibility you may have taken her into the bush?" he asked Steve. "If you have done this thing, I want you to tell me. It is much better you tell us the truth now and get it off your chest."

Judge Ferguson quickly became concerned with what sounded suspiciously more like a police interrogation than a medical query. "Who asked you to examine the youngster along that line? Anybody? It doesn't sound like an examination a doctor would take part in."

Addison replied that he suggested to Inspector Graham that he try to see if he could "get a story from the boy."

Later, the doctor tried to explain his actions. "After all, I was called out just to make a physical examination—"

"If you had stopped at that I would have a lot less trouble than I have, but you didn't, you see," the judge interrupted. "You took on the role of the detective before you were finished."

Addison admitted his account of his talk with Steven was not so much a faithful transcription as an impression of tone—as he put it, not the "exact words, but . . . the attitude I took." Steven's answers were not necessarily precise quotes but rather reflections of the boy's manner. For example, on the central issue of what, if anything, Steve did to Lynne, the doctor conceded he was a bit fuzzy about how he phrased his question.

"I am not positive [about] the word I used: 'molested her' or 'did this to her,' and Steve said: 'I might have' or 'I could have, but I can't remember.' It was the tone—the reason I can remember that is the tone with which he answered me.

"There was no life or fire to his reply," Addison concluded. "He didn't deny it at all. In my opinion, he didn't deny with enough enthusiasm."

Judge Ferguson was not impressed. "You sort of mixed up your evidence," he said at one point. By Tuesday, the judge was ready to rule.

"He wasn't there as the doctor looking after his patient in any possible sense of the word," he decided. "He didn't go in that role at all. He went there to make an examination on behalf of the police." The judge was also critical of the role inadvertently played by Dan Truscott. "Did anybody tell the father that the boy didn't have to answer? Nobody told the father that. Nobody told the boy that. . . . The boy could very well have been misled by the presence of his father."

But Ferguson reserved his harshest words for the police, chastising the OPP for not warning Steve he was, in effect, under arrest. "Every possible sort of inducement, everything to my mind contrary to the rule of the taking of statements took place between Dr. Addison and the boy. Under no circumstances would any court admit that statement in evidence against this accused boy, and I will exclude it."

Still, the judge ruled that the doctor's views on his physical examination of Steven and the boy's "demeanour" would be allowed. It was a door wide enough for the prosecution to get in as much compromising detail as possible.

With the jurors again settled in their seats, the local country doctor several of them knew and admired began to describe the scratches he found on the body of Steven Truscott the night he was in police custody.

"They certainly weren't recent scratches," Addison began. "They would probably be three or four days [old]."

Prosecutor Hays wanted more. "Can you be any more precise than that?" he asked.

"I wouldn't like to be more precise," Addison said with caution. "There is quite a difference on how little scratches will heal up. In a boy like Steven . . . I wouldn't like to put a definite time as to when he received those scratches." Hays did not have to worry; he would soon produce another doctor who would be much more willing to date scratches with remarkable precision.

Hays then moved Addison on to the more salacious topic of the sores on Steven's penis. The doctor informed the jurors he had never seen a penis as sore as Steve's, except for that of a man who had the misfortune of having a cow step on his genitals.

"Is it your opinion that these abrasions could have been caused by a boy this size and age trying to make entry into a girl age twelve?" the Crown attorney asked.

"Yes sir," the doctor said. "He is sexually developed, the same as any man, and trying to make entry could cause the sores on his penis."

Hays wrapped up his examination by enquiring about Steve's demeanour. "The boy appeared rather apathetic and disinterested," Addison reported. "Not too alarmed about the whole situation."

As soon as he rose for his cross-examination, Frank Donnelly pursued the issue of Steve's attitude during the long night of his arrest. Addison quickly agreed the boy was "quite calm," co-operative and not tense or nervous. Without explicitly saying so, Donnelly was trying to suggest that what some saw as apathy could very well have been a clear conscience and an absence of guilt.

Steven's lawyer then raised the delicate issue of the penis sores. Could masturbation have caused them, he asked.

"My opinion is no," came Addison's quick retort.

"Has that always been your opinion?" Donnelly pursued. "I suggest when you gave evidence here at the preliminary hearing, you indicated that masturbation could have been the cause?"

"At the preliminary hearing *you* indicated that might be a cause," the doctor insisted.

In fact, at the July hearing, the doctor, under intense grilling from Donnelly, had conceded there was a "very remote chance of masturbation" causing the sores. "Rubbing is one way," he said then.

Donnelly concluded his grilling of the family doctor by getting him to confirm that the scratches all over Steve's body were ordinary.

"There were no severe scratches or deep scratches," Addison said.

"Were they all very trivial, Doctor?" Donnelly asked.

"Well, that depends on your interpretation of trivial," the doctor responded. "I don't understand the question."

Donnelly again had to remind the doctor of his words at the preliminary hearing, when he himself had characterized the scratches as "all trivial."

"Just what you would expect in an active boy," Donnelly said.

"An active outdoor boy," the doctor agreed.

Tuesday, Wednesday and even part of Thursday's session in court were taken up with the testimony of the third medical expert, the chief health officer at the air force base, Dr. David Hall Brooks. Brooks had the advantage of being at both the autopsy on Thursday, June 11, and at the physical examination of Steven the following night. From the prosecution's vantage point, the loquacious doctor also had the advantage of being much more willing than the other medical witnesses to offer speculation.

Brooks began by telling the jurors that during the autopsy, he and the pathologist, Dr. John Penistan, held a jar of Lynne's stomach contents up to a single light bulb. Nothing could be more important for the prosecution's theory of the time of death than the stomach contents, and yet there were inexplicable differences between the doctors about what they saw staring at the same container.

Brooks saw "one piece that looked very much like pineapple"—a fruit that Penistan never mentioned. Brooks was certain "there were two kinds of meat," one brownish and the other whitish, "quite clearly poultry of some sort." It was a remarkably perceptive analysis, given that Penistan had testified that Brooks took notes during the autopsy at his dictation and the notes specifically said there was "no obvious meat." Did Brooks simply write down those three words and not inform the doctor standing next to him that he had indeed spotted obvious signs of two kinds of meat? Naturally, Hays did not pursue the contradiction; sadly, neither did Donnelly.

Unlike Dr. Addison, Dr. Brooks was eager to hypothesize about the age of the various scratches on Steve's body. A scab on his upper thigh was "two and a half to four days old," while vertical scratches on each kneecap were "certainly not more than five days old." Where Addison would only say that Steve's genital area was "a little cleaner" than the rest of his body, Brooks insisted Steve's private parts were scrubbed clean compared to the "filthy dirty" parts of the rest of his body.

"There was oozing," he said of the sores on Steve's penis. "By this time the oozing was stagnant." A curious choice of words since, by strict dictionary definition, oozing cannot be stagnant. Later, under cross-examination, the doctor appeared to be saying the oozing had stopped. "There was no oozing from them," he said. "It had got to the stage of being tacky, sticky."

"This is the worst lesion of this nature I have ever seen," Dr. Brooks said dramatically. And he left no doubt as to its origin—forcible sexual intercourse. Not just any kind of rape, but "a very inexpert attempt to penetration," the air force doctor said, in an expression clearly meant to suggest it was the work of an over-excited teenage boy. Brooks did not explain how an experienced rapist would differ from an amateur or how he could distinguish between the two by examining the damage to the victim's badly decomposed and swollen body.

Brooks had talked for almost an hour without the benefit of notes or much prompting. But in courts of law as in the outside world, pride goes before a fall. On Thursday morning, September 24, Frank Donnelly began his cross-examination. It would be one of the defence counsel's longest grillings of any witness, lasting twice as long as Hays' easy session with the doctor.

Donnelly's first serious challenge to Brooks was over his certainty that Lynne's hymen "was completely missing." Even Penistan, the pathologist, was not as categorical, suggesting that extreme decomposition might have made it impossible to see the hymen.

"Do you agree or do you not that there was a considerable degree of decomposition around the external parts of the vagina?" Donnelly asked.

"I am not a certified pathologist, sir," Brooks replied. "There was a degree of decomposition," was all he would concede.

Donnelly saved his sharpest barbs for Brooks's seemingly inexhaustible expertise on sores and scratches. Brooks had dramatically improved the precision of his timing skills over the summer. At the preliminary hearing in July, he had testified the penis sores were two to five days old—anywhere from Sunday to Wednesday, too wide a margin to tie Steven to the rape. But now at trial he had told Hays they were only "sixty to eighty hours" old—a much narrower window of twenty hours that put the origin of the penis sores squarely on the Tuesday Lynne disappeared.

"When did you come to that conclusion?" Donnelly wanted to know.

"This is a question of scabbing," Brooks said, avoiding the query.

"Would you please listen to my question," the lawyer rebuked him. "When did you come to that conclusion? Was it yesterday, or a week ago?"

"After the preliminary hearing," the doctor said.

"What did you tell us at the preliminary hearing?"

"That, I cannot remember," said the doctor who displayed such a sharp memory for other details.

"I will try and help you," Donnelly offered. He read the doctor's own words back to him and wanted to know why he narrowed his estimate so dramatically—from as much as five days to only sixty hours.

"I have since then been burnt once, and I have seen how long it takes a lesion to heal under ideal conditions," the doctor explained. He did not elaborate where he burned himself—presumably not on his penis—or why he thought a burn injury was comparable to the sores he found on Steve's genitals.

Donnelly now turned to a phone call the doctor made the day after examining Steve at the guardhouse. The call was made to Dr. A. H. Taylor, the jailhouse physician in Goderich.

"You phoned . . . and asked him to examine this boy to see if he was circumcised?"

"Yes sir," Brooks admitted, leaving in doubt how thorough his examination of Steve's genitals could have been if he was not sure of such an elemental fact.

But Donnelly did not know the worst of it. According to the Huron County Jail medical book entries, Dr. Taylor examined Steven at 1:20 p.m. on June 13. The doctor took his blood pressure and tested his urine. In 1966, legal investigators asked Taylor about his findings. "With special reference to his penis at the time of . . . examination," they wrote, "Dr. Taylor stated that he had not observed any injury or anything else out of the ordinary."

Taylor's was a startling observation, considering that just over twelve hours earlier, two other doctors had found what they considered large, oozing sores. Either the jailhouse doctor was so incompetent that he missed them, or the sores were not that severe and had greatly diminished by the next morning. No one will ever know. Donnelly knew nothing about Taylor's report, and the jailhouse physician was never called to testify.

Donnelly wrapped up his grilling of Brooks by asking him about the scratches on Steve's arms. He pointed out that at the preliminary, Brooks had dismissed them, saying it "would it be as if he had his arms around a tree and slid down."

"At the time that is what I said," the doctor admitted.

"And you don't want to change that?"

"Except that when I tried to do it since then, I have taken skin off and bled," the doctor said. "I have slid down trees since then, and I haven't been able to produce anything like this lesion."

The chief medical officer at RCAF Station Clinton appeared to have led a dangerous life over the summer, incurring burns that allowed him to test for penis sores and sliding down trees to see how his skin bled.

The final medical expert to testify for the Crown was Elgin Brown. Brown was a biologist with a bachelor of science from the University of Toronto who began work at Dow Chemical and had joined the attorney general's laboratory a year earlier. He was also a prosecutor's worst nightmare: a government expert who ended up being more helpful to the defence.

Hays handed Brown the underpants the police had removed from Steven in jail. The prosecutor was going to get as much mileage as he could from a pair of underwear Steve wore four days after Lynne's disappearance—even if his show had more to do with theatre than real evidence. Here at last was the physical proof "of very considerable significance" he had promised jurors on the first day of the trial.

"Will you hold them up?" he asked, trying for as much drama as possible.

The laboratory expert complied with the odd request and lifted Exhibit 57 in his hands. Even the judge seemed to find the display a bit tawdry. "All right, put them down," Ferguson said.

"What were your findings?" Hays began, after Brown explained that he'd examined them on Monday, June 15, two days after the police took them from Steve.

"They had a very heavy deposit of feces in the seat area," Brown said. "Investigations revealed that the yellowish brown discolouration in the fly area contained spermatozoa and traces of blood."

"How long had it been there?" Hays asked regarding the sperm. "Can you give an opinion of that?"

"No sir, I am unable to tell the length of time that had been there," the scientist replied.

That did not satisfy the prosecutor. "Can you give any estimate that it had been there for any period of time whatever?" Hays pushed.

But the government expert would not bend science to fit the prosecution's needs. He explained that the length of time sperm could be present "depends on a number of things," such as washing, bacteria in a moist area, dirt and the warmth of the body. "I have no way of determining . . . the probable duration of the deposit," Brown concluded.

Hays was not about to give up. If the biologist was not willing to be specific about Steve's sperm, perhaps he would be open to generalizations. "There is a certain well-known period of time in which these sperm may survive?" the prosecutor asked.

"Better than a year," came the reply.

Hays should have quit while he was ahead.

The biologist went on to describe his other findings, or rather lack thereof. He found bloodstains on Lynne's shorts and on her left shoe, as well as "heavy blood staining" on her undershirt near the arm openings. On Steve's shirt, jeans and shoes, however, Brown found not a drop. No blood, no pubic hairs, no hairs from anyone else, nor any traces of foreign fibres.

What Brown did find underneath Lynne's fingernails was a small quantity of debris. "I found that there were traces of blood present in the debris. There were some very short, white synthetic fibres and what appeared to be visible remnants of cells, skin tissues."

Hays, hoping to deflect the significance of this discovery—since they indicated an injured or badly scratched assailant—wanted to know if these deposits would normally be found under fingernails.

"I can't answer that to say what it was due from," Brown said.

Hays was in trouble and Donnelly sensed it. The judge adjourned the court for the day, but when court resumed Friday morning, Donnelly's cross-examination lasted three times as long as Brown's original testimony. Eager to milk the government biologist for everything he had to give, Donnelly made it his longest cross-examination of the trial.

To start, Donnelly wanted to exploit the absence of blood on any of Steve's outer clothing. He wanted to make sure that the jurors understood that the biologist did not even find traces of blood that would have been invisible to the human eye.

"Testing is very sensitive," Elgin Brown explained. "Just very small traces, small amounts can be detected."

"The size of a head of an ordinary straight pin?" Donnelly asked.

"That could be detected."

Knowing the prosecution might try to make an issue of the fact that Steve's mother washed his clothes the morning after Lynne disappeared, Donnelly also asked the biologist about the effects of doing the laundry. "It may remove the visible evidence of the blood," he asked, "but you can still detect the blood?"

"You may," Brown answered. He told the jurors that washing clothes in hot water helps preserve blood, while cold water disperses the blood traces.

For good measure, Donnelly also displayed various shirts and pants the police seized from Steve's room. The laboratory expert confirmed many of them were torn, ripped or showed "general fraying." To deflect the prosecution's theory that the tears in Steve's red jeans were proof he dragged Lynne over the barbed wire fence into the bush, Donnelly wanted the jurors to know holes and rips were common in most of the teenage boy's clothes.

Of all the pieces of Steve's clothing, it was his soiled underwear that was fixed in the minds of the jurors, Donnelly knew. Taken from Steve on Saturday, June 13, there was no proof that the feces-stained garment with traces of sperm was the same pair of underpants worn by Steve on Tuesday, June 9; indeed common sense would dictate otherwise. Still, Hays had tried to suggest the sperm was proof that Steve raped the girl, so Donnelly had to show this idea was scientifically unsound.

Under persistent probing, biologist Elgin Brown agreed that normal washing would remove blood and spermatozoa. "The presence of spermatozoa indicates it hasn't been washed since the deposit of spermatozoa." Brown also said that bacteria would attack and kill spermatozoa.

"How quickly will bacteria destroy spermatozoa under the most favourable circumstances to the bacteria?" Donnelly wanted to know.

"In a matter of hours," Brown said.

"I suggest to you a pair of shorts worn by a young man on a hot, humid day . . . would be ideal conditions for the spermatozoa . . . to be destroyed by bacteria. What is your opinion as to that?"

"It is the type of condition in which bacteria thrive," Brown said.

The defence counsel also asked Brown to give the jurors more details of what he found in Lynne's fingernail scrapings. The biologist repeated that he discovered traces of blood and remnants of "epithelial cells"—cells covering the outer skin.

"Is it a clear indication to you that this blood came from a scratching or scraping with those fingernails?" Donnelly asked.

"It came from contact with blood," Brown said, choosing his words carefully.

"Could it come from contact with blood on her own body?" the judge intervened.

"Certainly, Your Lordship," Brown replied.

But Donnelly was not about to let the judge ruin his line of argument. "The presence of blood in those skin cells puts a different complexion on it, does it?" he asked.

"In my opinion, the person scratching themselves would be expected to pick up a certain amount of skin cells and not necessarily blood," Brown conceded.

Prosecutor Glenn Hays had to recoup his losses. In his re-examination, he asked Brown if the debris he found under Lynne's nails "could be caused by scratching a mosquito bite?"

"Vigorous scratching could result in such a deposit," Brown hypothesized.

Justice Ferguson found this line of thought a bit of a legal stretch: "We haven't heard anything about mosquito bites in this case, or mosquitoes," he pointed out.

Hays' tactic was obvious. The Crown prosecutor had to downplay any suggestion that the blood underneath Lynne's fingernails came from her assailant. The jurors knew that Steve had no significant marks on his face, neck and chest. None of the doctors was willing to say definitively that the seemingly ordinary scratches on his arms or legs came from a struggle.

Curiously, no one asked Brown what type of blood he found under her nails or if there was even enough to test. If the blood was Type A—the blood type that both Steve and Lynne shared—a test would be inconclusive. But if the blood under her nails came from a different blood group, it would point to someone other than Steve as the killer.

There was no DNA technology available in 1959—a shame, because if the blood under Lynne's nails did come from her assailant, a simple test could have determined Steven's innocence or guilt once and for all.

## 18

# THE POLICE STORY

Police testimony often provides the framework for the prosecution in a long trial, connecting the dots in a complicated case. Aside from Inspector Graham and Identification Officer John Erskine, a dozen other OPP and air force police personnel trooped before the jurors during the course of the trial.

Prosecutor Glenn Hays used several of the officers to punch holes into Steven's claim that he could see a car at the highway from over thirteen hundred feet away at the bridge. Constable Trumbley recounted how he drove the boy to the bridge and asked him to point out where he was standing when he saw the car picking up Lynne. "I then walked over to the same point. I observed traffic going up and down Number 8 Highway. I still couldn't observe any licence numbers."

RCAF police corporal Keith Lipscombe, who accompanied Trumbley, told Hays the same story. "I saw automobiles going by, but I couldn't see any licence numbers."

But who had said anything about licence numbers? Steven had said he saw something yellow or orange on the bumper, possibly a licence plate. He never claimed he could read the numbers on the plate.

Trumbley also said that while he was standing on the bridge, a car passed by on the county road and made its way northward to the intersection where Steve said he had left Lynne. "I fixed my eyes on the licence plates and when the car stopped at Highway Number 8, I couldn't see the licence plates *at all*," he told the jurors. Trumbley was being less than complete in his account. According to his internal notes in the police files, he could see something on the rear bumper when the car stopped at the highway—if only briefly: "The licence plate appeared as a very small dot," he wrote. Only when he turned his eyes away and then looked back at the car could he no longer pick out the plate. Inspector Graham's official report to his superiors about Trumbley's impromptu test was also slightly different: "With this colour combination, a black spot (the licence) could be seen." These police notes never were revealed in court.

The testimony of the various police officers also offered an intriguing insight into the fallibility of human memory. In several instances, two police officers in the same spot at the same time portrayed events or conversations differently.

Flight Sgt. Frank Johnson of the RCAF sat in the back of the OPP cruiser while Const. Donald Hobbs questioned Steve on the Wednesday morning after Lynne went missing. Hobbs remembered Steve telling him he left the school with Lynne "between 7:00 and 7:30." Johnson recalled Steve giving a much more precise time of between "7:25 and 7:30."

The next day, Hobbs was joined by Sgt. John Wheelhouse as he interviewed Steven at school. Wheelhouse testified that Steven told them Lynne "was mad at her mother because she couldn't go swimming." Hobbs had made no mention of that fact. Wheelhouse also said Steven told the men whom he saw at the river and how long it took him to make the trip. Hobbs said nothing about these details in his testimony. "I am not out to make a note of every word the boy said," he explained, when asked by the defence to explain the omissions.

In his cross-examinations of the police officers, Donnelly pursued a common theme: the boy they drove around the base, questioned, probed and interrogated over three days was unflappably at ease and accommodating.

Hobbs described Steve as "quite co-operative." Another officer said he was "quite helpful, intelligent." Trumbley agreed with Donnelly that the boy showed "no signs of nervousness."

"Steven's story was the same to each of the officers, was it not?" Donnelly asked Sergeant Johnson.

"Yes, basically the same," the officer confirmed.

"And he appeared quite calm and normal, did he?"

"Yes."

With Cpl. Hank Sayeau, Donnelly had one of his testier exchanges. He began by questioning the rigour with which the police measured the all-important distances along the county road. Sayeau admitted he simply used his car speedometer.

"You could be out considerably on that?" the defence lawyer asked.

"I could be out."

"I suggest to you that you might be out over 200 feet on your measurement from the highway to the bridge?" Donnelly said, highlighting the crucial distance at which Steve claimed he could spot a car.

"I might be," Sayeau conceded. He was. Donnelly produced a surveyor map that showed the police were off by 284 feet.

Donnelly then showed Sayeau photographs of the bicycle tracks in the dry, cracked earth. At the preliminary hearing, Sayeau had readily agreed with Donnelly that the tracks were not fresh, but had been made "certainly before the 9th of June."

"These bicycle tire marks shown in the picture were made when the ground was soft," Donnelly said, simply repeating what he and Sayeau had agreed upon in July. "What do you say to that?"

"I don't know," the OPP man now replied.

"Are you able to express an opinion on the length of time these marks were there?"

"No, I am not," Sayeau answered. Now in front of jurors, the corporal, sadly, was much less forthcoming.

Donnelly also pushed Sayeau on the mystery of the golden locket Sandra Archibald found on June 19, ten days after Lynne disappeared. The defence lawyer asked if a large number of police searched the area where the locket was found before the 19th of June.

"Yes sir," Sayeau said.

"In the area where the locket was found?" Donnelly repeated for emphasis.

"Yes."

"And what is your opinion as to whether the locket was there when you made the search?"

"They didn't see it."

"Are they in a position to say whether it was there or wasn't there?"

"I feel if they knew it was there, they would have gathered it," Sayeau said with astonishing frankness.

"Mr. Donnelly," Justice Ferguson interrupted. "Let's be reasonable. You can search an area, you lose something, you miss it and you search again and find it. I see no relevancy in that."

But there was enormous relevancy in Sayeau's comment that the police "would have gathered" the locket if they knew it was there. If the police did not find the locket in the careful search of the area between June 11 and June 19, it was possible someone else—most likely the killer—had discarded it there after Steve was already in jail. With his dismissive comments, the judge had told the jurors, in effect, to ignore what might have been an important piece of evidence.

Ever astute, prosecutor Glenn Hays tried to have it both ways with the locket. Constable Donald Hobbs told jurors that Steve told him Lynne "was wearing a gold chain necklace. There was a heart with a RCAF crest *in* it." Hays suggested to the jurors that only if the boy had ripped the necklace from his victim would he have known what was *inside* the locket. Except that since the locket was made of Plexiglas, presumably the RCAF crest was visible through the plastic cover. That probably explains why, according to Hobbs at the preliminary hearing, Steve had told the police the locket had an RCAF crest *on* it, not *in* it—an important distinction that Hays kept from the jurors.

On the other hand, the prosecution also realized the locket raised more questions than it answered. If, as Hays implied, Steve took the locket from his rape victim as some sort of souvenir and then tossed it away out of fear or recklessness, why did the police not find it for more than a week?

That conundrum perhaps explained why Lynne's father, Leslie, was now reluctant at trial to confirm the locket belonged to his daughter in the first place.

"Lynne had one similar to it" was Harper's vague reply when defence lawyer Frank Donnelly asked him about the necklace.

"You identified that definitely, earlier, did you not?" Donnelly pursued.

"I don't recall," the flying officer said, asking the jurors to believe that a father would not remember identifying a piece of jewellery treasured by his slain daughter. In fact, as Donnelly pointed out to the jury, Leslie Harper had no such doubts at the preliminary hearing in July—even repeating his certainty when the judge asked him to identify the locket.

"All I am asking you is: did you or did you not make that answer on the 13th day of July?" Donnelly continued.

"I do not recall, sir," Harper responded.

Justice Ferguson seemed to sense that the witness was prevaricating: "Has anything occurred since July 13th which would shake your assurance that it is your daughter's locket?"

"No, my lord," Harper said, struggling to explain, "except there are no markings on it to distinguish it from one of many. It could be in the possession of other people."

"You have reasoned yourself out of it. This is what occurred?" the judge said, offering Harper a way out.

"More or less, my lord."

The locket was not the only piece of physical evidence over which the lawyers sparred in an effort to try to pin down where Lynne was killed. One curious anomaly was Lynne's blouse: there was a fairly large piece from the front—nine by ten inches—that had been cut out and gone missing. The prosecution argued Penistan probably was responsible for that when, during the autopsy, he snipped off the knot in the blouse under Lynne's neck. Unfortunately, Penistan himself denied the possibility. Donnelly suggested to the jurors that if such a large piece of the blouse was not found in the autopsy room or in the bush, Lynne must have been killed "at some other point—in an automobile . . . somewhere."

To counter that theory and show that Lynne was murdered in the bush, Hays entered into evidence a red button—matching one from Lynne's blouse—that police said they found next to her body. Donnelly tried to undermine this by securing from OPP officer Sayeau the embarrassing admission that the OPP only retrieved the button the day *after* they removed Lynne's body from the bush; Sayeau insisted he saw the button when the body was there but forgot to take it "because of all the distraction."

Glenn Hays' final witness was not a police officer, but the Crown treated him as if he were one. When Flying Officer Glen Henry Sage walked up to the witness box on Friday, September 25, the jurors probably could only vaguely recall that nine days and many witnesses ago, OPP identification officer John Erskine led off the prosecution's case. If the wide gap between the two witnesses was intentional, it was a stroke of genius; if it was not, it was a stroke of legal luck. Hays certainly would not have wanted jurors to remember that a police expert had dismissed the marks near Lynne's feet as "indistinct" because Flying Officer Sage was going to become the prosecution's new expert on footprints.

Sage had been the officer in charge of the small band of airmen who found Lynne's body. He stayed at the crime scene for several hours and helped the police protect the site. "Just about two or three inches from her left heel, there was this footprint," he told the court. "I noticed it right away and I bent down to scrutinize it very carefully. And this footprint, I got the impression there, after looking at it quite carefully, that it had been caused by what I know as a crepe-soled shoe."

Hays handed him a picture taken by Erskine that showed part of Lynne's bare leg and what looked like a dark mound, hole or impression hidden amidst the leaves and twigs. "Here was the outline of the foot," Sage explained. "This leaf obscures the actual impression. A very good impression of the instep and the heel."

Sitting in the courtroom listening to his fellow officer testify, George Edens, the man who actually found Lynne's body, could not help but squirm. After all, he too had stood guard over Lynne's body for four hours. Sage had not pointed out the footprints to him, and he was startled by Sage's detailed descriptions. "I was rather surprised," Edens said later. "He seemed to have seen more than I saw. . . . I couldn't validate any of it, really."

Edens recalls that he noticed "a kind of a smoothing in a little area" that could have been flattened from a footprint. "But I never drew any conclusions. I didn't associate it [with] any identified type of shoe or a tread. . . . I even had a bit of trouble associating it with a footprint. I thought, 'I'm not sure.'"

Wisely, the Crown never asked George Edens when he was on the stand to describe what he saw next to Lynne's feet. Nor did Glenn Hays ask the other searcher who took the stand, Lieut. Joseph Leger. There were several OPP officers hovering around the body for hours, but only one of them, Sgt. Charles Anderson, made a passing reference to footprints on the stand: "I saw two footmarks . . . immediately west of the deceased's body. They were marks in the earth." Hays never pushed him for details. Dr. Brooks had also said he spotted "two imprints of two shoes or boots . . . about six inches away from the deceased's feet."

Sage himself testified that he told three officers about the footprint, but Hays never asked police to corroborate this statement. Perhaps the Crown attorney knew that the word "footprint" did not appear in any police report.

Frank Donnelly was understandably suspicious of Sage's last-minute revelation. If Sage's sighting had been so eye-popping, why did he not testify at the preliminary? Donnelly did his best to undermine the flying officer's credibility. He began by asking him to confirm the depth of the print.

"Two to three inches," Sage said without hesitation.

"Well now, I suggest that Corporal Erskine said it had a depth of half an inch," Donnelly retorted.

Sage had no explanation for the difference. "I kneeled down in the presence of other people and observed it," he said.

How then, Donnelly wanted to know, did he explain the fact that he failed to spot a print next to the right foot? (Dr. Brooks claimed to have spotted it, and OPP expert Erskine even considered the mark next to the right foot to be a little clearer than the mark on the left.)

"Did you study or observe the print below the right foot?"

"No . . . I did not notice it."

"Did you not check it to see if there was a similar imprint?"

"No."

"What was the shortest distance between the marks?"

"I would say about twelve inches," Sage said, never making clear how he knew the distance to a mark he had just claimed he didn't notice.

"What branch are you in, in the service?" Donnelly asked pointedly.

"I am [in the] Telecommunications Office."

"Does that include the study of marks such as these?"

"I wouldn't say so, no."

Donnelly had done his best to control the damage done by Sage's claim of a crepe-soled footprint. But Steven's lawyer could have inflicted a lot more damage on Sage's credibility if he had the flying officer's original police statement. On June 26, at 10:12 a.m.—just fifteen days after so carefully scrutinizing the footprint next to Lynne's body—Sage swore out a detailed statement in front of Graham and Trumbley. He talked about spotting Lynne's underwear thirty-five feet away, northeast of her head. He mentioned her shoes, her socks, her blue shorts and her red headband. But not a word about footprints.

Years later, asked to explain this disquieting omission, Sage was perplexed. "I can't answer that, I don't know. I guess I wasn't asked." Hank Sayeau, who distinctly remembers Sage protecting the footprint at the scene of the crime for fear that someone would trample over it, says he "cannot fathom" why none of the existing police reports refer to the prints.

But Steve's lawyer knew none of this information. Frank Donnelly ended his rebuttals to Hays' witnesses the same way he began—with one hand tied behind his back, largely unaware of what most of the witnesses had told the police during the months of the OPP's investigation.

19

## WITNESSES FOR THE DEFENCE

"**M**ay it please Your Lordship and gentlemen of the jury, it is now my intention at this point to call certain evidence on behalf of the accused."

Frank Donnelly rose on Friday afternoon, September 25, to address the jury. For nine days, jurors sat through fifty-nine witnesses and seventy-six pieces of evidence for the prosecution. "The number of witnesses called on behalf of the defence will be very, very much fewer than the lengthy number of witnesses called on behalf of the Crown," Steven's lawyer said.

Donnelly's first witness was Joseph Calvert, meteorological instructor at the RCAF station who kept records of rainfall. It was not as odd a choice as it may have first appeared to the jurors. Calvert said the last precipitation before Lynne's disappearance occurred on June 1, with .01 inches of rain "as if a few raindrops had fallen, that is all."

"What about the 2nd of June?" Donnelly asked.

"No rain whatever."

"What about the 3rd of June?"

"No rain at all."

"And the 4th of June."

"No rain whatsoever."

"And the 5th of June."

"None whatsoever, sir."

"And the 6th of June."

"None whatsoever."

"And the 7th of June?"

"None whatsoever."

"The 8th of June?"

"None whatsoever."

"And the 9th of June."

"None whatsoever."

The repetition made Donnelly's point: the ground near the bush was much too dry in the first week of June to leave any traces. The bike tire tracks found in the bush laneway in all likelihood were made at least a week before Lynne was killed. In his cross-examination, Hays seemed to concede the earth needed to have been wet for tracks to have been made, so he got the meteorologist to explain that his measuring station was three-quarters of a mile from the base.

"Then it could be raining in Lawson's bush and not where you are?" Hays asked.

"Absolutely, sir," Calvert said.

Even if the bike tracks were old, Donnelly also wanted to explain why they might have looked as if they came from Steve's bike. He brought Leslie Spillsbury, a friend of Steve's, to the stand to tell jurors what the boys did one week before Lynne's murder.

"We went into the lane on the north side of Lawson's bush. At the far north, we built a tree fort," Leslie recounted. The boys parked their bikes at the corner of the bush.

Too smart a lawyer ever to miss a chance to score a point, however feeble, Hays asked Leslie under cross-examination if it was true that Steve sometimes went to Boy Scouts. "You had a little instruction on knots there, isn't that part of the Boy Scout training?" he suggested.

"Yes sir," the boy answered.

Donnelly also wanted to undermine Jocelyne's credibility, since her story of a secret date with Steve to look for calves in the bush was so key to the prosecution's case. Gary Gilks, a classmate of Jocelyne and Steve, told the court that Jocelyne approached *him* with the idea of a date in the bush in the weeks before Lynne disappeared. "Maybe we could go back and find some calves back in the bush," Jocelyne told him.

———

The Crown had called three medical doctors: a pathologist, an air force medical officer and a general practitioner. None of them was an expert in the areas of either the digestive system or rape. Berkely Brown, the sole defence medical expert, had knowledge of both. He had graduated from the University of Western Ontario in 1940, spent several years in the army during World War II and then four years in post-graduate work specializing in internal medicine and the digestive system.

Brown suggested that on average, the stomach of a twelve-year-old girl would take three to four hours to empty and even an hour more if the food was poorly chewed. But his main point was to emphasize the variables that influenced digestion, something Dr. Penistan barely mentioned. The stomach is a muscle, Brown explained, so disease, fatigue or emotional stresses affect it. Other factors included type of food and how well-chewed it was. A meal with a large amount of fat might take eight hours to digest, he said.

Donnelly then asked the key question—one upon which the entire case turned. "What do you say as to the practicability of attempting to fix the time of death by an examination of the stomach contents?"

"Well, I think that it is generally held by myself and experts in the field that [it] must be done with great caution because there are such wide variations and so many factors can enter into the situation," Dr. Brown replied, a point that was a sound opinion back in 1959 and one that medical science today accepts as an indisputable fact.

Donnelly then moved to the second major medical issue—the sores on Steve's penis. Brown explained that during his stint in the army overseas, he examined "many thousands" of penises. He had seen similar lesions; he discounted the importance of the alleged size of the sores because "stretching the skin would enlarge the lesion as well and make it appear larger than it actually was."

Could such sores be caused by sex with a young girl, Donnelly wanted to know. "I would think that it would be highly unlikely that penetration would produce a lesion of this sort," Brown offered. "It is interesting that the penis is rarely injured in rape, to begin with." When it is, he continued, the injury is usually to the head of the penis. Since the head is larger than the shaft, the shaft does not bear the same traumatic burn as the head; and unlike the skin on the tip of the penis, which is fixed and more likely to tear on heavy pressure in a tight opening, the skin along the shaft is durable and mobile.

What's more, he said, the hymen and surrounding genital area of a twelve-year-old girl would be "soft tissue" and thus "highly unlikely" to cause a burn. Instead, Brown concluded, the injuries on Steven's genitals were "consistent with masturbation."

Crown attorney Glenn Hays knew he had to destroy Dr. Berkely Brown on the stand. He had to demolish his testimony, even if that meant exploring sexual mores in a more explicit manner than jurors in 1959 were accustomed.

Would there not be "terrific pain" associated with the injuries on Steve's penis, thus ruling out masturbation?

Not necessarily, Brown insisted, arguing that "during moments of excitement" pain does not always register.

"You would expect that a subject would continue with masturbation to where he would bring about these terrific-sized lesions?" Hays continued, somewhat incredulous.

"That is my experience," said the doctor.

Would not the friction of a rape have an effect on the skin of the shaft since it is "tethered to that collar" of the penis head, Hays asked.

"I don't agree," Brown maintained. "The area where those lesions are described is immediately behind the head and the head has such a larger diameter. I don't see how friction could injure it."

Would not the doctors who examined Steve be in a better position to describe the wounds of Steve's penis, Hays asked.

"It depends on their past expertise, of course," Brown said, maintaining that his experience during wartime was more relevant than Brooks's quiet tour of duty in peacetime air force bases.

"What in the world would the difference be [between] the sexual act in Europe [and] in Canada?" Hays wondered.

It was too much for a staid courtroom in small-town Ontario. "I think we should draw a line here," the judge interrupted. Brown quickly explained that men overseas, deprived of girlfriends and wives, were more likely to "indulge in abnormal practices" and "there would be cases of rape."

Hays challenged Brown's contention that using stomach contents to determine time of death was not reliable. If stomach contents were so unreliable, why were they used so often in courtrooms, the Crown attorney wanted to know.

"Post mortems are a fairly crude examination, non-scientific examination," Brown answered with more forthrightness than most medical experts usually showed in court. It was perhaps too frank for the judge. Justice Ferguson jumped in to ask if autopsies were not performed precisely to determine the cause and time of death?

"Well, ordinarily the times of death are not the concern of the pathologist, except in the legal sense," Brown said, in one of the most understated and tragically ignored statements during the entire trial. It cut to the heart of how the police and the prosecution had misused Dr. Penistan and his pretence of precision.

For ten days, Steve's mother had sat behind her son as a spectator in the courtroom, wringing her hands, glaring at the police witnesses, whispering words of encouragement to her child seated in the prisoner's box, listening as doctors discussed intimate details about his body. Now, on Saturday afternoon, September 26, it was Doris Truscott's turn to speak.

She walked up to the witness stand with the same poise that had carried her through her summer ordeal, refusing to let any emotion sneak across her face. She calmly told her story of the chaotic week that started with Lynne's disappearance and ended with her son's arrest. She recounted how, on Tuesday, she asked Steve to rush to the store to get some coffee. "He came into the house and showed me he ripped his pants," she said. She described how he went out to play, returning home at 8:30 p.m. to babysit his younger brother and sister. The next morning, she threw a load of laundry into the washer.

"How often do you wash?" Frank Donnelly asked.

"Two or three times a week," Doris answered.

"Is there any reason why you wash so often?"

"Well, with four children, you do have a lot of dirty clothes," she explained.

If she had a dryer, why were Steven's jeans still on the line by Friday evening, Donnelly asked.

"The band at the top was still damp and the pocket lining was wet, and I just threw them over the line," she said.

Finally, Donnelly went into the seemingly minute details of Doris's laundry methods. He had prepared this terrain with his cross-examination of the government biologist Elgin Brown, who told the court that hot water and the alkali in most soap would fix any blood—even microscopic traces—in clothing.

So if there was any blood in Steve's garments, it should have been picked up by later tests, even after Doris cleaned Steve's clothes in her wringer washer.

"What type of water did you have?" Donnelly asked.

"Hot water."

"How hot?"

"Well, it is hot enough that I have to use a stick when I lift the clothes out."

"And what would you use in the water?"

"I always threw a bar of Sunlight soap in and a bit of detergent."

"Your witness, Mr. Hays," Frank Donnelly said.

Glenn Hays quickly zeroed in on what the police considered the most direct link between Steven's mother and the crime: her handling of his jeans. "Mrs. Truscott, that was a pretty small tear for Steven to draw to your attention, wasn't it?" Hays asked.

"His pants were new," the mother replied.

"Then the next Friday night, these same pants were the only item of clothing hanging on the clothesline in the basement when the police came in with the search warrant?"

"At the time—at that end of the line, yes. At the farther end there were more clothes."

"And you pointed the red jeans out to the police as being the clothing that Steven had been wearing on the Tuesday night?"

"Yes."

"And yet, Mrs. Truscott with that tear in them and its being in your mind, why did you not tell them about the tear at that time?"

"I guess because I was upset and I never thought of the tear."

"Then a full written statement was taken from you June 20th."

"Yes."

"And you never mentioned that tear in that statement either, did you, Mrs. Truscott?"

"No, I didn't. I never thought about it and I wasn't asked."

Hays moved on to another example of what he saw as a mother's attempt to cover for her son. When the police took Steven to the bridge on Wednesday after Lynne's disappearance, to show them where he had seen the '59 Chevrolet, his mother had volunteered her own interpretation of what her boy saw.

"You said, did you not, that probably what Steven meant was that it was a sticker on a car and not a licence plate that he saw?"

"I didn't say 'probably.' I said 'it could have been,'" Doris responded.

"Then Mrs. Truscott, wouldn't you agree that the reason for your statement was that . . . it was clear to you it was impossible to stand there at the
bridge and tell the colour of a licence plate on the highway?"

"No, I wouldn't."

"Why did you put in the suggestion that it might have been a sticker?"

"Because we have one on the back of our own car and I have noticed
them on several cars. From that distance, it could very possibly have been."

"You felt a sticker would be easier seen than a licence?"

"No."

"Oh, you didn't. What reason would you have to think that Steven had
meant a sticker when he said licence?"

"It just could have been," replied Doris Truscott.

Looking back years later on her battle with the prosecutor, Doris Truscott
is philosophical. "He was doing his job and trying to get me to say what he
wanted me to say," she remembers. "But he wasn't changing my mind, I knew
what was the truth."


As the jurors watched Steve's mother slowly leave the witness chair and walk
by the boy sitting in the prisoner's box, they must have wondered why her
son himself did not take the stand.

It was, of course, a defendant's prerogative not to testify. "You would
have thought a long time before putting a fourteen-year-old on the stand,"
Dan Murphy, Donnelly's colleague explains. "It was very, very common not
to put the accused in the witness box. I don't think any lawyer at the time was
surprised that Steven didn't testify."

But the jurors may have been surprised, or at least disappointed. A trial
by peers means just that—jurors are ordinary people, with the same fickle
attitudes and assumptions as most people. "I didn't like [his] look," said juror
Sidney Pullman, long after the trial was over. "We were all looking at him
quite a bit . . . to see how he reacts to different pieces of evidence." Jurors are
supposed to rule on the evidence, but Pullman was certainly not alone in
being swayed by appearances. "If it was me, I'd have been shedding tears,"
says Pullman. "He didn't show any signs of any sympathy. . . . He had a kind
of a grin on his face all the time. Kind of a hero type."

Reading facial expressions, of course, often says more about the person
doing the watching than the person being watched. George Edens, the airman

who found Lynne' s body and sat through much of the trial, had a completely different take on Steve's apparent lack of sorrow or worry.

"I used to see him sitting there, and I thought, 'Either he's nuts or he didn't do it.' If he did it, I expected him to show that he's terrified because he's caught. But I never got the impression that he did anything. He sat there with his arms up on the chair . . . with all this evidence coming up and not letting it bother him. He just made his mind up: 'I didn't do it, I don't have to worry. They'll get this over with and . . . I'll be back going to school and having fun again.'"

But George Edens didn't have a vote on the jury.

# 20

## THE BOYS AT THE RIVER

No defence witness was more important for Frank Donnelly to build up—and for Crown prosecutor Hays to destroy—than Dougie Oates. He claimed to have been within a few feet of Steve and Lynne as they crossed the bridge on the way to highway. With an excellent line of sight and no apparent reason to lie, Dougie provided seemingly unshakeable support for Steven's account of his whereabouts that evening.

Hays had shredded the defence's medical experts, bullied police and air force officers to get their story in line, and badgered Steve's mother. He was doing his job, and he was doing it well. Now the prosecutor faced an unassuming boy who had just turned twelve over the summer. It seemed an uneven match: a nervous school child and a veteran prosecutor.

But the duel turned out to be one of the surprising upsets at the trial.

"Do you understand what it means to take an oath in a courtroom?" the judge asked. "Yes sir," answered Dougie. "It means you are calling on God to watch you, and if you don't tell the truth then you are committing a sin."

The judge was not inclined to swear "a boy of this age," but defence lawyer Donnelly insisted the boy might give "some very important evidence." So again the judge turned to boy and asked him what taking an oath means. "It requires me to tell the truth," Dougie replied. The judge allowed him to be sworn.

Donnelly began by slowly taking his prize witness through the events of Tuesday night. Dougie left his home after supper to hunt for turtles down by the bridge over the Bayfield River. He was aided in his quest by an older boy named Ronnie Demarray and a younger girl, Karen Daum.

"Ronnie took his fishing rod and he snagged the turtle by the leg and brought it up and put it in . . . Karen Daum's [bike] carrier," Dougie recounted with precision. "After that, I saw one more turtle, it was quite small, and I went down to the bottom of the bridge and grabbed it."

Dougie made his way back to the top of the bridge. Ronald headed home, but Dougie lingered behind. "I stayed up on the bridge looking for a couple more turtles." Then, according to the turtle boy, two people came right by him on a bike: Steven Truscott and Lynne Harper.

"When they were coming by, I turned around and put up my hand and said 'Hi.' Steve was pedalling. She was sitting on the crossbar."

"What did Lynne do?" Donnelly asked.

"She smiled."

"What did Steve do?"

"I don't think he noticed me because he just kept on riding down."

"Which way were they going at the time?"

"They were going north, toward the highway."

Donnelly then produced a photograph of the bridge. Dougie pointed to a group of trees on the north side of the bridge, closer to the highway, where he saw Lynne and Steve. "They were right there along that group of trees."

Donnelly quickly wrapped up his examination by raising a key point on timing, which he knew Hays would zero in on.

"How long did you stay at the bridge?" he asked.

"I was there around until 7:30," came the reply, "because I got home at fifteen to eight."

"Your witness, Mr. Hays," said the defence counsel.


What was Hays to do? Dougie's testimony was filled with just enough flavour and detail to make it realistic and credible—and deadly to his case. The bridge was about two thousand feet past the bush where the body was found—and where the Crown alleged the murder had taken place.

Other defence witnesses who claimed to see Steven at the bridge were six hundred to eight hundred feet away and Hays could question their line of sight, but Dougie was too close. And since Dougie was too young to be in Steve's close circle of friends, Hays could not paint him as a conspirator trying to protect his pal.

So the Crown prosecutor decided to attack Dougie's memory of the time he saw Steven. "Other witnesses have told us of seeing Steven down there by himself at 6:30, Douglas," he started softly. "Is there a chance that that is what you saw?"

"No, it isn't, sir," came the firm reply.

"Did you simply add Lynne through things you heard after?"

"No, I saw him and Lynne."

"You did?" Hays said.

"Yes," the boy answered.

"Well, would you disagree with me that it was about 6:30?"

"Yes, I would" was Dougie's polite reply.

Hays sensed he was up against a little boy with a big backbone. So he pulled out his secret weapon: a typed copy of the statement Dougie had given to the police on June 13, four days after Lynne had disappeared. Hays quoted the boy as telling the police that he didn't know exactly when he saw Steve "but I think half an hour *either way* from seven o'clock." It looked as if Hays had his little adversary caught in a lie.

"Did you tell them that?"

"Well, I didn't say it was half an hour either way," Dougie responded. "I said it could have been a half an hour *after* seven."

"Constable Trembley read the statement back to you, but you wouldn't sign it. Is that so?"

"He didn't read it back to me, he gave it to me, and I never got finished reading it, though, and I didn't sign it because my mother said not to sign it unless she read it first," Dougie said.

"And why didn't you finish reading it?" Hays asked.

"He didn't give me enough time, sir," came the response. Dougie had slipped out of the trap; an unsigned police statement was next to worthless.

So Hays then tried another tack, seeking to prove that Dougie was down at the bridge earlier.

Dougie explained in detail how, after leaving home sometime after six, he first dropped by a friend's house and rang the doorbell two times, then talked to his friend's mother "for about five minutes." Then he headed down to the river, but was delayed.

"I stopped for about five minutes."

"Where did you stop for five minutes?" Hays asked.

"Beside the woods, near the beginning of the woods, to watch a couple of female cardinals," the nature lover explained.

Hays thought maybe he finally had him. Dougie had never mentioned these delays to the police. "But you didn't remember that when you were telling the inspector," Hays pushed.

"Well, he never asked me," came the boy's reply.

"He didn't ask you if you had watched two female cardinals?"

"He never asked me if I stopped."

Foiled again. Hays then tried trapping Dougie into speculating on times. But the astute boy knew if he was not sure about something, he was better off admitting it.

"What time did you get down to the river?"

"I guess I couldn't say for sure," the witness answered.

"Well, try, Douglas. You are pretty good at times."

"I don't know, sir."

"Well, then, Douglas, I suggest to you, if you don't know what time you got to the river, you don't know what time you saw Steve."

"I would say I got down there about half an hour after I left home, or fifteen minutes, anyway, somewhere in around there."

"Did you see Steven before or after Ron Demarray gave you the turtle?"

"I saw him after."

"And how long after?"

"I couldn't say, sir."

"You are very good at other times, Douglas," the prosecutor said, with more than a little sarcasm. "Couldn't you take a stab at that one?"

"No, I don't think I could," the boy answered, refusing to take the bait.

For more than fifteen minutes, Hays battered away at the schoolboy's tale, coming back again and again to the time he saw Steve. Could it not have been a half hour *before* seven, Hays kept asking; no—the boy stood his ground—it was *after* seven.

Eventually, even the judge grew tired of the relentless barrage. "Half an hour *after*. That is what he said," he finally interrupted. "It is the third or fourth time he said it."

219

Hays then quickly wrapped up his cross-examination and sat down. The prosecutor, so successful in unnerving adult witnesses, had met a brick wall in the form of a twelve-year-old turtle hunter.

More than forty years later, Douglas Oates recalls his grilling in the courtroom with a tinge of pride. "I don't remember it as being a real rough ride. I didn't really think it was that rough at the time," he says. Four decades have not shaken his certainty about what he saw that evening. "I know I saw Steve Truscott and Lynne Harper cross the bridge, heading north toward Highway Number 8, on that evening. And there's absolutely no doubt in my mind."

The confrontation between Dougie Oates and the Crown prosecutor was a sweet moment for the defence team, one of the few triumphs they could savour in a trial that was not going their way. Dougie stepped down from the stand late Friday afternoon and the judge adjourned the court, giving everyone some much needed rest over the weekend.

When court resumed on Monday morning, defence lawyer Frank Donnelly hoped the jurors were in a refreshed mood. He hoped to build on his success with Dougie by calling on his older brother, Allan.

The sixteen-year-old had stayed at home on Tuesday, June 9, to watch TV until 7:00 p.m., he told the court. Then he took his bike out for a spin around the base for about thirty minutes, before heading down toward the river. "On my way down there, I got about eight hundred feet away from the bridge and I saw Steven down there," Allan told Donnelly. "I just turned around and went back."

"Where was Steven when you saw him?"

"On the bridge."

"How was he dressed?"

"He had a pair of red pants on and a light-coloured shirt."

"What time did you say it was?"

"Between 7:30 and 8:00."

"Did you see Steven again that night?"

"No sir."

Allan's testimony was short and to the point, barely four minutes long. But his story provided confirmation that Steve was at the bridge, presumably after having dropped off Lynne at the highway. It was a story that Crown prosecutor Hays needed to discredit.

Hays struck first at Allan's weakest spot: the fact that he failed to report his sighting to the police and told it to a friend of the Truscott family only in the week after Steve's arrest.

"You knew that the police were all interested in finding out all about Steven Truscott's whereabouts," Hays asked. "Didn't you know that?"

"Yes sir," Allan replied.

"Why did you not tell this type of thing to the police at any time?" Hays asked. It was a legitimate query, and Allan's response was weak.

"I just never thought of going," he said.

Suddenly, Hays switched tactics, trying to throw Allan off guard.

"I suggest it was about 6:30, Allan, that you saw Steven down there, if you saw him at all," he began his attack.

"No sir," Allan said.

"Why are you so sure?" Hays pursued.

"Because I watch *Panorama* and it comes on at fifteen to seven."

"What programs did you see on the Monday?"

"Well, I watched *Panorama* and then I went outside, and then I came in and watched *The Danny Thomas Show* and *Cannonball*, too."

"And on the Thursday night, what did you watch?"

"I think I went to the show."

"On the 12th, on Friday, what show did you watch?"

"I didn't watch *Panorama*. I went outside, and I am not sure what was on that night."

"Saturday night," Hays asked, "do you remember the programs you watched that night?"

"Just the beginning of *Panorama*."

"Can you explain to the jury how you're able to recount programs you would watch every night in June?" Hays asked, hoping the jury would interpret the teenager's quick answers not as signs of a good memory but of purposeful fabrication.

"I watch them just about every night they come on" was Allan's reply.

Hays then tried to discredit Allan by suggesting his entire family was biased in favour of the Truscotts. Was it not true that three members of his family—Allan, Dougie and their mother, Genevieve—had come up from Ottawa for the trial? It was an unfair suggestion. As Donnelly later pointed out, the Oates family—who had been transferred out of Clinton—had no choice in the matter; they were appearing in court by subpoena.

Finally, Hays tried to set a trap for Allan.

"What kind of shirt did Steven have on?" Hays began.

"A light-coloured shirt" was the most Allan was willing to say.

"White?" Hays pushed.

"I can't say it was white," Allan answered cautiously.

"What about Exhibit 60?" Hays said, indicating a shirt. "Would that be it?

"No," Allan said with certainty.

"Take it over a little closer to him," the judge ordered. Exhibit 60 was a red shirt from Steve's closet, not the white shirt he wore the night Lynne disappeared.

"You are not prepared to say he had a white shirt, but it was a light shirt," the Crown counsel concluded. "Is that the best you can do?"

"Yes sir," said Allan.

Judge Ferguson now picked up the examination. It was unusual, but not unheard of, for a judge to directly question witnesses.

"Did your mother know you were in the house watching television?" he asked.

"Yes, she did," Allan said.

"She knew you were in the house?"

"Yes."

"Would she know where your younger brother, Douglas, was at that time?" the judge continued.

"Yes," Allan replied.

Allan and Dougie's mother, Genevieve, testified briefly for the defence at the trial. Neither the prosecution nor the defence had asked her to confirm the whereabouts of her children. It was an oversight that would later have serious consequences.

Dougie Oates insisted he saw Steve and Lynne cross the bridge around 7:30 p.m.; his brother Allan insisted he saw Steve alone at the bridge at around 7:45. Gord Logan's special value to the defence was that he combined both stories: he insisted that he, too, saw Steve and Lynne bike to the highway and then, a few minutes later, he saw Steve return alone to the bridge.

After he finished his paper route on Tuesday evening, Gord told the jury, he made his way down to the river, carrying his fishing rod and a bathing suit. When he finished swimming, he stepped out of the water onto a big rock in the bend in the river.

"And then what happened?" Donnelly asked.

"Then I saw Steve and Lynne go by the bridge on Steve's bicycle."

"How were they travelling?"

"They were riding double on Steve's bicycle."

"Where was Lynne sitting?"

"She was sitting on the crossbar."

"Facing what direction?"

"I am not sure. I don't remember."

"Did you see either of them again?"

"Yes sir," Gordon replied. "I saw Steve ride back to the bridge, and I saw him stop at the bridge."

"How long after you saw Steve and Lynne riding north . . . was it you saw Steven alone?"

"Five minutes."

Donnelly called it quits—perhaps a bit too quickly. Steve's lawyer could have made it clear to the jury that Gord's original statement to the police on Thursday morning, June 11, was all the more believable because he gave it to the police *before Steven ever needed a defence*. No one knew yet that Lynne's body was in the bush. Gord had no reason to lie or to cover for Steven. Crossing the bridge with Lynne, well beyond the bush, had no particular importance when Gord first talked to the police.

Hays quickly moved to attack Gord Logan on several fronts.

First, he cast doubt on the boy's line of sight. "Where were you standing?"

"Just by the bend in the river."

"I suggest to you, Gordon, that standing where you say you were standing, that you could not tell anyone on the bridge. That you couldn't tell a boy from a man or a girl from a woman," Hays pushed. "Do you agree or disagree?"

"I disagree."

"Would you agree that this is some six hundred feet east of the bridge?"

"No sir, I don't think it is," Gordon answered. He was wrong; Hays was right. The rock Gord stood on was 642 feet from the bridge.

"How was Lynne dressed?" Hays asked.

"I think she was wearing shorts."

"And which way was she facing?"

"I don't remember."

"So you don't remember which way she was facing, but you could see she was wearing shorts.

"I am not positive she was wearing shorts, but I think she was."

"Did you say anything to any of those boys [in the river with you]? 'There goes Steven and Lynne Harper?'"

"No sir, I didn't."

"Did you say to any of them, 'There is Steven down there at the bridge'?"

"No sir."

Hays was finished with his cross-examination, though not with Gord. He would devote much of his summation to attacking the boy's testimony.

In less than two days, the defence had finished calling its eyewitnesses. Under Canadian law, the prosecution has a right to rebut the defence's case after the defence lays it out to the jury. The Crown can re-summon witnesses and even bring in new testimony in an effort to shoot down major elements of the defence. It was clear who Hays' targets were: Dougie Oates and Gord Logan, the two eyewitnesses who provided the strongest proof of Steve's innocence.

Hays began his attack on Dougie's evidence by calling to the stand the stenographer who took down his first statement to police. Marjorie Jean Gardner had been a court reporter for seven years, trained in shorthand and transcription, and had worked as secretary in the Crown attorney's office in Goderich. She was summoned on June 13 to take notes when police questioned Dougie. The boy had insisted the police version of his statement was wrong—he said he had told them he saw Lynne and Steve cross the bridge between 7:00 and 7:30.

"What do your notes say?" Hays asked Gardner.

Quoting her transcription of Dougie's words, she read: "It might have been about seven o'clock. I don't know the time, but I think a half an hour either way from seven."

"So that exhibit faithfully transcribes what you took down in shorthand and what he said?"

"It does, sir."

Defence lawyer Donnelly was not to be deterred.

"Did the boy just stand there or sit there and tell his story, or was he questioned at all?" he began.

"No, he was questioned," the stenographer replied.

"Where are the questions?" Donnelly pursued.

"I did not take the questions and answers, sir."

"Did you take the questions down?"

"No sir. I took down a narrative," said the stenographer.

It was subtle but important point. It was standard police procedure to write up a witness interview in the form of a statement to be signed. But in this case, a faithful record of the dialogue between the police and Dougie would have revealed more about how specific the boy was about his time and how he responded to police queries.

Next, Hays tried to discredit Dougie by proving he had left the bridge at 6:30—at least, according to a new eyewitness.

Paul Desjardine had already testified about other activities down by the river, but now Hays recalled him to the stand to solicit an additional detail: Paul remembered seeing Dougie and Karen Daum when he arrived at the bridge around 6:25 p.m.

"Where were they?" Hays asked

"They were fishing off the bridge."

"And at what hour did they leave the road bridge?"

"They left at 6:30."

It seemed firm and unambiguous proof that Dougie must have been wrong about staying on the bridge late enough to see Steve and Lynne pass around 7:30 p.m. The defence lawyer knew he had to move fast and he had to move in for the kill. Donnelly got Paul to affirm that he was down by the river the entire time with his good friend Tom Gillette.

"Did Tom Gillette go home before 8:30?" Donnelly asked innocently.

"No sir," Paul answered.

Donnelly knew he had him. He reminded the boy that Tom had testified he left the bridge around 7:00 and came back later.

"Could you be mistaken?" Donnelly probed.

"Yes sir," the confused boy answered. "I don't remember too well."

"You don't remember too well," Donnelly repeated, making sure the jury got the point.

Paul also denied that another of his friends, Bryan Glover, went home during the evening; it was Wednesday night when that happened, Paul suggested.

"Well, he says it was Tuesday night, what do you say to that?" Donnelly asked, and then made his devastating final jab: "You don't know what night you are talking about, do you?"

"No sir."

"Pardon?" the lawyer asked, driving the point home.

"No sir," replied the boy sheepishly.

"Well, that is just fine," said Donnelly, pleased with his work.

"That is all, thanks, Paul," said Crown prosecutor Hays brusquely, eager to get his hapless rebuttal witness off the stand.

Hays fared little better in attacking the other key defence eyewitness, Gord Logan. The prosecution brought back Beatrice Geiger, one of the mothers at the swimming hole that evening, to cast doubts on Gord's ability to spot anyone on the bridge. Hays asked Geiger if she could see people on the bridge from her vantage point on the riverbank.

"I glanced up once or twice. There were people on the bridge. I couldn't tell whether they were men and women or children or boys or girls," Geiger replied.

"Why couldn't you tell whether they were men or women or children?" asked Hays, hoping for more.

"I guess I didn't pay too much attention" was the reply, not exactly what the Crown counsel needed. Undeterred, Hays pushed his luck, and broke a cardinal rule among trial lawyers: never ask a question to which you do not already know the answer.

"Could you have recognized a person on the bridge from where you were?" he asked.

"Had I been looking for someone I know, I imagine I would have recognized them," said Geiger.

Hays had just shot himself in the foot.

Trying to clean up the damage, the prosecutor called back OPP Const. Donald Trumbley. The policeman had taken Gord to the riverbank on the evening of July 6 to test what he could see from the swimming hole. Prosecutor Hays asked Constable Trumbley what he could see, standing next to where Gord was in the river.

"I couldn't make out the features of anyone on the bridge," he replied. He testified he spotted three boys on the bridge six hundred feet away, but his guess at their clothing did not match his examination of their attire when he walked up to them. In fact, Trumbley was being modest about his visual accuracy. He said one of the boys "appeared to have dark pants and light shirt" and upon closer inspection was found to be wearing blue denim trousers and a white T-shirt. The two others "appeared to have light pants and light shirts" and close up were discovered to be dressed in khaki trousers and white T-shirts. In other words, Trumbley basically got it right each time.

"Could you recognize any person's features, to know them from the bridge?"

"No sir," the officer maintained.

But then Justice Ferguson butted in. "Do you think you could recognize a man in a suit of clothes, if he had on a red shirt or white shirt, at two hundred yards?"

"Yes, I believe so," the police officer answered, lending weight to the defence claim that Gord could recognize a friend in red pants.

Trumbley's testimony continued to crumble under Donnelly's re-examination. The defence lawyer pointed out to the jury that the true test was not whether Trumbley could make out the features of strangers on the bridge, but whether Gord could identify someone he knew. It would have been easy for the police, Donnelly explained, to line up several of Gord's friends on the bridge to see if the boy could correctly pick them out. They didn't do that.

"Was there any test made of Gord Logan to see whether he could recognize anybody on the bridge?"

"No sir," the OPP officer admitted.

"Well, that is what you were there to see, to see whether Gord Logan could see, not what you could see. That was an important matter, wasn't it?"

"Yes sir."

"You could recognize somebody you knew, couldn't you?" Donnelly pushed.

"It is possible," officer Trumbley reluctantly agreed.

After Constable Trumbley stepped down from the witness box that Monday afternoon, September 28, there would be no more witnesses to call. Court reporter A. D. MacNeil was as exhausted as the jurors. The clerk had taken down between 350,000 and 400,000 words of the proceedings. Seventy-four witnesses and seventy-seven exhibits spread over eleven days of testimony. The trial had been complex, confusing and overwhelming.

The twelve jurors from Huron County now had to try to separate fact from fiction in order to decide on Steven's innocence or guilt. To help them make up their minds, there would be lengthy summations by the lawyers and then the judge's charge to the jury. Justice Ferguson decided to give everyone an all too brief respite.

"Gentlemen of the jury, the evidence has been of such a nature, counsel have asked me if they might have the rest of the afternoon to organize what they want to say to you," Ferguson said, adjourning the court until Tuesday morning.

That the lawyers—after a gruelling two weeks of trial—would accept only a few hours to prepare their summations for the next day was all too typical of the almost "frontier justice" that was so prevalent in the Canada of 1959, especially in smaller towns and cities. Ferguson was a circuit judge, a roving magistrate who came into town for a quick spell and then was off again to convene another high-stakes trial. Little wonder then that Ferguson obliged jurors to sit through two Saturday sessions, burdening them with a schedule no jury would suffer today.

The entire procedure went frighteningly fast, a legal locomotive that could not be stopped. Steve was jailed within twenty-four hours of the body's discovery, put on trial about ninety days later, and would be sentenced on a death penalty charge just two weeks after that.

The Crown had an army of police officers and government medical experts to help wage its battle. These foot soldiers interviewed dozens of witnesses and conducted a battery of scientific, medical and physical tests. Frank Donnelly may have been one of the most experienced and capable lawyers in the region, but he was no match for the State. In a case with a bewildering array of medical detail, confused times and garbled testimony from children, Donnelly had to labour all summer long by himself.

Today, on even an uncomplicated murder charge—for example, self-defence where no one disputes the facts, just the motive—a defence lawyer would be funded by legal aid if the client could not afford counsel. There likely would be enough money for the lawyer to hire a private detective, several experts and a legal researcher. The defence counsel would have months—perhaps even a year—to prepare the case.

The tragedy of the Steven Truscott trial was not that it was an exception in its rushed nature, its unequal tug-of-war between the Crown and the defence, but that it was par for the course. Dan Murphy, the young assistant who joined Donnelly's team only as the trial began, recalls that many murder trials of the time were wrapped up in as a little as four days. Who knows how many other cases of swift but sloppy justice went by unnoticed and unheralded?

As the jurors filed out of the Goderich courtroom on September 28, 1959, no doubt many were grateful that their ordeal was almost over. Perhaps many had already made up their minds about the guilt of the boy being led away from the prisoner's box. Perhaps some would wait until they heard from the lawyers and the judge. It would make little difference for Steven Truscott.

Some of the most egregious errors of justice were still to come.

**21**

THE DEFENCE SUMS UP

Frank Donnelly rose to face the jury at ten o'clock on Tuesday morning, September 29. Steven Truscott's lawyer knew that, in many ways, the hardest part of his battle still lay ahead. He had lost some of the confidence he showed at the beginning of the trial. True, the Crown had still not produced any direct evidence tying his client to the murdered girl. But Donnelly must have sensed that the jurors were appalled by the gruesome medical evidence, swayed by the carefully stage-managed prosecution witnesses and confused by the many arcane details of the case.

Could he spell out, in simple terms, a clear case for his client's innocence?

"It is impossible for anyone to have heard this evidence without having the very greatest sympathy for this poor, unfortunate girl," Donnelly began. "One cannot help but have sympathy for the parents. They have suffered a very, very severe loss." But emotion should not colour the jurors' objective evaluation of witnesses and exhibits, Donnelly urged.

Steven's lawyer then played a desperate card. He told the jurors they held not just the fate of Steve's innocence or guilt in their hands, but his very life. "If your verdict is guilty, His Lordship will have no alternative but to sentence this boy to be hanged by the neck until he is dead. Now I am not suggesting to you, gentlemen, that you have anything to do with the penalty. But

I raise this point to show the heavy duty that rests on me and the much heavier duty that is your responsibility."

Donnelly first attempted to deal with the mountain of physical evidence, photographs and tests the Crown had arranged against his client.

For starters, Steven's lawyer had to address the question of whether or not the boy could pick out the colour of a licence plate on a car, standing at the bridge thirteen hundred feet away. Donnelly dismissed the photographs produced by the police because "pictures can mislead you." Donnelly tried to bring the distances home to the rural jurors by using a farming measurement—a rod that measures a 16½-foot space between furrows in a ploughed field. "I do suggest that it is a simple matter to stand on one side of a farm and distinguish a small vehicle eighty rods away on a bright clear day." He also suggested that Steven quite possibly did not see a licence plate but a sticker or the sun's reflection on the back of the car.

"There is no direct evidence which in any way links this boy with that murder," the defence counsel went on. The tears and grass stains on Steven's jeans were not proof of anything except that "this was an active boy." He reminded the jury that Steve's mother had testified he ripped his jeans on a bicycle before Lynne disappeared and that almost every other piece of clothing the police had collected from Steven bore the holes and rips so typical of a teenage boy's clothing.

The bicycle tire marks in the laneway were also meaningless, Donnelly insisted, because the tracks were made when the mud was soft and not caked dry as the police photos showed. "Many of you are farmers," Donnelly added. "You can use your own good judgment as to how long it took for that land to become parched like that." And for good measure, Donnelly reminded the jurors that the Crown's own police expert had been far from definitive. "Corporal Erskine said that the marks he found in the mud were *similar* to the marks he made [from Steve's tires]. He did not say they were *identical*."

Considering how much the Crown had distorted this evidence and how heavily the prosecution relied on the bike tracks to put Steven at the scene of the crime, Donnelly perhaps could have stressed these points with even more force and detail. Still, it was a solid argument that the jurors would have to reject or ignore in order to find Steve guilty.

Frank Donnelly's next theme was the oral evidence of the Crown's trio of child witnesses—Jocelyn, Butch and Philip. He began with the girl the prosecution called its "most important witness." Donnelly stressed that she was "way out in her time," because Bob Lawson said she was on his farm almost an hour later than she claimed.

"Why in the world would this girl go to Bob Lawson's farm if she was to meet that boy down at the bush? I suggest that that, alone, proves that she is incorrect and that her whole story is wrong, because it certainly doesn't fit." He also reminded the jurors that it was Jocelyne who had tried to make a date to go looking for calves with another boy, Gary Gilks. It was likely that if Jocelyne and Steve did talk in hushed tones about going to see calves, it was Jocelyne and not Steve who initiated the chat, Donnelly argued. "Gilks gave her no encouragement and we have no more reason to believe that Truscott gave her any more encouragement."

It was a succinct refutation of Jocelyne's claims. But, again, taking into account how central she was to the Crown's case, perhaps Donnelly could have connected the dots more explicitly for the jurors. How could Jocelyne have been down at the lane looking for Steve around 7:15, as the prosecution claimed, if she had not even left Lawson's barn until at least 7:25? How certain was anyone that Jocelyne had been down at the bridge at all, allegedly looking for Steve, if not a single eyewitness except Butch put her anywhere near the river that evening? How certain was it that Steve called by her house before 6:00 p.m. if the police failed to produce a statement from the only other person who saw the face of her visitor, her younger brother who answered the door?

Donnelly took even less time dispensing with the Crown's second important child witness, Philip Burns. Philip testified he did not see Lynne and Steve on the county road that evening, but Donnelly noted that there were also at least two other children he did not see—Bryan Glover and Tom Gillette. Both boys travelled from the bridge to the base and then back down the river, giving Philip the potential of four chances to see them both. Yet he recalled nothing about them. He had only one brief opportunity of seeing Lynne and Steve. "In view of the very fact that he doesn't recall seeing these others," Donnelly argued, "you cannot rely on his statement." Once more, Donnelly's summary was accurate, but perhaps too concise for such a crucial

Crown witness. Donnelly's refutation of Philip's story took less than four minutes in a day-long address to the jury, easily forgotten by the jurors amidst the hours of testimony they were absorbing.

Donnelly summarily dismissed the third Crown child witness, Arnold "Butch" George, as an inveterate liar. "You should consider the fact that he gave three different statements to the police, and his evidence was given in this witness box after he studied and read over his statement ten times in the last two weeks," the defence counsel warned.

Curiously, Donnelly did not bring up the most revealing of Butch's lies. Butch had told so many children he had seen Steve take Lynne into the bush that it led to much teasing in the days after Lynne's disappearance. But in court Butch admitted that his stories were lies, since he testified over and over again that he had not seen Steven at all that evening until after 8:00 at his home. Donnelly never raised this glaring contradiction.

Donnelly's refutation of the prosecution's child witnesses' evidence was direct and to the point. He never paused, though, to give the jurors the bigger picture; he never allowed for a few minutes of oratory to batter the prosecution's edifice. Perhaps it was not his style; perhaps he felt it was superfluous. But in a case that relied so heavily on the testimony of children, the jury needed as much help as possible in sorting the tales from the truth.

Sensing that the mystique of science held the greatest sway over the jurors, Donnelly devoted a good part of his summation to rebutting the Crown's medical evidence. "The opinion of an expert is only as good as the facts on which it is based," Donnelly warned. "If the opinion of an expert is based on facts that are incorrect, then that opinion should carry no weight."

Nothing carried more weight with the jurors than John Penistan's remarkable ability to pinpoint the time of Lynne's death based largely on an analysis of her stomach contents. But how accurate was that analysis, Donnelly asked, if all Penistan and Brooks did on the night of the autopsy was hold a jar of her stomach contents to a dim light in a funeral home? "Turned it around like this, and looked at it. And they say they saw this and they saw that. Now, what in the world kind of examination is that on the contents of the stomach to base a time of death? To give evidence on a serious charge such as this?"

Donnelly reminded the jurors that his own expert, Dr. Berkely Brown, a specialist in the digestive system, had warned that stomach content analysis was "a quite unreliable and an unsatisfactory way of determining the time of death." It was a valid point—one that over the years would eventually become accepted forensic practice. But back in 1959, Donnelly would be unable to shake the jury's confidence in a man of science such as Dr. Penistan.

Next Donnelly tried to downplay the significance of the soiled underwear taken from Steve on his first day in jail. The defence lawyer suggested it was more than likely Steve stained them overnight in jail *after* Addison and Brooks examined him, since neither of the medical men noticed the underwear was filthy when the boy undressed in front of them. "They made no comment on the condition of the shorts," he noted.

The government biologist, Elgin Brown, testified that in hot, humid weather, bacteria could destroy sperm in two days, Donnelly reminded jurors. Even if the shorts Steve wore on Saturday were the same ones he wore the day Lynne died—an extremely unlikely scenario—the sperm "would certainly be destroyed."

Donnelly knew he had to address one of the most damaging pieces of evidence against his client: the sores on Steven's penis. Donnelly tried to discredit Dr. Brooks by reminding the jury that he had called the jailhouse physician to ask him to check if Steven was circumcised. "Now, isn't that an amazing thing?" Donnelly asked the jury. "It is difficult to conceive of any doctor making a full examination of the man and examining his penis and not knowing whether or not [he was] circumcised."

He suggested the doctors had described a brush burn type of injury, but Lynne had no pubic hair, there was no bony structure near her genitals, and the vagina was round, not oval-shaped. Steven's injuries were not caused by sex with Lynne, his lawyer suggested, but "probably caused by masturbation."

Donnelly then took a risky gamble—he argued that even if the injuries did come from intercourse, there was no proof the sex was with Lynne. "It might well be that this boy had intercourse with some other girl," he said. Donnelly realized he was treading on dangerous ground here with a jury made up of farmers, small-town merchants and labourers, and he added, "We must bear in mind that we are not trying the morals of this boy. He is not here on any charge that he was immoral with some other girl, or that he was guilty of practices of masturbation, which you do not condone. It is not an offence. Masturbation is not an offence. We must remember that the boy is not on trial for his morals; essentially, he is on trial for the murder of Lynne Harper."

It was a brave speech, an important point to make. But by raising the issue of morality, of masturbation and teenage sex, Donnelly also ran the risk of reinforcing some of the jurors' repugnance over the entire affair.

Donnelly tried to play on the sexual inexperience of Truscott, well aware he risked offending a largely rural jury. "I trust you will pardon me for speaking of things that you may think should not be discussed quite as openly, but this is a serious matter and my duty." Donnelly suggested a fourteen-year-old would likely experience premature or early ejaculation, and yet no sperm was found on Lynne's body; acid phosphatase was found in the upper regions of the vagina and not by the entry.

The point was dubious, but worse still, the defence counsel was painting a vivid picture in his own words about how his client could have been kneeling over the dying body of his victim while he was coming to an orgasm—premature or not. Not exactly the picture a defence lawyer would normally want a jury to remember.

Donnelly understood he had to win the war over the credibility of experts. Donnelly realized that many of the jurors knew and respected the local doctors, while they saw Brown, his medical witness, as an outsider. He emphasized to the jury that Brown had seen "many cases of rape," while the prosecution's doctors, Addison and Brooks, "had not one experience in connection with an examination of a man or a woman, either, raped, except this girl. In not a single, solitary instance did they have any experience."

Steve's lawyer then turned his attention to the footprint evidence. "With all due respect to Flying Officer Sage, I thought he got carried away," he said, arguing that Sage's examination was "much more casual, much less complete" than the study done by Corporal Erskine, who found the marks "indistinct." Donnelly noted that even if the jurors accepted Sage's description over Erskine's, no match was made between the mark and Steve's shoes.

As the morning drew to a close, Donnelly tried to give the jury the broader view of the territory he had sketched so far. "You can take all these facts from which some indication of guilt on the part of the accused may be possibly inferred, you can add them all up together and you still do not get that sufficient body of evidence to find that it is consistent with the guilt of the accused." It was hardly a high point with which to end the first half of his presentation; Donnelly in effect was conceding that the jury might find a lot of little things that made Steven look guilty, but he beseeched them not to add them all up into a single guilty verdict.

———

After the lunch break, Donnelly picked up the threads of his argument. Having demonstrated, at least to his own satisfaction, that the Crown had failed to prove his client guilty, Donnelly set out to show the jury all the signs that pointed to Steven Truscott's innocence.

He began by making explicit what he had only hinted at indirectly throughout the trial. "There is some evidence that the girl was not killed in this bush," Donnelly stated.

"It is very difficult to conceive of this girl permitting herself to be strangled in the manner indicated by the evidence without putting up a terrific struggle." He pointed out the ground where she was found was soft and yet police found only two small marks. "There isn't a single solitary mark in this area of any struggle between this girl and her assailant. And I submit that this is conclusive evidence that the struggle took place at some other point."

He suggested that if Lynne was raped in the bush, there should have been seminal fluid on the leaves under her crotch. Donnelly reminded the jury the police found Harper's white socks, neatly rolled up. In one sock, there were seven green blades and two brown blades of grass, and in the other sock more grass and some weeds.

"There was no grass in the area. Now where did this grass come from? I suggest to you gentlemen that the stockings were removed in a grassy area somewhere distant," Donnelly said. He noted that a government soil expert concluded the soil on Lynne's shorts "did not match any of the control samples" from the bush.

More proof, in Donnelly's mind, that the murder did not take place in the bush came from the fact that on a heavily travelled road in broad daylight, "nobody saw Steven Truscott and Lynne Harper go into that bush and nobody saw Steven Truscott come out of that bush. There is not a single solitary witness who gave evidence here that saw either of them go in or saw this boy come out."

Donnelly then moved on to the key question of time. Richard Gellatly, he reminded the jurors, insisted he met Steve and Lynne at the top of the road around 7:25 p.m. "So we have got them on the road at 7:25. Well, Steve was back at the swings at 8:00," Donnelly said. "I do earnestly urge you that in the thirty-five minutes available to this boy . . . he did not have time to commit this offence in the manner in which it was committed. He didn't have time to go there, attack the girl, struggle with her, rip the blouse, get the blouse around the neck and tie this nice neat knot. . . . The shorts had to be removed and they were apparently removed in a careful manner. . . . The socks were neatly taken off. Not hurriedly taken off. Taken off with care. . . . Then there were three branches—three trees broken off. It would take considerable time to break off those three branches, twist them off in that manner. . . . And I suggest to you that Steven Truscott could not have done all those things and been back at those swings at 8:00."

It was a powerful summation of the improbability of the prosecution case, and Donnelly capped it with the most illogical piece of the Crown's theory. If Steve killed Lynne, he said, "he would be terror-stricken, and the last place he would go would be over to this meeting place at this school where a number of people would be able to see him and observe him and observe anything unnatural or out of the ordinary about him."

"It is inconceivable that a boy fourteen years of age could cold-bloodedly murder a girl and come back and be perfectly normal and talk to his school chums," Donnelly said.

Donnelly also reminded the jury that there was blood on several pieces of Lynne's clothing, but not a drop on his client. "We have blood on the front of the right shoulder strap, we have blood under the armpits, we have a considerable patch of blood [behind the] shoulder, we have a few spots of blood on the front of the shorts. We have blood on the panties, under the shorts. We have blood on the left shoe worn by the girl," Donnelly said.

"The fact that we find the garments of this girl in this condition and we find the garments of the boy without blood is the strongest evidence in favour of the boy we could ask. If this boy attacked that girl, he would be bound to have blood on his garments, and that blood would have been fixed and it would not have been washed off."

The lawyer stressed to the jurors how Dougie Oates, his star witness, failed to crack under the withering attack by Crown prosecutor Hays. "Now there was a very bright young man, and he surely must have impressed you by the capable manner in which he gave his evidence. Cross-examination is the real test of the weight of a witness's evidence. My friend cross-examined that boy at length and he didn't shake that boy one iota. Not one iota."

Finally, Steve's lawyer stressed to the jurors what he saw as his client's unwavering truthfulness. "He has consistently told the same story," the defence counsel said. The very first time he was asked what happened to

Lynne—when he returned to the ball field at 8:00 p.m.—he told his friends he had dropped Lynne off at the highway; he told the same story to Lynne's father the next morning; again at 9:30 that morning to Constable Hobbs; again at 12:20 to Constable Trumbley and Sergeant Johnson; and again at 5:00 that afternoon to Trumbley. "So we have this boy telling this story on all those occasions, and at no time did they shake him."

Frank Donnelly had spent most of the day trying to raise reasonable doubt in the minds of the jurors. It had been a long, at times rambling and confusing address, perhaps a sign of how little time the defence attorney had to prepare a summation for such a complicated trial. He never clearly organized his themes or gave the jurors a guiding hand to explain what subject he was going to cover next. At times during his marathon presentation, Donnelly himself seemed to lose track of key trial testimony and could only hope the jurors had better memories. Donnelly could not even remember exactly what time Dougie, his most important witness, had seen Steven cross the bridge. "It is rather difficult to keep these matters in mind," he told the jurors, "but some of you will recall more clearly than I do what Douglas Oates said."

Donnelly wrapped up his summation in a somewhat apologetic tone. "I was much longer in my remarks than I had expected to be," he said, "but if I had been shorter I wouldn't have filled my duty to this boy on the defence of this most serious charge. I am confident that after careful attention that you can come to only one conclusion and one finding, and that is a verdict of not guilty for this boy. It is with confidence that I leave the fate of this boy in your hands."

Donnelly had been confident about his case from the beginning. He had told the Truscotts not to worry. He had successfully defended four people accused of murder in the past. Surely, with Steven Truscott, he could make it five in a row.

## 22

## THE PROSECUTION MAKES ITS CASE

I have the honour to be acting on behalf of the Crown. That means the State. That means the community," Glenn Hays began his summation, establishing a bond with the upright local citizens in the jury box and foreshadowing the cloak of morality in which he would wrap his case. He was on their side, against those who would threaten the standards of decency in Huron County.

With skill and aplomb, Hays proceeded to weave the thin strands of circumstantial testimony into a tapestry of guilt. His tactic was the same he had used so successfully in the trial: less is more. Make the evidence seem more than it was, drown the jury in details and fudge the facts when necessary.

It worked.

From the start, Hays addressed head-on what he knew was his case's main flaw: "There is no reason for anyone to ever discount the value or standing of circumstantial evidence," he told the jurors. Sometimes, he said, circumstantial evidence is much more reliable than eyewitness evidence because people are capable of "error and bias." It was a sly manoeuvre, since Hays neglected to point out that most of his circumstantial evidence also came from eyewitnesses and human beings who were not only capable of, but at times had been proven to show, error and bias.

"Dr. Penistan gave the time of death as from 7:00 to 7:45 p.m.," Hays explained, coming quickly to the guts of his entire case. "Now, who was with her during this time? What person or persons had the opportunity to kill her from 7:00 p.m. to 7:45 p.m.? I suggest that a review of the facts narrows those facts like a vise on Steven Truscott and no one else."

There, in a nutshell, was the entire case against Steven Truscott. Medical science—especially Penistan's analysis of the stomach contents, Hays reminded the jurors—had pinpointed the time of Lynne Harper's death to a forty-five-minute window, and since no one else was with Lynne at that time, Truscott had to be a murderer.

Who were the jurors going to believe on time of death, Hays asked? The outside defence expert, Dr. Berkely Brown "who never saw the stomach" or Dr. Penistan, whose "careful study" at the local funeral home nailed down the exact time of death?

Next Hays had to establish that Steve had the time to kill Lynne, so he skilfully pushed back Lynne and Steve's departure from the school as much as possible. He told the jury that the two Brownie leaders, Dorothy Bohonus and Anne Nickerson, had seen Lynne and Steve leave from 7:00 to 7:10 p.m., glossing over the fact that that was simply the time when the women said they turned away and stopped looking at Lynne and Steve, not necessarily the time that the youngsters headed down to the river.

Hays then engineered a stunning triumph of obfuscation. He described how two of the boys playing baseball, Stuart Westie and Warren Heatherall, had seen Lynne and Steve. "Both put that time about 7:00 p.m., and Richard Gellatly, southbound on his bicycle, met and passed them." It sounded so obvious, three boys supposedly confirming a 7:00 departure. Except that Hays was seriously misrepresenting their testimony. Only Warren said he saw Steve "about 7:00" and he said he was "not too sure." Stuart gave no time at the trial; he told police he thought Steve left "around 7:30 p.m.," give or take twenty minutes.

Richard had testified that he passed Steve and Lynne *not at 7:00 but around 7:25*. How was Hays going to explain why Steve and Lynne took twenty-five minutes to travel the short distance from where the boys were playing ball to where Richard met them on the county road near the school? The prosecutor performed a feat a verbal gymnastics.

"Now, Mr. Donnelly *quoted Gellatly as saying* 7:25," he began. "The boy is obviously—*if that is what he said*, he is obviously out. I think Mr. Donnelly conceded that was probably not reliable as the time." Hays knew that the 7:25 time was exactly what Richard had said. Hays knew Richard consistently gave that time from the beginning—in his police statement, at the preliminary under Hays' own questioning and at the trial. By referring to Donnelly "quoting" Richard, Hays was implying it was perhaps another dubious piece of defence evidence. But Gellatly was a prosecution witness; *it was Hays himself* who solicited the 7:25 time—twice—and at no time in the trial did Hays ever challenge or dispute that time. Donnelly certainly never "conceded" that the time "was not reliable."

Hays had made a bold gamble: when stuck with a glaring contradiction in your own case, forge on and hope the jury doesn't notice. Evidently, they did not.

To wrap up his timing scenario, Hays had to push back Steve's return to the school. He dismissed John Carew—the only youngster whose time estimate was backed by his parents—by noting he "wasn't wearing a watch," although the same could be said of most of the prosecution witnesses. Carew put Steve's return at 8:00; the other teenagers at the school thought it was about ten to fifteen minutes later. "Let us suggest that he's getting back some time . . . 8:00, 8:10, 8:15," Hays said as he prepared to tighten the noose of time around Steve's neck. "It puts him in the bush from 7:15 to let us say eight o'clock. Call it 8:10. Call it something *in that vicinity*. What does that give him? That gives him from three-quarters of an hour to one hour in that bush, and I suggest that is ample, most ample time for him to do what he is charged with doing."

It was a masterful stroke. The Crown's own witness, Richard Gellatly, had put Steven on the road as late as 7:25, and several witnesses put his return at close to eight o'clock, giving Steven at most thirty-five minutes to commit the crime. Yet in his summation, the prosecutor had succeeded in almost doubling the amount of time Steven Truscott could have had to rape and murder Lynne Harper.

Hays still had to get Steve and Lynne into the bush. With all the children, adults, bikes and cars going up and down the road, and with at least two teenagers—Butch and Jocelyne—insisting they were on a very specific hunt for Steve or for Lynne, somehow no one that evening managed to catch even a glimpse of the pair going into the bush. So Hays set out to convince the jury that the very fact that so many people *did not* see Steve and Lynne was, in effect, the equivalent of eyewitness testimony that they must have gone into the bush.

"Philip Burns, coming along behind Gellatly, is on foot," Hays explained. "Philip Burns testifies that he did not meet Steven and Lynne or either of them. I ask you, is that not pretty conclusive that Steven and Lynne turned off the county road into the bush? What other explanation is there? Where else could they have gone?" Another simple nugget, easy for the jury to grasp.

"I suggest to you in all seriousness, gentlemen, that if Steven, with his red pants and his green racer had been any place on the county road," Hays continued, "Jocelyne Gaudet and Arnold George would certainly have seen him because they were looking for him and neither one of them saw him." Hays used this point to prepare for one of the most theatrical moves in Canadian legal history. He turned away from the jury and faced the judge.

"I wonder, my lord, if I might have Jocelyne Gaudet step in?"

"Yes," agreed the judge, and the girl walked in.

Hays turned back to face the jury and pointed to the girl. "I realize, gentlemen, that there are so many children for you to remember," the Crown lawyer said. "That, gentlemen, is Jocelyne Gaudet." It appeared innocuous: bring a young girl into the courtroom to help the jury identify her. But Hays had a much darker motive for pointing out the girl.

The Crown prosecutor knew he had to make the most of Jocelyne Gaudet. "She is a key witness in this narrative," he explained. With the sight of Jocelyne fresh in their minds, the jurors listened as Hays pulled off a judicial coup that came perilously close to crossing the line of legal ethics.

Hays began by reminding the jury that, according to Jocelyne, Steve had come calling for her on the evening of Lynne's disappearance: "He called there but she was having her supper," Hays said. "And I suggest to you, gentlemen, that if they were late having their supper, it was God's blessing to that girl." Jocelyne, but for the grace of God, could have been the victim of the sexual predator sitting in the prisoner's box. Hays was effectively accusing Steven of wanting to rape, if not murder, Jocelyne; Lynne was just an unfortunate second choice. The Crown's manoeuvre played on the jury's sympathies and horror, but it was also a judicial sham. Steven Truscott was charged with the rape and murder of Lynne Harper and of her alone. There was no basis even to suggest he had intention to commit a crime against Jocelyne or anyone else. But Glenn Hays got away with doing just that.

After Jocelyne escaped Truscott's clutches, "I suggest he saw a substitute in Lynne Harper," Hays explained. "He missed his first prospect, and what more logical and likely person to accept his proposal to go with him on short notice than a girl he knows is fond of him, soft on him."

Hays also moved to bolster Jocelyne's credibility. "Pretty solid support for her account that she was looking for Steven comes from the evidence of Mr. Lawson. Mr. Lawson testified that Jocelyne went over to his farm looking for Steven, he said between 7:15 and 7:25. And he gave one of those times definitively, when he looked at his watch. So suggesting she is making the story up is pretty well refuted by that. She was there."

A more selective use of testimony would be hard to find. Of course, Jocelyne "was there" but the truth was that Lawson's evidence showed the girl was making up a large part of her story. She lied—or was seriously mistaken—about the time of her visit and she was wrong about how long she stayed at the barn.

Hays was painfully aware that he faced an even more serious credibility problem with Butch George as the boy's statements changed so often. Hays decided to turn Arnold's flip-flops into an advantage, claiming that his vacillations were not signs of unreliability, but of a change of heart. Butch was a shining example of a conspirator who had seen the light.

Butch lied to the police to protect his friend Steve, Hays said, "but when Lynne's body was found, the boy came to a realization that to protect a friend can just go so far, and then he gave a right statement."

Hays also used another tactic: taking outwardly innocent actions or facts and turning them into something much more sinister.

Steve's aimless wanderings on his bicycle along the county road in the hour before he met Lynne now became proof of evil premeditation. "What else could he be doing other than looking into the bush, planning things, just seeing that the coast was clear?" Hays suggested.

When he was taken into custody, Steve's legs and arms were dirty but his genital area was washed clean. "Why was he washed that way?" Hays asked. "Would it be to remove any signs of blood or sperm from that area?"

Simple scratches on Steve's knees and elbows, not unusual for a high school athlete, were leftovers of a crime, Hays informed the jury. "Obviously, those are positions that bear contact with surface during an act of intercourse.

The location may add just another fact or deduction linking him with the assault of that girl."

The defence had suggested that only an adult male could reach for three thick tree branches in the bush, cut them off and place them over Lynne's body. The police witnesses said the branches were three-quarters of an inch wide and conceded it would take "considerable effort" to break them. But the Crown counsel dismissed the thick branches as "sticks." He pointed to photographs of them and told the jury: "Look at them, gentlemen. A boy who wins the senior boys' award for sports, could he not take them off almost like matchsticks?"

"A young girl, no passion, dry area, gentlemen," Glenn Hays said, neatly summing up the sexual core of his case in eight words. Like defence counsel Donnelly, Hays prepared the jurors: "We have got to talk of things and you have got to think of things that are not even discussed in polite society, but this is a murder trial." But unlike Donnelly, Hays was happy to play the sex card in his summation. After all, any explicit talk about sex was bound to strengthen jurors' abhorrence of the young boy in the prisoner's box.

Hays began by describing the "brush burns" on Steve's penis "covering, I believe, some eighty per cent of the area"—a deliberately vague exaggeration. No doctor suggested the sores covered such a large part of the penis. Only Brooks had used the eighty per cent figure and in a confusing manner, saying the area involved was "slightly bigger than a quarter . . . that area was eighty per cent of an area larger than a quarter."

Hays also played loosely with the facts when it came to the soiled underwear the OPP removed from Steven in jail. The blood and sperm found in the underwear was "awfully strong complementary evidence involving this boy in the sex act with the girl." Crown prosecutor Hays encouraged the jurors to speculate that for some reason Steve wore the same dirty underwear for four days after he raped and murdered Lynne. "I suggest you will arrive at the conclusion he had it on for a good many days and that you may be able to make the deduction that . . . the sperm is from the attack on the girl."

With a careful mixing of selective facts and suggestive fiction, Hays painted a picture of how he thought the murder took place. He first had to deal with what Steven did with his bicycle, since Jocelyne never saw a bike when she was walking down the lane just ninety feet from where Steven, according to the Crown, was busy with Lynne. "Did he then conceal his bicycle? Did he put his bicycle through the fence?" Hays asked. "It would be no effort to put the bicycle through, under or over. And that wouldn't cause alarm to Lynne, possibly, if she were told now this is kind of a secret mission."

Next, Hays had to explain why Lynne's clothes were scattered so far from the body. "And then, did her attacker put his arm around her neck and choke her into unconsciousness? And when she was then limp on the ground, was she then dragged by her shorts through the fence, getting some cuts on her knees? And was a stop made some fifty feet in, while she was still unconscious, and her pants pulled off?" Hays speculated. "They were found about there. Were they dropped there? Taken off by her attacker, left there, and was the body taken on in?"

If Steve dragged a cut and bleeding body across barbed wire fences and through the bush, pulled off her clothes and strangled her, why was there not a drop of blood on his clothing? "If he went to the trouble of taking off her clothes when she was unconscious or dying and limp, in curiosity about her body, might there not be the action of taking off his own and putting them aside, to satisfy his desires? Only a matter of a minute or two to do that, and put them back on. Then there would be no blood."

"The Crown's case doesn't take the form of showing that she was dragged from the lane through the fence to where the body was," Hays cautioned. "The Crown's case is simply that she was murdered at or near where she was found." Yet he had succeeding in planting in the jurors' minds a terrifying picture of how that could have been done.

The experienced prosecutor knew jurors attached more credibility to things they could see and touch, such as bicycle tire marks and footprints. If jurors were going to condemn a young boy to hang, better to have something solid to hold on to, instead of only the confused memories of children. Hays, therefore, had to excel in what he had done so well so far: make something small appear much more important than it was.

He reminded the jury the police found tire marks along the tractor trail leading into the bush. "It would seem to be fairly strong evidence that that bicycle was down there," he said, acknowledging it was circumstantial. "You have a pile of facts, and if there is one or two that are not conclusive, you still have the conclusive proof of the facts that are there."

In other words, pile on as many facts as possible and even if "one or two" of them are not entirely proven, a high mountain of guilt is created. Consider, for example, how Hays handled the bothersome fact that it had not rained for days and that the police testified a bicycle would not likely leave a trace in the dry earth on June 9. The trees could have provided some shade, he told the jury. "There is plenty of rain in May and none in June, but there could be dampness," he suggested to the jurors. "That is only one of the great stack of facts that are amassing for your assistance."

To top off this growing "stack of facts," Hays added one final gem. "To put Steven at this scene there is something, I suggest, a great deal heavier, more conclusive," Hays told the jurors—Flying Officer Glen Sage's testimony about the footprints. Even Hays had to admit the marks were not "readily discernible" in the photographs. He also acknowledged that the airman saw what the OPP's footprint expert did not. "I am sure we can count on that there are some pretty bright people outside of the police force and just as capable of seeing something," Hays offered.

The marks came from "a crepe-soled shoe," the prosecutor insisted. "The evidence is clear. You can make the comparisons yourself, and you can evaluate it. These were Steven's shoes."

There was a dispute over whether the marks were clear footprints, and no evidence that they matched anyone's footwear. But Hays had turned what the police identification expert had called "scuff marks" into exact matches for Steven's shoes. It was a ploy that had a great impact on the jury, even many years after the trial. Juror Sidney Pullman told the CBC decades later, "The kind of shoes he had on were crepe soles, and the ground was damp, and his shoes left the marks from the damp ground."

Finally, Hays had to discredit the two boys who insisted they had seen Steven cross the river with Lynne that night—Gord Logan and Dougie Oates. Hays deftly turned the tables in his summation. Butch was praised for changing his story, while defence witnesses who never once budged on their testimony were unrepentant liars plotting to protect their friend.

Hays told the jury to disregard Gord because he was part of a carefully orchestrated cabal. "I submit that he is part and parcel with the Steven Truscott–Butch George conspiracy," Hays said, referring to Butch's allegation that he plotted to lie for Steven. "You can take it from the sworn evidence before you that Gord Logan got in on the same deal to tell the police a false story, but unlike George, he stuck to it." What "sworn evidence?" There was no evidence that Gord and Steve met in the days after Lynne's disappearance to cover up a murder.

Dougie Oates was also part of the plot, according to Hays. "He was prepared for a role and told where to hold the line, and in doing so he made himself out to be a little liar." Doug was not in court to hear that accusation. When shown the court transcripts years later, he laughed at the notion that he or any of the other youngsters would have the guts or the intelligence to plot a cover-up. "Where would we have had the time to conspire to say that we've seen them cross the bridge and get all our stories straight?" he says. "When you think about it logically, at the ripe age of eleven, we would have to have been extremely sophisticated to be able to put together stories like that. How much time would we have had to come up with these stories and where would we have gotten together to do this? It really doesn't make a lot of sense."

It was 4:35 in the afternoon. The many hours of testimony and summations were finally coming to an end. "I submit, gentlemen, that on all of the evidence there is only one conclusion that you can reasonably come to . . . and that is that the accused committed this crime," Hays said solemnly.

He sensed that the twelve men in the jury box might be reluctant to sentence a fourteen-year-old to hang: "I feel very sure that it will not have the effect of deterring you from doing your duty as you see fit. For to suggest that you be cowed or deterred from doing your duty in regard to your oath would reflect your integrity."

"The Crown asks you to find the accused guilty as charged."

Glenn Hays then sat down, after spending the entire day on his feet performing some very fancy footwork. Years later, Steven's father, Dan Truscott, reflected on how he felt as he sat in the courtroom watching Hays' performance. "We felt they had only circumstantial evidence," Dan told a newspaper in 1967. "We thought we had won the case until the judge's and the Crown's summaries."

When Hays finished, the jurors turned to the judge. "We are going to have [a few] minutes' recess, gentlemen, then I propose to charge you tonight on this case," Justice Ferguson told the jurors. "Let the jury retire."

It was another example—by today's standards—of the frantic rush to judgment. It was bad enough the jurors had to endure two weeks of testimony with not even full weekends to recover. Bad enough, too, that the judge gave the lawyers little time to prepare their summations. Now—after two exhausting days of closing arguments—the judge expected the jury to begin its deliberations that evening.

## 23

## THE JUDGE'S CHARGE

"Gentlemen of the jury, this has been a very long and difficult trial and you have been very patient," Justice Robert Ferguson said by way of introduction when the jurors returned from their ten-minute break. It was 4:45 in the afternoon.

"This is the most important duty that any citizen has to perform," he continued. "Your churches may be the lid of respectability in the community, but you, gentlemen of the jury, by the barometer of that respectability, you are the screws that hold the lid down and in place. The whole character of your community depends on the way you do your duty in this case."

Jurors may expect witnesses to lie and lawyers to twist facts to fit their theories, but they look to the judge for impartiality and guidance. A judge, in his concluding remarks to the jury, guides the jurors by summing up the evidence, clarifying matters of law and outlining what different weights to accord different types of evidence. But in Steven Truscott's case, the judge's charge to the jury played a significant role in sending him to the gallows.

To have such a young prisoner in the dock for the most serious charge in the criminal code was "so unusual as to be unheard of in this country," the judge explained. "One would think that only a monster could be guilty of such a killing." Lynne, he said, was killed "in the most shocking and revolting circumstances" and the accused charged with "this monstrous crime" was "just a lad of little more than fourteen years." Nevertheless, he warned the jurors, "You must not permit the fact of his youth in any way to prevent you from bringing in [a] verdict in accordance with your conscience." Justice Ferguson also cautioned the jury to weigh the evidence carefully. "Everyone who stands in that prisoner's box is presumed to be innocent until he is proven guilty beyond a reasonable doubt. . . . You must be able to say: 'I have no doubt. I am sure.'"

Since the case was for the most part circumstantial, the judge told the jurors they must be satisfied not only that the circumstances were all consistent with Steven's guilt, but also that they were inconsistent with any other rational explanation. He cautioned jurors not to take any estimates of time too seriously. "If you and I were asked where we were last night, you may remember that you went out for a walk. If you were asked the exact time you went out you would probably have the greatest difficulty in telling anyone what the exact time was, unless there were some very special circumstances at the time which would impress the time on you," he said. "I do not think you should get yourselves involved or tied up with a lot of 7:10, 7:15, or 7:20 or 7:25."

Ferguson also correctly warned the jury to ignore one of the prosecution's key pieces of testimony: Jocelyne's account of her secret date with Steven. "Because he made a date to meet Jocelyne at Lawson's bush is not to be used as evidence that he would take Lynne Harper there," the judge explained. "The evidence of Jocelyne Gaudet is perfectly good evidence to show why she went to the bush to look for Steve, but it is not evidence at all as to proof that the prisoner took Lynne Harper to the bush." No doubt defence lawyer Donnelly would have wished that the judge had not described Gaudet's tale—fraught as it was with contradictions and outright lies about her time—as "perfectly good evidence." But at least the judge had tried to prevent the jury from connecting any supposed date Steve and Jocelyne had with a plot to lure Lynne into the bush.

So far, so good. Having warned the jurors of some pitfalls, Ferguson then proceeded to lay out the facts of the case for the jury, or, at least, the facts as he saw them. It did not take long for the mistakes to start piling up.

He began with the bicycle tire marks. OPP Const. John Erskine, he said, testified that the marks were "similar" to the tires of Steve's bike. Then, he added, as if to drive the point home, "The bicycle is not a common one." Erskine, in fact, had only said that there was a series of vertical lines on the side of Steve's tires similar to marks in the photograph of the bike tracks. He never made a match and he testified the tire marks had to have been made "some time" ago when the ground was "wet and moist." The judge conveyed none of those important distinctions to the jury. Worse still, Steve's fancy racer not being a "common" bike was beside the point, since it was the tires, not the bike, that were in question. No suggestion was ever made that the tires on Steve's bike were anything but the most common tires found on the bikes of countless teenage boys in the area.

Justice Ferguson then moved on to Steven's movements on the night of Lynne's disappearance. He singled out the defence's emphasis on the testimony of Dorothy Bohonus, who saw Lynne doing most of the talking with Steve at the schoolyard. "This has very little to do with this case, if anything," the judge said, and then added: "It would not by any possible shade of reasoning justify or excuse a subsequent killing of the girl in any possible way, shape or form." It was the first of several statements by the judge that could only be described as bizarre. Bohonus's testimony was important for the defence case, since it helped contradict the prosecution theory that Steve had actively lured Lynne to her death. But no one had ever suggested Lynne's chatter justified her murder.

Ferguson moved on to the central issue of why Philip Burns failed to see Steve and Lynne on the road after they passed Richard Gellatly. "So what is the conclusion?" he asked. "Where did Steve and Lynne disappear to? Where did he disappear to after he met Gellatly? Do you think Steve and Lynne went into the woods in that interval? That is entirely for you to say. It is not for me to say." It was a loaded question. Steve and Lynne did not have to "disappear" anywhere if Philip only happened not to see them because he was too distracted or off the road when they began their bike trip. Furthermore, Steve and Lynne did not "disappear" at all, according to defence eyewitnesses who saw them cross the bridge, well past Philip Burns.

Justice Ferguson gave a cursory acknowledgment to this scenario when he asked, "Now then, did Steve and Lynne get over the bridge? Did they get over the bridge? That is one of the theories of the defence in this case, and they have brought forth evidence to justify it." But then the judge seemed to dismiss that possibility with his very next words. "Philip Burns said he didn't meet them. Looking at the map where could they've gone?" he asked, using the same suggestive phrase the Crown prosecutor had. "Where could they have gone after Gellatly saw them? Somebody will correct me if I am wrong, but there was very little room for them to manoeuvre unless they went into this lane."

It was, to say the least, a prejudiced account of the testimony. And it only got worse. Ferguson asked Dougie Oates to step into the courtroom so the jurors could remember him. "This is Douglas Oates. He doesn't quite say what hour he was at the bridge." That, of course, was not only not true, but it also cut at the heart of the defence case. For Dougie had insisted, despite an intense grilling by the prosecutor, that he was on the bridge after 7:00 p.m., when he could have seen Lynne and Steve pass. The Crown had to convince the jury that Dougie was wrong, and Judge Ferguson now stepped in to help the prosecution.

He reminded the jury that Beatrice Geiger had seen Dougie on the bridge at 6:30 and had also seen Steven there around that time. He then strongly suggested that Dougie was wrong about seeing Steve with Lynne after 7:00. "You would think what Douglas saw was really Steven down [there alone] just as Mrs. Geiger saw." Ferguson even went further than the prosecution in introducing a new attack on the testimony by Dougie and his older brother, Allan. Their mother, Genevieve, was not asked on the stand where either of her children were at that time. "Perhaps you will think, as I thought, that that was an extremely important omission," the judge suggested. "If she knew that her son Douglas was at the bridge between 7:00 and 7:30," the judge asked, "then one would have thought she would have sworn to it." She did not swear to it because neither the defence nor the prosecution ever asked her.

The judge went on to discredit the defence's next key eyewitness, Gord Logan. He reminded the jurors the bridge had a forty-inch cement railing. "You have to consider the nature of this cement railing and whether or not Logan could have seen all he says he saw."

Ferguson then took the unprecedented step of introducing an entirely new theory into the case. It was one thing for the judge, in his charge to the jury, to seem to favour a prosecution theory he felt merited more consideration over a defence version he found dubious. But it was highly unusual, in the closing minutes of a two-week trial, for the judge to suggest to the jury an entirely new way for the crime to have occurred.

Crossing or not crossing the bridge was crucial to whether Steve was innocent or guilty. The prosecution insisted Steven never made it very far down the county road because he turned off the road into the laneway to murder Lynne in the bush. The defence maintained that Steven was innocent because two witnesses saw Steve far beyond the laneway, crossing the bridge with the girl on their way to the highway and returning alone. It was one or the other. But Justice Ferguson now suggested that even if Gord and Dougie saw Steven and Lynne cross the bridge, Steven could still be the killer because he might have returned with her *after* they made it to the highway.

"If the accused boy drove or rode Lynne Harper to Number 8 Highway, then you must ask yourselves who brought her back, because somebody brought her back. . . . Is it possible that the accused brought her back?" the judge asked. "You'll ask yourselves, if this boy is guilty, why has he shown such calmness and apathy? Is it because there is an element of truth in his story that he took her to Number 8 Highway, because somebody brought her back? Did he bring her back?"

It was a preposterous idea, so outlandish even the Crown never dared to suggest it. The prosecution knew Steven did not have the time to bike more than a mile to the highway, then ride a half mile back up the county road, then go into the bush to murder and rape Lynne—all the while, never spotted by any of the many people at the bridge or on their long return voyage.

Ferguson made another serious mistake by telling the jury that police tests proved it was not possible "to see the numbers on a licence plate" from the bridge. The Crown, he explained, wanted the jury to dismiss Steve's story as "fabrication because you couldn't see the licence plate, much less could you read the numbers at that distance." At no time did Steven ever claim to have seen licence plate numbers on the car at the highway; yet six times in his charge to the jury, the judge would repeat the same grievous error about plate numbers.

The judge continued his barrage on the defence case by casting doubts on the children who—without exception—testified that Steven appeared normal, unscratched and unbothered when he returned to the school at 8:00 p.m. "It is for you to say," the judge continued, "whether at that hour of the night they were in a good position to observe his demeanour and the looks of his clothes." But it was not night—the sun didn't set for another hour on June 9, less than two weeks away from the longest day of the year. At 8:00 p.m., there was still enough sunlight in the sky for children to be swimming and playing baseball. There was enough light for Lyn Johnston to notice the colour of Steve's shirt, pants, socks and shoes from twenty-five feet away. Surely that was enough light for Steve's friends to have noticed any blood, scars or even sweat on the teenage boy a few feet away from them.

———

"There are certain points that are clear from the evidence," Ferguson said as he began wrapping up his charge to the jury. "First that they left the school somewhere around 7:00. Assuming that you believe these witnesses, *Gellatly particularly*, and Mrs. Nickerson and Mrs. Bohonus, they left the school around 7:00 and Steve returned alone at 8:00 and Lynne Harper was found dead in the bush." What was clear was that Ferguson either did not remember the evidence or was deliberately misrepresenting it. Richard Gellatly in particular did not say Steve and Lynne left the school around 7:00; he insisted it was closer to 7:25.

The judge also reminded the jury of another key defence point—that there were "no marks left by the boy" at the crime scene—before taking a swipe at it. "There were no marks, except there are two footmarks that fit the position [where Lynne was] lying." Justice Ferguson stressed to the jury that one of the searchers, Flying Officer Glen Sage, saw a print, and the judge seemed to chide the police expert for not being as sharp. "[Sage] said that he saw the marks, and one looked as though it had been made by a crepe shoe. One would have thought that Corporal Erskine would have been as observant."

On the debate over the soiled underpants that the police removed from Steven in jail, Ferguson also appeared to come down squarely on the side of the prosecution. "It is argued by the defence that if the underpants had been fouled and dirty and [had] blood on them, why didn't Dr. Brooks and Dr. Addison find them," the judge explained, referring to the extensive examination the two doctors made of Steven on the Friday night of his arrest. The judge told the jury not to worry about that niggling detail: "They asked the boy to take off all his clothes and they didn't examine the pants."

By any measure, Justice Ferguson's charge to the jury was shockingly biased and unbalanced. There was not necessarily anything legally wrong with the judge's directions; his explanation of the law was clear and concise. But in reviewing the case, he consistently attacked every single defence claim and, without exception, let the prosecution theories go unchallenged. His charge mentioned twenty-nine pieces of evidence and excerpts from witness testimony; fourteen could be considered defence points, fifteen prosecution positions. Ferguson made negative comments or raised critical questions on every defence item; his statements on all of the elements in the prosecution case were either positive or neutral. Worse still, he introduced new theories that completely gutted the defence's main case.

"You may bring in a verdict of not guilty or you may bring in a verdict of guilty as charged. There is no other verdict open to you in this case on this evidence," Justice Ferguson concluded. "You are now free to retire, gentlemen, and consider your verdict."

It was already five o'clock in the afternoon—but the day was far from over.

In a flash, defence counsel Frank Donnelly spoke up. "I have a number of objections, my lord," he said, trying to control his irritation. "I would have thought the objections should be made now, before the jury gets out."

"They are not going any place," Ferguson said curtly.

"But before they discuss the matter," Donnelly pleaded.

"I will adjourn for five minutes anyway," the judge answered. The jury had already been sent away. The judge stood up to go to his chambers. The guards led Steven away.

When the court resumed—with the jury absent—Frank Donnelly could barely contain his anger. It was bad enough sitting through a day of the prosecution's summation, watching Glenn Hays twist and turn the evidence to support his case. That was to be expected; it was part of the sport and sparring between lawyers. But to watch Justice Ferguson unravel and leave in tatters the defence case was too much for Donnelly.

Lawyers have the right to ask a judge to redirect the jury in order to clarify points in his charge. The lawyer raises one or two issues and a judge briefly calls back the jury to make the appropriate changes. But in the Steven Truscott case, nothing was simple. The jury would be called back so many times, they ended up playing an exhausting game of musical chairs.

Donnelly began his critique of the judge's charge with the simple point that Philip's testimony about not seeing Steve on the road was unsworn and uncorroborated.

"It is difficult to corroborate that, isn't it?" the judge said grudgingly. "All right. I didn't tell them. I should have."

Donnelly then noted that it would take Philip thirty minutes to walk home, so the timing of his meeting with Jocelyne seemed off. Other boys on the road, such as Bryan Glover, never saw Philip. "So my submission is that

Burns must have been off the road because Glover didn't see him," Donnelly explained in a clearer fashion than he ever had when the jury was present.

"All right, I will tell them that," the judge promised, but soon added, "I don't know the point you are getting at. What difference does it make?"

All the difference in the world, of course. The difference between the hangman and freedom. If Philip was off the road, perhaps already at the school, then no wonder he did not see Steve and Lynne on the bike—a linchpin of the prosecution case was gone.

Donnelly then moved on to the core issue. "I do submit to Your Lordship that your charge to the jury could leave them with no impression except to wipe out the theory of the defence that Douglas Oates and Gordon Logan saw this boy and girl go north across the bridge."

"I don't know where you got that impression," Ferguson said firmly. "I thought I made it plain [that] it is for them to decide and not me on those points."

Donnelly quoted the judge's strange words to the jury about Steven taking Lynne to the highway and then bringing her back. This was an unproven, new theory that cut the heart out of the defence case, Donnelly complained. ""There is no evidence to indicate that he brought her back," Steve's lawyer argued. "Any evidence would be that he didn't bring her back."

"Well, she was back. This is where they may draw the inference he brought her back," Justice Ferguson insisted, still not getting the point, "because she was back." Donnelly was forced to move on, but the issue would soon flare up again.

Donnelly asked the judge to consider that Steve seemed relaxed and natural after Lynne's disappearance not only to his school friends, but also to the police. "The police and various officers said he was very calm and co-operative and trying to assist and was just a normal fourteen-year-old boy."

"They [the jury] might think the person who committed this killing was capable of doing anything" was the judge's rebuttal.

"It is an important theory of the defence, my lord. There is no evidence that the person who committed this killing would be capable of talking quite normally to five or six police officers."

"I thought I mentioned it," said the judge. (He had not.) "But I can mention it again, if you wish."

Donnelly also pointed out how the judge had erred in telling the jury that Steven claimed to be able to read the numbers on a licence plate from his vantage point on the bridge. The judge was confused, Donnelly hinted politely.

Uncertain, the judge turned to the prosecutor. "Is that your recollection?"

"Yes, my lord," Glenn Hays admitted quietly.

"All right," the judge muttered, embarrassed.

But Donnelly was not through.

"And with the greatest respect, my lord, I submit that the jury listening to your charge could not help but get the impression that you consider a verdict of guilty was warranted on the evidence," Steven's lawyer said. It was as close to calling a judge biased as a lawyer could go.

The judge's five-word response was stunning.

"What is wrong with that?"

Donnelly could scarcely believe what he had heard. "I submit the matter should be left with the jury," he said, stating what should have been obvious in any court of law, "rather than put it that strongly to the jury."

"I didn't put it strongly to them at all," the judge protested. "I didn't put that strongly to them. I didn't take it away from them."

"It results, in effect, [in] taking the matter away from the jury and wiping out the defence theories," Donnelly said, standing his ground.

"I have heard that now," Ferguson said sharply. "I don't agree with you." "Thank you, my lord" was all Frank Donnelly said as he sat down. He had gone to the brink; he had pushed the judge and questioned his impartiality as much as he dared.

For the moment.

The judge turned to the prosecutor's table.

"Have you got any objections to this charge, Mr. Hays?"

The prosecutor, as pleased with the judge's charge as Donnelly was horrified, had only a few minor details to bring up and Ferguson readily agreed to them. "Recall the jury," he ordered, and the twelve men, somewhat confused, trooped back to the seats they had vacated about fifteen minutes earlier.

"During your absence, gentlemen of the jury, I have been requested to point out one or two other things to you and to correct one or two slips that I made," the judge began. "Now the first is that Philip Burns was, of course, not sworn, and he said he didn't see Lynne and Steve on the road as he went north, and no one corroborates him in that respect, so that his evidence is worthless so far as you can use it in convicting the accused boy."

It was a powerful correction, but the judge moved quickly to undercut it. "But you can hardly corroborate a statement that 'I didn't see somebody,'" he went on. "You may corroborate that [Steven] wasn't on the road, and I expect that is what Philip meant, that Steve and Lynne weren't on the road as he passed along it."

Ferguson got it completely backwards. The defence claim was not that Steve and Lynne were not on the road—that, after all, was what the prosecution was saying all along to prove that Steven was in the bush murdering her. The defence claimed that Philip may well have been off the road by the time Steve and Lynne began their bike ride down to the highway, so he never would have seen them.

Donnelly had also asked the judge to remind the jury how calm and relaxed Steven appeared, specifically to the police officers who interrogated him. Ferguson told the jury that Steven "was perfectly normal" throughout "all the interviews and all the statements he gave to one person and another, including his mother." The judge again had managed not to mention the police.

"I am asked to remind you that it is a theory of the defence that there was sufficient blood on the body of the girl that anybody who had attacked her was bound to show evidence of blood," Ferguson continued, and then he threw a characteristic counterpunch. "But don't forget that the evidence is that the blouse was pulled around the neck. If there was blood, and there would be, it wouldn't necessarily put blood on the attacker."

Ferguson then tried to correct one of his serious mistakes. He had misled the jurors by reporting that Steve claimed he saw the licence number of the car at the highway. In fact, Steve had told police only that he had seen the number 981-666 on the plate of another car that had passed right by him as he was biking down the county road.

"I made an error in telling you that the number Steve gave of the car was the car on Number 8 Highway," the judge admitted. "This was a car on the county road, but it was not the car on Number 8 Highway."

It was hardly the clearest of corrections. Not surprisingly, several jurors still clung to that wrong impression the judge—six times in his charge to them—helped plant in their minds about Steve's guilt.

"He says this car came along and she got into the car," says juror Sidney Pullman, "and he could see from where he was at this time on the bridge, when he looked back he got the number of this car."

Fresh with the judge's new clarifications, or new confusions, the jurors again retired to their chambers. Defence lawyer Donnelly was still not satisfied. "My lord, would Your Lordship not consider putting the theory of the defence in connection with those lesions [on the penis] to the jury?" he asked.

"All right," Justice Ferguson replied as he called back to jury a second time.

"I am sorry to have brought you back again, gentlemen." He reminded them about the defence theory that the lesions on Steve's penis could have been caused by masturbation. "They could have been caused by any roughness or a knothole or any mechanical device or anything of that kind," Ferguson said. "Now that is a matter that you will have to decide for yourselves, and you use your own common sense as to that phase of it."

It was 8:38 p.m.


During the long wait for the jury's verdict, Steve's parents grabbed a quick bite at a nearby restaurant with Frank Donnelly. Doris remembers she shot a glance at Inspector Harold Graham, as the man she blamed for her family's woes walked in. "He had such a smug look on his face, as if to indicate that everything was all set," she remembered.

For close to three hours, the twelve men of Huron County deliberated behind closed doors. They had supper brought into their chambers. A milkman, a barber, five farmers, three labourers and two merchants. They discussed, debated and pondered. No one but the twelve men knew exactly what went on in that room—what evidence they discarded, what testimony they clung to, what questions they asked. One thing was certain: they were stuck on the key issue that at least two boys had spotted Steven and Lynne crossing the bridge.

At 10:05 p.m., the twelve jurors returned to the courtroom. The guards escorted Steven Truscott back to the prisoner's box. He turned to the jurors who would decide whether he lived or died.

"Gentlemen of the jury," Justice Ferguson intoned, "have you agreed upon your verdict?"

The courtroom was silent. The news reporters, most of whom had not attended the trial because of the publication ban, now sat anxiously in the spectators' benches at the back of the courtroom, their pens ready for the big announcement.

It was not to be.

Clarence McDonald, the jury foreman, turned to the judge. "No, my lord, we have not."

"You have not?" said the judge, barely containing his surprise.

"We want some more information," McDonald explained. He held a piece of paper in his hand. "Can I read this?"

"Yes," Ferguson agreed.

"A redirection of the evidence, corroborated or otherwise," the foreman requested, "of Lynne Harper and Steven Truscott being seen together on the bridge on the night of June the 9th."

"Is that all?"

"That is it."

After all the testimony and arguments, after more than seventy witnesses and an equal number of exhibits, it all came down to two boys at a bridge: Dougie Oates and Gordon Logan, who insisted they saw Steven and Lynne cross the river together.

For the first time in the trial, Justice Ferguson came as close as possible to giving a fair, balanced and clear summary.

"You have the evidence of Douglas Oates, who says that in the neighbourhood of about 7:30, he and Karen Daum were fishing for turtles at the bridge, and while they were fishing for turtles and arranging them in their carriers, Steve and Lynne came by on a bicycle. 'I saw Steve and Lynne going by me on the bridge. I put up my hand and said "Hi."' Now that is the evidence of Douglas Oates.

"Allan Oates says he watched television from 6:00 until 7:00 at his home and then he went down the road toward the bridge, and when he was eight hundred feet away from the bridge, he noticed Steve on the bridge alone, without Lynne.

"Then you have Gord Logan who testified. He said he was swimming at 7:30, and then he saw Steve and Lynne go by on Steve's bicycle and they were riding double. She was on the crossbar. He said: 'They were on the north side of the bridge going toward Number 8 Highway, and I saw Steve drive back and stop on the bridge.'

"That is the evidence that they were on the bridge at 7:30," Ferguson concluded, before he turned to the prosecution's view of events.

"Jocelyne Gaudet and Arnold George were down there looking for Steve at that time, or around that time, and they saw nothing of him. Logan was fishing from the rocks 640 feet east when he saw this going on. It is suggested by the Crown that he could not have distinguished who the riders were, even if he had seen a bike. It is suggested by the Crown that when [Douglas] Oates says he saw Steve, he saw him alone at 6:30 and not at 7:30. It is suggested that Allan [Oates] would make a very shaky recognition of Steve at eight hundred feet. Then you of course won't forget Philip Burns's evidence that he left the river between 7:00 to 7:10 and walked up the road and saw nothing of Steve and Lynne."

It was the best presentation of both sides of the case Ferguson had ever made. "I have been over all this before and I don't want to repeat it too often," he concluded. "Is there any other branch of the evidence you would like me to go over for you?"

"That is that I was asked for, my lord," the jury foreman said. "I hope that covered it."

It could have ended there. The jurors could have gone back to the room to ponder the evidence of Dougie and Gord as Ferguson had just laid it out to them with clarity and concision. We will never know if events might have turned out differently.

But Justice Ferguson seemed determined to have one final word. He turned again to the twelve jurors. "That is the evidence with respect to the two of them being on the bridge together. They were there in the neighbourhood of 7:25 or 7:30," he began. Then he spoke the words that, once again, cut the ground from under all of the defence work: "But as I pointed out to you, you must reject the story that he went to Number 8 Highway and the girl got in a car there, you must reject that story to convict him. If you find that although he went to Number 8 Highway with the girl and he brought her back again—and she was back, somebody brought her back—you will have to find that he did bring her back again. Then the going back and forth across the bridge is of very little importance—very little importance because the question is: did he kill her? That is the point in this case."

It was not of "very little importance"—it was more important than anything else said in that courtroom. If Steven and Lynne crossed that bridge, he did not kill her. End of case.

But Justice Ferguson, in his final words to the jurors, had told them just the opposite. That even if they believed part or all of the testimony central to Steve's defence—that Dougie and Gordon saw him and Lynne bike across that bridge—they could somehow still conclude that Steven killed Lynne and find him guilty.

"If there is any other help I can give you, don't hesitate to ask me, gentlemen," Ferguson said. "But that is all I can say about it now."

The chairs scraped against the floor as the twelve jurors once again stood up and walked out of the box. As the door closed behind them, a frantic Frank Donnelly again stood up to address the judge.

"My lord, I know I raised this before, but I do submit that the evidence is that Steve came back alone. Logan's evidence is that Steve came back alone. No one said he came back with the girl."

"I didn't say he did," Ferguson retorted. "I said Steve came back alone and that Logan said he saw him come back alone."

"Then you said: 'If you find that he went to Number 8 Highway and then brought the girl back,'" Donnelly pursued. "I submit there is no evidence to warrant them finding that."

"Yes, there is," the judge insisted. "There is evidence that would warrant it: she was back. Dr. Penistan's evidence."

"The body was found in the bush," Donnelly conceded, but he pressed on. "She might have come back some other way. This is a most important piece of evidence and I do submit with respect, my lord, that it is one of the most important theories of the defence, and the way Your Lordship comments on it, it pretty well destroys the effect of that theory."

Ferguson was fuming. Dan Murphy, the young colleague who was sitting next to Frank Donnelly, later recalled that the judge's face turned red with anger. "Oh, he was furious. He put his hands on his desk so hard, he spun his chair right around," Murphy said, chuckling at the memory. "He was so upset at Donnelly."

"Call the jury back," Ferguson said sternly, once he had calmed down.

"I dislike having to bring you back so often and interrupt your deliberations, but I do it only at the request of counsel," the judge told jurors when they had returned to the courtroom for the fourth time. "I told you when you last were out here that if Steve brought Lynne back across the bridge, it doesn't make much difference whether he went over the bridge or not. But there is, of course, no eyewitness that says he did."

It was a grudging concession to Donnelly's pleas. But Justice Ferguson could not leave well enough alone. He decided to recapitulate, one more time, the eyewitness testimony. Dougie and Gord said they saw Steve and Lynne, he conceded, but he seemed to suggest that their stories did not matter. "They would also have been there at a time when Jocelyne Gaudet and Arnold George had an opportunity to see them, and they were the people who are looking for them. The others were not. That is all."

The jury retired.

And again, Donnelly rose to face the judge.

"I am very reluctant to make a further objection," he said. But he could not ignore what the judge had just done: in effect, he told the jury that the testimonies of the prosecution's witnesses were more reliable than the those for the defence, because Jocelyne and Butch had claimed to have been on a hunt for Steve.

Donnelly patiently tried to point out to the judge that at the bridge, Jocelyne and Butch could have missed Steve's return alone from the highway. "One of them went swimming and the other then went home. I do think it is important to correct the impression that Gaudet and George were ahead of Steve and Lynne on the road because that is not the evidence, my lord."

"I didn't give an impression, I don't think," Ferguson maintained.

"You said that Gaudet and George—"

But Judge Ferguson's patience had run out. He cut off the defence lawyer in mid-sentence and turned to the clerk. "Call the jury back. Please, will you."

For the fifth time, the jurors returned to the courtroom. After a judge has charged the jury, it is rare for a jury to come back so many times for clarifications; it was a reflection of the confusion and missteps in the Truscott trial that the twelve jurors had to make so many trips to and from the jury box.

"The last word I said to you, when I spoke to you before, was that Gaudet and George had an opportunity to see them. Well, Gaudet and George would not have been at the bridge when Steven and Lynne went on to Number 8 Highway," Ferguson said, making the point for which Donnelly had fought so hard.

But then, the judge added, "It is for you to say, but do you not think they would have had an opportunity to see Steve if he came back in five minutes?"

Not, of course, if Arnold was busy swimming in the river and not if Jocelyne had gone home, as they both testified they did. Donnelly had pointed this out but the judge pointedly ignored it. "Could [Steven] have got back without Jocelyne Gaudet and George having seen him? It is for you to say, not me."

It was now 10:45 p.m. The jury, as drained as everyone else in the courtroom, retired for the last time.

"Now," the judge turned to stare down Donnelly. "Have you any objection to that?"

Defiant to the last moment, Donnelly found the courage to make one more stab at it. "Just that I think George went to the river to swim," Steven Truscott's lawyer said. "He went down to swim and he wasn't hanging around the bridge, my lord."

The judge did not even deign to answer.

He turned to the guards. "Take the prisoner out," he ordered.

This time, they would not be gone for long.

**24**

THE VERDICT

Outside the courtroom, in the halls of the court building, they waited. The families, the friends, the police, the curious. They stretched their legs, shuffled their feet, rubbed their eyes and cleared their throats. Anything to avoid thinking about what was to come.

Lil Woodson, the neighbour who sat beside Doris Truscott through most of the trial, dashed to a phone to tell her husband she would be late because the jury had taken so long. She marvelled at her friend's resolve. "Doris was very solid. She never really broke down at all," she remembers. "She was a pretty tough lady."

Frank Donnelly, despite the rough ride the judge had given him, remained confident to the end. "After the summations were finished, I would say that most people thought for sure Steven would be acquitted," recalls Dan Murphy.

"Things are looking pretty good," Donnelly assured Steve's parents. "He had us fully convinced that it was going to go our way," Doris Truscott remembers.

Some of the OPP officers appeared to be the most nervous. "While we were out waiting for a verdict, none of us were sure," Hank Sayeau says. "We thought we had a good case—we didn't know if the jury would buy it against a fourteen-year-old. There's some anxiety about whether they are going to buy your case, about whether you have put the jigsaw together."

The anxiety did not last long. This time the jury stayed away for less than ten minutes. At 10:55 p.m., the twelve men walked back into the courtroom.

They were ready with their verdict.

Doris Truscott wrung her hands as the jury took their seats. For three months she waited as her son sat in a jail cell. For fourteen days, she and her husband had sat behind their son in the courtroom, not being able to see his face as he was called a liar, a rapist, a murderer. Now, finally, the moment of truth was near.

This was not Hollywood; it was not the judge who intoned the fateful words but the court registrar, Jean Clements, who spoke. "Gentlemen of the jury, have you agreed upon your verdict?" she asked.

"Yes, my lord," answered jury foreman Clarence McDonald.

"Do you find the prisoner at the bar guilty or not guilty?"

"We find the defendant guilty as charged," said McDonald stiffly, quickly adding, "with a plea for mercy."

"A hush fell on the crowded courtroom," reported the *London Free Press*. "It was broken later by the quiet sobbing of the boy's mother." Other women in the court also broke into tears. Steven Truscott was "ashen faced," according to one reporter. "He went white," his mother remembers. "He just looked like, 'This wasn't for real.'"

"My lord, may I have the jury polled?" Frank Donnelly requested.

"Poll the jury," the judge ordered. One by one, the twelve men of Huron County gave their verdict:

Harold Vodden, a merchant from Blyth: "Guilty."
Louis Frayne, a farmer in Grey Township: "Guilty."
Fred Thompson, a farmer from Goderich: "Guilty."
Carl Lott, a labourer from Wingham: "Guilty."
Gordon Dick, a merchant in Seaforth: "Guilty."
Wilmer Dalrymple, a farmer in Tuckersmith: "Guilty."
Walter Brown, a labourer from Wingham: "Guilty."
David Kyle, a mechanic from Hensall: "Guilty."
John Deitz, a farmer from Howick: "Guilty."

Anson Coleman, a farmer from Stanley: "Guilty."
Clarence McDonald, the foreman, a milkman from Exeter: "Guilty."
Sidney Pullman, a barber in Seaforth: "Guilty."

It had not been an easy decision, according to Pullman. "There was nobody in there to get him," he told a CBC researcher years later. "We found him guilty because none of us could come to any sense at all [about his story]. Not even one person argued [for his innocence]." Pullman's story that none of the twelve jurors pushed for an acquittal was confirmed by Graham, who learned, indirectly, from one of the jurors that "the guilty verdict was reached early in deliberations." It was only the qualms of one of the older jurors that delayed their deliberations. "An elderly juror didn't want to soon leave this world with a conscience troubled by sending a young boy to the gallows," Graham later reported. "Hence the mercy recommendation." Indeed, the prospect of sending a young boy to the gallows did seem to weigh heavily on the minds of many of the jurors. "He said it was a terrible decision to have to make," Wilmer Dalrymple's wife later told the newspapers. "We have three sons of our own, you know. But he was sure the lad was guilty, and he had to do his job."

But Justice Ferguson had made it clear to jurors they had no choice—they could deliver the verdict, but he alone could hand down the sentence. The judge turned to the boy in the prisoner's box. "Stand up."

"Steven Murray Truscott, have you anything to say why the sentence of this court should not be passed upon you according to law?"

The boy looked up at the judge and said softly, "No, Your Lordship."

The judge looked at Steven and the entire courtroom. "Steven Murray Truscott, I have no alternative but to pass the following sentence upon you. The jury have found you guilty after a fair trial. The sentence of this court upon you is that you be taken from here to the place from whence you came and there be kept in close confinement until Tuesday, the 8th day of December, 1959, and upon that day and date, you be taken to the place of execution and that you there be hanged by the neck until you are dead. And may the Lord have mercy upon your soul."

The words stunned the boy. "His eyes filled with tears, Steven Truscott gasped in the dock," according to the Toronto *Telegram*. The *Toronto Daily Star* said simply, "the boy turned pale."

Even some of the jurors were shocked. "It brought tears to our eyes," says Sidney Pullman. "I thought jail would have been enough, but to say to a boy of fourteen to be taken, hanged by the neck until he's dead, that kind of gets to your heart. When [the judge] came out with that it led me to think, 'I wonder if we should have said something different.'" Apparently, some jurors thought a verdict of guilty "with a recommendation for mercy" would spare the boy from the noose.

But it was too late for anyone to change the verdict. "Remove the prisoner, please," ordered the judge.

"It can't be, it can't be!" thought Doris when she heard the words "hanged by the neck until you are dead."

"He won't hang," Donnelly tried to reassure the stricken mother. "They wouldn't hang a fourteen-year-old kid."

"Everything has gone wrong, so who's to say what's to happen," Doris remembers telling him.

"Hanging. We just didn't believe it," her oldest son, Ken, remembers, upon hearing the news. "You're just sort of numb, you don't believe you have even heard it."

A crowd of about two hundred, according to one news report, stood in front of the county courthouse on the town square to get a look at the prisoner. "The Crown attorney was leery of any type of commotion or violence," OPP Corporal Sayeau recalls. "He wondered what we could do." Sayeau called the police station to send a vehicle out to pull up behind the courthouse.

"Steven, come on!" Sayeau called out, and he and the boy ran down three flights of stairs, out the back door and across the park into the car.

"We sure put it over on them that time," Sayeau says Steven remarked as the car sped away, avoiding the crowds. The comment shocked the OPP officer.

"I couldn't believe it, a fourteen-year-old kid, come out with that after just being sentenced to hang," he says. "I found it astonishing. I would have been on the floor crying and screaming."

But crying and screaming were not in the emotional lexicon of the Truscott family. "It's just my makeup," Steve explains. "I just wasn't brought up that way. It's not the air force way." Steve says he remembers hearing the verdict, but none of it felt real. "You kind of sit there stunned. . . . You couldn't understand how they came to that conclusion with what they had," he says. "It's almost like it's a fantasy world. I think it's just too much for any kid to really comprehend."

For the Harpers, still grieving three months after the loss of their daughter, the verdict meant closure—of a sort. Publicly, the family would always maintain they were satisfied with the verdict. "I've believed the original verdict was right and just," Leslie Harper said later. But privately, some members of the family revealed there were always lingering doubts about Steve's conviction. "It's hard on the family because they don't know who did it," says James Harper, Leslie's cousin. "They just don't know for sure."

John Erskine, the OPP identification officer who from almost the start of the investigation had his doubts about Steve's guilt, was crestfallen. "He was white. He couldn't believe it," recalls his wife, Dee. "He was quite emphatic that he was not guilty."

Even some officers who remained convinced of Steve's guilt were not necessarily overjoyed by the outcome. "I had mixed feelings," admits Hank Sayeau, who played a central role in gathering evidence. "I don't know where my sympathy lay there. I suppose toward the Harper family—Lynne was gone. At the same time, the Truscotts had a fourteen-year-old son who was sentenced to hang. I was glad that I wasn't in the Truscotts' position."

One OPP officer, however, was unwavering. Inspector Graham to the very end seemed determined to paint as dark a picture as possible of the boy he had helped send to the gallows. "When sentenced, his eyes were filled with anger, not with fear," Graham wrote in a memo after the trial. The OPP investigator must have had a better vantage point to peer into Steve's eyes than the journalists, who had reported a strikingly different picture.

To reinforce his assessment, Graham told his superiors, "Dr. J. Senn, superintendent of the Ontario Hospital, kept observation of the accused throughout the trial. His emotions were only slight and he could be best described as callous." In fact, Dr. Senn reported that "the boy showed little or no emotion" and did not give the impression that he was "happy being the centre of attention." He "flushed occasionally" during the more sexually explicit testimony and was "following the evidence quite intently." The word "callous" never appeared in Dr. Senn's available reports.

Graham's conviction that justice had been done was shared by many townspeople. "After the verdict most people just thought he was guilty," explains Henry Lamb, the garage station owner who watched most of the trial. While Lamb was shocked—"I couldn't believe it when they brought in the guilty verdict for that kid. The evidence they had wasn't even circumstantial"—he found that most of his fellow citizens did not share his outrage. "It was 1959 and back then we didn't put innocent people in prison," Lamb says. "The thing is, they wanted to have somebody and put them away so that everyone could let their little girls out to play again. People were just happy to have the case finished and over with."

That determination to quickly bury a disturbing trial was reflected in the major local paper, the *Goderich Signal-Star*. "The Truscott trial was the most important criminal case of the year in Canada. . . . Now it is a matter of history," the newspaper concluded, somewhat prematurely.

On the base, opinion was more divided. Allan Durnin's father, who sat through the trial, told his son he thought the evidence indicated Steve had to have been in the bush with Lynne. "And in my mind, when I got thinking about it afterwards, I thought he must have done it," Allan says. Allan recalled the confrontation at school he had with Steve on the following Thursday, when he questioned whether his schoolmate had really taken Lynne to the highway. "Why did he get so upset in that washroom if he had no connection at all with her?" Allan asks.

But for many of the children, especially for those who had taken the stand against their own classmate, the verdict was hard to take. "All we really knew was that he was our friend," says John Carew. "He was a nice guy, he played hockey and softball like we did, and he was like us. There was no thought that he was guilty. It blew us all away."

"When they read the sentence out, I just about collapsed," remembers Bryan Glover. "When they said he'd be hanged by the neck, shudders just went up my spine."

Doug Oates, who had stood up so vociferously against the onslaught of the Crown prosecutor, to this day cannot fathom why the jurors did not believe his testimony about seeing Steve and Lynne cross the bridge. "I was flabbergasted. I just couldn't believe that they could find him guilty," he recalls. "The fact that you can convict somebody with really no evidence other than circumstantial evidence—I think that's just abhorrent."

To his mind, the trial never resolved the mystery of what happened on June 9, 1959. "There are only three that really know: Steven, whoever did it and God."

The lawyers who had been sparring for two weeks over Steven's fate slipped quietly out of the courtroom through the door to the right of the judge's bench. Donnelly exited first, followed by Hays. Accompanying them was Donnelly's colleague Dan Murphy. Murphy recalls that Hays seemed concerned the Crown had a teenager on their hands condemned to hang.

"Well, what are we going to do now?" the prosecutor asked.

"That's your problem, not mine," Donnelly said curtly, and walked away. It was the only sign of bitterness Murphy ever saw from his colleague.

"The next day, it was business as usual," Murphy recalled. In the office the morning after the trial, Donnelly handed Murphy an insurance file to pursue and never talked to him about the Truscott case again.

Donnelly had been oblique when reporters had questioned him right after the trial about an appeal. "It is apt to be a few days before we are able to make a decision," he said.

But that "we" would not include Donnelly. Donnelly could not handle Steve's appeal. Two days after losing Steven's case, Donnelly got the promotion he had delayed accepting at the start of the summer—a judgeship on the Superior Court of Ontario. The move was "acclaimed by people of all walks of life," the Goderich newspaper reported in gushing terms. Hundreds of tributes came in the form of phone calls, telegrams and letters to "one of this country's outstanding lawyers."

The Truscotts were grateful for Donnelly's efforts. "I think he did the best that he could," Doris says, but with hindsight she adds, "I felt that had we had a big-time lawyer, he could have done better."

As Doris's son sat in the Goderich jail, Donnelly began what would become an illustrious career on the bench. Today, in the courtroom where Donnelly lost his most famous case, where Steven Truscott was sentenced to hang, a gold-and-brass plaque is mounted on the wall. Just above where the jury sits, the plaque pays tribute to "Frank Donnelly, Judge," the letters still shiny on the dark brown background.

## 25

### THE TROUBLE WITH TIME

Timing, in murder as in life, is everything.

Steven's innocence or guilt could be weighed by the credibility of the eyewitnesses: do you believe Dougie Oates and Gord Logan, or do you believe Butch George, Jocelyne Gaudet and Philip Burns?

But in the end, even if you believed that the children who claimed to see Steve and Lynne by the river were wrong or liars, you would still have to convince yourself that Steven had time to murder Lynne Harper. Theoretically, a timeline where Steven is guilty goes like this:

Steve leaves his house around 5:50 p.m. to get coffee for his mother. He dashes over to Jocelyne's house, a couple of minutes away, to see if she wants to go to the bush. He still has a few minutes to make it to the store and home before 6:00.

After supper, Steve bikes around the base and along the county road, until he makes it to the school around 7:00 p.m., where Lynne approaches him for a ride. They leave the schoolyard sometime between 7:00 and 7:10 and very soon cross paths with Richard Gellatly, on his way home from the river (meaning Richard is seriously off on his time by about fifteen minutes and that his father is also wrong about the time his son arrives home).

It takes Steve just over three minutes to get to the tractor trail from the school, according to a police test of bike times. Around 7:15, he and Lynne turn off the county road at the entrance to the tractor trail. According to the scenario suggested by the prosecution at the trial, Steve then walks down the laneway about three hundred feet with Lynne, somehow subdues her, carries her limp one-hundred-pound body—and his bike (since Jocelyne and other children never saw it)—into the bush over a barbed wire fence, scratches her badly but manages to avoid any barbed wire cuts on his own body, drags her ninety feet, strangles and rapes her, rolls up her socks neatly, zips up her shorts, drops her panties thirty-three feet away, breaks off saplings three-quarters of an inch to an inch thick, lays them over her body, puts back whatever clothes of his he removed, cleans himself off, takes his bike back to the tractor trail and bikes to the schoolyard to chat with his friends.

All of this supposedly within earshot of Jocelyne, who, according to the prosecution, is on the tractor trail at about the same time. All of this, without breaking a sweat, scratching his face or neck and not getting a single drop of blood on his clothes. And all of this within about forty-five minutes—depending on which witness you believe—or as little as thirty minutes.

As a fourteen-year-old, Steven would have to exhibit almost pathological nerves of steel to carry out a crime like this. Perhaps he snaps when he is in the bushes with Lynne, some sexual flirting goes too far, he strangles her in a moment of panic. Perhaps he even blocks the horrible deed from his mind and emerges from the bushes calm and collected. His penis sores will be discovered in a few days. When friends tease him, he makes up a story about looking for calves in the bush. When the police question him, he invents a car at the highway.

Is all of this possible? Mathematically, yes. But it stretches credulity and common sense beyond the breaking point.

On the other hand, is it possible to construct a more reasonable scenario that explains what could have happened on the evening of June 9 without distorting logic or the memories of most of the witnesses:

| | |
|---|---|
| 6:15 | Lynne Harper leaves home and makes her way to the school. Steven leaves his home a little later and is spotted by several children and adults biking around the county road. |
| 7:02 | Philip Burns leaves the bridge. |

| 7:11 | Philip reaches the entrance to the bush. He does not see Steven because Steven and Lynne have not left the school yet. |
| 7:14 | Philip meets Jocelyne at the south end of the bush and, shortly after, Butch George. |
| 7:15 | Jocelyne reaches the laneway, turns in and walks along the trail before turning back to the county road. |
| 7:16 | Jocelyne meets Butch at the entrance to the laneway. Butch heads down to the river, but Jocelyne—contrary to her testimony about going to the bridge—heads for Lawson's farm. |
| 7:20 | Richard Gellatly leaves the bridge on his bike. (He testifies it was "around 7:20 p.m.") |
| 7:21 | Jocelyne arrives at Lawson's barn and chats for a few minutes. In court, Lawson said "it was 7:25 when she left." She doesn't see Steve or Lynne because she is still at or near the farm. |
| Around 7:25 | Philip Burns reaches the school grounds. He does not see or notice Steve and Lynne. Steve glances at kindergarten clock as he and Lynne leave the school grounds. Steve and Lynne start their journey down the road. Shortly after, they pass Richard Gellatly. |
| Around 7:30 | Steve and Lynne cross the bridge. Police say it takes almost five minutes to bike from the school to the bridge. Both Dougie Oates and Gord Logan see Lynne and Steve cross the bridge. |
| 7:31–7:32 | Steve leaves Lynne at the highway. The police estimate the total time to ride a bike from the school to the highway is six minutes. |
| 7:34–7:35 | Gord Logan sees Steve return alone at the bridge. |
| 7:45 | Allan Oates see Steve standing alone at the bridge. Steve heads back to the school area. |
| Around 8:00 | Steve arrives back at the school grounds. |

This timeline matches the testimony of defense witnesses Gord Logan, Allan Oates and Doug Oates. It is also supported by the testimony of prosecution child witnesses Richard Gellatly, Bryan Glover, Michael Burns and even to some degree the testimony of Philip Burns and Arnold George. It corresponds to the testimony of most of the children who saw Steven leave or return to the school.

As for the adults, this scenario coincides with the memory of farmer Bob Lawson and of Richard Gellatly's father. It is consistent with the testimony of John Carew's parents and of Sgt. William McCafferty, the man who gave Philip the time at the river, and it matches most of the recollections of Beatrice Geiger. It is not inconsistent with the two Brownie mothers at the school, who saw Steve and Lynne between 7:00 and 7:10 but never saw them leave the school grounds.

Only two people have to be wrong for this scenario to work: Donna Dunkin has to be mistaken about seeing Richard and Philip leave together; and Jocelyne Gaudet lied or was mistaken about almost all of her times and about going to Lawson's farm before she went to the bush.

There is no absolute proof that this is how and when events occurred on June 9. But there is enough reliable evidence to indicate *it could well have happened this way*. That is what reasonable doubt is all about.

Of all the prosecution's theories about timing, nothing was more pivotal than Philip Burns's story. It was the central piece of evidence that allowed the prosecution to put Steve in the bush with Lynne. The logic went like this: Philip, on foot, and Richard Gellatly, on his bike, leave the bridge within moments of each other. Richard passes Steve and Lynne on the county road on their way down to the river. Philip makes it to the bush, without ever seeing Steve and Lynne. Therefore, they must have exited the county road at the tractor trail and gone into the bush. What if it was based on bad timing, incomplete eyewitness accounts and flawed logic?

For the Crown's timing to work, Philip obviously had to get to the laneway *after* Steve and Lynne had made it there. If he got there *before* or about the same time, he presumably would have bumped into them or seen them either on the road or turning into the bush. The county road offered an unobstructed view of the bush and the laneway.

The simplest calculations would have revealed the prosecution's numbers did not add up—or rather, they added up to a conclusion of innocence, not guilt.

OPP Constable Trumbley determined it took Philip *only six minutes* to walk 2,059 feet from the bridge to the tractor trail at the northern edge of the bush. For Steven to be guilty, *during the same six minutes* Richard had to bicycle from the bridge to the south end of the county road where he met Lynne and Steve, and then Lynne and Steve had to have enough time to make it into the bush without being spotted by Philip. Richard had to bike anywhere from about 3,800 to 4,200 feet from the bridge before he passed Steve and Lynne—the exact spot was never determined but it was somewhere between the end of the bush and O'Brien's farm, not far from the school.

Assuming Richard defied gravity and pedalled as fast going uphill towards school as he did going towards the river, according to police times it would still take him just over three minutes to reach Steven and Lynne, depending on where they crossed paths. Steve and Lynne would need an additional one and a half minutes to make it to the laneway. In all, more than four and a half minutes would have elapsed from the time Richard and Philip supposedly left the bridge together. In that time, little Philip, according to the police, *would be less than a minute and a half from the laneway, or about 440 feet*—with a clear line of sight to the trail. Once Steve and Lynne reached the laneway, they still had to get off their bike and walk along the trail, giving the rapidly approaching Philip even more time to spot them. In about eighty or ninety seconds, he would be right at the lane entrance, and Steve and Lynne could not have been very far down the lane as they made their way on foot along the rutted path.

This scenario is based on official police times. But the prosecution case weakens significantly if one factors in more realistic bicycle times. Richard himself told police it took about twice as long to get home from the swimming hole than to go down to the river from the base, because of the steady hill to climb from the bridge to the bush. The police also made the dubious assumption that Steve, carrying Lynne on his bike, would travel at the same speed as a single cyclist. In fact, one test later indicated it could take two people riding as much as twice as long to make the journey.

Assuming more accurate bike travel times and a meeting point with Richard halfway between the bush and the school, just over six minutes would have elapsed before Steve and Lynne arrived at the tractor trail— roughly the same time the police said Philip took to reach the entrance to the bush, In other words, *Philip should have bumped right into Steve and Lynne* just as all three approached the laneway.

———

It gets even worse for the prosecution if you take into account a serious mis-calculation the police made of Philip's walking time.

In court, no one doubted the accuracy of the OPP's timing of Philip's walk home. That was a shame, because a more scientific estimate of his jour-ney would have revealed a startling possibility—that Philip did not see Steve and Lynne on the county road *because he himself was not on the county road at the time.*

On June 20, Philip himself re-enacted his stroll home for the police, while Const. Donald Trumbley followed slowly in his police cruiser. According to Trumbley, Philip took twenty-four minutes to make the entire trip. Trumbley told the court it took Philip six minutes to go up the steepest hill of his journey—from the bridge to the laneway at the northwest corner of the bush. That would be an impressive pace of more than 340 feet per minute. He then apparently cut his speed almost in half, taking four minutes to meet Jocelyne at the far end of the bush. Philip, according to the police, then slowed to a crawl of one hundred feet per minute, taking two minutes to reach Butch George only a couple of hundred feet further along the road.

For the final leg of his journey, Philip apparently sprouted wings. By the OPP's calculations, it had taken Philip twelve minutes to get to Butch, about three thousand feet from the river. Yet the police claimed he would now take the exact same time—twelve minutes—to make it all the way to his home on Quebec Road, near Steve's house—a trek of roughly 4,400 feet, or about fifty per cent longer than he had walked so far. At that blistering pace, Philip would have beaten more than one thousand people in the New York Marathon.

The police timing simply made no sense. The OPP had Philip walking an average of 5.1 feet per second and sometimes as fast as 5.7 feet per sec-ond. The official Green Book of the American Association of State Highway and Transportation, used to design streets and crosswalks, recognizes 4.0 feet per second as the average speed of pedestrians, and small children obviously walk slower. There is no reason to believe Philip would be sprinting on that hot summer night.

In fact, independent tests carried out for this book show it would take a boy not twenty-four minutes as the police claimed, but closer to twenty-eight or thirty minutes to walk from the bridge to the Burnses' home, or an average of 4.1 feet per second—very close to the officially recognized speed for pedestrians. This thirty-minute estimate also coincided with the eyewitness testimony of when Philip arrived home.

"It was just two minutes past 7:30," Michael, his older brother, told the court. The boys' mother also told police that her oldest son told her Philip did not get home until 7:30 p.m.

If Philip arrived at his house between 7:30 and 7:32 and he took twenty-eight to thirty minutes to walk home, his departure from the river was between 7:00 and 7:04 p.m.—just about when the eyewitness evidence from the adults at the river suggests he left the bridge.

Getting an accurate assessment of Philip's walk was not legal hair-splitting. If Philip took about half an hour to walk home at a steady pace, instead of the frenetic changes the police timing implied, he would be off the county road around 7:25, making his way through the crowded school playground at about the time Steve says he left with Lynne. It was even possible Philip went around one side of the school while Steve and Lynne circled the other way. All of which easily explains why Philip would not have noticed two more children walking next to a bike amidst the dozens of other children at the school.

For the prosecution to put Steven in the bush, they not only had to have Philip do some impressive walking. They also had to match his departure from the river with Richard Gellatly's bike ride home. Without a simultaneous departure for both boys, the Crown had no "eyewitness" case.

The theory for both boys leaving the bridge at exactly the same time hinged mainly on the testimony of Donna Dunkin, the mother who drove four young boys to the river on Tuesday night. Dunkin told the police and later the court that as she pulled in to park near the bridge shortly after 7:00 p.m. she saw Richard and Philip "no more than ten feet" apart.

The only other adult who saw both boys at the river around the same time was Beatrice Geiger. She testified Philip and Richard left "within the same time period," but she was by the riverbank near the swimming hole, six hundred feet away from the bridge. Under cross-examination by Frank Donnelly, Geiger readily admitted she paid little attention to either boy once they left riverside and had no idea what they did or how long they took on the bridge.

"You didn't watch him go?" he asked about Richard.

"No."

"And Burns . . . he departed from the river and you don't know what he did after that; is that right?"

"Yes," she answered.

As for the two boys themselves, one would think that if, as Dunkin thought, the two boys were only ten feet apart, they would not have had a hard time spotting each other. Yet no matter how mightily prosecutor Glenn Hays tried, he could not get the boys to testify that they saw each other.

"Did you see Richard Gellatly at the swimming hole while you were there, before you left?" Hays asked Philip.

"No, I don't think so," the boy replied.

"Did you see him at the bridge?" Hays pushed, ever hopeful.

"I am not sure," said Philip.

"Well, did you see him at all, Philip, after you left the swimming hole?" Hays asked, seemingly losing patience with his witness.

"No."

Hays had no more luck with Richard. At the preliminary, the teenager confirmed he saw Philip down by the river but never saw him leave the bridge.

"Where was he when you left?" Hays pursued.

"I can't remember," Richard answered.

So the two boys who were supposedly just feet apart soon after they left the bridge together did not see each other. Donna Dunkin was undoubtedly right about seeing Philip, because the ten-year-old walked up to the car and spoke to her son. The timing of her sighting of Richard was more questionable. Perhaps she confused him with one of the many boys on bicycles. If Dunkin did see Richard, perhaps it was a few minutes later when she got out of her car and walked to the riverbank with her children, joining the other women there. "As I was walking along the bank, I saw Mrs. Geiger down the cliff beside the water at the swimming hole," she told the court. Glenn Hays asked Richard if there were any women he knew at the bridge when he left. "Yes," Richard answered. "Mrs. Geiger, Mrs. Dunkin and Mrs. Burke."

The biggest problem with the theory that Philip and Richard left at the same time was that there was much to suggest that Philip left close to 7:00 p.m., while Richard left around 7:15 or 7:20. Philip and two other witnesses—both of them adults—put his departure at around 7:00. Philip asked Beatrice Geiger for the time; she did not have a watch so she asked Sgt. William McCafferty, who was fishing with his young daughter. In his statement to the police, the sergeant said, "It was around 7:00 p.m. It may have been five or ten minutes either way." Geiger remembered it at about five to seven.

Philip dove into the water, swam to the other side of the river, got dressed and headed home. A departure around 7:00 p.m. coincides with his confirmed arrival time home at 7:30, for a walk that would have taken him twenty-eight to thirty minutes.

There was evidence to suggest that Richard only *arrived* at the bridge at about the time, or even *after*, Philip headed for home. Gord Logan told the police he got down to the river around 7:00 p.m., thanks to a ride from Richard. Robb Harrington confirmed that story: "Gordie Logan and Richard Gellatly came along from fishing," he said. "Before they came, Philip Burns swam over to the south bank, put on his running shoes and left." Richard said he stayed at the bridge "about half an hour" after he arrived.

"What time did you leave the bridge, Richard?" prosecutor Glenn Hays asked at the trial.

"About 7:20," the boy insisted. That coincided with his testimony that he passed Steve and Lynne on his way home around 7:25 p.m. Beatrice Geiger also told the court she thought Richard left "ten to fifteen minutes after seven."

Only one person—Donna Dunkin—was definitive about a simultaneous departure for Richard and Philip. Hardly a solid enough hook on which to pin a hanging sentence. Dunkin never retracted her statement, but after the trial she did express regrets about the way the prosecution used her entire testimony. "She told me she felt partially responsible for sending an innocent person to jail," her son Alan says. "She went to her grave thinking that she helped convict an innocent child."

There is no escaping it. Even accepting the dubious police estimates of walking and bicycling speeds, the prosecution's case for a timing that makes Steve guilty is mathematically shaky at best. If you jettison the OPP's fanciful account of Philip's walk home, it teeters on the precipice of impossibility. If you remove the questionable premise that Philip and Richard left the bridge at the same time, the entire prosecution timing collapses.

## 26

## THE MISSING WITNESS

D id Steven Truscott get a fair trial?

By today's standards, absolutely not. Rules of evidence today oblige the Crown and the police to disclose all the relevant information they turn up in the course of their investigations. This information includes potential leads and suspects discarded or never pursued, which can be vital for the defence counsel.

But in 1959, the authorities were under no such legal obligation to be as forthcoming with Steve's defence team. "There was no disclosure. None. Absolutely none," Dan Murphy explains. "They didn't give you anything. If police found something they didn't want to disclose, you would never find out about it."

That put Donnelly at a tremendous disadvantage, since the military authorities, the police and the prosecution kept from him numerous clues or statements that could have swayed the jurors. Some of that information was so fundamental to the jury's reading of the case that the Crown may well have violated their own ethical and legal guidelines—even as they existed in 1959.

——————

For starters, Frank Donnelly did not have critical information about Lynne's state of mind on the night she disappeared. It was a central tenet of Steven's defence that Lynne hitchhiked from the highway; it was a central principle of the Crown's case that Lynne was not the kind of girl who would do that. Donnelly did not have access to three separate OPP and military police reports that proved beyond a doubt that her parents' first fears on the night she disappeared were indeed that Lynne had hitched a ride to her grandmother's house in Port Stanley, Ontario.

Donnelly also did not know that Lynne's neighbour Betty McDougall told the police the girl was "in a sort of pouty mood" or that Brownie leader Anne Nickerson said that Lynne told her she did not want to go home because "her mother was cross with her." Had the jury heard these witness statements to the police, perhaps they would have come to a different conclusion about the credibility of Steven's story about the girl asking for a ride to the highway.

The defence was also impaired by what it didn't know about key witnesses for the prosecution. Jocelyne Gaudet, for example, told various—and at times conflicting—stories in court, but Donnelly did not have Graham's notes that show she first told police "she was looking for Lynne," not Steven. He did not have Jocelyne's first police statement in which she makes no mention of Steve's visit to her house. He did not have Bob Lawson's statement from June 25 that, contrary to what Jocelyne had told police and the courts, she told the farmer she went to the bush first, before visiting his barn.

The prosecution was adamant that Steve left the school shortly after 7:00 p.m., but held back statements from two young boys playing baseball who supported Steve's claim of a departure closer to 7:25. David Faubert, eight years old, told the police it was "between 7:15 and 7:30" when he saw Lynne and Steve leave. Darrell Wadsworth, nine, put it at "about 7:25 p.m." The Crown also withheld a declaration by Sandra Pleasance, who spotted Steven returning to the school from a bedroom window in her house between a quarter to eight and eight.

All these accounts would have helped Steve by narrowing his time away from the school—but Donnelly and the jurors never got to hear them.


If Steven didn't kill Lynne, who did? The jurors must have pondered this question, since the police or the prosecution never suggested any other legitimate suspect. They didn't know that on the same day Lynne disappeared, senior military medical officers met to discuss the deteriorating mental state of Sgt. Alexander Kalichuk, the alcoholic who had a history of "indecent acts" going back to 1950. They did not know Kalichuk had tried to molest a girl only nineteen days before Lynne went for a bicycle ride with Steven.

The 1959 Chevrolet that Steven said he saw stop for Lynne at the highway was central to his claim of innocence. Much of the trial testimony was taken up with a debate over what he could or could not have seen from the bridge. But what the jurors did not know was that there were at least three sightings of '59 Chevs that same evening in the Clinton area, including the car filled with young men who tried to pick up Arlene Strauman near the base just thirty minutes before Steven said Lynne got into a similar car.

Finally, three air force searchers told the police they spotted tire skid marks in the laneway leading to the bush on the afternoon they discovered Lynne's body. George Edens made a passing reference to the marks in his court testimony. But his sworn statement to the police—which Donnelly never saw—was much more detailed. "I had observed the tire marks on the crest of the approach to the road when I was coming out of the bush," he told the OPP. "They appeared to have been made by spinning wheels and weren't very fresh. They appeared to have been made when the ground was dry."

Lieutenant Joseph Leger told police he saw the same thing—a foot-long mark, eight feet from the pavement. "I saw another mark which appeared to have been made by a car spinning . . . more recent than the baked-in [bicycle tire] marks" he had seen farther down the laneway. "As I stepped up on the pavement, I noticed the tire tracks," added a third airman, Cpl. Harold Pudden. "They were quite deep and wide, and looked to me as if someone got their front wheels up on the pavement and gunned it and the rear tires had spun and dug in."

There can be no doubt that the Crown prosecutor knew about these marks and kept the information out of the courtroom. Police notes dated August 12—one month before trial—reveal that at a meeting in Hays' office they specifically discussed the car tracks. The minutes show that Sergeant Anderson, senior OPP officer in Goderich, and Constable Hobbs "saw spin marks."

Hays incessantly reminded the jurors of the bicycle tire marks that even several of the police officers dismissed as old and irrelevant. Why was the jury not told that three air force men and two police officers saw fresh car tracks?

Also unknown to the jury was that Steve may not have been the only person to see a girl hitchhiking by the highway on Tuesday, June 9. Out for a drive along the county road, an elderly couple identified in the police files as Mr. and Mrs. Fletcher Townsend made their way across the bridge and stopped at the intersection where Steve says he left Lynne. "Mrs. Townsend claimed she saw a girl standing by the stop sign," a police report says. "She commented to her husband that it was pretty late for a kid of that age to be hitchhiking."

Here was potentially vital corroboration of Steve's story, but the police did not share this information. Constable Trumbley interviewed the Townsends on Thursday morning, June 11, before Lynne's body was found. His notes or any statements from the Townsends are not available in the police archives. All that exists is a two-page memo written by Harold Graham seven years after the fact.

Graham claimed that Mr. Townsend, upon reflection, thought he and his wife were on the road on Sunday, June 7, not Tuesday, June 9. Graham dismissed the Townsends as simply "an aged couple who were trying to be helpful" in the investigation. "No further investigation was made."

Would the jury have changed its verdict if they had known about other potential suspects? Or if they had known about the other people who spotted 1959 Chevrolets or those who saw a young girl hitchhiking? What if the jury had known from Lynne's friends that she had a history of hitchhiking?

We will never know. We will never know how the jurors deliberated, or what evidence they debated as each juror struggled with his conscience and his vote. But we can be certain there was at least one key issue that troubled the jurors. Before they sent a fourteen-year-old to the gallows, the twelve men came back with only one question for the judge: clarification of the evidence "of Lynne Harper and Steven Truscott being seen together on the bridge on the night of June the 9th."

Two boys at the river—Gord Logan and Dougie Oates—provided the strongest corroboration of Steve's story. Clearly, the jurors understood their stories were central to Steven's innocence or guilt. Dougie's story was the most important because he claimed he was close to Steve and Lynne when they crossed the bridge around 7:30 p.m. Police notes in Graham's handwriting, not revealed at trial, show that in his first interview with the OPP, Dougie told them he saw Butch George at the bridge. If true, Dougie could only have seen him close to 7:30 when Butch arrived at the river. While Hays spent most of his cross-examination of Dougie battling to convince jurors that the boy was lying or just plain wrong about being at the bridge after 7:00, sitting next to him at the prosecution table was the police inspector whose own notes indicated the boy was at the bridge well after 7:00 p.m.

Hays held an even darker secret. What the jurors also did not know was that there was a witness who could verify Dougie's claim he was at the bridge after 7:00 p.m., when Steve and Lynne were biking down the county road. Everyone in the courtroom knew that Dougie Oates was not alone in his quest for turtles down by the river. He had mentioned a companion, nine-year-old Karen Daum. But only the Crown knew how important she was in verifying his story.

"We didn't hear anything from Miss Karen Daum, as to what she would have said," Crown prosecutor Glenn Hays said obliquely while talking about Dougie in his summation, as if to seal the boy's reputation as a "little liar." It was perhaps the most devious statement at the trial. At the very least, Hays' implication was that Karen Daum's story was unknown. At worst, Hays was suggesting that there was something nefarious about it all—that the testimony from Karen that they "didn't hear" perhaps contradicted Dougie's claim that he was on the bridge well past 7:00.

But the truth was that Glenn Hays was the only person in the courtroom—aside from the police—who knew exactly what Karen had to say. And he knew it was damaging to his case. Her story would remain hidden from public view for four decades.

Who was this mystery girl and why was she never called as a witness?

Her blonde hair came down just to her shoulders, and her bangs were short enough to give a full view of her dark brown eyes. Her school picture shows her biting down on her bottom lip with an impish grin. In the photo she wears a pretty, polka-dot dress. But Karen Daum wanted to get rid of that dress just as soon as the photographer's flash went off. Pedal-pushers and a simple shirt were more her style—Karen was a tomboy, and she could swing a bat or ride a bike as well as any of the boys.

"My brother Rodney was eleven. I hung around with him a lot, so his friends were my friends, and to stay in their gang, you wanted to do the same things they did," Karen explains. One of those things was catching turtles. Dougie Oates was good friends with Karen's brother Rodney; Dougie had called at the Daums' house on the evening of June 9, but Rodney was not home. Rodney had already left for the river with his sidekick sister. So it was only natural that when Doug went turtle hunting around the bridge that evening, he would find himself next to the cute blonde girl on a hand-me-down boy's bike.

"I knew I had to be home at 7:00. I had a very strict father and I was really worried about getting home. I was scared I'd get a licking," says Karen. Absorbed in their hunt, Karen lost track of time. When she finally turned to Dougie to ask him what time it was, he told her. "I can't remember what he said," Karen says today, "whether he said 7:15 and I started thinking I wouldn't get home until 7:30, or whether he said 7:25 or 7:30. But in either case, I was late!"

Karen hopped on her bike to make the dash home up the county road back to the air force station. She remembers being slightly ahead of Dougie as they left for home. Dougie's recollection of events differs slightly from Karen's on this point; it was the only discrepancy in the two accounts the eleven-year-old boy and nine-year-old girl independently told police. He told police Karen was under the bridge looking for turtles in the river when he saw Steve and Lynne go by him and that she was still *behind* him when he left the bridge.

Both children may have been partially correct, as Karen told police she *was* originally behind Dougie. "Doug and I left the bridge together, he was riding first and I was behind him on my bike," her statement says, "but he got his pant leg caught and had to stop, so I caught up to him and got ahead."

It was what she told the police next that was the bombshell. "Me and Dougie were coming up the river and going to go home, and I saw Lynne riding on the bar of the Truscott boy's bike," her statement continues. "We were going home and they were coming toward the river."

Karen was close enough to the older bike riders to remember their specific facial expressions and clothing. "Lynne and Steve looked happy," she said in her statement, which was taken by police on Sunday, June 14, the day after they jailed Steven. "Lynne was wearing a white blouse and blue shorts."

Karen was also very specific about where she saw Steve and Lynne. "Karen taken by Constable Trumbley to point out spot on road where she and Doug met Steve and Lynne." Then added in parentheses is this last line: "Point of meeting was just about railway tracks."

Karen remembers OPP Constable Trumbley taking her in his police cruiser along the county road and asking her to point out exactly where she saw Steve and Lynne.

"Are you sure this is where you saw him?" Constable Trumbley asked, according to Karen's recollection.

"Yes," she replied.

"I thought you said you saw them up here," the police officer said as they drove to a point closer to the school.

"No, I didn't say that, I said I saw him there," Karen insisted.

At least two times over the next few days, Karen says, Trumbley took her back to the road to repeat his questioning, to the point where Karen burst into tears. "I felt intimidated because I couldn't figure out if there was something I wasn't saying right or if they weren't understanding what I was saying," she recalls.

OPP Inspector Harold Graham's signature as a witness appears on the bottom of Karen's statement, signed on Friday, June 19. A week after he had jailed Steven Truscott, he had to know her account was extremely damaging to the prosecution's case. The railway tracks were about fifteen hundred feet north of the bush and just five hundred feet from the bridge. The Crown now had a third witness—besides Dougie and Gord Logan—who saw Steve and Lynne beyond the bush. Here was a third witness whose testimony meant Steve could not have been the murderer.

So why did no one in a courtroom ever hear Karen's story?

"I didn't testify because I was too young. I heard that from my father," Karen recounts. Her parents may have given her that explanation, but clearly the decision was not theirs to make—the prosecution decided who would be called to testify. Hays had no difficulty bringing a ten-year-old girl, Sandra Archibald, into the courtroom to testify about finding Lynne's locket. Other young children were allowed to testify before the jury at the trial, even if they were not sworn.

An inescapable and deeply troubling conclusion can be drawn: the prosecution consciously kept Karen Daum's statement from Steven Truscott and his lawyer. Hays was able to keep Karen's story secret because Steven did not recall meeting her on the road that night. He never mentioned seeing Karen to police or to his lawyers; as far as the defence team was concerned, Karen Daum barely existed. If the Crown made sure they stayed ignorant, it engaged in a deliberate suppression of evidence that was vital to proving Steven

Truscott's innocence. The only other more charitable explanations would be either that Karen's statement was somehow "forgotten" about or that for some reason, it was considered not reliable or not relevant to the case. Either way, the prosecution effectively sabotaged a key element in Steve's defence—that other children had seen him and Lynne near the river.

Today, Karen Daum is a self-assured, successful civil servant and is upset that she was never called to the stand to tell her story. Forty years later, she still vividly remembers her encounter with Steve and Lynne.

"They were having fun, giggling and laughing and smiling. Lynne was turning around, looking at him and talking," she recalls.

Suddenly, Steve veered toward the middle of the road to have some fun by scaring the little nine-year-old. Karen panicked and fell off her bike into the ditch on the side of the road. "They were kind of laughing about it, but all I could think of was, 'Now I am really in big trouble. I am going to be even later!'" Karen turned in anger to her two tormenters, but Steve and Lynne kept bicycling and never looked back. Karen got back on her bike and ped-alled home.

Karen's modern-day account differs from her 1959 statement in one sig-nificant way. As she recalls events today, she crossed Steve and Lynne not at the railway tracks but closer to the school, somewhere along Lawson's bush. Karen thinks by identifying the railway tracks in her 1959 statement as "the point of meeting," the police confused the spot where she caught up with Dougie and the point where she met Steve and Lynne.

If true, her revised story does not completely exonerate Steve, since she was south of the laneway that led into the bush when she met up with Steve and Lynne heading north. Conceivably, Steve could have turned off the road and taken Lynne into the bush right after he bicycled past Karen.

But Karen's modern version still helps the defence in another way. The prosecution and the defence agreed that Steven and Lynne were on the road sometime after 7:10 p.m. That meant one thing was certain: if Steve and Lynne passed Karen, Karen had to be on the road after 7:00 p.m. And that meant without a doubt the turtle-hunting companion she left back at the bridge—Dougie Oates—was most definitely still by the river, in a perfect position to see Steve and Lynne. Thus the prosecution was wrong and Dougie was right: he was on the bridge well past 7:00.

Karen's original police statement in 1959 about seeing Steve and Lynne by the railway tracks was one more eyewitness account that proved Steven was innocent. Her modern-day version of seeing Steven and Lynne south of the laneway was not completely exculpatory, but it still gave strong support to Steve's most important defence: Dougie Oates's claim of seeing him cross the bridge with Lynne. It was not her age but her story—so damaging to the prosecution—that kept Karen from the courtroom.

Did Glenn Hays break the law by withholding Karen's statement from the court?

Arguably, if Hays willingly hid Karen's story—as well as crucial information about other witnesses and evidence—he bent his ethical guidelines to the breaking point. The Law Society of Upper Canada only formalized its code of ethics in 1965, but the written guidelines were based on principles well known to lawyers in the years before that. "When engaged as a prosecutor, the lawyer's prime duty is not to seek to convict but to see that justice is done through a fair trial on the merits," the Rules of Professional Conduct state. "The prosecutor . . . should make timely disclosure to defence counsel . . . all relevant and known facts and witnesses, whether tending to show guilt or innocence." Karen's statement, and much of the other police reports and notes kept from Donnelly, certainly fall in that category.

Ethics are one thing. What about the law? The disclosure rules at the time meant that the police and prosecution were under no legal obligation to automatically divulge Karen's story to the defence, as they would have to today. But there were significant and well-known Supreme Court rulings in the 1950s that strongly suggest Hays was wrong in what he did.

In *Lemay v. The King* (1951), the court ruled the Crown need not call witnesses who assist the defence but "must not hold back evidence because it would assist an accused." Three years later, in *Boucher v. The Queen* (1954), the court argued there was an obligation on the Crown to "bring before the Court the material witnesses." Justice Ivan Rand—in language still quoted to this day—said that the Crown's role excludes "any notion of winning or losing" and that prosecutors "have a duty to see that all available legal proof of the facts is presented."

"All available legal proof." By that standard—one that existed well before 1959—Steven Truscott did not get a fair trial.

## 27

## DOCTORING THE MEDICAL EVIDENCE

It was bad enough the prosecution suppressed evidence and testimony vital to Steven's defence. But even some of the most crucial evidence the jurors did get to hear was tainted by half-truths and distortions.

"It is awfully important when this girl died," Crown prosecutor Glenn Hays told the jurors. "You can take with safety that this girl was killed from 7:00 p.m. to 7:45 p.m. on Tuesday, June 9." It was the single most important piece of evidence—the "vise," as Hays had called it that tightened on Steven and no one else. Hays took pains to remind the jurors of the "careful study" Penistan made of the stomach contents—a study, the pathologist indicated, he made only once: during the autopsy he and Brooks completed on Thursday evening, June 11. "The doctors told me that they were of the opinion that death occurred not more than two hours after Lynne Harper had last eaten," Graham claimed in a 1966 report.

The next day, on Friday June 12, the experts at the provincial laboratory confirmed that the food was in Lynne's stomach for "not more than two hours." Graham promptly had Steve picked up and arrested.

In that scenario, Penistan took the initiative, and his insightful findings on Thursday night were backed up by other experts on Friday. Medical science leads, the police follow. Hays surrounded his case with an aura of scientific objectivity.

The story sounded plausible and the jury believed it. But there is strong evidence to suggest that Penistan doctored his evidence on both the time of death and the contents of the stomach to help the police and the prosecution. In other words, he made the time fit the crime.

There is plenty of room for doubt about when Penistan made his exact determination on time of death and what he based it upon. That doubt comes from documents never seen by the defence or the jury.

Contrary to the official version given in court, there is every reason to believe that Penistan gave, at the most, a vague approximation of the time of death on Thursday night, June 11. At the key moments, there were four people in the small autopsy room at the Ball and Mutch funeral home in Clinton that evening: Penistan, Brooks, Graham and Sayeau. Brooks took notes at Penistan's dictation. Those notes have never been produced.

Sayeau's notebook from the evening, however, is available. He carefully logged every minute he received evidence from the doctors: 8:40 p.m., hair from scalp; 8:58 p.m., jar containing contents of stomach; 9:27 p.m., fingernail scrapings. Sometime between 8:58 and 9:27, Sayeau also entered into his notebook the following information: "Ate supper at 5:30 p.m., June 9th— consumed turkey meat, potatoes, peas, raw tomatoes, pickles, pineapple upside-down cake."

Presumably, Sayeau learned this information either by phoning the Harpers or from previous inquiries; he almost certainly communicated these facts to the doctors. That meant that Penistan knew *what* Lynne ate for her last meal and *when* she ate it. If he was so sure that night that Lynne died "not more than two hours" after eating, as Graham claimed, he would have given the police a firm time of 7:45 p.m. as he was completing his autopsy.

But Sayeau's logs show no such conclusion. Between 9:00 and 9:30 p.m., as Penistan was wrapping up his autopsy, Sayeau made the following inscription, which could only have come from the doctors: "Cause of death— Strangulation. Evidence of rape."

Nowhere in the pages from Sayeau's notebook that evening does any reference to a time of death appear. It is inconceivable that the OPP officer in charge of gathering exhibits in a murder investigation would fail to note such a crucial lead if the doctors did provide it. "I don't know if he said anything about that" is all Sayeau is willing to say today about Penistan's estimate of a time of death during the autopsy. "It wasn't directed to me to write down."

In a private document Penistan wrote several years later about the events that Thursday evening, he recounted that he told the police the food was "presumably recently ingested." He also gave the police what he called another "tentative observation." He told them "the food might well have been consumed at a later meal" than the supper Lynne had at home. In other words, the doctor was speculating to the police that Lynne might have eaten something *after* Steve had dropped her off at the highway around 7:30 p.m. Penistan stated that "following this observation" the police went to check local restaurants.

A log entry by one of the OPP corporals on duty that day, Donald Weston—the same corporal who first went to the Harper residence the night she disappeared—states that he "questioned restaurant personnel in [the] Clinton and Seaforth area." Inspector Graham himself confirmed in a 1966 report that "officers from the Goderich Detachment canvassed eating places in the district and exhibited a picture of Lynne Harper, with the view of determining her movements and the identity of her companion."

Clearly, if the pathologist had told Graham on Thursday evening he was certain Lynne had died before 7:45 p.m., the OPP would not have wasted their time canvassing restaurants that a dead girl could never have visited. If the OPP were checking restaurants on Thursday night, they must have believed—*even after the original autopsy was concluded*—that Lynne could have been alive past 8:00 p.m.

If Penistan did give the police a specific time of death beyond his vague estimate of a "recently ingested" meal, there is eyewitness and documentary evidence that his first guess was not 7:45, as the police and prosecution later claimed, but in fact 9:00 p.m. Dr. Brooks, the medical officer assisting Penistan in the autopsy, now says, in a surprisingly frank admission, that the doctors originally gave the police a much wider margin for the time of death: "Certainly it isn't falsely reported . . . that it could be stretched as far as nine o'clock and that that was the time we were thinking of."

The strongest documentary proof that Penistan gave a later time of death is Graham's General Information Broadcast (GIB) issued Thursday evening. It stated explicitly that Lynne's murder was "believed to have taken place about 9:00 p.m." The authorities were sure enough about that first presumed time of death that they broadcast it across the province. "Doctors set the time of her death about 9:00 p.m. Tuesday," the *London Free Press* reported on Friday morning.

There is every indication that Graham wrote the GIB mentioning the 9:00 p.m. time of death sometime after the autopsy was completed.

The GIB referred to the fact that Lynne was raped and that her killer probably had scratches on his face and neck—information presumably garnered from the autopsy. The bulletin also twice describes the car as white. Steve never mentioned that colour. But Vaughn Marshall, the airman Graham and Sayeau interviewed around 10:00 p.m. that Thursday night, said the '59 Chevrolet he saw on the highway near Clinton was white. Graham's bulletin about the car also refers to "witnesses" in the plural, not just the single witness they had in Steve.

By Graham's own account he arrived in Clinton at 7:45 p.m. and by 8:00 he was observing the autopsy. In the intervening fifteen minutes, he conferred with three officers and then travelled to the funeral home. It was hardly likely that he had time to scribble out the bulletin before the autopsy—and if he did, did he simply make up the 9:00 p.m. time of death?

The sun went down at 9:08 p.m. on Tuesday, so perhaps the police assumed Lynne was killed when it was dark, when the county road was quiet and after people had abandoned the river area near the bush. Still, it is hard to imagine the OPP would rely on something as flimsy as guesswork to fix the time of death in their first bulletin on a sensational murder. It is much more logical to assume that Graham chose the 9:00 p.m. time of death for his province-wide bulletin after consulting with Penistan during the autopsy on Thursday night.

More evidence that this was the case comes from the police and medical logs of what happened the next day, Friday, June 12. To get a better analysis of what Lynne ate before she died, Graham sent Sayeau to the attorney general's laboratory in Toronto with the jar of her stomach contents. A handwritten note from the biologist at the laboratory who received the jar contains this telling remark: "Found: 1:50 p.m. Thurs. June 11th Time Death—Path—maybe 40 hours." "Found" was a reference to when Lynne's body was discovered. "Path" was short for "pathologist," John Penistan. If the police were telling the laboratory experts that Penistan's guess for the time of death was forty hours before the body was found, that would put the time of death at sometime between 9:00 and 10:00 p.m.

The laboratory experts that afternoon told the police "that death had occurred not more than two hours after the girl had last eaten," Graham wrote in a 1966 draft report on the case. "This, of course, *for the first time,* placed Steven Truscott as a suspect."

For the first time? That would have to mean that Penistan and Brooks did *not* give Graham a time of death that pointed to Steven on Thursday evening. Perhaps realizing the problem with what he had written, Graham crossed out that last typed sentence and handwrote a new line saying that the laboratory's time "was consistent" with the time Penistan gave at the autopsy.

Therefore, contrary to what Hays indicated in court and what Graham has stated publicly ever since, all indications are that Penistan did *not* decide Lynne died by 7:45 p.m. when he completed his autopsy on Thursday night. When did he come to that conclusion?

Whenever it was, it was apparently not when Steven was picked up on the next day or when he was jailed. And not when he appeared in juvenile court on June 13 or by the time he appeared in court again several more times over the next two weeks. Even though a boy had been arrested, charged and sent to adult court for a hanging offence, there is no record of a single piece of paper from Penistan or a report from a police officer that contains any reference to the 7:15 to 7:45 time of death. In a detailed, six-page report Graham filed to his superiors on June 19, 1959—eight days after Penistan's supposedly pivotal autopsy, Graham says he has not received Penistan's report. The only reference to a time of death is a mention of a pending analysis of stomach contents by the attorney general's laboratory.

On June 30, a judge ordered Steven's preliminary hearing to begin by mid-July. At this point there is still no document available from the police files that fixes the time of death between 7:15 and 7:45 p.m. But the prosecution knew they had to convince a judge at the preliminary hearing to send the case against Steven to a full trial.

Finally, on July 6—almost a month after Steven had been arrested—the time of death so incriminating against Steven appears on the record for the first time. Graham on that date wrote his second report to his superiors and to Hays. "No evidence has yet been submitted to any court," he wrote, pointing out that the preliminary was days away. "The evidence of Dr. Penistan, who performed the autopsy, is most important in respect to time of death." If it was "most important," one wonders why it was never mentioned in any of Graham's reports or his notes until that moment.

Graham reported Penistan based his time of death on the state of decomposition of the body, the extent of rigor mortis and the stomach contents—particularly the large quantity of only partly digested food. Graham appeared to cite a note or report he must have received from Penistan, although he did not identify the source: "I find it difficult to believe that this food could have been in the stomach for as long as two hours unless some complicating factor was present, of which I have no information," Graham quoted the doctor. "If the last meal was finished at 5:45 p.m., I would therefore conclude that death occurred prior to 7:45 p.m. The finding would be compatible with death as early as 7:15 p.m."

One has to question how—a month after his autopsy—Penistan came up with the magic window so convenient for the police's case against Steven Truscott. Penistan never claimed he did any extensive study on the stomach contents after his June 11 autopsy. On that Thursday night, according to the documentary evidence, Penistan gave the police either no time of death, or perhaps suggested Lynne died around 9:00 p.m. One wonders in the intervening month between the autopsy and the preliminary hearing, what could have changed the doctor's mind to the point where he could select 7:15 to 7:45 as the absolute parameters for Lynne's death.

Penistan could cite medical texts to show that some experts believed the digestive process was usually well underway and the stomach starting to empty in about two hours—in Lynne's case, around 7:45 p.m. But that was a general principle only, not a hard and fast rule—the textbooks did not say all stomachs digest food in exactly 120 minutes. Penistan, to be safe, could have suggested 7:55 or 8:00 or 8:05—except that the police knew Steven was back at the school by then.

Penistan's selection of 7:15 p.m. as the earliest time for Lynne's death was even more capricious. There was little in the medical literature to suggest the stomach starts to empty at precisely ninety minutes after the last meal. Why not choose 7:12 or 7:05 or 6:58? The police, of course, knew that Lynne was alive and at the school until at least 7:10. It is interesting that in court Penistan initially suggested a time of death as early as 7:00, but in his final autopsy report he found it prudent to specify 7:15 as the earliest possible starting time.

It is simply impossible not to suspect that someone gave Penistan these crucial pieces of outside information about Lynne and Steve's whereabouts between 7:15 and 7:45 to influence his determination of the time of death.

The scenario gains credence because of one fatal flaw in the doctor's official autopsy report: it has no time or date. Penistan did not write his official report on the death of Lynne Harper that same night or even in the days, weeks or months to come.

When stuck during cross-examination at trial, Penistan referred to handwritten notes, not to an autopsy report. The Crown never filed his autopsy report as a court exhibit. No witness ever makes reference to seeing, reading or writing such a report. Penistan was still polishing his autopsy report even *after* the trial was over—he admitted later he revised the section that referred to "no obvious meat" in the stomach contents because "the wording was felt to be potentially misleading."

No one knows when Penistan finally got around to writing up his official autopsy report, but it could have been years later. Indeed a formal, typed report did not make it to the office of the chief coroner for Ontario until late in 1963—four years after Lynne was murdered. (Until 1965, provincial pathologists were not required to send a copy of their reports to the supervising coroner.) Even then, Penistan's "Report of the Post-Mortem Examination" bore his signature, but no time or date.

A journalist who saw that report in 1963 said the copy she saw then still made no mention of a time of death between 7:15 and 7:45 p.m. Finally, when Penistan's autopsy report was entered into evidence in the Supreme Court of Canada in 1966, it contained an asterisk on the front page referring to a section added on to the report entitled "Note on time of death."

That passage matched word for word—down to the commas—the "observations" of Dr. Penistan that Harold Graham quoted in his memo of July 6, 1959.

Since Penistan's final autopsy report was undated and not filed until years later, no one could be sure what and when he told police and the prosecution about Lynne's time of death. No one could be sure Penistan did not bend his times to suit a police agenda.

The autopsy report is supposed to be the official account of what an unbiased pathologist concludes about a corpse. The report is a medical snapshot of a crime, and as such it must be preserved and protected in its original state. A pathologist might amend an autopsy's findings for scientific reasons: for example, upon learning a crime victim had a certain illness or that a murderer used a certain poison, the pathologist might return to the body and carry out more tests.

But overall, the autopsy must be seen never to have been tampered with or altered in any way by subsequent events or pressures from the police, prosecution or any other outside forces. Police call this the "chain of evidence." A clue found at the crime scene must be carefully dated, labelled and tracked as it gets handed from one officer or doctor or lawyer to another. Unless that happens, testimony about that clue can be hopelessly compromised.

Penistan, by his own admission, was willing to revise his autopsy report because of misleading wording about stomach contents. It would not be a big step to make an addition about time of death.

Penistan is dead and cannot account for his actions—although several years after the trial he would make a stunning reversal in his findings. His colleague during the autopsy, the chief air force medical officer David Brooks, has only a vague memory of what went on that evening.

"I cannot remember the exact moment or the wording in which [Penistan] conveyed the idea of his findings" on the time of death, he says today. "I don't know whether Penistan felt pressure . . . to provide a medical opinion which would be of assistance." But Brooks frankly admits the doctors were under the gun. "I wouldn't say I felt seduced by the police force, but on the other hand, I think there was some seduction in our anxiety to get this over and done with as soon as possible. There was a certain amount of pressure . . . in the absence of knowing about anyone else who might be responsible [for Lynne's murder]."

If Hays and Penistan misled the jury into thinking the doctor came up with his exact 7:15 to 7:45 time of death by himself during the autopsy, the prosecution also bent the truth when it suggested the attorney general's laboratory fully backed that narrow time of death. Nobody from the laboratory testified at the trial, but Crown prosecutor Glenn Hays assured the jurors that the experts there endorsed Penistan's findings. He explained he did not bring the centre's biologist, John Funk, to the stand only because he had already filled his quota of five experts.

"I did not call Mr. Funk, but I made him available to the defence," Hays said in his summation. "You haven't heard from Mr. Funk. I only leave it to you to draw your reasonable inference." The inference was clearly that Frank Donnelly did not call upon Funk because the laboratory supported the prosecution's case on time of death.

Inspector Harold Graham also convinced the judge of the same thing. In a voir dire session held out of earshot of the jurors, Graham testified that it was not until he heard Jocelyne's story about her date with Steve and when he received the laboratory report that Steve "became a strong suspect."

"Friday afternoon, you had the report from the laboratory?" Ferguson asked.

"Yes sir," the OPP officer replied.

"I think I can properly infer whatever was in the laboratory report clinched the matter," Ferguson concluded later in the voir dire.

What exactly was in the report that "clinched" Steven's guilt?

John Funk himself would admit later he made only a "cursory examination" of the stomach contents that Friday afternoon. For a more extensive analysis, Funk brought the stomach contents to Dr. Noble Sharpe, the medical director of the centre. "He told me a young girl had been found after being absent from her home about forty-eight hours. That was all he told me," Sharpe recalled in a memorandum written in 1966. "At the time I had not heard the name Truscott, nor had I heard Dr. Penistan's estimate of the time of death."

Sharpe, an experienced and cautious pathologist, immediately told Funk he had "no wish to be involved in court on stomach contents alone." Sharpe was all too aware of what he called the "many variables" that influence digestion. His reluctance to rely too heavily on stomach contents in a murder case was significant. "I suggested to John Funk that the investigating officers should be advised to start focusing one hour after the last known meal to be on the safe side and not overlook anything," he wrote. Had the police spoken to Sharpe directly, the director said, he would have warned them "stomach contents may carry more weight in court than they are entitled to."

"The time I stated was a rough guide only," the medical director cautioned. "Had I been in court I think I would have said, 'I believe digestion stopped between one and two hours after the meal,' but I think I would have added, 'It might have been later.'" Words of caution, of course, that Penistan never used.

Sharpe made an oral report to Funk, who in turn spoke to OPP Corporal Sayeau. If Funk transmitted the medical director's hesitations to the police, the OPP did not absorb them. A handwritten note Funk wrote that day shows at one point he was only guessing at the stomach contents and the time of death:

Meat—ham?
Vegetable—tomato?
Pea?
Fruit—pineapple?

Funk would add cucumbers and potatoes by the time he finished his analysis later that summer and he would drop any mention of tomatoes. The thick, stewy nature of the contents, Funk wrote, "suggests an early state of digestion." Perhaps the biologist firmed up his opinions as the afternoon wore on. Somehow, by the time Sayeau wrote down in his notebook what Funk told him, the question marks were gone and the time was more definite:

Meat (either turkey or ham)
Tomatoes
Celery
Pineapple
Peas
"Early stage of digestion—food gulped. Death
within two hours of eating these foods."

The "two hours" appeared in Sayeau's notes but not in anything written by Funk. Sayeau telephoned the information to the Goderich OPP office. When Graham got the message, his notes show the inspector, in his mind, had enough to pick up Steven as his chief suspect: "Lab: . . . Died within two hours after eating."

If Funk did tell the police Lynne died "within two hours," he was being more precise on that Friday afternoon than he ever would be again in his life. One month later, at the preliminary inquiry in mid-July, Funk refused to give a time of death, even though by this time he had had four weeks to do a microscopic study of the stomach contents and not just a couple of hours. Funk insisted he did not "feel qualified." It is hard to imagine how Funk could have felt more qualified on June 12, when he had only completed what he described as a cursory examination.

Today, Hank Sayeau concedes that when Funk talked to him that Friday afternoon, the biologist may have said that he was not qualified to state a time of death in court. "Those guys, they didn't go beyond their boundaries," Sayeau says.

It was not the laboratory experts but the police—and later Penistan—who created an impenetrable barrier of time by suggesting Lynne died at 7:45 p.m. and not a minute later. "John Funk and Dr. Sharpe . . . had given the opinion that death had occurred not more than two hours after the girl had last eaten," Graham proclaimed in a March 30, 1966, report to the OPP.

But the words "not more" never appear in any notes available from Funk or Sharpe. If the Crown was so confident about the findings of the laboratory report, why was it never released? Graham had testified he received by telephone the news from the laboratory that led to Steven's arrest. It should not have been difficult to produce a written report to back up a scribbled phone message.

Funk completed his report on August 31. Graham would later claim that the Crown "provided laboratory reports to Mr. Donnelly promptly." In fact, the only record available in the files shows that on September 2, Hays wrote a letter summarizing the stomach contents found by Funk, but Hays did not include an official copy of the report.

Hays also never entered the crucial laboratory report into evidence. And for good reason. Funk's report was only one page long. It listed in detail what was inside Lynne's stomach. But—unknown to the jurors or the defence—it said not a word about time of death.

The implications are staggering. Imagine if Graham had claimed, on the basis of a phone call, that he learned the lab had confirmed a suspect's knife was the murder weapon, but then was unable to produce a written lab report to back up that claim. He would be laughed out of court. Yet that is exactly what the prosecution was allowed to get away with in the case of a much talked about but never seen lab report supposedly confirming time of death.

Even when Funk and Sharpe testified at the Supreme Court in 1966, neither said they told the police Lynne was killed before 7:45 and no later. Neither of them would endorse Penistan's narrow, thirty-minute window for the time of death.

But the Crown apparently convinced the jurors and the judge that they had.

Nothing illustrates Penistan's willingness to play the prosecution and police game more than his uncanny ability to change the contents of Lynne's stomach. You would think that if the prosecution was asking a jury to sentence a boy to hang—largely on the basis of a pathologist's con-clusion that stomach contents indicated a time of death between 7:15 and 7:45 p.m.—that the doctor would at least be certain of what those stomach contents were.

Penistan himself wrote in 1966 that on the night of the autopsy "several items [of food] were immediately and clearly recognized" but "other items were less easy to identify with certainty."

"He pointed out he couldn't say exactly what the food was," Harold Graham later admitted in a speech—words he never uttered before a jury.

What is remarkable is how Penistan's analysis of the stomach contents evolved to match closely the analysis being made at the laboratory by Funk—the only person to closely study the jar of digested food over the summer.

In his official autopsy report, Penistan noted only three vegetables in Lynne's stomach: "peas, onion, corn." The laboratory never found traces of corn and Penistan never made mention of this error again. Penistan admit-ted in court that his notes from the night of the autopsy said there was "no obvious meat."

Between the time Penistan completed his autopsy on June 11 and the time he testified at the preliminary hearing on July 13, Funk had told the police he found celery, pineapple and some kind of meat, "either turkey or ham," according to police notes. Lo and behold, at the preliminary, Penistan went from "no obvious meat" to "a little meat which I feel was probably ham."

As Funk completed his study by late August, he added potatoes and "two types of meat—probably fowl and ham." At trial in September, Penistan—who never indicated that he had re-examined the stomach since that evening of June 11—suddenly added the same ingredients to his list. Now he told jurors he found ham, white meat that was either chicken or turkey, and traces of potato.

The evidence is overwhelming that Penistan finessed not only his con-clusion about time of death, but even his analysis of the very stomach contents upon which he claimed he based that conclusion.

Thanks to the lack of disclosure laws, Hays kept all this compromising infor-mation from the eyes of Donnelly, the judge and the jurors. Time of death was crucial to Donnelly's defence of Steven and yet the defence lawyer was working blindfolded.

Donnelly did not have the all-important General Information Broadcast, which indicated the police first thought Lynne's murder was "believed to have taken place about 9:00 p.m." and not around 7:30 when Steve was with her. He did not have Sayeau's notebook, which indicated Penistan gave no precise time of death on the night of the autopsy. He did not have the notes from the laboratory the next day that indicated the police told the experts Penistan's estimate of death was forty hours before the body was found. He did not have access to Sharpe's opinions about the validity of determining time of death from stomach contents.

Medical science and justice are supposed to be about verifiable facts. Two crucial documents—Penistan's autopsy report and the provincial laboratory's report—were never presented at court. One was written after the trial and almost certainly adjusted to fit the police scenario; the other—despite the prosecution's misleading suggestions to the jury—said nothing about time of death. It was a case of bad science in the service of bad justice.

The irony is that Penistan could have given fair and balanced medical testimony without changing his opinion about stomach digestion—and without necessarily condemning Steven. But he, along with the prosecution and the police—deliberately or not—blurred the distinction between the stopping of digestion and death. In other words, Lynne's stomach could very well have stopped digesting her supper "within two hours" but she need not have died before 7:45 p.m.

The jurors never heard this important distinction from Dr. Penistan, but Dr. Noble Sharpe understood it very well. "Something stopped her digestion before it was complete and left the stomach," he said in his memorandum on the case. "It could be death *or fear* which stopped the digestion," Sharpe said. He explicitly criticized Penistan—well after the trial—for not mentioning "the variables which affect stomach contents" in his testimony.

If, as Steven claimed, Lynne got into a car around 7:30 p.m.—just about two hours after her supper—she very well may have faced a stomach-wrenching turn of events in the ensuing minutes or hours. If the driver or someone else shortly afterwards began menacing her or assaulting her, it would be only normal for the girl to suddenly stop digesting her supper. Fear could have gripped her but she could have remained alive for several hours longer.

It was a shame that Frank Donnelly focused only on Lynne's anger with her parents over swimming as a possible explanation for the interrupted state of her stomach contents, and did not seize on fear after she had left Steven's company as a good reason for jurors to have a reasonable doubt about stomach contents and the boy's guilt.

But then it was no less a shame that Donnelly did not know that Dr. Noble Sharpe had grave doubts about Penistan's willingness to pinpoint a time of death to within thirty minutes. "I criticized him for using definite times in place of saying one or two hours," Sharpe wrote. "Saying 7:15 to 7:45 sounds so absolute!"

One can only imagine the impact that the more cautionary testimony from the medical director of the attorney general's laboratory would have had on the jurors. "It is somewhat frightening to realize that any court could sentence a man to death on the basis of the testimony on the time-of-death issue," Sharpe wrote in a medical journal several years after the trial. "Medicine cannot be that precise and exact at the present time."

Yet Penistan—with the help of Hays—convinced a jury medicine can be that precise and exact. And that carefully staged and planned performance helped sentence a fourteen-year-old boy to hang for the murder of Lynne Harper.

## 28

### "BURN THE PICTURES"

**B**y October of 1959, the summer heat wave that had drawn the children of RCAF Station Clinton to the river by the bridge was a cold, distant memory. The fall wind swept away the leaves and everyone seemed eager to put the heat and the passions of the summer behind them. The jurors went home to their farms and their shops. The lawyers went back to their offices. The reporters went back to their typewriters.

Steven went back to jail.

In the *London Free Press* of October 1, the morning after Steve's trial ended, the story of his hanging sentence shared front-page billing with news that 50,000 people were expected to pack into Comiskey Park in Chicago to watch the White Sox take on the Los Angeles Dodgers. By the Night Final edition, news of Steven's death penalty was overshadowed by a banner headline announcing that the Chicago home team had won the series opener.

By the next day, the Truscott story was gone from the papers.

Steven Truscott was still on the mind of Inspector Harold Graham, who had some paperwork on the case to clean up.

"All the officers of the Goderich detachment worked long and anxious hours on . . . this case," he wrote in his formal report one week after the trial ended. "This entire case has been fraught with unusual difficulties."

Graham had one more vital duty to fulfill: endorsing an application by Flying Officer Glen Sage for part of the $10,000 reward posted for Lynne's killer—"dead or alive." Sage had not found the body; George Edens and Joseph Leger did. All Sage did was run over to the two men who were part of his twenty-five-member search team and take charge of the site. But Sage did perform one task that endeared him to the authorities—he testified about a footprint from a "crepe-soled shoe" that he spotted near the body in the bush. "Although the footprint was not positively identified as having been made by the shoe of the accused, the evidence was . . . one of the most important facts given in evidence," Graham noted in a lengthy memo. "Despite all vigorous cross-examination, the evidence of Sage was not shaken. I am sure he left a very good impression with the Court and Jury." Graham concluded that in his "respectful opinion, Flying Officer Sage should be given due consideration for a portion of the reward."

There is no record that Sage ever received the money he requested.

Justice Ferguson, meanwhile, penned a sixteen-page report to the Honourable Davie Fulton, the federal minister of justice. "The jury rejected the defence and, in my view, had good reason to do so," he said, heartily endorsing the verdict.

Remarkably, Ferguson continued to get key facts wrong. He noted that from the bridge Steven could not have discerned "the colour of a licence plate on a car, *much less the numbers* at that distance." He also stuck to his absurd theory that even if Steven crossed the bridge with Lynne "he brought her back, because nothing could be clearer than she was back, having been found dead in the bush."

Justice Ferguson made it clear he had little sympathy for the boy who sat in the prisoner's box in his courtroom for two weeks. "He sat throughout the trial without showing any signs of emotion," he wrote. "It was an awful deed—the act of a monster—and the person who performed it is capable of anything—in my opinion, quite capable of very little emotion."

Ferguson had sentenced the boy to hang, despite the jury's plea for mercy. He appeared to have no regrets or second thoughts. "I know of no reason, other than the youth of the prisoner, to recommend him for the Queen's mercy," the judge told Canada's justice minister.

———

It had not been an easy summer for Alexander Kalichuk, the air force sergeant with a taste for liquor and young girls. While Steve had spent the summer months incarcerated in the Goderich jail, Kalichuk was on the psychiatric ward of a London hospital. After several weeks of inconclusive tests and examinations, doctors released Kalichuk. It did not take long for him to return to the bottle.

On September 1, about two weeks before Steve's trial began, a social welfare officer in the air force recommended a transfer for Alexander Kalichuk from Aylmer to the Clinton base, or to the nearby Centralia installation, in order to allow the ailing airman to be closer to his family. The top brass at the Clinton base would have nothing of it. The last thing they wanted on their hands was a "sex deviate," as they described Kalichuk. They dug in their heels and effectively blocked his transfer. A memo written several weeks later spelled out their reasons. The Clinton commanders noted Kalichuk's attempt earlier that summer "to entice school girls into his automobile using female underclothing as bait." Referring to the Truscott trial, they also noted the Clinton air base was already embroiled in a "murder stemming from sex deviation of sorts, which caused severe problems and embarrassment to both the unit and the air force generally."

Kalichuk would not return to the Clinton base until 1965, but his drinking and sexual habits would cause the air force problems long before then.


By October, a new school year was well underway for the children on the Clinton air force base, but many of their classmates were gone. Lynne's two brothers had moved away, as had Steve's brothers and sister. Butch George went on to high school, but eventually he and his family departed from Clinton; it would be forty years before he was ever heard from again. Jocelyne Gaudet and her family transferred out and none of the children kept in touch with her.

But no matter how far they dispersed across the country, the children of Clinton could not shake the memories of the traumatic summer.

"The grief! It's like somebody reached in and took a piece of your heart out," says Michael Burns, looking back with horror on those first few months after the trial of his good friend. "Today, they have grief counsellors; we had nothing. Except parents telling you to shut up, it's over and done with."

"The aftermath of the whole thing was very difficult for everyone," agrees Yvonne Danberger, a friend of Lynne's. "We had to deal with it on our own. Nowadays if anything like that happened, there would be professionals at their disposal to help the children, the teachers and the parents.

"Instead we were under suspicion from our parents because they were horrified by everything that had happened. It negated everything in terms of friendship. It destroyed a lot of the confidence the kids had. No one wanted to have much to do with each other after that."

In some cases, the obsession with burying the memories of the summer ordeal went to rather dramatic extremes. Bryan Glover, who joined other boys teasing Steve on the bridge the night after Lynne disappeared, recalls the mood at his home. "I remember our parents telling us to burn the pictures so we wouldn't have any record of it. Any pictures we had of Steven and Lynne," Bryan says. "They didn't want us to have anything from it."

But purging the past would not be as easy as lighting a match to a few black-and-white snapshots of smiling children in happier times. Hank Sayeau, the OPP corporal who worked all through the summer of 1959 investigating the case against Steven, was one of the first to realize that forgetting the Truscott trial would not be easy. "I was relieved it was all over," he says. "But then it wasn't—and it never will be."

A fourteen-year-old boy sitting alone in a jail was about to confront his own ghosts. And his story would continue to haunt Canadians for decades.

# PART TWO

## THE BATTLE BEHIND BARS: 1960–1966

*"I didn't think he knew he murdered the girl.*
*I didn't think he knew that he had done an evil deed."*

—Prison psychiatrist Dr. George Scott

## 29

## GHOSTS OF THE GALLOWS

"**S**ENTENCE BOY TO HANG DECEMBER 8."

Across the country the media flashed the information that a Canadian jury had condemned a fourteen-year-old to death. The astonishing news reached into the highest chambers of power. On October 1, when the cabinet sat down for its meeting in the Privy Council chamber in Ottawa, Prime Minister John Diefenbaker confessed "he had been shocked to see that a fourteen-year-old . . . had been sentenced to hang." Diefenbaker—who as a lawyer claimed a client of his whom he thought innocent had gone to the gallows—had been a staunch opponent of the death penalty. He was also a pragmatist, fretting confidentially to his ministers that "the outcome would be reported all over the world and would undoubtedly reflect badly on Canada."

Diefenbaker was right. Steve's date with the hangman gave Canada a black eye on the world stage. In England, one newspaper called it "a shocking thing." In Germany, a teenager named Krista Severa read with horror the news that Canada was set to hang a boy about her age. When her parents announced they were planning to move to Canada, she protested in vain, "It's barbaric—they hang children there." Little did she know that years later her own life—and the lives of her children—would become intertwined with the boy who was awaiting the death sentence far across the Atlantic.

Back in Ottawa, Diefenbaker told the justice department to review the case "in order that the government could consider an immediate reprieve." But five days later, Solicitor General Léon Balcer put the brakes on any speedy help for Steve. He told cabinet he had not yet seen the trial transcripts or the judge's reports, but had consulted "press reports." The boy, he assured his ministerial colleagues, was not in a "death row" but in the Goderich jail, where "he did not seem unduly depressed." The solicitor general recommended cabinet defer any formal action until Steven's lawyers had filed an appeal.

Diefenbaker and the other ministers agreed that "premature commutation might well be criticized as setting an undesirable precedent for the future." So they stalled, leaving Steve in a judicial limbo where everyone assumed he would not hang, but technically—and legally—the noose still beckoned from the shadows.

Contrary to the assurances exchanged around the cabinet table, the tiny jail cell that had been Steve's home for four months had indeed turned into his death row cell. Now that he was a convicted murderer, the rules changed. No more regular meals at the tables in the common room outside the cellblock. No more regular doses of sunshine in the exercise yard. Guards let him out of his cell only once a week for a shower. Otherwise, he stayed on his metal cot, the only sign of daylight coming from the narrow slits in a small window.

The boy was now more alone than he had ever been in his life. His family and friends had always been there to support him during the summer ordeal. But a death sentence was his alone to face.

"Taken to the place of execution and hanged by the neck until you are dead." Justice Ferguson's words echoed in Steven's brain. And the boy who would not cry when a sliver of wood sliced into his body, the teenager who would never shed a tear in public when he was on trial because "it was not the air force way," now, in the dark solitude of his death cell, sobbed the sobs of a frightened child.

"At night time you lie there and cry," he admits today. "But it doesn't really accomplish that much. So after a while you even stop doing that. You kind of harden yourself up for what's to come."

The tears stopped, but not the fear. One morning Steve heard a noise outside the jail window. "I woke up one day and somebody was building something outside the wall. You could hear the hammering. I figured they were building scaffolding [for the gallows]. It's just kind of living in terror because nobody tells you any different and it's getting closer and closer to the date that they set."

Five decades earlier, they had been building a scaffold in the same county jail that held Steven to hang the murderer of another young girl. Like Lynne Harper, she was twelve years old. Her name was Elizabeth Anderson. Fifty summers before Lynne and Steve played baseball in the fields of Clinton, Elizabeth went missing from her home near Goderich on September 20, 1910. Her nude body turned up in the cellar of an abandoned home near the county fairgrounds, where eyewitnesses saw a man named Edward Jardine with the girl. A court found Jardine guilty the following spring.

"He broke down for half an hour but he recovered and walked to the scaffold, apparently without a tremor," the Goderich paper recounted. "Less than sixty seconds elapsed from the time the procession started from the cell until the trap dropped. It was eight minutes and a half after the drop when the heart stopped beating." If that seemed like a long time to dangle from the end of a rope, the newspaper assured its readers they need not worry. "Of course, death to all intents was instantaneous, Executioner Ellis doing his job well," the newspaper said, never explaining why it took Jardine's heart more than eight minutes to get the message.

Canada had executed more than seven hundred people since Confederation; there were no accurate records prior to 1867, but hundreds more were hanged. According to Frank Anderson in *Hanging in Canada*, by the start of the nineteenth century, there were more than one hundred offences—many of them minor—for which death was the ultimate penalty. On September 18, 1803, the noose claimed a boy named B. Clement, whose crime was stealing a cow. Authorities hanged another thief who had stolen a few potatoes, and executed three men for the theft of an ox in 1829. By 1833, governments reduced the number of capital offences to a dozen, but they still included crimes such as robbery, arson and burglary. The rebellions of 1837–38 saw the widespread use of political executions after the British authorities crushed the uprisings.

The first hanging after Confederation was a gala affair, according to Anderson. Admission was by invitation only to the execution of a Norwegian sailor condemned to die for murdering his landlady. Doctors, reporters, lawyers and students snapped up the tickets, printed with black borders. Organizers boarded up the bottom of the scaffold, presumably to hide the man's final death spasms. But the spectators insisted on a full show. "So great was the desire to view the last struggles that boards were torn from the sides," according to one report.

Canada's hangmen continued to perfect their technique, replacing a short rope with the "long drop" technique. A short rope meant the criminal died of strangulation, at times slowly and in agony. The "long drop," which Canada perfected twenty years before it was used elsewhere, ensured a faster death with an efficient dislocation of the neck. It was not an exact science, however, and there were always botched jobs. Decapitations were not uncommon, with spectators gasping as they got a much bloodier and more Gothic spectacle than they had bargained for.

The last known teenager to be executed in Canada was a sixteen-year-old named Archibald MacLean of New Westminster, B.C., hanged for the fatal shooting of a policeman in 1881. Not since 1875 had anyone as young as Steven been convicted for murder and condemned to death. In that year, a fourteen-year-old Native boy named Quanamcan was convicted of murdering a woman and her small son by bludgeoning them with rocks. The government later commuted his sentence to life. Before Christmas came in 1959, would Steve be the first fourteen-year-old to be executed in Canada in more than a century?

As Steven waited behind the historic walls of the Goderich jail for news about his execution date, he knew little of the history of executed prisoners who preceded him. He did not know he was sitting in the same jail, perhaps even the same cell, that Edward Jardine occupied before he was strangled at the end of a rope.

Steve had more immediate concerns on his mind—could that constant banging outside his jail cell really be the sound of his scaffolding being prepared? With relief, Steve soon discovered it was only some construction work going on near the jail. Still, the fear and uncertainty over his future lingered, and not just for him.

Pierre Berton, one of Canada's most prominent commentators at the time, broke the journalistic tradition of objective prose and penned a poem about Steven in his column for the *Toronto Daily Star*. Berton took no stand on the boy's innocence or guilt, but he recoiled at the notion of a legalized execution:

> The cell is lonely
> The cell is cold
> October is young
> But the boy is old;
> Too old to cringe
> And too old to cry
> Though young,—
> But never too young to die.
>
> . . . . . . . . .
>
> We've a national law
> In the name of the Queen
> To hang a child
> Who is just fourteen.

Berton's words unleashed a storm "more violent than I have yet known," as he wrote in a follow-up column. A man called to say he hoped one of Berton's daughters was raped. Another woman shouted into the phone that Steve should never have been brought to trial: "If I'd been his mother I'd have killed him myself," she screamed. A third person wrote in with another suggestion: "The child should be whipped before he dies."

"It is blood they want and blood they mean to get, and there is no reasoning with them," Berton wrote. He reiterated that it was not necessarily the guilty verdict he objected to, but the death penalty, "a law that belongs to the Dark Ages."

"It is not the hangman whom we must weep for, in this grisly matter, but the multitude who guides his hands—ourselves," Berton concluded. "Has no one got the point? Have we become so used to the extremes of cheap television, the blacks and whites of overblown westerns, the easy and lazy alternative of Mickey Spillane, that we see no other way out but death or anarchy?"

There were other signs of unease. Shortly after, the *Clinton News-Record* ran an uncharacteristically bold cartoon—not about Steve's case in particular but about the death penalty in general. Underneath the shadow of an executed man hanging from a noose, a police officer, a judge and a member of Parliament stare as Lady Justice rushes in holding a paper and screams, "Hold it—here's some new evidence." The caption read, "The sentence that is irreversible is not Justice!"

By law in the 1950s, the federal cabinet had to review any death sentence, though at times the process could be quite perfunctory. Decisions were "often taken quickly and simply on the oral report of the solicitor general," according to one *Globe and Mail* report. One unnamed but "particularly taciturn minister" thought cabinet wasted its time on such cases. "Whenever one arose," the *Globe* recounted, "it was his custom to demonstrate his feelings by gathering up his papers, declaring 'hang the bastard' and stomping from the cabinet room."

For Canada's youngest prisoner in nearly a century sentenced to die, there was little comfort when the first chill winds of November blew off the river that ran next to the Goderich county jail. Steve's execution date of December 3 loomed just weeks away. The assurances from lawyers and prison officials that Canada would never hang a teenager did little to calm the boy. He had been burned too many times already by legal promises of a smooth and quick end to his ordeal.

On November 20, Steve got a temporary reprieve. Justice Minister Davie Fulton announced he was postponing the boy's death sentence to give Steve's lawyers time to appeal. Steve's next date with the hangman was Tuesday, February 16.

Meanwhile, Steve had to endure another kind of trial. Dark nights in the shadow of the hangman's noose were not to be his only nightmares. Psychiatrists came to the Goderich jail to probe his mind, searching for proof of guilt in the twisted mind of the jailed teenager. It was a preview of what was to come in the following years, as Steven fought to keep his sanity and maintain his innocence in the face of a psychiatric onslaught.

Glenn Hays, the prosecutor who had successfully put Steven behind bars, was convinced that the boy convicted of Lynne's murder was undoubtedly psychologically disturbed. "The evidence of Jocelyne Gaudet," he wrote in a memo, "might indicate the accused had sexual designs not limited to the deceased girl and might be a potential menace. He seemed to me to be utterly without fear, and almost lethargic most of the time."

The authorities sent in psychiatrist J. P. Cathcart to investigate. On January 8, 1960, the doctor began his tests of the boy. Steven told him his father had cautioned him not to speak to anyone about his case, but the doctor assured the prisoner his interrogation "had nothing to do with his appeal." That did not stop the doctor from spending much of his time questioning Steve about the crime.

"How did you feel when you heard about the tragedy [of Lynne's death]?" the doctor asked.

"I didn't feel so happy when I heard she was dead," Steve replied, according to Cathcart's notes.

Did he read sex literature, the doctor wanted to know.

"No, most of the books I read are of mechanics and agriculture," Steve answered. "Claims no special interest in girls or sex curiosity or books on sex," the doctor noted.

But Cathcart was having difficulty figuring out the patient he called "an enigma."

"A puzzling item in the case," he admitted. "Prisoner does not seem to be the type—a lad busy in all kinds of sport and spending a lot of spare time after school and on weekends with neighbouring farmers and exhibiting boyish enthusiasm about driving tractors."

The doctor had Steven fill out more than 150 answers to the "family and group experience inventory." The boy answered "True" to such questions as "My father never gave me doubts about his love and affection for me" and "My mother was pretty happy when I was born." Steve checked off "False" to such questions as "I would be interested in reading a magazine called *Women and Crime*" and "Once in a while I like a good sexy story."

"He has all the right answers," Cathcart wrote. "But are they too correct? He claims innocence of the crime and acts the part? . . . I have a hunch that the lad is guilty but incapable of admitting it, perhaps even to himself."

Steven could not win. Even his good behaviour counted against him. Since coming to the death cell, the doctor reported, his jailers taught him to play cribbage, "which he has picked up so fast that he is now able to beat any of the staff guards."

"He accepts the close confinement without apparent protest—almost as if guilty and resigned or perhaps indifferent," the psychiatrist said.

Still, Cathcart could not end Steve's first major examination without a hint of optimism. "I cannot see him as a monster, as has been suggested, nor such a menace as to prohibit future parole," the doctor concluded, "and there is no reason to believe that he will be any trouble during confinement."

Steven, for his part, was beginning to form an impression about what these doctors were up to. "After the first couple of questions, automatically you go on the defensive because this guy is just like another cop—somehow or some way they are going to try to get something to prove that you're guilty," he says. "You know where it's going and what they're after. You're defensive—then they wonder why."

The psychiatrists Steve would encounter over the years would see this defensiveness as simply more proof, in their eyes, of the boy's guilt.

As the year drew to a close, the fourteen-year-old grew more and more despondent. "You don't even know if you're going to see Christmas," he remembers. "People wonder why you live day to day. Probably because you don't know if you're going to be alive the next day or not."

In the late fall, the governor of the jail invited Steve to his private residence inside the prison to watch a baseball game on television. Steve relished the break, but it lifted his spirits only for a while. By the time the holiday season arrived, Steve spent the first of what would be many Christmas evenings alone. Typically, he was sadder for his family than for himself. "You know your whole family is having Christmas, but you're not there, and you know it's not going to be the same for them."

Meanwhile, outside Steven's jail cell, his family turned to John O'Driscoll, a senior and well-respected lawyer in the province, to handle the boy's application before the Ontario Court of Appeal. The high court judges could not consider new evidence, only points of law. For three days, beginning January 12, 1960, five judges pondered the legal intricacies of the September trial. Opposing Steven's appeal for the Crown was William C. Bowman, the director of public prosecutions, a determined and skilled attorney who would fight Steven's case again in six years' time in a much more public and prominent arena—the Supreme Court of Canada.

O'Driscoll tried to convince the appeal court to set aside the jury verdict. He said that some of the child witnesses did not appreciate the nature of the oath. He kept his harshest words for Justice Ferguson, arguing "that the theories of the defence were not sufficiently and adequately placed before the jury." He attacked the judge for appearing to criticize Steven for his failure to testify on his own behalf. And most seriously, he said that Ferguson "in effect dismissed the theories of the defence and in fact took the matter from the jury and substituted his own finding on the facts."

O'Driscoll told the appeal court that the Crown prosecutor's reference to the statement Steven signed at the police station the night of his arrest was "highly prejudicial" and the jurors were likely to think Steve made a confession. Chief Justice Dana Porter did not disagree, but he wondered why "the defence counsel did not see fit to call for mistrial. . . . I think the defence counsel might have well thought it all right. He made no comment." It would not be the last time high court judges would make Steven pay the consequences for his attorney's decision not to push a matter.

The appeal court judges showed some disquiet on other issues as well. One judge commented that the evidence from Steven's clothing was "valueless" because police seized the clothes several days after the crime. Another judge felt the way Justice Ferguson twisted and turned to get Butch George to understand an oath was "highly improper." A third judge was critical of the way the police interrogated the boy. "I understand the police were of the opinion they were going to charge the boy, yet no warning was given," he said.

Crown attorney William Bowman argued that none of these factors was sufficient to overturn the verdict and the judges, in the end, agreed. They found the grounds for appeal were "without substance." The court conceded the Crown should not have referred to Steve's statement to the police, but took comfort from the fact that Hays never called it a confession. They concluded the incident did not cause any "substantial wrong or miscarriage of justice" because the controversy over the statement took place at the start of the trial, fourteen days before the jury retired to deliberate. It was a curious judicial logic, implying that even if something untoward had happened, the jurors with any luck had forgotten about it. Despite their other misgivings, the appeal court concluded the trial was fair. "Therefore, the appeal fails on all grounds and will be dismissed," the court pronounced on January 20.

It was a dismal birthday present. Two days before, on January 18, Steven turned fifteen. Was it going to be the first of many birthdays behind bars or perhaps the last birthday he would ever celebrate in his life? Steve did not know for sure. He was still scheduled for execution in less than a month—February 16.

Despite his tender years, Steven's odds for a reprieve were not necessarily favourable. Between 1920 and 1960, Canada executed twenty-one people under the age of twenty, according to one study cited by historian Carolyn Strange. In what she aptly termed a "lottery of death," Ottawa commuted the death sentences of only one in three young people.

At 10:30 on Thursday morning, January 21, the federal cabinet gathered around a table in Room 340S of the House of Commons. On the agenda was the pending execution of two convicted murderers: an adult named Marvin McKee and a teenager named Steven Truscott. Diefenbaker and his colleagues decided not to stop the hanging of the man but to save the boy. Clearly what weighed in the balance for Steven was not any consideration of the unfairness of his rushed arrest or a dubious prosecution—only his age mattered. "It was inconceivable to allow this boy . . . to hang," the cabinet had noted earlier. In other words, had he been eighteen, or perhaps even sixteen, he might well have hanged—innocent or guilty.

The following day, on January 22 at 12:23 p.m., a telegram from the deputy minister of justice arrived at the Goderich jail. The nineteen words brought both salvation and doom: "Governor general in council has commuted death sentence of Steven Murray Truscott to life imprisonment in the Kingston Penitentiary."

Steve would not die. But unless he got parole, the boy would spend the rest of his natural life behind bars.

O'Driscoll immediately announced he would make an appeal to the Supreme Court, filing his action on February 22. Two days later, the Supreme Court turned Steven down. As was typical in such cases, they gave no reason for their decision.

The Truscotts had exhausted all of their legal avenues. Eight months after he was arrested on the hot summer evening of June 12, Steven finally did leave the Huron County Jail in Goderich, but not in a way he or his family ever envisaged.

Steven walked down the same long, dark corridor of the jail he first entered in June as a naive boy. Now he walked out a condemned convict, wearing manacles and chains.

The boy had escaped death, but a life sentence behind bars was impossible for the fifteen-year-old to comprehend. "It's beyond your imagination to even think about," Steve says. "I was going to jail and I was going to be there for a long time."

## 30

## LESSONS OF REFORM SCHOOL

Deciding not to hang Steven Truscott did not end the government's predicament of where Canada was going to jail a convicted murderer who had just turned fifteen. A penitentiary, filled with adult criminals, seemed harsh and potentially dangerous. So the authorities came up with a novel solution. The Penitentiary Act allowed authorities to transfer a convict under the age of sixteen and "susceptible of reformation" to a reformatory prison in the province where he was sentenced. For one night, police would take Steve Truscott to a penitentiary in Kingston—thus technically satisfying the requirement to imprison him in a federal penal institution. They would then transfer him to the Ontario Training School for Boys, near Guelph.

The police in Goderich were not going to make it easy on the boy. Sheriff Nelson Hill and another officer escorted Steven in their cruiser, with leg irons clamped around his ankles and handcuffs on his wrists. Not once along the six-hour journey to Kingston did the police remove the restraints, even when they stopped for a bite to eat.

The patrons inside the small restaurant froze as the chains rattled on the floor. They looked up to see a thin boy boxed in by two burly, armed policemen. "I'll never forget the sound my chains made as they scraped along the floor of the restaurant," Steven recalls today with uncharacteristic bitterness.

The unlikely trio sat down to order their food, but the officers would not take off Steve's handcuffs when the meal came. Helpless, Steven stared at the meat on his plate, unable to use both a fork and knife with his wrists locked tightly together. A waitress, taking pity on the boy, came over to cut his meat.

"Thank you," Steven said as he manoeuvred the fork in his manacled hands.

Fear replaced humiliation as they approached the imposing grey walls of the Kingston prison complex. Don Patterson, a supervisor there, remembers his first glimpse of the teenager who had become Canada's most famous inmate. "His knees were shaking," he says. "You hear the darn bars shut behind you—clash, bang—that's enough to scare anyone."

Patterson looked askance at the shackles and handcuffs on the boy. "I thought it was kind of heavy," he says. "That was frightening for the young chap." Frightened or not, penitentiary officials were unsure what to do with a fifteen-year-old in one of Canada's toughest penitentiaries, even if his stay was only overnight. They finally decided to let Steven sleep in the prison hospital, away from the general inmate population. "He was very quiet and co-operative," Patterson says.

As he led Steven to his bed for his night behind the penitentiary walls, Patterson tried to calm the scared boy. "Don't worry about it, you'll be well looked after," he said.

The soothing words did not help. Steven slept fitfully. "I was so terrorized and pumped," he remembers. "You're in a state of shock . . . still expecting someone to come to your rescue."

The next morning—once again chained in leg irons and handcuffs—he began the two-hundred-mile drive from Kingston to what was to become his home for the remainder of his youth: the Ontario Training School in Guelph.

"I thought at first he was going to be a troublemaker."

Ray Nankivell was nervous. One of the guards at the school, Ray was a hefty, well-built man from Cornwall, England. He was mulling over the strict orders from his superintendent, John Bain. Earlier that day, the head of the boys' reform school had gathered his staff together to issue a stern warning. "We have a federal prisoner coming in. His name is Steven Truscott," Bain said. "If twelve boys escape, let the rest go, but get Steven because he's not our prisoner; he's a federal prisoner and he was sentenced to die. We have to keep an eye on this guy."

The Ontario Training School was, in effect, a maximum-security prison for young offenders, or "juvenile delinquents" as they were called in the 1960s. "We had anything that other jails could not handle," Nankivell explains. Still, they tried to make the boys feel as relaxed as possible. Surrounded by farmers' fields and a small river to the north, the red-brick, two-storey building looked not unlike a small high school—except for the bars on the windows and the barbed wire fence. The guards wore grey slacks, green jackets, ties and a white shirt. They were unarmed. The boys wore black boots, khaki pants and T-shirts.

When Sheriff Nelson Hill dropped off his shackled prisoner, his over-the-top tactics disturbed the prison officials in Guelph as much as they had in Kingston.

"We were shocked to watch this little boy with leg irons and handcuffs," recalls Les Horne, the school's librarian, who happened to be in the front office when Steve arrived. "The first thing we did was make the sheriffs take their guns off. They were a little reluctant."

Horne immediately took pity on the newest arrival. "He was a very bewildered, confused kid; it's a wonder he stayed sane." Steven had made his first friend.

Once the armed escorts had removed their weapons—and Steve's chains—the boy entered the prison facility through a blue steel door with a small bulletproof window. As one door shut behind him, the guards buzzed open another one until he was inside a long, barren corridor. Steve turned right and made his way to the check-in room, where he showered and prepared to be strip-searched and photographed.

The guard doing the honours was Dave Mills, a likeable fellow from Belfast who had lost little of his Irish brogue. Steve was soon to discover that most of the staff was from Ireland, Scotland or England, giving the school an air of old-world civility combined with an almost colonial paternalism.

"I had in the back of my mind that I couldn't treat him like the other guys," Mills remembered. "We were told he was 'high security.'" But he found the shy and polite boy charming. Following standard procedure for new arrivals, Mills put Steve in segregation in "C" block. He quickly tried to put the boy at ease by calling him "Steve" instead of the curt "Truscott" the boy was used to hearing from his jailers in Goderich.

"That's the first time [in jail] anyone had called me by my first name," Steve said. Within minutes, he had made a second friend.

Superintendent John Bain promptly wrote to the deputy minister in charge of reform institutions to inform him that Steven was adjusting well. The boy wrote two "quite cheerful letters"—prison officials monitored all correspondence—to his family and to the governor of the Goderich jail—to tell them he was okay. "He has been very quiet, making no requests or inquiries of any kind," Bain reported. He added that Canada's youngest federal inmate was still in segregation, but they planned to slowly integrate him into their organized activities.

Integration meant moving into one of the four cellblocks that housed the fifty or so juveniles at the school. Steve moved into "A" block on the first floor. There were twelve cells in each block; Steve's home was the third cell down from the showers. His quarters had a bed, toilet, basin and a small cupboard. His keeper was Ray Nankivell.

He recalls with genuine affection the boys under his charge. "It felt like twelve sons," he says. "We would treat them that way." But it was a strict family, with swift retribution. "If you give me a rough time—fighting or even for giving lip—I'll lock you up and put you on charge," Nankivell warned his Dirty Dozen. A charge meant a note on a boy's record—something Steven managed to avoid for his entire stay at the Guelph institution.

"He never did a thing wrong, never got charged," says Nankivell, who despite his superintendent's warnings took an immediate liking to Steve. "He was a gentleman, very respectful of authority. Always gave us a smile: 'How are you today, sir?' He got on well with the boys as well as the staff."

Nankivell woke up the boys around 7:00 a.m. They went down to the cafeteria to pick up breakfast, where Steve quickly befriended Alice Hebden, the cook with a plump figure and the hearty cuisine to justify it. "We have lots to eat; I've gained twelve pounds in the last two months and weigh 160," Steve told a visitor in March.

Hebden, remarkably alert and lively today at ninety-six, unabashedly admits she quickly began to love the good-natured new boy like a son. "He was very quiet. He would do anything for anybody," she says. "He never caused any trouble." Steve's mother, Doris, was grateful for the cook's maternal kindness. "She more or less took him under her wing," Doris says.

After the obligatory reciting of grace, the boys ate their meals and then headed off for work in the basement machine and carpentry shops. It was a long day—from 9:00 a.m. until 4:00 p.m., interrupted only by a forty-five-minute lunch break.

But Steven loved the shop work, soaking up the skills with an enthusiasm that would serve him well in his adult years. Steve always enjoyed working with his hands, and anything that kept him busy meant his mind did not have time to ponder the prospect of growing old behind bars.

In woodworking classes, Steve and his friends built a cornice decorated with carved doves for a local church, a two-storey spiral oak staircase for a Guelph resident and mahogany cabinets so grand that one guard proudly took them home. Steve's special talent, though, was with anything mechanical. "When I get out, I'd like to work in a machine shop," he told a visitor. The fifteen-year-old could not have imagined he would come very close to fulfilling that wish as an adult, just a few miles from where he was labouring as a juvenile inmate.

Despite his young age, Steve's height, strength and easygoing but firm character quickly made him a natural leader among the other boys. Once a week, the boys in the cellblocks at each end of the corridor would compete to see who could do the best cleanup. Steve was a team leader, and he imposed air force crispness. "They won every week. That place was spotless," says guard Dave Mills. "You got to watch TV, and you also got cookies and milk," Steve remembers today, still proud of his teenage victories.

There were less salutary rewards as well. The housecleaning champions, despite their age, also sometimes received rolling tobacco—this was, after all, long before public health campaigns against smoking. From a single pouch of the brown leaves, Steve could make fifty cigarettes, enough to last a week or more. Less than a month after entering the training school—and barely past his fifteenth birthday—Steve became a heavy smoker, a habit he has been unable to shake to this day.

Two nights a week, Steve took grade Nine classes in English, French and mathematics. Steve also picked up other lessons that were not exactly on the official curriculum. From his fellow inmates, he learned the tricks of making do behind bars. If the boys wanted to smoke and they had no matches or lighter, they would wrap toilet paper around a razor blade, unscrew a light bulb and gingerly jab the device into the socket. The resulting sparks and burning tissue did the trick.

Other fires were burning outside the reform school walls. Steve could carve wooden cabinets and wash the floors with the rest of the boys, but no matter how hard he tried to blend in with the other detainees, he could not change the fact that he was different. His case was a *cause célèbre* that continued to make ripples—small ones at first, but eventually a crashing wave that swept across the country.

One of the first cracks in the official wall of silence came in March of 1960, when George Wardrope, the Ontario minister for reform institutions, decided to pay a visit to the training school in Guelph. The minister chatted with the adolescent prisoner for forty-five minutes. "I just told him I didn't do it, that's all," Steven told a reporter at the time.

Holding out the prospect of parole, the minister indicated that a life sentence did not necessarily mean life. "Mr. Wardrope said it all depended on my behaviour so I am prepared," Steve said. "I'll do my best to obey the rules."

In the eyes of some authorities, it was bad enough a cabinet minister met with a convicted murderer. But a furor erupted when Wardrope publicly declared that he had "a great deal of doubt" about Steve's guilt. "I was able to size him up and I couldn't see he was hiding anything," the minister said. "He seems like just a normal teenager."

It did not take long for the wrath of the establishment to come down on the errant minister. Kelso Roberts, the attorney general who had posted the $10,000 "dead or alive" reward for Lynne's killer, promptly denounced his cabinet colleague's words as "entirely incomprehensible." The *Toronto Daily Star* warned his remarks were "bound to cause needless misgivings about our courts in the public mind."

Wardrope quickly fell into line. "I should not have commented on the matter of his guilt or innocence at all," he said, apologizing for any denigration "upon the administration of justice."

The issue died quickly, but not for Steve's father. He penned a poignant letter to the cabinet minister on March 29. "You have given us a great deal of hope," Dan Truscott wrote. "It means a great deal to us to know that someone is thinking along the same lines as we have always thought."

Dan ended his letter with a plea for help that, like the letter, was ignored. "I have used all my savings and am in debt trying to help Steven and to establish a new home for my family," he explained. "I do not know who to turn to for help now."

The Truscotts did not know it yet, but help for their cause was about to come from someone who deeply believed in their son's innocence. An inquisitive writer named Isabel LeBourdais had read about Steve's case and it piqued her curiosity. "I started off because I had a son the same age," she later explained. She originally felt such a young offender should have been tried in juvenile court and if guilty, needed treatment, not punishment. But as she investigated, she became convinced something had gone horribly wrong in that Goderich courtroom in 1959.

LeBourdais, whose work had appeared in national magazines such as *Chatelaine* and *Saturday Night*, came from a comfortable Toronto family with a long tradition of social activism. Her mother was a suffragette; her sister Gwethalyn Graham won Governor General's Literary Awards for two of her books, including one that skewered the "polite" anti-Semitism in so-called high society.

"To take on the establishment was not a thing that bothered her, but it was a time when far fewer women were doing it," says her son Julien, who remembers a mother active in the fight for mental patients' rights, ban-the-bomb protests and the early black civil rights movement. She was the only white member of the Toronto Negro Community Centre, so busy there her husband, Don —himself also an accomplished writer—once joked: "If I ever want a divorce I'll name the Negro Centre as co-respondent."

Now LeBourdais applied that same energy to a pursuit of the truth in Steve's case. She began by travelling to Clinton and met with families who knew the Truscotts—the Logans, the Gilkses and the Carews. Frank Donnelly, Steve's former lawyer, would not talk to her, but she did obtain the court transcripts—an important breakthrough since no outside observer had ever combed through the official record for inaccuracies or contradictions.

On April 22, 1960, Isabel LeBourdais wrote to Doris and Dan Truscott, introducing herself and announcing plans for an article in the near future about their son in *Chatelaine*. Steve's parents readily agreed to a meeting, telling her, "We always believed that Steven is innocent and feel that there has been a miscarriage of justice, but it is another thing to prove it."

That challenge made the quest all the more appealing to LeBourdais. Never one to shy away from an unpopular crusade, she was eager to take on what in 1960 was still sacrosanct: the infallibility of the police and the courts. "The criticism that Mother made of the legal system was shocking at the time," Julien LeBourdais explains. "And that it was [coming from] a woman, too, was a bit more of a shock. It was a bit unseemly. That didn't bother her; in fact she relished that."

While Isabel LeBourdais began sniffing around Clinton for proof of Steven's innocence, prison psychiatrists began probing the boy's mind for proof of his guilt. It was the onset of a decade-long battle that Steven would wage—largely alone and isolated—against the psychiatric and prison establishment. They would throw everything at him—interviews, tests, needles, drugs, truth serum and even LSD. All the boy had was his iron determination not to give in to the doctors' persistence that he confess to a crime he insisted he did not commit.

From the start of his incarceration at the Guelph reform school, half a dozen different psychiatrists, psychologists and social workers began filing regular reports to Ottawa.

J. P. Cathcart, the psychiatrist who had first examined Steven in Goderich, returned to probe the young prisoner in Guelph on February 19, 1960. The strongest indication of guilt he could find was a "remarkable change in tone of voice—including tremulousness" when he asked the boy about the crime.

Perhaps hoping for better evidence, the authorities brought in psychologist H. J. Breen for more examinations. After a brief conversation and a short test, Breen seemed to have cracked the mystery. "This would appear to be the case of a rather schizoid boy who is precociously developed for his age and hence lacks sufficiently strong ego resources to cope with his expanding physical (sexual and aggressive) drives. It seems entirely probable that he could commit an impulsive crime such as that of which he has been accused."

It was the kind of analysis that would unfortunately mark most of Steven's encounters with those out to delve into his mind. "It's hard to realize how much power they have," says Steven. "You have to be in that position [as an inmate] to see the power that they have. It was just so frustrating."

The man who would dominate Steve's psychological probing throughout his stay in Guelph was Dr. James Hartford, a consulting psychiatrist from Kitchener who saw Steven at least six times from 1960 to 1962. "On the surface he was likeable and generally co-operative," Hartford said in his first report. "And to an untrained person he would appear reasonably normal." Fortunately, the doctor pointed out, he was not so easily fooled: "I felt the boy was ill," he quickly concluded.

From the start, Hartford found the boy's memories of his life on different air bases "rather unusually superficial." When Steve complained that psychiatrists and psychologists had already grilled him, Hartford saw dark overtones to the teenager's mistrust. "He is defensive, guarded," the psychiatrist wrote.

Steve's unwavering insistence on his innocence seemed to trouble the doctor as well. "He completely denies any involvement in this of any kind," he said. "He feels that at the trial a good many people told stories that were not true and he was particularly angry with the police for some of their accounts of his evidence."

"It is difficult to give a diagnostic expression of my findings, to date, in connection with this boy," Hartford said, but then—as was customary in his profession—the psychiatrist had no difficulty finding the appropriate labels to affix to Steven. "There are some things that suggest a mild suspiciousness, some petulance and some psychopathic flavouring. . . . I would classify this boy as a mixed neurotic picture of almost borderline degree with mild paranoid and moderate psychopathic tendencies."

Social workers seemed to concur. Clare McGowan, assistant local director of the Children's Aid Society, wrote a two-page report that appeared to be based largely on gossip picked up from "confidential references" around the Clinton base. "Steve was interested in sexy 'comics' and was known to possess some obscene copies," she wrote. She added that Steve was a "pathological liar" and "the product of his home," a substandard home, in her opinion, since "the Truscotts did not attend church . . . and [Steven] apparently had no encouragement from his parents re: spiritual growth."

Another social worker, E. J. Brown, recounted bizarre statements from Steven that never appeared in any other reports before or since—declarations that Steven today fervently denies ever making. Steve allegedly told Brown he had an eighteen-year-old girlfriend and had sexual intercourse for the first time when he was thirteen—a remarkable thing to keep secret on a military base.

Indeed, if the social worker was to be believed, thirteen appeared to have been a busy age for the budding criminal. The boy, according to Brown, ran with a gang when he was in Vancouver—presumably while visiting his grandparents for a few weeks during the summer. "He learned how to make gunpowder from the gang he ran around with—they used it for blowing locks." These teenage hooligans "were up to everything—stealing, breaking and entering, robbery, etc. . . . The proceeds of their crimes were always split evenly between them all."

Brown's diagnosis was bleak. "This student has told lies so readily in the past—and got away with them—that he now lives those lies, and finds the truth hard to tell. He shows absolutely no sense of shame, appreciation of moral values or remorse for his past mode of conduct," he concluded. "Underneath this exterior of calm acceptance, I believe there is an effervescent, boisterous and quick-tempered boy with a contemptuousness for rules in general and authority in particular who considers himself clever enough to 'beat the rap.'"

There appeared to be two Stevens, a sort of teenage Jekyll and Hyde: the dark, devious and repressed troublemaker who emerged every time a social worker or psychiatrist closed the door in the interview room, and the happy-go-lucky, responsible and well-behaved boy that the guards, cooks, teachers, inmates and virtually everyone else at the facility saw every day in the reform school corridors.

Certainly the new superintendent of the school, Don Williams, had a radically different appreciation of Steven than the mind probers. In his first report, dated June 6, Williams noted Steve exhibited a "steady behaviour pattern" and was "well accepted" by all the boys. "One rather amazing feature of this boy's performance is his apparent emotional indifference to all situations. He has not received a single misconduct report, which is unusual," Williams wrote.

Two months later, the superintendent was still scratching his head. "Steven is still a difficult boy to fathom," he recorded on July 27. "He is a polite, quiet spoken and generally well-behaved boy. . . . There is very little criticism that one can offer." Perhaps sensing this was not what his superiors were expecting to hear about Canada's renowned convicted teen killer, Williams assured correctional authorities that his staff were on guard. "Sooner or later, one feels that this boy must find some medium of expression, be it mild or volatile. Of necessity he must be watched closely," he wrote. "The early prognosis has been favourable, but we should not relax our vigil."

But after another three months had passed, the vigil seemed only to confirm there was nothing to be vigilant about. In October, Williams reported it was hard to believe Steven had completed the first eight months of his sentence "without a misconduct report or having displayed some form of defiance or insolence. And yet this is exactly what Steven has done. We accept the situation and give him full marks for maintaining such a high standard of behaviour." The superintendent concluded, "It would appear that Steve has resigned himself to this situation, and that he intends to make the best of it."

The guards who worked and lived closely with Steven every day had a simpler explanation. "I never thought that Steve was guilty," says Dave Mills. "In all the time I worked here, they had more social workers, psychologists, psychiatrists that went to interview him. I used to go home wondering, 'They've been out to see this guy for six or seven months off and on—surely he's going to break down somewhere.' But not once. Not once. I never did think that he had committed murder."

Alice Hebden, the cook, agreed. "We all thought he was innocent. Everybody." As librarian Les Horne put it, "Most of the staff would have said, 'He's not the kid who could have done that.'"

Ray Nankivell, the supervisor who spent a great deal of time with Steven was equally adamant. "We all thought he had a bum rap." Nankivell remembers how sullen Steven looked every time he emerged from a grilling by the psychiatrists or psychologists. "He would just stare into nothing."

"You kind of develop an attitude that, 'I don't care what other people think,'" Steve explains. "You try to put up a barrier and you say, 'All that matters to me is what *I* think.' I knew I was innocent. There wasn't a doubt in my mind that I had absolutely nothing to do with this murder."

But for the mind readers, Steve's protestations of innocence were just more indication of his obvious guilt.

"Mom and Dad are coming," Steven told one of the guards, Ken Russell.

"I wonder what the heck they're going to bring this time," Russell replied eagerly. A tough, no-nonsense guard who would go on to become an OPP detective, Russell liked Steve, even if he felt the boy was reserved. "We used to have toe wrestles," Russell remembers, hooking their big toes together and pressing back to see who gave in first. "I would always beat him."

Russell and the other staff looked forward to visits from Steve's parents almost as much as the boy did. "They always had piles of stuff for the school—candies, cakes, a big bushel of apples," Russell says.

"We tried to carry on as if nothing happened," Dan Truscott wrote to a friend, reflecting his family's determination to keep a tenuous hold on normality despite the jailing of their son. Dan and Doris had settled in

Richmond, a small town south of Ottawa, close enough to the air force base and quiet enough to give the family some anonymity.

"It was hard on the kids," Doris admits, as the Truscott name had achieved national prominence—and for some, notoriety. "Different little things came out, like 'Oh, you're a Truscott,' said in a little slur."

"It was a strain," says Steve's older brother, Ken. "You're always wondering what people are thinking." But if Ken and his younger brother and sister ever winced under the burden of being Steven Truscott's sibling, they never let their parents know. "They felt we already had a lot of pressure," Doris says. "They didn't want to bring that home because it would upset us more."

Doris and Dan took their other children to see Steve at the training school, even if it was awkward to explain to ten-year-old Bill and seven-year-old Barbara what their older brother was doing behind bars. Making the three-hundred-mile trip was a financial strain for a couple still trying to cope with raising three children at home and paying down a mortgage. Dan got a part-time job four nights a week at a local racetrack; Doris worked weekends and sometimes once or twice a week at the Richmond bakery.

"It was a hard struggle to get through," Doris says. "I never begrudged it and I never moaned and cried about it, because it got us up to see Steve. I was just glad we could get there."

Getting there meant seeing their boy adapt to growing up behind barbed wire fences. "All in all he is bearing up wonderfully well and seems to get along well with the guards, and they always speak well of him," his parents wrote of Steve in May of 1960. They watched Steve and his fellow detainees play baseball against a team from Toronto. Steve, as he had under the freer skies of Clinton, always shone as a sharp third baseman with a wicked throw to first.

"He is quite happy now that he's able to be outside and play ball," his father noted. Dan perhaps did not suspect that for his jailed boy, sports had become more than a game. "People vent their frustration differently— I would do it in sports," Steve remembers. "You kind of throw yourself at it. Just about anything I went into I ended up winning." Steve's enthusiasm for sports as an outlet for his frustration left him with the usual battle scars. His medical record shows that, in addition to providing a prescription for glasses, doctors treated him for fractures to his left hand and a sprain to his right ankle.

In October, Steve's parents reported that their son was learning to play the trumpet—a gift from guard Dave Mills—and as section leader his cellblock came first in the clean up competition three months in a row. But as Steve created a new life for himself behind bars, his old life from Clinton seemed to be slipping away. One of his visitors at the training school was Gord Logan, one of the boys who insisted he saw Steven and Lynne cross the bridge on that Tuesday evening in June of 1959. The reunion was awkward for the two former school buddies, and Gord's father, Tom, had to do most of the talking. "I couldn't think of anything to say," Gord later told a reporter.

The chasm between Steven and his former childhood friends was to be expected. Steve was changing, forced to make friends with a much tougher crowd—boys like Mike McGuin, a troubled youngster who from the age of six until twenty-five would spend seventeen years in various institutions. Mike came to the Guelph reform school in the summer of 1960, and remembers Steve as a likeable kid who stuck to the code juvenile delinquents adopted behind bars: "You're in here and I'm in here, let's make the best of a bad situation and get on with our lives," McGuin explains.

At the end of the year, Steve spent his second Christmas behind bars. For Steve and his family, Christmas was always the saddest time of the year. His mother sent him fruit cake and shortbread. "It was hard to get it through your mind he was really serving a life sentence," Doris remembers. "You couldn't imagine he was there for that long a time for something he didn't do."

Doris had a few friends to turn to, but most of the time when she needed support, she turned inward: "I'd sit and talk to myself, and I was not ashamed to admit it. I felt I had to keep going because of the kids," she says.

Meanwhile, Steve's father, to take his mind off his son's imprisonment, plunged himself into one of his favourite activities—hockey. Dan took his son Bill to practices and games, and even refereed. Bill's team once lost a tight 1–0 decision because his father ruled a goal scored by his son's team went under the net. "I must say Bill doesn't think too much of his dad as referee," Dan wrote.

Looking back on a childhood dominated by his older brother's imprisonment, Bill Truscott marvels at his father's ability to devote time to all of his offspring. "Dad was always busy with hockey. I never felt I missed anything."

But Bill also remembers a father obsessed with clearing his son's name. "Every table in the house was covered with anything that he could find anywhere," he remembers. "It was just normal after a while. Dad would spend five or six hours a day clipping newspapers, writing, talking on the telephone to people to see what could be done."

"It always seemed like, 'Next month things will be taken care of' or 'six months from now,' or someone would say, 'By the spring something should be done,'" Bill remembers. But help for Steven always proved out of reach.

"A lot of times Dad wouldn't come out of the house for a weekend, upset over the whole thing," says Bill. "It would get to him, just wondering if he'd done everything, what else he could do."

For several months now, the Truscotts had left their trailer outside of the Guelph home of Alice Hebden. It made the long drive from Ottawa easier, and they could drop by the cook's house for cold drinks and warm company when visiting Steven. There was no toilet in the Spartan trailer, just a small stove and table that folded into a bed. With an air mattress and a sleeping bag, three people could fit into the cramped quarters.

Hebden had to go to work at six o'clock in the morning, but one night she remembers Dan stricken with grief over his son's plight. "I sat with him until 5:45 a.m. He cried all night long," she recalls. "His son was going through all this and he couldn't do a thing."

Meanwhile, Isabel LeBourdais was finding her challenge to get to the truth about Steven's case was also full of grief and aggravation. The publishing world would prove less than eager to publicize a controversial case that seemed to throw into question the underpinnings of Canadians' faith in the fairness of their justice system. By August, she told friends *Chatelaine* had decided not to print an article on the case. She then pinned her hopes on publication in the *Star Weekly*, but that, too, seemed elusive.

"If only someone will print your story, I feel certain that it will bring something out into the open," Doris Truscott wrote to LeBourdais.

By early 1961, LeBourdais set her sights on a bigger publishing splash—a full-length book. "McClelland & Stewart are definitely committed to publishing my book on the case as soon as I can get it written," she told the Truscotts. "This is the first time that we really have what looks like some solid, definite guarantee that efforts will bear fruit. I'll never give this up until we all have what we want—Steven free and completely cleared."

Speculating about a new trial, LeBourdais suggested the only person up to the task was Arthur Martin, one of Canada's most prominent defence attorneys. "I would do everything I possibly could to help make sure that he takes the case, when the time comes," she stated.

LeBourdais recruited various friends and acquaintances of the Truscotts at the Clinton base to do some of her footwork—measuring distances at the bridge, breaking off branches in the woods, testing how far sound travelled from the crime scene, and poking around the air base for information.

Tom Logan summoned the courage to give LeBourdais a copy of his son Gord's statement to the police. Gord's declaration would be one of the few pieces of paper from among the many dozens of witness statements that would see the light of day—until boxes of police and Crown files became available some forty years later.

LeBourdais also talked to Dr. David Hall Brooks, the chief medical officer at the base, in what he later described as a "stormy interview." According to LeBourdais' notes, he said he knew a boy had done the crime because Lynne "was too undeveloped to appeal to an older man." Brooks claimed the couple started "exploring each other" in the field by the woods and only later went into the bush.

The air force authorities were not going to make it easy for LeBourdais to pursue her investigation. Fear began to grip the military families who had welcomed the author into their homes on the Clinton base.

It had been two years since Steve's arrest, but by the summer of 1961 members of the military brass were unnerved to see a journalist sniffing around the base for clues and witnesses. On June 23, they issued a regulation in the daily routine orders that effectively banned base personnel from talking to LeBourdais. The directive used general terms about military staff not speaking to outsiders about personal matters, but the target was clear.

The air force made it explicit to the Logan family. Frances Logan wrote to LeBourdais to tell her an air force police officer said LeBourdais could remain at the Logans' "as a personal friend, but we're not to discuss the Truscott case." John Carew, one of Steve's classmates, remembers the atmosphere of intimidation he and his parents felt. "News travels around a base pretty fast," he says. "The administrative staff got wind that [LeBourdais] was staying there. They didn't like her purposes and they were worried about what she was going to say. They didn't want her on the base."

The strong-arm tactics of the air force worked. Grace Carew wrote to LeBourdais saying that if news got out her husband, Grant, was talking to her "they might just terminate his career and he would go out on a dishonourable discharge. . . . It's too bad it has to be like this, but I think you can understand why."

LeBourdais was livid. "It was ridiculous, incredible, idiotic," she bellowed, "and what in thunder did they all think they were doing anyway, trying to stop me from visiting friends?"

Steve's second summer behind reform school bars was proving to be as enjoyable as it could be in an institution that was a prison in all but name. "Steve is doing fine, he is allowed outside the fence now and takes care of the flowers, lawns and garden, so he is quite pleased," Doris wrote when she and the children visited him in early July of 1961. She also brought along a bushel of apples and four watermelons. By August, his parents were proudly reporting that Steve's wooden scale model of a school was going on display at the Canadian National Exhibition in Toronto.

Family visits were a mixed blessing. Steve missed his family terribly, but seeing them occasionally only reminded him of what he had lost. "It was the only time he was sad," guard Dave Mills recalls. "They were fairly close-knit. That family was really broken up by the whole thing."

"He used to get in his quiet moods—kept to himself," supervisor Ray Nankivell remembers. "Never saw him cry. That's the one thing we thought—there's something wrong—because he didn't show any emotion."

There were rare moments when the teenager expressed his bitterness. One of the other boys at the school was also serving time for a murder, but because the adolescent was tried in juvenile court, he obtained an early release.

"He got out in two years. What's wrong, Mr. Mills?" Steve complained.

He chafed at other restrictions. As a federal prisoner, Steve, as one guard put it, was "the only one who never saw daylight (outside the prison grounds) from the day he arrived to the day he left." Steve's cellmates—even the other boy charged with murder—made regular trips to a swimming pool at the local university and to a downtown hockey rink. But not Steve. Superintendent Williams even tried to lobby government officials to change their strict policy toward Steve, but he did not succeed.

"It's tough, Mr. Mills," Steve grumbled as he saw the others leave the confines of the institution for sports trips.

"Sure," the guard empathized.

"Well, I guess I'm different," Steve said.

"Well, I don't think that way about you, Steve," Mills said, trying to console his favourite detainee.

Escape attempts were not uncommon among the juveniles. The chain-link fence with a few strands of barbed wire on top was not an insurmountable barrier to an athletic and determined teenager. "Three big leaps up the fence and you're out," Steve recalls. Inevitably, the police and guards caught any runaway boys—with only open farm fields in the immediate vicinity there were not a lot of places to run. Steve, though, says he didn't entertain the possibility of making a break for it because he was convinced the justice system would eventually realize an innocent boy had been jailed. "I never thought of escaping because, in my mind, somebody was always going to come up and say, 'Sorry, we made a mistake,'" Steve says. It would take a while before Steve would have the courage to rid himself of the naive hope that the cavalry was right around the corner, just waiting to rescue him from a miscarriage of justice.

Steve's more immediate concern was surviving in a prison-like atmosphere. For all its trappings of grace before meals and unarmed guards, the Ontario Training School still housed some fairly disturbed boys charged with violent crimes, sexual assaults and other serious offences. "It was a pressure pot," says Les Horne. "Steve was physically able to hold his own without any bullying. . . . The way he carried himself, he developed a security in himself pretty early on. He got respect from the staff and other kids."

Ken Russell remembers there was only one time he ever saw Steve in a scuffle. He opened a door to see Steve, halfway down a back staircase, pinning a boy against the wall as if responding to a provocation. Steve and Russell made eye contact, and without a word, the boy knew what he had to do. "He just backed right off," Russell says. "Most of the time he just stayed out of trouble."

Indeed, more often than not, the staff called on Steven to diffuse any trouble.

"If you had a problem, you'd call on Steve," says Alice Hebden. She remembers the guards once called Steve down to the kitchen because the cook was having trouble with an unruly boy. "He knew how to quiet them down. He would just talk to them quietly."

"If he was in the [military] service, he would have been a leader of men," Ray Nankivell says with almost fatherly pride. "They all respected him. They looked up to him. If I ever had any trouble with any of the boys, I would say, 'Steve, have a word with so-and-so.'"

"Steve had leadership qualities that were unbelievable," says Dave Mills. "He didn't do things half-heartedly. If I had to have a boy, I would like to have a son like Steve."

Indeed, Mills saw Steve as part of his family. It was not unusual for the guards to bring their relatives to the school for holidays and to see shows put on by the boys. Mills' wife and his two young daughters got to know Steven well. "I was always struck by Steve's good manners," Mills remembers, adding he never once felt nervous having a convicted murderer play with his girls.

Steve's ease at winning over the hearts of guards and fellow cellmates was profoundly disturbing to the psychiatrists, who were still convinced they had a dangerous sex offender on their hands just waiting to explode.

"He has maintained, up until now, his facade of innocence, bravado and sureness of himself by playing the role of the lone wolf," psychiatrist James Hartford reported. "This has helped him maintain the kind of iron curtain of denial around him. But this kind of isolation is something that must be maintained at its full strength at all times, twenty-four hours a day. He cannot let down for a moment because if he does he might make a slip."

Hartford came up with a strategy to ensnare this patient who so adamantly maintained his innocence. For more than a year the psychiatrist had taken Steve's "lack of affect" as proof of guilt. But now he reversed positions and told the boy *not* to become too friendly and emotionally involved with others. "I told him that it was perhaps not a good idea for him to let down his guardedness," Hartford said. "In this manner I have him on a spot. If he withdraws from these involvements he will be doing so because I suggested it, and therefore will see me as being on his side. If he doesn't withdraw and they do produce a degree of disorganization in him, he will also see me as having foretold it."

On paper, it looked like an ingenious way to force what Hartford called "an impending breakdown of [Steve's] defences." But six months later, the doctor had to admit the patient seemed to have foiled his plot.

In a memorandum to the superintendent, the psychiatrist accepted grudgingly "the high esteem" the other boys had for Steve. "He has assumed the role of the benevolent leader and enlists strong loyalties and sincere respect. The boys apparently help to maintain his denial by feeling that he is a victim of injustice," Hartford complained. "This creates a dangerous

336

situation because it becomes a generalized sort of delusion in which everyone participates, but it is nevertheless unreal and will eventually force Truscott into a more and more godlike role."

Hartford apparently never stopped to consider that if everyone else thought Steven was innocent, perhaps the delusion was the psychiatrist's.

Superintendent Don Williams, for one, did not see Steven as "godlike" but he certainly seemed to describe him as practically angelic—at least from a disciplinary point of view. "An aura of mystery still surrounds this boy," Williams wrote in an assessment report in 1961. "He has been in this school over a year and has yet to be charged for misconduct. There have been occasions when his inner controls have been sorely tested by the daily strain of the situation—seeing the other boys come and go and the uncertainty of his own future. . . . We anticipate that one of these days Steve will have to give expression to these pent-up emotions, if for no other reason than to release the pressure."

That anticipated explosion never came. By the middle of the year, Williams was recording that Steven was participating in "all activities with plenty of interest and desire" and showed "sound leadership." By year's end, there was no change. "Steve continues to behave like a model student. His participation in all phases of our program is good and he has yet to be placed on charge for any form of misbehaviour. There are times when he could be likened to a robot."

Six months later—by June of 1962—Steve still had an unblemished record after almost three years behind bars. "Steve continues to exercise remarkable control of his emotions and general actions," the superintendent reported. "As yet Steve has not been on charge . . . and always manages to give a good account of himself."

The objective reality was too hard even for psychiatrist James Hartford to ignore. "[Steve] has been here two years and has adjusted himself so successfully that he is quite unique," he admitted in his final report on the boy he seemed determined to crack. "The following remarks embody my own speculations, which hopefully are based upon more than appearances," he wrote, perhaps sensing how thin his speculation was. "When Steven came here I was struck by his lack of affect," Hartford wrote. "He has changed. I fear that the changes we see are all on the surface. . . . His offence is dealt with a firmly defended denial and this primitive defence covers a good many of his conflicts. I would consider there to be considerable danger to other people when this denial is broken down."

The psychiatrist ended his report with a stern warning. "I still consider Steven to be egocentric, narcissistic, uninvolved with other people as with things. . . . I also consider him, as of today, potentially dangerous to other people."

Hartford would get one more chance to assess Steven in four years' time. But then it would be on a prominent national and very public stage—the Supreme Court of Canada.

For several months Steve's parents had been trying desperately to find out what Ottawa had in store for their son. In the spring of 1962, Dan Truscott learned that when his son turned eighteen at the start of the following year, prison authorities would transfer him permanently to a federal penitentiary in Kingston. The chairman of the parole board, George Street, told the Truscotts that as a matter of course they would be reviewing Steven's case since he was so young, but Street would not give Dan any commitments. "So I guess we'll have to wait and see and hope," Dan wrote.

Easter weekend that year gave Steven and his friends a chance to let off some steam after another winter of incarceration—and an excuse to show off some of their talents to families and invited guests from the community of Guelph. The boys put on skits and musical numbers. The program listed Steven in the choir's performance of "Milk and Honey" and "Open Your Heart." He also played guitar and sang an enthusiastic, if not altogether melodic, rendition of the Everly Brothers hit "Dream."

One of the couples in attendance was enjoying the show so much they telephoned their babysitter to ask her if she minded working a little later.

Not at all, said Marlene, the seventeen-year-old the well-to-do couple had hired. The daughter of a labour organizer from the working-class part of town, Marlene was only too glad to make some extra cash. When the couple returned home, they talked excitedly about the show they had seen at the institution.

"What is that place?" Marlene asked.

"It's a training school for boys," they told her. "There was even a boy out there who was in for a murder of a classmate."

Marlene went home and put the story out of her mind. "I never thought any more about it," she said. But in four years, she would get caught up in a very public battle over the boy who played guitar at the Guelph reform school talent show.

Steve's stay at the training school was coming to an end. Christmas Day in 1963—as in previous years—was a low-key affair, with no parties or presents, which could spark jealousy among boys in detention. Instead, there were only a few cards from family and friends, some mild revelry in the cell-blocks and then lights out. "Christmas just reminds you of everything you don't have, everyone you are not with," Steve recalls.

Five days before Christmas, there was a more sombre atmosphere at another jail in Ontario. For several years, it had been the practice of the government to commute all death sentences to life imprisonment when the jury had recommended clemency. But in two recent cases, the juries made no plea for mercy. Ronald Turpin was found guilty of murdering a policeman and Arthur Lucas guilty of stabbing to death another man. Ottawa made no move to stop their death sentences. In Toronto's Don Jail, they were executed, one after the other, in the early hours of December 20.

Turpin and Lucas were the last people to be hanged in Canada. Already there were limits on the use of capital punishment. "Bowing to public pressure" generated in part by Steven's case, says historian Carolyn Strange, "the Diefenbaker government introduced legislation in 1961 that provided a statutory prohibition against the execution of juveniles under the age of eighteen." In 1966, when Steven's case would again become the centre of public controversy, the death penalty debate resurfaced—and Canada took its first steps toward the complete abolition of capital punishment.

Steven had escaped the hangman's noose but for the jailed teenager another deadline loomed. He was only a month away from his eighteenth birthday, which meant he could no longer stay in the relatively benign confines of the Ontario Training School. For months, staff and administrators at the Guelph institution had tried to figure out a way to keep the boy with them, but their lobbying efforts failed. Prison authorities were determined to send him to Collins Bay Penitentiary in Kingston.

In early January Dan Truscott spoke on the phone to federal justice minister Donald Fleming. "He told me he was sorry," Dan reported, but there was nothing the minister could do. At the government's suggestion, Steve's parents took a tour of the federal prison with the warden. They were pleased to see the prison had a good training department, but the visit did little to assuage their panic. "Once he is sent to Collins Bay he is fingerprinted, photographed and given a number which will follow him the rest of his life," Dan wrote to Isabel LeBourdais.

"Don't worry," the writer tried to reassure Steve's parents, typing the next words in upper case to reinforce their resolve: "WE ARE GOING TO GET HIM CLEARED AND THE RECORDS WILL NO LONGER EXIST!"

On January 18, 1963, Steven celebrated his eighteenth birthday—a symbolic passage to manhood for most boys. But for Steven Murray Truscott, turning eighteen meant a one-way ticket to a high-security prison.

Jailed at fourteen and then sent to a reform school until he was eighteen, Steven never went to high school. No football championships, dates with cheerleaders or prom nights. Steve instead had spent his formative teenage years behind bars. He came into the Guelph reform school a frightened fifteen-year-old; he left as a chain-smoking, confident yet shy young man who had added both weight and sadness to his now muscular frame.

"I remember the sadness that befell us all when we finally had to surrender him to Collins Bay," says Les Horne, the librarian who was the first to see Steven when he had arrived in Guelph three years earlier. Indeed, Steven's case so moved Horne that a few years later, when he left the prison system to become the provincial child advocate in Ontario, he opposed every attempt to move a child defendant to the adult criminal system.

Alice Hebden wept unabashedly as she hugged Steven. "It was just the same as if I had a son," she says.

"The kitchen staff was crying, the female staff were crying, the teachers were crying," recalls Ray Nankivell, Steve's supervisor for much of his stay in Guelph. The male guards tried to keep their composure as they shook hands with their favourite young charge, but Nankivell confesses a little water came to his eyes as well.

"I was very sorry to see him go," Nankivell says, not just because he would miss Steve, but also because the veteran guard at the reform school knew the dangers that lay ahead for the boy: "He was going to prison."

## NUMBER 6730

"**H**ow would you like to go for a ride?"

Fred Smith, the warden at Collins Bay prison was asking one of the supervisors, Don Patterson, a question that was really an order.

"Sure, where to?" Patterson complied, always eager for an assignment that took him outside the drab walls of the penitentiary.

"Guelph," his boss explained. "Go up to Guelph, pick up Steven Truscott and bring him back."

As he stood in the warden's office, Patterson's mind flashed back to the day three years before, when he first saw the frightened boy who had come to sleep overnight in the Kingston penitentiary complex. Now his job was to bring that boy back for a much longer stay—in theory, for the rest of his life.

Patterson had to transfer not only the prisoner, but also his file. Once in Guelph, he met for two hours with the training school supervisors to get their assessment of his newest charge.

"He was an ideal inmate; we'd wish he'd stay here," they told him. "For a young chap, he was really well-motivated. He wasn't going to sit in a cell and mope all day."

Patterson then took a nervous Steven into a side room and introduced himself.

"You know where you're going?" he asked.

"Yeah," replied Steven.

"You're going right back where you were temporary before. Back to prison—only this time not in hospital," Patterson said. "There's two ways you can go back there: in handcuffs, or sit down beside me driving all the way back and enjoy the ride."

"Mr. Patterson," Steve said immediately, "you'll never have one bit of trouble with me."

And he didn't. "I never took the handcuffs out of my pocket," Patterson recalls. For Steven, it was a welcome contrast to the humiliating shackles the Goderich sheriff had put on him for his first prison transfer. This time, when Patterson stopped at a restaurant to treat Steve to a juicy steak dinner, there were no embarrassing chains or cumbersome handcuffs.

"That sort of broke the ice," Patterson said. As the teenager and his new friend made their way through the snow-covered southern Ontario country-side, Patterson tried to prepare his passenger for the hardships that lay ahead. He warned him about "muscle groups" that go after the youngest inmates. "They'll get him in there and he's their kid," Patterson explained—everything from sexual favours to more menial tasks.

"When you get there, any trouble at all, you come to me," Patterson tried to assure Steve.

The supervisor changed topics. "There's a machine shop there, are you interested?"

"Yup," the young man answered.

"Well, you'll meet a super guy who runs a small shop there with only about six other inmates," Patterson promised.

As the car sped along the highway on that cold winter day in January of 1963, Steven considered his uncertain future. Then, as Patterson pulled into the parking lot on Bath Street in Kingston, the aging stone walls of Collins Bay loomed in front of him. The red copper towers that sat atop the castle-like entrance earned the prison complex the name "Disneyland" among the locals. But the six hundred-or-so permanent tourists inside its thirty-foot walls would give it the more appropriate label of "Gladiator School."

Though technically a medium-security institution, the fortress structure and tough population of Collins Bay made it what the authorities called a "high-medium" prison. When the gate of heavy iron bars closed behind

Steven, he forgot all the reassuring words from Don Patterson: "It scares you half to death," Steve remembers. He later told his family it was like being put on a plane blindfolded and landing in another country where you don't speak the language.

Steven walked along a long hallway with a low ceiling and bland green and yellow walls. The corridor was called Gaza Strip, because inmates walked down one side, guards down the other. Steve's "drum" (living quarters) was on cellblock "C," third door on the right, Number 5. The two-inch-thick wooden door was only about twenty-two inches wide, with two solid fifteen-inch hinges and a tiny black metal slot to allow guards to peer in. The cell came furnished with a tiny sink in the right-hand corner, two metal shelves, a cot and a small window in the back.

Gazing at his new living quarters—one of two dozen cells on a range that housed murderers, thieves and hard-time convicts—Steve did not yet realize how lucky he was. "C" block was a choice location, sort of the upper-class neighbourhood of the prison, because the cell's solid doors—instead of open bars—afforded inmates a measure of privacy and quiet. His prison fatigues were appropriately drab black boots, grey pants and a white T-shirt. Only one thing distinguished his outfit from the hundreds of other incarcerated men: a label bearing the number 6730.

At the age of eighteen, Steven Murray Truscott's identity had been reduced to four digits.

"It was a grim place to go in," Doris Truscott says today, remembering her visit to see Steven in a penitentiary. "You hear those doors shut behind you and you think, 'Oh God, imagine this every day, every day—you're lucky to be sane when you come out of those places!' That was my thought."

Prison rules stipulated his parents could visit him only once a month for an hour, or twice a month for thirty minutes. Doris and Dan decided they would alternate visits by themselves with visits accompanied by the other children. "I believe that once Steve becomes acclimatized to this new system, he will get along fine," Doris wrote with her typical grin-and-bear-it resolve. "He seems very happy, was put right to work in shop and says they have wonderful equipment and instruction is very good."

That instruction came from a man who would become Steve's surrogate father figure, replacing the Guelph guards who had watched over him in the training school. Joe Fowler, a grizzled former World War II navy seaman, would put in thirty-eight years in the Collins Bay machine shop before he eventually retired in 1985. "You don't have to be crazy," he says, reflecting on his career as a prison instructor, "but it helped me."

He remembers the call he got one morning from Warden Fred Smith.

"Joe, I'm sending you a con that's coming down from Guelph," the warden said. "Keep an eye on him, he's a young lad." Fowler said he'd look after him.

"He looked like a scared boy, a very, very scared boy," Fowler remembered. "He seemed lost; he didn't know which way to turn. He was very quiet, kind of withdrawn, very bashful."

Fowler realized he had to connect with the boy right away. He knew Steve's father was in the air force, so the veteran seaman chatted away about the armed forces, and Steve lightened up at once. "He came right out of his shell," Fowler says. Not one to rush to judgment, Fowler says he waited two years before making up his mind about the convicted killer standing before him.

For the next few years, the grinding motors and flying sparks in Fowler's shop became the centre of Steve's life. Fowler taught the eager student arc welding, acetylene work, brazing and propane torch manoeuvres. Together, they fixed prison farm machinery, took care of kitchen equipment, replaced cellblock locks and did maintenance in the boiler room. Anything that broke inside the walls of Collins Bay, they fixed. Guards would even bring in their home appliances for quick repair work. For community groups, Steve built wheelchair lifts for vehicles. "That boy got an education in there that nobody else could have got—he's done it all," Fowler said. "He listened. That's why he was as smart as he was—he listened."

Fowler carefully watched over his new trainee—he was, after all, a convict charged with raping a child, not usually the most popular type of inmate in the prison culture. Don Patterson also regularly dropped by the machine shop to keep an eye on the teenager.

"Has anyone bothered you? How are things going?" he would ask Steven.

The new arrival never reported any problems. In fact, he quickly made friends with some of the other inmates. After the first month passed without incident, Patterson relaxed. "Once he got over that hurdle, he was okay."

Steve's fellow prisoners felt the same same way. One of the inmates at Collins Bay was Mike McGuin, who knew Steve briefly from the Guelph reform school. Mike had left the reformatory before Steve, but had been arrested on new charges and now found himself in a penitentiary. He was struck by how quickly Steve picked up the survival skills of prison life. "There's a code that you go by and I never remember anyone bothering Steve. Everybody liked him."

Mike's older brother Ted was also in the same prison. Both brothers were such regular offenders one prison official quipped they were doing life on the instalment plan. Hardened convicts like Ted were impressed that Steven, accused of raping a child, survived unscathed in a prison environment where sex crimes were rarely tolerated. "At that time there was some honour in the joint," Ted says. "It's like nobody touched him because . . . we all believed in his innocence." In McGuin's eyes, Steven had passed an important test. "He went to a tougher court than any court in this country, and he was found innocent in our court."

In Steve's mind, he had passed an internal mental test as well. For years, since his arrest in June of 1959, Steve had convinced himself that it was all a nightmare—the arrest, the jailing, the preliminary, the trial, the verdict, the death sentence, the reform school—that somehow, somewhere, someone would realize it was all a mistake and free him. It never happened, but Steve always clung to the hope that someone would rescue him.

Now, as the bitter winter winds swirled around the prison yard in Kingston, Steven finally accepted it would not happen. He was alone. "I knew I wasn't getting out. It sort of hits home that no one is coming to get you out," he says. "You sort of harden yourself up because you don't know what to expect."

While Steve was trying to find his way in the confines of a gloomy penitentiary, Isabel LeBourdais was trying to break down the no less daunting walls of a publishing industry that seemed determined to condemn her investigation to a silent death.

LeBourdais had signed a contract with McClelland & Stewart in late 1961. By the end of 1962, she was telling the Truscotts the publisher had returned her 350-page draft with "scathing criticisms . . . so I started all over again." As Steven was settling into Collins Bay, LeBourdais told his parents she had a September publication date. "There is still a lot of detail to be worked over but daylight is finally in sight," she informed the Truscotts, but quickly added a cautionary note: "During the past year I have had a series of disagreements with Jack McClelland."

345

In fact, McClelland was getting cold feet. Even a trip to Clinton with LeBourdais did not allay the fears of one of the most powerful publishers in Canada. Fearing lawsuits and a political maelstrom from a book that so brazenly took on the legal establishment, McClelland implored LeBourdais to tone down her book.

For the next two years LeBourdais battled to get Steven's story out while continuing to unearth new findings about the case. In 1963, she wrote to the chief coroner of Ontario, Dr. Frank Cotnam, to request a copy of Dr. John Penistan's official autopsy report. Much to her surprise—and Cotnam's—there was no official report on file. Cotnam wrote to Penistan asking for one; two weeks later he informed LeBourdais he still had no news, which he found odd, he told her, because it should have been as simple as putting a copy in the mail.

Finally, the typed, undated report arrived, and LeBourdais sat on a sofa in Cotnam's office to read it (he would not let her make a copy). She discovered that nowhere in the report she saw did Penistan specify the 7:15 to 7:45 time of death. "I was, in fact, astounded that the report gave NO time of death other than forty-five hours before the identification [of Lynne's body]," she wrote.

Someone else was also carrying out new investigations into the four-year-old case of Steven Truscott. Harold Graham of the OPP had quickly moved up the ranks after his headline-grabbing resolution of the Lynne Harper murder. By 1961, Graham had become the OPP's chief inspector. In 1963, with more than a hundred murder investigations under his belt, he was promoted to assistant commissioner, taking charge of the anti-gambling and anti-rackets squad in addition to the CIB. He furthered his reputation by heading investigations into allegations that gangland figures had bribed senior OPP officers.

Graham learned that Ken Russell, the guard who used to toe-wrestle with Steven at the Guelph training school, had become an OPP officer. In the middle of 1963, Russell got an unsettling message, asking him to come to Toronto headquarters to meet with Assistant Commissioner Graham.

"What have I done wrong?" worried the new recruit.

Russell duly reported to Graham's secretary. He waited for about fifteen minutes until Graham arrived, wearing a large overcoat. "Come in the office," his superior ordered. Once inside, Graham got straight to the point:

"You were at the Guelph training school?"

"Yes."

"You were a supervisor there?"

"Yes."

"Do you know Truscott?"

"Yes."

"I'm just going to ask you one question. During the time you were there, did he ever talk about it to you?" Graham said, referring to Lynne's murder.

"No, he never mentioned a word. As far as I know, nobody mentioned it to him and he didn't mention it to anyone else," Russell replied.

"Okay fine, thank you very much," Graham said, and the meeting was over.

Graham never asked Russell point-blank if he thought Steven was guilty or innocent. "It was hard to say—I wasn't too sure myself," Russell says. "To me Steve had a little bit of a curtain. There was a little bit behind that you didn't know about."

He did not find it curious that, four years after a court had supposedly settled Steven's guilt once and for all, Graham was still poking around the case. "He worked so many angles," said Russell.

Back at Collins Bay, Steve once again was facing some intensive grilling of his own, with a battery of psychologists and psychiatrists trying to break the young man's stubborn insistence on his innocence. Only now, the mind games would be much more extreme than at the Guelph school—going all the way to truth serum and hard drugs. And this time, the stakes were much higher. At Collins Bay, the psychiatrists were trying not only to unlock the supposed secrets buried inside Steven's brain; the doctors also held the key to his release. Without a psychiatric endorsement of Steve's rehabilitated mental health, the eighteen-year-old would never get parole.

For the next five years, Steve's nemesis would be Dr. George D. Scott, a small, unassuming man who seemed particularly keen on cracking the mystery of Lynne Harper's murder. "I have been interested in the psychological aspects of his case and feel he will require considerable psychiatric attention before any understanding of his offence can be postulated," he wrote to the National Parole Board in June of 1964. "In the next period of time he will be seen at some length from both the psychological and psychiatric point of view . . . to try and uncover the fundamental motives for his offence."

At their first meeting, Steve found the doctor friendly and outgoing. "But he had the same attitude as the others: 'I'm a prison psychiatrist. If you're not guilty you wouldn't be here,'" Steve says. "He had one mission when it came to me—to get a confession, and I always got the feeling that it was a big disappointment that he couldn't get an admission of guilt."

"He was like a scared rabbit," Scott says today. "He had a secret. . . . The secret was repressed by him—whatever it was." Scott speculated that perhaps Steven had attempted to kiss Lynne, and when she fought back he tried to stop her from screaming, accidentally strangling her. "At fourteen years old, it's a world of instant reaction," he says. "I didn't think he *knew* he murdered the girl. I didn't think he knew that he had done an evil deed."

One of the first full-time psychiatrists in the Kingston-area prisons, Scott says he was a "path breaker" in the use of electroshock treatment and what was called "narcotherapy"—softening up patients with drugs. "My life was spent doing things that were damn near innovative," he says. "I was the big honcho then."

In 1964, at forty-nine years old, Scott was perhaps also hoping the Truscott case would give his career a much-needed boost. His reputation had suffered a serious blow when an inmate named Léopold Dion, serving a life sentence for sex crimes, was paroled. "George came out unequivocally— this man does not represent any risk to the community," one prison official recalled. Within a year of his release, Dion murdered four boys in Quebec in 1963.

The psychiatrist would take no chances with the famous child murderer now under his care in Collins Bay. Scott determined that the best way to "uncover the motives" for Steven's crime would be to loosen the boy up with the help of some drugs. Within a month of filing his first report on Steven, the Truscotts got wind of the doctor's proposals. "Steve told me that [Scott] wished to administer some drug that would make him relax, and he refused to take it," Doris wrote in a letter to Isabel LeBourdais.

His parents went to talk it over with the warden and then wrote to Scott himself. "We certainly do not want Steve to refuse any treatment if it means jeopardizing his chances of parole, but we did tell him we did not feel this was the time for any truth serum," they said. "If he must, he must, but first we would like to talk to you."

On August 15 the Truscotts met with the psychiatrist, who convinced them of the wisdom of drug therapy, suggesting that the mind sometimes "blanks out" the memory of a criminal deed. They then reported to the doctor that they had "a very good talk with Steven."

"We were first quite concerned how to approach Steve and the subject of taking these injections, as we did not want to leave him with the impression that we did not think he was telling the truth," they said. "So we explained to him what Warden Smith had said regarding how the parole board [based] so much of its decision on the psychiatric reports. . . . We told him that the only way he could expect to be released was by co-operating."

Steven, according to his parents' account, pleaded for support. "Dad, what more do they want to know?" he begged. "I've already told him all I can."

Desperate to get their son out of prison, his parents authorized the drug tests. "Dr. Scott, we are more concerned than ever to get to the bottom of things," they wrote. "We hereby authorize you to carry out any test with Steve that you deem necessary to aid him in obtaining his parole."

The next entry in the psychiatric file is a handwritten note by Scott saying that Steven "at his own request . . . wishes to proceed with psychiatric treatment." The drug tests were scheduled to begin October 1.

It is not clear from the files if Scott spelled out to the Truscotts exactly what kinds of drugs he was planning to use, or their possible side effects. Typically, psychiatrists used some kind of relaxant, commonly known as "truth serum," which lowered an individual's usual psychological defences and theoretically made the subject more prone to talking and opening up. But Scott and many of his colleagues were also experimenting with a more powerful mind-altering drug called lysergic acid diethylamide—LSD.

Just 150 miles east of Kingston, at the Allan Memorial Institute in Montreal, one of Canada's leading psychiatrists, Dr. Ewen Cameron, was making widespread use of LSD in a series of terrifying experiments on unsuspecting patients. His work, financed in part by the American CIA, sparked an uproar years later when details came to light.

Dr. Scott was running a smaller-scale laboratory using prisoners as human test subjects. His extensive use of LSD on female inmates in Kingston during the 1960s prompted a federal government inquiry three decades later. "LSD with some people can glorify their problems—make them clear to them," Scott says by way of explanation. With luck, he hoped it would crack Steven's shell.

As early as 1961, descriptions of the toxicity and adverse effects of LSD had been reported in several medical publications. Sandoz, the company that manufactured the psychedelic drug, had warned psychiatrists of "possible abuse" in 1962. Still, drug therapy was a fairly common, if legally murky, practice in the prison system of the 1960s. Technically, all that was needed was informed consent. Scott persuaded Steve's parents to get Steve to consent; it is debatable that any of them made their decision in an "informed" way.

In any case, the supposed justification for the drug therapy—improving the chances for parole—was a non-starter. Steve and his parents rightly surmised that without the blessing of a psychiatrist, he would never get parole. What they did not know was that Steve could not get parole for some time. Under federal law, no inmate serving a life term after a commuted death sentence was even eligible for parole until spending ten years behind bars. Nevertheless, there was nothing to stop an inmate from applying for parole at any time. As early as January 1963—as Steve was being transferred from Guelph to Collins Bay—the parole board reported they "did not deem it advisable to grant parole." They ruled his case would come under review again in January of 1965 and so, in August of 1964, Steven filed an application.

"I know five years is not very long for a sentence like mine, but I was very young, and all I ask is just one chance to prove that I'm worthy of being allowed to mix with society," he wrote. "I have done my best to keep a clean record while I am serving my sentence. I have reached the stage where being locked up will be of no more good to me."

Then came the one sentence that would cause Steven much trouble in the years to come: "I have paid five years of my life but *this has taught me that crime does not pay*, so all I ask is please grant me one chance to make a success of my life and prove that *one dreadful mistake does not mean that I will ever make another one.*"

Those who believed Steven was guilty would later seize on those words as being tantamount to a confession, though Steven would give quite a different interpretation—that he was talking in general about the lessons of incarceration, not admitting to any specific crime.

In fact, there was evidence in his parole file to back up his claim. Two weeks after he wrote those words, Steve met with a parole classification assistant named W. J. Haggerty. The prison official, having read the dossier and interviewed Steven, came to a simple conclusion: "Truscott still claims innocence of the present offence but accepts his sentence with the feeling that nothing can be done now." One month later, another parole officer, J. Sullivan, met with Steven and reported the inmate's statement: "I do not think I am guilty."

Steve's parole file also included uncommonly strong words of praise from his guards. One official, identified only as Squad Commander Smith, wrote, "Without a doubt the most polite and co-operative inmate I have ever dealt with. . . . Although he is serving a life sentence, I cannot picture him as a criminal." Joe Fowler, the machine shop trainer, said, "This has been the most outstanding inmate I have ever had work for me. His work is excellent—and he produces with a minimum of supervision. You can depend on him to do his best at all times."

But Fowler and the rest of the prison staff were too gullible, as far as the psychiatrists and psychologists were concerned. In early September of 1964, Dr. A. Celovsky, a consultant psychologist, remarked that on the surface Steven showed "good outward control" and "a demeanour beyond reproach." But his testing purported to uncover something much darker. "On further scrutiny the test data point to an aloof, self-centred, peculiarly detached individual," Dr. Celovsky reported. "Keeping very much to himself, he manages to cover with a good cloak of control what would otherwise set him in an unfavourable light."

On December 1, chief prison psychiatrist George Scott reported that though he had seen the patient several times since June in "superficial" meetings, he had just completed the "prime psychiatric interview."

"I found this man polite and perfunctory," Scott said, noting the young inmate struck him as "somewhat sad." Scott laid out four possibilities for Steven: that he committed the crime and did not want to admit it; that he had "subconsciously forgotten the whole affair because it was so sordid"; that he was innocent but covering for someone who did the crime; and finally, that he did not commit the offence.

The doctor implied he did not think the last alternative was likely. "I wanted him to know that he could consciously be forgetting the whole situation because it was so traumatic," he said, holding out a carrot to Steven: "[I] further exhorted him that if he could remember it, the problems related to his case would be simplified."

Scott had originally planned to start using truth serum injections on December 15, 1964. Instead, the doctor delayed the drugs and questioned Steven about what he called adolescent experimentation with sex. Scott reported that Steven did not answer questions about Lynne Harper directly, except to say, "She wasn't that good-looking." Asked if he had sex with other girls, Steve said he could have if he wanted to, according to the doctor.

With or without drugs, Scott seemed confident he could wrest a confession out of the reluctant convict. "I would suspect that if we continue in this type of interview some astounding revelations will occur as time goes on," he boasted. The doctor felt 1965 was going to be a make-or-break year in the battle to unlock the secrets of Steven's mind.

By the time Steve marked his twentieth birthday in January 1965, he had been inside Collins Bay for two years. He barely noticed that outside the prison's walls, the sea change that came to be known simply as "the sixties" was beginning to dramatically alter the country he had left behind.

John Diefenbaker, the Conservative leader who had commuted Steven's death sentence, had gone down to defeat at the polls in 1963. Lester B. Pearson's Liberals ushered in a new period of reform, bringing in the new Maple Leaf flag, a national medicare program—and a young intellectual from Quebec named Pierre Elliott Trudeau, who, as justice minister, in a few years would get his chance to wrestle with a new Truscott controversy.

A telling sign of the times came via the small screen. Back in 1959, Steve and his friends had thrilled to simple-minded TV cop shows like *Dragnet*. By 1965, a hit new series was now in its second season. It featured David Jansen as *The Fugitive*, a wrongfully convicted man running from the police. Popular culture was not only suggesting the justice system sometimes made mistakes— it was making a hero out of someone railroaded by the police and the courts.

Inside the confines of the psychiatrist's office in Collins Bay prison, however, there was little room for such doubt. Dr. George Scott began the year questioning Steven if, in his imagination, "he ever decided how Lynne had died." Steve simply replied he never imagined what happened to her after he left her at the highway.

Did Steve not think she would scream, Scott asked.

Steve said he thought she would.

Was it possible he had forgotten the crime because the murder was so out of character for him?

"There was more anxiety" from Steven over this question, Scott reported, but "he does not think about the murder at all over the last few years and has put it out of his mind."

To get at the truth about the murder trapped in Steve's mind, Scott was now ready to use chemical inducements. Steven saw it as a necessary pact with the devil, a gamble he felt he was sure to win. "I wanted out and the only way I was going to get out was by him putting in a favourable report, and the only way he was going to [do that] was if I did all these tests," Steve explains. "I finally said to Scott, 'I'll do the tests providing when you're done, if you find nothing to prove that I'm guilty, you go along with my way of thinking about it.'"

A note in Scott's files confirms that the doctor assured Steven that through drug treatment he might be able to recall something related to the offence that could help "with his eventual release from [this] institution."

Never for a moment, Steve says, did he fear that the drugs would bring to the surface a secret so deep perhaps he did not even know he had buried it. "I knew I wasn't guilty, so I said okay. I had no hesitation. Whatever tests you want to do, I'll go along with them. And I did."

The first recorded use of drugs on Steven was on February 16, 1965, starting with sodium pentothal, a popular relaxant widely used after World War II as a sort of truth serum. The drug slowed the patient's heart rate and relieved tension and anxiety. Often, nitrous oxide—commonly known as "laughing gas"—was added as an anaesthetic.

Scott—who says he administered over five hundred such treatments in his career—had to use "a great deal of caution" with the drug—too fast, and his patient would slip into unconsciousness, too slow, and Steve would just be enveloped by giddiness.

"[It was] just to take the edge out of the brittleness of emotion," Scott explains. But it didn't work. If the serum helped Scott uncover any secrets in Steven's brain, he wasn't telling anyone. No findings appear in the available files for the next two months.

On April 9 and 10, over a period of "five hours of treatment," Scott gave Steven four hundred grams of LSD. More doses soon followed, and Scott noted he planned to use the drugs again "in about five to six months." Once again, the psychiatrist was disappointed.

"His reaction during the five hours of treatment was remarkably over-controlled," Scott reported. "He lay on the bed with eyes in an upturned position. He had a gentle smile on his face but he felt very little. . . . From time to time his back would straighten and arch tightly, raising his body on his toes and his head."

The medical staff kept a close watch on their drugged patient in the next twenty-four hours. The logs record Steve saw "many beautiful and desired memories together with gritty childhood recollections"—but no confessions to murder. Today, Steve remembers only a vague feeling of disorientation and a vision of bright, flashing lights.

Scott seemed unwilling to shake his belief the young prisoner was hiding something, despite turning up nothing on his drug-assisted expedition into the far reaches of Steve's unconscious mind. "At times I feel there is nothing to investigate in this case. . . . He [is] so controlled, so pleasant and so objective that certainly there must be in his subconscious a tremendous control for commanding details," Scott wrote in May of 1965. "The rapport between Truscott and myself is good, but I will have to continue to see him for some time yet before even the slightest break in the case occurs."

The good rapport appears to have been largely in Scott's mind; for his part, Steve was now increasingly alarmed about the psychiatrist's designs. "Was Dad able to reach him?" he asked his parents in early May, desperate for them to help him. "If so, what did he have to say about this next test he's going to do? He told me that he wasn't going to do anything until I said I was guilty, or if I could convince them that I didn't do this. I said that I'd go along with him . . . but only if at the end of the tests nothing comes up he would go along with me—and he didn't say anything. He's got his mind set that I'm guilty and there's no chance of me changing his mind."

Doris Truscott remembers her frustration. "The tests they gave him did not prove that Steve was guilty, but Scott said it did not change their opinion. Well, I thought, 'They've got their minds made up. Nothing's going to change their mind.'"

Still, on Sunday, May 23, Steve's parents spent an hour with their son, trying to convince him to keep co-operating with Dr. Scott. "I have always instilled in Steven the importance of staying in line," his military father assured an official in the Office of the Commissioner of Penitentiaries in Ottawa.

In his own calm way, though, Steve was holding firm against Scott. "Dad, no matter what I say to him I have the feeling that he thinks I am not telling the truth," he wrote. "Dr. Scott on one of his first visits told me that if I did not admit to the charge or that if I did not truly convince him that I did not commit the crime, he would not put in a favourable report to the parole board."

Increasingly convinced that the doctor he had authorized to use drug treatments on his son had a hidden agenda, Dan Truscott made a bold demand to prison officials in late May of 1965. "I request that Dr. Scott be taken off the case," Dan wrote, asking authorities to let an independent doctor chosen by the family examine their son.

The Truscotts wanted to bring in Dr. John Rich, a visiting lecturer in child psychiatry at Queen's University in Kingston, who specialized in adolescent problems. In principle, federal prison authorities did not raise any objections to the idea, but they seemed in no hurry to give an outside doctor access to Dr. Scott's patient. Months dragged on before the Truscotts got a straight answer.

Meanwhile, in June of 1965, Dr. Scott and Steven confronted each other in the small office on the second-floor hospital ward of the prison.

"It was pointed out to him that unfortunately he is looked upon as a guilty party," the psychiatrist reported. "As such he therefore committed an offence which he will not recognize." Scott told Steven that psychiatric treatment was directed toward getting him to face his guilt "squarely rather than keeping it away from his mind." Or, if he was erroneously convicted, "eventually some information will come up which will completely free him."

Scott recorded there was anger in Steve's voice as the inmate pointed out "what a difficult position he was in." Doctors were suspicious because he was so controlled, Steve explained, but getting mad and expressing himself would only make himself get into a worse position than he was presently in."

The young man's complaint about his Catch-22 situation seemed to have some effect on the doctor. "The psychiatric side of the case was not directed at trying to prove that he was guilty, but was trying to assist him in facing the facts so that eventually he could be released," Scott wrote.

The problem, of course, was that Steve disputed the very fact of his guilt that the psychiatrists wanted him to face. Over the summer, Scott and other experts he enlisted continued to probe Steven's psyche. A psychologist instructed Steven to draw pictures of men and women in what was called—in all seriousness—the "drawing a person test." Somehow the test conclusively showed that Steven exhibited signs of "egocentrism and narcissism," as well as "aggression toward the female figure and a strong identification with the masculine image."

At times, Scott contradicted himself: "He has not actually laughed in one interview that I have had with him over a period of years, although on many occasions I have found myself enjoying some of the conversation and laughing with him."

But to the Truscotts, the stranglehold the prison psychiatrist had on their son's future was no laughing matter. In September, a worried Dan

Truscott wrote directly to Prime Minister Lester Pearson, asking what would happen to Steve's chances of parole "if Dr. Scott . . . does not receive the answers he wants." He again pleaded for help in arranging Dr. Rich's visit to Collins Bay to examine Steven.

The prime minister's office forwarded Dan's letter to the justice minister. An executive assistant to the minister finally informed the cash-strapped family they could send in their own doctor "at your expense." Rich would finally meet Steven in February of 1966, nine months after the Truscotts had made the request.

As Steven's struggle with the prison psychiatric establishment continued, he took solace and strength from new friends and activities inside Collins Bay.

"You just live it day by day," he remembers. "You don't look ahead and you don't look back. What comes up today—that's what happens. There's no way you can plan ahead. You don't know whether you're getting out in five years, ten years or twenty years."

As he did in the Guelph training school, Steven displayed the ability to win over the hearts of usually hardbitten prison guards and officials. "Boy, he was great!" says supervisor Don Patterson. "Never got into a fight. He was cool, calm, collected. He had marvellous self-control for a young chap coming into prison. I thought, 'Well, maybe he had all these pent-up emotions and if he ever broke down, what would happen?' But that wasn't the case at all—he was in control of himself all the while."

As the months turned into years, Patterson's admiration turned into something deeper: an abiding belief in the young inmate's innocence. "You kind of study these people over the years; you get a pretty good handle on them," he says. "You see this person and you speak to him. You realize that you don't think he ever did it."

As a prison guard, of course, Patterson was used to convicts' tales of woe. "Inmates will tell you tales that long," he laughs, stretching his arms far apart. But Steve was different, he insists. "A lot of people had the same feelings about that young lad, yes indeed."

Joe Fowler, Steve's instructor at the machine shop, was coming to the same conclusion. "The warden had told me, 'He's just a kid, just another kid,' but he turned out to be a good kid," Fowler says. "He wouldn't do anything to hurt anybody. He wouldn't hurt a mouse. You'd trust him anyplace."

That trust took concrete form when Fowler worked with Steve for several months on a special project. Both teacher and student were tired of lugging their heavy toolboxes around the prison grounds. So they took a clutch from a stone crusher, a small motor from a lawn mower, metal and trimmings from discarded appliances—and fashioned an odd-looking cross between a dune buggy and a go-kart. Once completed, it had two seats, a small hood and—most important for the two busy repairmen—a trunk in the back to store their tools. Fowler and Steve drove everywhere in their contraption to make their repair calls, sparking waves and laughs from inmates and staff alike. "He looked like King Farouk," Fowler says, remembering Steve's proud smile.

Remarkably, Fowler even got permission to take Steve outside the prison walls in their vehicle. Just beyond the confines of Collins Bay lay a vast prison farm annex, where minimum-risk inmates raised animals and harvested some food for the penitentiaries in the area. Since Steve and Fowler frequently had to repair machinery on the dairy farm, their little car was the easiest way to make the journey. But it meant one of Canada's most celebrated convicted murderers was roaming around open fields with nothing standing between him and freedom except a small farm fence.

Fellow inmate Ted McGuin remembers watching Steve with envy. "He'd drive out that gate *every day* and go over to the annex. I'm sorry, you'd only have to give me *one chance* and I wouldn't have been back."

But Joe Fowler wasn't worried about Steve.

"I told him, 'Don't you try to run away!'" Fowler says.

"Oh, no, Mr. Fowler, I wouldn't do that."

And he never did. "I just knew in my heart he wouldn't escape," Fowler insists. "It wouldn't be hard for him to knock me off and run to freedom. But he wasn't going to run. I knew. I just knew—it's not very often you can say that. He was as true as he could be. Never lied to me."

As Fowler's respect for the boy grew, so did his doubts about Steve's conviction. One day, the machine shop instructor even made a trip out to Clinton to see for himself how far the bridge was from the highway. "How in the hell could the police say he couldn't see the car!" he says. "They tried to make a liar out of him—that's the way I kind of looked at it."

"I could not see the boy doing what they said he did," Fowler continues. "He didn't have the character for that. Not a mean hair on his hand. I guess that's what convinced me he didn't do that crime. I know in my heart he didn't kill anybody. I was too close to him, for too long."

When Steve wasn't working with Fowler in the machine shop, his favourite hangout was the radio room. From a small cubicle jammed with old records and even older equipment, Steve could broadcast news and music throughout the prison (every prisoner had a radio in his cell with the choice of two in-house stations). Every morning, Steve would get up thirty minutes before the other prisoners, fire up the system and put on some rousing music. Over the public address system, he told the inmates to get ready for the guards' count of the prisoners. Then he selected two local radio stations—country music was always a favourite—and plugged them in for the day. In the evening, Steven would read news bulletins from the administration, play records by request and announce upcoming sports activities.

His radio job gave Steven something to do in the evenings—the loneliest part of the day. "The ones that get in trouble are the ones that sit around and do nothing. And then what do you think about—the outside?" Steve says. His disc jockey career also provided the setting for Steven's only run-in with the administration in all of his years at Collins Bay. One night, a kitchen staff member made coffee for some inmates and had no milk; Steve gave him a can of milk they kept in the radio room. The next day, the kitchen helper returned the milk to Steve, who put it in his coat pocket and forgot about it. That night, during a frisking, guards found the milk and accused him of stealing it from the kitchen.

The following day, the deputy warden called the machine shop and told Fowler he was docking Steve thirty days of good time for the theft. "Tell him he can have all my good-time days," Steve joked to Fowler. Both of them knew that an inmate serving life did not get any time off for good behaviour.

Among the other inmates, Steve's closest friends were two other lifers, John and Chuck. Both men, in their early thirties, were serving time on murder charges. It was ironic that after drifting from one military base to another as a child without long-term friends, then spending three years at the Guelph reform school watching other juveniles come and go, Steven finally found a sense of permanency with convicted murderers.

But prison life had its own set of rules. "You didn't hang around short-timers because it hurt too much," Steve explains. "You meet a short-timer, he's in and out, so why become friends with him? You kind of form your friendships with someone who's in for the same time as you so that you know you've got a friend here for a long time."

Still, for all his success in building some semblance of stability inside prison, the one inescapable fact was that a normal life with his family and friends was passing him by. Steve tried hard to keep a grasp on familial ties. In his letters home, he asked about his brother Bill's hockey tournaments, his sister Barb's skiing classes and his older brother Ken's school work. But a few words scrawled on prison stationery were hardly a satisfying substitute for family life. Ken would move out of his parents' house and get married; Bill and Barb grew from the siblings Steve had to babysit into young adults. Except for brief chats in a barren prison visiting room, Steve would miss all of that.

John Carew, one of Steve's childhood friends, came by the prison while he was attending the nearby Royal Military College in Kingston. Any hopes for a warm reunion evaporated in the chasm that now separated the former baseball buddies. "The visit was embarrassing for both of us," Carew recounts. "I just felt so helpless that here was a kid that I played sports with and was a schoolmate. But it was just so awkward. Maybe if we'd been in touch before that it might have been easier, but everything was so different for each of us."

The twelve men who put Steven in prison appeared to show no regrets as the years passed. The jurors of Huron County who had sentenced Steven Truscott in 1959 organized a picnic several years later to keep in touch. "It was only a social gathering, it had nothing to do with the trial," explained the wife of jury foreman Clarence McDonald when the media got wind of the bizarre affair. "The men all became good friends at the trial and thought it would be a good idea to get together for picnics and things."

Former juror Wilmer Dalrymple defended the socializing, saying, "We got to know each other pretty well in the two weeks we were locked up together at the trial, and we thought our wives and kids should get together too." His wife said they received Christmas cards from several other jurors.

Pausing for a moment to think about the boy her husband had found guilty, Mrs. Dalrymple told a newspaper she thought Steven should be released from prison. "After all, he's not the only one to blame if he did it," she said. "It's his parents [who] were at fault in raising him the way they did."

But the jurors' satisfaction over their decision would be short-lived. Isabel LeBourdais' controversial book on the trial was about to be published.

As James King tells it in *Jack*, his biography of Jack McClelland, by late 1964 LeBourdais had grown disillusioned and bitter with Jack McClelland, especially after her mother died. "She died without ever knowing that the book was published, or that I had succeeded in doing anything to save the boy she had grown to care about so much," she wrote. The next year, McClelland told her, "We would like to publish the book, but only if you will stick to the facts and not tilt at windmills."

LeBourdais instead recruited a trusted friend and lawyer, Ted Joliffe, to help her break her contract with the reluctant publisher. She also arranged for Joliffe to visit Steven in prison. She explained to the Truscotts that Joliffe, a left-wing activist with strong ties to the CCF party, had vetted her manuscript and was now intimately familiar with the case. "He intends to stay on the job with us until Steven's conviction has been reversed and the truth has been proved."

LeBourdais then went to London, England, and had little problem convincing Victor Gollancz—a respected publisher with progressive sympathies—to publish her book uncensored and undiluted. He promised he would export copies to Canada, even if that meant he lost money. It was only at that point that McClelland & Stewart leapt at the chance to publish a Canadian edition. It was a sad and embarrassing moment—a story about a pivotal Canadian trial first had to find foreign support before Canada's own publishing industry took it seriously.

"I shall always probably feel somewhat acid about Jack McClelland because of his refusal to take a courageous stand on my book until after Gollancz had done so," LeBourdais noted to a friend.

But at least Steve's story would get out. "Progress!" LeBourdais announced triumphantly to the Truscotts. The book would be published in England on January 13, 1966, and soon after that in Canada. "This time, there will be no glitches and no cowardice on the part of the publisher or his lawyer," LeBourdais wrote. "With any luck, 1966 should see us making news."

In her wildest dreams, she could never have foreseen how right she would be.

# PART THREE

THE PUBLIC BATTLE: 1966–1967

*"I soon came to the conclusion that it wasn't
a sick boy who was guilty, but a perfectly normal
boy who was innocent."*

—Isabel LeBourdais

*"A bad trial remains a bad trial. The only remedy for a
bad trial is a new trial."*

—Supreme Court Justice Emmett Hall

## 32

## A NATIONAL DEBATE

I t did not take long for Steve's story to start making headlines.

*The Trial of Steven Truscott* was scheduled for release in Canada only in March, but the publisher sent advance copies of LeBourdais' book to newspaper editors and members of Parliament. "Book Disputes Evidence on Which Boy Convicted of Murder," the *Globe and Mail* reported in late January, a hint of the furor to come. "If there seems to be any merit in it, I'll look into it at once," Arthur Wishart, Ontario's attorney general responded in a declaration he would soon regret.

For Steven, who had just turned twenty-one behind bars, the publicity was heartening. "I read several articles in different papers about the book and they were pretty good," he wrote his parents in February. "So I'm praying that things work out okay, as I sure want out of here."

It was quite unlike anything the Canadian public—not to mention politicians and police—had ever seen. An investigative book was still a rarity in the 1960s. A book challenging the judicial system was unheard of; that the book was written by a female made it all the more unusual. In the quaint language of the times, many headlines referred to LeBourdais as a "woman writer" or even as a "widow."

A *Toronto Daily Star* columnist, Ron Haggart, captured the uniqueness of LeBourdais' work: "The new kind of journalism for Canada: the review of the judicial process by an intelligent, rational and inquisitive layman who sets out to re-investigate and re-try a case without the preconceived notions of the police and without the artificial and frequently stupid restrictions of the courtroom." Even if LeBourdais was wrong about Steve's innocence, he wrote, "the book is a terrible revelation of the bumptious elegance, the pretense and the ritualistic nonsense which afflicts the Canadian courtroom."

LeBourdais had gone back and carefully read the hundreds of pages of court transcripts—something no reporter covering the trial in 1959 ever thought of doing. She interviewed many of the child witnesses and talked to families on the air base. Basic journalistic methods—but in the uncritical mindset of the times, few observers saw the police and the courts as fair targets of scrutiny. LeBourdais changed the rules.

Her book exposed for the first time some of the glaring problems with Steve's conviction: the constantly changing stories of Butch George, the improbabilities in Jocelyne's tales, the contradictions in the medical testimony, the dubious police tactics and the bias of the presiding judge. One of her most frightening revelations was the prejudice some of the jurors felt toward Steve from almost the opening of the trial.

"I knew the boy was guilty right from the start," one juror admitted to Isabel LeBourdais when she interviewed him a year after the trial. "I had no doubt from the beginning, but I did not form any conclusions until the end," said another. Perhaps the mood of the twelve men from Huron County was best summed up by the angry words of the juror who admitted, "I knew by the third day no one was going to prove that young monster innocent. If we'd had to stay there all winter to convict that fiend, I'd have stayed."

A passionate appeal for justice by a passionate crusader, the book had an openly partisan approach that rankled even sympathetic reviewers. Arthur Maloney, a former MP and head of the Canadian Society for the Abolition of the Death Penalty called LeBourdais' book an "eloquent plea" in his critique for the *Globe and Mail*, but noted "she is guilty of the biased emotional approach" she decried among the jurors. Kildare Dobbs in *Saturday Night* magazine felt the book was "marred by bias." Still, its power impressed him. "We see clearly that the Truscott trial was a solemn farce," he wrote. "At best the Truscott trial was shockingly careless."

Unaccustomed to such bold challenges to their traditionally sacred profession, the defenders of the legal system—even those with no direct stake in the Truscott case—fought back with surprising venom. Joseph Sedgwick, one of Canada's leading criminal lawyers, denounced the book as "an unwarranted attack on the processes of justice" in a front-page article in the *Toronto Daily Star*. At a panel discussion on the book in Toronto, Clay Powell, a prosecutor with the attorney general's department, warned the book "could lead to the eventual destruction of Canada's judicial system."

Not unexpectedly, *The Trial of Steven Truscott* struck a particularly sensitive nerve in Goderich and Clinton. The *Goderich Signal-Star* accused LeBourdais of carrying out a "vicious vendetta" against the county. According to one headline, jurors denounced her as a "City Author Chasing a Buck." Referring to the biased justice in the racially torn southern United States, one city official complained, "The worst thing is that people are liable to think this is some kind of Dallas—you know, Goderich, the Dallas of Canada."

"Residents freely admit that many . . . felt a hostility toward the young suspect and his parents at the time," the *Globe and Mail* reported. "But they say also that none of those feelings influenced the jury into deciding the fourteen-year-old boy was guilty."

What seemed to frighten many people was the unsettling prospect that if their community had erred about Steven in 1959, it exposed a much wider crack in their belief system than they were willing to contemplate. "If we can't have confidence in our courts, what kind of country have we got?" asked John Livermore, the clerk treasurer of the town of Clinton. "As far as I am concerned, it's closed." Others, however, were willing to consider the unthinkable. An unnamed lawyer told a newspaper he felt a "sense of hurt" over the case: "A hurt for what has happened to Steven, of course, but more than that I think, a hurt because that system of justice in which we all believe showed its fallible human side and let us down by erring."

A reporter came across former juror Sidney Pullman, engaged in a debate with his business partner, Lorne Dale. The two men confessed they argued all the time about the merits of the case. "As long as I live, I'll never believe he did it," Dale said. "I think the boy's trial was unfair. There's a lot of things that were never brought out at the trial, things that should have helped that boy."

Pullman, on the other hand, defended his colleagues on the jury as "a fine group," although he was not above admitting there was a fair amount of bias against Steven. "Even if they might have felt the boy was guilty when they went into court," he said, "I think they were fine enough to judge the case on the evidence."

"I still think he was guilty and my conscience is clear," said his fellow juror, Anson Coleman. "I am getting sick and tired of it," added juror John Dietz. "You'd think we were the guilty ones."

In a front-page editorial, Wilma Dinnin, the editor of the *Clinton News-Record* called for "personal soul-searching." Describing LeBourdais' work as "well-documented, well-researched, well-written," she was all too aware that many of her fellow citizens were not keen on reopening old wounds.

"There will be those in this area . . . who will say: 'Why do they have to go into all that again?'" she wrote. But Dinnin had a ready answer. A young man has just turned twenty-one after spending six years in prison, she pointed out, "and to him, we believe 'all that' is important."

Certainly, some of the young people in town agreed with her. Over 190 students from Clinton's Central Huron Secondary School signed a petition calling on the federal solicitor general to take action. One of the petitioners was Gord Logan, the boy whose testimony about seeing Steve and Lynne cross the bridge the jurors refused to believe.

This was the 1960s, after all, and the dawn of a new anti-establishment activism among young people unheard of during the conservative times when Steven was arrested. Other students in Ontario quickly rallied to the cause. In Toronto, fifty-five students from Victoria Park Secondary School signed a petition protesting that "a boy of our generation" may have been wronged. At a conference of the Ontario Older Boys Parliament meeting in Lansing, Ontario, a grade Twelve student spoke out on Steven's behalf, and his classmates agreed to write to the prime minister. Five student leaders received wide press coverage when they arrived in Ottawa in late March to present one of many petitions to the House of Commons. The prime minister's parliamentary secretary told them Pearson had a "personal interest" in the case—and gave them a letter for their principal asking that they be excused for missing school.

Within a few weeks, LeBourdais' book had sold almost sixty thousand copies and its influence began to spread beyond the borders of Canada. The *New York Times* highlighted the story in early April. In England, the *Sunday Telegraph* called the book "brilliant," and concluded "the elaborate system of criminal justice has plainly broken down." The *Sunday Express* told readers the book was "most disturbingly convincing."

Controversy and publicity were well and good, but what Steven needed was action. The pressure mounted as ordinary citizens debated the trial in local riding associations, community centres and churches. "We like to think that our courts are always just, if not infallible," said the *United Church Observer*. "We expect that publication of this book will start things happening."

It did. The Ontario legislature entered the fray when a Toronto newspaper interviewed Dr. John Addison, the family doctor who questioned Steve the night of his arrest. Addison said he told the boy "to confess, to tell the truth, that it would be a lot easier for him if he did." That bothered one Liberal MPP, who wondered if it was normal practice for a doctor to interrogate a patient for the police. It was not, replied Arthur Wishart, the Ontario attorney general, who—despite his pledge in January to look into the case if it had merit—now insisted that the controversial dossier was entirely a federal matter. "I have no authority," he said, even though it was an Ontario police and court system that jailed, tried and sentenced Steven.

It did not take long for the whirlwind to hit Parliament Hill. On March 7, James Byrne, a Liberal MP, called on the solicitor general to hold a royal commission into the Truscott trial, insisting the "cards were stacked" against the boy. "I personally am so convinced of this boy's innocence that I am prepared if necessary to stake my seat in the House of Commons on the outcome of an inquiry or a royal commission," he vowed. Ralph Cowan, a fellow Liberal, denounced Byrne's declaration, condemning him for bringing the entire House into disrepute.

For the next month, there was a relentless barrage against the government from all three opposition parties. Tory opposition leader John Diefenbaker joined the call for some kind of inquiry. NDP House leader Stanley Knowles became Steve's most outspoken defender, visiting him in prison and proclaiming on national television his faith in the young man's innocence. "Sensing the kind of lad that he is and hearing him answer all my questions quite freely and quite straightforwardly . . . convinced me that he didn't commit the crime, indeed convinced me that he couldn't possibly have committed it," he said.

James Byrne joined Knowles and Isabel LeBourdais on Betty Kennedy's popular radio show in Toronto for a ninety-minute special. "I lost faith in the Canadian courts," Byrne proclaimed. "I have lost faith in the legal profession."

LeBourdais gained even greater celebrity status when she appeared on *This Hour Has Seven Days*, the most talked-about TV show of its time. The irreverent current affairs program on the CBC, hosted by Patrick Watson and Laurier LaPierre, was so controversial the network's top brass eventually yanked it off the air. The program featured a lengthy interview with the book author they billed as "the defender of a boy murderer."

"He had some scratches on his body?" the interviewer asked delicately, going through the evidence that helped convict Steve.

"He had injuries on his penis, if you want to call it by its right name," LeBourdais said boldly, becoming perhaps the first person to use the word on national television. She then explained the conflicts and inadequacies of the medical testimony.

By confidently making such a bold accusation of a miscarriage of justice, was she not asking readers to believe that her judgment was better than that of the judges, jury and appeal court, the TV interviewer asked.

She had had more time than they did to investigate the intricacies of the case, LeBourdais responded. "I soon came to the conclusion that it wasn't a sick boy who was guilty, but a perfectly normal boy who was innocent," she said.

Viewers then saw a brief, touching interview with Steve's mother. Her hair up in a beehive style, Doris Truscott patted the armrest of her sofa nervously as she talked about her only moments of intimacy with her son in a crowded visiting room at the prison.

The camera then cut to a visibly shaken Laurier LaPierre—this was still in the days when most network television was live, not taped. "Steven Truscott was sentenced to hang by the neck until dead," the host said, as he moved his hands up to wipe away the tears forming in his eyes. "Doubts about his innocence, ladies and gentlemen, give urgency to the movement to abolish capital punishment," he continued, his voice cracking. "Next week in the House of Commons the abolition bill will get first reading."

That display of journalistic non-objectivity earned LaPierre a severe reprimand from his bosses and gave the corporation's executives one more nail for the coffin of the show they were desperate to kill.

LaPierre's words reflected how the debate over Steve's fate became inextricably linked with another issue gripping the country—the abolition of capital punishment. "Truscott Furor Boosts Anti-hanging Hopes," said the headline in the *Toronto Daily Star*, over a story that noted Steve's case assumed a "new national significance" as Parliament prepared to debate the death penalty.

The timing was accidental, yet it was only natural the two debates merged. Reviewers of LeBourdais' book had emphasized how close Canada came to hanging a fourteen-year-old that many people now believed was innocent. "If a case of such importance can be so badly bungled, even more alarming travesties of justice must be commonplace," *Saturday Night* noted. "That we should retain the death penalty in a country where no one in a courtroom can be relied on to do his job conscientiously is incredible." When the *Globe and Mail* canvassed public opinion in Clinton, an unnamed church minister told the paper: "Perhaps there is a lesson here for those about to consider the question of capital punishment in Canada. Human nature is susceptible to error. Think of the horror of discovering that error when it is too late to do anything about it."

"I pray that never again in Canada shall a fourteen-year-old hear those dreadful words 'to be hanged by the neck until you are dead,'" said one letter writer to the *Toronto Daily Star*.

Oddly enough, while the death penalty debate split the country, it was probably the only issue upon which Steve Truscott and the father of the girl he was accused of murdering agreed. "There shouldn't be any," Steve told a newspaper interviewer when asked about the death penalty. "Not just because of myself but because spending years in jail is a lot worse. You suffer in jail."

Leslie Harper, considering the depth of his grievous loss, showed surprising compassion. He told the press he personally opposed the death penalty, calling it barbaric. He said a murderer should be forced to contemplate his deed every day from the confines of a jail cell. "[Lynne's] death affected him tremendously," recalls Leslie's cousin James Harper. "After he retired from the military he went on to work with young offenders. I think it was because he wanted the connection with young people."

Capital punishment was so contentious there was even a debate about the debate in Parliament, as politicians wrangled over how to proceed. It was not the first time Parliament had wrestled with the issue. Between 1954 and 1963, individual MPs had introduced private abolition bills in each parliamentary session, each time ending in failure. This time there were six private members' proposals, but the government also indicated some support. When Prime Minister Pearson decided to allow for a free vote on hanging, cheers erupted in the chambers.

The Commons, like the country, was evenly divided. One poll showed that fifty-eight MPs favoured outright abolition and another forty-three were for abolition with exceptions (for the murder of prison guards and police officers). Only eighty-four were firm retentionists or leaning that way. Ralph Cowan, the outspoken Liberal backbencher who opposed any review of the Truscott case, wanted to abolish hanging but replace it with the gas chamber. The remaining sixty-one MPs were undecided or undeclared.

On the weekend before the debate, Stanley Knowles visited Steve in prison and made no secret of the fact he saw the dispute over hanging and over the Truscott trial as one and the same. "This was one of the reasons I developed a particular interest in the case, and decided to go down and see him," he said. "The discussions behind the curtains and in the lobbies [of Parliament] yesterday indicated there was a widespread feeling of 'Thank God we didn't hang this guy.' I heard one Tory say that there were 'lots more like him.'"

Prison officials were infuriated when Knowles published an account of his visit with Steve in a Toronto newspaper. The distinguished parliamentarian asked the convicted murderer if he harboured any bitterness. "No, not now," Steven told me, "but there were times when it was more than a human being could take."

Steve had only one question for his visitor. "What do you think of the chances of a public inquiry into my case?"

Knowles replied he thought they were good, but he would not predict the outcome of such an inquiry.

"I am not worried about that," the young man said confidently. "I know if there is an inquiry, it will prove that I am innocent."

Knowles was not the only politician suddenly making a trip to see the young man at the centre of a new political controversy. In the week prior to the capital punishment debate, James Byrne visited Collins Bay, and so did the prime minister's parliamentary secretary, John Matheson.

It was all too much for the authorities. On March 23, Ottawa announced it would bar any more MPs from visiting Steven, even though it was a traditional practice to allow politicians access to prisoners. Penitentiary officials insisted they made the decision in Truscott's best interest. "We just cannot have a succession of people going in to see him," the warden said.

Back in Parliament, after a stormy and emotional debate over the death penalty, a compromise position won out. The Pearson government introduced and passed Bill C-168, limiting capital murder to the killing of on-duty police officers and prison guards. It would be another decade before Parliament tried again to completely abolish the death penalty—this time, under the leadership of Prime Minister Pierre Trudeau.

Behind the grey walls of Collins Bay, Steve only caught glimpses of the public furor over his trial and capital punishment. Except for the occasional newspaper article or radio report, he was sheltered from the controversy. Prison officials would not even let him have a copy of the LeBourdais book. "The warden explained to me that other inmates would steal it and might get fighting, taking sides over whether Steve was guilty or not," Doris Truscott told the press. "When I told Steve, he said, 'Yes, I see that.'"

"Don't let these people get on your nerves," Steve later wrote to his parents, telling them he was glad the book was selling so well, "so the more people that read it can see just how crooked the law can be when people put a little pressure on the police."

The pressure was about to mount against Steve as well. The next year would see him rise to the pinnacle of public acclaim and crash to the depths of private despair. He was lucky that just at this time he made a new friend in prison who would help guide him through the turbulent days ahead.

Malcolm Stienburg was a rarity in a penitentiary—a prison chaplain with heart and brains. After graduating from Mount Allison University with a major in English and psychology, Stienburg went to Queen's University for his master's of divinity. Once ordained as a United Church minister, Stienburg served in small towns in Saskatchewan and southern Ontario. But he quickly tired of what he called the "pink tea circuit," and at thirty-two years of age he jumped at the chance for a more exciting challenge inside prison walls. He did so with no liberal illusions about reforming lost souls. "If you lean a little bit toward the inmates you're a con lover, if you lean too far toward the administration you're a joint man," he says. "So you can't win. It's a very tough line to walk. You burn out very quickly."

Collins Bay had never had a full-time chaplain, and in early 1966, Stienburg was determined to make his post more than a house call from God. "I need about half a dozen inmates who I can trust to tell what kind of programs they need," he told the administration. One of the inmates suggested Steve join the group. Stienburg took an immediate interest in the boyish-looking inmate with the constant smile.

"Steve was a very quiet kid, polite, with a bit of that wry sense of humour," Stienburg remembers. "He was always at Sunday service. It wasn't terribly important for him in terms of his own personal faith or beliefs, but it got him out of the 'drum' Sunday morning." Steve became a regular visitor to the Protestant chapel at the far end of the prison courtyard, playing endless games of cribbage and four-hand euchre, talking the hours away with the padre.

In one of his first encounters with Steve, Stienburg asked his new card partner a simple question. "I said, 'How could you possibly make the adjustment from a fourteen-year-old boy riding your bike around the community to a convict facing life in prison?' And his answer was, 'You either adjust or you die.' And he adjusted."

Adjusting to prison life was one thing; adjusting to being one of Canada's best known inmates was quite another. As the winter's snow began to melt from the prison yards, Warden Fred Smith wrote to Steve's parents, advising them their son was "pale and strained." He told the *Globe and Mail* the publicity around the case was unnerving the prisoner: "I was worried about the effect that all this pressure might have on the boy," Smith said.

In fact, the more serious pressures on Steven had to do with psychiatry, not publicity. His long-running private battle with the prison psychiatrists was coming to a head. On March 22, NDP member of Parliament Andrew Brewin showed reporters a copy of the letter J. R. Geoffrion, executive assistant to the justice minister, sent to Steve's parents in the previous fall. "The penitentiary authorities are hopeful that Steven may be encouraged to abandon his so-called defence strategy when discussing his offence and be absolutely frank with the psychiatrist, who is only acting with a view to help and assist the patient," the cabinet aide wrote, in effect saying Steve should 'fess up and come clean.

To avert any scandal, A. J. MacLeod, federal commissioner of penitentiaries, assured the media that prison psychiatrist George Scott never tried to force Steven into admitting guilt. "I know Dr. Scott well, and pressure would not be an appropriate word." Warden Fred Smith also denied there was any problem. "This is ridiculous. There has been absolutely no pressure."

But Scott's private records from the time reveal a more complicated story. Scott had been trying to convince Steven to consider going to

Penetang, an institute for the criminally insane, for a period of five to six months. "They will never get me to go to any bughouse except in a box," Steve told his parents.

"Scott sometimes had a cavalier attitude that he was one hundred per cent sure [about an inmate]," Malcolm Stienburg remembers. "He would say to the inmate, 'I think your problem is this, this and this. I want you to go away to think about that for a while.' Amazingly, the inmate comes back next month with a great penetrating insight—'Yes sir, Dr. Scott, you're right on the nose.' Scott would then write down that the inmate has developed insight into his problems."

But Scott's easy formula was not working with Steven, and his dismay was evident in his log entry for February 22, 1966:

> The problem of his innocence or guilt plays a role in my particular attitude toward [him]. He states that he is not guilty of the offence and this must be accepted as his statement. The fact that he was found guilty in the traditional courts of Canada is a factor of extreme importance. If he's guilty and is not admitting it then this implies that there is a complete repression of the problems involved.
>
> This case presents an extreme dilemma from the psychiatric point of view because no matter what is done by psychiatry in this case, it is going to be suspected of forcing this man into the admission of guilt whether he's guilty or not.

Increasingly frustrated with the obstinate young prisoner, Scott wrote the head of medical services in the Office of the Commissioner of Penitentiaries. Scott had tried to treat Steven with all the available techniques, but now he wanted to call together a psychiatric panel of leading experts to figure out what steps to take next. It was partly a therapeutic exercise and partly an attempt to cover his political backside.

By late March, Scott had pulled together an impressive panel of experts: Dr. Ronald Briggs, the director of the child and adolescent psychiatric clinic at the Kingston General Hospital; Dr. Robin Hunter, the head of the department of psychiatry at Queen's University; and Dr. John Pratten, the superintendent of the Ontario Hospital. Another penitentiary psychiatrist, Dr. Robert McCaldon, would chair the panel. Each man was to interview Steven separately and then meet with his colleagues for an evaluation.

Scott asked the board to determine if they would "recommend further probing to enable Truscott to come to grips with his problem." Among the possible avenues of treatment, Scott suggested more truth serum and nitrous oxide, a transfer to the Penetang institution, and group therapy with another convicted young murderer who admitted his offence. In one particularly revealing question, Scott asked his fellow doctors, "Do you agree that the LSD treatments and the pentothal [truth serum] should not be recorded on his prison file, as they are distinctly privileged relationships?" It is certainly possible that the only distinct privilege Scott wanted to preserve was his right to administer drug treatments without controversy.

If Scott was hoping for a collegial endorsement of his efforts to get Steven to crack, he was sorely disappointed. The experts instead found a normal boy reacting with strength and resolve to a situation of stress—a stress aggravated to a considerable degree by prison psychiatrists determined to prove his guilt.

Dr. Robin Hunter found Steven to be "very direct and co-operative." Unlike other analysts who concluded Steven lacked affect, he noted that the young man smiled, blushed and laughed. "I did not concern myself with the question of his guilt or lack of it, but merely approached the matter by telling him that I was a doctor and not a law enforcement officer and that I had been asked to see him in order to try and understand him as a human being," Hunter said. "He puzzles endlessly about what happened to him but can find no adequate answer. He sometimes feels angry but does not know who to blame except that, by and large, he has no affection for the police," the doctor reported. "He spontaneously told me that he certainly was not guilty of the crime for which he had been put in prison and that . . . there had been a miscarriage of justice. He feels that if he were to confess, that things would go easier for him, but he cannot do this and would not think of doing so merely for the advantages that he has been told would accrue to him."

Hunter's final evaluation was explicit: "There are no psychotic indicators nor indicators of behavioural disorder."

Hunter's colleague at the adolescent clinic of the Kingston General Hospital, Dr. Ronald Briggs, concurred. With more insight than most of the other doctors who had analyzed Steven over the years, Briggs described him as "a young man who suffered a very traumatic experience, culminated by his stay in the death cell. . . . Initially he appears to have reacted with bewilderment and then hostility. He continues to make a conscious effort at enforcing control and aloofness." Briggs thus found Steve's reactions to be healthy, "solidly based in reality." Steve told the doctor he did not trust him, but that he should not take it personally. "Everyone he met in prison started from the assumption that he was guilty and proceeded to try and prove it," Briggs recounted. "I see no evidence of any psychotic process."

Steve made the same complaint to the third psychiatrist, John Pratten. "He rather resents the opinion expressed by many people that there must be something wrong with him because of the crime for which he was convicted, which he very definitely denies," Pratten reported. Pratten found his subject to be polite, intelligent and wry. "I did not detect any evidence of sickness nor did I feel that he is in need of any specific form of treatment."

Little wonder, faced with three almost identical appraisals, that panel chairman Robert McCaldon said he was "somewhat baffled as to [Steve's] management" by Scott. Steve co-operated with all drug tests and remains convinced of his innocence, McCaldon said. "He sees himself as a relatively normal boy who has always felt completely innocent of the charges against him," the panel chairman concluded. "He recognizes it might be easier for a psychiatrist to make a recommendation for release if he were to admit guilt and show remorse, but he states he cannot do this when he does not honestly believe it."

Scott insists today he did not see the consultants' report as a rebuke of his practices. "Not at all, not at all," he says, dismissing their comments. "That was just part of the passing parade." Scott says there were many things about Steven the outside doctors weren't able to understand. "I had been stuck with the job, to put it mildly—it gave me an intimacy with him," he says.

Still, by any measure, the panel's conclusions were in stark contradiction to Dr. Scott's views. Far from endorsing Scott's ideas for more drug tests, group therapy and LSD treatments, the panel of experts implied that one of Steven's problems was the way psychiatrists had been treating him.

Scott was unrepentant, even letting slip his own opinion about his patient to the media. "Was Steven Guilty? I Know the Truth," ran the headline in the *Toronto Daily Star* in mid-April of 1966. "I know whether Steven is guilty or innocent," Scott coyly told a reporter. "But that's all I can say. If Steven wants to get up and make a statement of course he can. But he hasn't."

"Adolescence brings out the fantasies of anger, cruelty, mastery, pride, heroism, which can bring killing in an instant of hostility," he said in the article.

Steve's parents were outraged by Scott's very public declarations. Members of Parliament had already urged the government to take steps to make sure Steven was not pressured into admitting "a crime of which he consistently says he is innocent." The federal commissioner of penitentiaries stepped in to assure critics he would be talking to Scott "in the next few days."

As a sign that prison officials were warming to their celebrity inmate, the warden told the Truscotts he was exempting them from the rule limiting visits to two thirty-minute sessions a month. They could come see their son any time they wanted.

When Steve saw his parents the week after his battery of interviews with the experts, he recounted once again how he had stood his ground about his innocence. "Dad, it's the truth and it's the same under drugs as before," he told his father.

"Don't expect a miracle," Doris told Steve. "It's not going to happen overnight. There may be hard battles ahead. It's better to walk out an innocent man a year from now than to be paroled, still guilty, today."

Steve's mother knew that proving her son's innocence would be hard. She had no idea just how hard a battle the police would wage to prove that the arrest they made in 1959 was the right one.

## 33

## AN "AGONIZING REAPPRAISAL"

I f there was one person in Canada troubled by all the renewed attention
around the Truscott case it was Harold Graham. By 1966, Graham had
been assistant commissioner of the force for three years. The man who
first soared to national prominence when he jailed Steven Truscott was on his
way to capturing the top job—head of the OPP—in just seven more years.

Still, Graham could not seem to shake the ghosts of Clinton. "It bothered him badly," says Dennis Alsop, the identification officer who worked
with Graham in 1959 and would help him again in 1966. "This case is all
done and gone, and all of a sudden it comes into the limelight again. He did-
n't know why they're paying attention to one person who was a born liar."
Alsop's characterization was directed at Steven, but it could just as well have
described Graham's feelings toward Isabel LeBourdais.

"He was going to shoot this LeBourdais down," Alsop recalls. "He didn't
like the criticism the press was giving the case."

When *The Trial of Steven Truscott* hit the headlines in March, Graham went
on the warpath. He fired off three lengthy memos to his superiors in one
month, totalling thirty-eight pages. "Columnists and editors . . . have already

given wide acclaim to the book," he noted with alarm. "Mr. Diefenbaker has asked the prime minister for a royal commission."

Graham wanted to set the record straight. He made a detailed criticism of errors he said plagued LeBourdais' book. Some were minor (surnames spelled incorrectly, but taken from trial transcripts where the original errors appeared). Other inaccuracies were hardly LeBourdais' fault, given her lack of access to police and military files; she erroneously reported, for example, that the police took no action the night Lynne disappeared. Most of Graham's condemnation was based on differing interpretations—he took the Crown's view on the evidence, she took a perspective favourable to Steven.

But Graham made some errors of his own. At one point, he wrote that after questioning Steven at the OPP detachment in Goderich, "he was returned to the guardhouse"—a tepid description of what the trial judge decried as an arrest and interrogation that violated legal standards. Graham took exception to LeBourdais' portrayal of his grilling of Steven as an "inquisition." He told his superiors, "I was fully aware of the views of some jurists regarding the questioning of juveniles and for that reason, arranged for the boy's father to be brought to the guardhouse." What Graham did not say in that memo was that he chose to ignore the guidelines for juveniles, first questioning Steve alone and only calling for his father two and a half hours after the police picked up the boy.

Graham did more than write apologias for his actions. He took an active part in top-level strategy sessions with senior provincial and federal government officials to plot a counter-attack to this unprecedented onslaught against the justice system. How things had changed since 1959, when the police could jail a boy and the prosecution could win a sentence for hanging with little fear of criticism from a timid press corps and a placid citizenry. But the turbulent sixties had altered all that. LeBourdais' message, amplified by newspaper columnists and TV commentators, had touched a chord in a populace waking up to the possibility that not everything the police, the courts and the judges did was necessarily right.

As this storm buffeted the legal establishment, a worried group of men huddled around a conference table in a government office in Toronto. On Friday, April 1, 1966, Harold Graham sat down with Don Christie, the director of criminal law in the federal department of justice; A. R. Dick, Ontario's deputy attorney general; and William Bowman, the province's director of public prosecutions, who had successfully blocked Steven's appeal in 1960. Joining Graham from the OPP was Hank Sayeau, the corporal who had helped him in Clinton and now had risen to the rank of inspector. It was as senior a gathering of judicial heavyweights as possible; the top lawman in the country—federal Solicitor General Lawrence Pennell—would have attended were it not for another commitment in Ottawa.

Harold Graham and the other officials debated how the government would resist these unprecedented and unwelcome challenges to their power. According to Graham's account, unearthed in documents obtained from the government, the men were worried not so much about the legal implications of the Truscott affair, but were more concerned with the wider political fallout. They feared if a full inquiry were held, "the administration of justice would be attacked." What's more, LeBourdais had the support of the NDP, Graham observed, "and it was more than a coincidence that this book came on the market at the same time as the debate of capital punishment in the House of Commons." To make matters worse, Graham noted, "there has also been talk in Ottawa about compensation in the event the boy is ruled innocent."

Clearly, this would not do. Graham's memo offers a fascinating glimpse into the mindset of the beleaguered police and justice officials. "It was agreed by both the federal and provincial governments that there must be a rebuttal to the book," the assistant commissioner wrote.

The federal justice minister or Solicitor General Pennell "should make a speech in the House of Commons indicating that after a detailed study by the law officers, it was found that there had been no miscarriage of justice," suggested A. R. Dick, the deputy provincial attorney general. It was a remarkably premature recommendation, considering LeBourdais' book had been on sale for only a few weeks before the meeting and there was no evidence the police had yet completed such an extensive study endorsing their 1959 operations.

The senior police and justice officials discussed appointing a jurist or a lawyer to write a report. "A rebuttal could be accomplished by the appointment of a royal commission set up by both the federal and provincial governments," Graham wrote. Presumably, a royal commission was supposed to find the truth; Harold Graham had already decided the inquiry would accomplish a rebuttal to his detractors. But even Graham acknowledged that a royal commission could lead to more attacks on "the administration of justice."

The meeting ended without any definite solutions. Graham reported the federal solicitor general would confer with his provincial counterpart. Within three weeks, Ottawa announced its decision.

On April 19, there came a remarkable victory for the boy who had grown up to become a man behind prison walls. "It has been decided that a review of the case should be made," Solicitor General Larry Pennell told the House of Commons. He quickly cautioned: "It should be stressed that the government, in coming to this decision, is not prejudicing the case or the correctness or otherwise of the allegations that have been made concerning the Truscott case."

Pennell did not immediately clarify what form the review would take. Confidential minutes of cabinet meetings now reveal just how sharp the debate was—and how powerfully the cabinet realized they were dealing with a political, much more than a legal, time bomb.

Pennell had presented his colleagues with several options: a royal commission or another form of inquiry, a new trial, a reference of the case to the Supreme Court of Canada, an outright pardon, or simply non-interference. A new trial was risky, Pennell said, because it "would be tantamount to stating that there had been a miscarriage of justice." On the other hand, Pennell warned his colleagues they had to find a way to resolve the Truscott controversy "in such a way as to allay public concern and at the same time remove the cloud of suspicion which has been cast over the judicial process."

Most outsiders favoured some sort of new investigation, rather than a trial. LeBourdais said she thought only a politically neutral royal commission could thoroughly review the case and "bring justice to the boy." But perhaps heeding the April 1 warning from Graham and other senior officials that such an inquiry would lead to an attack on the administration of justice, Ottawa chose a safer route. The government would sidestep any inquiry into a bungled police investigation and pass the controversial dossier to the highest court in the land.

On April 26, the federal cabinet spelled out its reference to the Supreme Court, asking if, based on new rules and new evidence, the Supreme Court would come to a different conclusion than it did six years earlier, when it first turned down Steven's appeal. In 1960, the highest court in the land could hear an appeal only if there was a dissent by a judge in a lower court of appeal, or if there was a question of law to be settled. In July 1961, an amendment to the Criminal Code widened the right to appeal on grounds of fact, as well as law. Now, in an unprecedented move, Ottawa was going one step further, allowing the Supreme Court to hear new evidence in the case.

In its ninety-one-year history, the Supreme Court had never heard live testimony from witnesses. But Steven was not getting a new trial. The nine Supreme Court justices could not declare him innocent or guilty. They could only decide if the original trial was fair and, if not, they could recommend a new one.

While Ottawa was announcing an open "review of the case" its top officials had secretly come to the conclusion that much of the key medical evidence that underpinned Truscott's conviction was in shambles.

Don Christie, Ottawa's director of criminal law who had sat down with Graham to plot strategy, took it upon himself to consult two top pathologists: the first from inside the federal government was J.R. Jackson, head of the laboratory at the department of veterans' affairs; the second was D.H. Starkey, a pathologist at the Queen Mary Hospital in Montreal. According to secret memos Christie wrote to the deputy minister on April 4 and April 6, both experts concluded that the many of the so-called scientific conclusions presented at Truscott's 1959 trial were either "absolutely wrong" or "not possible."

Jackson told the federal justice officials that there was "no justification" for Penistan's conclusion that Lynne died within two hours of eating dinner, given that there is always a "a great variation" in how people digest food. The most that Penistan could have said, Christie wrote, was that "the child *might* have been killed" before 7:45 p.m. but the coroner "would have to say it could be later."

The experts also scoffed at the testimony of Penistan and Dr. Brooks that the lesions on Truscott's penis were caused by a "blind, furious thrust of the male organ." One of the doctors consulted two other experts—a dermatologist and a urologist—who concluded the prosecution's experts were "entirely and absolutely" wrong about the scabbing on Steven's penis. "There is no reason at all for doubting the boy he had not had any sexual intercourse," they said.

Starkey also blasted Penistan for his analysis of the acid phosphatase in Harper's vagina, which he used to confirm the rape, noting that Penistan's tests were "so far off the correct figures as to make one wonder if Dr. Penistan knew what he was talking about."

381

It was all extremely damaging to the prosecution's case. But none of this information ever saw the light day for thirty years until these documents were uncovered in the government archives early in 2005. What is worse, federal officials were not the only ones keeping vital facts away from the public and Steven Truscott. Provincial prosecutors and the police engaged in much more serious cover-up about Penistan's findings—only what they kept hidden were not criticisms from outside experts but from the good doctor himself.

It was bad enough that Harold Graham, assistant commissioner of the OPP, had to face the prospect of the Supreme Court re-examining his most famous case. Three weeks after Ottawa made its unprecedented decision, Graham received a disturbing private letter that threw in doubt much of the medical evidence used to convict Steven Truscott. The letter was not from the Truscott family, a defence lawyer or an outraged citizen. It came from none other than Dr. John Penistan, the pathologist who seven years earlier had worked so closely with Graham in helping to secure a conviction against a fourteen-year-old boy.

Penistan, still the chief pathologist at the Stratford General Hospital, appeared troubled. Perhaps the intense public scrutiny of the case prodded him into reflection. Maybe he felt twinges of unease about his role in presenting his medical testimony to help the prosecution.* There was also a good chance he had gotten wind of the stinging criticisms levelled at his work by Dr. Noble Sharpe, who was still the medical director of the attorney general's laboratory. Sharpe had drafted a three-page memo on the case for public prosecutor William Bowman, and Sharpe was unsparing in his rebuke of Penistan. He singled out Penistan's failure at trial to stress the variables that affected stomach contents, rigor mortis and decomposition.

For whatever reason, Penistan in the spring of 1966 was clearly having serious second thoughts about his 1959 testimony—or at least, the way it was used and interpreted. He wanted to get those doubts off his chest by publishing a review of his autopsy findings in a professional medical journal.

---

* Penistan's daughter Julia came forward in 2004 to say that she felt her late father had been pressured to support the police theory that Truscott was guilty. "I know, just from my dad's body language and his quietness, that he took an awful lot of heat for what he found," she said. "I'm sure he suffered internally for it."

On May 19 Penistan sent Graham a draft of his article with the following comment, which must have unnerved even the normally unflappable OPP veteran: "One is tempted to refer to it as an 'agonizing reappraisal' in the current jargon: the adjective is probably better justified here than in most cases."

Sensing that he was treading on dangerous ground, Penistan seemed nervous about admitting the consequences of his reassessment. "I do not believe I have changed any of my essential conclusions as a result of my review . . . but I must depend on someone else to assess whether there has been any significant change in the expression of these views."

The pathologist was being disingenuous. He knew he was reappraising the rigidity and certainty of his testimony about the time of death—and he knew on the eve of a Supreme Court review this new review was dangerously explosive stuff.

Penistan titled his paper "Autopsy on the Body of Lynn Harper—A Review of the Pathological Findings." He got the spelling of Lynne's first name wrong in the draft, but it was also evident he was worried he got a lot more than that wrong in his trial testimony. From the start of his draft article, Penistan seemed determined to extricate himself from the verdict against Steven. He tried to argue that his autopsy could be used only to exclude a suspect, not point the finger at anyone. "If the evidence were to show that Lynne could not have died at the only time Truscott had access or opportunity, his innocence would be established," he wrote. "The corollary, however, is not true. If the autopsy shows that she did, or could have died at such a time, this fact per se bears no relevance to him as opposed to any individual, which must depend on altogether other evidence."

Theoretically, that was true, but the pathologist was ignoring the reality of his testimony in 1959. By using phrases like "could not have died" and "could have died," Penistan was suggesting a cautious medical approach he never displayed at the trial. The issue was not that his evidence showed whether Lynne could or could not have died by 7:45 p.m., but the absolute certainty with which Penistan determined the time of death in the eyes of the jurors. He knew that by testifying Lynne had to have died before 7:45, he was fingering the only person known to have been with her at that time.

But with hindsight too late for Steven, Penistan was now chipping away at almost every major aspect of his testimony. At trial Penistan shocked jurors by testifying Lynne's vaginal injuries were produced "by a blind, violent thrust of the male organ." The prosecutor used the vaginal lesion evidence to link Steve's penis sores to the rape. Seven years later, Penistan was no longer so sure. "The labial lesion was not of obvious causation," he wrote, even speculating that "in theory [Lynne's injuries] could have been inflicted with a blunt instrument," not necessarily a penis.

Steve's defence lawyer, Frank Donnelly, had suggested the decomposition of the body could account for much of the swelling and damage to the genital area. He pleaded with the judge that "it would be extremely dangerous" for Penistan to express any opinion about the injuries because of the post-mortem changes. But the judge overruled Donnelly's objection, and Penistan went on to assure the jurors the swelling and other damage to Lynne's vagina "all indicate a large degree of violence." Penistan's description was crucial to the prosecution, who could hardly accuse Steven of rape without this evidence.

But now the pathologist had changed his mind about the post-mortem, or autolytic, transformations. "The initially expressed view that the severity of the vagina changes reflected a corresponding degree of violence, while quite possibly true, did not sufficiently discount the autolytic changes," he wrote.

On the crucial question of time of death, Penistan had told jurors the state of decomposition and the extent of rigor mortis suggested that "death had occurred some two days previously"—when Steve was with Lynne. But in a direct reversal of his trial testimony, Penistan widened the window appreciably: "The state of decomposition in Lynne's body is considered fully compatible with death about forty-eight hours prior to autopsy, but it is *not incompatible with death a day previously or a day later*." The doctor was now saying Lynne could have died as late as Wednesday! As for rigor, Penistan now claimed it was compatible with death about forty-eight hours previously, but "compatible also with death *some hours later than that*." And when it came to the all-important stomach contents, Penistan now added qualifying words that he never used at the trial. He said "the impression" he got while inspecting the stomach was that the food showed little sign of digestion and was "therefore *presumably* recently ingested" (his emphasis).

Penistan's conclusions in 1966 were dramatically more open-ended than in 1959. "All findings are compatible with death within two hours of Lynne's last meal," he wrote, standing by his original testimony—but then adding a word he never spoke at trial: "However." That single word indicated a new flexibility in Penistan's interpretation of the autopsy's findings.

"However," he wrote, "the degree of rigor and decomposition are compatible *also with death at a later time*," he said. "The state of the stomach contents is also compatible with death at a later time, provided that digestion and emptying were delayed by some physical or psychological episode occurring within approximately two hours of the last meal"—at last making the distinction he never made at trial between digestion stopping and death occurring.

In another version of his draft, Penistan went even further: "All findings are compatible with death within two hours of Lynne's last meal. *They are not incompatible with death at a later time (up to twelve hours or even longer).*"

To make a case for his innocence, Steve did not need the twelve-hour time frame Penistan now seemed willing to give for the time of death—just twelve minutes would have put the boy in the clear. The Crown convinced jurors Penistan's definitive time of death before 7:45 p.m. tightened the vise on Steven alone. In that courtroom in Goderich in 1959, if Penistan had stated death could have occurred "twelve hours later" or "a day later"—as he now wrote in his proposed article—more than one juror might well have had a reasonable doubt about Steven's guilt.

On the eve of a Supreme Court review, Penistan's rethink was a disaster for Harold Graham and for the legal team preparing the Crown's case. Handwritten at the bottom of Penistan's letter to Graham is a note indicating Graham sent Crown prosecutor William Bowman a copy.

The letter Penistan attached to his report concluded, "I would be glad if you would read the draft critically and advise me if you find anything in it which is at variance with the facts or which is ill or misleadingly expressed." Graham and Bowman certainly would have found much in Penistan's new position that was at variance with what they wanted to hear. But they had a more urgent problem—keeping a lid on the draft opinion of this wavering soldier in the prosecution's ranks.

It was not going to be easy. Just a hint of Penistan's views had leaked out several weeks before his private letter to Graham. "Key Evidence Now in Doubt," the Toronto *Telegram* headlined over a story based on a brief interview with the doctor in late March. The newspaper, on its own, had gathered opinions from three pathologists not connected with the case who concluded it was "almost impossible" to determine the time of death from stomach contents alone.

"I am in general agreement with their comments," Penistan told the newspaper. He regretted he could not say more because Ottawa was reviewing the case, but he made it clear he hoped he would get a chance to testify at any inquiry "to give my full statement on my findings." Penistan never got that chance, even though Steven's defence team was clearly interested in what he had to say.

By late April, Bowman was reporting that Ted Joliffe, one of Steve's lawyers, was interested in "Penistan's own views which . . . may be inconsistent with original evidence."

In early June, Ted Joliffe met with Penistan under the watchful gaze of Graham and Bowman. "In this company, Dr. Penistan was more guarded than on other occasions," Joliffe reported, indicating that the defence team had managed to have previous meetings with the pathologist, and that perhaps he had been more forthcoming.

"At one point he conceded that death could have occurred after 8:00 p.m., but he did not really retreat from any of his statements in 1959," Joliffe said. "My observations were not intended to be definitive," Penistan said— and that was as far as the pathologist was willing to go.

Bowman and the Crown team worked hard over the summer months to circle the wagons around Penistan by recruiting top international experts to their cause, experts who could bolster Penistan's 1959 conclusions—and ultimately, replace Penistan as the chief defender of his own autopsy. Chief among those experts was Keith Simpson, who ran the department of forensic medicine at Guy's Hospital in London, England, and edited the respected *Principles and Practices of Medical Jurisprudence*. Simpson had reviewed LeBourdais' book in a British journal, dismissing her medical references as outdated and her arguments as biased. He told reporters he was outraged that "a disgraceful kind of publicity" sparked by the book had forced the government's hand into questioning sound medical and legal practices.

By early June, Simpson was preparing briefs for the Crown counsel. A Crown lawyer flew over to London to meet with Simpson and Dr. Milton Helpern, an American pathologist who would also eventually testify at the Supreme Court.

While never going to the extremes that Penistan did in his reappraisal, Simpson did advise the prosecutors that defending the original autopsy conclusions was not without its challenges. "It would not be difficult for critics to point to many statements from various writers (including myself) . . . indicating the caution one must exercise in using stomach emptying time in estimating the approximate time of death."

A particularly irksome matter was the recognized medical fact that fear or shock could easily slow stomach movements. Simpson came up with a simple way to deal with the fear factor—he dismissed the chances that Lynne experienced any fear or shock. "These last factors cannot have operated in this case," Simpson boldly proclaimed, insisting that strangulation must have killed Lynne rapidly. "Lynne Harper was not dragged screaming into the [bush], spending some time in fear of death before dying. It seems likely that she went willingly, may even have undressed herself and suffered only a few moments . . . of such high emotional disturbance before dying." The British expert did not explain how he gained such insight into Lynne's final moments.

The closest Simpson ever got to Clinton was Toronto, when Bowman organized a planning session and a lunch party in July for the visiting medical dignitary. Simpson got a chance to meet Penistan and other members of the government team. Simpson called it a "masterful manoeuvre." The day after the gathering, Penistan wrote to the Crown office to tell them he would "awfully like to have a copy" of Simpson's report on the case. The Crown obliged, and by the end of the summer the British medical celebrity penned a letter to Penistan guaranteed to boost his morale.

Simpson told the pathologist that the Crown's team had contacted two other world-renowned authorities "both of whom back your findings solidly, entirely without reservation. . . . This is only what I expected but it is yet more backing which must entirely restore your confidence in the views you expressed from the very first." The fact that Simpson felt it was still necessary in September to "restore" the pathologist's confidence—three months after Penistan had sent in his reappraisal to Graham—indicated how worried the Crown was about Penistan as a potential loose cannon.

Even Simpson had to admit to Penistan they were going to have to fudge things more than the pathologist had at the original trial. "We are of course prepared to admit that [under] wider special conditions . . . the stomach might not empty normally," he wrote in his letter. "This is a matter of probabilities, not a mathematical deduction." The problem was that at Steve's trial in 1959, Penistan's talk about a thirty-minute window for time of death sounded much more like mathematics than probabilities.

Simpson need not have tried so hard to calm his doubting colleague. A handwritten note on stationery from the Ontario attorney general's office, dated August 9, 1966, indicates Bowman had already made up his mind to

387

keep Penistan far away from the courtroom. The note runs through a list of seven potential expert witnesses. All the major experts would testify—except the last name on the list. Penistan's name is circled, then followed by three question marks, the single word "No" and a thick exclamation point. The Supreme Court justices and Steven's defence counsel would never hear about Penistan's "agonizing reappraisal."

Two years later, long after the Truscott controversy had died down, the article that Dr. Penistan had sent to Harold Graham in May of 1966 was finally published in a medical journal. Without exception, every major contentious passage from his original draft had been deleted. Penistan's admission that Lynne could have died hours after Steve left her—important information for Steve's defence before the Supreme Court of Canada— would remain secret for more than thirty years.

Penistan was not the only doctor who testified for the prosecution at the original trial who was now having second thoughts. In August, Bowman made an entry in his notes concerning John Addison, the family doctor who examined and questioned Steven the night of his arrest. Addison met with Dr. Charles Danby, a dermatologist who treated Steven in Collins Bay and who would testify at the upcoming Supreme Court hearing about finding oozing, crusted eczema on Steve's body—a possible explanation for the sores on Steven's penis, especially since Steven had told Addison the sores appeared four to five weeks before his arrest. "Danby . . . told him about skin condition—shook his confidence in Truscott guilt," Bowman noted.

Trying to do damage control with Dr. Penistan was only one of Harold Graham's challenges in that busy spring and summer of 1966. Once it was clear the Supreme Court was going to re-examine the case, the OPP had their hands full. Letters, phone calls and tips came in from across country, and police followed up leads on more than a dozen potential suspects. All of the clues appeared to be fruitless, but at least the police were casting a wider net than they had during their twenty-four-hour "lightning" investigation in 1959.

Graham's men also set about finding whatever new information they could on the boy they had sent to prison seven years earlier. In what looked like an increasingly desperate operation, Graham's men tracked down tips on everything from a secret stash of pornography to a putative prison confession—only to find their efforts to dig up any real dirt come to an embarrassing failure.

"Inquiries were made with a view to developing the report that pornographic literature which implicated Steven Truscott was found hidden in the house formerly occupied by the Truscotts in Clinton," Graham told prosecutor Bowman. The porn hunt began when G. A. Duguid of the OPP's Criminal Investigations Branch interviewed a former RCAF officer on June 17. He said a friend who moved into the Truscotts' former home on the base discovered "a bundle of letters" written to and from girls. "It makes Peyton Place look sick," the man allegedly said.

But two days later, the OPP discovered the pornography comprised only two small notes written to Steven from a girl saying, "I miss seeing you, I will be coming in town, I love you Steven." The woman who found the letters told the police, "there was nothing smutty or dirty about them."

The OPP were more excited when it looked like a fellow inmate could finally give them the goods on Steven. Graham himself travelled to Burlington police headquarters on September 22 to secure a signed statement from Carl Glover, an ex-prisoner from Collins Bay. Out on parole after serving four years for passing bad cheques, Glover had been nabbed once more for fraud and was to appear in court the next day. He doubtless hoped his co-operation with the police would work in his favour.

From the start there were anomalies in Glover's story that should have rung alarm bells for Graham that his informant was more interested in a deal than in the truth.

"I first met Steven Truscott about September 22, 1962, when he arrived at the penitentiary," claimed Glover. "In September and October, 1962, I often talked to Truscott on the sports field." Glover had to be talking to ghosts, because Steven did not arrive at Collins Bay until 1963—four months after Glover alleged the compromising conversations took place.

"You are the smart punk that goes around raping young girls," Glover said he told Steven.

"Well, we're all in the same boat here—what the hell can they do about it?" Steven supposedly replied. "I done it and I didn't need any help to do it."

"He never went into detail about his crime but he often said he did rape the girl and he didn't need any help," Glover recounted. "He said he did it for kicks and he was in a frenzy." Glover told Graham Steve made these confessions "many times when eight or nine inmates were around." As dubious as Glover's story may have been, the police dutifully tried to track down other witnesses to Steve's incriminating boasts—presumably some of the names Glover gave them himself. Not surprisingly, they had little luck.

An October 1 telegram from the OPP in Barrie, Ontario, revealed that another ex-inmate told the police he "never overheard Truscott ever talk about the crime." On October 2 came a report from the Burlington OPP that six other former prisoners said the same thing. The prison barber who cut Steve's hair said the boy was "the quiet type [who] never said anything about the case." A friend of Steve's who worked with him in the radio room for two years told the OPP "he had discussed the case with him many times. Truscott always maintained he was innocent."

In the end, Graham had to accept his quest for someone to back up Glover's tale of a jailhouse confession was hopeless. An inspector informed him that the police had no luck with the twenty names supplied by Glover. "All that could be located were interviewed but none will corroborate [his] statement."

Graham quietly dropped the matter. In the meantime, the OPP hoped they could come up with something new from a series of tests they were conducting in Clinton.

The police went back to the evidence of the bicycle tire marks found in the dry, cracked earth near the crime scene in 1959. In 1966, the OPP identification unit contacted two professors at the University of Guelph who specialized in soil analysis. Both men, unfortunately, said the photographs indicated the tire tracks were made after a heavy rainfall of at least a quarter of an inch. The last recorded rainfall of that amount occurred May 31, more than a week before Lynne disappeared.

New footprint evidence looked more promising for the police. In May of 1966, Dennis Alsop—the same identification officer Graham recruited at the last minute before the 1959 trial, hoping to get a match from the scuff marks found near Lynne's body—began another series of tests. He made enlargements from the negatives and found the vertical ridges on the outside edge of the sole of Steve's right shoe were "consistent" with the marks near the body.

"It is my opinion that the characteristics found in the impression at the scene could have been made by the shoes that I received . . . on September 11, 1959," Alsop, now a detective sergeant, wrote. A second identification expert, Cpl. M. I. T. Peer, determined the marks "appear similar to the lines . . .

Steven at the Ontario Training School in Guelph, where he was kept from 1960 to 1963.

**ABOVE:** The Truscott family visits Steve at the Ontario Training School. From left to right, back row: Steve, Ken, Doris and Dan, and in the front row: Bill and Barbara.

Steven at the Ontario Training School in Guelph.

Dan and Doris Truscott read Isabel LeBourdais' book, *The Trial of Steven Truscott,* as they await the decision of the Supreme Court.

Arthur Martin, called by his colleagues "the greatest criminal lawyer Canada has ever produced," represented Steven before the Supreme Court of Canada.

Marlene, the young woman from Guelph who took up Steven's cause and eventually became his wife.

Steven and Isabel LeBourdais at the farm annex outside Collins Bay Penitentiary in 1968.

Steve escorts his daughter, Lesley, to her wedding in September 1994.

**ABOVE:** Julian Sher (right) with Steven Truscott during the filming of his interview with *the fifth estate*.

**BELOW:** Steven and Linden MacIntyre on the county road during the filming of *the fifth estate* documentary.

Marlene and Steve Truscott celebrate Canada Day in 2006 with 160 supporters at their home. The picture was taken by the daughter of Cpl. John Erskine, the one police officer who raised doubts about the rush to condemn Truscott back in the 1950s.

imprinted into the earth." He concluded they were made by Steven's shoe or—in an important qualification—"by shoes of a similar type of manufacture." It was far from conclusive, but it was the best the OPP was going to get.

The police also carried out research for the two key visual debates at the trial. First, could Gord Logan, standing 642 feet away at the swimming hole, see Steven at the bridge? Second, could Steven see the colour of a licence plate on a car thirteen hundred feet away at the highway?

On June 16, provincial constable A. Twaddle, standing where Gord Logan said he spotted Steve and Lynne, was able to identify nine different vehicles crossing the bridge, what colour they were, and at times even the number of occupants in the cars. When two young girls came to the bridge on their bicycles (much like Steve and Lynne did) Twaddle could see one girl wore pink slacks and a brown coat, while the other wore black slacks and a white sweater. "The girls at this time would possibly have been recognizable to us if they were previously known, mainly due to clothing," he said.

Perhaps dismayed by this apparently strong endorsement of Gord's claims, the police dispatched another team to redo the same test on July 14. They reported that this time all four officers present "agreed that it was impossible to identify anyone on the road or bridge."

That same day, the police also ran tests from the bridge. They found two civilians, gave them notepads and told them to mark down what they saw as an OPP officer drove by the spot where Steve said he saw Lynne get in the car. The officer drove a light grey 1959 Chevrolet Biscayne, on which he affixed different-coloured licence plates in six separate tests. "The tests proved to all observers that it is impossible to see the colour of any licence plate," Inspector R. A. Ferguson reported.

The statement was not quite accurate. The first observer noted glare on the rear bumper three times. Steve's lawyer had suggested the yellow markings Steve claimed to have seen could have been reflection from the sun. The second test subject saw the glare twice. He also easily spotted the driver (Steve had said he could make out at least one person in the car) and once he thought he saw an orange plate (it was yellow). When a police corporal tried the test, he did even better, choosing colours that were close or matching three times out of five. All the observers could easily make out the year and model of the vehicle.

The Crown never entered any of these police tests into evidence before the Supreme Court. It had not been a rewarding summer for the OPP investigators.

———————

For all his fervour in pursuing the Lynne Harper case against Steven Truscott, Assistant Commissioner Harold Graham did not pick up the trail of one of the most suspicious men around the base at the time of the murder: Sgt. Alexander Kalichuk, the alcoholic airman who had been arrested shortly before Lynne's disappearance for attempting to pick up a young girl in his car.

Since his release from a psychiatric hospital in the summer of 1959, Kalichuk's thirst for liquor had shown no signs of diminishing—and there were signs that his appetite for little children remained as well. Kalichuk's farm was only twenty minutes from the Clinton air base, but his attempt in the fall of 1959 to get a posting there had been rebuffed by the Clinton brass, who did not want the known predator on their base in the midst of all the publicity around the Truscott trial. Kalichuk settled for the nearby Centralia station, and it did not take long for problems to re-emerge.

"Police Warn Parents: Young Girls Molested," ran the front-page head-line in the local paper, the *Exeter Times-Advocate*. The Goderich OPP issued a bulletin on "a male person attempting to entice young girls into his car on township and county roads." Sergeant H. T. Barker said the police were inves-tigating two recent incidents: a thirteen-year-old who ran away from a man to avoid abduction, and a seven-year-old who was "forced into [the man's] car, but released after she screamed and yelled at length."

"Molesting Continues," the newspaper reported one month later, noting that "police remain concerned about continuing attempts . . . to pick up young girls." There had been four incidents involving girls ranging in age from six to fourteen. The police were never able to identify a suspect, but the air force certainly had its suspicions. J. J. Young, the social worker who had handled the Kalichuk case in 1959, made reference to the community's con-cerns when he updated the airman's file in the 1960s. "The number of report-ed incidents were frequent enough that the local papers were reporting them," he wrote in a report on Kalichuk. "At that time, I let the then commanding officer at Centralia know." Apparently, nobody on the air force staff bothered telling the police they thought they knew the identity of the molester.

Kalichuk eventually got his transfer to RCAF Clinton in early 1965. And it was there that Willard "Bud" Longley stumbled across his file. Longley was a flight lieutenant and the personnel administration officer at the base. "I discovered a misfiled psychiatric report on an airman . . . which filled me with foreboding," he says. Longley was curious why Alexander Kalichuk had been traumatized by guilt and hospitalized so soon after Lynne's murder. "I briefed my commanding officer on what I had found, and he authorized and encouraged me to investigate the individual to whatever depth it might take to determine whether this airman might be the real murderer."

Brigadier General K. W. Greenway, now retired, confirms he gave his assistant the go-ahead to launch an investigation. "Longley was very good at documenting things," he says. Longley says he spent fifty hours a week tracking down Kalichuk's records, his whereabouts before and after Lynne's disappearance, the sale of his car shortly after the girl's murder, and his hospitalization. "I became totally obsessed with this case," he remembers. "My investigation was peculiar. I couldn't come right out and ask questions. I had to keep it a secret so no one would know I was asking about him."

After three months, Longley felt he had amassed "a mountain of material . . . that pointed a very accusing finger at the airman." Longley claims Harold Graham then came to the Clinton base for a long meeting to discuss his findings. "I explained all the facts and concerns we had and, in fact, I opened the whole book to him," Longley recalls. "I gave Inspector Graham the best . . . briefing that he could ever have been given."

But according to Longley, the OPP officer was not impressed. "Graham indicated the information was all really redundant and would make little difference to Steven's situation because, as he put it, 'Truscott had had his day in court,'" the air force investigator says. The meeting ended badly. "I lost my patience. . . . He was telling me to keep our noses out, and I was suggesting he should pull up his socks and do his job better. We didn't shake hands. I was disgusted."

Harold Graham, for his part, denies he ever met with Longley at the Clinton station or anywhere else. "I would pick up on any sex offenders that came to my attention that might be of some interest," he told *the fifth estate*, "and I don't remember Kalichuk, the name, nor the meeting that somebody says I had with him."

Edith Baker, who worked as a secretary for Longley and Greenway, says, on the contrary, she distinctly remembers Graham coming to the base and walking past her desk to their offices for a meeting. Greenway, for his part, did not attend any meetings on Kalichuk but says of his officer, "Knowing Longley he would have kept the OPP involved." The OPP says it no longer has

Graham's datebook for that period. The air force says it no longer has log-books to show who visited the Clinton base at that time and it has no trace of any report being filed at military headquarters. So no official record is available to prove if a meeting between Graham and Longley ever took place.

There is one intriguing piece of official correspondence from that time, however. On April 4, 1966, Kalichuk's social welfare officer, J. J. Young, took the unusual step of writing a confidential memo to the commanding officer of RCAF Station Centralia about Kalichuk's "aberrations when he had been at Clinton." Military censors have whited out most of the document. Still, it was curious the air force brass would be discussing Kalichuk during the very weeks the Harper affair was once again hitting the front pages with news that the government was about to re-open the case.

No further action was taken by the air force, and the Kalichuk file slipped into obscurity, where it would remain for another three decades.

For Steve and his family, meanwhile, the summer and fall of 1966 was an upbeat, if anxious time. Isabel LeBourdais cheered them with news she was launching the Steven Truscott Defence Fund "because we know that Steve's case must be handled without any thought of the cost." The tireless campaigner assured the family, "This time Steven will get the strongest, fullest, and the most competent representation that it is possible to provide." Usually a political cynic, LeBourdais allowed herself a brief burst of optimism. "Several years ago, I gave [Doris Truscott] my word that I would not stop until Steven's name was cleared and he was home with her," she wrote. "I think we are within sight of achieving this objective."

Not without a cost, however. Steve's father suffered two minor heart attacks in the spring. "The doctor told him if he didn't slow down, the next one would be fatal," Doris wrote to LeBourdais. "But he'll never change in any way." Dan and Doris took a short break from their battles to celebrate a happy family event in July: the marriage of Steve's older brother, Ken.

If Steve was saddened as he watched his siblings grow up without him, he was not showing it. "The change in the past month is clear—he is far more self-confident and less immature," Isabel LeBourdais reported after a brief visit in September. "The support of the lawyers and everyone else has pulled him out of his imprisoned teens."

Steve was upbeat in a letter he penned to his parents that month:

Dear Mom and Dad,

I hope that you and the family are all fine and in good health. I read some stories in the paper the other day and was glad to see that things are starting to get underway. At last I guess I'll be going to take the stand. . . . I sure hope the truth will come out this time.

I hope to see you all soon, so long for now.

Love,
Steve

When his parents came to visit, Steve informed them he had resumed playing trumpet and he had promised the other inmates he would blast it loudly on the day of his release. "The guys certainly are behind me on this thing," Steve said. "They all wish me the best of luck. Even the guards have said they're keeping their fingers crossed for me."

Malcolm Stienburg, the prison chaplain, could sense the groundswell of support for Steven. "An overwhelming percentage of inmates were really cheering for him, hoping that he would get released, and [so did] many, many of the guards as well," the minister remembers. Stienburg tried to caution the young inmate as he sat across the table, playing cards in the prison chapel. "I said, 'Look Steve—this is a court, and while I don't think the courts would ever do anything deliberately dishonest, I think that they are very reluctant to change, too. Just don't get your hopes built too high.'"

But Steven could not help but have hope. "I want to testify and clear my name once and for all," Steven told his mother. "He told me he'd come back and spend a few days cooking . . . when he got out," Doris told reporters. "I warned him not to build his hopes up because he wasn't out yet. You just don't know—some funny things can happen."

Despite Doris's worries, the papers reported that she, Dan and Ken came out of the prison happy, smiling, and confident that this would be one of their last visits to Steven in jail.

**34**

HIS DAY IN COURT

The country sat transfixed as one of the most controversial legal dramas in the nation's history played itself out on the national stage. A CBC documentary took viewers into the home of the Truscotts, where Dan and Doris proudly showed off the needlepoint, leatherwork and woodwork—including a dresser with a mirror and two desks—their son had crafted for them behind bars.

"He has certainly missed the best years of his youth," Dan said, describing the past period as "years of blankness."

"He missed going to a show with a girl, dancing, playing with other children," Doris added. "I don't know any ways society could pay back to Steve the years he has put behind bars."

The program ended with Steve's parents making their way up the wide steps outside the Supreme Court of Canada. "I do feel that now that we have the highest court in the land dealing with the case, he will get a fair break at last," Dan said optimistically. Doris, ever the cautious realist, added: "All we can do is hope and pray."

Ottawa's decision to put the fate of Steven Truscott into the hands of the nine most senior judges in the country had as much to do with politics as the law. The preamble to the federal cabinet's reference to the Supreme

Court made no secret of the fact that the public outcry sparked by LeBourdais' book had forced the government's hand: "There exists widespread concern as to whether there was a miscarriage of justice in the conviction of Steven Murray Truscott, and it is in the public interest that the matter be inquired into."

At least one of the Supreme Court justices saw the influence of the public in the matter as a "dangerous precedent." In a confidential memo, Justice John Cartwright expressed unease at the political time bomb that had landed on the court's front doorstep. "We know the reference has been made to satisfy an aroused public opinion to the effect that Truscott's trial was unsatisfactory and that he may well be innocent," Cartwright said. "Unless every latitude is given to the defence, public opinion will be left unsatisfied. I cannot escape a feeling of regret that the government, having yielded to Mrs. LeBourdais' cry for an inquiry, did not also accept her view that this court is not the proper tribunal to conduct it."

Justice Cartwright's memo was a sign that—even before proceedings began—some of the Supreme Court justices might have been worried about the consequences of overturning Steven's conviction. Four of the sitting judges had been on the court in 1960 when it refused Steven's first appeal. If the court now ruled that Steven deserved a new trial, the justices in effect would be criticizing not only the original trial judge, but also their own decision in 1960.

The stakes were high—not just for Steven, but for the credibility of the entire justice system. On October 4, the evening before the first day of public hearings into the Truscott case, Steve's parents went to the Ottawa airport to meet the woman who, in the words of one newspaper, "aroused the nation and the government" to give their son a second chance. "It's good to see you," Doris said with a smile, as she embraced and kissed LeBourdais while the flashbulbs of the news photographers popped and reporters jostled for a quote. "This time, I'm sure the truth will come out," Doris said, confidently telling the press that her son would be "home for Christmas."

Publicly, Isabel LeBourdais stayed positive and assured the Truscotts she was confident of victory. But the longtime warrior against the status quo had her private doubts. "Unfortunately, there is a grave danger that the desire not to upset the establishment apple cart . . . may be much stronger than the desire to do justice to one boy," she wrote to a friend.

"What do you think this is—a circus?"

The Supreme Court clerk was outraged at all the spectators who had invaded the august chambers of high justice. He ordered the pushy onlookers to leave the overcrowded public benches in the courtroom or the hearing would not resume. One newspaper reported thirty-seven people, most of them women, rushed through the doors and grabbed all the available public seats. Steven "caused a stir among the crowd, particularly among the young women."

"I think I saw him," gushed twenty-year-old Nancy Thiverge. "He was smiling. Oh, it couldn't be him." She was one of three secretaries from the justice department across the road who had taken time off from work to watch the hearing. Lucille Mercier, eighteen, another one of the lucky people to get a front-row seat to history, said, "I never realized it, but he really is a human being."

The object of the young women's attention was whisked into the Supreme Court building in an unmarked car through an underground garage. At first, Steven found his sortie out of Collins Bay to Ottawa exhilarating. It was his first trip outside the prison grounds since his transfer from Guelph in 1963, and the noise and bustle overwhelmed him. "It was fascinating seeing cars go past," he remembers, having not seen late-model vehicles except on TV. Steven even got a taste of a real-life car chase, as one intrepid news photographer tried to snap a picture of the famous prisoner. "I can remember racing down the highway and a newspaper guy hanging out the car window and banging on our car window so I would look," Steve says. "I thought he was crazy."

The novelty of the excursion quickly wore off. After three years of stability and routine, Collins Bay had become his new and—by prison standards—fairly comfortable home. Suddenly, he found himself confined to the Ottawa county jail, where he stayed during the Supreme Court hearing. Whereas in Kingston, Steven had been busy all day and had accumulated the perks and privileges that came with seniority behind bars, in Ottawa he was stuck in a cramped and dingy cell.

The courtroom was his only reprieve, but the stares from the public gallery, the reporters and the judges unnerved Steven, who was accustomed to the anonymity of prison life. On the morning of Wednesday, October 5,

1966, he entered the room wearing a light brown suit made in the tailor shop at Collins Bay Penitentiary, black shoes, a white shirt and a grey tie. If the eager spectators were hoping to hear Canada's most renowned convicted murderer testify, they were going to have to wait a couple of days. The Supreme Court hearing began with—and would largely be dominated by—the dry, often technical testimony of medical experts debating stomach contents, body decomposition and time of death.

But sparks would soon fly, thanks to the presence of some of the sharpest legal minds in the country. For the Crown, William Bowman, the director of public prosecutions since 1957, was in command. He had successfully defeated Steve's appeal in 1960 and had worked closely with Graham and the police to prepare the case this time around. "He has a dry wit, a beguiling chuckle," one newspaper reported. For the direct questioning of witnesses, the Crown hired Donald H. Scott, a successful forty-two-year-old Niagara Falls lawyer who grew up in Seaforth, the small town next to the Clinton air base. "There's more than a casual touch of the traditional about tall, dark Donald Scott," the *Globe and Mail* reported. "He believes profoundly in the dignity of the law and the proper trappings which tradition commands."

Assisting Ted Joliffe with Steven's defence was Arthur Martin, at fifty-three already a legend in legal circles. "His Clients Never Hang," a headline in *Maclean's* once proclaimed in the 1950s. By the time he retired in 1988, Martin had defended sixty clients accused of murder—not a single one was found guilty. When he died in 2001, his colleagues hailed him as "the greatest criminal lawyer Canada has ever produced" and "the most brilliant lawyer of our time."

Martin's often incisive, if not brutal, cross-examinations were more useful than classes for many law students, who flocked to watch his courtroom performances. "Emotion does not work," he explained to one newspaper. "It only clutters up a good case and in the poor one it is well to remember that tears dry quickly. Facts are all that really count in the end. . . . Only as a last resort is an emotional appeal advisable, and even then it is useless without at least one fact."

Over the next five days in October before the Supreme Court, Martin would reveal many new facts about the 1959 murder and trial. But he would find, much to his dismay, that facts—no matter how startling—were not always enough to move the judges of the Supreme Court of Canada.

———

It was fitting that the first witnesses called before the Supreme Court were the two medical experts who never got a chance to testify at Steve's original trial. In 1959, Crown prosecutor Glenn Hays had strongly implied to the jurors that the analysts at the attorney general's crime laboratory in Toronto fully endorsed Dr. John Penistan's conclusions on the time of Lynne's death. Now speaking publicly for the first time since Steve's conviction, what would the lab's scientists say?

"I made only a cursory examination," John Funk, the biologist who first took the jar of stomach contents from the OPP on June 12, 1959, told Crown lawyer Donald Scott. "I noticed what I thought to be at the time some meat, some vegetable in the form of peas, and what appeared to be pineapple."

"Did you make an exhaustive examination of the contents of the stomach?" defence lawyer Arthur Martin pushed when it was his turn to question the witness.

"I would say not," Funk replied.

The man the OPP claimed had told them Lynne's stomach indicated she died "not more than two hours" after supper, as Harold Graham insisted, was making no such claims under oath. In fact, he was insisting his analysis the day police arrested Steve was so preliminary he could not even be sure what the stomach contents were. Neither lawyer asked Funk to speculate on time of death—rightly so, as that was not the biologist's job.

That expertise did fall within the purview of Dr. Noble Sharpe, the medical director of the government laboratory since 1951. "Mr. Funk brought the jar to me with a special request. He wanted me to make an examination in order to advise the investigating officer of an hour, if I could, from which they would commence to focus in their investigation," Sharpe recalled. He found the stomach contents had a strongly acidic, thick consistency of a recently digested meal. "It was in my opinion they had been there one or two hours after eating," he concluded.

On the surface, it appeared to be an endorsement of Penistan's findings. But unlike Penistan, Sharpe saw these times as guidelines, not immovable goalposts. "The time based on . . . these examinations is at most an approximation, an inspired or educated guess," he told Arthur Martin. "It is more likely only a probability or a hunch. It is of use to the investigator but of much less value to the court."

Steve's lawyer was able to secure that important admission by quoting from a revealing public article about the frailty of time-of-death testimony

Sharpe had published in a scientific newsletter. What Martin did not know—like Donnelly seven years before—was how strongly Noble Sharpe had admonished Penistan in private. Martin never saw the three-page memo Sharpe wrote around the time of the Supreme Court hearing in which he criticized Penistan for being "so absolute."

Martin, of course, had an even more serious handicap when it came to the medical evidence. He had little inkling just how much Dr. Penistan himself had made a reappraissal of the central planks of his own testimony.

The next medical witness was Elgin Brown, the analyst in the government's biology department who had testified at the trial on the evidence of Lynne's blood-soaked undershirt and Steven's soiled underwear. Crown lawyer Scott had a different agenda for Brown this time, though. At the original trial, much had been made about a large section of Lynne's blouse that was cut and went missing; the piece was never found at the crime scene or the autopsy room. The defence suggested that it could have meant Lynne was killed elsewhere or that her real assailant perhaps took the piece as a souvenir. The prosecution argued Penistan himself had cut the blouse when he snipped off the knot in the blouse under Lynne's neck, although Penistan himself disputed that is what happened.

Now, seven years later, Scott found himself in the odd position of trying to prove, with Elgin Brown's help, that Penistan had been wrong. In front of the Supreme Court judges, Brown had an assistant put on a pink blouse over her clothes. He then ripped it up the side, knotted it tight enough so that she winced, and cut the knot. A sizeable piece of cloth fell to the floor in what one reporter called a "Perry Mason" performance.

On the less dramatic front of hard science, however, Brown conceded his tests found nothing to incriminate Steven. From all the material seized from Steven's bedroom—pyjama bottoms, pillowcases and bedsheets—no hair fibres, or stains from blood or semen were found.

"You did not find on the clothing or material which the accused had been in contact with any hair or fibres from the deceased?" Martin asked Brown.

"That is correct, sir."

"You did not find on the clothing or on the deceased girl any hair or fibres or material attributable to the accused?"

"No sir, I did not."

Martin wrapped up by asking about the underwear taken from Steven after his first night in police custody—four days after Lynne's disappearance.

At the original trial, the prosecution had made much of the semen traces Brown had found, despite any evidence Steve wore those underpants the night he gave Lynne a ride on his bicycle, and despite overwhelming scientific evidence on the short lifespan of sperm.

"You do not know the age of the stain or how long it was there?" Martin asked bluntly.

"No sir," came the scientist's unequivocal reply.

At Steven's trial, Crown prosecutor Glenn Hays devoted a lot of time to convincing the jury the soiled underwear was of "considerable significance" in Steve's guilt. The Supreme Court hearing dispensed with it in less than fifty seconds.

The final witness of the morning was OPP identification officer Dennis Alsop. Alsop could not testify at the 1959 trial due to a limit on the number of expert witnesses. This time, the OPP would finally get a chance to put their best physical evidence before a court.

Alsop told the nine Supreme Court justices how he used Steven's right shoe to make a mark in the earth, and photographed the imprint. He then enlarged the pictures of the marks found near Lynne's left foot to "as great a magnification as I could get at that particular time." When he compared the two photographs, he found the straight vertical indentations from the crime scene photo resembled the ribbing of Steve's right shoe. He also discovered that "wavy lines" from the crime scene that he said came from the lift of a shoe were consistent with the arch platform of Steve's runners.

"It is my opinion that the shoe that I wore to make the impression . . . made the marks that are shown," Alsop told the justices, but then quickly added a caveat: ". . . or another shoe that would have the same characteristics could have made the same marks."

It was hardly the definitive match needed for a capital murder case. And Martin's vigorous cross-examination exposed a flaw with the evidence. Since Cpl. John Erskine had failed to put a ruler next to the scuff marks at the crime scene before taking the original photographs, Alsop had no accurate measure. In other words, the marks left by the killer could have been from a similar shoe to Steve's—but in a size much smaller or larger.

"I found by enlarging this photograph to a certain size that the indentations shown . . . are the same height," Alsop explained to Steve's lawyer.

"You're just enlarging the one to get to match the other?"

"That is correct."

"Anybody can do that. . . . The fact that these impressions are the same distance apart or the same height doesn't mean anything?" Martin asked. Alsop did not have a ready answer.

"In other words, any shoe of that kind can make it?" the lawyer pushed.

"Yes sir, with the same characteristics."

"You have no idea how many shoes . . . were made in Canada of this kind?"

"No sir, I did not."

Doris Truscott, like many in the courtroom, was not impressed. She "turned to her husband, wrinkled her nose and shook her head disdainfully," according to one newspaper report. Even the Crown attorney later conceded in his summation to the justices the footprint evidence was "not demonstrable. It is not conclusive."

Martin spent the rest of the afternoon and most of the following morning trying to remove another plank in the OPP's testimony against Steve. Several police officers told jurors in 1959 it was difficult, if not impossible to identify a car on the highway, much less a licence plate, from the bridge where Steven claimed he saw Lynne get a lift. Martin did something Frank Donnelly had neither the money nor perhaps the foresight to do: he hired private detectives to conduct independent visual tests from the bridge. They held five different-coloured cards—blue, white, orange, yellow and red—next to the rear bumper of a 1959 Chevrolet. Various people standing at the bridge could distinguish almost all of the colours correctly. All of the participants were able to identify the make of the vehicle as well. Martin also produced a photography expert from the University of Toronto who explained that the police had used an incorrect focal length for the pictures they presented to the jurors. The car in the police photo was one-third the size it should have been.

On the footprint and car evidence, Martin had scored well. But now he faced a more daunting challenge.

"I now call Steven Truscott."

With those five words, Arthur Martin invited Steven to tell his story in a courtroom for the first time. It was ten minutes after noon on Thursday, October 6, 1966.

"A dark, lean-faced man, his black hair glistening with oil, stepped through the double doors at the rear of the courtroom," the *Star Weekly* reported. Steven was not shackled or handcuffed. "There was a slight smile on his face. Led by a guard, he walked to the front of the court, his brown suit bunched over his high, square shoulders. He stood erect at the witness table." His parents said their son looked "pretty shaky"; the slight upturn on his lips, they said, was a "nervous smile."

Steve's parents had spent twenty minutes with him before he took the stand. "He had the butterflies. I was a little nervous and sort of excited at the same time," his mother told reporters. "Steven is very much like me. Our emotions do not really show outwardly. You feel them inwardly, a certain excitement and tension. We told him to keep his chin up. We told him how nice he looked in his new brown suit."

"Sure, he was tense," said his father. "I know I would be if I had to get up in front of nine judges in a packed courthouse like that."

Steven stood in a makeshift witness box with a chair and a desk. Doris, wearing a pale blue coat with an artificial flower in her lapel and a brown hat that matched her dress, never took her eyes off her son during his ninety-minute testimony. Dan dabbed his eyes occasionally, leaning forward with one hand on his knee.

Arthur Martin started with simple biographical questions. Yet, from the beginning, there were worrying signs that Steve's memory was fuzzy at best.

Was Steve's older brother about twenty-two years old?

"I think he is, yes."

"Do you remember where you were when you first went to school?"

"I don't recall just where I was," Steve said in a voice so faint the justices could barely hear.

"You'll have to speak louder so the court may hear you," said Chief Justice Robert Taschereau. "I hear fifty per cent of what you said."

("It's a little hard for my son," Doris later told reporters. "He's not used to raising his voice. They don't talk that loud at Collins Bay." Steve told his parents his knees had felt like buckling, but at least standing up had helped him project his voice.)

As Martin proceeded to lead Steven through the events of 1959, his memory did not improve. "I was at one party where Lynne Harper was. . . . I believe it was her birthday party." (He was wrong; it was Lorraine Wood's

404

party.) He remembered he was wearing red pants the night Lynne disappeared but could not recall anything about the rest of his attire.

"I don't remember what colour shirt I had on," Steve said.

"I stopped at the end of the school and I was watching the Brownies who were having a meeting there," Steve went on. "Lynne Harper came over to the bicycle and asked me if I was going down by the river, and I replied that I was, and she asked me if she could have a lift down to the highway. And several minutes later we proceeded to the county road and I gave her a ride."

What time was it, Martin asked.

"It was one minute either way of 7:30," he said, a slightly different time than the "about 7:25" estimate he gave police in 1959.

"How do you know that?"

"There is a clock in the end of the school."

As they headed down to the river, Steve recounted, Lynne asked him about fishing by the river. "She also mentioned that she was mad at her father for not letting her go swimming. . . . She also mentioned she was going down to the white house where they have ponies." Steve could not remember passing Richard Gellatly, but he told the court he saw Douglas Oates, Butch George and Gordon Logan. He described the 1959 Chevrolet that picked up Lynne: "It had a lot of chrome on it and also, when it pulled out, there appeared to be a yellowish-coloured—it appeared to be a licence plate."

Martin then asked Steve to explain the conversation with his friends at the bridge on the day after Lynne disappeared, when they told him Butch was spreading a story about Steve taking Lynne to the bush. "I went over and asked Arnold George, and he said he had never told anybody that," Steve said.

"Were you in the bush with her?"

"No sir," Steve said, insisting he and his pals were "more or less kidding with each other."

"Did you make any statement that you're not in the bush, you had just been at the edge of the bush looking for calves, or anything of that nature?" Martin asked.

"No sir."

"Had you been anywhere near the bush looking for calves with Ms. Harper?"

"No, I wasn't."

"Do you remember any discussion about that time about calves in the bush?"

"No sir."

After a lunch recess, Martin asked Steven about Butch George's story that the two friends plotted to mislead the police.

"Did you at any time ever request Arnold George to say he had seen you when, in fact, he had not seen you?"

"No, I didn't," Steve said.

Then Martin approached the issue of the sores doctors found on Steve's penis the night of his arrest. "They were well on the way to healing," Steve insisted. "Dr. Addison described them as oozing and there was no oozing whatsoever."

"I want you to listen to this next question quite carefully and apply your mind to it," Martin said slowly. "What did the condition of your penis look like when you first noticed there was something unusual existing there?"

"It was about six weeks before I was picked up," Steve said. "And it started off, what appeared to look like blisters, and continued to worsen from there until it was in the state it was when I was picked up."

"What caused it to worsen? How did its appearance change?"

"Well, one blister would break and it just seemed that more would appear."

"Now, when you first noticed this condition that you describe, did you tell your father about it?"

"No, I didn't." Steven answered. "I was too embarrassed." Steven told the court the first people he told about his condition were Martin and his colleague Ted Joliffe in Collins Bay Penitentiary. It was another example of how Steve's dreadful memory even led him to get things wrong that would have helped him. On the very night of his arrest, in fact, Steve told Dr. John Addison the sores had been on his penis for "four to five weeks," according to the doctor.

Martin, knowing he was going to use Steven's struggles with the psychiatrists later in the hearing, asked Steven about his opinion of them. "The majority of them wanted me to admit I was guilty," he told the nine Supreme Court justices.

"What did you do?"

"I would not admit to it."

But Martin also knew Steven was vulnerable because his detractors saw his 1964 parole application—with its mention of "one dreadful mistake"— as a confession. "Did you intend to make any admission of guilt?" he asked.

"No, I didn't."

"What did you mean by that?"

"Well, when you are sent to the penitentiary it is considered that you're paying for the crime that you have been sentenced for. This is what I meant when I asked that I had paid five years of my life. And from observing all the people in the penitentiary, it was obvious to me that crime didn't pay," Steve answered. "I decided that it wasn't going to benefit me by arguing any more. . . . It would be in my benefit to more or less go along with them on their terms in order to get out."

To conclude Steven's testimony, Martin asked him a simple five-word question that no one had ever heard Steven Truscott answer publicly.

"Did you kill Miss Harper?"

"No, I didn't."

"Your witness," Martin said, giving Crown attorney Donald Scott a chance to grill Steven Truscott about his story. Steve continued to display a dismal memory of the most basic events surrounding the crime. Steven denied even the most innocuous of events. For example, several people spotted him on the county road before 7:00 p.m. Steve had told Kenny Geiger he had just passed his mother, Beatrice, on her way down to the bridge. But in front of the Supreme Court seven years later, Steven denied it all.

"Did you see him at any time?" Scott asked, in reference to Kenny.

"No, I didn't."

"Am I correct here, Mr. Truscott?" Scott said in disbelief. "You did not see Mrs. Geiger, you did not see Ken Geiger, you did not see Paul Desjardine?"

"That's correct," Steve said. He could have said he did not remember seeing them, but by refusing to acknowledge these encounters even took place Steve was damaging his credibility when it came time to refute much more damning testimony. Steve told the court he never asked Butch to lie for him, and he denied Jocelyne Gaudet's story that he had dropped by her house. But would the nine justices believe him if he denied the obvious fact he met several people along the county road?

Scott asked Steve if he met Richard Gellatly—the only person on the county road Steve had singled out in his police statement. If anything, meeting Richard gave Steve important support because Richard claimed they crossed paths around 7:25 p.m., around the same time Steve said he left the school.

"No, I didn't," Steve said, inexplicably.

Even once Scott read back Steve's conversations with police officers about meeting Richard, Steven stuck to his denial: "I don't recall that, sir, no."

Scott asked Steve if he recalled various people testifying at the trial—Paul Desjardine, Beatrice Geiger and Kenny Geiger. Always, his answer was the same: "No sir." Steve even said he did not recall knowing schoolmates like Bryan Glover.

"I was wondering, frankly, Mr. Truscott, bearing in mind the nature of the evidence that I have read to you . . . and bearing in mind the nature of the charge against you, why you cannot even recall these people giving evidence?"

"I don't recall them giving evidence."

"I know that, sir. My question was: why don't you recall?"

"Because I have forgotten," Steve said, finally offering an explanation that implied he was not lying about certain incontrovertible encounters—but he had limited memory of events from a traumatic, jarring few days in his boyhood.

"And what was your reaction, if you recall, when that evidence was being given?" Scott continued.

"I don't remember," Steve said simply.

Scott went on the attack against one of Steven's most vulnerable stories before the court—that he had told no one about the sores on his penis until seven years later when his lawyers asked him. Scott asked if Steven had told his father about the apparently long-lasting injuries after the two doctors testified about them at the preliminary hearing in July.

"I don't remember whether I told him anything or not," said Steve.

Scott wanted to know what happened when the sores became such an incriminating issue at the trial in September 1959. "Even at that time you did not tell your father or anyone how they occurred?" Scott asked.

"No, I didn't," Steve insisted.

Scott, having inflicted the maximum amount of damage, turned to the nine justices. "That concludes my cross-examination, my lords." Steve's defence lawyer, Arthur Martin, added, "I have no questions in re-examination, my lords."

Steven Truscott's one and only day in court was over.

"He was wonderful," said his father. "I am very pleased with the way he carried himself and the way he answered."

"We're very proud of him," Doris Truscott told the press. "We feel just the way he does. We know that he did not commit this crime. There has never been any doubt in our mind."

With conviction, Steve stuck to the core of the story he first began telling police the morning after Lynne disappeared, a story that had barely changed in the days and months after the murder and in the years of prison. But in other regards, especially his limp answers in the cross-examination, it was a lamentable performance. The best that could be said was that Steve's memory was so uniformly—rather than selectively—poor that he certainly did not come off as crafty and calculating. After all, he denied not just incriminating testimony but also events that were neutral or even helped prove his innocence, such as meeting Richard Gellatly on the county road.

With the benefit of hindsight, Steven today says his own lawyers did not adequately prepare him. "I wasn't even given a copy of my [original police] statement to go over to remember," he says. "So at the Supreme Court hearing when they started asking you questions, you don't remember clearly."

As he did at his 1959 trial, Steven felt he was a bystander in a high-stakes legal contest that was entirely out of his grasp. "You had prominent lawyers and they were going to handle this. This was a legal matter, you are off to the side."

Malcolm Stienburg agreed. The chaplain from Collins Bay had travelled to Ottawa to lend support to the most prominent member of his prison flock. "This was all like a big whirlwind swirling around him. He was sort of standing outside watching it happen," he says. "It was a pretty draining experience."

With his mercifully short testimony at the Supreme Court over, Steven returned to Collins Bay for the three-day Thanksgiving weekend. At least he was back in familiar surroundings, with people he knew.

He had no idea how many more years prison would be his home.

## 35

## A BATTLE OF SCIENCE AND EGOS

S teven's brief appearance before the Supreme Court justices was the exception in a hearing dominated by experts. Steven was, in fact, the only non-
specialist to testify—the other twenty-three witnesses were police officers,
detectives or scientists. No less than sixteen of them had medical or psychiatric
credentials.

Arthur Martin relied on three doctors to try to prove a surprising new
defence theory that Steven's penis sores did not come from raping Lynne or
even excessive masturbation, but were signs of a skin irritation to which Steven
was prone. Dr. Emilian Marcinkowsky, a medical officer at the Guelph reformatory told the court he treated Steven several times for dermatitis in his ears
and armpits and once for "an inflamed cyst of the dorsum of the penis." Dr.
Charles Danby, a dermatology specialist in Kingston, testified to treating Steven
at least six times at Collins Bay for skin ailments that were "oozing and scaling
and crusted." On one visit the doctor noticed "a large, patchy nummular type
of eczema" on his shoulders, face and ears. Nummular, the doctor explained,
means coin-shaped—"small or large round areas in the skin that are reddened
and marked by innumerable small blisters which opened and ooze."

It sounded strikingly similar to the sores "the size of a quarter" that doctors first noticed on Steven's penis at the station guardhouse on June 11,

1959. Danby said the injuries were not typically caused by intercourse. Rather, the dermatologist suggested, it was a case of herpes simplex, commonly known as cold sores, aggravated by secondary bacterial infection and irritation from urination and wearing underwear and jeans.

For more support, Martin called on Dr. Norman Wrong, a senior dermatologist to the Canadian army during World War II and a past president of the Canadian Dermatological Association. He said it was "extremely unlikely" that intercourse would cause lesions on the side of the shaft of the penis.

"I think either it was simple herpes plus infection or . . . irritation from sweating and the skin surfaces rubbing together," he said. He explained that while it would be unusual for simple herpes to affect both sides of the penis at the same time, such an infection could easily be aggravated in a teenager who was frequently riding his bike, wearing rough jeans and collecting dirt in his clothes.

It was a bold yet plausible explanation for what had always been a prosecution trump card.

The dermatologists were just a precursor to the real medical war—a no-holds-barred legal slugfest as some of the top experts in the world fought it out over the intricacies of stomach contents. It was a war of science, of egos, of international heavyweights bragging about how many autopsies they had done. But more often than not, their own expansive boasts and quick judgments tripped them up.

First up for the defence was Dr. Charles Sutherland Petty, the assistant medical examiner for the state of Maryland. A tall man, wearing glasses and a bow tie, he said he performed four hundred autopsies per year. Martin began by asking him to estimate the time of Lynne's death based on contents of her stomach.

"I would find myself completely unable to pinpoint any time," Petty replied.

"What would be the limits either way?" Martin asked.

"Several minutes, twenty, thirty, forty minutes . . . perhaps as long as eight hours," Petty replied. He criticized Penistan for not taking into account the many factors that alter digestion. Penistan also did not take into account how hot weather influences rigor mortis, delaying its onset and speeding up its disappearance.

Petty also stressed the absence of certain telltale signs of decomposition he expected to see in a body that had been dead for forty-eight hours or longer: bloating, the outline of clearly delineated veins, and slippage of the skin. He estimated the time of death at "less than forty-eight hours" before the autopsy—in the neighbourhood of thirty or thirty-six hours, possibly forty hours. In effect, Petty was saying Lynne probably died on Wednesday, not on the Tuesday evening when she was with Steve.

Martin also used Petty to prepare the terrain for a scientific challenge to another aspect of the 1959 conviction: the place of Lynne's death. Much of Petty's theory rested on hypostasis, the discolouring as blood tends to settle in a dead body. In the autopsy photos, Petty noticed a blanching on Lynne's left arm, her left breast, and on the left side of her face, particularly on her forehead and cheek. "I believe this body lay on its left side for a period of time after death and was moved at a later time," he concluded, a potentially shocking determination that—if true—would rule out Steven as the killer.

Petty gave other reasons why he thought Lynne was not killed in the bush. Dr. Penistan told jurors the marks on Lynne's back were proof her body had been pressed against the twigs on the ground, but Petty insisted the twigs would have snapped under her weight or made small linear scratches, instead of the tiny holes found on her torso. He also speculated the little scratches on the outside of both her legs—with no apparent bleeding—indicated her killer had taken hold of the upper part of her body and dragged her backwards through the bush.

Donald Scott began his cross-examination with the kind of testy sparring that would mark most of the medical skirmishes at the Supreme Court. Was it not true that Dr. Penistan found "very little" food had left the stomach to the intestines?

"Well, sir, my car took 'very little' gas yesterday. Is that one gallon or ten?" Petty retorted.

Scott then read from a medical textbook that stated the bulk of a meal leaves the stomach in one or two hours. It sounded definitive—until Petty insisted the lawyer read the entire passage, which concluded: "That emptying may not be complete for three to five hours or even longer."

Unshakeable, Petty stroked his chin and gazed at the ceiling during much of his grilling. But then Scott scored several damaging blows. Petty's theory of a lingering rigor mortis, and therefore a more recent death, was based in part on an arched back and a stiff finger he spotted in one of the photographs. Scott pointed out the finger's apparent stiffness came simply from resting on another digit, and suggested the arching of Lynne's body was a natural occurrence.

Scott also tried to undermine Petty's claims that the blanching on Lynne's left side indicated the body had been moved long after Steve was safe at home. Was it not true, the attorney asked, that simply transferring the body from the ambulance to the funeral home to the autopsy table could cause different shadings as the blood settled?

"No, sir, I do not agree with you on that," Petty said, insisting that no momentary change in position would have any effect after twenty-four hours had passed between death and when the body was moved.

Petty's theory got support from the next medical expert, Dr. Frederick Jaffe, the assistant pathologist for Toronto Western Hospital and regional pathologist for the government since 1951. He, too, saw "a peculiar pattern" on the left cheek, the left side of the nose and forehead and the left shoulder and upper arm. "This type of pattern is frequently caused by the dependent portion of the body resting upon clothing or cloth of some sort, the folds of cloth producing this type of pattern," he said, suggesting significantly the pattern occurred within the first hour of the blood settling.

Crown attorney Donald Scott countered that the different angles, distances and lighting in the autopsy photographs made them unreliable indications of blanching. He also suggested that as long as Lynne's blood remained fluid, the discolouration on her skin could continue even in the autopsy room. Jaffe—in an important concession—agreed that in many strangling deaths, blood might re-liquefy after clotting.

Like the other defence witnesses, Jaffe warned the Supreme Court justices that stomach contents were a most unreliable guide to determine time of death. "Two equally competent observers looking at the same stomach contents may get very different impressions and therefore arrive at very different conclusions regarding the time of death," he explained. "This makes it basically an almost useless method." But based on the absence of changes in the decomposition of the body lying in a hot and humid bush, he hypothesized Lynne died perhaps "halfway between twenty-four and forty-eight hours" before the autopsy—again, on Wednesday, not Tuesday.

———

The Supreme Court was now halfway through the fourth day of its hearings, but the most acrimonious duel of doctors still lay ahead—between two medical giants from the other side of the Atlantic. Dr. Francis Edward Camps, described as England's foremost authority on the medical aspects of crime, was the director of the department of forensic medicine at the University of London medical school and the co-author of a standard text on forensic medicine. He was so outraged by what he saw as the shoddy medical evidence at Steve's first trial, he wrote to LeBourdais' publisher early in 1966 to offer his help.

On Tuesday, October 11, Dr. Camps found himself in the chambers of Canada's highest court. Martin wanted this renowned pathologist to reinforce the defence assault on the medical science used to convict Steven. While conceding that "one has to be very, very cautious interpreting photographs," Camps agreed with Martin's other witnesses that the autopsy pictures showed a consistent difference in contrast on the face and the upper part of Lynne's breast, indicating her murderer kept her body on the left side for some time before placing her in the position she was found. He also concurred there was evidence the sexual assault occurred elsewhere than the bush, since investigators found no semen or acid phosphatase on the ground near her body.

Martin asked him specifically about Penistan's 7:45 p.m. cutoff for the murder. "I would say it is quite impossible and, in fact, I would say it could be dangerously misleading to the investigating officers," Camps told the Supreme Court justices.

When it was his turn to grill the witness, Donald Scott took direct aim at the doctor's dismissal of Penistan's estimate of the time of death. "Do you agree in this case this girl could have died within that period?" the Crown lawyer asked.

"This girl with the stomach contents could have died within two hours, could have been nine, ten, eleven hours. But I do not think you can say she died fixing the time within half an hour," Camps maintained.

Surely pathologists can give the police some kind of guidance about the time of a murder, Scott wanted to know.

"I can only say from my experience over a number of years that I have been so far off centre that I am almost afraid to indicate this to the police officers," Camps informed him with surprising humility. "It becomes a matter of a guess. You can twist to get on either side as much as you like."

But then came the doctor's most embarrassing moment. Scott read excerpts from a letter Camps wrote about the LeBourdais book stating the prosecution's medical evidence could not stand up to scrutiny. Did that not show the reputed doctor had made up his mind "long before" he had examined first-hand the medical testimony, Scott asked.

Camps had been caught. The doctor stumbled, called the question "misleading," and said he did not like anyone questioning his integrity. But when it was over, Scott had efficiently deflated the defence's star medical witness. Little did Scott know that his own top performer would soon suffer an identical fate.

Keith Simpson also came with a high medical pedigree, and an eagerness to flaunt it. A fierce rival of Camps, he told the press, "In some thirty years, I have completed some 100,000 autopsies." A remarkable achievement, requiring over three thousand autopsies a year, or more than nine every day—weekends and holidays—non-stop for three decades.

When Simpson repeated that claim in front of the nine Supreme Court justices, he raised his voice to a near shout, according to the *Toronto Daily Star*, and an "incredulous murmur" spread through the courtroom. Justice Cartwright, perhaps taken aback by the prospect of a single doctor examining that many corpses, interrupted to say he was not quite sure he had heard the doctor's words. Simpson reassured the court he had personally performed and not merely supervised the 100,000 examinations.

Based on that expertise, Simpson gave Penistan high praise for carrying out a "very competent and conscientious investigation" of the crime. "He was right to conclude that it was likely that death had taken place somewhere up to two hours after eating that meal," Simpson said, choosing his words carefully, since "somewhere up to two hours" was still much less precise than Penistan's down-to-the-minute snapshot of the time of death. Simpson said there was a general consensus in the medical literature that the bulk of a meal leaves the stomach inside of two hours.

"This girl's death must have taken place within two hours after taking that meal," he concluded.

Scott then proceeded to use Simpson to discredit the main tenets of Martin's new theories. The doctor said there was "a very simple explanation" for the discolouration or blanching on Lynne's body. Just before the autopsy, the doctors placed her body on its side on some kind of sheeting or covering. As long as the blood was fluid when this took place, discolouration could appear, Simpson said, and blood could remain liquid in a dead body for a long period of time.

As for the penis sores, Simpson conceded he found them "perplexing" and agreed they were not the ordinary kind of injury produced from forced sexual intercourse. (Privately, Simpson had told the prosecutors in a letter before the trial that "other explanations" for the sores "would be acceptable in an adolescent boy—masturbation perhaps most of all.") So he came up with an ingenious way to undercut Martin's new evidence. Simpson accepted that a pre-existing skin irritation could have started the lesions, but perhaps they were rubbed "in some way which caused them to become more sore or to weep or crust"—rubbed, Simpson suggested, as part of a sexual assault.

When it came his turn to question Simpson, Arthur Martin realized it would be his most important cross-examination. He wasted no time in launching his attack. Was it not true that in his published review of LeBourdais' book, Simpson had defended the medical evidence as "surprisingly sound," even though he had never seen it or read the trial transcript? "I formed the opinion from the book," Simpson was forced to admit, revealing the same sort of bias that had humbled his rival, Francis Camps.

Martin then proceeded to use Simpson's own writings to devastate his testimony. Simpson's textbook on forensic medicine had gone through five editions, yet Martin noted that nowhere did the illustrious doctor even mention stomach contents as a reliable guide for the time of death.

"No sir," Simpson agreed. "That is, as may be evident to you, a short book for the student."

"It would not have made it much bigger to put in a sentence indicating that stomach contents were also a reliable guide," said Martin, in a biting reply that showed why his cross-examinations were required reading in law classes.

"I think you may expect the next edition, sir, to contain some reference," Simpson said, in an attempt to recover.

Never one to miss a chance to skewer a witness, Martin held up Simpson's book. "I will throw this away and buy the next edition," he promised. (Martin could save himself the expense. Contrary to his pledge in court, Simpson never did make a reference to stomach contents in any subsequent editions.)

The defence counsel was not finished humiliating the prosecution's star witness. Martin quoted from another book Simpson edited, which said that the "state of digestion of contents of the stomach ... are wholly unreliable." Simpson could only reply that there was a "sharp difference" between state of digestion and stomach contents.

Martin then offered Simpson more of his own words to digest—one of his books featured the autopsy of a woman, strangled to death, whose stomach showed meat fibres, peas and potatoes as late as nine hours after her death. Simpson conceded the parallels with Lynne's murder were striking—the cause of death was the same and the stomach contents were remarkably similar. The doctor said he knew little about the facts regarding the case in his book that could account for the exceptionally slow digestion time.

"You do not know what the facts were with respect to Harper?"

"No, sir; I am saying this is—"

"So, we have another parallel," Martin cut in quickly.

Based on all this, how could Simpson agree with Penistan's attempt to pinpoint the time of death between 7:00 and 7:45, Martin asked.

"To start with, 'pinpoint' is not a word one could use to establish the time of death from one observation," Simpson said. "It is always an approximation."

"The words Dr. Penistan used were that he would put the time of death between 7:00 and 7:45," Martin pushed. "Those are relatively narrow limits."

"I do not think it was pinpointing," Simpson insisted.

What about rigor mortis, Martin barrelled on. Did Simpson's own book not say in high temperatures it could disappear in eighteen to twenty-four hours? If that were the case, Lynne could have died on Wednesday. Yes, the doctor admitted. Simpson also agreed that he would expect to see green staining on the abdomen about forty-eight hours after death. "The fact that you do not find it ... tends to put the time of death later rather than earlier?" asked Martin.

"Yes, I think you put that very fairly, sir."

Martin wrapped up his cross-examination of Simpson by pushing him on the place and even the cause of death. "If you get a pattern of purplish discolouration on both sides, it would indicate the body lay first on its face and then on its back?"

"Yes sir, that is possible."

"And if the front or the face was pressing against something, you would get a blanching, wouldn't you?"

"Yes sir," Simpson replied, conceding that several autopsy photographs showed there was blanching on the face and arms.

"Have you ever seen a pattern like that from an arm resting on wrinkled clothing?"

"Yes sir."

"On a car seat, perhaps?"

"Yes, I have seen it lying on cloth."

"Normally you would expect a pattern like that to become established by the body lying on it within an hour after death?" Martin continued.

"Yes sir, at any time after death when the blood is still fluid," Simpson agreed.

"But normally that . . . would be within an hour or two after death?

"No sir, it may remain fluid for a day," Simpson responded, trying to dig himself out of a hole. He had already accepted there was blanching and a pattern on Lynne's skin. Now he had to somehow attribute those marks to the funeral home where doctors examined her. He suggested Lynne's blood may have clotted for two days and then unclotted precisely around the time her body was moved in the autopsy room.

At best, this was dubious scientific speculation, but it was the only way Simpson had to explain his theory that the patterns on Lynne's skin came from the autopsy room and not elsewhere.

Finally, Martin introduced the possibility that even the cause of death was worth re-examining. Lynne's thyroid was fractured, but Simpson agreed that that was "extremely rare" when a killer strangled the victim with a cloth or rope instead of hands. He also agreed other signs usually found in victims of strangling—petechiae, or round, purplish red spots caused by bleeding under the skin, as well as tension spots in the eyelids and the undersurface of the scalp—were absent.

"Would that indicate other factors being involved in the death of this girl?" Martin asked.

"I think it is possible, sir."

Were all these circumstances not inconsistent with the death having occurred elsewhere, Martin asked.

"I can't exclude that, sir," said Dr. Keith Simpson.

It was a major breakthrough. Martin had one of the chief prosecution experts agreeing that Lynne—murdered perhaps "later than earlier"—could have been killed elsewhere, a pattern forming on her skin as her body lay on one side, perhaps in a car.

It had been an impressive duel, certainly more full of sparks than any of the medical debates during the trial in 1959. At least one person in the courtroom seemed to be enjoying the show. When the hearing recessed for lunch after Simpson completed his testimony, Steven winked at his mother as the guards led him out.

The testimony of the final two medical experts for the Crown was almost anti-climactic, but it, too, illustrated the frailties of scientific pontification in a court of law. Dr. Milton Helpern, the chief medical examiner for the city of New York, also played the numbers game, telling the court he had performed approximately twenty thousand autopsies. His conclusion on Lynne's demise was precise. "Death had occurred no more than two hours after the food was ingested. I think that is the rule in these cases."

But Helpern ended up eating his own words when Arthur Martin quoted a book Helpern had written on legal medicine and pathology. The book warned stomach contents should be treated "with caution," and any opinion about the time of death "should be guarded."

Samuel Robert Gerber, a Cleveland doctor and a coroner since 1937, was equally definitive when Scott asked him how long the food had been in Lynne's stomach: "Less than two hours," the expert said without hesitation.

But in one of the most devastating cross-examinations in the hearing, Martin succeeded in showing the futility of trying to narrow time of death to exact minutes using stomach contents. He subjected Dr. Gerber to the kind of grilling Dr. Penistan was lucky to escape in 1959.

"You say less than two hours. How much less than two hours?" Martin began.

"It is less than two hours. And since I know that the child had eaten at 5:45, and that child had been seen around 6:30, so therefore it had to be between 6:30 and 7:45."

But Martin was not going to stand for that. He pointed out the doctor only knew Lynne was not dead by 6:30 because eyewitnesses had seen her. "I want to know on the basis of the stomach contents, how much less than two hours?"

"I couldn't give you any exact minutes," Gerber said.

"You are purporting to say how long the food was in the stomach from the stomach contents," Martin said, in a question that could well have been asked of all the Crown witnesses. "How long from the appearance of the stomach contents alone has this food been in the stomach?"

"My answer is less than two hours," Gerber said. "I cannot define it in minutes."

"Why did you strike at two hours, why not two hours and five minutes?"

"I can give you five minutes," the doctor said, suddenly transforming science into a poker game.

"Ten minutes?" Martin upped the ante.

"No, I am not going to give you ten minutes."

"What makes the difference between five and ten? What would the stomach have to look like to give you that extra five minutes?"

Martin did a wonderful job of exposing the folly of relying on something as variable as digestion to pin a girl's death—and a boy's life—down to a few minutes.

After spending nearly three days debating details of Lynne's lifeless body and the contents of her stomach, the Supreme Court moved on to hear rival psychiatrists battle over the contents of Steven Truscott's mind. For the Crown, the chief witness was James Joseph Hartford, the consultant who first saw Steven at the training school in Guelph.

"I found him to be generally an intelligent, rather likeable boy, but I also found he was very guarded," the psychiatrist said. "I think, to an untrained person, he would appear to be reasonably normal." But as a trained professional, the doctor was not tricked; he determined that what he saw as Steve's flat emotional level meant "the boy was ill."

Martin leapt at the doctor's facile diagnosis. "Would you not expect a fourteen-year-old who was been through a murder trial and found guilty and sentenced to be hanged, and under sentence of death for at least three months, and removed from his family into an institution, to be somewhat traumatized by that experience?" he asked.

"I would expect him to be very traumatized," the doctor admitted.

"You would not expect it to reduce his emotional level and his involvement with people in this new environment?"

"No sir," said the psychiatrist.

Martin pointed out that the superintendent at Guelph praised Steven for his good sportsmanship, fair play and emotional control, and described him as "a splendid example to other boys." But Hartford insisted Steve was a very suspicious, even paranoid boy with "psychopathic tendencies."

How did he define these tendencies? Martin read aloud to the court one of Hartford's reports about what he termed Steven's "psychopathic flavouring." "This latter is indicated by his apparent philosophy that guilt is something that has to be proved and the onus is not upon him to establish his innocence," Hartford said. The nine Supreme Court judges broke into smiles upon learning the prison psychiatrist had taken one of the fundamental principles of Canadian justice—innocent until proven guilty—and turned it into proof of mental illness.

Martin then introduced several psychiatrists who painted quite a different picture of Steven. The experts had been part of the panel that George Scott, the chief psychiatrist at Collins Bay, commissioned in March of 1966. But Scott never expected the panel's conclusions would indicate the real sickness was with the way psychiatry was practised in the prisons.

Dr. Robert McCaldon, who chaired the panel of psychiatrists, said the unanimous evaluation of all four consultants was that Steven was not suffering from any psychiatric or behavioural disorder. He also told the court the psychiatrists concluded in their final report "that Truscott's admission in his parole application was not necessarily a direct admission of guilt, but rather, a carefully worded application designed to favourably impress the parole board."

The panel also made a not-so-veiled criticism of the years of harassment Steven endured at the hands of doctors such as Scott and Hartford. "It was agreed that the primary orientation of psychiatry and the use of psychiatric techniques should not be to extract confessions from inmates."

All Crown lawyer Donald Scott could do in his rebuttal was argue that these psychiatrists had seen a twenty-one-year-old Steven in 1966, not the "psychopathic" teenager Hartford was treating in 1960.

But then, as a closing expert—the last witness to address the Supreme Court of Canada—the defence called Dr. John Rich, the psychiatrist and adolescent specialist the Truscotts had tried for months to get into Collins Bay prison to see their son. Rich studied Steven's entire medical file—reports from prison doctors, teachers and other officials going back to 1960—and interviewed him twice in 1966.

He found Steve's "lack of spontaneity," which so fascinated the prison doctors, to be not only "completely understandable in the light of his experience," but also typical of most training-school boys and jailed adolescents.

"One of the striking things about all the records is that [they] . . . are not only inconsistent with psychopathy but actually contradicted [it]," Dr. Rich said. "I find it hard to believe that he was a psychopath or psychotic on a number of discrete occasions and no other occasions."

It was a final blow against the psychiatric presumptions of the doctors who for so many years had tried to pigeonhole a boy because he refused to admit his guilt.

Round One—the unprecedented public hearing with witnesses—was over. Over five days, the Supreme Court justices had sat through the sometimes extremely technical testimony of twenty-four witnesses. Still, there had been important revelations: a new explanation for the sores on Steve's penis and fresh theories about blanching and other signs that Lynne might not have died in the bush. The validity of using stomach contents as a test for time of death came under much more vigorous fire than in 1959.

Perhaps most importantly, a fourteen-year-old boy who had sat silently during his murder trial in 1959 spoke out in his own defence, now as a young man of twenty-one. Steve's father had followed the other witnesses with nervous attention. "Dan Truscott's mouth tightened and he shut his eyes as if in pain," the *Toronto Daily Star* reported at one point. But when his son stood up to testify, Dan Truscott was a proud father.

When the public sessions were over and Steven exited the courtroom, Dan "once more took leave of the son who had grown up in prison," the newspaper reported. He put his hand on Steve's shoulder.

"I'll be seeing you, son," he said.

A flicker of a smile crossed Steven's face.

"See you," Steve said, and he was gone.

## 36

# THE LAWYERS SQUARE OFF

The public glare diminished after October, but the legal battles intensified. With the unprecedented hearings from witnesses behind them, the Supreme Court justices turned to more familiar terrain. In December, the lawyers submitted their written briefs. For four days in January, the judges heard oral arguments.

The long months of waiting and constant media attention were beginning to wear on the Truscott family. Doris admitted to a reporter she was taking tranquilizers. She recounted one visit to Kingston, waiting to meet one of Steve's lawyers: "We were in a motel restaurant. I tried to raise the cup of coffee to my mouth. I couldn't."

Still, she put up a brave front. "Like Steve, we're saying we haven't built up our hopes," Doris said. "But inside we have. We have no doubts about the outcome, no doubts at all." Amidst all the tension, Dan Truscott found time to think of the other family traumatized by the case. "It's awful for the Harpers," he told one newspaper. "Everything brings back things for them. After all, she was their daughter, and they went through hell, too. I've always felt pity for them."

At Collins Bay, Steven returned to the reassuring stability and anonymity of his daily routines. "We don't take sides," a new warden named John Meers told reporters, when asked how the prison was dealing with its high-profile inmate. "In this case, he is guilty until proven innocent." But some newspapers reported otherwise. "We're rooting for Steve," an unnamed senior penitentiary official told the Toronto *Telegram*.

Doris had told the press in the spring she hoped her son would be home by Christmas. It was not to be. "Well, of course we're disappointed," she said, consoling herself with another holiday visit to a penitentiary. "We have nothing special planned, however, since all we will be allowed to do is to talk across a table," Doris added.

Birthdays behind bars were also becoming a ritual for the Truscott family. On January 15, Steve turned twenty-two—his seventh birthday in jail. His parents, sister and two brothers sent him cards—penitentiary rules did not permit gifts.

Ten days later, his lawyers began their final fight to free Steven from prison.

On Wednesday, January 25, 1967, Arthur Martin stood before the nine justices to begin one of the most important legal arguments of his career. For the next two and half days, the gifted orator would try to convince the robed arbiters of Steven's fate why the evidence did not justify a conviction.

Martin's first task was to try to convince the justices that—even on the basis of the 1959 evidence—there were reasonable grounds to throw out the guilty verdict as unfounded. He began with an attack on the chief prosecution child witness, Jocelyne Gaudet. "The evidence is subject to a number of frailties and improbabilities," he argued. "But even if her evidence is accepted at its best value, it does not show an intention on the part of Steven Truscott to lure her into the bush . . . and it was not admissible on trial anyway." Jocelyne's times were so off-base the prosecution had to throw them out for her testimony to be of any use, he reminded the judges. No other witness aside from Butch George supported her story about being down at the bridge looking for Steven.

Martin questioned Steve's supposedly hush-hush plot to lure Jocelyne into the bush. He wondered where the requisite secrecy was if Steve talked to her in classroom with the teacher present, and then went by her house "where her mother and father would be aware that he was the person who had called for her if anything happened to her." He noted that Steven's departure from the school with Lynne in full view of the Brownies and ball play-ers was "inconsistent with harbouring any secret or evil design."

Martin raised a thought-provoking hypothetical legal quandary to illus-trate his point. If Jocelyne had told her mother on Tuesday afternoon about Steve's alleged advances and she called in the police, would there be enough evidence to charge Steven with attempted indecent assault? Hardly. Yet the prosecution at Steven's trial used the same shaky evidence to suggest Steven had a criminal intent toward Jocelyne and then, in her place, Lynne.

"Surely it is not a criminal intent to go out on a date with the girl?" asked Justice Douglas Abbott.

"No, it is not," Martin answered, "but the prosecution, in my submis-sion, called it a criminal intent by saying it was God's blessing that this girl was late for her supper and the other girl went to her doom."

"Are you suggesting that the Crown went so far as to say that there was a proof of intention, that the accused intended to rape?" Justice Cartwright asked.

"I submit so, my lord; if this was not the suggestion, what was the sug-gestion? That they were there to pick the violets?" Martin answered with his usual wit.

"Do you see any responsibility in the trial judge to have stopped Crown counsel . . . in his tracks when he started to tell the jury about Jocelyne nar-rowly missing her doom?" Justice Emmett Hall asked.

"It would have been better if he had," Martin agreed. "It would have brought home to the jury more emphatically that this was not to be used for that purpose."

Martin quickly dismissed Butch George, noting the wide discrepancies in his constantly changing tales made it "very dangerous to act on his evi-dence." Martin was equally dismissive of Philip Burns, insisting his testi-mony about not seeing Steven "is of very little weight." Philip also did not see Richard Gellatly, Martin reminded the judges—did that mean Richard was not on the road?

Other children were equally unreliable, Martin said. When Steve's friends testified about their "boyish horseplay" at the bridge on the Wednesday evening when they teased him about being in the bush with Lynne, each witness had a different version of the conversation, even though the boys were only about five feet apart from each other.

"Caution should be used in approaching the evidence of these children, even under the most favourable circumstances," Martin warned. He reminded the judges that two of the witnesses—Butch George and Tom Gillette—read over their police statements many times just before entering court. Fumbling on the stand, Tom even tried to take his statement out to read until the judge stopped him. "It is dangerous to act upon the uncorroborated evidence of children of tender years, even when sworn," Steve's lawyer said.

Martin then did something before the Supreme Court justices that Donnelly never did before Judge Ferguson in 1959: he tried to disprove the prosecution's case about what happened on the county road by taking a cold, hard mathematical look at their numbers. Donnelly had made a fatal flaw in 1959. He tried to attack the credibility of Philip Burns, but he never challenged the police and prosecution timings that determined Philip should have met Steven before he reached the entrance to the bush.

Martin wanted the Supreme Court justices to understand that this prosecution theory collapsed if it could be shown that by the time Steve passed Richard and made it to the bush entrance, Philip was so close to the laneway he would have seen or bumped into Steven.

Martin first gave the judges various scenarios assuming different speeds for Steve and Lynne's bike ride and several possible spots where they met Richard on the road. By one calculation, Philip would be only thirty-seven seconds away, about 210 feet north of the laneway when Steven and Lynne got there. "He would have a view of Steven Truscott as he turned down the trail," he announced.

In another scenario, assuming slower travel times and a meeting place closer to the school, Philip would have been almost five hundred feet *beyond* the laneway—south of the entrance to the bush—making his evidence about not seeing Steve irrelevant.

"It is really doubtful whether Burns was observing people. He had no reason to note who passed him or who he passed," Martin continued, making an obvious but vital point.

"Your theory is that Burns in fact . . . did pass them?" asked Justice Cartwright.

"Yes," Martin said.

"And that he didn't notice them or forgot them?"

"Yes, that is my submission."

Whether the justices accepted Martin's mathematics remained to be seen, but at least the defence's criticisms of the county road evidence got a fairer hearing than in 1959.

Steven's counsel then moved on to the medical testimony. "I do respectfully submit that looking at the medical evidence as a whole . . . is to raise the gravest doubts as to whether it is possible with any degree of certainty to place the time of death," Martin began.

He reminded the judges that even the Crown experts at the Supreme Court hearings were less rigid than Penistan about a 7:45 p.m. outside time limit for Lynne's murder to have taken place. Simpson, for example, said death had very likely occurred within a period of *about* two hours. "I should just like to point out that that is not the way Dr. Penistan gave his evidence at the trial; he put the death *within* that precise period," Martin said. The warm weather also hastened the onset and departure of rigor mortis, Martin argued. Simpson agreed the lack of greening on the body "tends to put the time of death later rather than earlier."

As for the blanching on Lynne's skin, Martin reiterated that the defence experts testified it likely occurred within the first one or two hours of Lynne's death, and not necessarily at the place where her body was found. He argued that Simpson's explanation for the pattern on her skin was far-fetched: "The Crown has to rely on the simple coincidence of the blood having previously clotted, reliquifying and clotting again during the interval when the body was turned on its face," Martin said.

No Crown witness was able to point to any medical literature suggesting that sexual intercourse, rather than a skin irritation, could have caused the sores on Steve's penis, Martin argued. Even the Crown's star expert, Keith Simpson, called them perplexing. Martin admitted, however, that Steve kept his sores secret and that even upon discovery on the night of his arrest, he did not tell his father about his long-standing skin problems.

Justice Wishart Spence found it unusual that a boy faced with a serious criminal charge would not overcome his embarrassment about such an incriminating sore. "What is more natural than the boy should tell his father?" he asked.

"I agree, my lord; I think I must face up to it that the failure to disclose this at that time is unusual," Martin replied.

Spence pursued the point, noting—incorrectly—that Steven kept his secret until he talked to his lawyers "years and years later."

427

"Oh, I quite agree . . . that is undoubtedly an unusual thing," Martin had to concede, "but it is not unusual to suppress such things."

It was a shame the Supreme Court accepted at face value Steve's misinformed testimony about not telling anyone in 1959 that the sores pre-dated his arrest by several weeks. The Supreme Court judges seemed to forget— and Martin failed to point out—that the transcript from the original trial showed clearly Dr. Addison testified Steve informed him the sores had been around for four to five weeks.

Finally, Martin went on to challenge the physical evidence. There was no evidence Steve wore the stained underwear the night Lynne disappeared, and in any event, any sperm released on Tuesday night would have vanished by the time the laboratory analysis began five days later. As for the footprint near Lynne's body, there were three markedly different accounts. "Identifying Officer Corporal Erskine could not find any mark that he could attribute to anything. Flying Officer Glen Sage said he thought he saw what was a footprint pointing toward the body and Detective Sergeant Alsop said he thought he saw a footprint pointing away from the body," Martin summarized.

Moreover, according to laboratory analyst Elgin Brown, Steve's shoes "had splits in the soles at two places, one near the toe and one near where the sole joined the heel. There is no suggestion of any mark being made on the ground that had been made by a shoe with a split in the sole."

Martin reminded the judges that blood was widely spread over Lynne's undershirt, even though the only wound seeping blood was under her left shoulder. "I do not know how that blood could get so distributed from the one injury unless there was some sort of struggle going on or unless somebody carried her," Martin suggested. "That being so, one would think the assailant would necessarily get some blood on him, especially the upper part of his body." He noted there was no blood, hair or fibres from Lynne on Steve's body and vice versa. The blood under her fingernails was consistent with scratching her assailant, but police found no comparable markings on Steven.

Finally, the police photographs of what Steven could see from the bridge were "extremely distorted," misleading the jurors into thinking the car was farther away than it really was, the defence counsel said.

For all these reasons, Martin concluded, the evidence presented at the trial in 1959 did not support a conviction. "I respectfully submit that for the above reasons, the court should find that the verdict on all the evidence was unreasonable," he said.

"Mr. Martin, you did not deal with the application for parole signed by Truscott in which he said he had committed a terrible mistake," Chief Justice Taschereau jumped in, before Martin had a chance to sit down.

Another judge, Justice Joseph Fauteux, stepped into the breach: "What Truscott said . . . in his application to the parole board was not intended to be taken as an admission but was something he felt he had to say in order to be successful in his application?"

"Exactly, my lord," Martin said, grateful for the unexpected assistance from the bench. "Your Lordship has expressed my submission very succinctly."

"When did she die?" Justice Fauteux asked. "You may not want to answer the question. It may be an unfair question."

No, it is not an unfair question, Martin said, but the burden was on the prosecution to prove Lynne died before 7:45 p.m. "It was an interval of considerably less than forty-eight hours between the time she died and the autopsy," he estimated.

"That would make it possible for her to have died the day after," Fauteux calculated.

"Around midnight," Martin agreed, noting his experts gave a range of thirty to thirty-six to forty hours prior to the autopsy. "She might have spent several hours in a car, captive. One does not know," he added. "When one gets down to possibilities, the evidence favours a later time of death."

Martin argued that the spinning tire tracks found on the laneway near the county road, the pattern on Lynne's left arm—which even Simpson agreed was consistent with a body resting on cloth or on a car seat—and the "remarkable arrangement of the clothing" in the bush all suggested Lynne was murdered elsewhere and carried into the bush. "These things are completely unknown, but I do submit to the court there is a rational explanation emerging from the evidence itself—not just on speculation or theory—which is consistent with the innocence of the accused," he said.

Up until this point, Martin had concentrated on trying to convince the judges that the old evidence at Steve's original trial did not justify a conviction. In addition, Martin now argued, the fresh evidence presented before the Supreme Court—the tests showing Steven could have seen a car from the bridge, an alternative medical explanation for his sores and the new medical insights into time and place of death—gave even more weight to a dismissal of the guilty verdict.

429

What is more, Martin concluded, Justice Ferguson did a dreadful job of presenting the defence case fairly to the jury. He did not point out there was strong evidence the bike tracks along the trail were made long before Lynne's death; he speculated it would have been hard for Steve's friends to judge his appearance upon his return to the school "at night" when, in fact, there had been still an hour of daylight remaining; he consistently confused jurors by suggesting Steven had claimed to have seen licence plate numbers; he allowed certain child witnesses with a dubious understanding of the importance of an oath to be sworn; and, perhaps most grievously, he introduced a new theory of the crime at the closing stages of the trial.

"It is obvious from the question asked by the foreman of the jury that the jury was giving serious consideration to the evidence of Logan and Douglas Oates that Steven and Lynne had crossed over the bridge together," Martin reminded the judges. Justice Ferguson suggested that it made no difference who saw Steve because it was possible that Steve returned to the bush with Lynne even after taking her to the highway. "It did make a great deal of difference. If he did take her down to the highway, he is virtually excluded," Martin insisted. "The theory propounded by the trial judge . . . removed a serious obstacle in the minds of the jury in arriving at a verdict of guilt."

After two and a half days, Arthur Martin finally completed his marathon presentation. "I thank you, my lords, for the very lengthy and patient hearing I have had," he said, and sat down.

It was Friday afternoon, January 27. Donald Scott had questioned the witnesses for the Crown, but William Bowman, the director of public prosecutions, would make the prosecution's summary. Bowman would accomplish his task in just over a day.

He started with the timing of the county road evidence, realizing that Martin had punched serious holes in the prosecution's calculations by showing that—even accepting the police times for Philip's walk and Steven's bike ride—Philip should have been close enough to the bush to see Steve or even bump into him. To challenge Martin's scenarios, Bowman had to do some fancy footwork. Philip met Jocelyne "somewhere in the area" of the southern edge of the bush, "roughly in the area where Gellatly met Truscott," he said. Since it took Philip ten minutes to meet Jocelyne, and Richard took only two to four minutes to get to roughly the same spot,

Jocelyne must have been six to eight minutes behind Steve, giving him plenty of time to scurry into the bush.

To the judges' ears, it must have sounded much simpler than Martin's complicated calculations of feet per second and exact measurements along the road. But Bowman had made assumptions that differed with the evidence in two ways.

First, by all accounts, Richard did not meet Steve "roughly in the area" where Philip met Jocelyne. Philip had insisted he met the girl walking toward the school about a hundred feet from the southern tip of the bush. Richard and Steve both agreed they crossed paths between the southern edge of the bush and the school—anywhere from about eight hundred to twelve hundred feet farther than where Philip met Jocelyne. So Bowman's version chopped off about a thousand feet of bicycle travel distance.

Second, Bowman's timing proof was extremely selective. He accepted the times given by Jocelyne, Butch and Philip as accurate and dismissed Richard and Steven's estimate that they met closer to 7:25. Little wonder Bowman's times ended up making Steven look guilty.

"Whatever the time Truscott took Lynne Harper north on the county road, it is clear that Gaudet and George were behind him seeking him out," Bowman stated. But only a guilty scenario needed Jocelyne and Butch to be behind Steve. In fact, if Bob Lawson's account of Jocelyne's visits to his farm was accurate, she was at his barn and Butch was already at the river when Steve left the school around 7:25, as he claimed.

Bowman told the judges the police timing of Philip's walk home was "realistic." In fact, as shown in Chapter 28, the OPP's timing was completely out of whack; they had the little boy slowing to a crawl at some points and racing at a marathon pace at others. Bowman also insisted that a boy on a bike with a girl "would have been an extraordinary sight for Philip." On the contrary, two people riding on a bike was not a momentous event on a summer evening in Clinton. According to the testimony in 1959, Beatrice Geiger rode double with her daughter down to the river, and Kenny Geiger got a lift on Robb Harrington's bike. What's more, Bowman and the court never considered that there was a good chance Philip was already near or at the school grounds when he crossed Steven and Lynne. If that happened, Steve and Lynne would not have been on the bike at all, but walking across a crowded playground.

Perhaps sensing he could not rely entirely on Philip's walk home, Bowman told the Supreme Court justices that other people on the road would have spotted Steve and Lynne if they had stayed on the county road. "He would be in plain view all the way."

"You say because he had red trousers?" Justice Spence asked.

"Red trousers, my lord," Bowman readily agreed, not sensing the trap.

"Could he have seen then a licence plate which was yellow?" Spence queried.

"I don't know," Bowman said.

Bowman tried to recover by suggesting Steve cleverly diverted the police with a fanciful tale of a car, obliging them to hunt for her abductor and diverting their search from the bush.

"He was a pretty clever fellow, wasn't he?" Spence interrupted.

"That was his intention, to divert the search from Lawson's wood," Bowman parried.

"Where in your submission is Truscott's bicycle when he walked over the tractor trail?" Justice Cartwright queried.

"It is in the woods somewhere," Bowman replied, repeating the scenario favoured by prosecutor Glenn Hays in 1959. But Bowman might have realized the improbability of Steven dragging Lynne and his bike across the barbed wire, so the Crown now came up with a new theory. Perhaps Steve went into the bush not along the laneway, but directly from the county road in the area where the locket was found. "It would not be too difficult to get into the woods from the county road," Bowman suggested. This entry point would help explain the troublesome locket, and would also fix some of the difficult timings by having Steve and Lynne off the road even earlier. Except that, in this unlikely scenario, the pair had to enter the bush straight from the county road, not via the tractor trail, and anyone on the road in that vicinity would have seen them.

Justice Spence sounded a note of skepticism. He reminded Bowman that the prosecution in 1959 insisted Steve went into the bush along the laneway, using the bicycle tracks as proof. "I am surprised when you say they went directly into the woods from the county road," he stated.

The prosecutor then moved on to what he hoped was firmer ground— the medical evidence, well aware that he had to counter Martin's challenges to the time and place of death. Bowman insisted the autopsy photographs that appeared to show signs of blanching on Lynne's body—seized upon by defence experts as indications the murder took place elsewhere—were not as reliable as the eyewitness accounts by Penistan and Brooks, who examined the body directly.

432

"What is the evidence as to the latest time this girl might have died?" Justice Cartwright wanted to know.

"7:45, my lord, on the evidence," the prosecutor answered.

But Cartwright wanted more. "I said 'at which she might have died,' but not the time you submit at which she did die."

"It would seem the weight of the evidence is . . . that she died within two hours after ingestion of her last meal."

"Could it be asserted with confidence on the medical evidence that the girl died before eleven o'clock that night?" the judge asked.

"I think so, my lord," Bowman agreed.

Such an admission left open the possibility Lynne could have died after 8:00 p.m., when Steve was at the school with friends, or later, when he was at home babysitting. Again, it was a concession Glenn Hays had never made.

Bowman knew one of the strongest cards he could play would be Steven's poor memory when he testified before the Supreme Court justices. He detailed Steven's embarrassing denials of meeting just about anyone on the county road. He zeroed in on Steven's testimony that he told no one the real cause of his penis sores until years after the trial, calling it "unbelievable," but ignoring once again Addison's testimony to the contrary.

The Crown counsel also seized on Steven's 1964 parole application as proof of his untrustworthiness. "It can be considered a confession," he said. "He lies at all times, and did throughout this proceeding."

Bowman's eagerness to paint Steve as a liar got the better of him another time. He tried to suggest that when Butch George met Steve after Lynne's disappearance, "it would look as though it might be primarily Truscott's idea" to mislead the police by telling them Butch saw Steve at the river. But Justice Spence stepped in to point out that the only evidence about the conversation came from Butch, and he had always insisted it was his, not Steven's, plan to lie.

Undeterred, Bowman came up with another example of Steve's deceit: his claim that he spotted the plates on the car at the highway. Bowman noted that a car stopping to pick up a hitchhiker would simply pull over on the highway, not back up onto the county road. Yet Martin's private detectives parked their test car not on the highway, but on the county road, giving someone on the bridge a much better view of the rear bumper. "Truscott said nothing about the car [having] backed in, but just described

433

it as swerving in off the highway and picking up the little girl and going away," the lawyer stated.

But it was Bowman, not Steven, who was being loose with the truth. If Bowman had checked the police record, he would have discovered that OPP Const. Donald Trumbley duly noted Steve telling him on Wednesday—before Lynne's body was even discovered—that the car pulled in from the highway onto the shoulder, then crossed the county road and parked on the right side, with its rear fender facing the bridge.

In any event, Justice Spence was inclined to believe Steve's claims—and not those of the prosecutors of 1959 or 1967—about what he could see from the bridge. "I would have been quite surprised if Truscott had admitted that he could *not* see the yellow plate," said Justice Spence to Bowman. "As you leave the building, look a quarter of a mile east and see if you can tell the yellow plates on the Quebec cars parked around here."

"That is quite so, my lord," the chastened Bowman was forced to admit.

Still, Bowman went on to imply that Steve could deceive even without talking. He suggested the boy's apparent calmness and normality when he returned to the school was not proof of innocence but rather another example of what psychiatrist James Hartford had labelled Steve's "particular mental make-up."

Justice Spence jumped in to voice his doubts once more. "And six years later a group of five psychiatrists found no evidence of paranoid tendencies," he said. "One would have thought it would have developed considerably in six years."

There had been no evidence on that, Bowman said.

"I know they weren't asked," Justice Spence retorted. "I am simply, perhaps, using a little common sense."

By midday on Monday, January 30, 1967, Bowman began wrapping up, and the nine Supreme Court justices began to wrestle with the challenge before them. As Bowman himself pointed out, the preamble to the reference explicitly cited the "widespread concern" about a possible "miscarriage of justice."

"There seems to be some indication that the real question for this court is guilt or innocence to be decided here, if it can be," Bowman concluded.

It was not something with which the esteemed judges were necessarily comfortable. "Supposing we find . . . that we think Truscott probably is guilty but we do not think we can affirm that beyond a reasonable doubt. What is the position then?" Justice Cartwright wondered aloud.

Justice Fauteux crystallized the dilemma, noting that, unlike traditional appeals, the nine judges were hearing fresh testimony for the first time. "We are the judges of the first instance on the evidence heard before us," he said. "That does make it different from the ordinary case of an appeal."

It was not a matter the judges were going to settle in public.

"We will reserve our decision," Chief Justice Taschereau announced—and the extraordinary session of the Supreme Court of Canada was adjourned.

How did the hearing of 1966 and 1967 compare to the trial of 1959? The two were not strictly comparable, since the first was a full-blown trial while the second was a special hearing without all of the witnesses and their testimony. Still, Steven's lawyers were clearly better prepared and more skilful this time. The defence was able to produce an impressive array of expert witnesses and credible new theories. The judges also showed less outward bias against the defendant than Justice Ferguson displayed in his summation. The media were present throughout much of the Supreme Court session, giving the public an independent account of the proceedings, and insight into the moods and performances of the key players.

But in one fundamental and serious way, the same flaw—lack of full disclosure—crippled both the trial and the Supreme Court hearing. Legally, the police and prosecutors were still under no obligation to divulge the details of their investigation. From the start, it was clear that lack of full access to the police files badly impeded Martin almost as much as it had Frank Donnelly in 1959. Disclosure laws would not fundamentally change until 1991. Many essential elements of the 1959 police case—as well as new information or opinions—remained secret.

At one point, when the Supreme Court was examining Butch George's various statements to the police, Justice Spence asked, "Has this statement ever been produced?" It was a good question, since few of the police witness statements had ever been scrutinized by outsiders.

"No, my lord," Martin replied.

"So we can't tell what has changed," the judge noted.

In describing Lynne's mood on the night she disappeared, Martin quoted her mother's account that Lynne "wasn't annoyed, but was resigned" to her parents' refusal to let her go swimming. Martin knew nothing of the three separate OPP and military police reports that revealed the Harpers' initial suspicion that their daughter was a hitchhiking runaway. In his brief to the court, Martin told the judges that according to the testimony of Brownie leader Anne Nickerson, Lynne "seemed quite normal." Steve's lawyer had no idea that Nickerson told police a rather different story about Lynne not wanting to go home because "her mother was cross with her."

As Martin described to the judges Steve's trip down the county road, he could not tell them about the two younger baseball players who put Steve's departure from the school at close to 7:30 p.m., much later than the times cited by prosecution witnesses. He pointed out the numerous "frailties and improbabilities" in Jocelyne's tale about her hunt for Steve, but Martin did not know she and two other witnesses told the police originally she asked about Lynne's whereabouts.

Martin tried to convince the Supreme Court justices of the importance of the blood under Lynne's fingernails. He could have made an even stronger case if he had a copy of the OPP bulletin the night Lynne disappeared, telling police to be on the lookout "especially for scratches on face, neck, hands and arms" on the assailant.

A key theory of Martin's defence was that the murder could have taken place somewhere besides the bush. Martin reminded the judges there was "some supporting evidence" for this idea from George Edens, the corporal who found the body and testified about seeing skid marks from a car at the end of the laneway near the county road. What Martin did not know—and the judges never found out—was that two other airmen at the crime scene gave the police similar leads about tracks "made by a car spinning" as if someone "got their front wheels up on the pavement and gunned it."

Martin did get some nuggets out of the prosecution before the hearing. For instance, Steve's lawyers requested and received the police statement of Karen Daum. In the end, however, Martin decided not to make any use of her testimony. The lawyer had made the strategic calculation not to challenge the accounts of the children and adults on the county road; he reserved most of his fire for the medical testimony, perhaps hoping scientific fact would sway the Supreme Court judges more than the confused memories of children.

But by employing that strategy, Martin was severely hindered by the silence imposed on Dr. John Penistan. The Supreme Court devoted most of its hearing to the testimony of world-renowned medical experts debating the validity of Penistan's 1959 autopsy. The prosecutor produced several witnesses to praise what Keith Simpson called Penistan's "very competent and conscientious investigation." Bowman told the Supreme Court judges that Penistan had more credibility than his critics because they were forced to rely on imperfect photographs, while Penistan had seen the actual body at the crime scene and on the autopsy table.

You would think, for all those reasons, Bowman would want to bring in Dr. Penistan himself to testify before the Supreme Court about what he saw. Penistan had made it clear he was willing and quite eager to talk before any inquiry. But the man at the very centre of the Supreme Court debate over the medical evidence that condemned Steven was curiously absent from the proceedings.

The tragedy was that the court, in the end, would rush to endorse the very findings about time of death that Penistan himself had begun to question and undermine.

## 37

## THE·DECISION

T here was nothing to do but wait.

The Supreme Court justices would take almost four months before issuing their decision in early May. The country, meanwhile, was in the throes of centennial year jubilation. Everywhere, schoolchildren were bellowing out the refrain from Bobby Gimby's "CA-NA-DA" song as hundreds of thousands of people were getting ready to attend Expo 67 in Montreal. South of the border, Americans were in the grips of political turmoil over race relations and the Vietnam War; in less than a year they would watch in horror as assassins gunned down Martin Luther King Jr. and Robert Kennedy.

Largely sheltered from the news and furor outside the prison walls, Steve spent several mercifully quiet months back in Collins Bay. The psychiatrists left him alone. It was a more anxious time for his parents and their supporters as they continued their campaigns of letter writing, lobbying politicians and speaking to the media. Isabel LeBourdais tried to assure Dan and Doris that everything had gone well at the Supreme Court. "The more I think back on the actual arguments and material presented by the two sides, the more I am sure we will win," she wrote. Privately, she was less confident.

"This period is truly nerve-racking," Isabel LeBourdais told a friend in a February letter, fearing the Supreme Court's decision would be political and have "nothing to do with the obvious weight of evidence and argument on Steve's side."

The two red leather chairs on one side of the courtroom were empty. The Supreme Court clerks had set them aside for the Truscotts. But Dan and Doris did not show up. Nor did Isabel LeBourdais. Instead, they waited to hear the news in a private home in Toronto, along with lawyer Ted Joliffe.

In Collins Bay, Steve had accompanied Malcolm Stienburg to the Protestant chapel at 8:30 that morning to await the decision. "It was a difficult two hours, a lifetime, but Steve kept a stiff upper lip," the chaplain reported. Shortly before the deadline for the announcement, they walked solemnly across the prison courtyard to the warden's office to get the news.

In Ottawa, about forty journalists and a dozen members of the public packed into the courtroom to hear Justice John Cartwright read one of the most eagerly awaited decisions in the court's history at 10:30 a.m. on the morning of May 6, 1967.

Dan and Doris heard the news on their portable radio. Dan's eyes filled with tears. Doris was stunned.

"Maybe we got it wrong," he said, gripping his wife's hand so hard she winced.

"God, how much evidence do they need?" Doris said, in an anguished and angry cry.

By a majority of eight to one, the highest court in the land had ruled against Steven Truscott. Eight judges found no reason—either on the basis of the evidence presented in 1959, legal principles or new testimony—to set aside the original verdict. Justice Emmett Hall was the only judge to dissent.

Weeping, Doris Truscott went to the phone. "I must tell him. Do you think they'll let me speak to him?"

Joliffe assured her it had been arranged. "Yes, dial direct," he said. At the other end of the line, her son took the phone.

"Hello, son. Have you heard the news?"

"Yes. Eight to one."

"Keep busy, son, we're not quitting," Doris said. "We'll be down to see you soon."

She passed the phone to LeBourdais. "Remember that promise I made to you?" she asked, referring to her pledge never to stop until she helped clear Steve's name. "I intend to keep it."

Steve asked to speak to his father.

"No. No. He can't come to the phone," Doris explained. "He's taking it hard." Dan was so shaken by the verdict he had left the room.

Steve's younger brother, Bill, seventeen at the time, remembers the devastating impact the verdict had on his parents. "It was almost like they got run over by a car—like, that was kind of the end of it and nothing had changed."

When Dan returned to the living room, he asked his wife, "Did you call him? How is he taking it?"

"Fine. He's taking it well," Doris assured him. "He took it like a man. It was so hard . . . so hard."

In the warden's office at Collins Bay, there was a deathly silence. "What do you tell a guy at a time like that?" Malcolm Stienburg later recalled. "I would love to have turned from the phone and said 'Steve, you're free,' but . . ." His voice trailed off.

By all accounts, Steve took the defeat with the stoic reserve that was his emotional trademark. "There was little change in his face," said Warden Ross Duff. "[He] asked to be taken back to the shop and we took him back to work."

Steve walked back across the prison yard, accompanied by the chaplain who had become his friend and mentor. "He didn't cry—but it didn't mean there weren't tears in his eyes," Stienburg says. "He eyes were filled with water—but he had control so he didn't break down."

Showing little emotion, Steve softly uttered a single phrase to Stienburg: "The Supreme Court made a mistake."

"After all the evidence given on the reference, the issues are still the same as those which faced the jury—who raped and killed this girl?"

The eight Supreme Court judges posed the question succinctly in their majority decision. And in their minds, it was clear the answer was Steven Murray Truscott. On all the important issues, they sided with the Crown's interpretation of the evidence and rejected most of Arthur Martin's pleas for a fresh look at the case. But it was also apparent that the judges had to ignore some glaring contradictions to justify their stand.

The eight justices devoted two thirds of their decision to the new medical evidence presented before them. They accepted "there was diversity of opinion" over the key issue of stomach contents, but decided to simply split the difference. Seven experts testified on the issue and, according to the judges' mathematics, the Crown won out four to three.

It was bad math and bad medicine. The problem was not whether Lynne could have digested her meal in two hours, but whether her time of death could be determined within minutes based on her stomach contents. By that standard, Sharpe clearly did not support the Crown theory. He explicitly told the court that the time of death based on these examinations was "an inspired or educated guess . . . only a probability or a hunch."

On other medical issues in contention, the judges appeared to throw up their hands and side with Penistan, who had an "overwhelming advantage" over the experts who were debating photographs that were seven years old. The defence experts saw evidence Lynne was killed elsewhere because of patterns of blanching on her skin, but Penistan made no note of this. They also accepted Dr. Penistan's evidence that rigor mortis had almost passed off because, unlike the Supreme Court witnesses, he was present at the autopsy. The justices did not know that Penistan had since revised his views and now concluded—much like the defence witnesses—that rigor mortis was "compatible also with death some hours later" than Tuesday evening.

"The effect of the sum total of the testimony of the expert witnesses is, in our opinion, to add strength to the opinion expressed by Dr. Penistan at the trial that the murdered girl was dead by 7:50 p.m." But ironically Dr. Penistan himself was now changing his opinion, writing in words that could have come out of the mouths of the defence experts: "All findings are compatible with death within two hours of Lynne's last meal. They are not incompatible with death at a later time (up to twelve hours or even longer)."

When faced with new medical evidence that supported Steve's claims of innocence, the Supreme Court justices refashioned it to fit a guilty scenario. They acknowledged, based on the testimony of the dermatologists, that a pre-existing skin irritation could have caused the penis sores. But the judges took refuge in the Crown's theory that even if that were true, intercourse could have aggravated the sores.

On the other crucial debate before the court—the evidence of who was where at what time on the county road—the judges also accepted as fact the theories of the Crown from 1959 and 1966. Yet every one of their affirmations was debatable—at least to the level of reasonable doubt. They said Steve's departure was "fixed with reasonable certainty" by the evidence of the Brownie leaders at the school at no later than 7:15 p.m. Yet the one woman with a watch said she was "not positive about my time" while the other said she "didn't have any way of telling the time." And neither actually saw Steve and Lynne leave the school grounds.

"Then, on his own admission, Truscott met Richard Gellatly between the schoolyard and Lawson's bush," the judges wrote. "He did not meet Philip Burns, as he should have done if he had continued on his way to the highway," they said. "He was not seen by Jocelyne Gaudet and Arnold George as he would have been if he continued on to the highway and returned alone from the intersection to the bridge," they concluded.

For the judges' timing to work, they had to make mutually contradictory statements. They insisted that Philip and Richard "left the bridge at about the same time . . . between 7:00 and 7:15 p.m."—except that one boy had to leave at the top of that fifteen-minute window and the other at the bottom for each of them to arrive home when witnesses said they did.

The majority decision admitted there was "obviously something very wrong with Jocelyne Gaudet's times." Yet they seemed to accept the rest of her story uncritically. The judges reported "she and George were both looking for Steven Truscott and they had a brief conversation" at the bush, even though Butch told police Jocelyne was looking for Lynne, not Steven.

Even when the judges were forced to admit a point in Steve's favour, they found a way to spin it against the defence. The eight justices conceded that new tests from the private investigators showed it was possible to pick out a coloured licence plate from the bridge. "The evidence upon this topic would seem to weaken the Crown's submission to the jury . . . that Truscott could not have seen from the bridge what he alleged he had seen," they wrote. But they argued the Crown used this "to attack the credibility of Truscott" and since "parts of his testimony . . . simply cannot be believed," the new evidence about the car sighting "becomes of much less importance." Stripped of legal niceties, the judges were saying, in effect, that they believed Steve was a liar, so the fact that they now knew he was not lying about being able to see a car did not really matter that much.

But it did matter. For most of the other evidence at the trial, jurors had to choose between warring witnesses who gave different stories or interpretations. But for the debate over what Steve could see from the bridge, the

Crown used police photographs as objective, incontrovertible evidence—evidence the Supreme Court was now dismissing as dubious.

In the end, the Supreme Court judges largely blamed Steven for his own fate. They found his story about not telling his father about having sores on his penis weeks before his arrest "impossible to accept." They cited proven encounters with friends on June 9 and conversations which Steve denied in his testimony before the Supreme Court. In the most damning sentence of their decision, they wrote, "There were many incredibilities inherent in the evidence given by Truscott before us and we do not believe his testimony."

The eight Supreme Court justices concluded the original verdict could not be set aside because it was unreasonable or unsupported by the evidence and that the verdict could not be overturned on any question of law "or on the ground that there was a miscarriage of justice."*

In his dissenting opinion, Justice Emmett Hall took a starkly different approach. Rather than concentrate on the minutiae of some of the testimony, he stood back and took a wider view of what he saw as a fundamentally flawed and ultimately unjust trial. "Having considered the case fully, I believe that the conviction should be quashed and a new trial directed. I take the view that the trial was not conducted according to law. Even the guiltiest criminal must be tried according to law," the jurist wrote.

"That does not mean that I consider Truscott guilty or innocent—that was for a jury to decide," Hall stressed. Still, he made it clear he did not think the Crown had met the standard of proof. "The evidence failed to establish that her death occurred prior to 7:45 p.m. on June 9. If she was murdered later than this time, Truscott could not be the guilty person. It is as simple as that."

For Hall, the trial went off the rails almost from the start. The most

---

* The Supreme Court of Canada was far more divided over the case than it let on and was also fearful that the chief justice, who was suffering from alcoholism and bad health, could be a public embarrassment during the Truscott hearings, according to a new book by political scientist Frederick Vaughan. In *Aggressive in Pursuit, The Life of Justice Emmett Hall*, Vaughan wrote that at least two of Hall's colleagues told him they would support his dissent but then backed out at the last minute. The book also revealed that Chief Justice Robert Taschereau walked around his home in a dirty bathrobe and torn slippers, surrounded by discarded liquor bottles, dirty dishes and leftover meals. He resigned two months after the Truscott hearings concluded.

serious problem arose when Jocelyne told the Crown—and repeated to the judge—that Steve insisted she not tell anybody about their secret date. "This was when the damage was done. These two last answers were wholly inadmissible," Hall insisted. The evidence had no value in proving Truscott murdered Lynne, and the judge should have rejected it.

Hall pointed out that Justice Ferguson seriously misled the jurors by repeatedly saying Steven had claimed to see numbers of licence plates from the bridge. He noted that the Supreme Court had the advantage of new evidence that showed the unreliability of photographs and the fact that the colour of a plate could be seen from the bridge. If jurors had this information in 1959 he concluded, "the jury could reasonably have taken an entirely different view of Truscott's story and of his credibility."

Hall chastised Ferguson for allowing the Crown to introduce dubious or irrelevant evidence. Hall said the photographs of the dry earth in the laneway and the testimony from the meteorologist completely ruled out the bicycle tire marks as evidence implicating Steve, and the judge should have excluded them. The judge let prosecutor Hays get away with the "fanciful theory" that Steven had the cunning to plant Lynne's missing locket on the barbed wire fence to mislead the police "without one iota of evidence." The Crown also exploited Steve's claim that while riding on the county road, he saw a car with the licence plate 981-666. The Crown paraded before the jurors several car owners with plates closely matching the numbers to show Steven had "a guilty state of mind." Hall said the judge only made matters worse by telling the jurors Steven might have fabricated the evidence to better hide his crime. In fact, Hall insisted, Steve only told police he saw the car somewhere along the road and never offered it as proof that he had taken Lynne all the way to highway. Therefore, it was irrelevant and the judge should have ruled the entire subject inadmissible.

Ferguson let Dr. Brooks get away with his claim that the rape was the work of "inexpert penetration," Hall said. "He was testifying as an expert as to a matter which was not in his special knowledge and the evidence was prejudicial to the prisoner." Hall objected to the judge's instruction to the jurors that the sperm on the underpants seized from Steven in jail were "consistent with an attack on this girl." Hall said that without the slightest proof Steve wore those underpants on the evening of June 9, these remarks were "prejudicial in the extreme, based as they were on something that was not in evidence at all. Those underpants should never have been marked as an exhibit or shown to the jury."

Commenting on Steve's demeanour during the trial, Ferguson had asked the jurors: "You ask yourselves the reason if this boy is guilty, why has he shown such calmness and apathy." Hall said the description "was purely gratuitous . . . highly damaging to the accused." Even more outrageous in Hall's mind was Justice Ferguson's last-minute introduction of a bizarre new theory. The majority of Supreme Court judges simply dismissed this gaffe as "unnecessary," but Hall was much more scathing. Ferguson's new theory "came wholly out of thin air," but it eliminated "the most vital issue in Truscott's case."

Several times in their decision, the other Supreme Court justices cited the fact that since Steve's lawyer did not object to certain dubious evidence, it supported their argument that there had been no damage or injustice. Hall took strong exception. "The consequences of defence counsel's failure to object at the trial do not fall upon counsel, but upon the client, in this case a 14½-year-old boy on trial for his life," Hall said. "I appreciate that after nearly eight years many difficulties will be had if a new trial is held . . . but these difficulties are relatively insignificant when compared to Truscott's fundamental right to be tried according to law."

Hall's dissent was powerful—and not just because it highlighted specific faults in the trial. He also challenged the entire approach his majority brethren took. They were splitting hairs to see if the new evidence could buttress the original guilty verdict—in Hall's words, they "attempted to direct a massive and detailed structure of evidence and argument to confirm a verdict that has no lawful foundation upon which to rest." But Hall argued the very way that verdict was reached was corrupted and twisted by bad law and bad evidence. Crown prosecutor Glenn Hays, Hall said, pursued a "planned course of action that included the subtle perverting of the jury to the idea that Truscott was sex-hungry that Tuesday evening and determined to have a girl in Lawson's bush to satisfy his desire, if not Jocelyne, then Lynne." Nothing that happened before the Supreme Court "can give validity to an invalid trial," Hall said forcefully. "A bad trial remains a bad trial. The only remedy for a bad trial is a new trial."

Hall's closing words went down in legal history as one of the finest pleas for justice to prevail in the most difficult of circumstances. "It was inevitable that this horrible crime would arouse the indignation of the whole community. It was inevitable that suspicion should follow on Truscott, the last person known to have been seen with Lynne in the general vicinity of the place where her body was found," he wrote. "In cases like the present one, when passions are aroused and the court is dealing with a crime which cries out for vengeance, then comes the time of testing. It is especially at such a time that the judicial machinery must function objectively, devoid of inflammatory appeals, with the scales of justice held in balance."

The power and eloquence of Emmett Hall's call for justice was quickly lost in the bedlam of the moment. It was a knockout blow—eight to one—and that was all the country needed to know. When Justice Cartwright finished reading the verdict, the reporters dashed to the telephones in a nearby lounge. One of the judges smiled at the unseemly behaviour of the scribes. Arthur Martin, his efforts defeated, "appeared glum and shaken," according to news reports.

"'Do Not Believe His Testimony,' Court Rejects Truscott Appeal," ran the headline in the *London Free Press*. Many papers carried a picture of the Truscotts, their lips tightly drawn, their eyes heavy with rejection. "I'm not going to quit, by God!" Dan exclaimed. "I'm out of the air force now. I'll have lots of time. I will go clean across the country getting signatures if I have to."

Steve eventually made his way to the radio room after hearing about his defeat. The warden sent some guards over to check on him. "I remember a couple of them coming over and asking if everything was okay," Steve says. "They showed a genuine concern."

Stienburg kept watch as well. "He was quieter that day. He was down but I am not sure he was down for himself. He was down because it was a real heartbreak for his parents," the chaplain says. "The system had done the worst to him but he saw the system doing the worst toward his parents—it was just a cold, heartless system and this was just more proof for him."

"They've already sentenced me to hang, they've thrown me in jail, they keep throwing psychiatrists at me," Steve says he thought at the time. "What more are they going to do to me? But they can still hurt my family."

The next day, Steve's mother drove three hours to see her son, accompanied by a reporter. She rapped twice on the knocker of the heavy steel door outside Collins Bay. A guard answered and let her in. When she emerged an hour and ten minutes later, she told the newsman that indeed her son was understandably upset—not for himself, but for his parents. "He felt his father and I were going to be so disappointed he wasn't coming home," she said. "He's strong and courageous. Steven needed to know we're standing by him."

It was the latest step in the delicate emotional tango Steve and his mother had been dancing since the catastrophe of his arrest, each of them putting up walls to protect the other. "You put up a barrier: I am not going to let my folks feel bad by seeing that it's really getting to me, and my mom was the same way," Steve says. "These people are not going to get to me. You break down—they've won. They've accomplished what they set out to do and there's no way you're going to let them get the best of you."

Doris returned to her neat, three-bedroom bungalow, where Bill and Barb greeted the mother who had been a pillar of strength through all the years of legal defeats. "We won't leave this house until Steve comes home," she said.

Steve, as always, seemed to accept his fate. He wrote Isabel LeBourdais to ask her to send a message to his lawyers. "I never got a chance to thank them for a wonderful job they did," he said. "I don't think anyone could have done as well as what they did."

The woman who more than anyone had stirred the public's passions over the Truscott case was defiant to the end. "We didn't lose, we were defeated, and there's a difference," LeBourdais told reporters. "The judgment of the land's highest court cannot change my own personal view. I'd be hypocritical and inhuman if I change my opinion about Steven's innocence now. I won't give up trying to prove he's innocent.

"I want him to be cleared more than I want him free," LeBourdais continued. "What good is it for him to come out with a record like that? Who would give him a job? Who would welcome him into their homes? Who would let him date their daughters?"

Others involved in the case had a different view. For Leslie Harper, the father who had suffered the irreplaceable loss of his daughter, the Supreme Court's decision was "purely anti-climactic." He told the press, "I've believed for almost eight years the original verdict was right and just." Lynne's mother held her grief in private. "Mother doesn't want to make any comment," Lynne's brother Barry, now twenty-five, said at the doorstep of his parents' home. "She's quite upset by it all."

The key legal players from the 1959 trial were equally mum. "I'm through with it now," said Justice Robert Ferguson. "It's somebody else's responsibility." The once opposing lawyers—Frank Donnelly and Glenn Hays—had both since been promoted to the bench. "I'm not free to discuss it," said Donnelly, a judge on the Ontario Superior Court. When reporters caught up with Glenn Hays, a magistrate in Goderich, he paused for a moment and then said simply, "I have no comment."

Harold Graham, the police officer responsible more than anyone else for Steve's arrest, was slightly more forthcoming. He told the press he took "no joy over it either way" but could not resist a small self-congratulatory note. "The case was carefully investigated by all concerned and we felt all along there was sufficient evidence to support the verdict reached," the OPP assistant commissioner said.

For the jurors in Huron County who reached that verdict, there was relief in the confirmation of a job well done. "The best news I've heard in a long time," said Walter Brown.

"We expected that. I couldn't see how they could do anything else," commented Harry Vodden.

Many people in Clinton, fed up with the bad name the entire affair gave their town, were also pleased. "Clinton Sighs with Relief," the *Toronto Daily Star* proclaimed. John Livermore, the town clerk treasurer, echoed the views of those who saw the Supreme Court decision as a much-needed assurance the justice system was working properly. "If we can't trust these things, what can we do?" he asked. "Now we can only hope that case is finally closed."

The Truscott case was far from closed, precisely because if the Supreme Court decision restored some people's faith in the law, it shattered the trust of many other citizens. The Truscott affair cut to the core of Canadians' attitudes toward the judicial process, and for that reason the political storm it unleashed could not be contained. Many people—for and against Steven—felt it was not Steven Truscott but the justice system that was on trial.

In that sense, the Supreme Court ruling was as much a political verdict as a legal one. Ralph Cowan, the federal MP who so fervently opposed his government's decision to refer the case to the Supreme Court in the first place, understood the significance of the verdict. It was the only decision the high court could make, he said. "Otherwise, it would have condemned the system of justice we have in Ontario and the dominion of Canada." The *London Free Press* underscored what was at stake: "It would be regrettable indeed if public emotionalism or hysteria were permitted to denigrate or subvert our judicial processes."

"Public emotionalism" was getting out of hand. Network TV showed pictures of dozens of young people protesting in Ottawa, carrying signs calling for "Justice for Steven Truscott Now." "We felt the trial still left a reasonable doubt," a college student said. "We feel the cabinet should take it upon itself to free the boy now."

On Parliament Hill, the demand for the government to do something about Steven was intense, cutting across party lines. "He certainly is not going to benefit by further incarceration, and I feel there should be no delay in granting to him a release on parole," Conservative opposition leader John Diefenbaker said. The NDP's Stanley Knowles—probably the politician who had lobbied the hardest for Steve's release—was crushed by the adverse ruling: "The boy will be out before long on good behaviour. This is not good enough. I'm still convinced he's innocent." Liberal James Byrne, who vowed to stake his seat on Steve's innocence back in March of 1966, called the Supreme Court decision a terrible disappointment. "I don't plan to give up my seat," he said. "It may be contempt, but I remain convinced that he should have been exonerated."

Monday, May 8, was the first day Parliament was back in session since the court ruling, and Steven Truscott's fate was front and centre of the debate. Diefenbaker opened Question Period by asking Pearson if he was considering including Steven in the expected commutation of many prison sentences for Canada's centennial year. Pearson said he would discuss it with the solicitor general and his newly named justice minister, Pierre Trudeau.

The NDP's Andrew Brewin wanted the House legal affairs committee to study the questions the Supreme Court ignored, such as the unequal resources available to the defence and the Crown in 1959 and the community bias against Steven. Pearson refused.

Pearson, Trudeau and the rest of the cabinet had several choices—they could grant Steven an immediate pardon, speed up his parole, order a new trial or do nothing. The easiest thing for the politicians to do was to hide behind the rules. Parole regulations stated that a commuted death sentence required a prisoner to serve at least ten years. That meant Steven would only be eligible for parole in June 1969.

The NDP countered that cabinet made rules and could change them. "Government thinking on the matter is that would create a dangerous precedent if the cabinet were to change its own regulations in the face of this campaign," the *Toronto Daily Star* reported, revealing that—as always—the Truscott case was as much about politics as it was about law.

The precedent for the government granting clemency in a high-profile case was not good. The only other recent parallel with the Truscott case was the trial of Wilbert Coffin. A Quebec court found Wilbert Coffin, a trapper, guilty of the 1953 slaying of three Pennsylvania hunters in a controversial trial. "L'affaire Coffin," as it became known, stirred the passions of the province. Much like the Truscott trial, Coffin's condemnation was seen as quick and shabby justice, a rushed verdict designed to placate the interests of the American tourism industry. Under intense pressure, the federal cabinet in 1955 asked the Supreme Court to rule on the original decision of the Coffin case. Unlike Steven's review a decade later, the Court could not hear new witnesses or testimony.

In January of 1956, the Supreme Court agreed with the guilty verdict in a seven to two decision. (One of the dissenters, ironically, was Justice John Cartwright, who was still a member of the court when Steven's case came up ten years later. Two other justices who decided Coffin's fate—Abbott and Fauteux—also would sit in judgment over Steven.) The cabinet decided there would not be a new trial and declined to alter Coffin's death sentence. He was hanged on February 10, 1959.

Years later, the controversy of the execution of Coffin still simmered. Jacques Hébert, a future senator, wrote a passionate bestseller with the provocative title *J'accuse les assassins de Coffin*. In 1965, the solicitor general in Quebec laid contempt charges against Hébert. The journalist was defended in court by his good friend, a young law professor named Pierre Trudeau.

Two years later, Trudeau was justice minister. Perhaps he thought of Hébert's campaign as he pondered what to do about Steven Truscott. If he did, it did not seem to influence his opinion of the Truscott case.

Trudeau, Solicitor General Lawrence Pennell and Pearson would not grant Steve clemency or an early release. The prime minister announced his cabinet's decision to the nation: "It is not our intention to take any action at the present time."

Steven Truscott would stay in jail, a convicted murderer, until at least 1969, when he would get his first real chance at parole. Isabel LeBourdais visited Steven in prison shortly after the decision. "It may be a long haul still, but Steve . . . can stick it out," she wrote to a friend. "He has a tremendous strength of character."

He would need it. He would over the next years grapple with the breakup of one family and the birth of another. His battles were far from over.

# PART FOUR

## THE PRIVATE BATTLE: 1967–1997

*"I never once doubted him. Never once.*
*He stood his ground for what he believed in and*
*that was the truth.... And he always instilled that in*
*us—that if you wait and you're a good person,*
*it'll all come back to you someday."*

—Ryan Truscott

## 38

RELEASE

I f Steve thought his life had hit rock bottom with his defeat at the Supreme Court in May of 1967, he was wrong. Just as he began to settle back into his routine at the machine shop at Collins Bay, his world crumbled. A few weeks after prison chaplain Malcolm Stienburg had told Steven about his legal setback, he had to deliver more bad news—but this time, the news struck much closer to home.

Stienburg got the call on a Saturday night. It was from Steve's aunt in Windsor. "Look, I got something I think you should know and perhaps you want to do something about it. If not, he's going to hear from other sources and it's going to be destructive for him," she told Stienburg. Steve's parents, Dan and Doris, had separated, their marriage irrevocably shattered. "Will you tell Steve tomorrow?" the aunt asked.

"I had the night to think about it, because I had chapel services the next morning," Stienburg says. The chaplain felt that Steve probably had an inkling all was not well on the home front; his parents had already begun visiting him separately in the last few weeks. Still, Stienburg feared the breakup would deeply affect the young man who depended so much on his family as a lifeline to the outside world. "I knew the strength of those ties and how much they meant for him," he says.

The dilemma weighed on Stienburg's mind as he delivered his Sunday sermon—he usually kept them short, he says, because "some of those inmates had the attention span of a louse"—while Steven sat in the stiff chapel chair, blissfully unaware. Stienburg walked up to him after services and quietly broke the news to him.

"It was like being hit over the head with a bat," Stienburg recounts. "He had a wounded, hurt look. It was the toughest thing I have had to do." Stienburg could see a thin film of water forming in the young man's eyes.

Stienburg also saw that Steve was more concerned for his parents than for himself. "I don't think there was much self-pity. It wasn't 'Poor me'—it was 'Poor Mom, poor Dad.' And there was an element of 'if it wasn't for me, they'd be together.'"

"It probably hit me harder than everything except the original trial," Steven admits today. "I only saw my parents once a month. The only thing that means anything to you in the whole world is your family."

After the Supreme Court defeat, Steve could retreat inside himself, comforted by the fact that he knew he was innocent and it did not matter what others thought. But he had no such refuge for this crisis. His parents' looming divorce filled him with sadness and the nagging guilt that he was somehow responsible.

"No way," his mother insists. "I think he felt he was maybe to blame, but it just wasn't so." Doris concedes the long battle to free her son was a great emotional and financial strain on the family, but her marriage simply fell apart when she and Dan stopped loving each other. "I don't think it [Steven's case] had anything to do with it all. We just didn't get along," she says.

Doris had endured her son's ordeal with stoic resolve. But Dan's emotions were much closer to the surface, and his passion to help Steve—while remaining a devoted father to his other children—exacted a heavy price. In the early 1960s, he had a mental collapse and spent a few weeks recovering at a psychiatric hospital in Quebec. It was not the first time; according to his air force medical record he had had a nervous breakdown in 1955.

Then, shortly after his breakup with Doris, Dan again sought psychiatric help. By late July, he wrote to Isabel LeBourdais that doctors had discharged him from the hospital "with a clean bill of health and one month's supply of pills" (although he would seek more treatment within a couple of years).

The rest of the family did their best to pull together. Steve's younger brother, Bill, who remained closest with Dan after the split, says the pressure

454

of the unrelenting battle to free Steve "probably had quite a bit to do" with the strain in his parents' relationship, since it dominated so much of their lives. "That became pretty much their whole life; it was pretty much all they talked about," he remembers. "It just felt like you were in a hole and couldn't get out."

By this time seventeen, Bill drove down to the prison whenever he could to see his brother. "He always looked the same—upbeat about everything," Bill said. "He never complained about anything."

Steve's older brother, Ken, meanwhile, went into a management training program at Woolco and landed a job as a department manager at one of the company's Kingston stores, serendipitously located just across the street from the Collins Bay prison. "It felt a little funny but it was handy for me to go visit," Ken says. Ken tried not to feel he was drifting away from Steve, but it was hard to have a conversation about everyday life with a brother who had grown up behind bars. "You're not on the same track," he remembers. "You don't have as much in common when you're having a conversation. You've outgrown building airplanes out of balsa wood."

Meanwhile, Dan Truscott, once released from hospital, quickly plunged back into his efforts on Steve's behalf. Dan kept in touch with sympathetic MPs on Parliament Hill; he also collected letters and petitions protesting the Supreme Court decision from across the country. "But all the petitions will not help," he told LeBourdais. "What is needed is new, concrete evidence."

In the wake of defeat at the Supreme Court, Steven's supporters tried to dig up more evidence. The Steven Truscott Defence Committee placed full-page ads in the *Huron Expositor* newspaper appealing to eyewitnesses to come forward. "If anyone saw Lynne Harper that evening Steven Truscott can still be proved innocent!" the ad said, inspired by unconfirmed reports that Lynne had been spotted in Seaforth on the evening of June 9, 1959. "Do you know the names of those who said they saw her? Do you have any information?"

No one came forward with new information. LeBourdais became convinced the only way to free Steve was to launch a new investigation to track down the real killer. But she could not convince any media outlets to invest the enormous time and money needed. Both *Canadian Magazine* and the *Star Weekly*, two major national publications, turned down her requests.

"I'm going to have to chicken out," Peter Gzowski, then editor of the *Star Weekly* wrote to her, expressing "enormous admiration" for what LeBourdais had accomplished so far. "What you are onto is possibly the greatest magazine story of all time. But it's also the most expensive. . . . I don't think [we] . . . can afford to take the kind of calculated risk you require."

LeBourdais even approached private investigators, only to discover the cost would be prohibitive. "They are quite frankly not at all encouraging," she informed the Truscotts.

Doris did not want to abandon the fight to clear her son's name, but she felt helpless. "What could you do? It really wasn't an option," she says. "We didn't have the money, that's for darn sure. How are you going to do it? You just can't."

One person who did not want to give up the battle was Marlene, the young woman from Guelph who five years earlier, in 1962, babysat for the Guelph couple when they went to see Steven and the other young offenders perform at the reform school's Easter show. Marlene grew up just a few miles from the reform school, in a working-class neighbourhood in the north end of Guelph. Her father, Leslie, was a union organizer for the United Steelworkers. "I can remember him coming home and getting books and magazines from us to take to the men that were on strike," she says. "I lived in a house where supporting the underdog was always prevalent."

Though a quick student with a photographic memory, Marlene did not care much for studying and left school in grade Eleven. She easily found work as a receptionist and bookkeeper in small firms around town. "I knew that I could quit, start saving, get a car, meet someone and get married," she says. Marlene would indeed get married and start raising a family within seven years of leaving school—but reality would prove less tranquil than she had imagined.

Born just four days later than Steven, Marlene had an interest in his case that was casual at first. As a fourteen-year-old, she remembers the summer of 1959 more for the fact that she bought her first sailor blouse at Reitman's for $3.98 than for the trial of a boy her age in a small town a hundred miles away.

But that all changed in the spring of 1966. Marlene's mother showed her daughter the front cover of the *Star Weekly*, featuring a picture of Steven. "You should read it," her mother said. "You should read about what happened to this boy."

At twenty-one, busy with work and a hectic social life, Marlene initially paid scant attention. But a couple of days later, she came into the living room, picked up the magazine article and read it all. "I was horrified," she remembers. She dashed out to buy LeBourdais' book, but both bookstores downtown were out of stock. She eventually laid her hands on a copy on a day she was getting her hair done. "I couldn't wait to get under the dryer so I could start reading it," she says.

Marlene was possessed. A few weeks later, she borrowed her father's car and drove two hours to Clinton to see for herself what a boy could see from the bridge. She started clipping every newspaper article she could find on the case. She began writing letters to Isabel LeBourdais. On the eve of Steve's appearance before the Supreme Court, Marlene penned a poem, put it in a simple frame and sent it to his parents. It read, in part:

> Stand up to the public—both brave and bold
> Tell them your story, which has never been told.
>
> . . . . . . . . . . . .
>
> Although you have missed the best years of your life
> Do not let the remaining years be years of strife.

Dan Truscott sent Marlene a short thank-you note, which she treasured. Marlene's steelworker father, more used to political battles with the establishment than was his newly activist daughter, tried to temper her enthusiasm. "They won't let him win," he told her. "They don't like to admit they're wrong."

At work as a receptionist in a real estate company the day the Supreme Court decision was announced, Marlene was so shocked by the eight to one verdict she called a local radio station to get confirmation of the news. "My father was right," she thought to herself. "I was sad, but I was angry more than anything."

The defeat only made Marlene more determined. She drew up a petition asking Ottawa to call for a new trial, and quickly gathered over three thousand signatures. "I can remember taking it everywhere with me, everywhere," she says. "This thing took over my life. I could tell that my dad was proud. He thought it was great that I was standing up for someone other than myself."

But by the end of the summer of 1967—when it was clear the government was not going to do anything but let Steven serve out his term until parole—Marlene had no choice but to end her crusade—at least for the moment. She had written a personal letter to Steven, but she got it back unopened. The prison authorities told her she was not on his official list of correspondents.

———

On August 22 and 27, the ABC network aired the concluding two-part episode of *The Fugitive*, at the time one of the most highly rated TV finales. Sitting in Collins Bay, Steven could find little solace in the fact that it had taken Dr. Richard Kimble four years and 120 episodes to prove he had been wrongfully convicted.

So far, Steve had spent twice as many years behind bars as the fictional character had been on the run—and he had no idea how many more years he had left. Steve turned to music, blasting away the blues on his trumpet or joining a jam session playing guitar with a few of the other inmates in a small music room near the prison gym. "You can't just say, here's ten years of my life, it didn't exist," he says. "It existed and you make the best of it. You were in a situation where if you were going to make the worst of it, you would have never come out of there."

Like other inmates, Steve learned to savour the small victories. For New Year's celebrations, the convicts would make home-brewed alcohol from potatoes and sugared water. The guards would find a few of the makeshift stills, but never all of them. "They'd stumble across an obvious place, but there would be others," Steve says with a grin.

"Steve fell in with a good bunch of inmates," Malcolm Stienburg explains. "One was in for safecracking and two for murder. I know it sounds strange, but they were a good bunch of inmates. The fact is that none of them came back to prison once they were released."

Ross, a veteran safecracker and an older convict who watched over Steve, was released in late 1967. But Steve still had fellow lifers Chuck and John for company. And in the spring of 1968, he and John got their big break—a transfer out to the farm annex, where Steve used to cut grass with Joe Fowler. Spreading from behind the walls of Collins Bay about a mile south almost to the shores of Lake Ontario, the farm provided food for the prisons in the area and served as a sort of transition zone for better behaved inmates. "The more you get them to trust you, the more freedom they give you," Steve explains.

Steve and the other farm helpers slept in rooms, not cells. It was a completely open-door policy—Steve and John headed out to the fields in the morning and returned only for meals. If they were baling hay, they might go back out after supper and work until dark. The only thing stopping them from running away was a four-foot-high fence.

For Steve, these were the glory days in prison. If he drove his tractor out to the far southeast corner of the fields, he could watch the drive-in movie playing across the road. "It was fascinating just to be sitting there," he remembers. "You'd sit and watch until the boss of the farm would come out and tell us it was time to go."

In a small creek that runs through the farm, Steve and John would sneak in a little fishing, using flies made by other inmates. In the barter system behind bars, Steve's handcrafted leatherwork was a valuable commodity that he could swap for fishing gear or other goods.

Standing under the sun, Steven—now a well-built twenty-four-year-old—could easily close his eyes and imagine he was back on Lawson's farm. The police had snatched him on a hot summer day as he made his way home from the farm. A decade later, he was working on a farm again—but ten years of his life had been ploughed under. Steven preferred not to think of the time and memories lost.

"You move on, one day at a time, and you kind of close that chapter," he says. "If you remember everything in the past, it hurts too much."

As a well-behaved prisoner with an excellent record, Steve also earned the privilege in 1968 to leave the penitentiary grounds to attend classes at Queen's University. "That was a complete shock," Steve says, recalling the campus scene at the height of the turbulence of the late 1960s. "I was used to people in authority with uniforms, a shirt or tie—the whole bit. Here, the professors walking around were dressed worse than the students."

Steve signed up for English and political science classes; no one knew who he was except the professors. He enjoyed the freedom, but felt out of place in the academic world, where principles seemed more important than reality. "I used to get into arguments all the time with the political science professor," he remembers. "Everyone knows how it should be," the convict would challenge him. "Let's go on to how it is."

"You have to give him a great deal of credit," says one of his instructors, Barry Thorne. "It's not easy if you're relatively uneducated to start up a university course. It's a daunting and tough prospect and he managed to do it. That impressed me."

A shy person at the best of times, Steve avoided his fellow students, who were younger, more carefree and preoccupied with finding either a good book, a good beer or both. "You didn't really mingle with them because you knew where you were going to be that night," Steve says, "and you knew they weren't going to be there."

———

That night, as every other night, Steve was back in prison. But at least he no longer had to worry about the psychiatrist.

Dr. George Scott, perhaps burned by the scathing testimony at the Supreme Court, largely ignored Steven for two years. When he began filing reports again in May of 1968, it seemed—almost magically—that the troubled, tortured inmate Scott talked about in years past had disappeared. "There was not rancour or hostility from any supposed problems which arose in his case in the past," Scott wrote, not specifying if by "supposed problems" he was referring to his own diagnosis of Steve's mental health or the public furor that erupted over his handling of the case. The doctor noted Steven was "without the obvious defensive air which he had some years ago."

By June, Scott reported Steven seemed to be "doing quite well." By October, he was "gaining much more confidence in his abilities to communicate." In November, a Rorschach test revealed "a sensitive, intelligent young man having good ties with reality." On December 24, 1968, Scott filed a Christmas present of sorts, telling the warden Steven was "doing quite well. . . . I do not think we're going to have any major problem."

It was the last significant analysis Dr. George Scott filed on his star patient—except for his parole papers. After almost a decade of reports from him and more than a dozen other psychiatrists, the serious mental disorders they said had afflicted Steven had somehow disappeared. "That kind of makes you angry," Steve says today. "These are official documents, [and they say] 'schizophrenia,' 'paranoid'—you name it, if it was in the psychiatric book, I was it. Now what did all these people do to cure me of all these sicknesses?"

Around the same time Scott was giving Steven a clean slate for his mental health, another doctor closely connected to the case, pathologist John Penistan, was doing a bit of housecleaning himself. In January of 1969, the president of the Canadian Society of Forensic Science wrote to William Bowman, still Ontario's director of public prosecutions. He wanted to publish the doctor's article about the Lynne Harper autopsy, in order to "provide Dr. Penistan with a discreet forum in which to present his finding."

Bowman did not object, but he warned, "the press may pick up the matter again. If this did occur, it would undoubtedly open up the old wounds." He need not have worried. By the time Penistan's article appeared in print in September 1969, the pathologist had removed all of his major reversals in the draft he had sent to Harold Graham in May of 1966. Still, Penistan did manage to squeeze in a few cautionary notes he had neglected to stress in court. Ten years after he helped condemn a boy to hang on the basis of a precise time of death for a "violent, brutal" rape, Penistan now talked only of a "superficial abrasion" in the vagina with no specified cause, and concluded that, based on stomach contents, "death had *probably* taken place within *about* two hours of the girl's last meal."

The 1960s were coming to an end, as was the decade Steven had spent behind bars. And now, finally, he had a tangible ray of hope for his freedom. Steven was eligible for parole in June of 1969—subject, of course, to recommendation by the parole board and final approval by the cabinet.

In the months following Steve's defeat at the Supreme Court, his supporters had tried, unsuccessfully, to jump-start the process. In the fall of 1967, NDP MP Stanley Knowles introduced a private member's bill to parole Steven. Terry Nugent, a Progressive Conservative backbencher from Edmonton, blasted his fellow MPs for supporting Knowles' proposal as "unwarranted attacks on the administration of justice." Solicitor General Lawrence Pennell silenced the debate by affirming the cabinet would not consider parole for Steven until he had served the minimum ten years required by law.

Steven bided his time and in September of 1968 filed his formal application for parole, beginning the arduous process about nine months before his eligibility date. His mother visited him on the Labour Day weekend and told reporters she was optimistic. "He couldn't have a better record," Doris said.

"He doesn't want to build up his hopes this time," Dan Truscott cautioned, "and we certainly don't." The newspapers noted Steve's father was unemployed and surviving on an air force pension, having been "in and out of hospital for a year with bad nerves."

Steven had a special ally in his fight this time—his parole officer was Malcolm Stienburg. In July of 1967, the prison chaplain, while still remaining a United Church minister, changed jobs and became a parole supervisor. Stienburg was eager, as he put it, "to get away from the frustration of the walls" that came from working with inmates in isolation. He wanted a chance to work outside the prison with parolees and their families.

Stienburg began pushing the mountains of paperwork through the system. He wrote fair but overwhelmingly positive evaluations, confident he could help get Steve out. "Truscott maintains that he is not guilty of the offence," Stienburg wrote in one of his reports to the National Parole Board. He noted that Steve's guards and prison instructors gave him top marks. "Truscott's institutional record is unblemished," Stienburg stressed.

Even Dr. Scott was on board for Steven. "He has not reflected any signs [of] any known psychiatric disability whatsoever," the doctor now proclaimed. "His conviction was based upon an alleged offence which he has consistently denied."

Stienburg had earlier told the press that, once released, Steve would live under his real name. "Anything else Steve would consider dishonest," he said. Now Stienburg regretted those words, because the parole board decided Steve had no choice in the matter. "We came to the decision that he would come out with an assumed name because we were concerned with what the media would do to him. It was a clamour at that point, and we just figured that was the best way to handle it."

Steve objected, Stienburg recalls, but not too strongly. "If he had his preference, he'd have come out as a Truscott," he says. Sitting at a picnic table on the farm annex, just outside the prison walls, Stienburg and Steve began thinking of possible names. Johnson was a simple one that came to mind. They also considered Steve's mother's maiden name, which he could easily remember and respond to. No firm decision was taken right away.

There remained one intractable problem, however—where would Steven live? His parents were divorced. His father had been seeking medical care. His mother had begun a new relationship with another man (whom she would eventually marry). Stienburg and the parole officials were also worried that if Steven moved in with either parent, the media could easily track him down. "The press would know where he was and the publicity hounds were going to be riding herd on him," Stienburg feared.

It was not a decision that sat well with Doris. "Steve and I weren't given a choice," she says. "I think he would have been better to come home."

The June 1969 deadline for Steve's eligibility for parole came and went, as the paperwork and decision-making dragged on. At a parole board meeting in Ottawa, frayed nerves led to testy exchanges. Someone suggested sending the all-too-famous inmate to live in the student residence at a university.

"You have to be out of your skulls," Stienburg interjected. "Taking him out of one institution and putting him in another!"

Out of frustration, one of the committee members asked why Stienburg did not take Steven home to live with his own family.

"I may do just that," the minister blurted without thinking.

There was a pause when no one said anything, too stunned to react.

"Are you serious?" one of the parole board officers finally asked Stienburg.

"Well, look," Stienburg said more slowly this time, "I better check with my wife first." He left the room to call home. His wife, Mary, had met Steve a few times when Stienburg had brought her and their two young sons to visit his favourite inmate at the farm annex.

"If that's what you decide, that's fine with me," Mary said without hesitation.

"I hung up and that was the end of it," Stienburg says.

Parole officers might take their work home with them—but not the ex-inmates themselves. But over the years, Stienburg had developed a much deeper bond with Steven than he ever had with any other inmate: "Personally, I had a great deal of trouble believing that he was guilty. He's a very gentle person. And I don't see that type of emotion in him that would lead him to commit that type of offence."

Gentle enough to win the hearts of Stienburg's two young boys. To prepare his family for their new houseguest, Stienburg had Andy, aged three, and Trevor, aged seven, visit Steven at the farm about a half dozen times over the summer and fall. They tossed a ball back and forth and played on the swings. "It was his first introduction to real life with kids," Stienburg recalls. His children quickly took to the tall man they called "Uncle Steve."

By early September of 1969, the National Parole Board finally sent in a favourable recommendation for Steven to the federal cabinet. "Once the board recommends parole, the cabinet rarely turns it down," Stienburg assured Steven. "But the Lord alone knows when it will make the decision." Steve would just have to wait.


On Tuesday, October 21, Steve was working on the farm when he got a message to go to the warden's office. Still in prison garb, Steve made his way to the administration building. "I didn't have a clue what they wanted," he remembers.

The minute he opened the door and saw Malcolm Stienburg and the warden with a sheaf of papers on the desk, he knew he was one step closer to freedom.

"Well, if you just sign these papers, we can be on our way," Stienburg told Steve.

"I'll sign them," Steve said immediately.

Standing in the office was Don Patterson, the prison supervisor who had first greeted the frightened fifteen-year-old who came for an overnight stay at the Kingston prison complex in 1960. And Patterson had also driven eighteen-year-old Steven from the Guelph training school to Collins Bay in 1963. Now, as he stared at the twenty-four-year-old man in front of him, he saw only traces of that fearful child.

"He was taller," Patterson recalls. "He'd filled out a bit. But that face you'd recognize right away." And that face, Patterson remembers, instead of being etched with fear or apprehension, now displayed a beaming smile.

"He walked out of there more of a gentleman than probably any con that came out of prison—with his head high," says Joe Fowler, his machine shop instructor. The man who taught Steven welding modestly insists that he had nothing to do with welding the boy's character as well. "Maybe I did a little by showing him trust and faith," Fowler says. "He grew up in there. He could have become like another con," Fowler says. "But the system never took hold of him. He just held a line and never changed from that line; he was going to do things right and he did things right. He turned out to be a pretty decent boy."

Steve's departure was so rushed, he did not have time to say goodbye to Fowler or to his two friends, John and Chuck. Even his mother was not told about his release. Prison officials knew that the news would leak out, so they arranged for Stienburg to ferry Steve out the back gates in his steel-grey 1964 Volkswagen Beetle.

"I looked out front and there were reporters all over the place," Don Patterson remembers.

Patterson escorted Steve and Stienburg across the prison courtyard to the southwest exit and waved as the car sped away.

"It's a success, he's gone," Patterson told the warden. Then he walked outside the prison gates to the hordes of newspapermen.

"What are you chaps waiting for?" he asked.

"Truscott!" they exclaimed.

"You're a little bit late, he's already gone," Patterson told the disappointed scribes.

And to himself the prison guard who had seen a young lad grow up behind bars whispered a silent prayer:

"Good luck there, boy!"

## 39

STARTING OVER

Steve was utterly stunned, almost paralyzed by a curious mixture of joy and fear. "One minute you're in jail, then suddenly you're outside. It's such a shock to the system," he says. "You're off in another world, you can't believe it."

He and Stienburg drove along a small road that cut between the western wall of the prison and the farmland. They reached the main city road and turned left. A light snow had started to fall.

When Steven first walked into a jail in June of 1959, the Russians had put the Sputnik satellite in orbit, Elvis ruled the airwaves and Diefenbaker's Conservatives ruled the country. By the time he had emerged in late 1969, the world was unrecognizable. Neil Armstrong had walked on the moon, the Beatles had come and were almost gone, two Kennedy brothers had been assassinated and Pierre Elliott Trudeau was starting his transformation of Canada.

Steven had missed all of that and more. His kid brother and sister were now adults. His older brother was married. His parents were divorced. Steve left prison without a stitch of clothing except the prison uniform he was wearing. In a red wooden toolbox, he carried his trumpet, a lighter, some photographs and personal letters.

———

The original plan was simple. Malcolm Stienburg had wanted to keep Steven under wraps in an isolated cottage on Bob's Lake, about forty miles north of Kingston, until the initial press fury died down. But that was a summer scheme, hatched when Stienburg assumed Steven would be out of prison in June. Now it was the onset of winter, and the two men arrived at a creaky cabin that had little heat and less insulation.

"Mac"—as Steve began calling Stienburg—piled charcoal into an old wood stove to generate some heat. Stuffing themselves with bacon and eggs, the two men sat down to watch the fuzzy images of a black-and-white TV set. "We're listening to the news and they're reporting that Steve has been taken to an unidentified city in western Canada," Stienburg remembers. "We're sitting back there killing ourselves laughing."

Two hundred miles away, in her living room in Guelph, Marlene, the young woman who had worked so hard to get Steven released after his Supreme Court defeat, was watching a hockey game. The news flashed that Steven Truscott had been freed from prison. "Oh, isn't that great!" she exclaimed. She wrote Steven a Christmas card, sent to Isabel LeBourdais' attention, wishing him the best in his new life.

Back in the cold cabin, an exhausted Steve had gone to bed. "Truscott's in there sleeping like a baby and I'm up all night stoking the old wood stove," Stienburg laughs. He woke up his young companion the next morning with an urgent proposal: "We've got to get out of here or we'll freeze to death." The snow had made the steep hill leading away from the cabin treacherous, so the minister told Steven to get in the front seat of the Volkswagen, while Stienburg started spreading sand.

"Suddenly, the engine was bucking and the tires were spinning," Stienburg recounts. "I forgot—he'd never driven a car!"

With Mac at the wheel, the two refugees of winter managed to make their way to the nearby village of Moscow, Ontario, where Stienburg's mother-in-law had a home. They expected her to be there, but upon finding the house empty, Mac and Steve had no choice but to enter by strongly pushing in an unlocked basement door.

"Truscott, we've been out one damn day and already you've got me involved in a B and E," the minister said only half jokingly. "Steve was standing back killing himself laughing," Stienburg remembers. "He thought it was a hoot."

The two men rested at the house until Friday, when Mac decided to treat Steven to a hockey game at Maple Leaf Gardens. They caught an early train out of Kingston to Toronto at 7:00 a.m., because Mac figured the chances were slim of meeting anyone he knew at that hour. But he ended up running into a friend of his anyway.

"Good morning," Mac said nervously. Pointing to his somewhat awkward-looking young companion with the crewcut—he muttered, "This is a friend of mine, Steve, uh, Rogers," using the first name that popped into his head—the name of a used-car lot where he had recently purchased his Volkswagen.

"Geez, I see Truscott got out," Mac's friend commented, as he scanned the headlines in the morning paper he was carrying.

"Yeah," Mac answered nonchalantly, hoping the conversation would die.

"Did you know him?" the man pursued.

"Oh, yeah."

"How well did you know him?"

"Oh, I knew him pretty well," Mac answered, elbowing Steve as the two of them tried to stifle their laughter. The man had his newspaper in front of his face so he could not see the huge grins on his fellow travellers' faces.

After a weekend in Toronto, Stienburg felt media interest had faded sufficiently to make it safe to bring Steve to Westbrook, a small bedroom community just outside of Kingston, where Mac lived with his family. The minister had prepared the terrain a few weeks earlier by canvassing his neighbours, asking them what that they thought about Steven Truscott getting parole. No one raised objections.

"Well, that's fine for you—you figure he's going to be a thousand miles away," Mac pushed. "What if he came to your neighbourhood?"

"It wouldn't make a difference," his neighbours told him, including one who was an OPP officer. "A lot of people knew Steve was there," Mac remembers, "and not one said a word."

Steve settled quickly into the Stienburg household. "Oh, hi, Uncle Steve," Andy and Trevor said when they saw him at the kitchen table. Andy, the younger boy, took a special liking to the new houseguest. "His smile is like a clown, because it's ear to ear," he told his parents.

A Super 8 home movie shows a smiling Steve on the verge of tears, as the two boys, Mac, and his wife, Mary, surround him in mid-January for his twenty-fifth birthday—his first outside of prison since 1959. Steve told Mac he always wanted to celebrate with champagne, so the minister took him down to the liquor store to buy a fourteen-dollar bottle of Mumm's. "He wanted to uncork it—damn thing blew off, left a mark in the ceiling, foam all over the carpet," Mac recounts. "Poor Steve, he was so embarrassed."

"They treated me just like a son, the boys treated me like an older brother," Steve remembers. "It was really important because it was a family atmosphere, and it made me feel at ease." Steve made brief visits to see his father and his mother, but it was clear his new home—at least for a while—was with the Stienburgs. "I only wish I could get the family back together," Steve wrote to Isabel LeBourdais about his separated parents. "But I guess it's best the way things are, as everyone seems quite happy now."

As an ex-con, Steve began to make the difficult adjustment to life on the outside. "All of a sudden you're thrust out—every decision you make is your own," Steve explains. "I had never been in a restaurant for years, never dialled a phone."

"Little things bothered him," Mac remembers. He noticed Steve, like other recently released inmates, preferred to pay for a coffee with a five-dollar bill even if he had coins, because he was too nervous to count out the exact change.

"He always felt bad about not having good manners, never knowing just what to do," Mac says. During one visit with neighbours, Mac remembers the ex-inmate trying to manoeuvre a teacup, saucer and cookies in his clumsy hands. "It was just like watching a bear cub—awkward as the devil," he says.

There were more practical concerns as well. Mary took Steven to buy him a pair of jeans and a wallet. Mac went to a government office in Kingston and arranged for Steven to get a social insurance number under his assumed name. In Steve's file, his real name was also listed, so when it came time to retire he could claim his pension. The manager at the government bureau was so eager to help he took it upon himself to drive to Ottawa to make sure the paperwork got done efficiently and discreetly.

Stienburg also had to run interference for Steve at work. One day, an irate citizen phoned the parole officer to complain. "Well, I sure would hate to hire a babysitter and know that it was Truscott looking after my kids!" she said. Stienburg smiled to himself, knowing at that moment Steven was home taking care of his two young boys while Mary was in hospital.

Another time, one of Stienburg's bosses at the National Parole Board called in a panic.

"Where's Truscott?" he wanted to know.

"He's at my house," Stienburg answered.

"Are you sure?"

"Well, he was this morning. Why?"

"He's been positively identified in Winnipeg by the police there."

"Well, if you want to hold the line, I'll verify," Mac said, and switched lines.

"Truscott—where are you?" he asked Steve.

"What?" Steve said, bewildered.

"You're not in Winnipeg then?"

"No."

"All right, I'll explain it to you tonight," Stienburg said. He returned to the nervous parole supervisor to assure him Canada's best-known parolee was not on the run.

In case of future trouble, Stienburg suggested Steve keep a diary of where he was every day. "For a long time, if there's another type of offence like this, you're going to be questioned," Mac warned.

Steve had escaped the hangman's noose. But he was beginning to realize that being branded a convicted child slayer would follow him around for the rest of his life. The judge's words "until you are dead" took on another layer of meaning.

As Steven was feeling his way in the uncertain world outside prison walls, he was about to meet face-to-face with one of his most ardent supporters—and a woman who would change his life. Isabel LeBourdais had given Steve the Christmas card Marlene, the Guelph campaigner, had written to him. "I will write to the girl who has put so much effort into helping," Steve told LeBourdais in a letter, "as I appreciate the thought and work that everybody has done."

In late January, LeBourdais called Marlene and asked if it was okay to drop by soon for a visit. "I've got someone here I'd like to bring down," she said. "Actually, it's Steve, and I want to put him on the phone."

After a nervous hello, Steve could not seem to muster much beyond a few words. "I know people in Guelph," he said.

"I'm thinking, 'What should I say?'" Marlene remembers. "This guy doesn't know what to say to me."

"It was the first girl I had talked to in years," Steve recalls. "It was all new territory for me."

Marlene, still living with her parents at Kristen Road, ran out to pick up some fried chicken for the visitors. A couple of hours later, the doorbell rang, and Marlene got her first look at the young man she had read so much about. Steve wore a long navy blue raincoat, a black turtleneck and slacks. Despite his short hair, he had a sort of James Dean rakish look about him. "I can remember feeling bad," Marlene says. "Here's this person that I know so much about—so much private stuff. You don't usually meet a man when you know things about his body parts and his whole life."

Marlene's father was the first to speak to the visitor at the door. "He probably recognized fear," Steve jokes today. Marlene's parents, LeBourdais and the two twenty-five-year-olds finished up the chicken and dessert in the living room while engaging in some awkward chit-chat. Then Marlene offered to take Steve to a local car club—she'd heard he was a mechanical whiz.

They got into Marlene's 1962 white Chevrolet Impala and drove through the streets she had roamed as a teenager, the same town that had been Steve's home a decade earlier—except he had been an adolescent prisoner behind a reform school fence. Realizing she was going to have to introduce her companion to her friends, Marlene turned to Steve.

"What name are you using?" she asked.

"Steve, uh, Johnson," he muttered, using one of the aliases Mac had come up with.

Marlene remembers feeling odd as she stared at the man who had been the centre of her political attention for the previous three years. "All of a sudden he's a real person."

At the end of the evening, when it came time for the uncomfortable goodbyes, Marlene was not quite ready to let go of the shy young man.

"You'll have to write and tell me how you're making out with your life," she suggested. "You have my address?"

"Yeah," Steve said in his usual monosyllabic parlance.

Marlene babbled on about her summer plans. "I'm going with a friend out west."

"Where you going?" Steve dared to ask.

"Vancouver."

"Well, I'll be out there too," Steve said. Stienburg and Steve had decided that by the spring, Steve would be ready to leave the safe confines of the parole officer's home. He would move out west to live with his grandparents near Vancouver.

Steve gave Marlene his grandparents' phone number and they said goodnight. Marlene quickly dashed off a letter to Isabel LeBourdais.

"Here was a boy who I knew so much about and always thought of as a young fourteen-year-old, and all of a sudden he appeared at my home as a man of twenty-five (and a handsome one at that)," she confessed in her letter. "I am just fascinated by him—he is just a wonderful person in every respect—he is soft-spoken, well-mannered and humorous—three good characteristics."

"Steve is just great! His parents must be so proud of him," she concluded. "It is just too bad he is going away, though."

Going away for Steve meant saying goodbye in early April to Mac and the Stienburg family, who had nurtured and sheltered him in the first few trying months of freedom. Steven hugged Mary and the kids and boarded a train to British Columbia.

When Stienburg went upstairs to Steve's room, he discovered the red toolbox Steve had carried out of prison. "The box was there, with his lighter, shoes, prison release clothes and his trumpet. He left everything that reminded him of the prison," Stienburg says. "He never explained it and I never asked."

It was the last house on a small street on a cliff in Burnaby, perched over the Second Narrows Bridge. Just across, the Georgia Strait waters flowed steadily toward the Pacific, and the snow-capped mountains reached for the blue skies of a West Coast spring. After the grey vistas of his prison years, the view from his grandparents' home was nothing short of liberating for Steven Truscott.

Marlene had driven out to Vancouver with some friends and kept trying to call Steve, never getting an answer. "I almost gave up, and then one time his grandmother answered and I asked for him," she says.

"Do you remember me?" she asked nervously.

"Oh, yeah," Steve answered, using as few words as possible.

"Do you want to come over sometime?"

"Okay."

Steve did not have a car—he didn't even have a licence. But he began dropping by Marlene's apartment in downtown Vancouver to play cards or Parcheesi with her and her girlfriends. Marlene usually drove him home.

"It was more of a friendship thing," Marlene says. "He was a desperately lonely person."

One evening, overcoming his shyness, Steve asked her if she wanted to go out for dinner. "Have you ever been to the Ship of Seven Seas?" he asked, referring to a floating eatery on the other side of the Second Narrows Bridge. Marlene hated seafood but readily agreed to go.

They stared out at the Vancouver skyline across the inlet and to the west, up river, they could see the towering trees of Stanley Park. They talked about school, about growing up in Ontario, about family.

"I felt, 'This is a lost person.'" Marlene says. "He was quite in tune with what was going on in the world, but he just needed somebody emotionally and physically."

As the weeks progressed, she saw Steven slowly gain confidence. Her father came for a visit for several weeks in July and spent long days walking through the city with Steve while Marlene worked as a bookkeeper. One evening, as the summer was winding down, Marlene and Steve walked around Stanley Park and Marlene stopped to sit on a swing.

"I just remember him standing, looking at the water, and I'm looking at him. And everything changed," she says. "Before he had been a name, then a cause, then a friend. But then I realized I had a different feeling— I saw him without the case behind him, someone I wanted to be a companion to."

Steve, for his part, says there was "no moment when a light bulb went on. I just felt really confident with her." That confidence blossomed into an unshakeable love.

By fall, the two had married in a private ceremony. No family, no guests, no pictures. They were afraid that somehow word would leak out and the press hordes would descend. For Marlene, who had always dreamed of a big wedding, it was a crushing compromise—the first of many she would have to make over the next years.

"It was the happiest and the saddest day of my life," she says.

Marlene and Steve also decided to move back east, to Guelph. Steve, who had been born in Vancouver, loved the sea and mountains. But his aging grandfather was more than a decade older than the "Pop" who took the young boy fishing on his boat. "I had grown up so much that the things you remember when you were a kid were just not the same," Steve says.

He was also having trouble finding steady work. Marlene was homesick and was convinced Steve needed to be closer to his family in Ontario. They arrived in Guelph on a Friday, and by the following Monday Steve had found a job as a millwright—a general mechanical repairman—at a local plant called Linreed. He would stay there for nearly two decades.

For a while, the new couple lived with Marlene's parents, and Marlene helped Steve make the transition to daily life. At restaurants, Steve always waited for Marlene to order first and then asked for the same thing, still not used to having a wide choice of meals. He shied away from crowds, and would not go to a movie if there was a long lineup at the theatre. He hated talking on the phone.

"There was still so much that I hadn't done. It was really tough," Steve says. "Marlene really helped me adjust. I don't know how I could have survived."

Marlene had to do some adjusting of her own. For starters, she had to deal with a somewhat shell-shocked mother-in-law. Doris Truscott had seen her young boy snatched away from her, but Steve did not end up living with her after a decade in prison. And then—less than a year after leaving jail—he married a girl in what must have seemed like impetuous haste. "We didn't know what she was like or anything," Doris says. "It was a little upsetting."

The two women—equally iron-willed and unbending—slowly got to know and respect each other. "She said to me, 'I don't know how you could go through what you did,'" Doris remembers. "I told her, 'You have to adjust yourself—there are other kids.'"

"She was the one who kept the family going," Marlene says of Doris with admiration. "She kept the other children back from it—one child had been hurt, she wasn't going to have the rest all hurt."

Marlene understood that choice, but she still yearned to launch a public fight to clear her husband's name. "Why did it stop? Why did it just disappear after the Supreme Court?" she asks. "It just died. It shouldn't have. I'm like my dad—a fighter." She had come to the Truscott case as a fiery, tireless campaigner. Now married to the man she had fought to free, she suddenly found she had to restrain her combativeness.

To make matters worse, while Steve was thrilled to be out of the penitentiary, Marlene found Steve's parole restrictions suffocating. He could not leave town without notifying the authorities, so a last-minute decision to go see his family on the weekend meant scrambling to reach a parole officer.

"I was a free spirit, used to doing what I wanted—I was going crazy," Marlene says.

Being a free spirit—and the daughter of a labour organizer in an NDP household—didn't stop Marlene from being very traditional in many ways. She had worked since she was sixteen, but her life's ambitions were simple. "I didn't want a career—I always wanted a family," she says.

"That's all I ever wanted—a white picket fence around my house, and kids."

The kids would come, but Marlene would find that raising a family was a lot more challenging than she ever dreamed when you are the wife of Steven Truscott.

## 40

## WHAT TO TELL THE CHILDREN

He stood there quietly, cradling this strange treasure in his arms. The rough hands that had chiselled wood and welded metal in prison now felt the softness of a newborn's skin. For all his awkwardness in the outside world beyond the prison walls, Steven seemed to take to fatherhood as if it was his natural calling.

It was the late spring of 1971 and Marlene had just given birth to a healthy eight-pound girl named Lesley. "I am still to this day overwhelmed—it was like he had had ten other kids," she remembers. There were complications after the delivery and Marlene spent six weeks recovering.

Steve was up every night bottle-feeding Lesley, then out to work at the crack of dawn and back by the early afternoon for more baby care. Over the next few months, Steve took his daughter on walks in the summer, sleigh rides in the winter and for the inevitable first pictures with Santa Claus. "Lesley would just go wild when she saw Steve," Marlene says. "He was just everything to her."

Lesley was named after Marlene's father, who had died of a heart attack just a month before. Steve's father, Dan, made regular trips from Ottawa to see his new grandchild. Divorced, and still heartbroken he could not do more to clear his son's name, Dan fawned over the baby girl. "Lesley was his world," Marlene says.

A first child is something special for every father, but for Steve, Lesley was much more—a testament that he had survived, that after losing his freedom, his name, his childhood, here at last was something he could hang on to.

"I just can't believe I have her—it's something that can never be taken from me," he told Marlene as he held their young child in the hospital room.

"I can remember thinking at the time: 'I wonder if your mother thought that when you were born,'" Marlene says. "Mind you, they took him from her."

When Steve and Marlene drove out to the Kingston area to show off Lesley to Malcolm Stienburg and his family, Steve's parole officer suggested Steve come watch Mac and some of his friends at a ParticipACTION baseball game.

What Steve did not know was that Mac played on a police team, and the game was at a diamond right outside the walls of the Collins Bay Penitentiary. When they arrived, the ballplayers—who had no idea of Steve's real identity—suggested the new father join them on the benches, where he would be more comfortable holding his daughter. At one point in the game, Mac found himself as a runner on second base, and from his perspective he could see Steve surrounded by off-duty police officers—with the prison walls as backdrop.

"I just burst out laughing," he remembers. "I couldn't help it."

Steve could get away with it because, while his name was notorious, his face—at least as an adult—was virtually unknown. His story was back in the news in the fall of 1971 with the launch of a new book called *The Steven Truscott Story*, written by Bill Trent, a Montreal journalist who was a staff writer with *Weekend Magazine*. A three-part series of excerpts from the book ran in the popular magazine distributed free across the country as an insert in many daily newspapers. "Behind these walls a fourteen-year-old sat waiting to be hanged," the cover story said, accompanied by a gloomy picture of the Goderich jail. "Steven Truscott tells his story of growing up in jail."

Trent had spent several weeks talking and even living with Steve shortly after his release and wrote the book as a first-person narrative. It had little of the shock value of LeBourdais' revelations and some of the passages purporting to be Steven's exact words seem too flowery or literate to have been uttered by the usually reserved Steve. Still, the book gave Canadians personal insight into what Steve and his family had gone through during his arrest and long years behind bars.

Trent's book was controversial enough for the trustees in Huron County to strike it off the recommended reading list for the secondary schools in the area where Steve had been tried and convicted. "The book was not an unbiased overview of the incident," the director of education explained. "[The trustees] did not feel that its use would add anything to the education program." At least two of the school officials would have had good reason to be upset by the book. One was jury foreman Clarence McDonald; the other was Dr. John Addison, the family doctor who had testified against Steven.

In 1975 a shadowy figure in the Truscott affair passed away. Air force sergeant Alexander Kalichuk had continued his downward slide into an alcoholic haze of mental collapse throughout the late 1960s and into the 1970s. One of his colleagues, Sgt. John Lawson, was serving as a custodian in a psychiatric institution in Goderich after retiring from the air force. Lawson had known Kalichuk as the base drunk, but was still shocked when he saw the dishevelled and sunken man muttering to himself and walking aimlessly in the corridors. "I guess his brain is all pickled with alcohol," a nurse commented.

Few people mourned when Kalichuk was buried in a small plot near Seaforth. Today, weeping willows droop over his abandoned farmhouse just twenty minutes away from Clinton. The shingles are falling off, rags are stuffed into holes in the wall, and weeds push up through a rusted old car in the field. Whatever secrets Kalichuk might have had about where he was on the night of June 9, 1959, he took with him to his grave.

The year 1975 also saw the release of a fictional movie inspired by Steven's story called *Recommendation for Mercy*. The poster showed a forlorn boy on a cot behind bars, and two jagged newspaper headlines screaming "BOY 14 SENTENCED TO HANG!" and "GIRL 13 SLAIN." The names and many of the facts were changed, but the movie served to generate even more sympathy for Steven's experience. "I've always felt the boy was innocent," producer and director Murray Markowitz said.

The film also sparked Steven's first foray onto the public stage since his brief appearance at the Supreme Court. Following the buzz around the movie, Steven did a forty-five-minute interview with reporter Brian Thomas of CHUM radio in Toronto, and excerpts were widely rebroadcast on television and quoted in the newspapers. "I definitely am not and I will never say that I was guilty," he said.

Steve described to the radio audience the LSD and truth serum treatments he endured. "I was tested for two years by at least a dozen psychiatrists—with pretty much every test they could think of—trying to get a confession out of me, which they never got."

Steven stated that it would be his first and his last interview. "And so now, as quickly as he reappeared, Truscott has gone back into anonymity," one television report on Steven's brief public sortie concluded.

But not quite. Steve could seek anonymity, but echoes of his appointment with the hangman were not far from many people's minds when Canadians grappled with the debate over the abolition of the death penalty. A decade earlier, at the height of the controversy over Steve's conviction, Parliament had restricted hanging—for a five-year trial period—to slayers of on-duty police officers and prison guards; the trial period was renewed for another five years in 1972.

In April 1975, Justice Emmett Hall, now retired from the Supreme Court of Canada, led a delegation to Parliament Hill urging that the death penalty be completely abolished. Hall explained that his delegation—assembled by the Canadian Civil Liberties Association, and including religious leaders, broadcasters and authors—was a "response to the growing demand for the restoration of capital punishment."

Indeed, Solicitor General Warren Allmand, a strong abolitionist, was under intense pressure to bring back the noose. One convicted killer was scheduled to be hanged the following month for the slaying of a Toronto policeman during an armed robbery. The Association of Municipalities of Ontario, representing 535 towns and cities in the province, called on Ottawa to reinstate the death penalty for murder committed during robbery and any premeditated killings.

Canada's official hangman, deprived of business by the commutation of death sentences since 1962, called for Allmand's resignation. "I am definitely against him holding that position," the anonymous state executioner said in a radio interview, insisting his criticism was not motivated by monetary concerns, since he was paid an annual retainer by the federal government whether or not he slipped the rope around anyone's neck.

By the time Allmand and the Liberal government were ready for a formal parliamentary debate on capital punishment in May of 1976, there were eleven men in Canada sentenced to die. The bill proposed to abolish hanging and substitute it with a life sentence to be served for a minimum of twenty-five years before parole. Allmand read a letter from Pauline Maitland, the widow of the slain Toronto policeman. She urged the government to do everything it could "to prevent this terrible second crime"—the execution of her husband's murderer. "The killing of this man would be completely foreign to all the moral standards of my late husband and myself," she said.

Before it was over, 119 MPs spoke their minds, taking up forty-six hours of Commons time. Erik Nielsen, a powerful Tory, was a strong retentionist, as were many others in his party. Andrew Brewin, so active in the campaign to free Steven a decade earlier, assured Parliament the sixteen members of the New Democratic Party would vote to abolish capital punishment.

Prime Minister Trudeau insisted his opposition to the death penalty was based not on principle, but on practicality—it was not an effective deterrent. Still, he spoke with his usual rhetorical flourish: "To kill a man for punishment alone is an act of revenge—nothing else. Some would prefer to call it retribution because that word has a nicer sound. But the meaning is the same," he said. "Are we, as a society, so lacking in respect for ourselves, so lacking in hope for human betterment, that we are ready to accept state vengeance as our penal philosophy?"

In the end the vote was extremely close. In what the newspapers described as a packed, sweltering and divided House of Commons, politicians voted to abolish the death penalty by the slimmest of margins. The bill passed the all-important second reading on June 22 by 133 to 125.

Trudeau called it "one step further from violence and barbarism." NDP deputy leader Stanley Knowles, the parliamentarian who perhaps more than any other had fought for Steven's freedom, called it "a great day in the history of civilization."

Ironically, John Diefenbaker, who had commuted Steven's death sentence and fought hard for his early parole, was angry. All his life he was against the death penalty. But he turned against the bill to abolish it because it also did away with hanging for treason, rebellion and the murder of the monarch. "Thugs from all over the world will know that it's come one, come all—it's open season for all of you," the venerable politician blustered. "Now they will assassinate whomever they please, when they please."

After more wrangling in committee, Parliament gave the abolition bill final approval on July 15 with an even closer tally—only six votes separating the two sides. Allmand announced that all eleven convicts sentenced to die would have their sentences commuted immediately.

By abolishing the death penalty, Canada became the eleventh Western nation to do away with capital punishment. The British Parliament had rejected a move to restore the death penalty in December 1975. Other Western countries without a death penalty at the time included Denmark, Finland, Sweden and West Germany.

Interestingly, just as Canada formally put a stop to state executions, the United States was moving in the opposite direction. In 1976, the American Supreme Court ruled the death penalty—which had not been used for some years—was constitutional, provided the states implemented certain safeguards. Thirty-six of fifty American states would eventually bring back the death penalty, killing 944 people between 1977 and 2005.

In Canada, the issue refused to die quietly. Two years later, in 1978, Diefenbaker led a rump group inside the Tories to force new Conservative leader Joe Clark to accept a national referendum on the issue. Some polls showed eighty-eight per cent of voters wanted a referendum and sixty-eight per cent would favour a return to hanging.

The prime minister would have none of it. "The 1976 vote settled the issue," Trudeau said with characteristic defiance. "We don't plan to reopen it."

Back in Guelph, Steve and Marlene were more preoccupied with domestic concerns than national debates. They now had two children—Lesley, who was turning into a bright, inquisitive schoolgirl, and Ryan, born in 1974.

Steve continued to be a devoted father. "The minute Steve came through the door, my day was over with those kids," Marlene says. "He fed them, he changed him, he bathed them, he put them to bed. He just loved them."

After spending his childhood moving constantly from one air force base to another, then his teenage and young adult years in prison, where cellmates and friends would come and go, Steven yearned for stability. "All my life, everyone came in and out of your life," Steve says. "It was important for me to put down roots somewhere."

Once he and Marlene settled in Guelph, they never left. Steve would work in the same factory for seventeen years, leaving only when the plant shut down. He quickly found another job, where he works to this day.

"Every day at 3:30 after work his car pulled in—you could count on him," says Olga Samson, a neighbour and friend of the Truscotts. "He is without a doubt the best father that I have ever seen in my life," her husband, Gary, adds. "He has such great rapport with his children. He never raises his voice, ever."

But the joy of raising a family also posed a dilemma to Canada's best-known, but most private, convicted child murderer: what to tell the children about his past—and when. Steve and Marlene had not made any conscious decisions about what to do and they were caught between two countervailing pressures.

On the one hand, Steve did not want go out of his way to conceal himself. Steve never legally changed his name. He and Marlene married under the name Truscott.

"There's a big misconception—we've never hidden," Steve says. "If somebody asked, 'Are you Steve Truscott?' I told them."

On the other hand, Steve's foremost concern was protecting his new family. "If the children had to have the name Truscott, from the word go they wouldn't have had the chance to have a normal life. It had nothing to do with them," he says. "For me, my family is my life. So everything else is secondary—even my own life." That's why Steve's passport, his social insurance number, his bank accounts and driver's licence—everything to do with his public identity, including the surnames of his children—were all under his assumed name.

Not that Marlene accepted their enforced anonymity meekly. She still detested Steve's parole restrictions, everything from his need to report in regularly to the requirement to get permission for any travel outside of town. When five years outside of prison passed without incident, Steve was placed under reduced parole supervision. After his parole officer came by the house with the official papers, Steve promptly went upstairs to sleep.

"But I was up all night in the kitchen, jumping and excited and dancing a jig," Marlene says. "Yes, I'm free of those people!" she shouted.

Marlene wanted to scream to all who would listen what the real name of her husband was, and why he was innocent—but not while her children were small. "I was waiting for those kids to grow up," Marlene says. "But I knew it was going to happen, come hell or high water, something's going to give here."

Steve and Marlene—along with their co-workers, neighbours and friends—walked a fine line between privacy and pride. One of Steve's best friends at work, Ray Hatton, knew his real identity, as did many other employees. "The guys would never say anything out of respect," says Ray's widow, Maureen, who became a close confidante to Marlene. "The guys were very protective of Steve. They figured he's been through enough. If he wants to talk about it, he will."

Maureen found out about Steve's identity at a card game, when some of the men pointed him out to her.

"Do you know who he is?" one of them said, revealing Steve's real name.

"Are you serious?" Maureen gasped.

"Yeah—but he wasn't guilty," the man assured her.

An energetic woman with eight children, Maureen soon moved next door to Marlene, and the two women quickly formed an unofficial "breakfast club," grabbing a coffee at a local diner after they dropped their kids off at school.

"[Steve's situation] was never a subject until she wanted to bring it up," Maureen says. "I didn't think it was any of my business."

Other neighbours felt the same way. Butch and Joan Brock met the Truscotts at a Labour Day picnic, and warmed to their folksiness and good humour. Butch took Steve hunting; the Brocks' teenage boys babysat for the Truscott children. "We knew who he was, but whenever we got together we never talked about it," says Butch.

Neighbours with smaller children were equally nonplussed. Pat Corbit lived near to the Truscotts in the 1970s, and Steve often took care of her baby daughter along with Lesley. When Pat later discovered who he really was, she wasn't upset. "I didn't say, 'Oh my God, my daughter has been in his house.' It didn't bother me at all," she says. "I knew Steve and I knew the kind of man he was."

Oddly enough, the one neighbour who did panic over Steve's notoriety only did so because she didn't know who Steve really was. Christa Severa had been the teenager from Germany who in 1959 was horrified her parents were immigrating to Canada, where they sentenced young boys to hang. Twenty years later, in the spring of 1979, she was a mother of two moving into a new home in Guelph.

"You know the guy next door has been convicted of rape," a relative told her, without ever mentioning the name Truscott.

"That's really great, that's what you want to hear when you move into a new house," Christa recalls. "It really disturbed me. I had a daughter and it was a scary situation."

The driveways and backyards of the two families were separated only by a small fence, and Christa's daughter Tracey quickly became friends with Lesley, much to her mother's disquiet. Lesley's father—whom Krista knew only by his assumed name—did not seem dangerous. "I thought it was strange that he wasn't mean," she recalls. "I was never afraid when the children were outside, but when my daughter was out of my sight, the hair at the back of my neck stood up."

Finally, her fear overwhelmed her, and Christa suggested Tracey find a new friend. She stopped her daughter from going to Lesley's birthday party. Marlene's heart sank. She figured Christa had discovered her husband was the notorious Steven Truscott, convicted murderer and rapist, and was convinced of his guilt. It was Marlene's worst nightmare—that her children should have to pay for the alleged sins of their father.

And they did pay. In July of 1979, Steve's father went into the hospital with stomach cancer, and within two weeks Dan Truscott was dead. Lesley had been the apple of her grandfather's eye, and she adored the playful, kind man who would cover himself with acorns to make her laugh. But the family decided the eight-year-old girl should stay away from the funeral.

"I was not allowed to go, and I felt I should have. I felt I was old enough," Lesley says today. "They wouldn't let me go for fear of reporters. They didn't want pictures taken of us. And I can remember just crying and crying, wanting to go to my grandfather's funeral. And I couldn't."

Perhaps the decision was wise. Outside the funeral home, photographers tried to grab a shot of the elusive Steven Truscott. Inside, family mourners caught reporters taking notes. Steve—normally calm and even-tempered—was outraged. "I didn't want the press to have anything to do with this. This was my family—stay the hell away!" he remembers. One of his brothers escorted the newsmen out.

More publicity was stirred up in October 1979, when journalist Bill Trent came out with an updated version of his 1971 book. This time it was entitled *Who Killed Lynne Harper?* The book consisted largely of his original first-person account of Steve's life, with Justice Emmett Hall's dissenting Supreme Court opinion as an addendum.

But Trent also added about fifty new pages as an introduction, speculating on various possible suspects. The leads were tantalizing but nebulous—

anonymous sightings of Lynne in Seaforth after she left Clinton; an unnamed nurse who phoned an open-line radio show claiming she knew "it was an adult on the base who killed her"; a plumber from Kitchener who insisted he had the real story.

Trent also included the story of the "Three Painters" who were working on gas station signs in the Clinton area at the time of Lynne's murder. One of the men had died, but the other two, brothers named Ronny and Russ, had served time in Kingston Penitentiary for armed robbery. In a transcript of a taped interview from the 1960s with an unnamed interrogator—almost certainly Dr. George Scott or another psychiatrist at the prison—Ronny says his brother may have killed a girl named "Linda Harper." But later, when asked to sign a statement, Ronny said he "could have been making things up."

The *Toronto Star* later tracked down the two brothers out on parole. Russ said they were indeed painting signs in the area at the time "but we had nothing to do with it. If we had, the police would have questioned us." He said his brother Ronny had been mentally unbalanced ever since being shot in the head in an aborted bank robbery.

What neither the *Star* nor Trent knew was that as far back as November of 1967, the authorities had been aware of the story of Russ and Ronny. A letter from William Bowman, who represented the Crown at Steven's Supreme Court hearing, revealed that he and other officials met with psychiatrist George Scott just weeks before Steven's new hearing. They discussed Scott's "frequent examinations" of Ronny, with and without drugs. Bowman reported that Ronny claimed his brother "showed him the body of a young girl whom he said he had assaulted. . . . [Ronny] further indicated that he thought that the body was that of Lynne Harper." Bowman said both brothers "may be described as pedophiles." For some reason, though, Bowman concluded that "there was no connection between [these] statements and the Truscott case." Any investigation of the "Three Painters" quickly died.

Trent's book created enough renewed interest in the Harper affair that the press again began hovering around the Truscott home. That Steve was living under an assumed name in the community was one of Guelph's best-known "secrets."

To make matters worse, the book came out just days before Halloween, and Marlene was in a panic the night Lesley and Ryan were supposed to go trick-or-treating. "We were scared to answer the door," Marlene remembers.

"What were we going to do? I just didn't want the reporters to come to the door and say something in front of the kids." She decided to shut off all the lights in her home, bundle the children into a car and drive them to a friend's house at the other end of the city.

Lesley recalls being puzzled as she and her brother Ryan were not allowed to go trick-or-treating in their own neighbourhood. "I knew that something was wrong; I just couldn't figure it out," she says.

"They were disturbed because they couldn't understand why they were whisked away without any real explanation," Marlene admits. But she was tortured. How could she explain to her five- and eight-year-old children that their father had been convicted of raping and murdering a girl, that he did not do it, but the newspapers still wanted his picture.

To satisfy the public's thirst for more news on the Truscott story, Marlene agreed to do a series of radio interviews in Toronto with Bill Trent—a convenient way to speak out publicly while maintaining a fair degree of privacy. Marlene also appeared on *Canada AM* with her back to the camera.

Marlene knew she was pushing the limits of the code of silence by which Steve, his mother and siblings had chosen to live. "Steve said it was fine for me to go, but you don't want to drive a wedge into the family," Marlene recalls.

"I felt that if I did anything that caused any problems, then I'd really be in trouble," Marlene admits. "Yet I felt that I couldn't sit still on this. It was very hard on me. I felt alone—I was for a long time."

Her brief media exposure had two unexpected effects. In Toronto, Marlene met a young radio reporter named Trish Wood. "She was very pushy, and I liked her because of that," Marlene says. The two women exchanged phone numbers, and over the years Wood kept in touch with the Truscotts. That encounter in 1979 would eventually have immeasurably profound consequences for the entire Truscott family twenty years later.

Marlene's concealed appearance on TV also caught the attention of her neighbour, Christa Severa. She recognized Marlene's voice instantly and realized the "rapist" living next door was none other than Steven Truscott—the boy whose case she had followed even while in Germany, and in whose innocence she had always believed.

When Marlene returned home, there was a knock on the door and Christa stood at the entrance.

"Marlene, I saw you on TV," she said.

"Oh, really," Marlene muttered.

"I recognized your voice," Christa explained. "So Steve is Steven Truscott."

"I thought 'Oh my God, here we go again,'" Marlene recalls. "I was so afraid she wasn't going to talk to me, that she was going to ask me to move."

Instead, Christa explained her story—how she always sympathized with Steven Truscott—and apologized profusely for keeping her daughter away from Lesley. "What can I do to help?" she asked. As Christa got to know Marlene better, she discovered that underneath the normal bustle of a stay-at-home mother was a seething anger and frustration.

"We can't do what normal people do," Marlene once confided to Christa, who had just returned from a Florida vacation. Steve's reduced parole restrictions still barred him from entering the United States without declaring at the border that he was a convicted murderer. "Nobody knows what we had to go through, how our life has been affected by all this over the years."

"She was never going to give up," Christa recalls. "Marlene said, 'If it's the last thing I'll do, I'm going to fight for Steve.'"

Marlene's best friend, Maureen Hatton, elaborates: "You've got to realize where she is coming from. She is totally devoted to her husband. She's like a mother bear with cubs. Steve never answers the phone—she is so protective of him. 'You don't touch my husband and you don't touch my kids.'"

"It's a matter of your name, your pride, of holding your head up high," Maureen remembers Marlene telling her one day. "There have been a lot of tears; there are days when she has been down. I think she dug in her heels years ago and promised she was going to clear her husband's name. If she does nothing else she will do that—that's her whole mission."

In 1980, Marlene and Steve had their third and final child, Devon, a rambunctious boy who quickly grew into such a playful rascal his parents were sometimes tempted to replace the last two letters of his name with an *i* and an *l*.

"With Devon you never knew what to expect when you walked into that house," Marlene says. "The place could look like a bomb—believe me, Devon could do it, and Steve would just walk in and pick him up and hug him as if nothing had happened."

Steve today is philosophical about it all: "Things didn't bother me, after what I had gone through."

Marlene remembers one incident in particular, when Devon, as a toddler, smashed a carton of eggs on the kitchen floor.

"Look at the mess he made!" Marlene complained when Steve arrived from work.

"Oh, it's only eggs, it's no big deal," Steve said calmly.

But with Devon's older sister and brother, Lesley and Ryan, fast approaching their teenage years, Marlene and Steve had more pressing worries than broken eggs—they had to figure out soon when and what to tell the children about Steve's past.

"When is the right time?" Steve asks himself today. "You kind of have an age in mind, but have you waited too long or are you going to tell them before they even understand?"

"It is one of those things where you say to yourself: we'll know for each one of them," Marlene says. "I sort of got it in my mind that it would be fourteen—because if their dad could go through with what he did then, they could listen to it—they could go through it too."

The children were already curious about why their name was different than so many of their cousins, aunts and uncles on Steve's side of the family.

"How come they are all Truscotts?" they asked.

"Well, your grandmother married twice," Marlene replied. While not a lie—Doris had remarried—it was hardly an explanation. Marlene realized it would only satisfy the children for a while. "I knew they had to know soon because they were getting too old not to know."

As it happened, it was in school that Lesley first discovered the truth. Browsing through the library one day, she stumbled across Bill Trent's book, *The Steven Truscott Story*. "I recognized the last name from my aunts and uncles," Lesley remembers. "I took it out, read the back, leafed through it. I started looking at the pictures, and I recognized my grandmother, my aunts, my uncles and I'm thinking, 'Oh my gosh! This is my dad!'" Lesley was twelve at the time.

Lesley kept her discovery to herself until two years later, when her mother called her into the living room one day. "She had all the books out on the table, and she said, 'I have to talk to you about something,'" Lesley says.

"Mom, I already know," Lesley said, surprising her mother. "I don't believe it—I don't understand it, how could they have done this?" Lesley asked about the jailing and sentencing of her father.

Three years later, when Ryan turned fourteen, Marlene broached the subject with him as well, only to discover that he too had seen the book. But for Steve's oldest son there was a special poignancy about being fourteen and discovering his father's story. "I thought of all the things I got to do when I was fourteen that he missed. I thought of having my family taken away, having my friends taken away, the place that I lived, all my belongings, all my clothing, everything taken away from me," Ryan says. "And to be able to live through it to tell about it."

Devon, the youngest child, did not find out until he was an adolescent in the mid-1990s, when a more cynical generation had grown up surrounded by legal scandals in real life and many tales of wrongful convictions on movie and TV screens. The teenager had only one question for his mother about his father's dramatic life at fourteen:

"Tell me he didn't wear red pants," Devon quipped.

Marlene had made a conscious decision to talk to the children about their father's past without Steve present. "I just felt I was the better one to tell them, because there were things I could say about him that he couldn't say about himself," she explains. "There's just no way I would have married him if I thought [the accusation of murder] was true, and I sure as hell would have found out over the years."

Steve was relieved his children, once they were old enough to understand, had learned the truth. "I didn't want to burden them with what happened to me years ago," Steve says, "but I think they accepted me for who I am."

Indeed, if anything, the discovery of what their father went through seemed to raise Steve's stature in the eyes of his children. "I think I myself would be very angry. And he's not. Not at all," Lesley says. "He's an absolutely incredible father. I can't believe they would even think of blaming something like that on him."

"I never once doubted him. Never once," says Ryan. "He stood his ground for what he believed in and that was the truth. I'm sure that he had opportunities where he could have gotten a lesser sentence by admitting to something that he didn't do, and he didn't. He stood his ground. And he's always instilled that in us—that if you wait and you're a good person, it'll all come back to you someday."

Knowing the full story of their father's past did not make things much simpler for the children—it just meant they were now part of the game of keeping the family secret. "You couldn't tell certain people your name, and you had to be very careful when it got to family trees or things like that at school," Lesley says. "So we always kind of skirted around problems like that."

One day in a grade Eleven class on law, Lesley found herself squirming in her seat as her teacher launched a discussion about the famous case.

"I hear he lives in Guelph," one student said.

"I hear he has kids here," another added, as Lesley grew increasingly uncomfortable. When class was over she approached the teacher.

"Please tell me that we're not going to do any more on this subject," she said.

"Why?" he asked. "Does it bother you?"

"Yes, it does."

"Well, it bothers me too, to see an innocent man sit in jail for ten years for something he didn't do."

"Well, it bothers me for a different reason—he's my father," Lesley blurted.

"His chin must have hit the floor," Lesley remembers.

"You're kidding!" the teacher gasped. "Oh my gosh, I can't believe it!"

"Do you want to meet him?" Lesley offered.

"Are you kidding? Are you serious? I can meet him?" the teacher asked.

"Sure," Lesley said, with not a little pride in her voice. "You know, he's just my dad."

The next day after school, Lesley brought Steve over to the school. "It's a pleasure to meet you, sir," the teacher said, still somewhat in shock.

As an involved parent, Steve spent a lot of time at his children's schools. He and Marlene often volunteered for special days and activities. Steve particularly enjoyed going on ski trips with the students. When Ryan graduated from elementary school, the Truscotts had the entire school staff—more than thirty teachers—over to their house for a party.

"He'd play with kids all the time. He was always out there, with his kids, the neighbourhood kids," says neighbour Gary Samson. "I think in part it was to get back into his childhood, to get back things he missed."

Joan Brock, another neighbour, recalls that Steve was never shy about showing his affection—always hugging and embracing his children. "Loving is touching," she says. "He would not have had a lot of that while in jail. He was a hands-on father."

Ryan, Steve's oldest son, agrees. "He always tried to do things with us that I think he missed," he says. "He was always very involved with our lives as we were growing up."

Steve's children also realized they could exploit that soft spot in their dad. If Marlene grounded them for misbehaving, Lesley and Ryan would try to get their father to reduce the sentence. "Somehow or another they'd work their way around him and he'd say, 'Oh well, you know, they're young and you should let them go,'" Marlene recalls. "I think it was because he was confined as a teenager. He wanted them to have a lot of things he didn't have."

While Steve was entirely devoted to his children, he did manage to find time to indulge himself in two passions he forfeited as a young man: motorcycles and planes. In the fall of 1980, Steve's brother Bill brought him a beat-up black motorcycle someone had abandoned. Steve spent the entire winter in his basement rebuilding the bike to perfection—only to discover that once assembled, it was almost impossible to get the machine up the stairs and outside.

The tinkering suited Steve's mechanical bent, but speeding along the highways also gave Steve a rush, a sense of exhilaration. It was as if he were also trying to race back in time to become an eighteen-year-old showing off his new bike to the girls at the drive-in diner.

Perhaps Steve daydreamed too much about those lost days while cruising down the road. After one especially nasty spill, Marlene forced him to sell the bike. He did, only to buy a bigger one at a garage sale. He kept that bike—a red Yamaha 750—until the early 1990s.

As a young kid on an air base, Steve had also dreamed of being a pilot. But his arrest in 1959 curtailed that dream. Twenty years later, while driving by an airstrip outside of Guelph, Marlene noticed Steve longingly looking at the small planes taking off from a local flying school.

"Geez, I knew he would just love to fly," Marlene says. "He would never tell me—he would never do that. But I always knew that was his passion." As a Father's Day present, she bought him a gift certificate for a lesson. Steve put more money aside for the expensive lessons—not easy to do while supporting a family on a single salary. Never a disciplined student in Clinton, Steve started cracking the books and staying up late to master the theory and technical requirements. He thrilled at every chance he got to fly the Cessna planes with an instructor. A year later, out of more than thirty students, he was one of a handful who made the grade and graduated from flying school.

To Steve's everlasting regret, he was never able to take his father up for a ride. Dan Truscott—bursting with pride when he learned one of his sons was going to be a pilot—died just two weeks before Steve finally got his licence. But Steve took almost every other member of his family for a spin. He teased his friends and neighbours by buzzing perilously close to their rooftops and waving his wings. "You're cutting the grass a little low," one of his instructors commented wryly when he caught sight of Steve's daredevil moves.

"To be up there alone, he feels free—away from everything," Marlene says.

Steve's sense of freedom as he soared over the skies of Guelph had little to do with escaping the daily pressures of raising a family. It was not even the freedom from the confinement he felt in prison. The feeling was of freedom from his jailers—the police, the judges, the jurors, the doctors and the guards—those who, for too long, held the keys to his life and his future.

"You're up there by yourself," he sighs, "and you're the one in control of your destiny."

Destiny also meant accepting that one day, the children he so cherished would grow up and leave home. In September 1994 Steve had to go through a rite of passage that is a milestone in a father's life—the marriage of his daughter.

At Guelph's Trinity United Church—just three blocks away from the house where Steve and Marlene first met in 1970—Lesley walked down the aisle accompanied by her father, dashingly handsome in a tuxedo with a white carnation in the lapel. After the ceremony, more than 150 guests packed the local legion hall for some speeches, laughter, singing and dancing.

"Marlene didn't have the wedding that she dreamed of, so she gave it to Lesley," said the Truscotts' friend Gary Samson.

"You're happy, but you're sad," Steve says, remembering the day the daughter he had cradled in his arms twenty-three years earlier became a married woman. Prison kept him from his older brother's wedding, countless family birthdays and Christmas celebrations. He did not want to forget this special family moment for a long, long time. "You don't really know what you've missed until you're out of prison."

At Lesley's wedding, as Marlene took to the floor with Steve, alongside the bride and groom, Ryan and a friend sang one of Lesley's favourite tunes from the recently released movie *Aladdin* entitled "A Whole New World."

A whole new world was indeed about to begin for Steven and the Truscott family, as changes in the legal landscape in Canada, a bold decision to break a forty-year silence, and a dramatic television program would alter their lives forever.

# PART FIVE

## THE FINAL BATTLE

*"What they did was wrong. And that's all I want them to do: say they were wrong. I'm not asking for the world. Go over all the information. Investigate it. Let the people know all the evidence. . . . I'm not afraid of that. Why are they?"*

—Steven Truscott

## 41

## OUT OF THE SHADOWS

The dam broke in the summer of 1997. As with most floods, it began as just a trickle, a small crack in the wall of silence.

"One night we were sitting outside," Marlene remembers. "It was dark out and we were drinking coffee."

"I want to ask you something," Marlene said to her husband.

"Yeah?" Steve answered.

"Did you really think they were going to hang you?" his wife asked.

"Yup," came the simple reply.

"You would know that they wouldn't do that to someone so young, wouldn't you?" Marlene pursued.

"Every time my lawyer said they weren't going to do something, they did, so why would I think anything different about hanging?"

"Oh, for years I wanted to ask him—I was dying to know," Marlene explains today. That first question on the front porch was the start of countless probes she made into her husband's memory. "I started to ask him more questions and more questions," Marlene says. "All I knew is that there was something desperately wrong with the case."

There had always been a sort of unwritten rule in the Truscott household: they would talk about Steve's case when they had to—when the Trent book or the fictionalized movie came out, for instance, or when the children asked. Generally, however, the subject was avoided. The priority was on raising the family in safety and in privacy.

But by the late 1990s, the two oldest children, Lesley and Ryan, were in their twenties and Devon was almost eighteen. Canada had matured too—people no longer believed that the justice system was infallible. In fact, several high-profile scandals had revealed just how tragically wrong the police and the courts could be.

Not long before the porch talk, in July of 1997, Steve and Marlene watched the TV news in amazement: DNA testing had exonerated a man from Saskatchewan named David Milgaard, jailed for almost a quarter of a century for a murder he did not commit.

If it worked for Milgaard, maybe it could work for Steven. "It was the number of years in the Milgaard case that got us," Steve remembers. "That kind of sparked the hope that there was a chance."

David Milgaard was only seventeen when police arrested him in 1969 for the sex slaying of Gail Miller, a nursing aide in Saskatoon. He spent twenty-three years of hell behind bars. He was raped, tried to commit suicide, escaped twice and was even shot once. After a relentless campaign by his mother, Joyce, to clear her son's name, the Supreme Court of Canada finally ordered a new trial in 1992, and the charges were then stayed until DNA cleared him.

Milgaard's case was the latest in a series of wrongful conviction cases. In 1983, the Nova Scotia Court of Appeal acquitted Donald Marshall Jr. for a 1971 murder, after he had spent eleven years in prison. Marshall had been just sixteen when police arrested him. News stories and talk in the community eventually led the police to discover that one of the chief witnesses who accused Marshall of stabbing a friend actually had been the one who wielded the knife. A royal commission, concluding that "the criminal justice system failed . . . at virtually every turn," made sweeping recommendations to reform the justice system.

In 1986, Guy Paul Morin was tried for the murder of his nine-year-old neighbour, Christine Jessop, in Queensville, Ontario. Morin, who had spent almost a year in custody, was acquitted at his first trial, but police arrested him again when the Court of Appeal reversed the jury's verdict. A second jury found Morin guilty in July 1992, after a nine-month trial with more than a hundred witnesses. The Ontario courts condemned Guy Paul Morin to prison for life. Morin's supporters and a group of dedicated Toronto lawyers set up a defence committee, and by early 1993 they scored an important victory—Morin was released on bail.

The defence committee held a party to wind down their activities. But one of the lawyers there—James Lockyer, an outspoken advocate with a mane of curly hair and a booming voice—pulled a couple of his friends and colleagues aside. "You shouldn't be closing down," he said. "We should be expanding."

Lockyer had been practising law in Canada since 1977, but he still had enough of a British accent to give away his University of Nottingham days. The accent wasn't the only thing that endured. "I've always been interested in miscarriages of justice," he says. "It goes with my left-wing politics from university on."

Lockyer sat down to draft the objectives of a permanent organization devoted to uncovering cases of injustice, and in May 1993, the Association in Defence of the Wrongly Convicted (AIDWYC) was born. Theirs was a novel approach. Glaring examples of judicial screw-ups made headlines, but the public and the news media generally regarded these cases as isolated, if somewhat horrific. AIDWYC challenged that comfortable illusion.

"We were suggesting that wrongful convictions are not an uncommon occurrence," Lockyer says. "There are all sorts of systemic problems within the trial process that helps produce them."

Over the next few years, AIDWYC organized a series of public conferences. While the association has become a credible lobbyist for government reforms, its most useful function is as a sort of clearing house for expertise and resources on overturning wrongful convictions. An AIDWYC review committee of three lawyers examines prospective cases, and, if deemed suitable, a legal team is assembled. That's important, Lockyer explains, because most defence lawyers, by definition, think first of defending: throw something at them, they try to deflect it.

"They are not used to the role—and therefore they don't play the role—of carrying the case," he says. "When you're trying to expose wrongful convictions, you are really the prosecutor. You're the one who has to satisfy everyone beyond a reasonable doubt."

It did not take long for AIDWYC lawyers to produce results.

Lockyer headed up Guy Paul Morin's appeal and in January 1995, DNA testing exonerated Morin—almost ten years after police first charged him. Lockyer's next high-profile case was that of David Milgaard. In July 1997, the science of DNA finally proved Milgaard was innocent. Milgaard's mother, Joyce, became an active director of AIDWYC.

Milgaard, Morin, Marshall. They all became household names in Canada, very public symbols of justice gone awry. But AIDWYC says its conservative estimate is that at least forty other people are currently serving sentences of life imprisonment for crimes they did not commit.

In 1959, Steven Truscott's arrest and subsequent death sentence elicited barely a murmur of protest over the speed of the conviction or the justness of it. Four decades later, the mood in the country had changed dramatically. Investigative journalists were digging into dubious trials. Committed lawyers were defending the wrongfully convicted. Science had developed sophisticated DNA tests that—given the proper and available evidence— could prove guilt or innocence.

It was time for Steven to step out of the shadows.

The 1996–97 TV season for *the fifth estate*, the CBC's flagship current affairs program, had been a busy one, with exposés on everything from Big Tobacco to Karla Homolka. At one point in the mad rush to research stories, film interviews and make deadlines, Trish Wood, one of the hosts, approached me about the possibility of producing a documentary on the Truscott case. I wrote a memo proposing "a fascinating piece about Canada before Morin, before Marshall . . . the case of a brutal slaying and the lingering controversy." Executive producer David Studer and senior producer Susan Teskey quickly endorsed it.

Wood had kept in touch with the Truscotts ever since she had first met Marlene in 1979. "She kept phoning and phoning," Marlene says, "and we were waiting for the kids to get older."

When Wood approached her in 1997, Marlene finally agreed to discuss the possibility of doing a TV program with Steve. She also agreed to talk with a researcher from *the fifth estate*, Theresa Burke.

The Truscotts knew that if they were going to take the plunge, *the fifth estate* was the natural place for them to turn. Aside from their connection with one of the hosts, the show had a wide national audience and a well-earned reputation for hard-hitting journalism.

The show also had begun to earn a track record for examinations of wrongful convictions. In the 1990s, *the fifth estate* had produced documentaries on the cases of David Milgaard and Guy Paul Morin. For the 1997–98 season, Trish Wood and producer Harvey Cashore were beginning work on the controversial case of a Nova Scotia man, Clayton Johnson, who had been imprisoned in 1993 for murdering his wife. Lockyer and AIDWYC had uncovered serious flaws in his conviction. Eventually, AIDWYC helped win a review of his case and Johnson was released on bail.

In principle, the Truscotts knew *the fifth estate* was the right choice, but after thirty years of anonymity, Steve was not going to make up his mind about going public overnight. Disagreements began to emerge between Steve and Marlene about how far they would go.

On the simplest level, Steve and Marlene had radically different perceptions of the media. "I felt without the press he had nothing," Marlene says. "I think the media have been damn decent."

Steve was more cautious. "You have to remember at the trial what the news did to me," he explains, still smarting from the uncritical coverage that portrayed him as a sexual monster. "My level of trust was very low."

But the differences between Steven and Marlene ran much deeper than that. "I always wanted this, it's here now, I have my opportunity to fight—I don't give a damn what everybody thinks, this is what I am going to do," Marlene says.

For too long she had restrained herself, even though she longed to campaign openly for her husband's innocence. Marlene felt that Steve—to his own credit but also to his disadvantage—had sacrificed himself in order to save Doris and his brothers and sister the agony of another public controversy. They, after all, still had the Truscott name; he, Marlene and the three children lived under an assumed name.

"It was a very touchy thing. I always felt that Steve—and it wasn't for his own reasons—didn't want anything brought out. You didn't want the flak from the family, right?"

"Yeah, pretty much." Steve admits.

"I'm not knocking that—I understand that," she says. "But it was not going to happen with our family—it's my children, my husband, it's my life—and he's a big boy. He's in his fifties, he's not fourteen."

"I don't want to start anything—it only causes problems. There are people that can be hurt," Steve told Marlene.

499

"It's about time you looked after number one instead of everybody else," she answered.

Steve sympathized with his wife's frustration. But he had been burnt too often in the past, proclaiming his innocence to psychiatrists who would not listen, to a Supreme Court that rejected his pleas. "I got nowhere. Nobody would listen, nobody cared," he says. "Up until that point, nobody gave a damn. The turning point was *the fifth estate*."

Marlene convinced Steven *the fifth estate* would give a damn. But even as Marlene patiently nudged and prodded her husband, Steven wanted to get permission from his three grown children. "If I thought for a moment it would harm the kids, it would end," he says.

"You don't ask them, you tell them," Marlene said to her husband. "You've asked too many people too much in your life what to do. For the first time in your life, tell family members what *you* want to do. You're going to fight this thing and you're going to win it."

In the end, Marlene and Steve compromised. They met with their children, not to ask for approval to go forward, but to consult with them over the risks and benefits. To Steve's relief, far from being nervous, his children were tremendously excited about the prospect of a renewed public battle.

"He's getting older and we are getting old enough to realize how much of a problem this is," Ryan says. "He really needs to have somebody help him so that he can go on and live the rest of his life knowing that somebody has admitted to being wrong in this case."

"It's always got to be there in the back of his mind at all times. Nobody's ever proven him innocent." Lesley says. "And I think for a sense of peace— just to put it to rest—I think he deserves it."

As senior producer at *the fifth estate*, Susan Teskey was in charge of the day-to-day operations of the show. A veteran field producer with a reputation for being both scrappy and dogged, Teskey had put together the documentary that helped garner wide public sympathy for Guy Paul Morin's innocence.

Teskey agreed with the Truscotts that there might be a chance some DNA traces were still available from the Lynne Harper crime scene. But to make the formal request for evidence and launch the long legal battle over DNA, the Truscotts were going to need a lawyer. Due to his success with DNA evidence in the Morin and Milgaard cases, James Lockyer was the logical choice.

Lockyer drove to Guelph to meet Steve and Marlene. In the cool of an autumn evening, James Lockyer asked Steve to step outside with him. The two men turned south to the end of Steve's dead-end street and entered a park that ran along the Eramosa River. It was a time of assessment for both men. Steve was wary of lawyers who, however devoted to his case, never seemed to include him profoundly in their plans and deliberations. Lockyer, for his part, had to size up this potential new client.

"I laid it on pretty thick," Lockyer recalls. "I told him I was very confident we could find DNA samples." In fact, Lockyer had little idea what the chances were, but he needed to test Steve's resolve. "I made it very clear that the perpetrator would have left behind his DNA," he says, "and the fact that forty years had passed was neither here nor there."

"If they've got DNA samples, I can guarantee you a result," Lockyer told Steven. "And if it's you, if you're the one who killed Lynne Harper, you're being suicidal to go ahead with this. Because I'll prove it in no time—simplest thing in the world."

"Let's go for it," Steve said without a moment's hesitation. "I have nothing to hide—go for it."

Steven decided to retain Lockyer as his lawyer and the hunt for DNA officially began in the fall of 1997. There was, at first, every reason to hope that if the evidence and exhibits were preserved, some of it might contain DNA from Lynne's killer. The most likely source would be the bodily fluids taken from the girl's vagina. There were also fingernail scrapings from Lynne containing "traces of blood," possibly from her assailant. Some of the blood found on her clothing and on leaves and twigs near her body might have come from her attacker. Her underpants and other clothes might also hold clues.

Lockyer wrote to the Centre for Forensic Sciences—the successor to the attorney general's laboratory that had done the tests in 1959—to see if they had specimens, including the microscopic slides prepared by Penistan, the cotton-tipped applicator used to collect fluids, and a bottle with seal number 2205 containing material from Lynne's vagina.

"They're looking. They might be somewhere or they might not," an official with the Ontario solicitor general's office told reporters. "Until they've run out of places to look, they'll keep on trying."

News of the DNA search leaked out in the *Toronto Sun*, and the sudden re-emergence of the Truscott case created a flurry of media interest.

"Talk of the Town Again—DNA twist has small town buzzing anew about Steven Truscott" was the headline for a *London Free Press* article about Clinton. Most residents interviewed seemed genuinely enthusiastic. "At the time I thought he was guilty," said Anna VanderHeyden, a fifty-five-year-old florist. "Now I have my doubts. I hope we'll finally know the truth."

On the other hand, there were the usual naysayers. The *Toronto Star* contacted their veteran crime reporter Gwynn "Jocko" Thomas, who had always been on good terms with the OPP's Harold Graham. "There's no chance of this being a travesty of justice," he said. "It was a very strong case of circumstantial evidence."

At OPP headquarters in Orillia, D. I. Jim Wilson started a new file on October 27, 1997, and began keeping track of the media coverage on the Truscott affair. Wilson insisted it was normal procedure. "Any information that is received, you look at," he said. Still, it was hard not to grasp the irony: the case that his former boss—Harold Graham, the head of the OPP—had cracked as a young homicide detective in 1959 had come back to haunt the force once again.

So intense was the media frenzy, lawyer James Lockyer had to issue a press release. "Mr. Truscott and his family appreciate the interest shown by the media, but now request that their anonymity be preserved and their privacy respected," he urged, at least until the results of the hunt for DNA were known.

It did not take long to discover that the DNA trail was cold. Nothing remained from a forty-year-old case that, after all, had long been settled in the eyes of the law. The final tally on the evidence list was clear—next to all of the items appeared the words "Presumed Destroyed."

There was some confusion, nevertheless, on exactly what happened to the evidence. "All exhibits in this case are now destroyed," reported a September 1962 OPP memorandum. "The officers stayed until everything was consumed by fire." But some medical evidence might have survived, because in February of 1968, Graham was writing to Keith Simpson, the British medical expert who testified for the Crown at the Supreme Court, stating that he was looking for microscopic slides from the Harper autopsy. "I have been unable to find them in Canada," Graham said.

"We knew it was a 50-50 thing," Marlene says. "It wasn't a huge disappointment."

Still, it was a crushing setback for the lawyers. DNA is the "magic bullet" in any legal appeal. It would have been the fastest, most conclusive way to prove whether or not Steven Truscott killed Lynne Harper. "That would have been the end of the case," says Lockyer. "That was a simple task. It became a very complicated one."

Now *the fifth estate* investigators would have to do a lot more digging to find the truth.

Through his lawyer, Steven filed a request with the Ontario government to obtain thousands of pages of documents from court transcripts, police notes and Crown records—most of them never before seen by any member of the public. In the 1960s, author Isabel LeBourdais and lawyer Arthur Martin had read the original trial transcripts and a couple of police witness statements, but they had no access to anything as vast as this treasure trove of secret files.

"When some of that stuff came in, I couldn't believe it," Steve says.

"Oh, it was so real—it all came at once," Marlene recalls. "The boxes came on a Saturday. We were supposed to go to a wedding and I didn't even want to go." She remembers the excitement of capturing a snapshot of history.

"Oh my God—look at Harold Graham's writing!" she exclaimed upon seeing one document.

For the first time, here were the many confusing police statements made by Jocelyne and Butch. Here were the witnesses the police and prosecutor had kept from the defence and the jurors. Here was the memorandum from Dr. Noble Sharpe criticizing Penistan's narrow window for the time of death. Here was a handwritten police note about Jocelyne claiming she was looking for Lynne; another about a possible 9:00 p.m. time of death; yet another note concerning Lynne's hitchhiking. Marlene discovered that most of the important witness statements given to the police were signed by the children themselves. Butch George's and Steven's were not.

The leads opened up many new avenues for investigation. Marlene devoured each document, committing most to memory. Like well-known activist Erin Brockovich, Marlene had the ability to instantly recall the most minute and arcane detail.

"It was all bottled up inside; now I can really get into it," she confided in her friend Pat Corbit.

"She would jump up and cry, 'Look what I found!'" Maureen Hatton, another good friend, recounts. "I don't think a lawyer can even get close to the way she fine-tooth combs everything. I swear to God she must think about this case twenty-four hours a day."

Marlene explains that everyone with blood ties to Steve—his parents, his brothers and sister, his own children—had no choice about getting involved in the case. They were born into the Truscott family. Marlene is the only family member who made a conscious decision.

"I chose to get involved with the campaign in 1966 and I chose to marry him," she says. "I knew what I was getting into and I wanted it."

For all her obsession with the case, Marlene created a protective barrier in her mind between the boy caught up in the whirlwind of 1959 and the man she married. Sometimes, she would be explaining to Steve a new piece of evidence she had discovered in the boxes, only to catch herself talking about him in the third person—"Steve did this" or "Steve did that."

"Steve?" her husband would interrupt her. "That's me."

"I still see a boy on a bike that I never knew," Marlene says. "There was this ten-year gap—I had heard about this young boy and then I got this man that I married, but there was something missing. I needed to make that separation. If I didn't, it would be harder on me."

Marlene's hunt for clues also got the better of her as days of research turned into weeks, the weeks into months, the months stretching over a couple of years. "You live and breathe those boxes, Mom, but there's other things going around that you're missing," Ryan warned her when his sister, Lesley, was pregnant. "She's having a baby, she's very excited, and you sort of put her on the back burner."

"It was then that I realized I was putting too much into it," Marlene admits. She cooled her efforts, if only slightly.

In general, though, the children were thrilled with the buzz around the case. Steve himself could sense the difference. "We were finally where Marlene wanted to be in the first place—we were finally talking about things," Steve says. "It was exciting. After all these years, we were finally out."

More excitement came in January 1998 when Susan Teskey brought a special visitor to the Truscott home—Guy Paul Morin. It was hard to tell who was more in awe—the young man whose recent victory in the courts made his name synonymous with bad justice, or the fifty-three-year-old who for decades had been a symbol to many Canadians of a troubled trial.

"He is a pioneer of the wrongfully convicted," says Morin. "Hearing about him all those years, and then for me to even have the honour to meet him and see him—wow!—I was taken aback. He's got strength about him in such a calm way. I think it's what carried him through."

The two "vets from the war of injustice," as Morin put it, connected instantly. There seemed to exist a kind of emotional radar between two men who had spent years behind bars protesting their innocence. Over a lasagna dinner, they swapped stories about Kingston's jail cells, prison life and the striking similarities in their cases.

The judge who presided over Morin's second trial was James Donnelly, the son of Frank Donnelly, Steve's first lawyer. The chief pathologist in Morin's case had to admit he missed rather obvious injuries in his autopsy. And jurors in both trials seemed to be convinced of guilt in part because of the way the defendant behaved. One juror at Morin's trial told *the fifth estate* he was disturbed by the fact that Morin "never once looked at us."

"If I was innocent, I would have been hollering and screaming," the juror said, eerily echoing the words of a juror in Steve's trial four decades earlier.

"The parallels are uncanny," concluded Morin. As he gripped Steven's hand to say goodbye, Morin urged him to keep his wits about him.

"Always have confidence. You know yourself. You know you're innocent," he said. "Justice will prevail." They were surprisingly optimistic words considering the legal history of the man who uttered them.

"The Guy Paul Morin case is not an aberration," warned Judge Fred Kaufman, appointed by the province to investigate what went so disastrously wrong with Morin's prosecution. "Science helped convict him. Science exonerated him," he said. "One can expect that there are other innocent persons, swept up in the criminal process, for whom DNA results are unavailable."

Steve knew he was one of those people who could not count on DNA evidence. One evening, Marlene and Steve were having another of their late-night porch chats.

"*The fifth estate* will get into this and they'll find something," Marlene assured her husband. "I think this is what you need."

"I hope it happens in my lifetime," Steve said, in an uncharacteristically emotional moment.

"I found that very sad," Marlene remembers.

In the summer of 1998, the filming of the Truscott story hit an unexpected roadblock.

Trish Wood, the journalist assigned to the story, and James Lockyer, Steven's lawyer, began a personal relationship. The CBC, like most media organizations, had very strict conflict-of-interest guidelines. It would hardly do for the journalist on such a controversial story to be involved with the protagonist's lawyer.

CBC management decided that Wood would have to give up the story to another journalist. She initially opposed the idea of withdrawing from a story that had been close to her heart for so many years. The dispute led to other differences with *fifth estate* senior executives, and CBC management did not renew Wood's contract. She eventually worked out a settlement with the corporation.

Only after a year-long hiatus did the CBC resume production on the documentary, this time with Linden MacIntyre as the host.

It was now the early summer of 1999, but it would be almost another year before the CBC would broadcast the finished program. Many people assume when they watch a TV documentary that the producers decide which pictures they need, then go out and film those sequences, get quotes from various people, and stick it all together more or less according to a pre-set plan.

The reality of investigative journalism is far more complex and frustrating. For every minute shown on television, a crew can film anywhere from thirty to sixty minutes. The completed Truscott documentary was about forty-seven minutes long, but the team had over forty-five hours of interviews, visuals and archives on tape. In addition, there were hundreds more hours of unrecorded interviews and research.

The *fifth estate* team tracked down and spoke to twenty-four child witnesses, three jurors, more than fifty people from the Clinton area and a dozen military and police officials. Pathologists, rape specialists and medical experts on stomach contents were consulted, as were lawyers and legal historians.

The team proceeded without any preconceived notions of Steven's innocence or guilt—at times, for the sake of thoroughness, even presuming guilt and trying to prove the case for the prosecution. Only when holes could be punched in every element in that theory could a solid and balanced case for miscarriage be made.

Accordingly, the CBC followed many leads, even if they seemed unfavourable to Steve's cause. One such lead was the possibility that Philip Burns, the ten-year-old boy in 1959 so crucial to the prosecution case, had changed his story. The Crown convinced the jury, and later, the Supreme Court, that Philip did not spot Steven and Lynne on the county road because they must have gone into the bush. Forty years later, Philip was saying he might indeed have seen Steven and Lynne walking near the bush, a new story that had the potential to be much more damaging to Steven.

"I remembered seeing two people back at the corner of the woods pushing a green racing bike," Burns told the CBC, "and . . . it jogged my memory that Steve had a green racing bike." But when pushed, Burns admitted he could not make out the faces of the children "a good quarter of a mile" away. "Whether they were two boys, boy and a girl, two girls I have no idea," he said.

If Burns did see someone, it likely was not Steve and Lynne. During the interview, Burns pointed to a map to indicate where he said he saw the two people: at the far northeast end of Lawson's field where the tip of the bush approaches the river—nowhere near where the body was found or where the prosecution implied Steve dragged Lynne into the woods.

Burns also could not explain why, minutes after seeing these two children, he told Jocelyne and Butch that he had not seen Steve or Lynne. Furthermore, Burns had no explanation why just days later, under intense questioning from the police, he denied seeing Steve and Lynne near the bush—only to recall the vision later.

The making of the documentary was a pursuit of many such false leads, dead ends, recalcitrant or confused witnesses, mixed in with just plain luck—good and bad. Several key witnesses had died just months or sometimes even weeks before *the fifth estate* managed to locate them or their families. After many months, Theresa Burke finally tracked down Butch George, and contacted him through a family member, but he refused to be interviewed. None of the surviving police officers wanted to talk at the time, and the two doctors still alive—Dr. Addison and Dr. Brooks—declined to be interviewed on camera.

Burke spent long weeks tracking down other people; in one case, more than two thousand people across Canada with a common surname were contacted in what turned out to be a wasted attempt to locate a possible witness (the name provided by a former base resident had been wrong). The Internet proved invaluable in finding children who had lived on the Clinton air force base in 1959, but then had scattered across the country, married, and sometimes changed names. Through chat groups and reunion pages on the Web for Canadian "military brats," *the fifth estate* appealed for help, information and even home videos. Local museums came up with photographs and other memorabilia from the era.

Some filming took place in the early fall, even while the research was ongoing. The Clinton area had changed little over time: the road Steve bicycled down, Lawson's bush, the bridge and the river were all much as they had been in 1959. Student volunteers from the local high school—many of whom had studied the Truscott case in class—helped with the re-enactments. They wore fifties-style clothes, rode creaky old bicycles and played with ancient-looking baseball gloves and skipping ropes. The program producers decided to film these black-and-white sequences with old film stock, rather than modern videotape, to give the scenes a grainy, textured look.

A highlight of the filming came when Steven consented to return to Clinton with Linden MacIntyre, to amble across the schoolyard where he played as a child, travel down the county road he biked on so often as a boy, and walk to the bush where Lynne's body was found. A grey-haired grandfather, he stood on the same bridge where he often came as a teenager, and told the TV cameras about the last time he saw Lynne Harper on June 9, 1959.

Meanwhile, *the fifth estate* crew was turning up new leads. By late 1999, a young journalist with a law degree, Dallas Brodie, joined the research team. She contacted surviving jurors and medical experts, and helped co-producer Theresa Burke dig into an intriguing mystery—the file of Sgt. Alexander Kalichuk. Willard Longley, the retired air force officer who had stumbled across the file in the 1960s, had been in contact with *the fifth estate* since the fall. He talked about his chilling discovery of a "sexual deviant" in the Clinton area, but declined to give up the name of the suspect and was reluctant to get involved any further; he then left for an extended motor home vacation in Mexico.

The researchers at *the fifth estate* hoped that documents related to Longley's investigations might be located in the records of the Department of Defence, even without a name of the suspect. So they filed an Access to Information request; the military came back empty-handed, insisting they had no records of any correspondence between Longley and headquarters about the Truscott case. What's more, the military had transferred all their old files over to the National Archives in Ottawa, where archivists said they would be unable to look through tens of thousands of boxes of personnel records without a name.

Dallas Brodie then phoned and faxed every trailer park in Mexico until she located the wayward Willard Longley, who finally called back and gave up the name of the suspect. The archivists then went through the boxes from the Clinton air force base. But to everyone's surprise, nothing was found. What no one knew at the time was that Longley had misspelled Kalichuk's name—and furthermore, Kalichuk's file was with another air force station.

By February 2000, Gary Akenhead, a talented film and videotape editor, began the daunting task of cutting hours of pictures and interviews down into a television story—even as final research continued. Typically, a *fifth estate* documentary will go through about a half dozen "cuts" or versions before the final cut is approved. The Truscott program went through more than ten revisions over a period of two months before senior producer Susan Teskey gave her thumbs-up. With so much good material that couldn't be used, the show decided to build a Web site, featuring everything from Philip Burns's new story to Glen Sage's sighting of the footprints and Harold Graham's confidential memos.

Up until the last minute, there were dramatic additions to the documentary. Steve and Marlene had nervously agreed to let the cameras film a family get-together, but they were adamant that they did not want their children interviewed. The producers believed viewers would want to hear what it was like growing up in the Truscott household. Finally the Truscotts relented and Linden MacIntyre travelled to Guelph to interview Lesley and Ryan. Their story was among the most riveting material in the documentary.

Also in the final days before deadline came the big break in the Kalichuk file. Andrew Whorl, an intrepid researcher at the National Archives, decided to check through the boxes from the Aylmer base, which was located not far from Clinton. It did not take him long to find the Kalichuk records—and a file that had been hidden for forty years was about to make news across the country.

In their small living room on March 29, 2000, Steve and Marlene Truscott gathered around the television set with their children. Most of their friends assumed they had already seen the program, but CBC policy forbids participants in a documentary from getting an advance screening or having any say in content.

Steve, forever mistrustful of the powers-that-be, continued to doubt the show would make it to air. "I figured right up until the night that it aired that something was going to happen and they weren't going to put it on," he says.

Even the advertisements in *TV Guide* did not convince him. "I was more shocked that it came on, than what was in it," Steve says.

When the program was finally broadcast that Wednesday evening, over 1.4 million Canadians tuned in to watch Steven emerge from the shadows. "His Word Against History: The Steven Truscott Story" was one of the highest-rated documentaries on the network that year. It touched a deep chord with Canadians who had grown up with the story, and reached out to younger citizens who had never heard the name Steven Truscott.

"In a Goderich, Ontario, jail cell, he awaited the hangman," MacIntyre's voiceover began over sombre black-and-white pictures of the brick prison walls and the bleak, dark cell. "He was fourteen."

Pierre Berton read excerpts from his moving poem about a boy "too old to cringe and too old to cry, but never too young to die." Then, in a dramatic moment, black-and-white footage of a little boy bicycling down a road in the 1950s dissolved into colour footage of running shoes on bike pedals. As the camera slowly revealed the feet and body of the cyclist, Canadians caught their first glimpse of Steven Truscott in three decades.

He spoke his first words about breaking the silence: "It's important to me. I know that they got the wrong person," he said. "My kids are all grown up. We've discussed it as a family and we figured it was time to come out."

The documentary then proceeded to lay out the evidence that there had been a miscarriage of justice: the contradictory tales of Butch and Jocelyne, the eyewitness testimony of Dougie Oates, the dubious medical conclusions. Dr. John Butt, the former chief medical examiner for the province of Nova Scotia and one of the pathologists *the fifth estate* consulted, explained that modern science has completely discounted stomach contents as a reliable indicator of time of death. "The definition by time in this case is wrong," he stated categorically.

Then Steven should never have been found guilty, MacIntyre asked.

"If that was the linchpin, the answer is, he should not have been," Butt replied. "If that was what was used to wrap the parcel, it should have fallen apart."

A highlight for many viewers came when Lesley and Ryan talked about their father. Did they ever have any doubts about his innocence, MacIntyre asked. "Never," Lesley responded with a smile. "My dad is the most laid-back, relaxed person I've ever met in my life. I'm sure everything that he went through with all the time in jail has really moulded the wonderful person that he's become."

"I guess I just couldn't imagine having all of my rights taken away from me," Ryan added. "People talk about heroes all the time. And who do you admire, and who's your hero in your life. And we don't even have to go anywhere but our house."

The documentary revealed that all the evidence with potential DNA had been destroyed, so Steve had little chance of proving his innocence conclusively. "No one will ever know beyond a reasonable doubt who killed Lynne Harper," MacIntyre said as his narrative drew to a close.

Why, MacIntyre asked Steve and his wife in the documentary's final scene, was it so important for them to pursue their battle since Steve was long out of jail?

"He is not scot-free," Marlene said. "He goes to bed every night as a convicted murderer, and he wakes up every morning as a convicted murderer. Why should he be?"

The camera cut to Steven. "I want to see justice done. Justice hasn't been done," he said. "Not to the Harper family and not to my family. So I mean for both families. It's all I want. After forty years I don't think that's too much to ask."

With a freeze-frame on a tight close-up of Steve's face, the documentary ended. And so did an entire chapter of Steve's life.

## 42

A NEW HOPE

T he boy was nervous and more than a little scared.

He walked down the small street in Guelph, turned up the walk to the second house on the right, and knocked hesitantly on the side door of Steven Truscott's house.

Eleven-year-old Skylar Hurst had the hip haircut, loose-fitting jeans and flashy sneakers that are the uniform of the MuchMusic generation; a far cry from the military crew cut, red pants and simple canvas runners that a teenage Steven wore in the 1950s.

Yet the boy in the year 2000 seemed to reach across time to connect with the boy from 1959 as Skylar sat down to watch *the fifth estate* documentary on the Truscott story with his mother. "I was just really sad and mad that he got charged like that, so I thought it would be cool if the other kids in my class could hear how unfair that was," Skylar said. He decided to prepare a speech for his grade Six English class and wanted to interview Steven. He knew the famous ex-prisoner lived in his city, but he didn't know where, so he simply wrote on the envelope, "Steven Truscott, Guelph."

The letter got to its recipient. The *fifth estate* show had made Steven a minor celebrity. Hundreds of letters poured in from across the country, many of them with only a name. Canada Post gave Steven the special treatment usually reserved for the likes of Santa Claus, and delivered every envelope straight to his door.

Of all the letters, Skylar's intrigued Truscott the most. "I'm really sad that you had to go through all that," Skylar wrote. "Don't worry, I'll understand if you don't want talk about it, but if you phone and I am not home, keep trying. I am probably out playing sports so keep calling."

Skylar was often outside on the streets, fooling around on his mountain bike. Four decades before, another schoolboy had been inseparable from his new green racing bike. Perhaps Steven Truscott saw a little of himself in the kid from across town. As luck would have it, when the phone call came Skylar was indeed outside on his bike, but the Truscotts made arrangements with his mother and invited the Hurst family for a visit and an interview.

"Innocent or guilty? You decide," Skylar told his classmates as he began his presentation. At fifteen minutes, his speech was much longer than it was supposed to be, but the usually restless students of Guelph's Central Public School listened intently and peppered him with questions. In the first year of a new century, grade Six children were enthralled by a murder case that made headlines when most of their parents were schoolchildren. The Truscott story has always fascinated Canadians. Now it had gripped a new generation.

Skylar received a mark of 99.5 out of 100 for his speech.


Over five hundred people sent e-mails and letters to the CBC, an exceptional response to a single program. The messages, almost all of them sympathetic, came from strangers, from children who grew up at the Clinton air force base, even from former inmates.

In Prince Albert, Saskatchewan, tears came to eyes of Ted McGuin when he saw Steve's children talk about their father as a hero. McGuin, like his brother Mike, was a tough veteran of reform school and Collins Bay, and had admired Steve's stamina and principles behind bars. Thirty years later, he found himself watching Steve's story on TV with his wife and nine of their foster children.

"He's not a bad man?" one of the children asked.

"No, he was not," McGuin replied, explaining that Steve did not belong in prison.

Then came the question McGuin knew was coming but he dreaded just the same. "Did you belong there, Dad?" his children asked.

"Yes, Daddy belonged in prison back then," McGuin told his family. "But that man was innocent."

After the show, McGuin sat down in front of his computer to send a message to Steve, identifying himself by name and by number—ex-inmate number 1486.

"You need to know, Steve, that I, like my brother, will go to our graves believing in your innocence," he wrote. "I know that might not be much comfort to you, coming from guys like us—guys that were in there because we belonged there. But I always believed you to be innocent. I still do. . . . I knew you. I looked into your eyes. I saw the innocence they failed to see.

"Steve, you're a lucky man to have kids that are that proud of their father," he concluded. "Hold your head up, man."

Even some police officers—active and retired—were upset by the show's findings. "I personally take pride in my own police work," wrote one thirty-two-year veteran of the Ottawa-Carleton police force, "and would not jeopardize any investigation 'to get a conviction at any cost.'"

In addition to the e-mails to *the fifth estate*, the Truscotts also received about four hundred letters and cards in the weeks following the show (and another one hundred Christmas cards at the end of the year). "We accused him and threw him away, hoping that we would never have to hear about his case again," said one letter writer. "What an injustice we have done to you and your family."

"Like it or not, Steven Truscott, you have become a Canadian icon," wrote an Ottawa schoolteacher. "For young people, you do not have to clear your name."

A number of people seemed eager to do something to make amends for what they saw as Canada's mistreatment of Steven. Mary Yanchus, a teacher from Guelph who grew up in Clinton, volunteered to stuff envelopes, make calls or circulate petitions to help Steven get a new hearing. "Know that, like millions of others, I care about you, pray for you in my way and earnestly wish you success."

Traci Bell of Alberta was inspired to build a Web site with an online petition, calling on the federal justice minister to take action. "This is my opportunity to help see justice done," she explains. "Sometimes you have to stand up for something you believe in."

At Steve's workplace, only about a quarter of the roughly four hundred employees had known his real identity. Steve took a few days off before and after the *fifth estate* broadcast, but the day after it aired he and Ryan stopped by the plant to pick up his paycheque. Ron Charbonneau, Steve's supervisor, says it took the new TV celebrity an hour to make it from one end of the factory to the other, as his workmates cheered him, clapped him on the back and saluted his courage. For Steve, it was a moment of supreme pride and relief to be accepted for who he was. "The guy's a gentle man," Charbonneau says when asked how Steve's work buddies see him. "Talk to me until you're blue in the face, you'll never convince me that he's guilty."

More and more people were coming up to Steve in public. Sometimes they gawked or pointed fingers at him; one woman nearly fell into the frozen food bin as she stared so intently at the man whose image had appeared on TV and in the newspaper. Often people came up to him to shake the hand of a man they admired.

It was a novelty for Steven to experience directly the passions his case engendered. "I missed all the publicity in the past," he says. "I never saw all the letters, the media interest. This is a first for me. And I'm sort of overwhelmed by it."

Slowly, imperceptibly at first but then unmistakably, *the fifth estate* broadcast and its aftermath began to have a profound effect on Steve. "I noticed a change in myself," Steve admits. "I wasn't outgoing [before]. The house, our close friends, that was basically it. All of a sudden things started opening up. People who we never knew or met came to the door. I can now stand there and talk to a complete stranger and it doesn't bother me. It was very positive what it's done to me."

The children and Marlene saw a more relaxed, more open Steve, as if pressure and tension building up over decades had finally been released.

"It has taken the heat off me. Because now he'll answer a telephone and talk to anybody," Marlene says. "I was the one who had to talk to everybody first. He's more confident now."

Across the country, the story reignited passions around the case that refused to die a quiet death.

"Truscott Issues Plea for Justice—show makes strong case for his innocence," ran the headline in the *Globe and Mail*. "Truscott Wants Vindication—

CBC documentary raises new doubts," said the *Gazette* in Montreal. "Stunning new proof in Steven Truscott's 1959 sex-slaying case," the *Ottawa Sun* said on its front page. "Was there a cover-up?" The documentary would go on to earn the Canadian Association of Journalists' top prize for Best Investigative Report of 2000, and was part of a package of *fifth estate* exposés on the justice system that won the prestigious Michener Award for "meritorious public service journalism."

"Thank you, Steven Truscott, for having the courage" to come forward after all these years, wrote *Edmonton Journal* columnist Duart Farquharson. "Your case has troubled a lot of Canadians. It shook my faith in our criminal justice system; it still does." It was, he said, "time for Truscott to get justice."

On Parliament Hill, some MPs seemed to agree. Peter MacKay, justice critic for the Progressive Conservatives and a former prosecutor, raised the affair twice in Question Period. "The Truscott case, as we know, has been a festering wound on the psyche of this nation, and casts a shadow over the entire criminal justice system," he said. "Based on what could be the most egregious miscarriage of justice in Canadian history, will the minister agree that it is incumbent upon her department to conduct a full public inquiry into this situation?"

Justice Minister Anne McLellan sidestepped the question of an open inquiry and instead limited her reply to a strictly legal matter. "If and when we do hear from Mr. Truscott or his lawyer, we will take any allegations or any submissions made very seriously," she told the House on March 30, the day after *the fifth estate* broadcast.

McLellan did not have to wait long to find out Steven's plans. Any time after a convicted person—in or out of jail—has exhausted all other legal avenues, section 690 of the Criminal Code allows for a direct approach to the justice minister for a review. On May 16, six weeks after *the fifth estate* show, reporters packed into a press conference in Toronto. They were there to hear AIDWYC lawyers formally announce they were applying for a 690 review— and to get their first look at Steven Truscott in person. Steven appeared somewhat shell-shocked as flashbulbs clicked, television cameras whirred and journalists scrambled for position.

Marlys Edwardh, one of the lawyers who worked with AIDWYC, opened by describing the Truscott affair as "a painful doubt that has stayed with the administration of justice over the decades." She said AIDWYC would ask Ottawa to review the case with the "hope and expectation that his conviction will be overturned."

Philip Campbell, another AIDWYC lawyer, explained to the news media that in 1959, medical science thought it could narrow the time of death to a very small window based on the contents of the stomach of a deceased person. "If Lynne Harper died between 7:00 and 7:45, Steven Truscott killed her. The Crown was right. It's the science that was wrong," he said.

"Judges, juries, lawyers, police officers—we all long for science to give us the exact answers to relieve the agony of uncertainty and confusion that surrounds so many murder cases. And science wants to oblige. And in 1959 it thought that it could oblige," he said.

Campbell recalled Crown prosecutor Glenn Hays' claim to the jury that Penistan's medical evidence tightened like a vise on Steven. The "vise that gripped Steven Truscott was a tissue of error, but nobody could see that at the time," he said. "The vise has held him tight for forty-one years. This generation of scientists can try to correct the errors of the past generation. So can this generation of courts and lawyers and police officers and ministers of justice."

Finally, it was time for Steven to speak. He read briefly from a prepared statement. He thanked Isabel LeBourdais for her pioneering work in the 1960s and *the fifth estate* for its work in modern times. "It's hard for me to comprehend the issue of capital punishment when there is a growing number of wrongfully convicted people in Canada," Steve told reporters. "It's horrible to think that these now-famous innocent people could have been put to death. . . . I have often wondered if I had been eighteen, I probably wouldn't be here today."

What surprised many reporters was Steve's lack of anger. Several times journalists pressed him: Your youth was stolen, you were taken away from your family, how could you not be bitter?

"I don't think you can be bitter and raise a family," he said, pointing to Ryan and Marlene, who were sitting in the back of the room. "I've moved on, I have a pretty good life. I'm not really wanting for anything except to have my name cleared."

Ryan smiled, prouder than ever of his father, now a hero not just in his eyes but also in the eyes of many Canadians.

Also present at the press conference was Rubin "Hurricane" Carter, the executive director of AIDWYC. Found guilty in two separate trials for a triple slaying at a bar in Patterson, New Jersey, Carter spent nineteen years in jail before clearing his name. A Bob Dylan song and a Hollywood movie starring

Denzel Washington made the story famous. Disenchanted with the United States, Carter had made Toronto his home, where he became active in the movement to help other wrongfully convicted prisoners.

Shortly before the press conference began, Carter had taken Steve for a coffee to calm his nerves. As with Guy Paul Morin, Steve hit it off immediately with the boisterous and talkative Hurricane. Carter, for his part, remembers a "soft, warm person" sipping coffee across the table from him.

"We talked about surviving," recounts Carter. "And in order to survive, you have to stop being a victim." Carter told Steven he was impressed by his "courage to re-open old wounds" by stepping into the public spotlight. "He's doing it for the same reason I did it," Carter explains. "I refuse to be condemned by history. 'Talk to me, listen to me' is what we're saying."

"Hang in there," Hurricane told Steve as they finished their thirty-minute chat. "Believe in yourself."


Steve has reason to believe that maybe this time he will win. His legal arsenal, drawing on talent from three different Toronto law firms, is impressive. His AIDWYC lawyers have been associated with all the major victories against wrongful convictions in Canada. Marlys Edwardh had worked on the Donald Marshall case and with Guy Paul Morin. Philip Campbell helped win a section 690 for Clayton Johnson. James Lockyer had secured DNA acquittals for Morin and Milgaard.

To help them research and coordinate the massive Truscott file, they recruited Jenny Friedland, an articling student at the firm of Pinkofsky Lockyer. Her father, a law professor, had done research for Arthur Martin in preparation for the Supreme Court case. "I heard about Steve's case as a child," Jenny Friedland says. "I never thought I'd get a chance to work on it thirty years later." She began spending hours at the archives of the Ontario government and the Supreme Court, combing through the documents on Steve's case, looking for more clues.

For a legal undertaking of such breathtaking proportions, the work of Steve's lawyers has the outward appearance of confusion. In a cluttered conference room in a nondescript downtown Toronto office building, documents and boxes lie strewn across a large table and in corners on the floor: a police file here, a witness statement there, a trial transcript buried somewhere else. Lockyer writes his drafts in longhand on yellow legal notepads.

He may be on the cutting edge of defence work, but he steadfastly refuses to join the computer age, and does not even have a personal e-mail address. But the apparent disorder and lack of modernity are deceiving—Lockyer is known for his sharp legal mind and powerful eloquence.

Just a few blocks away, in the offices of Sack Goldblatt Mitchell, Philip Campbell plows through his set of boxes of documents, dictating his thoughts into a tape recorder for transcription later. Campbell, a Maritimer and son of a preacher, sports black-rimmed glasses, a beard, blue jeans and a loose-fitting shirt. Beneath his casualness lies a ferocious attention to detail and a keen sense of the law.

"You put it all together and you say to yourself, 'The jury did not get anything like the full story,'" concludes James Lockyer. "If the jury did not hear anything like the full story, there goes the conviction. It has to be quashed. The problem is that it doesn't prove he's innocent. We believe he's innocent, but unfortunately, with no DNA it is very hard to establish it."

In the cases of Canada's famous reversals of wrongful convictions—Marshall, Morin and Milgaard—defence lawyers had DNA, the real killer or both. With Steve's case they have neither. Steve lost not only in front of a jury in 1959, but also at the Ontario Court of Appeal and the Supreme Court in 1960 and then at the full Supreme Court in 1967. In all, fourteen out of fifteen judges who heard his case sided against him.

But far from seeing the legal cards stacked against him, Lockyer sees Steven's case in a much more optimistic light than his previous battles for frequently unknown and unloved clients. "We're starting from a very good position," he explains. "The public knows all about the case and the majority think he's innocent. That's a stronger position than I've ever started with."

"We as lawyers may criticize the justice system, we may question it," Philip Campbell says, "but in the end we have to have some faith that it works—that it is capable of distinguishing the guilty from the innocent."


The odds of anyone winning a section 690 review are not good.

About fifty to seventy people file requests every year. AIDWYC estimates only one per cent of the applications lead to the overturning of a conviction. Department of justice statistics indicate between two and three per cent of the total applications are approved for review, but the department insists many of those requests are not complete enough for the minister to even consider. By April of 2001, there were 105 applications in the system; only one case made it to a final decision in 2001 and it was rejected.

Critics of the process say that applicants face "almost impossible hurdles," as AIDWYC argued in a lengthy brief to the government about the problems with the review system. Appeals can be costly—in effect, lawyers have to re-investigate and re-argue the entire trial. Access to public funding in many provinces is limited. Delays can be extreme—one case took eight years.

Lawyers for the applicant and even government officials reviewing a case have no right to subpoena records or witnesses, seriously hampering an investigation. The reviews "are conducted largely in secret," AIDWYC states. "The applicant is rarely aware of the progress and is not invited to participate in interviews of witnesses." The minister is not even obliged to give a reason for turning down an application.

A successful section 690 application, according to guidelines set out by the government in 1994, must be based on "new matters of significance" that either were not considered by the court or that arose after appeals—much like the information revealed in this book that was hidden from the jurors and judges. At the same time, the applicant "need not convince the minister of innocence," or even prove "conclusively that a miscarriage of justice has *actually* occurred." Rather, all that is needed is a demonstration that "a miscarriage of justice *likely* occurred."

Steven Truscott's case certainly appears to meet those standards. Dr. Penistan's pivotal estimate of the time of death was scientifically unsound. Worse still, there is no evidence he even came up with that time of death by himself on the night of the autopsy. The prosecution got Lynne's parents to tell the jurors their daughter did not hitchhike, but they told police the opposite the night she disappeared. The jurors never heard that the Townsends at one point told police they saw a young girl hitchhiking on Tuesday night, nor did they hear that Cpl. Arlene Strauman was harassed by men in a 1959 Chevrolet thirty minutes before Steve says a similar car picked up Lynne at the highway. The prosecution argued Steven could not see a car from the bridge—something tests presented to the Supreme Court proved was possible. The prosecution argued Gord Logan could not have seen Steve at the bridge, but police tests in 1966 showed he could. The prosecution said Dougie Oates was not at the bridge past 7:00 p.m. but Karen Daum, the witness they kept hidden, proved he was.

How, given all that was kept from the jury, could a miscarriage of justice not have occurred?

In many ways, Steve has already won, at least in the court of public opinion. Coming out into the open on national television—and seeing the widespread support he has among Canadians—has been a vindication for the man who kept his silence all those years.

Marlene, for her part, is hungrier to go beyond the moral victory they have won and secure a landmark legal one with a successful section 690 application. For Marlene, the reason to hope Steven's case gets a full review is accountability.

She draws an important distinction between the tragedies that befell the Harper family and the Truscotts. "It was a far more awful thing that happened to Lynne Harper because they don't have Lynne any more; Steve's family has him," Marlene says. "But you have a sick person who commits a crime like that—[people like that are] out there and we do not have any control over them. But we should have some sort of control over what happened to Steve," she continues. "The people that were in charge of investigations that go wrong, they're supposed to be trusted people that are employed by us. But we don't have control over them either. Who was out there controlling the police for what they were doing? Nobody."

Steve also wants the police to be held accountable. But, given his past defeats on the legal battlefield, he is cautious about his chances of victory. "I've never really had that great of a rapport with the justice system," he says. "I've made my life, no thanks to them. They did nothing to contribute to my life; Marlene and I made that," Steve says. "So as far as them coming out and saying 'We believe you're innocent,'—I don't care what they believe. I know I'm innocent. Nothing anybody is ever going to say or do is going to erase that. So for me the one thing left is for them to say, 'We were wrong.'" What he needs—and wants—is for the authorities to admit they made a mistake.

"There was no test that I wasn't willing to go through. I applied for DNA; it sure wasn't because I thought I was guilty. I did truth serum tests in the penitentiary, LSD tests. I went through all that," he says, a tinge of frustration rising in his voice. "Nothing came out to indicate that I was guilty. And it's always me having to prove that I didn't do it."

"What they did was wrong. And that's all I want them to do: say they were wrong. I'm not asking for the world. Go over all the information. Investigate it. Let the people know all the evidence, and let them judge for themselves, not just what the police want you to hear, but all of it. I'm not afraid of that. Why are they?"

## 43

## LESSONS LEARNED

More than forty years after it began, the Steven Truscott story continues to leave its mark on Canada. Those most deeply affected were the children of Clinton—scarred by the trauma of the murder of one schoolmate and the arrest of another. "All of our lives changed abruptly," says Michael Burns. "Your best friend goes to jail, is sentenced to hang for a crime you don't think he committed. Your whole opinion of police, the justice system, takes quite a shock."

Douglas Oates, the turtle hunter who stood his ground against the unrelenting assault of prosecutor Glenn Hays, works in the air traffic control centre in Edmonton. But he too cannot shake the memories of a guilty verdict he saw as a travesty. "I carried that around all my life," he says. "I really don't trust the judicial system. I certainly wouldn't want to bet my life on it."

Steve's childhood friend, Karen Allen—who told the OPP Steve kissed her at a party and then was grilled so intensely she cried—lost touch with Steve after he was jailed. But Karen never left the Clinton area and the guilt never left her. "To this day I cannot drive down that [county] road without remembering and feeling unsettled," she wrote in an e-mail to *the fifth estate* after the broadcast of Steve's story. "Over the years, I have often wondered if there wasn't something I could have done besides defending his innocence when the conversation came up.

"I hope Steven will realize that many, many people in this area always believed in his innocence, and for many of us, he was never forgotten," she concluded. "The fact that we did nothing, even though we didn't really know what we could do, is something that we have to live with."

Karen got in touch with Steve and they renewed their friendship. Somehow, that bond seems to have given Karen a peace of mind she has not felt for years.

Butch George settled in London, Ontario, where he became a painter. Like his former friend Steven, Butch has aged well. When he answers a knock at his door, he appears fit and relaxed, his thick hair flecked with more paint than grey, his eyes deep and his face handsome. But he adamantly insists he does not want to talk about anything that happened in 1959.

Jocelyne Gaudet became a nurse. When she did her training in Quebec, she made three-month rotations in various hospital wards. In the mid-1960s, while doing psychiatric training at St. Mary's in Montreal, she roomed with another nurse, Sandra Stolzmann. "She was trying to go by another name— the name she was using was Kim—but everyone knew she was Jocelyne Gaudet," says Stolzmann.

According to Stolzmann, Gaudet's Clinton past came back to haunt her in 1966. Isabel LeBourdais' book put the trial back on the front pages and eventually in front of the highest court in the land. Jocelyne was never called as a witness, but apparently feared she might be.

"She was hysterical because there was a Supreme Court hearing coming up, and she told us that she had to testify," Stolzmann says. "She kept moaning to everyone that she knew Steven didn't do it."

Whatever secrets Jocelyne might have been hiding she kept to herself. Jocelyne to this day still goes under the name of "Kim" and lives in a small town in Alberta.

Steve also continued to influence lives, even of people with whom he spent the darkest years of his life. One day in 1998 he heard from John, the inmate at Collins Bay who worked with Steve on the prison farm. Seriously ill in hospital, with no friends or family by his side, John desperately wanted to speak to the one friend he still cherished—Steven. Before long, the two former inmates were talking on the phone.

"I'm in tears," John said. The two ex-inmates chatted briefly, then said their goodbyes. Steve has not heard from his prison pal since.

In the fall of 2000, Steve and Marlene's children surprised them with an open-house party for their 30th wedding anniversary. Among the eighty guests who showed up were modern-day neighbours and childhood friends from Clinton such as Bryan Glover and Karen Allen. Bob Lawson came with his wife, Anne, as did Steve's former teacher from the air base, Maitland Edgar. It was a cross-section of the people whose lives were touched by the Truscotts over the decades.

"It was really amazing," says Krista Severa, their neighbour from the 1970s. "They really deserved it."

The key legal players in the saga—Frank Donnelly, Glenn Hays, Justice Ronald Ferguson, Arthur Martin, Emmett Hall and his eight other colleagues on the Supreme Court—all died without ever having made any major public comment on the Truscott case.

Shortly before Dr. John Penistan died in June 1973, he deposited "additional reading material" from his files with the Perth County Archives in Stratford, Ontario. What was unusual—and perhaps indicative of how tortured Penistan was over his role in the trial—was the preface he penned to his archive collection. "Whether Steven Truscott did murder Lynne Harper is not known; nor will it ever be known unless further and incontrovertible evidence on the subject is obtained," the doctor wrote. Eight weeks later, Penistan was dead. It was a surprising final statement on the case coming from the medical expert whose testimony on time of death convinced a jury that there was indeed "incontrovertible" evidence of Steven's guilt.

Dr. David Hall Brooks, the chief medical officer at the air force base who assisted Penistan at Lynne's autopsy, is more talkative. But today, the man who seemed so eager to convict Steven during his testimony shows signs of recanting. He told jurors in 1959 the sores on Steven's penis pointed clearly to an "inexpert attempt at penetration." Now he is less than certain. "Looking back on this, it would have been very fine if my ideas of 'enthusiastic amateurs' and young people [were] not . . . as highly powered as I thought," he says. He is also far more equivocal about Steve's guilt. "In the absence of DNA, I don't think it will be settled."

Perhaps Brooks' newfound sympathy for Steve stems from his own run-ins with authorities over sexual allegations. Brooks left Clinton in 1959 and eventually became medical director of the Forest Hill Rehabilitation Centre in Fredericton. In 1966, the Canadian Physiotherapy Association deferred approving the centre for its interns when one of the therapists reported Brooks "has been witnessed in several acts of exhibitionism in front of patients and staff (and) there is doubt as to his ethical procedures when examining female patients." The Medical Council of New Brunswick investigated. It found there may have been "carelessness on exposure" in one instance but exonerated the doctor in August of 1967.

Or so it seemed. The following year, the council refused Brooks' request for a "Statement of Good Standing"—in effect, blocking him from practice. The official minutes record the health minister at the time, Dr. Peter Weyman, wanted every provincial medical council in Canada "to be alerted to the conduct of this man." The minutes also indicate the RCMP began an investigation. Brooks left the province for the United States. He is now retired and lives in New Jersey.

Dr. George Scott, the prison psychiatrist who tried truth serum, LSD and a battery of psychological tests to get a confession out of Steven, ran into embarrassing problems of his own. In 1995, the Ontario College of Physicians and Surgeons revoked Scott's licence to practise medicine for "professional misconduct" when he pled guilty to having sex with one of his female patients. He began counselling her in 1965 while he was also handling Steven's case. Under Scott's care, her psychiatric treatment—along with "regular sexual intercourse"—continued until the mid-1970s.

George Scott is retired now and lives not far from the prisons in Kingston where he served for so long.

For opponents of the death penalty, Steven Truscott remains a living example of what is wrong with capital punishment. Had Steven's sentence not been commuted, Canada would have hanged a boy many are convinced is innocent.

"Capital punishment is unjust. . . . It is final. It is irreversible. Its imposition has been described as arbitrary. Its deterrent value has been doubted." Those words come not from a lobby group but from the Supreme Court of Canada. On February 15, 2001, the court reversed a position it had taken a decade earlier, when it allowed two American prisoners in Canada to be sent back to the United States to face possible death sentences. This time, the court ruled unanimously that the federal government must not extradite people to countries that still practise capital punishment.

The highest court in the land specifically cited five cases of wrongful conviction in Canada: Donald Marshall, David Milgaard, Guy Paul Morin, Thomas Sophonow and Gregory Parsons. (Four of those five cases were won with AIDWYC's assistance; all five were fought with help from lawyers who are now working on Steve's case.) The Supreme Court of Canada stated forcefully that: "The recent and continuing disclosures of wrongful convictions for murder in Canada, the United States and the United Kingdom provide tragic testimony to the fallibility of the legal system."

One group of people is not prepared to admit—or even discuss—their fallibility. The children of Clinton, now grown up, have wrestled with their demons. The Supreme Court's opinion on the death penalty has evolved; the justice department says it is "very aware" of the potential of a miscarriage of justice in the Truscott case. But the Ontario Provincial Police remains steadfast in its unconditional refusal to budge an inch from its 1959 stance.

Only two of the many OPP and air force police officers involved in the case are still alive. "As far as the investigating officers on that case, there's no one who thinks he's innocent," says Dennis Alsop, the identification officer called who testified as a footprint expert before the Supreme Court. "That's a pretty solid case. That's what the job is about and they had the right man. Not a doubt."

Hank Sayeau, the corporal who acted as second in command on the Harper murder case, is still furious at what he sees as biased reporting by *the fifth estate*. "You made us look as if we screwed this kid," he says. "He's gone through every process in our courts and you made him into a male Joan of Arc."

Harold Graham retired as commissioner of the OPP in 1982. More than seven hundred friends attended the testimonial dinner, including the Ontario premier, William Davis, nine other cabinet ministers and the chief justice of Ontario. The master of ceremonies was Attorney General Roy McMurtry.

Graham refused all invitations to talk about his role in arresting and convicting Steven Truscott. "It's been years," he said in a telephone interview in 2000. "When are we going to let this thing go?"

"Graham doesn't like to be reminded about how this case keeps coming up," said his former associate Hank Sayeau. "I think it's always on his mind. He's always thought about the Truscott case."

The first signs of spring were unmistakable in Guelph. A couple of students from the university jogged along a path that winds past the old reform school, which later served as a maximum-security jail before being shut down. The dogs were out romping in the park along the Eramosa River. Up the road from the river, outside the Truscott home, a bird feeder dangled from the branch of a tree. A half-used bag of salt lay on the porch, the only souvenir of the dreary winter just past.

Ryan Truscott, who lives in a basement suite in his parents' home, was thinking of getting some new lawn furniture for the backyard, which is enclosed by neighbours' fences on two sides and with the walls of the Truscotts' house and garage on the other sides. But Steve didn't like the idea.

"It's too confining," Steve said. "I like it out front. It's open. You can see." Then he added, referring to his prison days: "I don't like the walls."

"Dad," Ryan exclaimed, "that's the first time I have heard you say anything like that."

A year after their lives were turned upside down by *the fifth estate* broadcast, the Truscott family was returning to normal—except it was a different kind of normal. Steve now wore his pride on the outside, voicing feelings he kept inside for so many years.

Life has been good to the Truscotts. Steven's tastes and living style have always been simple. More often than not, especially in warm weather, Steve bicycles the few short blocks to work. Ryan is a successful manager for a cosmetics dealer. Lesley works part-time at a restaurant and is raising her three children. Devon, who inherited his father's passion for and ease with anything mechanical, works at an automotive shop and puts all his extra cash into remodelling his truck.

Steve's two brothers, Ken and Bill, are firemen in small southern Ontario towns, with families of their own. Barb runs a small business outside of Ottawa. Doris Truscott lives not far from the home in Richmond where she waged her relentless battle to free her son. "Well, I survived this long," she says when asked if she thinks Steve will finally win this time with his section 690 appeal. "I hope I survive to see the end of it."

Malcolm "Mac" Stienburg, the United Church minister who was Steve's prison chaplain, his parole officer and now is his friend, sees at last in Steven a man at peace with himself. "The fact that he doesn't live under that secrecy, I think he has found that liberating," Stienburg says.

"He's the best person that he knows how to be," the pastor says. "He's not a church person, but I think he's basically a very moral person, a very good person. I don't think he's one bit more callous or more hardened now than he was when he went into prison."

But for Steven and his children, there remained one last step to take to complete their journey. "In the whole time I've been married to Steve, he would never say the name 'Truscott,'" Marlene says.

"It's hard to get over the protection thing," Steve says, suggesting it was hard to shake the assumed name to which he had grown accustomed.

His wife disagrees. "It wasn't out of habit—he just wouldn't say the name."

That, too, changed after *the fifth estate* broadcast. Steve began introducing himself to more people as Steven Truscott, abandoning the surname he was obliged to take as a condition of parole.

"To live under an assumed name is not an easy thing," he says. "I'm proud of my name; I have nothing to hide and nothing to be ashamed of. It really is a big relief."

"It was something that we've always dreamt of since we've been married," Marlene adds. "Sometime or another everything would come out and we could be back to who we're supposed to be. It's a long time coming but I think it's finally here."

Lesley took her husband's name when she married. Ryan, at twenty-seven, legally changed his surname to "Truscott," and his younger brother, Devon, plans to do the same.

"I think now that it's really important because we're proud of who we are, we're proud of my dad and we're proud of my mom for the work that she's done in helping him," Ryan says. "There's nothing to hide from. It's sort of exciting. It's something that you thought about all through life—when was this going to happen? Or would the day ever come where it would be accepted enough that we could say, 'This is who we are'? And it feels great. We're still the same people, but it's just nice to have that name on paper."

For Steven, it is one final proof that, in the end, he has won. "The children grew up with me, so they know what I'm like every day," he says. "Year after year they know I'm innocent. But I think it's a relief to them to say, 'Hey, I'm his son. I stand behind him.' And this gives me a lift that I don't think anything else ever would."

At fourteen years of age, a young boy was arrested. He lost his freedom, his youth and—by order of the parole board when he finally was released from prison—his name. Now, as a father and a grandfather, Steven Truscott has reclaimed his dignity—and his name.

## 44

## RETURN TO CLINTON

T he chrome on the tail fins of the Chevrolet Bel Air, the Ford Fairlane and the yellow T-Bird convertible glisten in the afternoon summer sun. The chords of Elvis Presley's hits echo from loudspeakers. The fairgrounds in Clinton are full of children eating hot dogs and drinking Coke— and Steven Truscott is having as much fun as everyone else.

Only Steven isn't a fourteen-year-old high-school student. It is 2000 and Steven is fifty-five, walking through the fairgrounds with his three children and three grandchildren. Going against conventional wisdom, Steven was proving that you can go home again.

The town of Clinton had organized a 150th reunion, and the classic car show was one of the weekend's highlights. Steven had been to Clinton a few times in recent years to visit the Lawsons and once to film with *the fifth estate*, but those trips had been made discreetly, and Steve was always nervous. "Steve wouldn't get out of the car if there was a stranger's car in our driveway," Bob Lawson says.

This time, in the wake of the publicity after the TV show, the entire family decided to go to Clinton together. At reunions there, Steve met former teachers and classmates such as Cathy O'Dell and Michael Burns.

At the car show, a photographer from the local newspaper caught sight of

Clinton's best known former resident and asked Steve to pose for a picture—strikingly, in front of a classic car from the 1950s.

Two women came up to him and introduced themselves as children who grew up in the area around the time of the trial. "We all thought you were innocent," one said. "But no one would believe us because we were just kids," the other added.

When Steve told them about his lawyers' plans to file for a section 690 review, the women encouraged him. "Go to court, go for it—don't ever give up," they said, ending the encounter with hugs and tears.

"It was really uplifting for me to meet people from forty years ago and to know that they felt that way about me," Steve says about his decision to come back to Clinton so publicly. "It was something that I needed to do."

"It was good for Steve to see the whole town was not against him," Marlene adds.

Steve's mother, Doris, was on hand as well, watching her grown boy play with her great-grandchildren. "We had a lot of good times here in Clinton," Doris says. "It's important that Steve remember those as well."

The Clinton reunion took place on a holiday long weekend in Ontario, and the tourists were out in numbers. In nearby Goderich, the first sign that greets visitors on Highway 8, which leads into the town, announces tours of the "Historic Gaol." Inside the grey walls, you can get a picture of yourself on a Wanted poster and see the leg irons once used on prisoners. You can also tour the cells, a flyer says, that once housed "famous" prisoners like Steven Truscott.

Four decades after being a headline about hanging, Steven had become a tourist attraction.

The prim and proper military neighbourhood where Steve and his friends grew up has given way to the trappings of modern suburbia. Private developers took over the land from the former air force base. TV antennas and satellite dishes dot the roofs, and minivans cram the driveways.

The old corner store where the air force children once swarmed for ten-cent Oh Henry! bars and blackballs now rents videos and sports a stern warning sign on the door: "Due to a large increase in theft, only three students at a time, no backpacks, no loitering. We will prosecute on a first offence. Surveillance system is in use."

Down the county road from the farm, the bridge where Steve and his friends hung out still crosses the Bayfield River. But the river is too dirty to be a swimming hole any more. There are no more bikes and baseball gloves and fishing rods scattered about, no more sounds of children splashing and laughing.

There are only faint echoes of that hot June evening in 1959 when a young girl died—and with her, the innocence of many other children and the illusions of an entire country.

Much has changed since that summer in 1959. Some things cling, however tenaciously, to the past. From his barn, Bob Lawson slowly eases out his tractor, rattling with age, its colours long faded.

"It's still running," Steve says, the mechanic in him impressed.

"That's the tractor you used to drive," the farmer points out proudly.

"Well, some things are newer," Steve says, glancing at the refurbished barn and across the street at the expanded school grounds, "but some are older, just like we are."

"I think maybe we've aged a little," says the sixty-two-year-old farmer.

Steve pauses for a moment. Perhaps he is thinking of the last time he stood on the tractor, a fourteen-year-old working in the fields with Farmer Lawson on a Friday evening, his last hour of freedom before the police came to pick him up.

"Yeah," he finally says, "we all aged a little bit."

Just over a year after their reunion alongside the tractor, Bob Lawson sat quietly in the back of a packed room in Toronto. He was there to watch Steven Truscott on one of the most important days of his life. At a press conference carried live across the country on CBC Newsworld, Steven Truscott stared at the phalanx of a dozen television cameras and jostling reporters and calmly called on Ottawa to formally reopen his case. "I want my name cleared," he said.

It was the climax of a tumultuous fall in 2001 that proved to be a pivotal period in the Truscott saga.

Just a few weeks before the press conference, in early November, retired OPP commissioner Harold Graham died at the age of 84, taking to his grave many unanswered questions about his most famous case. "It haunted him all throughout his term and through his retirement," a friend of Graham's told a *Globe and Mail* reporter. "But to his death, I'm sure he thought [Truscott] was guilty."

Yet we will never know why Graham stayed silent while the Crown suppressed crucial testimony from nine-year-old Karen Daum that she saw Steve and Lynne cycling to the highway, especially when he himself witnessed and signed Daum's statement. We will never know why, after Dr. Penistan's autopsy on Harper's body, Graham issued a handwritten police bulletin estimating the time of death at 9 p.m. but insisted at trial that the evidence pointed to a time of death two hours earlier. And we will never know why, on the eve of the Supreme Court review in 1966, he and the Crown kept secret Dr. Penistan's "agonizing re-appraisal" on the time of death.

Graham may have died convinced of Steven's guilt, but many others are not so sure. When the first edition of this book hit the stores in October 2001, newspaper columnists and editorialists called on the justice minister to re-examine the case. "The book provides a long list of points that raise doubts about the validity of the conviction," said the *Kitchener–Waterloo Record*. "Truscott deserves [a] review. So does the judicial system."

The revelations generated renewed public enthusiasm for Steven's story—not the least in the place where it all started. In Clinton, several hundred students, teachers and citizens jammed themselves into the auditorium of the local high school to hear the author of this book talk about the town's most famous boy. And in Goderich—the town that had vilified the accused fourteen-year-old rapist four decades earlier—more than one hundred citizens came out on a chilly fall evening to discuss what had gone so wrong.

Paul Steckle, the Liberal MP from the riding that includes both Clinton and Goderich, told me the mood has changed in the community that once rushed to judgment. "There is a large acceptance that this man could not have been guilty. There's no doubt that's what you'd find in the street," he said.

Across the country, the story was the same. In Vancouver, a woman called an open line show to say that she grew up always knowing her father was convinced Steven had been railroaded by the police. Her father was Cpl. William A. Webb, the air force officer who first reported on June 9, 1959, that Mr. Harper suspected his daughter had run away from home by hitchhiking.

In Steven's adopted hometown of Guelph, three hundred people packed into a church to hear news of the case. They gave Steven, Marlene and their children a standing ovation. One of those in attendance was Mary Yanchus, the teacher who had written Steven, after seeing the *fifth estate* program, offering to help. Now she took it upon herself to organize a postcard campaign to urge the justice minister to take action. She printed up more than ten thousand cards—and ran out quickly. "I felt strongly that there were all kinds of people out there who wanted to do something about this," Yanchus said. "Let's hope it ends with Steven's exoneration."

Exoneration was precisely what was on the mind of the hard-working team of lawyers from AIDWYC on November 29, 2001, when they announced the submission of a near seven hundred-page brief to the justice minister. Reporters were surprised to find that more than a legal unveiling, the press conference turned out to be a testimony to the wide scope of people who had been touched by Steven Truscott over the decades. On hand to support Steven from his Clinton years were fellow students Gary Gilks, Bryan Glover and Karen Allen, alongside vice-principal Maitland Edgar. From his prison years, former inmate Mike McGuin came to express his solidarity. From his Guelph years, neighbours and co-workers hugged and clapped Steven on the back.

Through it all sat the two powerful and driven women who had stood by him all those decades—his mother Doris, still a firebrand in her seventies, and his wife Marlene.

At a table in the front of the room, flanked by the legal team, Steven spoke briefly, urging Ottawa "after 42 years to finally do the right thing." To the surprise of many jaded reporters, Steven stated unequivocally that he was not interested in financial compensation. "I want my name back, I want closure," he said. "It hurts, it's something that never goes away."

AIDWYC lawyer Philip Campbell was categorical: "There is, in our view, not a single part of the case mounted by the Crown that isn't called seriously into question, if not utterly devastated, by the evidence that we've retrieved from the Ontario archives and other sources."

The section 690 appeal written by Campbell, James Lockyer and Marlys Edwardh, with research assistance from Jenny Friedland, was indeed sweeping. It revealed several new potential suspects from the current OPP case file, in addition to Alexander Kalichuk and the other men revealed in this book. One man was an accused sexual offender from the area whose daughter said years later she had seen him taking "the limp body of a young girl" out of the trunk of his car. Another man stationed at the Clinton base in 1959 was discovered in the 1980s to have a large collection of child pornography, a transcript of the entire Truscott trial—and a strange alibi for his whereabouts on the night Lynne vanished. "Each of these men is a likelier sex killer than a fourteen-year-old who, neither before nor since his arrest, betrayed the slightest tendency to antisocial behaviour," the brief said.

AIDWYC's report also revealed new information about key witnesses. Sandra Stolzmann, the nurse who had befriended Jocelyne Gaudet in the 1960s, said in an affidavit that Joycelyne blurted out "that she had lied on the witness stand." Another nurse remembered Jocelyne saying "she lied because she was angry at Steven and wanted to get back at him."

The AIDWYC brief prompted more public cries for action. In Ottawa, a dozen politicians from the Commons and the Senate formed a coalition to push for "a full re-examination of this case." Then Peter MacKay, at the time Tory justice critic, rallied the entire Conservative caucus behind the cause. "We strongly believe that everything possible should be done to correct what appears to be a miscarriage of justice," said then party leader Joe Clark.

In Steven's hometown of Guelph, the city council endorsed his appeal. The *Guelph Mercury* was unequivocal: "It has been made perfectly clear that Truscott could not have committed the crime for which he was jailed. The evidence simply does not hold together."

"The air needs to be cleared, not just for Steven Truscott, but for the sake of this country and our justice system," echoed the *London Free Press*.

And the *Globe and Mail* would soon add its national weight to what it called the issue that "haunts the Canadian imagination."

"This country's justice system will avoid future miscarriages of justice only if it has the stomach to revisit and analyze its most egregious wrongs," the editorial said. "Enough evidence has been found to suggest the system went horribly wrong in this case.

But if the justice system went horribly wrong, it would take a lot longer— three justice ministers, two governments and five more years—before the system would be ready to seriously consider that a dreadful mistake had been made. Everyone—not just the Truscotts—thought that some kind of resolution of the case that had festered for more than five decades was just around the corner.

It was not to be that immediate. But one way or the other, the final chapter of the Steven Truscott saga was about to be written.

**45**

## THE FINAL CHAPTER

The first, faltering glimmer of hope came on January 24, 2002, when the new federal justice minister, Martin Cauchon, made public what his predecessor, Anne McLellan, had already set in motion. Ottawa named former Quebec Court of Appeal justice Fred Kaufman to investigate the case and advise the government about "the granting of a possible extraordinary remedy because of the circumstances of this case."

It was an extraordinary victory, because few appeals to the justice minister are powerful enough to convince the federal government to re-open a case. The choice of Fred Kaufman also seemed to be an inspired one. Though a pillar of the judicial establishment, Kaufman had proven himself to be an unflinching critic of its abuses. He had probed failures in the Nova Scotia Public Prosecution Service and authored the devastating inquiry into the wrongful-murder conviction of Guy Paul Morin. "There is now a greater awareness that things can go wrong—maybe the system does make mistakes," Kaufman said. "The justice system must not be afraid to take a second look at things."

"Of course we are thrilled," Marlene Truscott told reporters. "It's a very happy day for us. There's a time for everything and I think Steve's time has come."

But time had bedeviled Steven Truscott since 1959, when police, witnesses, lawyers and judges began picking apart those fateful minutes on the county road. And now Steven would learn that if the justice system wasted little more than two weeks to convict him, it would take a lot more time to even consider changing its mind.

No one expected Kaufman's inquiry to be quick, but it would be eighteen months before he handed in his report to a new justice minister in the summer of 2004. True, he had to review thousands of pages of evidence from the 1959 trial and the Supreme Court hearing of 1966. But a big part of the delay was due to the decision by the Ontario attorney general's office to dig in its heels and oppose Truscott every step of the way. Truscott's lawyers from AIDWYC had been used to the stiff resistance from the OPP; they figured the police were not going to rush to the front of the line to admit they had jailed the wrong person, all the more so since the man responsible for that arrest, Harold Graham, was an OPP legend.

But the opposition from the attorney general was disappointing. The Crown lawyers owed no personal allegiance to the prosecutors who operated in a 1950s court system much different than today. It was not their reputation at stake. Perhaps they felt some kind of institutional loyalty to the administration of justice at all costs; or perhaps the top prosecutors in Ontario in the twenty-first century looked at the rush to judgment in 1959 and decided— despite all the new evidence—there was nothing wrong: Steven Truscott was indeed guilty. Whatever the reason, Crown lawyers wrote a 254-page brief, urging Ottawa to reject Truscott's appeal. They took a swipe at AIDWYC, the CBC and this book, stating that "over the forty-four years since his conviction, [Mr. Truscott's] advocates have assailed the verdict on any number of fronts"—all of them without merit.

It all meant more work for Truscott's lawyers and for Kaufman. The Crown representatives challenged every bit of new evidence, every new revelation. Kaufman's inquiry was not a trial but a one-man investigation: no jury, no judge, no cross-examination by defence or Crown lawyers. The lawyers on both sides could only submit briefs and make recommendations on possible avenues of research. Kaufman had a police investigator to hunt down witnesses and evidence and the power of subpoena to oblige the reluctant ones to come forward. In all, Kaufman interviewed twenty-one witnesses under oath including Steven Truscott, several other children from Clinton at the time, police officers, medical experts, plus two journalists—

Julian Sher, the author of this book, and research associate Theresa Burke. When his report was finally released in 2004, at the request of the Crown and the defence, some sections remained confidential, but there were a few revealing insights.

For the first time in forty years, the two chief child witnesses against Truscott—Arnold "Butch" George and Jocelyne Gaudet—were heard from again. They had kept silent since the 1959 trial. George apparently changed his story again and told yet another version of what happened—his fifth, if one counts his three differing police statements and his trial testimony. His account to Kaufman was not made public but even the Crown admitted it was "inconsistent" with what he said in court.

Gaudet—who seemed to be in an unstable state of mind and who littered her new testimony with profanities—was the only witness who did not come forward voluntarily. She had to be subpoenaed by Kaufman. Her memory was spotty at best: she remembered playing dolls with Lynne but not the names of any other of her friends. She did not recall her home address. She did not remember Steven calling at her house on the evening of June 9, as the prosecution alleged, nor could she say if she was looking for Lynne or Steve as she walked up and down the county road. In fact, according to the report, "she does not remember a trial, although she remembers being there."

Of Steven, she said he was a "jock" but "she was not into boys and thus did not pay any attention" to him. She stuck to her story that Steven had asked her to meet him on the night of June 9; she was "shocked" but figured: "What the hell . . . I will go for it." Still, she said he was so gentle he once warned her that picking up a lizard by its tail would hurt the animal, so when the police asked her if she thought Steven could have killed Lynne, she answered: "How could he? He can't even kill a fly. I thought: 'What a dumb question.'"

Gaudet got the most agitated when asked about her dealings with the police. She complained about being woken up at midnight and questioned "without the presence of her father" in a room with three officers: "They kept trying to change my words," she said without providing any specifics. "Here's this twelve-year-old kid, half asleep, and these bastards are trying to change my story."

When Kaufman had excerpts of her statement to police read back to her, she interrupted angrily: "Remember [the police] were trying to get me to change my shit. They kept trying to change my words."

Steven himself testified twice under oath in front of Kaufman, once in August 2002 and again in March 2003. He recounted, as he did in the *fifth estate* program and for this book, his activities on the night of June 9, his shock at being arrested and his bewilderment as the adults around him—his lawyers and parents—told him not to worry as he kept sinking deeper and deeper into the pits of the justice system.

When Kaufman asked him if financial compensation was a factor in his decision to go public and ask the government to re-open the case, Truscott said he had "not really given it much thought."

"My main interest is clearing my name," he said. "I want my kids to go through life with a name that they're proud of, not something that has a stigma attached to it."

For their part, the Ontario attorney general's lawyers had argued vociferously that Steve's "version of what happened to Lynne Harper on the night of June 9, 1959, is not worthy of belief." They highlighted his dismal performance at the Supreme Court, whose judges seemed distinctly unimpressed with Truscott's memory and story. Kaufman, on the other hand, found that Steven's testimony back in 1966—even when he forgot evidence that was favourable to his case, such as meeting Richard Gellatly on the county road—indicated that "Truscott was a poor, but not necessarily a deceitful witness." After reviewing the extensive record of Truscott's police statements and the trial transcripts from 1959 and 1966, Kaufman came down solidly in favour of Steven's credibility: "On the totality of the available evidence, Truscott's evidence on the critical events is not incapable of belief."

Kaufman also interviewed enough modern-day pathologists to conclude that there was a wide consensus in medical circles today that the examination of stomach contents upon which Dr. Penistan had relied so heavily to pinpoint a time of death was a "highly unreliable" method. "Simply put," Kaufman wrote, "modern science has removed the time of death as a piece of circumstantial evidence favouring Truscott's guilt."

Kaufman's inquiry also looked into some of the outstanding mysteries surrounding the case. He examined the other sightings of strange cars on the evening of June 9* and found they would have given more credibility to Truscott's story if known to the jury. More importantly, he said, "to the

* See pages 92–95

extent that these sightings were summarily dismissed or inadequately investigated by the police" the jurors might have thought twice about the "quality of the investigation."

The same went for the long list of other suspects that were ignored. Kaufman looked at the case of Alexander Kalichuk, the airman who had tried to lure young girls into his car and whose name was raised in the mid-sixties to OPP investigator Harold Graham "but was dismissed in somewhat peremptory fashion." The Kaufman inquiry also heard of a salesman in the area who drove a 1957 Bel Air and later pled guilty to various crimes; of a man who had four convictions of assaulting females and males and who allegedly told his doctor on his deathbed that he had done "the murder that Steven Truscott went to jail for;" and of a military man stationed at the base between 1958 and 1959 who was a member of the search party but later for some reason felt the need to mislead police by claiming he was "miles away" when they discovered the body and who bizarrely named his own daughter Lynne after "a little girl that had to die."

None of these possible other suspects necessarily proved a miscarriage of justice, but in Kaufman's mind they raised the spectre of "tunnel vision" on the part of police and prosecutors. "This investigation—rightly or wrongly—quickly focused on Truscott . . . Traditional police work such as the identification of local sexual offenders may not have been pursued with vigour, or at all."

After sifting through the evidence, Kaufman then had to weigh important legal issues. He realized there was a danger in imposing modern-day standards on all verdicts of the past. Disclosure rules were almost non-existent back in 1959.* As Kaufman noted, the "constitutional right to full disclosure of the investigative file . . . did not exist in 1959 or in 1966." But even by the standards of 1959, Kaufman concluded, there was still an over-riding obligation for police and prosecutors to be fair. He cited a recent Supreme Court decision that long before tougher new obligations came into force in 1991, "the duty to disclose all relevant evidence to the defence had already been recognized at common law as a component of the accused's right to a fair trial."

Kaufman then went on to argue that lack of disclosure of key evidence "deprived the defence of a considerable amount of information that could

---

* See Chapter 29

have been used to impeach the credibility of witnesses, cast doubt upon the prosecution's theory of the case, or support the defence case. In some instances, the evidence would have made it possible to discover and explore new avenues of investigation." He was also convinced that the withholding of several witness statements "significantly reduced the ability of the defence to properly challenge the Crown's case." Taken together, he said, "this undisclosed evidence . . . could reasonably be expected to have affected the verdict." The conclusion was inescapable: these problems "contribute to a reasonable basis for concluding that there was a likely miscarriage of justice."

Those three words—"miscarriage of justice"—were in and of themselves a long-awaited and hard-fought victory for Steven Truscott. For the first time—except for Supreme Court Justice Emmett Hall's powerful but largely ignored dissent—somebody in judicial authority was listening to his complaints—and largely agreed.

But that was as far as Kaufman was willing to go. "The evidence presented to me, taken at its highest, does not demonstrate innocence, but only that there is a reasonable basis to conclude that a miscarriage of justice likely occurred." What, then, would he recommend the justice minister do?

"The issue of remedy is complex and unique," Kaufman warned.

Indeed.


Kaufman handed in his seven hundred–page report to the new justice minister, Irwin Cotler, in August of 2004. The Truscotts, through their lawyers, knew the content of some of his findings but not his final recommendation. For three months, Kaufman's decision remained a secret as Cotler—who had been a prominent civil rights activist for many years—patiently read the report and pondered what to do.

As word leaked out late in October that an announcement was imminent, nerves began to fray. "Although Steve appears to be holding up well, I can tell you that I have seen him age in the last while and I am concerned about his health," Marlene Truscott wrote her growing number of supporters in an e-mail. "The waiting has caused stress and is proving to be very difficult on him and other family members."

Peter MacKay, who had met Steven and Marlene several times and by now was deputy head of the Conservative Party, called any further delay "inexcusable." "Steven Truscott and his family have been living in purgatory," he said. "The tortuous pace of the minister is taking a tremendous toll on them." But like many, he was optimistic: "I'm very hopeful that this is going to result in a full exoneration." Liberal MP Paul Steckle shared that optimism, telling reporters he had presented the justice minister with a copy of the 2001 edition of this book when Cotler took over the portfolio. "We are all hoping for a very positive outcome of this," the member of parliament from Steven's original hometown of Clinton said. "This is the worst case of miscarriage of justice in Canadian history."

On Friday, October 22, Truscott made another of his increasing number of public appearances at a panel on the wrongfully convicted—this time before a group of law students in Windsor. Truscott told his audience that the justice system back in the 1950s "was completely different from the way it is today."

"There was no disclosure, so our lawyers didn't know what the police had or what the Crown had," he said. "Back then, there was nobody who would fight for anybody that was in jail."

On Wednesday, October 27, the night before Justice Minister Cotler's scheduled news conference to unveil his decision, Marlene was nervous but excited. The 34th anniversary of her marriage to Steven was just three days away. She allowed herself to dream the campaign she had been waging since the 1960s to clear Steven's name was finally over; she shared her hopes with the man she had shared a life and a life-long battle:

"I told Steve that I firmly believed that this was the last night he would go to sleep as a convicted murderer."


Thursday, October 28, 2004, turned out to be one of those gorgeous sunny days when fall seems to forget winter is coming and pretends it is still summer.

The small street in Guelph had been invaded by a media army. The TV satellite trucks from all the networks lined up outside the Truscotts' simple bungalow; dozens of reporters camped outside, waiting nervously to hear the live broadcast from Ottawa and then capture the Truscotts' reaction. Only close family and friends were allowed in the house. Steven's three children and his grandchildren were on hand. On the kitchen counter lay a white celebration cake, with the word "juSTice" decorated on the top—the "S" and "T" capitalized to stand for Steven Truscott.

The Truscotts and their supporters were hoping desperately for a victory. The fact that they had gotten this far was remarkable—almost all appeals to the justice minister to re-open a case are turned down. The worst case scenario for Truscott would be if the justice minister dismissed his case and found no merit to his appeal. As a middle ground, if Cotler felt there had indeed been a miscarriage of justice, he could refer the case to another court—either the Supreme Court again or, more likely, the Ontario Court of Appeal. That still meant, in effect, that Steven was guilty and, like any other appellant, he was asking a higher court to review the verdict against him.

Under the law, even if he felt it was appropriate, the minister did not have the power to direct an acquittal—in other words, to unilaterally declare that Steven was innocent. So the best option Truscott and his lawyers had pushed for was a new trial. That had the advantage of quashing Steven's conviction, since a man could hardly be put on trial if he is already guilty. In this scenario, Truscott would walk into the same courtroom in Goderich where he faced the noose more than forty years ago. The judge would read out the charge and ask Truscott how he pleaded.

"Not guilty, your honour," the adult Steven would say.

Then the Crown—in the best case scenario—would announce that they have no new evidence to present and the case would be dropped.

"Only then," said James Lockyer, "[would] Steven have the chance to rid himself—we hope—of demons that must have lived with him for now 45 years."

That, at least, was the hope.

---

The phone rang by mid-morning that Thursday and Steve picked it up quickly. Cotler had called his lawyers earlier and now Lockyer was passing on the announcement to his client.

"I will never forget the look on Steve's face and I knew that it was not the news we expected," said Marlene. "Steve, being the courageous and caring person he is, turned to all the family in the room."

They sat hushed as an ashen-faced Steven said: "I am used to disappointment and I am sorry to have to give you this news."

---

Outside the journalists huddled around the satellite feeds and across the nation Canadians watched as the justice minister issued his decision at a press conference covered live on several networks.

"I have determined that there is a reasonable basis to conclude that a miscarriage of justice likely occurred in this case," Irwin Cotler said.

That was the good news. The highest justice official in the land had agreed that most probably something had gone terribly wrong in that Goderich courtroom so many decades ago.

But his solution was not what the Truscotts had been waiting to hear. "I'm referring the case to the Ontario Court of Appeal." Cotler said. "I believe this is the most just and appropriate remedy."

Instead of dismissing Truscott's appeal, as the Ontario attorney general's lawyers wanted, or quashing the conviction and ordering a new trial, as Truscott's team had pushed for, Cotler had taken the safer, middle ground.

That was what Fred Kaufman had recommended. "The passage of time makes a retrial in his case unrealistic," Kaufman had written in his report to the minister. He acknowledged that a review by the Ontario Court of Appeal "would be cumbersome and prolonged" but it was the only way to prove Truscott innocent in the eyes of all. "The innocent are entitled to their public exoneration," Kaufman said. The "existing record"—in other words, the new evidence as presented to him—was enough to raise doubts about how fair the trial was but not enough to definitively prove Truscott innocent. Kaufman's job was not to hold an open trial; neither the Crown nor the defence had a chance to cross-examine the witnesses. The federal government's logic was that now justice must not only be done, it must be seen to be done in some form of open court.

Cotler repeated those arguments to reporters and bristled at any suggestions that he had taken the easy way out. He said that if he ordered a new trial, the Ontario prosecutors—who showed no signs of accepting Truscott's innocence—would have either argued the issue aggressively and dragged on the case or they might have decided to stay the murder charge because the evidence and witnesses were so old, or no longer available—which would have left Steven in a kind of legal limbo.

"That would not have given Mr. Truscott the exoneration that he seeks," Cotler said. "I'm guided by one principle only, and that is: What is the right thing to do?"

It didn't seem like the right thing to do in the Truscott home. There were tears, but not the tears of joy they were expecting. The champagne bottle was left corked, the victory cake, uncut.

"It was tense. It was sad. It was anger. It was a lot of different emotions rolled up into one," said Lesley, Truscott's daughter and by then the thirty-year-old mother of his three grandchildren. "It was a letdown. I don't think we were prepared for it, because it was built up so much that we were expecting a new trial," she said.

Marlene Truscott could not contain her disappointment—and her fury: "It's a disgrace; I think it's a cop-out."

Typically, it was the man at the centre of the battle who took the setback the best. After all, he had been used to seeing the justice system crush his hopes. "It's a bump on the road," Steven said stoically. "Once they sentence you to hang, what else can they do to you? They had sentenced me to death once, so anything else is a plus. You get up in the morning; you look around; you breathe. It's another day. I'll be vindicated. It will just take longer."

Ryan, who lived with his parents and had been the most active in their public battle, was overcome with disappointment. It was his father who came downstairs to console him. "Don't worry, we'll turn around," Steven told his wife and children. "We'll fight and we'll keep going."

"Dad always told us we had to be a close, tight-knit family because he never got to enjoy that family life at all," Ryan said. "The justice system took that away from him."

After they had wiped their tears and put aside—at least publicly—their anger and disappointment, the Truscotts walked outside, surrounded by their legal team to the waiting hordes of journalists. James Lockyer announced that Steven would not speak to the media that day.

"Steven Truscott is proving today that he is a formidable man with an extraordinary character," Lockyer said. "The fact is Steven Truscott did not kill Lynne Harper and the shame of our justice system is that more than 45 years have passed since he was convicted of a crime that he didn't commit. It now looks like it's going to be 46, 47, 48 years before he is finally exonerated."

"Everyone's going to be older, perhaps quite a lot older . . . when Steven Truscott's reputation is returned to him. But we'll all be here," Lockyer concluded. "We'll be here if we all have to live to 100."

Throughout the afternoon, Truscott's three grandchildren had been scampering around in white T-shirts that student supporters had made. The T-shirts listed the names of other wrongly convicted men in Canada—Guy Paul Morin, David Milgaard, Thomas Sophonow—with a red check in a box next to each name under the title "Cleared." But "Steven Truscott," at the bottom of the list, had no check mark yet. The grandchildren would have to wait a few more years to see it, but their mother, Lesley, said she had learned patience from a father who spent four months on death row and ten years behind bars.

"It's a new fight. As we talked about it, we figured it's going to be okay in the end," she said. "It's going to take us longer, but we may even get a better result in the end."

In the Senate on Parliament Hill, Conservative Senator Marjory Lebreton—who had worked with John Diefenbaker, the prime minister who had commuted the fourteen-year-old Truscott's death sentence—declared her "profound sadness" at yet another delay on Steven's long ride for justice.

"We all know that Mr. Truscott was convicted on highly questionable and circumstantial evidence in a trial that lasted only a few weeks," she said. "Any fair-minded, straight-thinking person would surely conclude that what we have here is a travesty of justice."

In a *National Post* column, media magnate David Asper denounced the "investigative mischief and incompetence" that had seen Truscott railroaded by a justice system unwilling to admit its faults. Asper was not just shooting from his editorial hip: as a lawyer, he had helped fight to clear David Milgaard, wrongly convicted of the 1969 murder of a Saskatoon nursing aide. He had seen Saskatchewan prosecutors battling feverishly to uphold the original conviction.

Now, Asper warned, Ontario Attorney General Michael Bryant was doing the same thing. "The spectacle of the system trying to defend the indefensible will unfold once again unless Bryant calls off his dogs. Why force a court to review that which has already been painstakingly reviewed? Unfortunately, Bryant seems more likely to play out his department's weak hand rather than admit what everyone knows."

That is precisely what happened. The provincial legal dogs were not called off. If Bryant had backed off and acknowledged—as his federal counterpart Irwin Cotler did—that there was a strong likelihood of a miscarriage of justice, the appeal process could have been settled within months. But Bryant refused to budge, stating that the issue of guilt or innocence "is not going to be determined by the court of public opinion but by a court of law." For the next two years, his prosecutors fought Truscott's lawyers over every detail, every point of law. Endless briefs and counter-briefs were filed by both sides, re-hashing much of what had already been explored by Kaufman. In the end, the Court of Appeal would not begin its hearings until late June 2006—almost two years after Cotler had promised a speedy, public resolution to Truscott's plea for justice.

In the meantime, Steven Truscott's supporters were not going to sit back and quietly watch the justice system drag its feet. In the Guelph home of Mary Yanchus, the teacher who had launched a postcard campaign for Truscott, more than two hundred people showed up a few weeks after Cotler's decision. By now Yanchus had exceeded her original print run of 16,000 and was planning to send 20,000 protest cards to Attorney General Bryant.

At the Humberview School, in Bolton, the grade Twelve law class researched and studied the Truscott case; then the class argued the case in front of Peel Region judges at the Brampton courthouse. They took on the roles of the defence, the prosecutor and the witnesses—and this time Truscott was found not guilty. The students didn't stop there. They launched an online petition and began selling bracelets for five dollars that read "juSTice now" to raise money for AIDWYC. "[The campaign] allows us to say this is terrible and then do something about it," said Alex Sinclair, a seventeen-year-old law class student. Steven and his family came to a public symposium the students organized. On June 10, 2005, the students marked the 46th anniversary of what they called Steven Truscott's "Fight for Freedom" by handing over their petition to Ontario Progressive Conservative Party leader John Tory—their local MPP—who then personally handed the thousands of names to the attorney general.

That same anniversary weekend, Steven found himself in Newfoundland for an AIDWYC conference that featured some of Canada's best-known wrongly convicted personalities. He was joined on stage by David Milgaard, Ronald Dalton and Gregory Parsons. All but Truscott had been exonerated after serving prison time.

"I'm still waiting. It's getting there slowly and we'll stick at it because of people like this," Truscott told the crowd, nodding to the men next to him. "Because of people who have yet to come."

Steven was becoming a reluctant celebrity. Still shy and unassuming, the man who had rarely traveled far from Guelph was now speaking to law faculties, and at public events—even to a gathering of prosecutors. His local newspaper named him Newsmaker of the Year. Still, Steven remained first and foremost a family man, going to work every day as a millwright at the local factory and spending the weekends with his grandchildren or friends. He shunned the spotlight as much as possible. It was Marlene who still answered the phone at his house most of the time; Marlene who wrote the e-mails and kept fanning the flames of the public campaign.

By the time Christmas rolled around in 2005, Truscott had spent almost a decade in a public battle to clear his name. The Court of Appeal hearing was still at least a half year away. As the snow piled up outside his home, Steven pulled a very special gift from under the Christmas tree. It was a carefully gift-wrapped pizza box.

Steven tore open the wrapping.

Inside were the documents that his youngest son, Devon, now twenty-five, had filled out to legally adopt his father's surname—Truscott. "You could never ask for more," Steven told the local paper. "That was totally unexpected, but it was probably the best thing he could have ever given me."

Ryan had taken his father's name proudly three years earlier; Lesley lived under her married name. Now Devon was completing the circle.

"That's the name I was born with," Truscott said. "It's my name."


His final chance to clear that name came in June of 2006 when the Ontario Court of Appeal finally set a date to hear his case.

If Truscott's new appeal would dig into long-buried truths and secrets, it seemed only fitting that it would be foreshadowed by the very real unearthing of long-buried bones. On Thursday, April 6, the body of twelve-year-old Lynne Harper, buried for forty-seven years, was exhumed by the coroner's office for DNA testing. It must have been a gut-wrenching experience for her family, contemplating the disruption of a grave of a girl who never saw her teenage years. The Crown, presumably, was hoping to find traces of Truscott's sperm or blood that would prove his guilt once and for all. On hand to observe the procedure for the defence was Edward Blake, a DNA expert from California, whose investigations for AIDWYC helped clear David Milgaard and Guy Paul Morin.

Dr. Blake worked on more than fifty post-conviction exonerations through DNA work, including people on death row. But this was the first time he had ever seen an attempt to secure DNA evidence from a body buried so long ago. "A body that has been buried fifty years has significant challenges," he said. He recently examined blood stain evidence from the Sam Sheppard case of the 1950s—the famous slaying that inspired *The Fugitive* TV series and movie. But he stressed that blood samples were quite distinct from bones. "When you take a body out of the ground, that is a totally different thing," he cautioned.

In the end, Blake was right: Lynne's body was too badly decomposed to give up any evidence about her killer. Dr. Michael Pollanen, Ontario's chief coroner who had been asked to supervise the new examination, said Harper's remains were "skeletonized" and of little forensic use.

As the day neared for the hearing to begin, the media contacted many of Steven's old friends. Malcolm "Mac" Stienburg, the parole officer who became Steve's mentor, was, as always, blunt: "To me, it was never an issue of just a wrong conviction," he said. "It was a case of a court system, a justice system or a country even that could find a fourteen-year-old child guilty of murder and sentence him to hang." Cathy O'Dell, a classmate of Truscott's who now lived in Montana and went by the name Beaman, was anxious: "I'm hoping they do what they should have done years ago—and that's exonerate him," she said.

"I'm really hoping that they listen."


The listening began on Monday June 19, 2006, in the ornate chambers of Courtroom 1 of the Ontario Court of Appeal at Osgoode Hall in downtown Toronto. Forty-seven summers ago, on an equally hot day on June 13, 1959, a frightened teenager had stood in a courtroom to hear the charge of murder read out to him; then a few months later that same teenager would hear the judge condemn him to hang by the neck "until you are dead."

That teenager had become a tall, proud grandfather, who strode into the courtroom, looking every bit the calm hero he had become to so many Canadians. Dressed in a simple grey suit with a maroon shirt, unbuttoned at the collar, Steven sat under a majestic chandelier in the front row of the public benches. On his left, was a determined Marlene, who by now probably knew more about the case than any of the lawyers in the court. On his right were his two grown sons, Ryan and Devon.

"We were up all night," said Ryan. "It's what you've been waiting for and then the day finally it arrives. It's hard to take in."

It *was* hard to take in: nearly five decades after he became Canada's most famous convicted murderer and a decade after he had first gone public to clear his name, Steven Truscott was finally getting his day in court. This would be his last, best chance. No more campaigns, no more legal arguments, no more waiting. This was it.

Going up against an array of Crown attorneys were three of AIDWYC's most experienced and combative lawyers: James Lockyer, Phil Campbell and Marlys Edwardh, assisted by Jenny Friedland who had done much of the legal research on the case as an articling student but was now a full-fledged lawyer in her own right.

It was not a new trial: Steven would not testify, nor would the key child witnesses against him, Jocelyne Gaudet and Arnold "Butch" George. The Court of Appeal could only hear new, fresh evidence. Still, it was an historic, unprecedented event. After all, the court was re-opening a case that had already been settled by the highest court in the land back in 1967. And while usually appeal hearings were limited to dry debates between lawyers over fine points of law, this time the court would spend three weeks hearing live, oral testimony from an array of witnesses—most of them medical and scientific experts, but also a handful of people from the Clinton area back in the 1950s.

"Court is now in session," the clerk intoned as the five judges walked in to take their seats on the dais in front. "Please be seated."

If the first witness was any indication, Steven had a fair shot at vindication. As Ontario's chief forensic pathologist, Dr. Michael Pollanen usually testified for the prosecution. It was Pollanen who conducted the second autopsy of Lynne Harper's remains after her body was exhumed. The Crown had also asked him to go beyond her remains to look at other material—including the black-and-white photographs of her body taken at the crime scene, Dr. Penistan's 1959 findings and the microscopic slides made from tissue samples removed during the original autopsy.

Dr. Pollanen's conclusions were so unfavourable to the prosecution he was called as the first witness not by the Crown but by Truscott's defence team. Pollanen had made a name for himself in the world of pathology exhuming bodies in East Timor, examining skeletal remains in Cambodia, and studying torture victims in Kazakhstan. He had also written and lectured extensively about the "pitfalls of pathology" as he called them, to "make sure these pitfalls don't enter the justice system."

Sounding like a character from TV's *CSI*, he said pathologists had to take an "evidence-based approach" that looked at the global picture and not just one piece of the puzzle. Narrowing a time of death based mainly on stomach contents is "fraught with difficulty," Dr. Pollanen testified, because digestion was more a process than an event that could be pinned down to specific moment. But even if the state of her digestive system suggested she could have been killed sometime Tuesday evening, Pollanen explained, one had to look at the "real world implications" of that conclusion.

And in the real world, if Lynne had died between 7:00 and 7:45 p.m. on Tuesday, June 9, as Dr. Penistan had insisted, that meant her body had been lying for two days under a blazing June sun before it was found. But if that were true, one would have expected her body to be in a more advanced state of decomposition, Dr. Pollanen explained. Yet putrefaction, which would normally set in quickly in the hot and humid conditions of Clinton at the time, was "nil" even according to Penistan's own findings. Lynne's remains showed "remarkably little" decomposition and there was no indication her heart muscle or brain had started to break down, Pollanen said.

Taped to the wall of the courtroom next to the witness were pictures of slides taken from the autopsy samples of 1959 showing the state of autolysis—the process by which injured or dying cells self-destruct—for the Lynne Harper's liver and kidney. "I was quite surprised to find the liver so well preserved," Dr. Pollanen said. "The liver should not be in such pristine condition" for a body that supposedly spent two days exposed to summer's heat, he said.

For Pollanen, the conclusion was inescapable. Dr. Penistan's estimate was far too precise and too dependent on unreliable stomach contents. If the state of her digestion indicated she may have been murdered on the evening of June 9, the other medical evidence pointed to a much later period. "The time of death window must be broadly inclusive, to encompass June 9 and June 10," Pollanen told a packed courtroom.

It was a stunning appraisal. Back in 1959, they were arguing over minutes—for if Lynne Harper had died any time after 8 p.m., everyone agreed Steven was innocent. Now they were talking of days. The top coroner in the province was saying Harper could just have easily been killed on the Wednesday as on the Tuesday evening when she was last seen with Steven.

There were more pathological time bombs to come that first day in court. As part of his questioning of Dr. Pollanen, defence lawyer James Lockyer revealed that new documents uncovered in the government's archives in 2005 included two earlier, partly hand-written versions of Dr. Penistan's autopsy report. In the first, he wrote that Lynne's time of death was within forty hours of her body being discovered—which put her demise at around 12:15 a.m. on Wednesday. In a second version, he revised that estimate downward to between thirty and thiry-six hours, which meant she was killed between 4:15 a.m. and 10:45 a.m., early Wednesday.

Needless to say, neither of these versions ever made it into court in 1959 or when the Supreme Court re-examined Penistan's conclusions in 1966.

Dr. Penistan's conclusions—so central to Truscott's conviction—took more of a beating the second day from another expert. Dr. Nicholas Diamand, a University of Toronto professor with forty-five years experience as a specialist in the "disorders of the gut," dismissed Penistan's analysis of stomach contents as an "entirely useless" way to estimate the time of death. Today few doctors would categorically rule that the stomach empties within two hours, he said. It usually takes a person three to four hours to digest a meal, but a number of factors—ranging from the person's age to the type of meal—can slow down or speed up the process.

Cognizant that any pathologist can be made to look bad after almost fifty years of medical progress, Marlys Edwardh wanted the court to know if Penistan's pinpoint time of death was acceptable, given the extent of medical knowledge back in 1959. So she asked Diamand: "Was it tenable *back then* based on what he knew?"

"No," came the quick response, "There was enough evidence at that time that you could not limit it to that time period."

"Looking back with today's knowledge it is completely untenable?" the lawyer pushed.

"Yes," said the doctor.

One of the court of appeal judges, Justice David Doherty, asked Diamand what a reasonable estimate of Lynne's time of death would be considering she ate her last supper at about 5:45 p.m.

In the five- or six-hour range "or beyond," said Dr. Diamand, again putting it well after the period she was with Steven.

This was not good news for the Crown, desperately trying to argue—in 2006 as it did in 1959—that Steven Truscott was unquestionably guilty.

The original prosecutor, Glenn Hays, had famously told the jurors that Penistan's precise determination of the time of death narrowed "like a vise on Steven Truscott and no one else." Now that vise was cracking open, by hours if not days.

To try to salvage the credibility of Penistan's testimony, the Crown brought in Dr. Werner Spitz, an American pathologist with decades of experience who had worked with the congressional committee that reviewed the autopsy of U.S. President John F. Kennedy. "When I look upon the work of Dr. Penistan, I'm in awe of him," Spitz told the five appeal court judges. "He was way ahead of his time." He praised Penistan for collecting insects near the body—a rare practice at the time—and for other swabs and measurements he made. In that context, he said, Penistan's estimate of a time of death between 7:00 and 7:45 p.m. on June 9 seemed justified and accurate.

But under a withering cross-examination by Phil Campbell, Dr. Spitz conceded he had not seen the two other autopsy reports by Penistan, where he variously put time of death approximately at 12:15 a.m. or as late as 10:45 a.m on June 10. Nor had he seen Penistan's "agonizing reappraisal" in which he questioned his own narrow time of death conclusions. Spitz could not explain the wide variations, except to say that Penistan did the best he could with what "little" he had.

"He may have made a mistake," he said.

To explain away the surprisingly few signs of decomposition which had bothered Ontario's chief forensic pathologist, Dr. Pollanen, Spitz argued Lynne's body may have been exposed to cooler temperatures in Lawson's bush.

"Can you point to anything in the material you reviewed that would characterize the temperatures around Lynne Harper's body as cool?" Campbell asked, noting the temperatures had hit a high of 92°F and a low of 64°F between the night Harper went missing and the day she was found. "Can you realistically describe those as cool temperatures?"

"The environment in the forest, in my view, was classifiable as cool, because I've been to forests. I've seen cases come out of forests," said Spitz.

"You were not exposed to the body of Lynne Harper or Lawsons' Bush?

"No, I was not."

"Let's go to a witness who was. Dr. Penistan. Dr. Penistan described the weather as hot and damp. Do you, Dr. Spitz, have any better evidence than that?"

"How can I sit here in 2006 and second-guess somebody who was on the premises?" Spitz answered.

But the truth was that the Court of Appeal—like the Supreme Court had done thirty years before it—was in fact second-guessing Dr. Penistan's work in condemning Steven Truscott, or at least taking a serious second look at his work. And while the experts in front of the Supreme Court were evenly split, this time round, Penistan's critics seemed to outnumber and outclass his defenders.

There would be more battering of the medical evidence used to convict Truscott over the three weeks of the appeal hearing, but in between the testimony of experts, the five judges also heard from several witnesses who had stories to tell from the 1950s and 60s.

The first to take the stand was Harry "Hank" Sayeau, the corporal who helped lead the investigation of Truscott and who eventually retired as an OPP Chief Superintendent. Under a barrage of questions by defence lawyer Maryls Edwardh, he could not explain why he dismissed statements from two key witness that contradicted the Crown's case.

As a nine-year-old girl, Karen Daum was at the bridge with the turtle-hunting Dougie Oates on that fateful night in June 1959. Like Dougie, she told police that she saw Steve and Lynne on his bike close to the river—a crucial support of Steven's story. But Sayeau told the court he wrote in his notebook: "She was a cute little girl, but she had to be wrong. She's not credible as far as the Crown was concerned."

Another child, Daryl Wadsworth, had told police he remembered seeing Steven leave the schoolyard at about 7:25 p.m, much later than the Crown's theory that Truscott set off on his bike ride closer to 7:00. Sayeau characterized Daryl's evidence as "imaginative. Wouldn't consider his story at all."

Sayeau also testified that his team did not contact any other OPP branch in the area about a possible child rapist or sexual predator in the area. Sayeau said at the time he had never heard of Alexander Kalichuck, the heavy-drinking airman who had tried to lure young girls into his car two weeks before Lynne was murdered.

"There was no follow-up as far as I was concerned," said Sayeau.

One of the appeal court judges, Justice Michael Moldaver, wondered why the police never considered that a sexual psychopath might have been responsible for Lynne's rape and murder before narrowing their focus on fourteen-year-old Steven Truscott.

"Did the thought ever cross your mind that, for someone to . . . strangle her then sexually assault her, you might want to be looking for someone who is more of a pervert, more of a sexual psychopath?" he asked. "Did you ever talk about that with your colleagues?"

"I don't recall that," said the eighty-four-year-old Harry Sayeau.

Several days later, Karen Daum—now going by her married name Jutzi—took the stand herself. The last line of her statement to the police back in 1959—which was never shown to the defence—read: "Point of meeting pointed out was just about railway tracks." That would have put Steven and Lynne well past Lawson's bush and helped support Steven's innocence. As she had first explained in the 2001 edition of this book, Karen Jutzi told the appeal court that the police got it wrong: she had told them she ran into Steve and Lynne much higher up on the county road, close to the tractor trail entrance to the bush.*

That version was much less favourable to Truscott's case, so defence lawyer Phil Campbell set about to discredit it. He pressed Karen Jutzi on how accurate her recent memory could be compared to the at-the-moment statement she gave police in 1959. He also wondered how the police could have so badly misunderstood her story, considering that the account they wrote down was so damaging to their own case against Truscott.

Campbell noted that the girl's father, a "by-the-book" military man, accompanied her when she met police repeatedly and must have heard her recount her story at least three times.

"Wouldn't you expect your father, being the kind of man he was, to correct the statement [if it was inaccurate]?" Campbell asked.

"Yes, he would," Karen replied.

She remembered Steven veering toward her on his bike, knocking her off. But Campbell showed her pictures of the road which sloped sharply near the bush where she now said she ran into Steve and Lynne—making it difficult if not impossible for her to see anyone heading toward her. Karen then pointed to another spot on the road, in effect coming up with a third version of where she might have been standing. "All I remember is, when I fell off the bike, I looked up and the bush was there," she said.

---

* See pages 285–86

"Is that an actual memory of yours, of getting on your bike and riding up to the [railway] tracks, or are you just reconstructing?" he asked.

"I'm just reconstructing," the witness replied.

Karen was just one of several key witnesses who testified for the first time in a court of law to what they had initially revealed in the 2001 edition of this book. By coincidence, Bob Lawson turned seventy the day he took the stand at the appeal hearing, and the Clinton farmer took the judges back to the night Lynne disappeared. He told them that he saw a mysterious red convertible parked near the bush late that evening, but when he reported it, the authorities were not interested because they had already arrested Steven. Lawson also repeated his startling account of how Jocelyne Gaudet had come to him during the trial to ask him to change his testimony: she had testified she had come by his farm looking for Steve around 6:30 p.m. when in fact the farmer—and Gaudet—knew it was closer to an hour later, around 7:30 p.m.*

Jocelyne Gaudet's falsehoods were further explored at the appeal hearing when Sandra Stolzmann reiterated her story, as she did in the first edition of this book, that Gaudet told her in the 1960s that she had lied at Steven's original trial.† Stolzmann and Gaudet were both nursing students in Montreal when the Supreme Court hearings brought the Truscott case back to prominence. "They've got the wrong guy, they've got the wrong guy," Gaudet kept repeating.

Another nursing classmate at the time, Elizabeth Hulbert told the court that Gaudet said: "I was one of the witnesses at the Steven Truscott trial and I lied." When her classmates urged Gaudet to go public and tell the truth, she refused. "She wasn't going to testify to recant her earlier statement," Hulbert said. "I'll get myself admitted to a psychiatric facility" to avoid testifying Gaudet told her friends.

Catherine Beaman—who as Cathy O'Dell was a best friend of Lynne's—recounted how she and Harper would hitchhike regularly to Clinton.‡ Harper's parents had said at the 1959 trial their daughter did not hitchhike (even though in their first report to police the night their daughter disappeared they feared she had hitchhiked to her grandmother's house).

---

* See page 175
† See page 524
‡ See page 22

Beaman—who was never questioned by police back in 1959—testified that she and Lynne thumbed rides "at least 15 to 20 times."

Outside the court, Beaman told reporters she missed her friend Lynne but also hoped Steven would be able to put the ghosts of the past aside: "Steve needs justice as does Lynne, because it's as much about justice for her as it is for him."

The final week of hearings was dominated by—of all things—bugs.

At one point, all five judges of the Ontario Court of Appeal were passing around a box of flies, preserved and pinned like historical artifacts. In their briefs filed with the court, Truscott's lawyers argued new evidence from the field of forensic entomology—the study of insects in criminal investigations—could be "decisive" in determining Steven's innocence.

Dr. Penistan had collected samples of newly hatched maggots found around and inside Lynne's body. It sounds grisly but the speedy growth cycle of flies allows experts to measure them when a corpse is found, then basically count backwards and calculate when the eggs or larvae were first laid on a dead body—and hence, determine the time of death. In this case, Harper's time of death.

Elgin Brown was the biologist who received the maggots back in 1959 and he was still alive in 2006 to tell the appeal court his findings. During the original trial, Brown was asked about the grass stains on Steve's clothes and the blood under Lynne's fingernails—but not about his lab notes and the bugs. The original coroner, Dr. Penistan, assumed the insects he found were blowfly maggots, varying between 1/16 and 1/4 of an inch long. To reach such a size their eggs would have to have been planted before sunset on June 9—in other words, when Steven was with Lynne.

But Brown told the modern-day hearing that back in 1959 he grew samples of the bugs into adulthood in the attorney general's lab in Toronto. The smaller insects, at 1/16 of an inch, were indeed blowflies, but he found the larger ones, at 1/4 of an inch, were in fact flesh flies. That was significant because female flesh flies do not lay eggs—instead, they grow their offspring inside their bodies and then leave larvae on corpses.

After consulting with other experts at the Ontario Agricultural College and the author of a textbook on the subject, Brown concluded the flesh flies began to infest Lynne's body sometime on Wednesday, June 10—which meant that Lynne had to have died after the sun went down on June 9 because these flies are not active at night.

The sun set at 9:08 p.m. on June 9—putting Steven in the clear.

Brown's new testimony—considering he was the biologist who actually handled the maggots back in 1959—was extremely damaging to the prosecution case. So to counter him before the new court of appeal hearings, the Crown brought in Dr. Neal Haskell, a forensic entomology professor at Purdue University in Indiana, who had testified at seven hundred criminal trials around the world. Haskell insisted that the bug evidence did indeed point to a time of death when Steven was with Lynne. He based this largely on his conviction that flesh flies do not deposit their hatched larvae into a body until twenty-four hours after death. Indeed, in more than two decades of experience in the field, he had never seen a lag time of less than a day, the Crown's expert told the court.

It seemed like an ironclad conclusion, until under cross-examination defence lawyer Phil Campbell pulled out a report Haskell himself had written about a triple homicide in Thornhill in the summer of 1992. It was a different year, but the same province, the same geography and the same hot season. Except in that case Haskell concluded that the flesh flies had begun colonizing the body of a woman less than twelve hours after she died.

"Is that your opinion?" Campbell asked.

"I guess it must have been in 1992," was all Haskell could reply.

Haskell came under more fire two days later when another American entomologist testified there was "no scientific credibility" to his theories. Rich Merritt, head of the entomology department at Michigan State University, is the kind of expert who gets called in by the Hershey Company when a customer finds a bug in a chocolate bar: he uses science to determine if the insect got into the snack at the manufacturing plant or the store. On the more serious issue of life and death—in particular Lynne's death and the life of the maggots on her—Merritt studied the growth of the insects on her body, the temperatures around her and the amount of energy and hours it would take for the flies to reach their size. Like all the other experts except the crown's Haskell, he concluded the insects began to infest Lynne's body on the morning or afternoon of June 10, 1959—or perhaps even later.

He said science all but ruled out the possibility that Lynne's body was in Lawson's bush before it got dark on June 9, the only time Steven could have left it there. "You would expect to see larger larvae in this area of the body," Merritt testified.

The medical and forensic testimony that was used to convict Truscott was looking shakier as each day of the hearing passed. By the final day of testimony, it had almost collapsed. The last witness before the Court of Appeal—a world-renowned doctor who literally wrote the book on pathology—derided as "ludicrous" and "suspicious" the findings that helped condemn a fourteen-year-old to be hanged. Dr. Bernard Knight's book is one of the standard textbooks for pathologists. A professor at the University of Wales, a forensic expert in the UK for fifty-one years and a barrister for thirty-eight years, he is also the author of twenty crime novels. By the time he finished his testimony on Friday, July 7, it seemed as if Truscott had been found guilty on the basis of bad fiction instead of good scientific fact.

The Truscott affair, Knight said, is "known worldwide to every forensic pathologist"—but not in a positive light. Rather, he said, the case is generally seen as a "mishap" in the profession. He called stomach content analysis virtually useless. ("It's so inaccurate it is hardly worth doing," he later added outside the court. "There are so many errors in it that it's impossible to give an accurate time of death.")

He found it "suspicious" that Dr. Penistan fixed the time of death at precisely the half hour when only Steven could have committed the murder. "It seems very strange that he happened to land upon the very window of opportunity of access by Mr. Truscott to Miss Harper," Dr. Knight told the judges.

"Any doctor who tries to pin time of death down to a half hour is uninformed or incompetent," Knight said.

Harsh words to end what had been three weeks of harsh testimony.

Steven Truscott's days in court in 2006 were a lot different than those the justice system offered him in 1959 or 1966.

Unlike the 1959 trial, this time round, Steven had legal representation that at least had all the firepower—if not more than that—of the Crown. Steven had some of the best lawyers in the country who had the time and resources to mount a full investigation. There was full disclosure; in fact some of the biggest bombshells, such as Dr. Penistan's earlier versions of his autopsy report, came from documents the defence received from the government.

Unlike the 1966 Supreme Court hearing, where half the expert witnesses and almost all the judges endorsed Penistan's conclusions on stomach contents and the time of death, this time the shoddy reliance on stomach contents got the thrashing it deserved. This time, science seemed to line up squarely behind Truscott: medical and forensic practices had made great strides in four decades and they pointed away from, not toward, a time of death that fingered Steven.

Ever cautious and always a man of few words, Steven allowed himself a brief hint of optimism. "It's very enlightening for everybody to finally hear some of this information that has been there for a lot of years and nobody has ever brought out," he told reporters on the steps of the courthouse. "We're glad it's to this point, anyway, [but] there's still a lot more to go."

There was a lot more to go. The defence lawyers and the Crown were scheduled to return in January 2007 for three weeks of oral arguments before the judges. Truscott's team was planning to present even more arguments than they did during the summer hearings with live witnesses, trying to make the case that the mountains of undisclosed evidence revealed in the past few years would have meant a much different trial result back in 1959. A final decision was expected from the five judges probably sometime in the spring of 2007.

That will be ten years after Steven Truscott, the adult, first approached journalists in his bid to go public and clear his name. Almost fifty years after Steven Truscott, the teenage boy, was found guilty after a two-week trial. If there had been a rush to condemn a boy to hang in 1959 one could hardly say the justice system moved with same alacrity to get to the truth in the twenty-first century.

Still, one way or the other it will all be over. Nineteen judges since 1959 had ruled against Steven. Will these five be any different?

The Court of Appeal can either uphold or quash Steven's conviction. If the judges conclude there was nothing wrong with the original conviction, they can simply dismiss his appeal—an outcome difficult to imagine given the weight of new evidence, but Steven has learned the hard way never to put much faith in the courts.

If, however, the appeal court feels there was a miscarriage of justice, they can quash his conviction. That leaves them with three different kinds of remedies. They can order a new trial—a seemingly unlikely solution considering that many of the witnesses are dead and most of the evidence lost. But the Crown might push for this if the prosecutors feel the judges are not willing to dismiss the case outright. Second, the appeal court judges can issue a powerfully worded judicial stay of proceedings—perhaps explaining their criticisms of Steven's original conviction and his inability to defend himself because of the non-disclosure of key evidence. Stays are often used by the Crown when they are forced to stop a prosecution but don't want to concede the defendant might be innocent. But coming from the bench, it has the same clout as a verdict and has become a remedy to correct serious legal wrongs in what the law calls the "clearest of cases." Finally, they can enter an acquittal—a final verdict of "not guilty." This is obviously Steven's favoured choice since it is the strongest endorsement of his innocence. But it is a fluid arrangement: in any of three options the court could make it clear it feels there was an overwhelming unfairness in Steven's ability to defend himself against the charges.

No matter which of the three remedies the court offers, anything but an outright dismissal of the appeal would be a decisive victory: Steven would no longer be a convicted murderer.

That is certainly what most Canadians want, if the chatter on the radio hotlines and the letters to the editors following the public hearings are any indication. "Does anyone really think Truscott was guilty?" asked the *Orangeville Citizen*. "Our suspicion is that not one in ten Ontarians who have been following the daily disclosures to the five-judge panel would support the conviction. Mr. Truscott was the victim of a pathetically biased and inadequate police investigation that was buttressed by selective disclosure of evidence to the boy's lawyers."

There was nothing Steven and his family could do but wait, as they had done for so long already. As the appeal court hearings were wrapping up, the Truscotts held a Canada Day party at their home in Guelph. More than 160 people showed up—from Niagara Falls, London, Hamilton, Toronto, Stratford and, of course, Clinton—to show their solidarity. The guests all carried around little badges with the Canadian flag in the corner and the slogan in the middle: "My Canada Rights its Wrongs."

Marlene Truscott, the devoted wife and mother without whom the case would likely never have gotten this far, had been bitterly disappointed when the justice minister opted to send the case to the Court of Appeal. But being the soldier that she was, she buckled down and got her husband, her family and their troops ready for the last fight.

"Hopefully it will be worth it in the end," she told her supporters. "The majority of the country is watching."

The country is watching, perhaps more intently now than ever before. For in a strange way, it is not Steven Truscott who is on trial this time but the justice system. Unlike many victims of wrongful convictions, Steven is not a broken man, in jail or desperate, begging the court to set things right.

He has a life. He has a family. He and his children have taken back his name with pride. He is hero to many Canadians. In their minds, it is the justice system that now stands accused of a grievous wrong, not Steven. It is the justice system that has to make amends, not Steven.

Two crimes were committed that hot week in June of 1959. A girl of twelve had her life snuffed out. A boy of fourteen had much of his youth taken away.

He has grown up; she never did. The only question is whether the justice system—and the country—has grown up enough to admit a terrible mistake.

# ACKNOWLEDGMENTS

This book would never have come to be were it not for the teamwork that went into producing a documentary for CBC television's *the fifth estate*, where it was my privilege to work for ten years. The crew for "His Word Against History: The Steven Truscott Story" included cameramen Colin Allison and Michael Savoie, soundmen Larry Kent and Alistair Bell, editor Gary Akenhead, researcher Dallas Brodie, archivists Jim Bertin and Diana Redegeld, production manager Alex Powell, and, on the original team, Trish Wood and Joseph Couture. David Studer, as executive producer, made it all possible. Susan Teskey, as senior producer and mentor, was a driving force and inspiration to me.

Theresa Burke worked tirelessly as the co-producer on the program. Her title as "research associate" for this book hardly does justice to her long hours, patient interviewing and endless cheerfulness. I owe her a debt of gratitude that can never be repaid.

Letting a journalist into your life can be an invasive process, but the many members of the Truscott family accepted me with warmth and openness. Doris Truscott and her children, as well as Steve's children—Lesley, Ryan and Devon—were forever patient. Steve and Marlene Truscott put up with hours and hours of endless questions. They had the generosity to let me into their home and private lives and the courage to never impose their views or any limits on my investigation.

The legal team of James Lockyer, Philip Campbell, Marlys Edwardh, Jenny Friedland and Brian D. King were kind enough to share their thoughts and analysis, without ever expecting me to necessarily agree with their opinions or conclusions.

In the publishing world, I would thank my agent, Michael Levine, for his sage advice; Louise Dennys for her encouragement and support; Pamela Murray for her sharp lead pencil and even sharper eagle eye; and especially Diane Martin, my editor, for the idea, the confidence, the unflinching criticism and unflagging optimism.

Dr. John Butt, the former chief medical examiner of Nova Scotia, gave me invaluable advice on medicine and insight into how pathologists work; Patrick Healy of McGill's faculty of law tried to teach me law; Graham Ospreay of G. P. Ospreay Associates, was kind enough to share his top-notch handwriting expertise; Kevin McGarr, formerly of the Montreal Urban Police, helped me analyze police tactics and procedures and gave me a perspective into how good detectives think; and Mary McFadyen, senior legal counsel in the federal department of justice's Criminal Conviction Review Group, tried to explain section 690s to me. All these people deserve credit for what I get right. The blame for any errors or omissions rests entirely with me, although I have tried to be as accurate and fair as is humanly possible.

I hope this book builds upon the fine journalism that has come before it. Isabel LeBourdais' 1966 work, *The Trial of Steven Truscott*, remains a classic. I am especially grateful to her son, Julien LeBourdais, for his permission to hunt through her personal archives and quote from her correspondence. Bill Trent's two books, *The Steven Truscott Story* (1971) and *Who Killed Lynne Harper?* (1979) were also useful, as was Jack Batten's *Mind Over Murder*. For accounts of events in the 1960s, I relied on the fine reporting of many journalists for daily papers and magazines, including Peter Sypnowich, Gordon McCaffrey, Frank Adams, Phyllis Griffiths and Ron Haggart. Special thanks to Pierre Berton for permission to quote from his poem.

The complete transcripts of the trial of 1959 and the Supreme Court hearings of 1966 and 1967 are available for anyone to read. Through Access to Information I also obtained cabinet minutes from 1959 to 1967 dealing with the Truscott case and examined thousands of pages of police notes, Crown prosecutor's files and prison records.

# ACKNOWLEDGMENTS

For a taste of what cultural life was like in the 1950s, I consulted Alexander Ross's book, *The Booming Fifties*. For a history of the death penalty in Canada, I am indebted to Frank Anderson's *Hanging in Canada* and Carolyn Strange's article "The Lottery of Death: Capital Punishment 1867–1976" in the *Manitoba Law Journal*, January 1996. Research assistance also came from Virginia Smart at the CBC; Daniel German, Paul Marsden and Andrew Whorl at the National Archives in Ottawa; Dan Bryant at the Ontario Public Archives; Philip Malcolm at the air force museum in Clinton; and Sgt. Russ Koopman, RCAF (retired) Secretary-Treasurer of the Air Force Telecom Association of Canada.

The Truscott saga has become part of my life for the past decade. I could never have survived the challenge of bringing this book to life without the patience and love of my two children, Myriam and Daniel, who for most of their childhood watched their father leave on airplanes yet remained constantly curious about what I was doing; and without the support and help from my loving wife and writing partner, Lisa Fitterman, who tolerated late night and early morning computer vigils and kept me sane by forcing me to run all those hills.

Julian Sher
julian@sher.com

# INDEX OF PROPER NAMES

## INDEX OF PROPER NAMES

JULIAN SHER is the author of several books, including the upcoming *One Child at a Time: The Global Fight to Rescue the Victims of Web Porn*. Sher also co-wrote with William Marsden two national bestsellers, *Angels of Death: Inside the Bikers' Empire of Crime* and *The Road to Hell: How the Biker Gangs Are Conquering Canada*. He has worked on investigative projects for the CBC, the *Globe and Mail*, the *Toronto Star* and the *New York Times*.